# Handbook Of Frogs And Toads

HANDBOOKS OF AMERICAN NATURAL HISTORY

ALBERT HAZEN WRIGHT, ADVISORY EDITOR

# Handbook of Frogs and Toads

ALBERT HAZEN WRIGHT AND ANNA ALLEN WRIGHT

# HANDBOOK OF
# Frogs and Toads
## OF THE UNITED STATES AND CANADA

BY ALBERT HAZEN WRIGHT

PROFESSOR OF ZOOLOGY, EMERITUS, CORNELL UNIVERSITY

AND ANNA ALLEN WRIGHT

THIRD EDITION

Comstock Publishing Company, Inc.

ITHACA, NEW YORK, 1949

PRINTED IN THE UNITED STATES OF AMERICA BY THE

VAIL-BALLOU PRESS, INC., BINGHAMTON, NEW YORK

This volume, meant to serve the public, the scientist, and the group treated, is dedicated to the four American women who, in addition to serving the public and science generously, have in the last half-century contributed most notably to the study of this group:

Mary Hewes Hinckley, 1845–1944
Mary Cynthia Dickerson, 1866–1923
Helen Dean King, 1869–
Helen Thompson Gaige, 1889–

# Preface

NINETY YEARS ago John Le Conte in the prefatory paragraphs to his "Descriptive Catalogue of the Ranina of the United States" (Gen., 1856, p. 423) wrote:

> Before I begin, it is necessary to observe that all the Ranina which I have ever seen have more or less the power of changing color at will. The character of color, therefore, of so much moment in the description of many other animals, is here of very little value; for none of the marks dependent on it are constant. In consequence, it requires numerous specimens, living subjects and long study to produce any description that approaches perfection.
>
> How far I have succeeded in my attempt remains to be seen. I have been long and sedulously engaged in my researches. Every description has been made from living specimens.

In conclusion (p. 431) he observed:

> These are all the species of this family of reptiles which I have been able to see in a living state. I hold it to be impossible for any one to make a correct description of an animal which has the power of changing its color at will, unless he has it alive; and this power they all possess in a greater or less degree; when preserved in alcohol they fade. The difficulty of procuring descriptions made on the spot where the objects are found, has rendered this part of natural history as confused and unsatisfactory as the researches of botanists who draw up their accounts of plants from dried specimens.

In all our portrayals we have sought to emphasize the living animal by photographs from life, by color descriptions from life, by journal notes from the field, and particularly by excerpts from others' work pertaining to live frogs. In many regions we have been transitory visitors and the resident naturalists can tell a more complete story. Our notes and the notes of others, which in the two earlier editions were merged under the heading "Notes," are here expanded and designated "Journal notes" and "Authorities' corner."

We have the warmest feelings for the countless friends and strangers who have helped us at different times and in different places. We have seen most of the preserved materials of the important collections and we thank their custodians. An especial effort has been made to secure live material and many people have contributed. The first group constitutes individuals at most of the large zoos of the country. These people offered to loan or in some instances gave us much needed material. In a similar spirit specialists or workers—one hundred or more—in many places and institutions served us in countless fashions. The supply houses and biological bureaus were very eager and willing to help. The list of old students who have mailed or shipped us live frogs would be hard to compile. Many have contributed to these almost weekly surprises through many years. The limits of this book forbid such a list. When we recall that, in California colleges alone, we have some twelve to fifteen teachers of biology, old students, we realize the size of our obligations. Throughout this book will appear the collectors, helpers, comrades—our creditors.

For the typing of this work we extend our thanks to Mrs. Katharine Kapp, Dr. Ann L. Dunham, Mrs. Frankie Culpepper Goerges, and Mrs. R. F. Darsie. Two associates who have helped us particularly are Professors W. J. Hamilton, Jr., and Edward C. Raney. We are also indebted to Cornell University for the Faculty Research Grant to help in typing, purchase of specimens, visits to museums, and trips for specimens.

ALBERT HAZEN WRIGHT
ANNA ALLEN WRIGHT

*Ithaca, New York*
*December, 1948*

# Contents

# Handbook of Frogs and Toads

# General Account

IN THE TREATMENT of each species, the topical outline is as follows: Common names, Scientific name, Range, Habitat, Size, General appearance, Color, Structure, Voice, Breeding, Journal notes, and Authorities' corner.

**Common names:** We of the United States and Canada have concerned ourselves little with distinctive names for the amphibians. Most of the common names of the salamanders and frogs are collective. Just as all salamanders are generally called water dogs or lizards, so also the frogs are known by a few common names (toads, frogs, or tree frogs). Some people use the word "peeper" indiscriminately for several small frogs that call in the early spring. Others call peepers lizards.

Normally we expect common names to come from the people at large, but with amphibians and reptiles most of the common names in literature are really bookish names. Many are translations of the scientific names. The names may come from widely different sources, of which the following are a few:

(1) The person after whom the species is named. Example: Couch's spadefoot. *Scaphiopus couchii* Baird.

(2) The person who named the species. Example: Viosca's tree frog, *Hyla avivoca* Viosca.

(3) The person who first collected it. Example: Taylor's toad. *Hypopachus cuneus* Cope.

(4) A country. Examples: Canadian toad, American bell toad, Mexican toad.

(5) A state or province. Examples· Sonora hyla, Winnipeg toad, California red-legged frog.

(6) Habitats. Examples: River-swamp frog, pond frog, house frog, salt-marsh frog, canyon tree toad, desert tree toad, crayfish frog, gopher frog, wood frog, savanna cricket, cliff frog.

(7) Habits. Examples: Chameleon tree frog, solitary spadefoot, grasshopper frog.

(8) Structural characters. Examples: Ribbed toad, narrow-mouthed toad, toothless frog, femoral hyla, thick-skinned frog.

(9) Voice. Examples: Bell frog, screaming frog, pig frog, rattler, chorus frog, cricket frog.

(10) Color. Examples: Three-lined tree frog, striped tree frog, ornate tree frog, green toad, cinereous hyla.

(11) Seasons. Examples: Spring peeper, shad frog.

(12) Miscellaneous sources of many kinds. Folklore: example—charming toad (legend says this toad, *Bufo terrestris*, turns your eye green). Use (bait): example—pickerel frog. Weather signs: example—rain frog. Odor. example—mink frog.

**Present classifications:** This work has primarily the purpose of presenting the living animal. Through our forty years of study and teaching we have realized the inadequacy of vertebrae, skull, pectoral girdle, sacral diapophyses, teeth, disks, and other structural characters (largely osteological) in the classification of a smooth (scaleless) group. We early sought to work out our North American life histories to supplement this lack but doubt if we will ever have knowledge enough to undertake the task or to clutter up scientific literature with preliminary suggestions. One of the serious attempts in this country has been Dr. G. K. Noble's doctoral dissertation, *The Phylogeny of the Salientia,* wherein he attempts to employ musculature as a supplement to osteology, as has been done for birds and mammals. And his study will surely have to be considered in the final analysis. But many forms need to be canvassed and many life studies undertaken before we rely too implicitly on any set of morphological characters. In the past many morphological osteological criteria have been overworked and overemphasized, and we are in a state of judicial suspense awaiting a nonhasty synthesis Therefore we have temporized by employing Stejneger and Barbour's check list with no particular emphasis of our own devising.

**Scientific name:** Any consideration of the scientific name that an animal bears implies an understanding of the scheme of classification. All living things fall into two groups or kingdoms. The plants are treated in the science of botany, the animals in zoology. The animal kingdom has several major subdivisions or phyla, the last being the *Vertebrata* (vertebrates). In the vertebrate phylum, the various classes are known as fishes (*Pisces*), amphibians (*Amphibia*), reptiles (*Reptilia*), birds (*Aves*), and mammals (*Mammalia*). We designate the study of fishes as ichthyology, that of birds, ornithology, that of mammals, mammalogy, but we group together amphibians and reptiles in the science of herpetology. This merging of the two groups is in a measure due to our inability to designate infallible characters of separation. A fish has fins, a bird, feathers, a mammal, hair, but reptiles and amphibians have no one positively distinctive character.

The amphibians, to which the order of frogs (*Salientia* or *Ecaudata*) belongs, have been variously defined. Some fifteen to twenty characters have been employed. Most living amphibians have naked skin and a larval aquatic stage. Normally, as tadpoles or larvae, they breathe with gills air dissolved in the water; and as adults they breathe with lungs. Two of the membranes about a developing mammal are absent in amphibians. There are three living orders:

Apoda (caecilians) are limbless, blind, and wormlike. None occur in the United States or Canada.

Caudata (salamanders) are, as adults, tailed.

Salientia (frogs) are, as adults, tailless.

Seven families of Salientia or ecaudate amphibians are represented by 99 species or subspecies in the United States and Canada. Family names in zoology and botany end in *idae*. These seven families with the number of species and subspecies in the United States and Canada are:

| | |
|---|---|
| 1) Bell toads, Ascaphidae | 1 species |
| 2) Spadefoots, Scaphiopodidae | 7 species and subspecies |
| 3) Toads, Bufonidae | 21 species and subspecies |
| 4) Tree toads, Hylidae | 30 species and subspecies |
| 5) Robber frogs, Leptodactylidae | 7 species |
| 6) Frogs, Ranidae | 28 species, subspecies and phases |
| 7) Narrow-mouthed toads, Brevicipitidae | 5 species |

Some of these families are divided into subfamilies. The ending for subfamily names is *inae*. Thus, the true frogs considered in this work belong to the family *Ranidae* and the subfamily *Raninae*.

The family is divided into genera and the genera into species.

Ordinarily a scientific name consists of three parts: the first name is the generic name, the second the specific name, and the third the author or describer who first gave the name. The specific Latin name serves as an adjective agreeing in gender and number with the generic name, which is treated as a noun. This is the binomial system of nomenclature. The meadow frog might serve as an example. It is called *Rana pipiens* Schreber. The generic name is written with a capital and the specific name with a small letter. If the species be divided into one or more subspecies or races, the name may consist of four parts, namely, genus, species, subspecies, and authority. Such a name is an example of trinomial nomenclature. The swamp cricket frogs, *Pseudacris nigrita* (Le Conte), may be divided into several subspecies written thus, *Pseudacris nigrita nigrita* (Le Conte); *P. n. septentrionalis* (Boulenger), etc. Notice that abbreviations may be employed after *Pseudacris* and *nigrita* have been spelled out once.

## CATEGORIES

| | | | |
|---|---|---|---|
| Kingdom | Animal | Subfamily | Raninae |
| Phylum | Vertebrata | Genus | *Rana* |
| Class | Amphibia | Species | *boylii* |
| Order | Salientia | Subspecies | *sierrae* |
| Family | Ranidae | Authority | Camp |

Name: *Rana boylii sierrae* Camp

[*Note:* Observe that we use in this edition another example, *Rana boylii sierrae* Camp. In the 1942 edition, we used *Rana pipiens burnsi* (Weed) with a purpose. Never have we been queried by youthful or elder scholars on any other issue as on this example. We employed it to stimulate work; unlike most of the critics, we saw these frogs in the field. Never did we seriously hold it to be a valid form, but in a book of this sort evidence ought to be presented with not too much youthful certainty or elderly obstinacy.]

**Specific evaluation of our North American forms.** About 70 of our 99 species or subspecies are, in our opinion, established on firm grounds. If all the recently described forms were as certain as *Ascaphus truei* Stejneger, *Rana virgatipes* Cope, *R. septentrionalis* Baird, *R. catesbeiana* Shaw, and *R. heckscheri* Wright, no hesitation would be manifest.

We have included accounts of all the forms of Stejneger and Barbour's check list. The last species, *R. heckscheri*, we never would have dared to describe from preserved specimens alone had we not first seen its queer tadpoles and heard its peculiar voice. Nevertheless, we frankly put it in the list of forms for which more evidence is needed. In other words, we need field studies and much more ample material on at least 29 forms. They may all be tenable, but calm judgment dictates that material alive and preserved, life histories, and other evidence be at hand before they rank with established forms like *A. truei, Scaphiopus couchii, Bufo debilis, Hyla gratiosa,* and *R. virgatipes.* The 29 forms that need more attention are as follows:

1) *Scaphiopus hammondii bombifrons*
2) *Scaphiopus hammondii intermontanus*
3) *Scaphiopus holbrookii albus*
4) *Bufo boreas nelsoni*
5) *Bufo californicus*
6) *Bufo exsul*
7) *Bufo compactilis* (of Southwest)
8) *Bufo hemiophrys*
9) *Bufo insidior*
10) *Acris crepitans*
11) *Pseudacris nigrita* (6 subspecies)
12) *Pseudacris occidentalis* (probably nonexistent)
13) *Hyla cinerea evittata*
14) *Hyla crucifer bartramiana*
15) *Hyla wrightorum*
16) *Hyla versicolor chrysoscelis*
17) *Hyla versicolor phaeocrypta* (*avivoca* may be the same)
18) *Eleutherodactylus augusti*
19) *Syrrhophus campi*
20) *Syrrhophus gaigeae*
21) *Rana areolata* (subspecies)
22) *Rana boylii* (subspecies)
23) *Rana cascadae*

24) *Rana pipiens burnsi* (color phase)
25) *Rana pipiens kandiyohi* (color phase)
26) *Rana pipiens* (subspecies of the check list)
27) *Rana sylvatica latiremis*
28) *Microhyla areolata*
29) *Microhyla mazatlanensis*

The 99 species and subspecies have been established on different criteria and degrees of variations. It is the age-old problem. What is a species or subspecies? Are similarities in measurements indicative of relationship or of the same environment (e.g., short mouths and short legs in northern forms in contrast to longer mouths and hind legs in southern forms)? Are rugosities (*Pseudacris, Acris, Microhyla, Scaphiopus*) sufficient for species or subspecific distinctions? Are they inherent or are they peculiar to certain southern or southwestern areas?

Is the absence of spots (*R. p. burnsi*) in a form derivative from a spotted form (*R. pipiens*) sufficient for a species, or is it a mutant, a recessive, or a metachroistic phase? We were of the group who had doubts regarding *R. p. burnsi* and *R. p. kandiyohi*, yet they were two types found among thousands of live frogs. Had they come as a few specimens (preserved material) in a collection from distant countries, we might with less knowledge have described them and accepted them readily.

The 29 forms listed above are some of the most interesting and engaging ones for future study, and extended comments upon each appear under the species accounts.

**Range:** Maps 1 to 3 give life zones of geographical distribution and rainfall. Maps 4 to 37 show species distribution. The core of this information will be found in *A Check List of North American Amphibians and Reptiles* by Leonhard Stejneger and Thomas Barbour (Cambridge: Harvard University Press, 1943). We have added our own records through the years and such records as we have found in some of the smaller collections.

The ranges were compiled from dot maps of all records for each form. They outline the outer bounds of each form but can in no way give all ecological evaluations each critic might wish. They are meant to give the layman a macroscopic view of the range of a species or subspecies without portraying individual dot records. Sometimes the map unavoidably includes a state in which there is no published or known record. Our ranges whenever they enter Mexico must be interpreted as approximate.

Geologic speculations: Many features must be weighed in a study of distribution. Tolerance of drought and of high or low temperatures, as well as the type of food and shelter available, must be considered. The respective ranges of tolerance of concentrations of salt, sulphur, borax, potash, or gypsum must be noted. The susceptibility of either tadpoles or adults may limit the range. Frogs are probably very responsive to the rock structure of their abodes, their

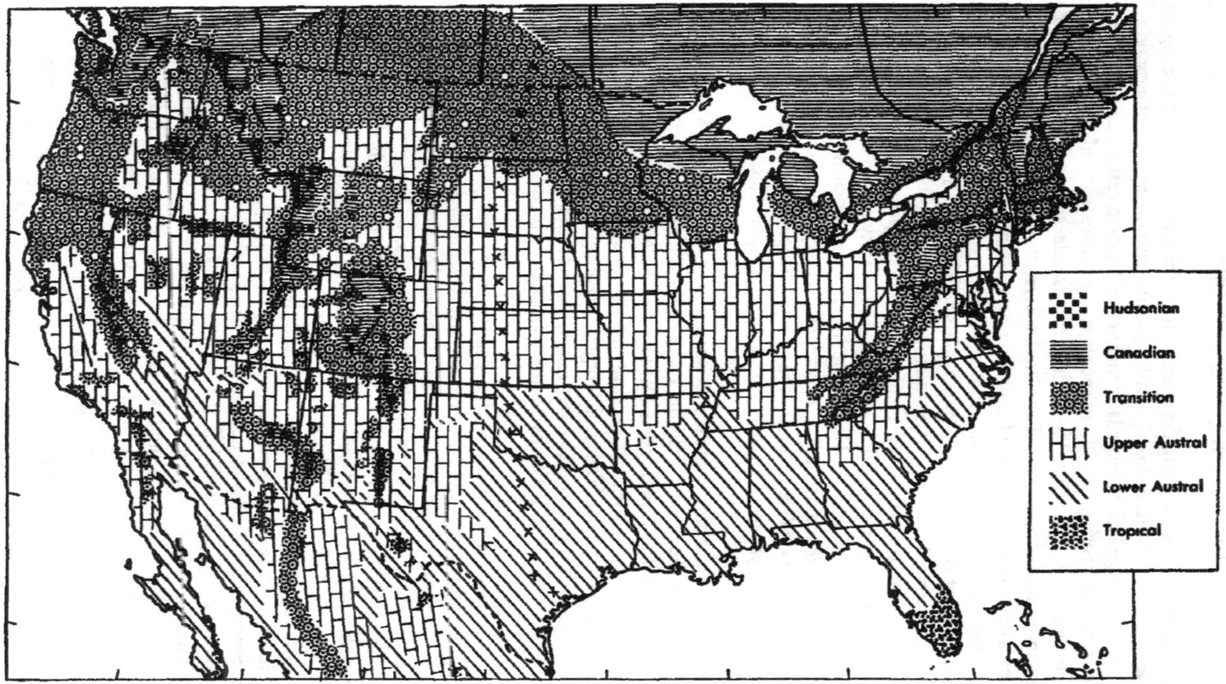


*Map 1.* Life zones. The humid sections of these zones are east of the line of crosses. (After Merriam.)

breeding spots, at least, being dependent upon the surface water of the region.

Do *Pseudacris* (cricket frogs) dislike granitic and other igneous situations? There is a strange lack of records of these small frogs in eastern Canada on the crystalline Laurentian Shield, although one form extends above the Arctic Circle west of Hudson Bay. The widespread *Pseudacris n. triseriata* (Map 18) stops short at the lava plains of the Snake River in Idaho but extends a knob of occurrence into the corner of that state near Montana where Carboniferous and Algonkian rocks occur and into northeastern Utah where there is limestone. Look at the range of *P. brachyphona* (Map 16). Those frogs seem to enjoy the carboniferous Pennsylvanian rocks of western Pennsylvania, West Virginia, corners of Ohio and Kentucky—the Allegheny Plateau. *P. n. feriarum* (Map 17) of Carlisle, Pa., occurs in the vicinity of Brunswick shale and other shales and limestones. Do marine limestone and marine shell marl help produce the rougher skin of *P. n. verrucosa* (Map 17)? Do those same marine limestones of Key West influence the color of *Scaphiopus h. albus* (Map 7), vary the *Microhyla* species (Map 37) of the region, or affect the ventral color of *Rana pipiens?*

Look for a moment at *Rana p. pretiosa* and *R. p. luteiventris* (Map 35). The latter tolerates the tertiary volcanic rocks of the Columbia River Plateau and ranges through the lava-infested Snake River Valley and its tributaries into northern Nevada, while *R. p. pretiosa* prefers the continental deposits in and west of the Willamette Valley of Oregon, crossing Washington and coming down, behind the *R. p. luteiventris* range, through the area of the Bitterroot Mountains and Grand Tetons to the Wasatch formations of northeastern Utah.

Does *Hyla c. evittata* live at the fringes of the range of *H. c. cinerea?* Around Washington, D.C., the first seems to be crowded onto the Cretaceous rock formations, leaving *H. c. cinerea* to the east on the marl, alum bluff, and limestones of the Miocene and on the alluvial sands.

We would all like to know more about finding the delicate little *Syrrhophus marnockii,* which chooses soft soil under stone or log shelter for habitat. Around San Marcos and Helotes, Tex., are Austin chalk, Eagle Ford shale, Edwards or Fredericksburg limestone, and the limestone to clay of the Washita group in close association. In Tom Green County, where this frog has been found, occur similar structures with the possibility of San Angelo sandstone and Blaine gypsum added. In Green Gulch, Chisos Mountains, we again find Eagle Ford shales, Fredericksburg limestone, Chisos sandstone tuff, touches of Washita group, and varying amounts of Austin chalk in close proximity. Does the different combination help vary the frogs' structure and pattern a bit, giving us *S. gaigeae?*

What does the robber frog (*Eleutherodactylus latrans*) like? Its distribution is surprising. For years it was known only from the region of San Antonio, Tex., and from Madera Canyon in the Santa Rita Mountains in

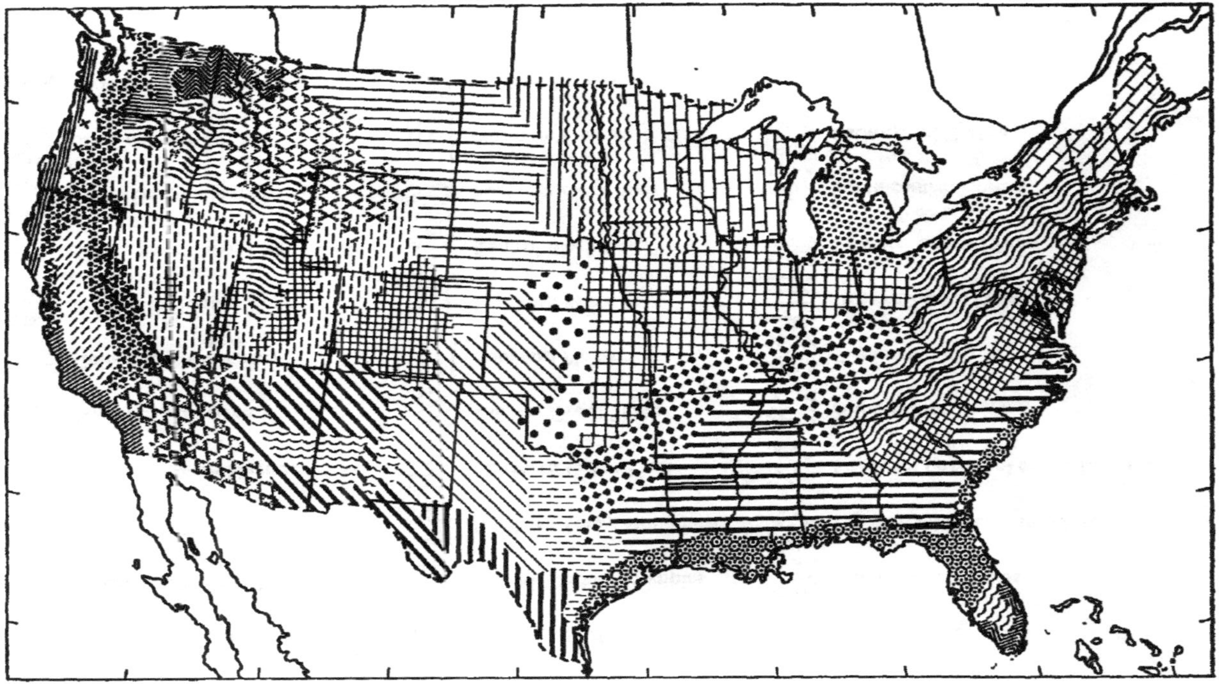

*Map 2.* Life zones. (After Van Dersal and Mulford.)

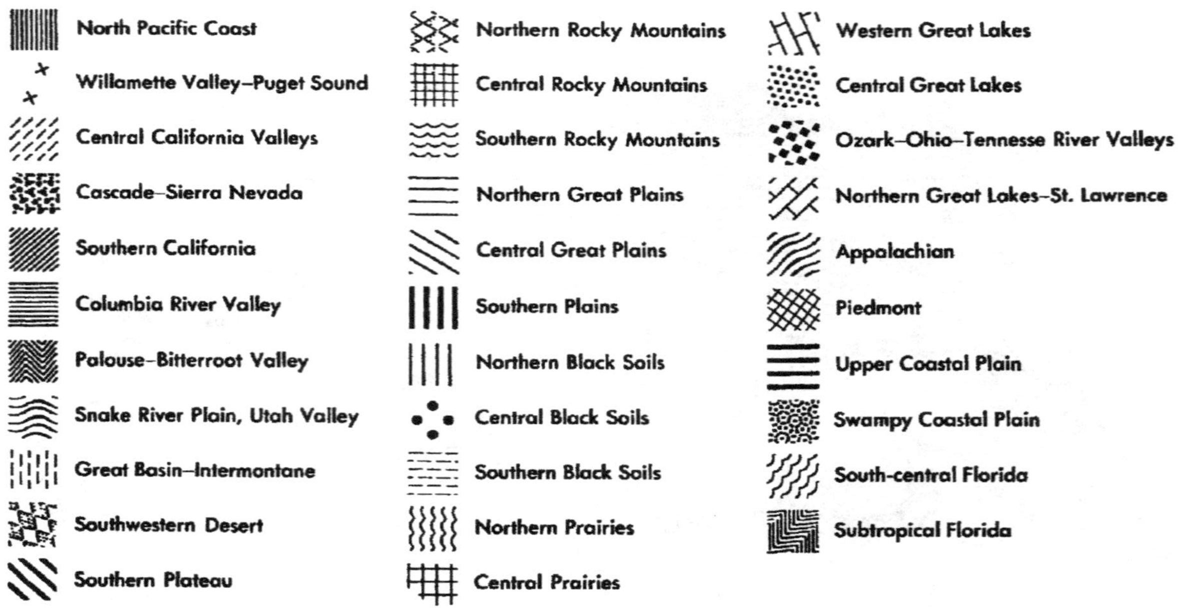
North Pacific Coast
Willamette Valley–Puget Sound
Central California Valleys
Cascade–Sierra Nevada
Southern California
Columbia River Valley
Palouse–Bitterroot Valley
Snake River Plain, Utah Valley
Great Basin–Intermontane
Southwestern Desert
Southern Plateau
Northern Rocky Mountains
Central Rocky Mountains
Southern Rocky Mountains
Northern Great Plains
Central Great Plains
Southern Plains
Northern Black Soils
Central Black Soils
Southern Black Soils
Northern Prairies
Central Prairies
Western Great Lakes
Central Great Lakes
Ozark–Ohio–Tennesse River Valleys
Northern Great Lakes–St. Lawrence
Appalachian
Piedmont
Upper Coastal Plain
Swampy Coastal Plain
South-central Florida
Subtropical Florida

Arizona, a separation of almost 1000 miles. It has recently been found in New Mexico near Carlsbad, a limestone and gypsum country, and is reported in Arizona north of Roosevelt Lake, from Parker Canyon, where there is also limestone. There are unusually good combinations of rock conditions around Helotes, Hondo, and Uvalde, Tex., to make desirable homesteads for this notional form. The breaks of the Balcones Fault occur at the front of the limestones of the Edwards plateau allowing water to come to the surface, and there is plentiful underground water. The several kinds of limestone conserve the water, and gypsum content easily washes out, leaving caves, cavities, and worn rock ledges readily available for shelter.

"Distribution of the Flora and Fauna of Louisiana in Relation to Its Geology and Physiography" (*La. Acad. Sci.*, 8, 11–73 [Dec., 1944]) shows well the interlocking of habitats, and Percy Viosca, Jr., explains (p. 55) how two forms, *Acris g. gryllus* and *A. g. crepitans*, may live in one pond separated by an invisible barrier, the one at the inlet where acid water from pinelands is present, the other at the outlet where the alkaline influence of the tide is felt.

Similar intimate studies of particular spots must be made before we can understand the apparent separation into broken spots and the apparent meeting of ranges of closely related forms.

**Habitat:** This topic usually refers to nonbreeding habitats, but at times allusions are made to breeding localities as well.

**Size:** The phrasing we have employed is: adults 3⅛–6⅝ inches (males, 80–156 mm.; females, 87–165 mm.). These are the measurements of the large Colorado River toad, *Bufo alvarius* Girard. They mean that breeding adults [illegible] from 3⅛ to 6⅝ inches in length of body from tip to snout to rear end [illegible] back of th[illegible] 3⅛ inches or 80 mm. is the smallest size at [illegible] ma[illegible] mature, and 6⅝ inches or 165 mm. is the largest size of any measured female. Almost invariably the lower measurement in inches will be that of a male, and the maximum adult measurement, the size of a female.

Jordan and Evermann considered the two killifishes, *Heterandria formosa* and *Lucania ommata*, the smallest vertebrates of North America. We have collected many of these tiny fish, but confidently pronounce the little chorus frog, *Pseudacris ocularis*, much smaller. Cuba, we understand, has a still smaller frog.

Most of the seven families have extremes in size. The tree frog adults vary from 7/16 inch (11.5 mm.) in the little chorus frog (*P. ocularis*) to 5⅛ inches (130 mm.) in the Key West tree frog (*Hyla septentrionalis*). The robber frog adults vary from ⅝ inch (15 mm.) in Camp's frog (*Syrrhophus campi*) to 3½ inches (90 mm.) in the Texas cliff frog (*Eleutherodactylus latrans*). The adult toads vary from ¾ inch (19 mm.) in the oak toad (*Bufo quercicus*) to 6⅝ inches (165 mm.) in the Colorado River toad (*B. alvarius*). The adult spadefoots vary from 1½ inches (37.5 mm.) in Hammond's spadefoot (*Scaphiopus h. hammondii*) to 2¾ inches (72 mm.) in Holbrook's spadefoot (*S. holbrookii*

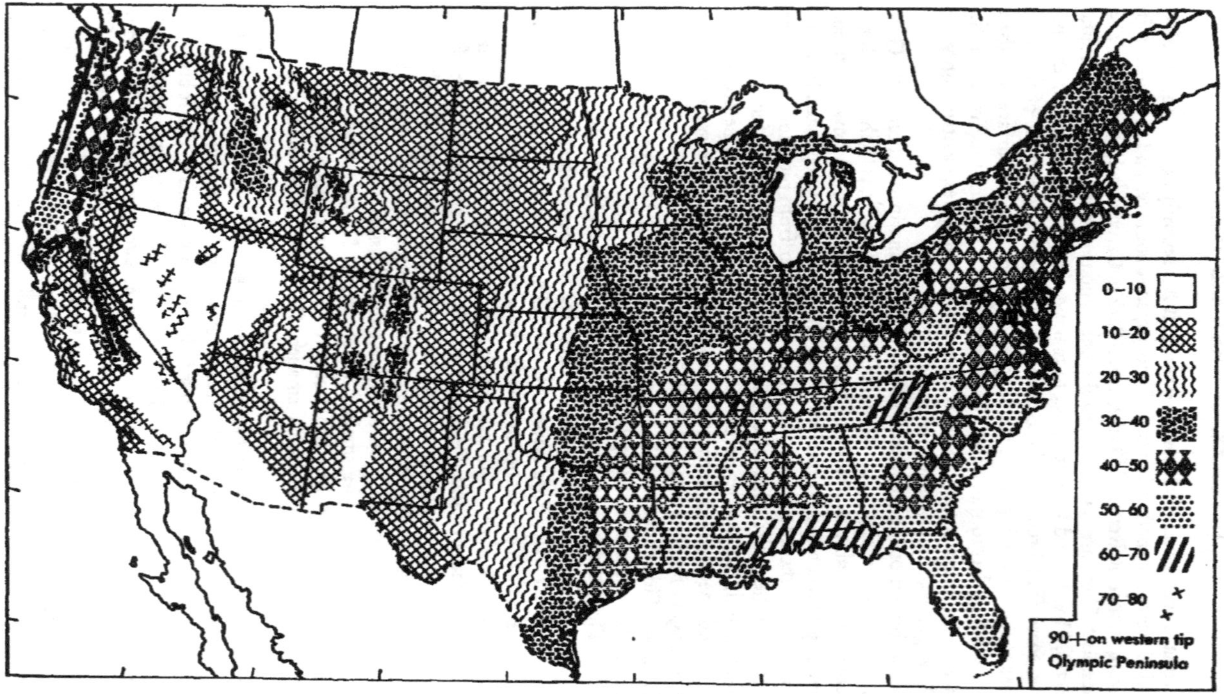


*Map 3.* Rainfall. (After Gannett.)

*holbrookii*). The adult frogs vary from 1⅜ inches (36 mm.) in the northern wood frog (*Rana s. cantabrigensis*) to 8 inches (200 mm.) in the bullfrog (*R. catesbeiana*). Two groups have little variation in their extremes. The narrow-mouthed toads vary in adults from ⅘ inch (20 mm.) in the Texas narrow-mouthed toad (*Microhyla olivacea*) to 1⅝ inches (41 mm.) in Taylor's toad (*Hypopachus cuneus*). The one species of ribbed toads (*Ascaphus truei*) varies from 1⅛ to 2 inches (28–51 mm.) in length.

**General appearance:** In most cases these accounts were written with a live specimen or specimens in hand. Each gives the form of body (habitus) of the animal, the color of the animal, and some of the other outstanding characters. Often the animal is compared to a closely related species or to the common type of the group.

**Color:** A consistent effort has been made to secure a color description from live specimens mainly in the field or occasionally in the laboratory. Each sex is described. It must be remembered each description is of a particular specimen. The description follows the Ridgway code (2d ed.), and his spelling. Any description not following this code is marked "non-Ridgway."

**Structure:** This section is meant to supplement the characters given under "General appearance" or to add to characters used in the keys. Whereas "General appearance" is written from living animals, "Structure" is added from examinations of preserved specimens and from published descriptions. Unless otherwise stated, all measurements in descriptions or keys are relative to the body length (represented by L.). "Structure" is written in the abbreviated form preferred in scientific descriptions. Very frequently the original description appears in this section.

**Voice:** Early travelers often commented on the frog music of our country. Witness the following:

"'There be also store of frogs, which in the spring time will chirp, and whistle like birds; there be also toads, that will creep to the top of trees, and sit there croaking, to the wonderment of strangers!"

"'To the stranger walking for the first time in these woods during the summer, this appears the land of enchantment; he hears a thousand noises, without being able to discern from whence or from what animal they proceed, but which are, in fact, the discordant notes of five different species of frogs!"

Previous to my coming to this country, I recollect reading the foregoing passages, the first in a history of New England, published in London, in the year 1671; and the other in a similar production of a later date.

Prepared as I was to hear something extraordinary from these animals, I confess the first frog *concert* I heard in America was so much beyond anything I could conceive of the *powers* of these *musicians*, that I was truly astonished. This performance was *al fresco*, and took place on the night of the 18th instant [April 18, 1794, Philadelphia], in a large *swamp*, where there were at least ten thousand *performers;* and I really believe not two *exactly* in the same pitch, if the octave can possibly admit of so many divisions or shades of semitones. An hibernian musician, who, like myself, was present for the first time at this *concert* of *antimusic,* exclaimed, "*Begorrah,* but they stop out of tune to a *nicety.*"

I have been since informed by an *amateur,* who resided many years in this country, and made this species of *music* his peculiar study that on these occasions the *treble* is performed by the tree-frogs, the smallest and most *beautiful* species; . . . their note is not unlike the chirp of a cricket: the next in size are our *counter tenors;* they have a note resembling the *setting* of a *saw.* A still larger species sing *tenor;* and the *under part* is supported by the bull-frogs; which are as large as a man's foot, and *bellow* out the *bass* in a tone as loud and sonorous as that of the animal from which they take their name.—William Priest, *Travels,* London, 1802, pp. 48–50.

Doubtless all males have voices, yet one has to be careful in such records. One of the phases of Pacific Coast frogs and toads about which all workers have the least evidence is the voice and vocal sacs; and it is a striking fact that *Rana boylii, R. aurora, R. pretiosa,* and *Bufo boreas* have no vocal sacs apparent in preserved specimens or particularly apparent in live individuals. Are they like some eastern forms, namely, *R. clamitans, R. catesbeiana,* and *R. sylvatica?*

The impression that Boulenger gives and the layman has, namely, that females are mute, is not exactly the situation. Let anyone pick up a female solitary spadefoot (*Scaphiopus holbrookii*) and squeeze it, and he might think he had a male. Those who know the species would recognize the difference between the male and the female voice. Or lay this same female on her back and stroke her belly, and she will speak vigorously, possibly not so strenuously as a male but nevertheless the voice is there. All spadefoot females can and do croak some. In the same way females of spadefoots, frogs, and some other groups can open the mouth and give a cry or scream note just as young bullfrogs have alarm notes as they go skipping to cover. Any field naturalist, if he has heard the peculiar cry of frogs and toads when in the grip of a snake or turtle, very well knows females can make themselves heard. The mercy cry of a toad or frog (like *R. catesbeiana, R. pipiens, R. p. sphenocephala, R. grylio,* or some Hylas) can be and is as likely to be that of a female as a male. Miss Dickerson is quite right in saying that females are not necessarily voiceless. Doubtless in time we will find many species with more or less vocal females.

Some of the adjectives employed in describing American frog notes are bubbling, weird, plaintive, hoarse, woeful, mournful, complaining, nasal, incessant, musical, pleasant, whistling, prolonged, mellow, tremulous, squawking, shrill, deafening, ventriloquial, peeping, metallic, resonant, twittering, loud, guttural, snoring, snorting, gurgling, clacking, explosive, grating, and sweet.

Man has attempted to characterize the voices of frogs since Aristophanes, but with varying success. Voice has been one of our most valuable clues on life histories, yet we must say it is hard for us to describe a call as others do. One's vehicle of description may be figures of speech, or it may be musical, phonetic, mechanical, graphic, or biological. Frog voices can be portrayed by tonal graphs. They are also presented on phonograph records, such as "Voices of the Night" (Comstock Publishing Company, Inc., Ithaca, New York).

Each species usually has its distinctive type of breeding song, yet each species may have several variations. *Hyla gratiosa* may bark in the high- long-leaved pines, but "coatbet" in the breeding pools. A peeper on its way to the pond might possibly call differently from one with the chorus. One might call differently in cold or warm weather, dry or rainy spells. The breeding song is usually typical, but one needs to beware of believing it is the same at all times. The main thing is to learn the quality of the song in order to be ready for its variations. Frogs can be as individualistic in this regard as are other animals.

It is a rather remarkable fact that one of the most frequent observations of earlier travelers (100 or 150 years ago) in this country was on the frog music of North America, but in the scientific names none suggest voice except in the early spring peepers (cricket frogs or savanna crickets, *Acris gryllus, A. crepitans;* chorus frogs or swamp cricket frogs, *Pseudacris*) and in three of the largest frogs, *R. clamitans, R. grylio,* and *R. pipiens.* In the same way common names suggesting voice are not frequent. None of the vociferous spadefoots, toads, and narrow-mouthed toads have common names suggesting their voices.

Several Hylas and others have come to be recognized as rain indicators.

If one knows the frog notes, he can in one night do more work on frog distribution than he might otherwise do in years. In one favorable night of auto riding from Lakehurst through southern New Jersey we located many colonies of *R. virgatipes* which might have escaped us entirely under other circumstances. The first record of a new form usually comes from a voice record. We never would have found our first *Microhyla* near Richmond, Va, or *H. andersonii* and *R. virgatipes* on an overnight camp near Everett Pond, N.C., without first hearing them. This was our method near San Antonio in 1925, namely, to go along the roads and listen until midnight or later and then pursue the species newly heard or most commonly calling that night.

The choruses of the Southeast are immense. Sometimes as many as five to eight species may be breeding in one place. At a distance it may be a perfect din but to wade among the performers one encounters a deafening concourse scarcely imaginable. Often we would have to devise methods of culling out predominant voices to catch others desired. Sometimes we would vary the pressure of our own ear openings or cup our ears to sift one particular call out of the chorus, e.g., *Hyla femoralis* would drown out *Bufo quercicus.*

**Vocal sacs** (Plate I): Doubtless all the males of our eastern species of frogs do croak and most of them have vocal sacs. Both males and females occasionally open their mouths to cry when in distress from teasing, alarm, injury, or capture, but all croaking males of the United States and Canada keep their mouths closed whether in air or under water.

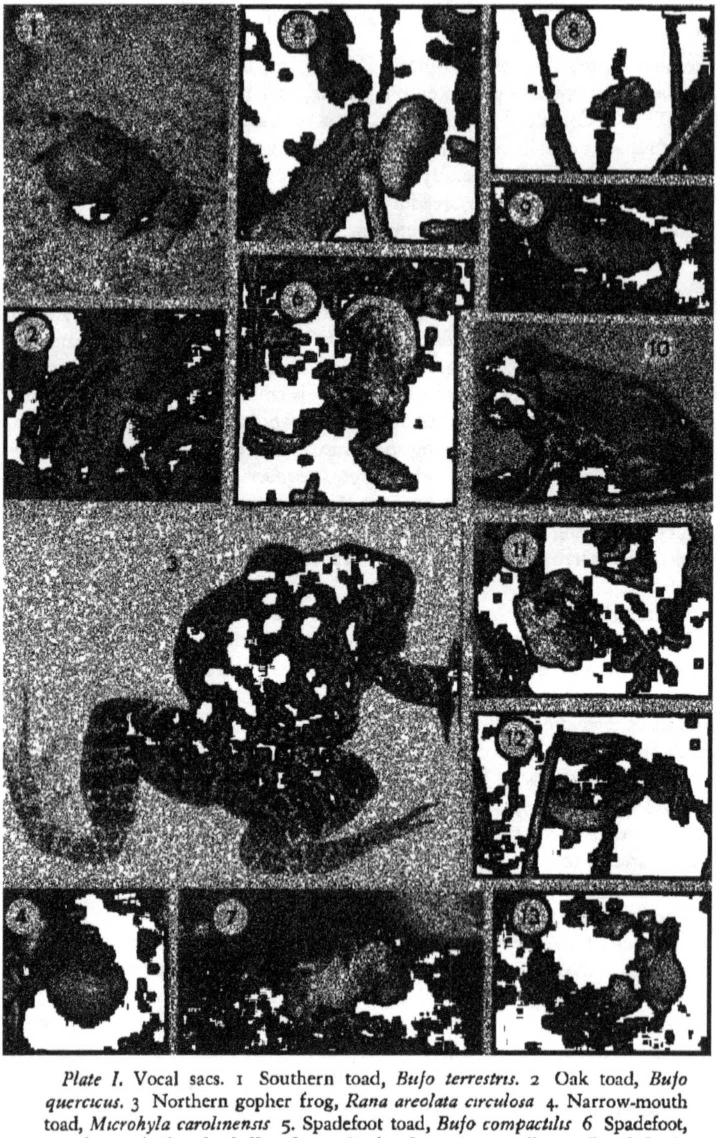

*Plate I.* Vocal sacs. 1 Southern toad, *Bufo terrestris.* 2 Oak toad, *Bufo quercicus.* 3 Northern gopher frog, *Rana areolata circulosa* 4. Narrow-mouth toad, *Microhyla carolinensis* 5. Spadefoot toad, *Bufo compactilis* 6 Spadefoot, *Scaphiopus holbrookii holbrookii.* 7. Cricket frog, *Acris gryllus gryllus* 8. Little chorus frog, *Pseudacris ocularis.* 9. Pine woods tree frog, *Hyla femoralis.* 10. Barker, *Hyla gratiosa.* 11 Gopher frog, *Rana capito* 12. Southern bullfrog, *Rana grylio.* 13 Sphagnum frog, *Rana virgatipes.*

Two of our students have made a study of vocal sacs. In 1931 Miss Rachel E. Field made a detailed portrayal (unpublished MS) of the vocal sacs of our eastern forms, and in 1935 Dr. C. C. Liu examined our American forms and made comparisons with world forms. Dr. Lui found the following: [1]

Vocal sacs and vocal sac openings absent (5):

*Ascaphus truei*
*Bufo halophilus*
*Rana aurora aurora*
*Rana boylii muscosa*
*Rana b. sierrae*

Median subgular internal sac and slitlike openings (17):

*Scaphiopus couchii*
*Scaphiopus hammondii*
*Scaphiopus holbrookii*
*Bufo alvarius*
*Bufo americanus*
*Bufo boreas*
*Bufo californicus*
*Bufo canorus*
*Bufo cognatus*
*Bufo hemiophrys*
*Bufo marinus*
*Bufo punctatus*
*Bufo terrestris*
*Bufo valliceps*
*Syrrhophus campi*
*Syrrhophus marnockii*
*Hyla femoralis*

Median subgular external sac and slitlike sac openings (24):

*Bufo compactilis*
*Bufo debilis*
*Bufo fowleri*
*Bufo quercicus*
*Bufo woodhousii*
*Acris gryllus*
*Hyla andersoni*
*Hyla arenicolor*
*Hyla avivoca*
*Hyla baudinii*
*Hyla cinerea*
*Hyla crucifer*
*Hyla gratiosa*
*Hyla regilla*
*Hyla squirella*
*Hyla versicolor versicolor*
*Hyla v. chrysoscelis*
*Pseudacris brachyphona*
*Pseudacris nigrita*
*Pseudacris ocularis*
*Pseudacris ornata*
*Pseudacris triseriata*
*Microhyla carolinensis*
*Microhyla texensis*

Median subgular sac internal and round sac openings (1):

*Hyla septentrionalis*

Median subgular sac external and round vocal openings (0).

Paired subgular sacs internal and slitlike openings (0).

Paired subgular sacs external and round openings (0).

Paired subgular sacs internal and round openings (1):

*Rana palmipes*

Paired lateral sacs internal and slitlike openings (2):

*Rana sylvatica latiremis*
*Rana septentrionalis*

[1] The names are those used by Dr. Liu in his thesis.

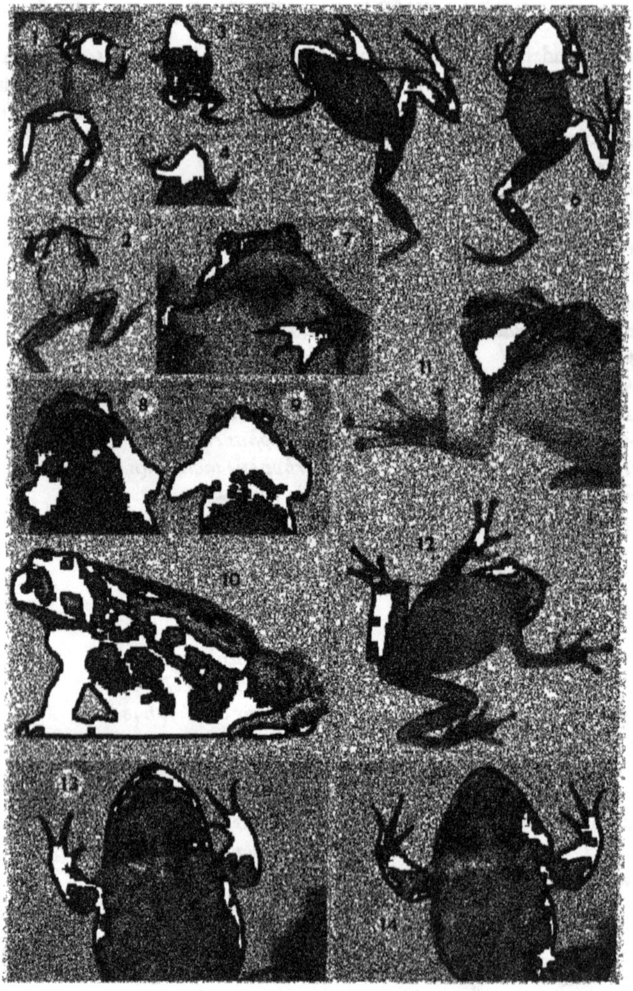

*Plate II* Throat differences in male and female 1. Cricket frog, *Acris gryllus crepitans,* male. 2. Cricket frog, *A. g. crepitans,* female. 3. Narrow-mouth toad, *Microhyla carolinensis,* male. 4. Narrow-mouth toad, *M carolinensis,* female. 5. Eastern chorus frog, *Pseudacris nigrita feriarum,* female 6. Eastern chorus frog, *P. n feriarum,* male 7. Spadefoot toad, *Bufo compactilis,* male (rear throat with pleats or lappet) 8. Southern toad, *Bufo terrestris,* female 9 Southern toad, *B. terrestris,* male. 10. Great Plains toad, *Bufo cognatus,* male (rear throat dark). 11. Barker, *Hyla gratiosa,* male 12. Barker, *H. gratiosa,* female. 13. River-swamp frog, *Rana heckscheri,* female 14. River-swamp frog, *R. heckscheri,* male.

Paired lateral sacs internal and round openings (9):

*Rana boylii boylii*
*Rana catesbeiana*
*Rana grylio*
*Rana palustris*
*Rana pipiens*
*Rana pretiosa*
*Rana septentrionalis*
*Rana sphenocephala*
*Rana sylvatica*

Paired lateral sacs external and round openings (5):

*Rana aesopus*
*Rana areolata*
*Rana clamitans*
*Rana draytonii*
*Rana montezumae*

These two were careful workers, yet we wish more information on live males to answer such inquiries as the following:

1. Why should *Bufo boreas* and *B. b. halophilus* be in different categories? Or *Rana aurora* and *R. a. draytonii*? Or *R. boylii* and *R. b. sierrae, R. b. muscosa*?

2. Why is *Bufo cognatus* out of the *B. compactilis, B. debilis, B. quercicus* class?

3. Why is *Hyla femoralis* unlike our other Hylids (except *H. septentrionalis*)?

4. Why is *R. sylvatica* unlike *R. s. cantabrigensis* or *R. s. latiremis*?

**Color of throat** (Plate II): In *Ascaphus truei, Syrrhophus campi, S. marnockii, Eleutherodactylus ricordii, E. latrans, Bufo b. boreas, B. b. halophilus, R. s. cantabrigensis, R. aurora, R. boylii, R. pretiosa, R. sylvatica,* the color of the throat of the male is little different from that of the female. These are forms with no prominent vocal sacs. In *R. palustris, R. pipiens, R. p. sphenocephala, R. capito,* and *R. areolata,* forms with lateral sacs, only slight differences occur in the throat color. In the narrow-mouths each sex may have a dark throat. Usually the male's throat is darker, but it is often difficult to use this criterion. Sometimes in *Scaphiopus holbrookii* and *S. couchii* the difference is not readily recognizable. In *S. hammondii* enough of the dark slaty or bluish cast appears in the male's throat to distinguish it.

The pronounced differences in throat coloration come in the Hylidae (except *Pseudacris ocularis*), Bufonidae, and Ranidae. Only seven of the twenty-one forms of *Rana* have this marked difference. These tend to have yellows (sulphur yellow, maize yellow, sulphine yellow, oil yellow, lemon yellow, olive ocher, aniline yellow, primuline yellow, or barium yellow) in the males, and in the females lighter washes of yellow or white; e.g., the green frog (*R. clamitans*) male has a barium yellow throat, the female a white throat. If each has the same yellow the male may have dark spots or some other equally striking character.

The whole throat of some species of toads will be discolored or darker than the rest of the venter, or only the lower part of the throat may be thus colored, as in the sausage group (*Bufo cognatus, B. quercicus, B. compactilis*).

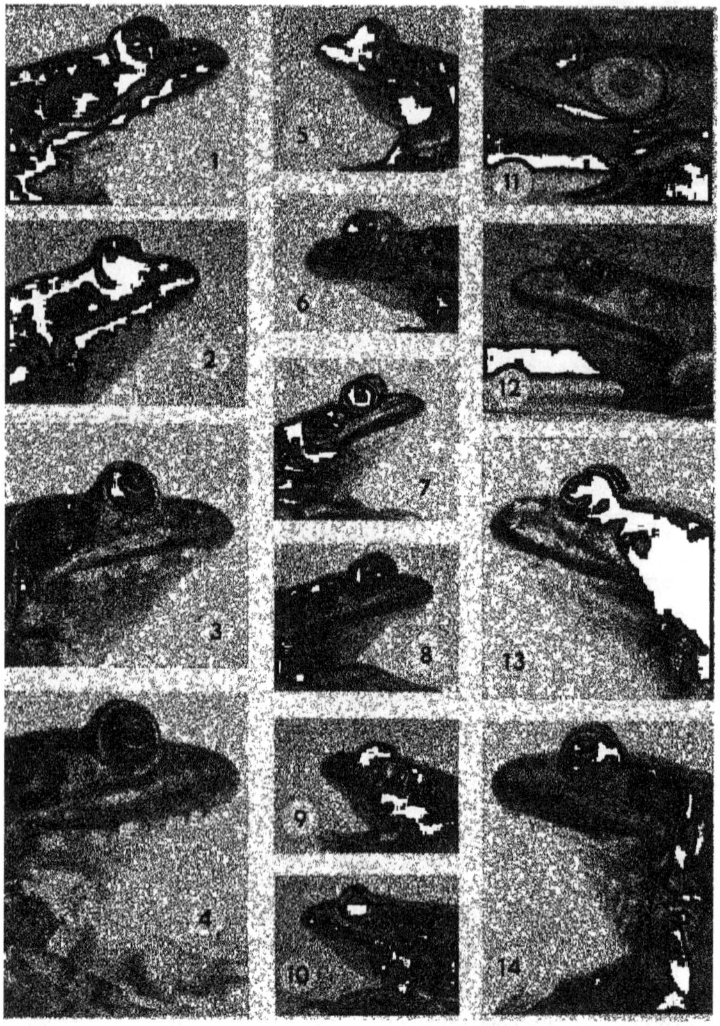


*Plate III.* Enlarged tympana in male Ranas (seven species) 1 Green frog, *R clamitans,* male 2. Green frog, *R clamitans,* female 3 River-swamp frog, *R heckscheri,* male 4 River-swamp frog, *R. heckscheri,* female 5 Mink frog, *R. septentrionalis,* male 6. Mink frog, *R septentrionalis,* female 7 Sphagnum frog, *R. virgatipes,* male 8 Sphagnum frog, *R virgatipes,* female 9 Nevada frog *R. fisheri,* male 10 Nevada frog, *R. fisheri,* female. 11 Southern bullfrog, *R grylio,* male 12. Southern bullfrog, *R grylio,* female. 13. Bullfrog, *R. catesbeiana,* male 14 Bullfrog, *R catesbeiana,* female.

In the Hylidae, *Pseudacris* (except *P. ocularis*), *Acris*, and *Hyla* have the throat dark and the female has the throat white or like the rest of the venter. In the group to which *Hyla cinerea cinerea*, *H. c. evittata*, *H. gratiosa*, and *H. andersonii* belong, the males have the whole throat or most of the throat dark or green, but the females have green on either side of the throat below and ahead of the angle of the jaw. In the two subspecies of *H. cinerea* females the color varies in degree of extension of green on sides of throat. In *H. gratiosa* females the green extension is more or less demarcated on the throat side with a prominent white border, and in *H. andersonii* this white border becomes clearly defined in females.

In general, males, being more active, are inclined to darker colors on the dorsum than the females. In a mated pair this is often quite noticeable, but even in those not mated the contrast may be very pronounced. This discrepancy is marked in early spring breeders but also obtains for later breeders. So also old males incline more to self-color (witness *Rana*, etc.) than the females, which may be more spotted. Or if a pattern be common to each, it will be bright in the female (e.g., *Scaphiopus holbrookii* females may have yellowish or buffy stripes or spots on back and the males may be almost uniform).

**Enlarged tympana, males** (Plate III): The seven species of frogs (*Rana*) in which the throats of the males may be differently colored from those of the females have even more marked differences in the tympana. These seven species first breed at about 41 mm. for *R. virgatipes*, 44 mm. for *R. fisheri*, 48 mm. for *R. septentrionalis*, 52 mm. for *R. clamitans*, 82 mm. for *R. heckscheri* and *R. grylio*, and 85 mm. for *R. catesbeiana*.

## BREEDING SIZES

| *Name* | *Males* | *Females* |
|---|---|---|
| | *mm.* | *mm.* |
| Ascaphidae | | |
| *Ascaphus truei* | 29–43 | 28–51 |
| Scaphiopodidae | | |
| *Scaphiopus h. bombifrons* | 38–56 | 43–56 |
| *Scaphiopus h. intermontanus* | 40–59 | 42–63 |
| *Scaphiopus h. hammondii* | 42–52 | 44–52.5 |
| *Scaphiopus h. hurteri* | 43–73 | 44–82 |
| *Scaphiopus couchii* | 48–70 | 50–80 |
| *Scaphiopus holbrookii* | 54–72 | 50–71 |

| *Name* | *Males* | *Females* |
|---|---|---|
| | Bufonidae | |
| *Bufo quercicus* | 19–30 | 20–32 |
| *Bufo debilis* | 26–45 | 31–52 |
| *Bufo insidior* | — | — |
| *Bufo punctatus* | 40–68 | 42–74 |
| *Bufo a. copei* | 40 | 75 |
| *Bufo w. fowleri* | 41–74.5 | 56–82 |
| *Bufo b. nelsoni* | 42–68 | 46–89 |
| *Bufo terrestris* | 42–82 | 44–88 |
| *Bufo californicus* | 44–58 | 44–68 |
| *Bufo exsul* | 44–59 | 46–65 |
| *Bufo canorus* | 46–64 | 45–74 |
| *Bufo cognatus* | 47–95 | 60–99 |
| *Bufo compactilis* | 52–78 | 54–91 |
| *Bufo a. americanus* | 54–85 | 56–110 |
| *Bufo valliceps* | 53–98 | 54–125 |
| *Bufo hemiophrys* | 56–68 | 56–80 |
| *Bufo w. woodhousii* | 56–99 | 58–118 |
| *Bufo b. boreas* | 56–108 | 60–110 |
| *Bufo b. halophilus* | 62–101 | 60–116 |
| *Bufo alvarius* | 80–156 | 87–165 |
| *Bufo marinus* | | –220 |
| | Hylidae | |
| *Acris g. gryllus* | 15–29 | 16–33 |
| *Acris g. crepitans* | 17–30 | 20–35 |
| *Pseudacris ocularis* | 11.5–15.5 | 12–17.5 |
| *Pseudacris n. septentrionalis* | 19–32 | 19–35 |
| *Pseudacris n. clarkii* | 20–29 | 21–31 |
| *Pseudacris n. nigrita* | 21–28 | 22–30 |
| *Pseudacris n. feriarum* | 21–30 | 22–35 |
| *Pseudacris n. triseriata* | 21–32 | 20–37.5 |
| *Pseudacris n. verrucosa* | 22 | 30 |
| *Pseudacris brimleyi* | 24–28 | 27–32.5 |
| *Pseudacris brachyphona* | 24–32 | 27–34 |
| *Pseudacris ornata* | 25–35 | 32–36 |
| *Pseudacris streckeri* | 25–41 | 32–48 |
| *Hyla crucifer* | 18–29 | 20–33 |
| *Hyla squirella* | 23–36 | 23–37 |

| *Name* | *Males* | *Females* |
|---|---|---|
| | *mm.* | *mm.* |
| *Hyla femoralis* | 24–37 | 23–40 |
| *Hyla wrightorum* | 24–38 | 24–42 |
| *Hyla regilla* | 25–48 | 25–47 |
| *Hyla v. phaeocrypta* | 28?–33 | 32?–36 |
| *Hyla avivoca* | 28–39 | 32–49 |
| *Hyla arenicolor* | 29–53 | 29–53 |
| *Hyla andersonii* | 30–41 | 38–47 |
| *Hyla v. versicolor* | 32–51 | 33–60 |
| *Hyla v. chrysoscelis* | 36–43 | 35–49 |
| *Hyla c. evittata* | 36–47 | 32–47 |
| *Hyla c. cinerea* | 37–59 | 41–63 |
| *Hyla baudinii* | 44–71 | 44–89 |
| *Hyla septentrionalis* | 46–75 | 52.5–95 |
| *Hyla gratiosa* | 49–68 | 50–68 |
| | Leptodactylidae | |
| *Eleutherodactylus r. planirostris* | 15–25 | 17–30 |
| *Syrrhophus campi* | 15–23 | 15–25 5 |
| *Syrrhophus gaigeae* | 21 | 28 |
| *Syrrhophus marnockii* | 21–33 | 22–39.5 |
| *Leptodactylus labialis* | 35? | –49 |
| *Eleutherodactylus latrans* | 48–74 | 57–90 |
| | Ranidae | |
| *Rana s. cantabrigensis* | 29–50 | 34–56 |
| *Rana sylvatica* | 34–60 | 34–68 or 82 |
| *Rana b. boylii* | 39–67 | 40–75 |
| *Rana virgatipes* | 41–63 | 41–66 |
| *Rana fisheri* | 44–64 | 46–74 |
| *Rana b. sierrae* | 44–72 | 48–84 |
| *Rana onca* | 44–68 | 51–84 |
| *Rana a. aurora* | 44–63 | 52–87 |
| *Rana p. pretiosa* | 44–75 | 46–95 |
| *Rana p. luteiventris* | — | — |
| *Rana b. muscosa* | 45–66 | 47–81 |
| *Rana palustris* | 46–64 | 49–79 |
| *Rana septentrionalis* | 46–71 | 48–76 |

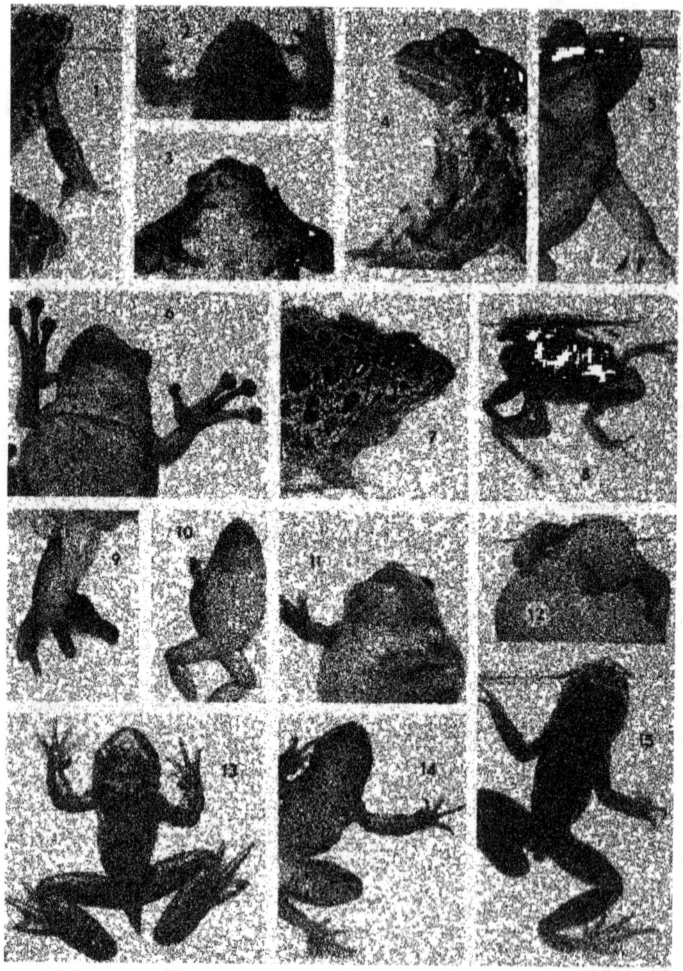

*Plate IV.* Secondary sexual characters. 1 Enlarged thumb, single pad, *Rana pipiens pipiens,* male. 2 Horny excrescences on thumb and first finger, *Bufo americanus americanus,* male. 3. Enlarged thumb, double pad, *Rana boylii muscosa,* male 4 Enlarged forearm, *Bufo boreas boreas,* male. 5 Horny excrescences on thumb and first finger, *Scaphiopus holbrookii holbrookii,* male. 6 Prepollex, *Hyla septentrionalis* 7 Plaited lateral vocal sac, *Rana areolata circulosa,* male 8 Dimorphism in mating pair, male smaller, darker, female larger, lighter, *Hyla crucifer crucifer* 9. Horny excrescences on arm and fingers, *Bufo alvarius,* male 10. Longitudinal throat plaits, *Pseudacris nigrita feriarum,* male 11 Double throat sac, *Hyla baudinii,* male 12. Apron over concealed lower throat sac, *Bufo cognatus,* male. 13. Tail and thumb pad, *Ascaphus truei,* male. 14. Excrescences on thumb pad and forearm, *A truei,* male. 15. Anal tube, *A. truei,* female.

| Name | Males | Females |
|---|---|---|
| | mm. | mm. |
| *Rana p. sphenocephala* | 49–78 | 53–82 |
| *Rana cascadae* | 50–58 | 52–74 |
| *Rana p. pipiens* | 52–80 | 52–102 |
| *Rana clamitans* | 52–95 | 58–100 |
| *Rana tarahumarae* | 58 | –113 |
| *Rana a draytonii* | 63–100 | 58–136 |
| *Rana capito* | 68–101 | 77–108 |
| *Rana a. areolata* | — | — |
| *Rana sevosa* | -84 | -92.5 |
| *Rana grylio* | 82–152 | 85–161 |
| *Rana heckscheri* | 82–131 | 102–131 |
| *Rana catesbeiana* | 85–180 | 89–200 |
| Brevicipitidae | | |
| *Microhyla olivacea* | 20–28 | 19–29.5 |
| *Microhyla carolinensis* | 20–30 | 22–36 |
| *Microhyla areolata* | 24–28 | 23–30 |
| *Hypopachus cuneus* | 28–37.5 | 36– |

## SUMMARY OF SECONDARY SEXUAL CHARACTERS

(Plate IV)

A. Thumb enlarged in male (Ranidae and *H. septentrionalis*)
  B. Enlarged tympana (*Rana clamitans* group)
    C. Males have external vocal sacs; males 41–71 mm., females 41–76 mm. (*Rana virgatipes* group: *R. fisheri, R. septentrionalis, R. virgatipes*)
    CC. Males without external vocal sacs; males first breeding at 82–85 mm., females 82–89 mm., except *R. clamitans* males 52–95 mm., females 58–100 mm. (*Rana catesbeiana* group: *R. catesbeiana, R. clamitans, R. grylio, R. heckscheri*)
  BB. No enlarged tympana
    C. Base of thumb swollen but no prethumb expansion (prepollex)
      D. No external vocal sacs
        E. Thumb pad in two parts with oblique groove (*Rana boylii*, 3 subsp., and *R. aurora* group somewhat, 3 forms)

EE. Thumb pad or enlargement not in two parts; web of hind foot of male more or less convex (*Rana sylvatica* group: *R. s. sylvatica, R. s. cantabrigensis, R. p. pretiosa*)

DD. External lateral vocal sacs; webbing margin of hind foot not modified in male

CC. Base of thumb enlarged with a striking prethumb expansion or prepollex (*Hyla septentrionalis*)

AA. Thumbs not enlarged nor ball-like nor padlike at base

B. Black or dark excrescences on first, second, and third fingers

C. "Tail" in male; excrescences on breast and inner edge of forearm; fore limb and hind limb enlarged, and hind foot also in male (*Ascaphus truei*)

CC. No "tail" nor excrescences on breast or forearm

D. No median vocal sac or darkened throat in males, with heavy forearms (*Bufo boreas* group; *B. b. boreas, B. b. halophilus*)

DD. Median vocal sac present in male

E. Vocal sac in lower throat (in alcohol, apron or biblike), darkened in male (*Bufo cognatus* or sausage group: *B. cognatus, B. compactilis, B. quercicus*)

EE. Vocal sac not principally from lower throat

F. Throat slightly discolored and finger excrescences not very prominent (*Bufo punctatus* group: *B. punctatus, B. debilis*)

FF. Excrescences normal and throat discolored (*Bufo americanus* group: *B. a. americanus, B. w. fowleri, B. terrestris, B. w. woodhousii, B. hemiophrys, B. valliceps*)

FFF. Arm broader in male; excrescences cover whole of upper fingers and first finger excrescence extends onto wrist (*Bufo alvarius*)

FFFF. Excrescences on top of fingers, not inner edge primarily; throats little discolored (*Scaphiopus* group)

BB. No black or dark excrescences on fingers

C. Throat of males with median sac—revealed in alcohol by wrinkles, folds, plaits, or darker color (Hylidae, Leptodactylidae)

D. Throat not discolored in male or particularly unlike that of female (Leptodactylidae, 5 species)

DD. Throat discolored in male or particularly unlike that of female (Hylidae: *Acris, Pseudacris, Hyla*)

E. Distinctly discolored (*Acris, Pseudacris,* some Hylas)

EE. Not so distinctly colored in male (Hylas)

F. Females with green on throat (*Hyla cinerea* group)

G. Green edged inside by white line (*Hyla gratiosa, H. andersonii*)

GG. Green not so edged (*Hyla cinerea cinerea, H. c. evittata*)

FF. Females with throat like rest of venter (*Hyla avivoca, H. arenicolor, H. crucifer, H. femoralis, H. squirella, H. versicolor*)

DDD. Throat discolored in male and female, less so in latter (*Microhyla*)

CC. Males with paired vocal sacs below angles of jaw (*H. baudinii*)

**Ovulation** (Plates V–IX): The vast bulk of frog species are in the South and Southwest, the warmer climes. In the North activity begins with the going out of ice or the first warming of spring and moisture. Most of our texts have been written for the northeastern states where few species occur, and so many writers have concluded that all frogs breed in early spring because *Rana sylvatica, R. pipiens,* and *Hyla crucifer* do. In the same way, many thought all salamanders breed in early spring because *Ambystoma maculatum, A. jeffersonianum,* and *A. tigrinum* do.

It is hard to classify species on one set of observations in one locality or region. A species may be a short, early breeder in the northeastern states, e.g., *Rana pipiens,* yet lay eggs in July in Devil's River, Tex. A bullfrog may lay normally in June or July but, under peculiar circumstances, lay in February in San Antonio, Tex. A *R. sphenocephala* might breed early in February or almost any month in the South, and we might think it would be restricted in the North; yet we find it breeding in Wabash Valley, Ill., in September. Even in the North *Bufo americanus, B. fowleri, Scaphiopus holbrookii,* and *R. clamitans* stretch the ovulation periods—a condition more normal in the South and Southwest.

The spadefoots, toads, small tree frogs such as *Acris* and *Pseudacris,* some larger tree frogs (*Hyla squirella, H. femoralis, H. crucifer, H. regilla*), and a few Ranas spawn in transient pools, impermanent situations, roadside ditches, and temporary floodlands, and often the loss must be immense. In the North *Rana sylvatica, R. s. cantabrigensis,* and *R. pipiens* masses may be caught by the surface ice of spring freezes. Next to the losses in toads and spadefoots, we believe the species with small surface films suffer the most from complete drying up of pools, thus being hung up by evaporation above a pond's level.

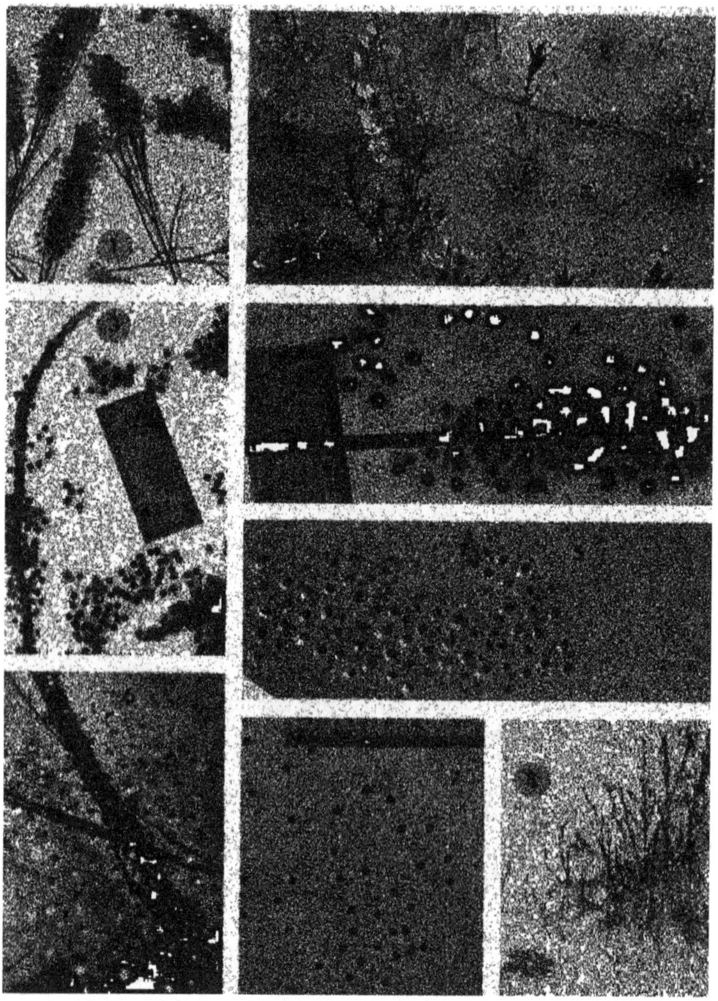

*Plate V.* Eggs. spadefoots, narrow-mouth toads (*Scaphiopus, Microhyla*). 1,8. Hammond's spadefoot, *S hammondii hammondii*. 2,4. Spadefoot, *S holbrookii holbrookii*. 3. Couch's spadefoot, *S. couchii* 5 Texas narrow-mouth toad, *M. olivacea*. 6,7 Narrow-mouth toad, *M. carolinensis*.

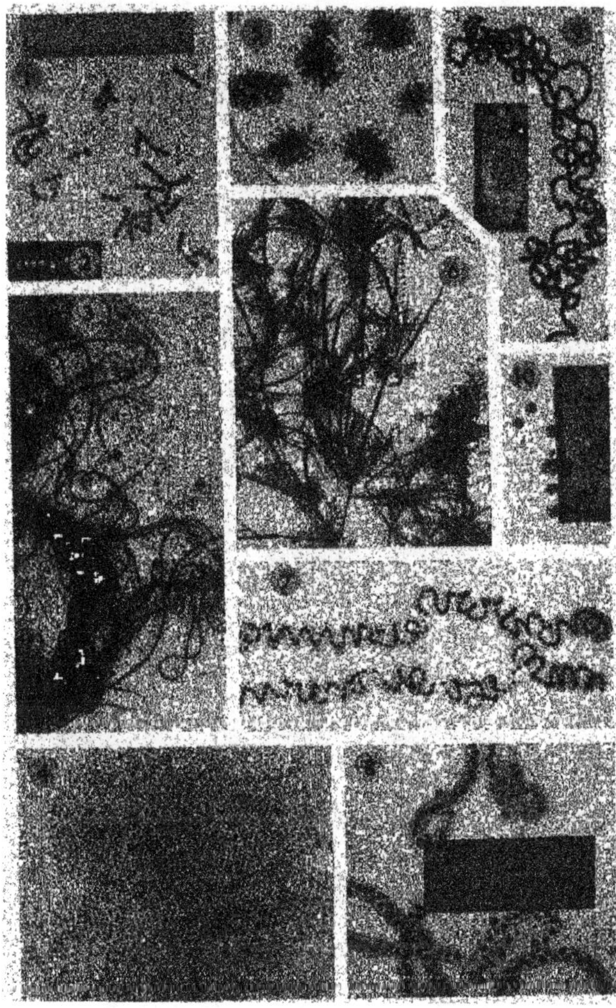

*Plate VI* Eggs. toads (*Bufo*) 1,2,5. Oak toad, *B quercicus* 3,8. Nebulous toad, *B. valliceps*. 4,10. Spotted toad, *B punctatus* 6. Southern toad, *B. terrestris*. 7. American toad, *B. americanus americanus*. 9. Spadefoot toad, *B. compactilis*.

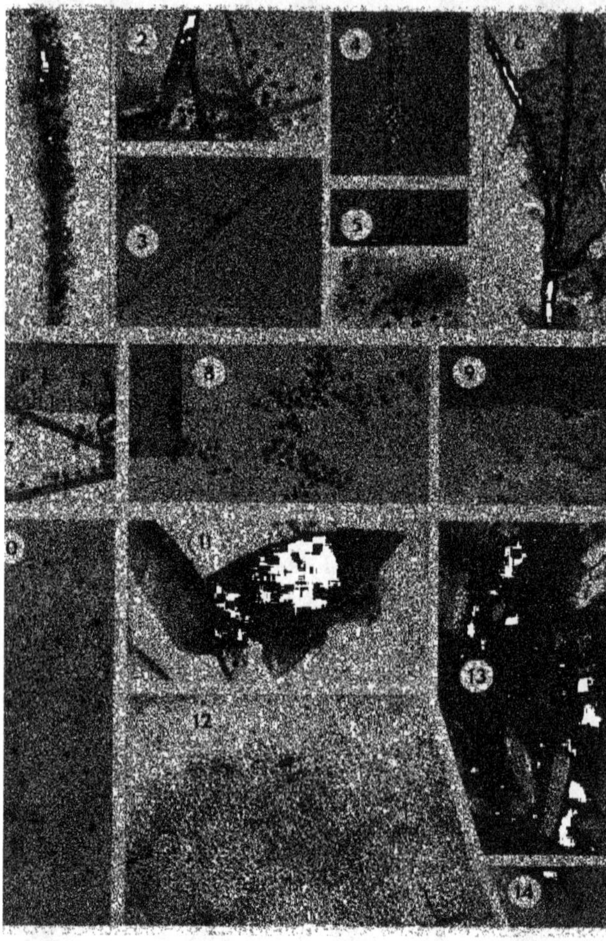

*Plate VII* Eggs: cricket frog, chorus frog, tree toad (*Acris, Pseudacris, Hyla*). 1. Little chorus frog, *P. ocularis* 2,5. Eastern chorus frog, *P. nigrita feriarum.* 3. Cricket frog, *A gryllus gryllus* 4 Clarke's chorus frog, *P. n. clarkii.* 6. Striped tree frog, *P n. triseriata* 7 Peeper, *H crucifer crucifer.* 8 Squirrel tree frog, *H. squirella.* 9. Green tree frog, *H. cinerea.* 10,13. Pine woods tree frog, *H. femoralis.* 11 Common tree toad, *H versicolor versicolor.* 12,14. Barker, *H. gratiosa.*

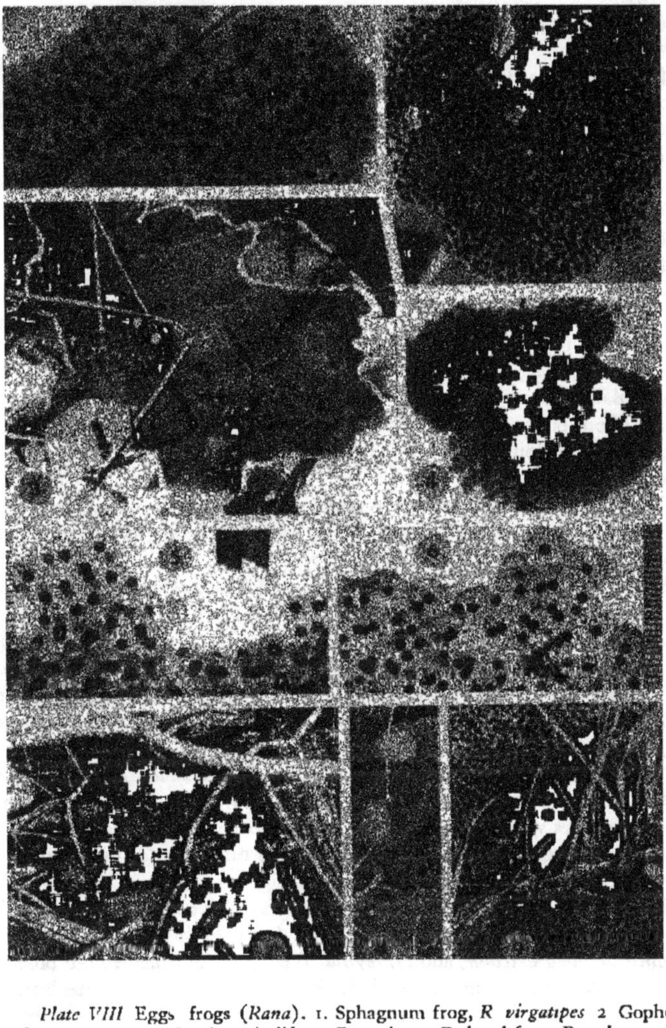

*Plate VIII* Eggs frogs (*Rana*). 1. Sphagnum frog, *R virgatipes* 2 Gopher frog, *R. capito* 3 Southern bullfrog, *R. grylio* 4 Pickerel frog, *R palustris.* 5. California yellow-legged frog, *R. boylii boylii.* 6. Nevada spotted frog, *R. pretiosa luteiventris.* 7. Bullfrog, *R catesbeiana* 8 Wood frog, *R. sylvatica sylvatica.* 9. Green frog, *R clamitans.*

*Egg-laying process:* The egg forms may be summarized as follows:

(1) Single eggs each singly ovulated after movement of pair, e.g., *Hyla crucifer.*

(2) Single eggs, several strewn at one time followed by movement, e.g., several Hylas.

(3) Single eggs laid as in (2) or small egg packets at surface, then movement by pair, e.g., *Hyla cinerea.*

(4) Small packets of eggs ovulated at one time at the surface, movement by pair, e.g., *Hyla versicolor.*

(5) Small packets of eggs ovulated at one time, no movement of pair and a resultant large film at the surface, e.g., *Rana catesbeiana.*

(6) Eggs laid in two rosarylike strings, e.g., *Ascaphus truei.*

(7) Files (three- or two- or one-rowed), movement from place to place by pair, e.g., Bufos.

(8) Bands, later swollen to cylinders, regular or irregular, like two films coalesced or two oviducal emissions merged; movement from bottom or base of stem to tip, e.g., *Scaphiopus.*

(9) Balls, lumps, spheres, or plinths, merged oviducal emissions; maintenance of one position by pair during entire process or for many emissions, e.g., meadow frogs, gopher frogs, wood frogs, Pacific Coast frogs; *Rana virgatipes* and *R. septentrionalis.*

The series is not so simple as it is given above because of movement or nonmovement, surface or submerged laying, size of frog, egg complement, and season.

**Eggs:** The species of the United States and Canada whose eggs are not recorded are *Scaphiopus holbrookii albus, Bufo californicus, B. exsul, B. hemiophrys, Hyla avivoca, H baudinii, Syrrhophus campi, S. gaigeae, S marnockii, Rana boylii muscosa, R. heckscheri, R. fisheri, R onca, Microhyla areolata, M. mazatlanensis*—15 in all. Breeding notes have been made but egg descriptions are lacking for *Bufo boreas boreas, B debilis, Pseudacris ornata, P. nigrita nigrita, P. n. septentrionalis, Hyla cinerea evittata, H. wrightorum, H. versicolor chrysoscelis, Eleutherodactylus latrans, Rana areolata areolata, R. sylvatica cantabrigensis, R. cascadae*—12 in all. Of our 99 or more forms we thus have 27 species whose eggs and ovulation habits need more attention. In this country we know the eggs of about 70 species minutely. Of these almost 50 species have been seen in the field.

In the synopsis of egg characters we have drawn in part on the work of Dr. Tracy I. Storer for *Rana aurora draytonii, R. boylii boylii, Bufo boreas halophilus, Hyla arenicolor,* and *H. regilla.* We have supplemented our observations on *Scaphiopus couchii* and *S. hammondii* with Dr. Ortenburger's records. For *Ascaphus* and to some extent *Syrrhophus marnockii* notes, we have used Mrs. Helen Thompson Gaige's collections and observations. E. R. Dunn's and R. F. Deckert's studies on *Eleutherodactylus ricordii* and Noble and Noble's work on *Hyla andersonii* have been incorporated in the synopsis.

Relatively, the egg vitelli of the robber frogs (*Syrrhophus campi* and *S. marnockii,* 3–4 mm. in diameter for yolk), in which the whole development occurs in the eggs, are the largest, with *Ascaphus* next. Actually, the largest vitelli are those of the bell toad, *Ascaphus truei,* in which yolks of 5 mm. occur. The smallest are those of the tiny swamp cricket frog, *Pseudacris ocularis,* with vitelli 0.6–0.8 mm. in diameter.

The size of the adult or parent does not determine the size of the egg or, more strictly, its vitellus. The bullfrog, the largest, has vitelli 1.2–1.7 mm., little larger than those of the narrow-mouthed toad, *Microhyla carolinensis* (1.0–1.2 mm.) or of the tree toad, *Hyla arenicolor,* and smaller than those of Ricord's frog (*Eleutherodactylus ricordii planirostris,* 2 mm.). The bullfrog eggs are only 0.6–0.9 mm. bigger than those of our smallest species, *Pseudacris ocularis.* Within one group wide variation takes place. Why has the canyon tree toad (*Hyla arenicolor*) vitelli 1.8–2.4 mm., almost twice those of its relative, *H. femoralis,* 0.8–1.2 mm.? Or why should one of the smaller frogs, the wood frog *Rana sylvatica,* have eggs 1½ times larger than the largest, the bullfrog? In the Northeast we concluded (in 1914) that the bullfrog had the smallest vitellus in proportion to its adult size and that *Pseudacris n. triseriatus* and *Rana sylvatica* had relatively the largest vitelli. In the Okefinokee region, Geo. (in 1929), we concluded that *Bufo quercicus, Pseudacris ocularis, P. n. nigrita, Acris gryllus,* and *Microhyla carolinensis* were largest in vitelli relatively, and *Rana grylio* and *R. catesbeiana* were the smallest.

The season of breeding for species in the North has its beginning and end clearly marked. Each species needs four or five weeks, except *Bufo a. americanus* and *Rana clamitans.* The exceptions may require two or three months for ovulation. In the southeastern states, when once a species has begun, its season of breeding may extend throughout the summer or even into the early fall, depending upon the high crests of precipitation. These species, although of a swampy region, wait for the rains, and in this reliance on precipitation they suggest our desert species of Texas and Arizona. Those that do not begin until June have at least eight to ten weeks of ovulation. This minimum period for a species of the South is the maximum period for a northern form. Species such as *R. p. sphenocephala, B. terrestris,* and *Acris gryllus,* which begin early in the season, breed during 25–30 weeks of the year, if not longer, or from February to October or November.

When one comes into a town in the Big Bend country of Texas or in the desert region of Arizona during a rain, after a dry period of six, nine, fifteen, or more months, one wonders how it is that spadefoots and toads are ready that instant for their congress of mating and ovulation. We can only explain it by supposing that the ovulation period of these species extends over the whole spring and summer and that all individuals are not ready at one particular moment, those appearing being only a small part of the population. Perhaps the frogs aestivate or hibernate with life processes slow, and the eggs in this condition may linger almost ready for ovulation for a long period.

In the mountainous regions of the Far West the season of ovulation is dictated by the short term of four or more months. Forms like *Rana b. sierrae* and *Bufo canorus* have a very short season for ovulation and tadpole development. If *B. canorus* did not come from a group of short larval development—small tadpoles—we would not be surprised at its wintering over as larvae, as must some *R. b. sierrae*. In the same way one wonders if some larvae of *R. s. cantabrigensis* in the North may not be occasionally forced into this same condition. In the North ice goes out so late that ovulation and development periods are considerably restricted.

The number of eggs in a complement may vary from 6 in *Syrrhophus campi* and *S. marnockii*, or 35–51 in the bell toad, or 100 in the smallest species, *Pseudacris ocularis*, to 20,000 in *Rana catesbeiana*, the largest form. The range in tree frogs (Hylidae) is from 100 (*P. ocularis*) to 2084 (*Hyla gratiosa*); in the toads (Bufonidae) from 610 (*Bufo quercicus*) to 16,500 (*B. b. halophilus*); in the frogs (Ranidae) from 349 (*R. virgatipes*) to 20,000 (*R. catesbeiana*). The complements of the narrow-mouthed frog (*Microhyla carolinensis*) and the spadefoot (*Scaphiopus holbrookii*) are, respectively, 869 and 2332.

The eggs of eight species, *Hyla cinerea, H. femoralis, H. versicolor, Rana catesbeiana, R. clamitans, R. grylio, Microhyla carolinensis*, and *M. olivacea*, float on the surface of the water; the eggs of 30 or more species (*Acris, Pseudacris, Ascaphus, Scaphiopus, Bufo*, 14 species of *Rana*) are submerged. In northern or southeastern states no form with buoyant eggs lays before May 10, yet in Texas *Microhyla olivacea* may breed in March or *Rana catesbeiana*, rarely, in mid-February. The 19 or 20 normally early breeders have submerged eggs. These eggs usually have firm jelly envelopes, except those of *Pseudacris* and *Scaphiopus*, which have a consistency intermediate between the firm jellies of early breeders and the loose surface films of late breeders. One form, *M. carolinensis*, although it lays at the surface, has the most beautifully distinct, firm eggs of all the species considered, yet its Texan relative, *M. olivacea*, has indistinct loose-jellied eggs.

We had eggs laid in camp and in the laboratory by mated pairs caught in the field. Later the eggs in the field were determined by these original checks. Whenever possible the process of egg laying was observed in the field. Two species, one of the North and one of the South, were identified by the positive elimination of all the other resident forms.

The measurements and color descriptions are based on the fresh eggs of average adults, not of very young females. Later these forms were checked with preserved material. For the eggs with loose outer envelope the outer margin is indicated by dots (Plate IX). In one species the vitelline membrane is far separated from the vitellus, and the space is indicated by cross hatching. A summary of the egg characters of each species follows in the accompanying synopsis (pp. 36–46).

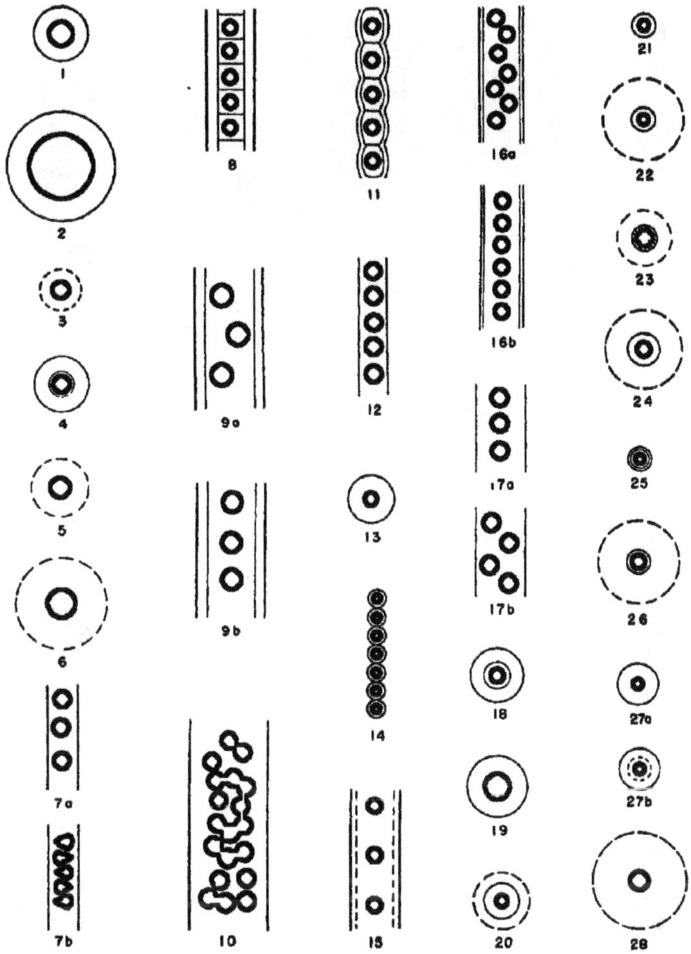


*Plate IX* Diagrams of eggs (×2½) From R. L. Livezey and A. H. Wright, *American Midland Naturalist*, 37, 213–216 (1947) 1 *Eleutherodactylus ricordii planirostris.* 2. *Ascaphus truei* 3 *Scaphiopus couchii* 4. *Scaphiopus hammondii hammondii*, the only species of *Scaphiopus* with two envelopes 5 *Scaphiopus holbrookii holbrookii.* 6. *Scaphiopus holbrookii hurterii* 7a,b. *Bufo alvarius* Note odd wedge-shaped vitelli in b, a common condition in this species 8. *Bufo americanus americanus* 9a,b *Bufo boreas halophilus* 10 *Bufo californicus* 11. *Bufo cognatus.* 12. *Bufo compactilis.* 13 *Bufo punctatus.* The only Bufo that deposits eggs singly 14 *Bufo quercicus.* 15. *Bufo terrestris* 16a,b *Bufo valliceps.* 17a,b *Bufo woodhousii fowleri.* 18 *Hyla andersonii.* 19 *Hyla arenicolor.* 20. *Hyla cinerea cinerea.* 21. *Hyla crucifer.* 22. *Hyla femoralis.* 23. *Hyla gratiosa.* Vitelline capsule far removed from vitellus * 24 *Hyla regilla.* 25. *Hyla squirella.* 26. *Hyla versicolor versicolor.* 27a,b. *Acris gryllus.* Rarely laid as in b. 28. *Pseudacris brachyphona*

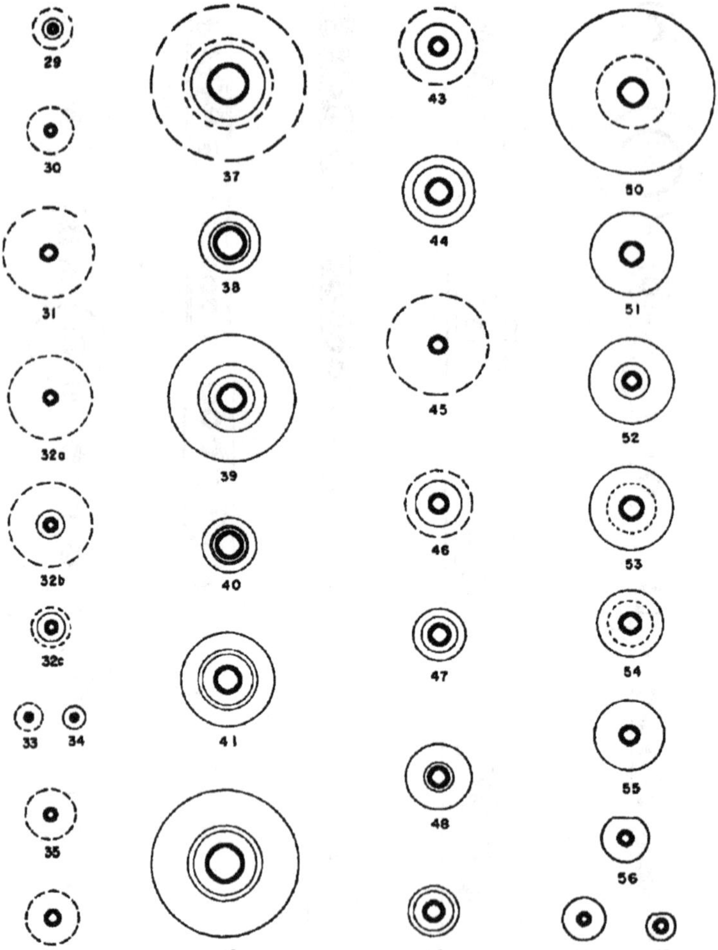


29. *Pseudacris nigrita clarkii* 30. *Pseudacris n feriarum*. 31 *Pseudacris n septentrionalis*. 32a,b,c *Pseudacris n triseriata* Figure a is probably the true appearance of the egg, c is after Smith's (1934) description, b is a composite of a and c 33. *Pseudacris n. verrucosa* 34 *Pseudacris ocularis*. 35. *Pseudacris ornata* 36. *Pseudacris streckeri*. 37 *Rana aurora aurora* 38 *Rana areolata circulosa* 39 *Rana aurora draytonii* 40 *Rana boylii boylii*. 41 *Rana b sierrae*. 42. *Rana cascadae* 43. *Rana clamitans* 44 *Rana capito*. 45. *Rana catesbeiana*. 46 *Rana grylio*. 47. *Rana palustris*. 48 *Rana pipiens pipiens* 49. *Rana p. sphenocephala* 50. *Rana pretiosa pretiosa*. 51 *Rana p. luteiventris*. 52. *Rana septentrionalis*. 53 *Rana sylvatica sylvatica* 54 *Rana s. cantabrigensis*. 55. *Rana virgatipes*. 56 *Microhyla carolinensis carolinensis*. 57. *Microhyla c. olivacea*. 58. *Hypopachus cuneus*.

* No vitelline capsules are shown, except in this figure, *Hyla gratiosa*.

## SYNOPSIS OF EGGS OF UNITED STATES FROGS[a]

A. Eggs unpigmented.

a. Laid in water Rosarylike string in circular mass, yolk 5 mm. in diameter, capsule 5·8 mm A tadpole stage. Egg complement 35–49. Season May to Sept. 21. *Ascaphus truei*

aa. Laid on land or in moist situations. (Whole development within egg, no larval stage ) (No data for *Eleutherodactylus latrans*.)

b. Egg complement small, 6–10.

c. Complement 6 or 7. Yolk 3–3 5 mm., av 3 0. Season April to May. Ovarian evidence. *Syrrhophus campi*

cc. Complement 6–10, yolk about 4 mm. Season April to June or July. Ovarian evidence. *Syrrhophus marnockii*

bb. Egg complement large, 12–25. (R. F. Deckert and Dunn ) Yolk 2 mm. in diameter, outer envelope eventually 4 mm. Season April to August *Eleutherodactylus ricordii planirostris*
Plate LXXVIII–5,7

AA. Eggs pigmented (upper dark pole and lower light pole) Laid in water

B. Eggs deposited singly

a. Envelopes two.

b Outer envelope, diameter 1.4–2.0 mm., inner envelope, diameter 1.2–1.6 mm , vitellus, diameter 0 8–1 0 mm., eggs brown above and cream below. Egg complement 942 Season June 10 to Aug 21. *Hyla squirella*
Plates VII–8, IX–25

bb. Outer envelope, diameter 3.5–4 0 mm.; inner envelope, diameter 1.9–2.0 mm., vitellus, 1 2–1.4, vitellus dark brown and creamy white, strewn among sphagnum. Egg complement 800–1000. Season May 1 to July 20. *Hyla andersonii*

aa. Envelope single.

b. Envelope 2.3 mm. or more.

c Envelope 6 7 mm more or less, loose, sticky, eggs single, tandemlike, often *Bufo* fashion or lattice work or irregular. Vitelli 2 3 mm , black above and white or gray below. Season April to July. *Scaphiopus h. hurterii*

---

[a]See R L. Livezey and A H Wright, "Synoptic Key," *The American Midland Naturalist*, 37, 179–222 (1947).

cc Envelope 2.3–5.0 mm; not *Bufo* fashion, frequently single and irregularly arranged.

d Vitellus 0.9–1.8 mm

e. Vitelline membrane far from vitellus, appearing as inner envelope 1.6–2.0 mm, outer envelope loose, glutinous, indefinite in outline, 2.3–5 mm., vitellus 1.0–1.8 mm. Egg complement 2084. Season March 3 to Aug. 21

*Hyla gratiosa*
Plates VII–12,14, IX–23, LXIX–6

ee. No inner envelope or appearance of one, envelope firm, indefinite in outline, 2.3–3.6 mm

f. Vitellus 0.9–1.0 mm., upper pole deep brown, buffy olive lower pole, rarely the appearance of an inner envelope Egg complement 241. Season April 15 or earlier to Sept 1 Sometimes in masses.

*Acris g. gryllus*
Plates VII–3, IX 27a,b.
*Acris g. crepitans*

ff Vitellus 1.0–1.3 mm, upper pole black, lower pole white, envelope 3.2–3.6 mm Egg complement 1000 to 3000. Season April to September. *Bufo punctatus*
Plate VI–4,10

dd. Vitellus 1.8–2.4 mm, jelly envelope 3.8–5.0 mm. Season March 1 or earlier to July 1 or fall. *Hyla arenicolor*

bb Envelope 1.2–2.0 mm.

c. Vitellus 0.6–0.8 mm Egg complement 100 Season January to September *Pseudacris ocularis*
Plates VII–1, IX–34

cc. Vitellus 0.9–1.1 mm. Egg complement 809–1000. Season March 30 to May 15. *Hyla c. crucifer*
Plates VII–7, IX–21, LXVI–4

BB. Eggs deposited in a mass.

a. Egg mass, a surface film.

b Single egg envelope a truncated sphere, the flat surface above, egg vitellus black above and white below

c Envelope 2.8–4.0 mm., outline always distinct, never lost in the mass, eggs firm and distinct like glass marbles, making a fine mosaic, vitellus 1.0–1.2 mm. Egg complement 869 Season March to Sept. 3. *Microhyla carolinensis*
Plates V–6,7; IX–56, CXXV–5

cc Single envelope 1 5–2.0 mm., vitellus 1.0 mm. Egg mass a loose raft. Egg complement 700. Season April to October. *Hypopachus cuneus*

bb. Egg envelope outline indistinct, more or less merged in the jelly mass; jelly glutinous, envelope not a truncated sphere.

c. Egg brown above, cream or yellow below.

d Egg packets small, masses seldom if ever over 20 sq. in (125 sq. cm.), or 4 × 5 in in diameter (10 × 12 5 cm ).

e. Inner envelope large, 2 2–3.4 mm., outer envelope 3.2–5.0 mm.; vitellus 0 8–1 6 mm Egg complement 343–500. Season May 19 to Aug. 21. *Hyla c cinerea*
Plates VII-9, IX–20

ee Inner envelope small, 1 4-2 0 mm , outer envelope 4–8 mm.

f Packets small, seldom over 30–40 eggs, vitellus 1.1–1 2 mm. Egg complement 1803 Season May 10 to Aug. 13. *Hyla v. versicolor*
Plates VII–11, IX–26; LXXIII–5

ff Packets large, sometimes 100–125 eggs, vitellus 0.8–1 2 mm., av. 0.95 mm. Egg complement 708. Season April 2 to Aug. 21. *Hyla femoralis*
Plates VII-10,13; IX–22, LXVIII–4

cc. Eggs black above and white below.

d. Egg mass small, outer envelope loose, irregular, does not look like a mosaic; somewhat merged, inner envelope possibly present close to vitellus, vitellus 0 8–0 9 mm Outer envelope 2.8–3 0 mm., not truncate Egg complement 645 Season March 15 to September *Microhyla olivacea*
Plates V–5, CXXVI–3

dd. Egg packets large, loose, glutinous films, 35–675 sq in (218–3721 sq cm ) (Suspect *R heckscheri* is in this class )

e Inner envelope absent, vitellus 1 2–1 7 mm., egg mass 144–675 sq in (900–3721 sq. cm.) in area, or 12 × 25 in (30 × 61 cm ) in diameter, egg masses among brush around the edge of ponds encircling *Pontederia*-like vegetation in mid-pond. Egg complement 10,000–20,000 Season March 15 to Nov 8 *Rana catesbeiana*
Plates VIII–7, IX–45, XCIV–6

ee. Inner envelope present, 2.8–4.0 mm., vitellus 1.4–2.0 mm

f. Egg mass seldom 1 sq ft (35–144 sq in. or 218–900 cm.) in area, or 5 × 7–12 in. in diameter, usually around edge of ponds, inner envelope elliptic, pyriform, or circular, av.

3.05 mm., vitellus 1.4–1.8 mm., mode 1 4 mm., av. 1.5 mm. Egg complement 1451–4000. Season May 23 to Aug 21. *Rana clamitans*
Plates VIII–9, IX–43; XCV–4

ff. Egg mass over 1 sq. ft. in area (144–288 sq. in. or 900–1800 sq. cm ), or 12 × 12 in to 12 × 25 in. in diameter, usually in mid-pond, inner envelope av. 3.45 mm , vitellus 1 4–2 0 mm., mode 1.8 mm., av. 17 mm. Egg complement 8000–15,000. Season March 4 to Sept. 15
*Rana grylio*
Plates VIII–3, IX–46

aa. Egg mass submerged.

b. Eggs in files or bands

c. Eggs laid in bands which soon become loose cylinders extending along plant stems or grass blades

d. Envelope 2 5–5.6 mm., vitellus 1.4–2 0 mm , vitelli throughout jelly cylinder, if stalklike on almost imperceptible short stalks. Egg complements 1000–3000

e Envelope 3 8–5 6 mm , vitellus 1.4–2 0 Egg complement 2332. Season March or earlier to October
*Scaphiopus h. holbrookii*
Plates V–2,4, IX–5, XXI 5

ee Envelope 2 5–3.5 mm Vitellus 1 4 1 6 mm Egg complement 1000–3000 Season April to August. *Scaphiopus couchii*
Plate XVII–5

dd Envelope 1 5 2 0 mm , vitellus 1 0–1 6, eggs in bands or cylinders on ends of grass stems, along vegetation stems, etc Eggs near periphery of cylinder more or less on stalks 5 10 mm. long. Egg complement 1000–2000. Season mid-February to August.
*Scaphiopus h. hammondii*
Plate V–1,8, XVIII 7

cc Eggs in files.

d. Files short (4–10 mm. in length), 4–8 eggs in short beadlike chain or bar, or many such files radiating from one focus, vitellus 0 8–1.0 mm , tube diameter 1.2 1.4 mm. Egg complement 610, 766 Season April 1 to Sept 5. *Bufo quercicus*
Plates VI 1,2,5, IX–14, XL–5

dd. Files long (several feet in length or often a meter or more long).

e Vitellus 1.0–1.6 mm , tube diameter 1.8–4 6 mm.

f. Inner tube absent.

g. Envelope more than 5 mm. in diameter (5–6 mm.), firm, distinct; vitellus 1.2–1.6 mm., black above, white or gray below; 35 eggs in 30 mm. (1 3/16 in.) Season May and June. *Bufo californicus*

gg. Envelope less than 5.0 mm. in diameter (1.8–4.6 mm.)

h. Envelope 2.6–4.6 mm., distinct and firm, vitelli crowded in the files at first in double row, later more spread out but still crowded although at times in single row, 22–25 eggs in 30 mm. (1 3/16 in.). Season March to May. *B. woodhousii*

i. Egg complement smaller, 5000–10,000, egg envelopes possibly smaller. Eastern Missouri eastward. Season April to mid-August. *B. w. fowleri*
Plate IX–17a,b

ii. Egg complement larger to 25,000, western Missouri westward. Season March to July. *B. w. woodhousii*

hh. Envelopes 2.4 or less (1.8–2.4 mm.)

i. Envelope slightly scalloped in appearance, tube tightly coiled; 1.8–2.4 mm., narrow, vitelli crowded, vitelli grayish or greenish brown above, cartridge buff or sulphur yellow below, 14–30 eggs in 30 mm., vitellus 1.2–1.6 mm. Season May 1 to July 10. *Bufo compactilis*
Plates VI–9, XXXIII–4

ii. Envelope not scalloped, rather loose but distinct in outline, vitelli black or deep brown above, tan or white below, 1.1–1.7 mm. in diameter. Season March to Aug. 25. Egg complement 7500–8000. *Bufo alvarius*

ff. Inner and outer tubes present (2 in number)

g. Partitions apparent between eggs.

h. Outer envelope distinctly scalloped, envelopes laminated, outer envelope 1.7 mm. at emargination, 2.0 mm. at widest diameter if in single row, or 2.0 mm. and 2.6 mm. if eggs in double row, inner envelope 1.6 mm. Vitellus 1.2 mm., black above, white below, complement to 20,000. Season April to September. *B. cognatus*

hh. Outer envelope not scalloped, 3.4–4.0 mm. in diameter, usually not two rows, inner tube distinct 1.6–2.2 mm., vitellus 1.0–1.4 mm. black or dark brown above, white below, 18–20 eggs in 30 mm. (1 3/16 in.) Egg complement 4000–20,000. Season March to late July. *Bufo a. americanus*
Plates VI–7, IX–8; XXV–6

gg. No partitions between each individual egg.

h. Eggs in a single row within the jelly tube. Outer envelope 2.6–4.6 mm; inner tube close to the outer tube, inner tube 2.2–3.4 mm; outer tube inclined to be slightly scalloped, distinct space between eggs; vitelli 1.3–1.4 mm.; 7–8 eggs in 30 mm. (1 3/16 in.) Season last of February to September *Bufo terrestris*
Plates VI–6, IX–15

hh. Eggs usually in a double row within jelly tube, more crowded

i. Vitelli small, 1.2 mm., outer envelope small, 2.8–3.2 mm., purplish black and white, inner envelope 2.6 mm., close to outer tube, 10 eggs in 30 mm. (single row), or 25–27 eggs in 30 mm. (double row), rarely single eggs. Season March to Aug. 25
*Bufo valliceps*
Plate VI 3,8

ii. Vitellus larger, 1.50–1.7 mm., black and white or cream, outer envelope loose but distinct, large, 4.9–5.3 mm. in diameter, vitelli double- or triple-rowed, inner tube 3.5–3.8 mm., not very close to outer tube (*boreas* group).

j. Vitelli larger, 1.65–1.75 mm. Season January to July *Bufo boreas halophilus*

jj. Same, except vitelli average smaller though their range is 1.5–1.75 mm. Season March to September. *Bufo b. boreas*

bb. Eggs an irregular mass, jelly loose, envelope 3.2–6.7 mm., vitellus black above and white below

c. Single envelope 3.2–3.6 mm., vitellus 1.0–1.3 mm., egg mass submerged film on bottom or loosely strewn on bottom. Season April to September. *Bufo punctatus*
Plate VI–4,10

cc. Single envelope 6.3 mm., vitellus 2.3 mm., egg mass various patterns, single, tandemlike, *Bufo*-like, lattice work, etc., at or near surface attached to vegetation. Season April to June.
*Scaphiopus h. hurterii*

bbb. Eggs in lumps.

c. Egg mass a firm regular cluster.

d. One jelly envelope. (At times *R sylvatica*, *R. s. cantabrigensis*, and *R p. pretiosa* appear in this category )

e Egg mass a plinth or sometimes globular, firm No indistinct inner envelope.

f Vitellus 1.4–1 8 mm , black above, sulphur or primrose yellow below, envelope 4 9–6 9 mm., av. 5 4 mm , eggs farther apart than in *R pipiens* or *R. p. sphenocephala;* egg complement 350–500 eggs, egg mass 1.5 × 2 to 3 × 4 in. New Jersey, southward Season June 21 to Aug 11
*Rana virgatipes*
Plates VIII–1, IX–55

ff. Vitellus 1.8–2 2 mm., black above, light tan below, envelope 5–7 2 mm., av 6 3, egg complement 2000–3000 eggs Egg mass 3 x 3 to 8 x 6 in Northern Nevada northward and westward. Season March to May
*R pretiosa luteiventris*
Plate VIII–6

ee. Egg mass a sphere, inner envelope indistinct (See dd Two or three jelly envelopes *R s sylvatica*, *R s. cantabrigensis*, *R. p pretiosa*.)

dd More than one jelly envelope

e. Two envelopes

f Egg mass a sphere 2½–4 in (6 35–10 cm.) in diameter, containing 2000–3000 eggs, outer envelope distinct.

g Eggs black above and white below, inner envelope apparently absent, slightly evident under lens, 3 6–5.8 mm., av. 3.8, outer envelope 5 2–9 4 mm , av 6 4, vitellus 1 8–2 4 mm., av. 1.9 Egg complement 2000–3000. Season March 19 to May 1. *Rana s. sylvatica*
Plates VIII–8, IX–53, CXIX–5

[h Is *R. s cantabrigensis* thus: vitellus 1.50–1 8 mm , av 1 65, inner envelope 3–4 mm , av. 3 5 mm , outer envelope 4 2–5 4 mm., av 5 mm.?]

gg Eggs brown above and yellow below, inner envelope distinct, 2 3–3.0 mm , outer envelope 3.6–5.0 mm.; vitellus 1.6–1.9 mm Egg complement 2000 to 3000. Season April 6 to May 18 *Rana palustris*
Plates VIII–4; IX–47

ff. Egg mass a plinth, complement large, 1000–10,000 eggs, eggs black above and white below.

g. Outer envelope large, 10–15 mm., inner envelope indistinct, sometimes absent, 5.0–6.0 mm., vitellus 2.2–2.8 mm., black and white, far apart in mass like *R. sylvatica;* egg complement 1000–2000 eggs in masses as large as 8 × 6 in. Northwest. Season March to May.

*Rana p. pretiosa*

gg. Outer envelope smaller, 7.0 mm. or less, inner envelope 1.4–4.0 mm., vitelli 1.4–2.5 mm., black and white, close together like *R. pipiens* masses. Except for *R. pipiens*, east of Rockies.

h. Vitellus av. 2.0–2.4 or 2.5 mm.

i. Vitellus av. 2.5 (range 2.4–2.6 mm.). Outer envelope 4.5–5.0 mm., distinct, inner envelope 3.2 mm. Masses larger, 5000–10,000 eggs. Midwest. Season March to May 15.

*Rana areolata circulosa*

ii. Vitellus av. 2.0 mm. (range 1.8–2.4 mm.), inner envelope 3.1–4.4 mm., outer envelope 4.4–6.0 mm., mode 5.2 mm., av. 5.3 mm. Egg complement 5000 or more. Southeast. Season March 13 to Nov. 3. *Rana capito*

Plates VIII-2, IX-44, XV-1, 2, XCII-4

hh. Vitellus av. 1.4–1.7 mm. (range 1.3–2.0 mm.), inner envelope 2.3–3.2 mm., outer envelope 3.4–6.6 mm. Egg complement 1000–5000.

i. Av. outer envelope 5.0 mm. or larger.

j. Av. outer envelope 6.3 mm. (5.6–6.6 mm.), inner envelope 2.4–3.0 mm., av. 2.75 mm., vitellus 1.4 av., range 1.3–1.6 mm., vitellus black or brown above, white or yellow below. Egg complement 800–1500. Season June 25 to July 30.

*Rana septentrionalis*

Plate CXVIII-3

jj. Av. outer envelope 5.1 mm. (range 4.2–6.0 mm., mode 5.0 mm.), inner envelope 1.5–3.4 mm., av. 2.25 mm., vitellus 1.7 mm., range 1.3–2.0 mm. Egg complement 3500–4500. Season March 30 to May 15. *Rana p. pipiens*

Plate IX-48, CI-3,4

jjj. Av. outer envelope 3.8 mm. (range 3.4–5.4 mm., mode 4.0 mm.), inner envelope 2.4–3.2 mm., vitellus 1.4–1.8 mm., av. 1.6 mm., egg complement 1084. Season January to December. *Rana p. sphenocephala*

Plate IX-49

ee. Three envelopes.

f. Outer envelope 3.8–4.5 mm , av 4 0 mm., firm, middle envelope 2 6–3.4 mm., av 2.8 mm., inner envelope 2.3–3.0 mm., av 2 5 mm. All envelopes distinct Vitellus 1 9–2 5 mm , av 2.2 mm., black and white. Mass compact 2 X 2 X 1.2 in. to 2 X 4 X 2.4 in. Eggs firmly attached to each other. Egg complement 900–1100. Season March 1 to May 1 *Rana b. boylii*

Plate VIII-5

ff. Outer envelope 6 4–14 0 mm

g. Egg mass small, 400–500 or less, all envelopes distinct.

h. Outer envelope 6 4–7 9 mm., av 7.2 mm., middle envelope 4.2–5.0 mm , av 4 6 mm , inner envelope 2.75–4 8 mm , av 3.9 mm , vitellus 1 8–2 3 mm., av 2.2 mm , black above and light gray tan below, plinthlike mass 28 X 40 mm with eggs ¼–½ in apart Egg complement 100–400 eggs High Sierras Season June, July. *Rana b. sierrae*

hh. Outer envelope 1 1–1 2 mm , middle envelope 5–6 mm., inner envelope 4 9 mm , vitellus 2 25 mm , black above, cream below Mass 400–425 eggs. Washington and northern Oregon. Season last of May to July 1. *Rana cascadae*

gg. Egg mass large, 750–4000. Envelopes quite distinct or indistinct.

h. All envelopes indistinct, especially the middle one Outer envelope 10–14 0 mm , middle envelope 6.2–8 0 mm , av. 6.8 mm., inner envelope 4 0–6.7 mm., av. 5.7 mm , vitellus 2.3–3 6 mm., av 3 0 mm , black above, creamy white below 750–1400 eggs in a flat mass 6 X 10 in across, vitelli ¾ in apart Principally northwest Oregon northward. Season February to May *Rana a aurora*

hh All envelopes quite distinct, middle one particularly dense and distinct, outer envelope 7.5–11.8 mm , av 8 5 mm , middle envelope 3.9–6.4 mm., av. 4.40 mm., inner envelope 3.9–6 4 mm , av. 4.4 mm. Vitellus 2.0–2.8 mm., av. 2.1 mm., black and creamy white, egg complement 2000–4000 eggs in a soft, viscid mass 2 6 X 4 X 3 inches to 6 X 4 X 4 in. Principally California and Lower California. Season January to March. *Rana a draytonii* cc. Egg mass a loose irregular cluster, sediment-covered.

d Egg mass small, generally about or less than 1 in. (2.5–3.5 cm.) in diameter, normally 10–25 or 40, rarely 100 or more in one mass.

e. No inner envelope

f Smaller species 19–37.5 mm (19–32 males, 19–37.5 females). Egg or vitellus 0.625–1.2 mm., av. below 1.2 mm (except in *P. n. septentrionalis*, 1.2–1.4 mm ) single envelope 2.6–5.0 mm normally, rarely to 7.8 mm.

g. Vitelli 1.2–1.4, envelope larger. Season May and early June *Pseudacris nigrita septentrionalis*

gg Vitelli 0.625–1.2 mm., envelope 2.6–5.0 mm normally Season early February or earlier to May.

h. Envelope 2.2–2.4 mm or more, vitellus 0.625–.9 mm Season March 20 to May 20. *Pseudacris n. clarkii* Plates VII–4, L–4

hh Envelope 2.6–2.8, vitellus 0.9–1.0 mm Florida to Georgia. Season February to August 15. *Pseudacris n. verrucosa*

hhh. Envelope 3.0–5.0, sometimes more.

i. Envelope 3.2–4.0 mm., vitellus 0.9–1.1 mm. Vitellus black and cream or slightly yellowish Season February to May. *Pseudacris n. feriarum* Plates VII 2,5, LI 4

ii Envelope 3.0–5.9, sometimes 7.8 mm , vitellus 0.9–1.2 mm. Egg complement 500–800 Season March 19 to May. *Pseudacris n. triseriata* Plates VII–6, IX–32a,b,c, LIII 4

ff Larger species 24–48 mm. (24–41 males, 27–48 mm females). Egg or vitellus av. over 1.2 mm. (range 1.2–2.0 mm ). Single envelope 3.0–8.5 mm Masses 10–100, rarely 200 in a mass.

g. Envelope 6.0–8.5 mm., vitellus 1.6 mm. West Virginia to Ohio to northern Mississippi and Alabama Season March to July. *Pseudacris brachyphona*

gg. Envelope 3.0–7.25 mm , av. normally under 6.0 mm.

h. Vitelli 1.6 mm Envelope 3.2–4.2 mm., av. under 4.0 mm Southeast. Season November to March. *Pseudacris ornata* hh. Vitelli 1 2–1 3 mm. (Bragg, 1 2–1 8 or 2 0, Strecker's material), envelope 3 0-7.25 mm, av. over 5 0 mm. Texas to Oklahoma Season December to late May.

*Pseudacris streckeri*

ee. Inner envelope 1 4 2 7 mm.

f. Outer envelope smaller, 2 2–3 0 mm, vitellus smaller, 0 65–1 2 mm, inner envelope 1.4–2.1 mm.

g Outer envelope small, 2.2–2 4 mm. or more, inner envelope 1.4 1 8 mm., vitellus 0 65–0 9 mm, mass smaller, 13–30 eggs, egg complement, 150–300 eggs. Season March 5 to mid-August.

*Pseudacris n clarkii*
Plate VII–4, L–4

gg Outer envelope larger, 3 0–5 0 or 7 8 mm, inner envelope 2 1 mm., vitellus 0 9-1 2 mm Mass 15–300 eggs per mass Egg complement 500 1500 eggs Season March 20 to May 20.

*Pseudacris n. triseriata*
Plates VII–6, IX 32a,b,c, LIII–4

ff Outer envelope larger 4 7–6 7 mm, inner envelope 1 8 2.7 mm.; vitellus larger 1 3 1 35 mm, vitellus light brown above and pale white, yellowish, or greenish below Masses 9–75 eggs, rarely single. Egg complement 600–1500 *Hyla regilla*

dd Egg mass an irregular cylinder 1 6 in (2 5–15 cm) in length, extending along plant stem or grass blade, envelope single, 3 8–5 6 mm, vitellus 1.4-2 0 mm Egg complement 2332 Season April or earlier to August 17. (See also d, dd, e, ee under c Eggs laid in bands which soon become loose cylinders extending along plant stems or grass blades)

*Scaphiopus h. holbrookii*
Plates V–2,4, IX–5, XXI–5

We never described in detail our results from work in Texas during 1925–1935. The Florida group of Carr, Goin, and Van Hyning have added much to our knowledge of the Florida forms. H. M. Smith in 1934 did a good study of the Kansas forms. J R. Slater of Tacoma has described the forms of the Northwest (still in manuscript), and A. and R. D. Svihla and K. Gordon have also added data about that area. But the group which has been most vigorous is the Oklahoma group (from the University of Oklahoma—Bragg, Trowbridge, Ortenburger, and others; and from Oklahoma A and M. College, the Moore group).

**Tadpoles** (Plates X-XV: lateral views, X-XI; mouth parts, XII-XIV; development, XV): Some 25 to 30 species of tadpoles of the United States and

Canada need to be described. Most have been found but were not described, and the tadpoles of 15 forms are yet unknown to science. The life histories of the robber frogs we know in our country indicate no free tadpole stage, the whole development being in the egg.

In discussions of the size of tadpoles *quite small* is 1 inch (24 mm.) or smaller; *small*, 1–1⅖ inches (24–35 mm.): *medium*, 1⅗–2 inches (40–50 mm.); *large* 2⅖–3⅖ inches (60–86 mm.); *quite large*, 3⅘–4 inches (95–100 mm.); *very large*, 5⅖–5⅘ inches (135–145 mm.). Some of the toads and swamp cricket frogs may have tadpoles a little less than 1 inch (23 or 24 mm.) in length, whereas bullfrogs may have tadpoles 5⅘ inches (145 mm.) or even larger.

The tadpole has a body and a tail. The body has sensory lines, a breathing pore or spiracle, a vent or anus, eyes, nostrils, and a mouth. The mouth is wholly unlike the adult mouth. It usually has a disk called a labium (with upper and lower labia). Generally about the edge of the labium are tubercles or papillae. At the inner edge of each labium or at the very portal of the mouth opening itself are horny crescents called upper and lower mandibles. On the upper and lower labia are horny ridges of teeth or combs for scraping food. The tail has two parts: the axis consists of muscle segments; and the fin consists of upper and lower crests.

The narrow-mouthed toad tadpole has no mouth disk, no labial teeth, no papillae, no horny beak. The spiracle is next to the vent. The eyes are on a lateral ridge. These tadpoles are small black flattened creatures with some white on the tail axis or body.

The ribbed toad (*Ascaphus*) has a mouth disk, an upper mandible only, papillae on the lower lip or labium, upper labial teeth at least two rows to a ridge, labial tooth ridges two to three above and seven to ten below, a spiracle in the middle of the venter nearer the hind legs than the snout, and eyes straight back of and close to nostrils, dorsal, and equidistant from middorsal line and lateral outline when viewed from above The tail is spatulate and rounded as in some mountain stream tadpoles. The tadpoles are black or brown with white tips.

The spadefoots have the vent in the middle position, the spiracle below the body axis and on the left side, the papillae completely around the labium except for a small interval above (absent in one species), the papillary border not emarginate on the side, labial teeth three to six ridges above and four to six ridges below, eyes dorsal and nearer middorsal line than lateral outline, and muscle segments of the tail plainly visible.

The toads usually have small blackish tadpoles with anus median, papillae confined to the sides of the labium, upper and lower edges of the labium toothed, sides of labium emarginate, labial teeth two ridges above and three ridges below, and eyes dorsal and slightly nearer the lateral outline than middorsal line. The spiracle is on the left side and is small.

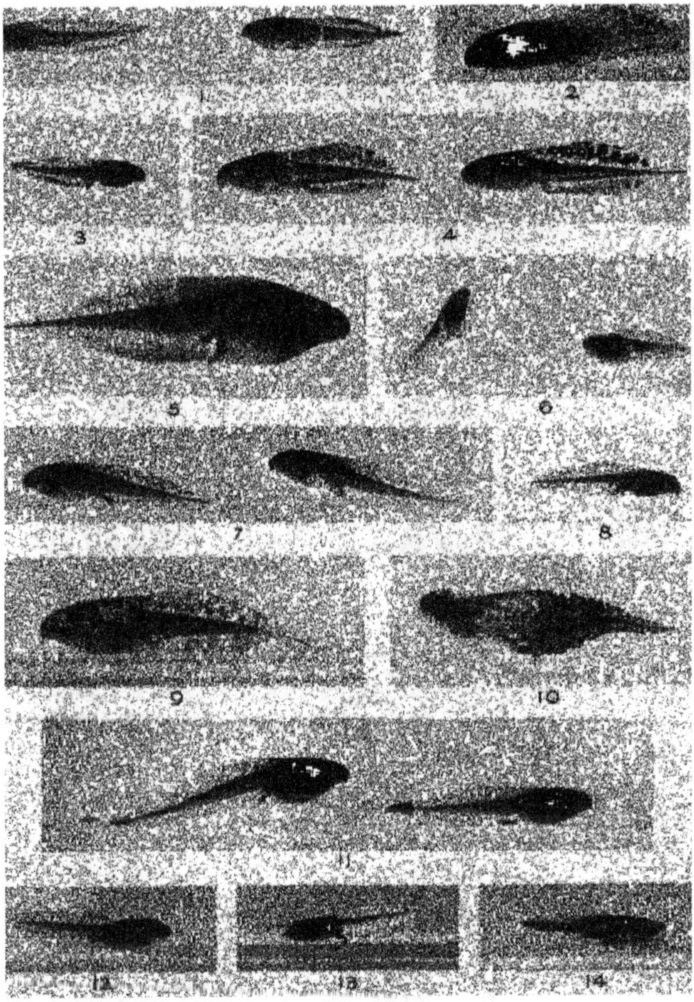


*Plate X* Mature tadpoles (×1) 1 Anderson tree frog, *Hyla andersonii* 2 Green tree frog, *Hyla cinerea* 3 Peeper, *Hyla crucifer crucifer* 4 Pine woods tree frog, *Hyla femoralis* 5,6 Barker, *Hyla gratiosa* 7 Squirrel tree frog, *Hyla squirella* 8 Little chorus frog, *Pseudacris ocularis* 9,10 Common tree toad, *Hyla versicolor versicolor* 11 Cricket frog, *Acris gryllus gryllus* 12 Spadefoot, *Scaphiopus holbrookii holbrookii* 13 Oak toad, *Bufo quercicus* 14 Narrow-mouth toad, *Microhyla carolinensis* (Wright, Gen., 1932, pp. 46–47.)

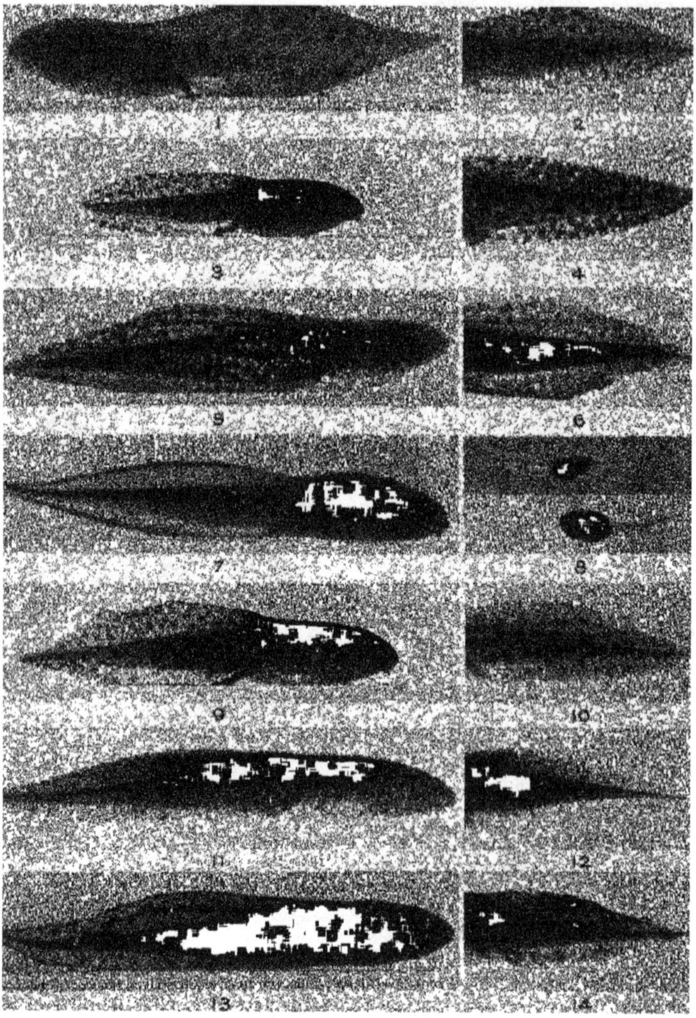


*Plate XI* *Rana* tadpoles (mature ×1). 1,2 Gopher frog, *R capito.* 3,4 Green frog, *R clamitans* 5,6 Southern bullfrog, *R grylio* 7,8 River-swamp frog, *R heckscheri* 9,10 Southern meadow frog, *R pipiens sphenocephala* 11. Mink frog, *R septentrionalis* 12. Meadow frog, *R p pipiens.* 13 Sphagnum frog, *R virgatipes* 14 Pickerel frog, *R palustris* (Wright, Gen., 1932, pp. 45–47.)

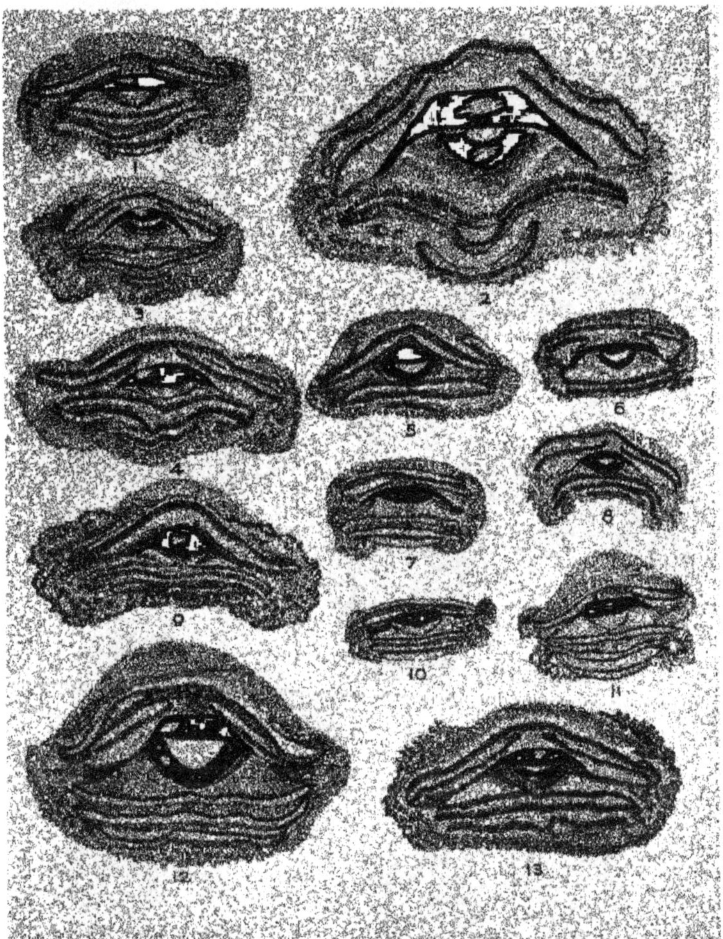


*Plate XII* Tadpole mouth parts (*Hyla, Acris, Pseudacris, Bufo*) 1 Peeper, *H crucifer crucifer.* 2 Barker, *H gratiosa* 3 Anderson tree frog, *H andersonii* 4 Green tree frog, *H cinerea* 5 Eastern swamp cricket frog, *P nigrita feriarum* 6 Cricket frog, *A gryllus gryllus* 7 Fowler's toad, *B woodhousii fowleri* 8 Little chorus frog, *P ocularis* 9 Squirrel tree frog, *H squirella* 10 American toad, *B americanus americanus* 11 Southern toad, *B. terrestris* 12 Common tree toad, *H versicolor versicolor* 13 Pine woods tree frog, *H femoralis* (Wright, Gen , 1932, pp 54–55 )

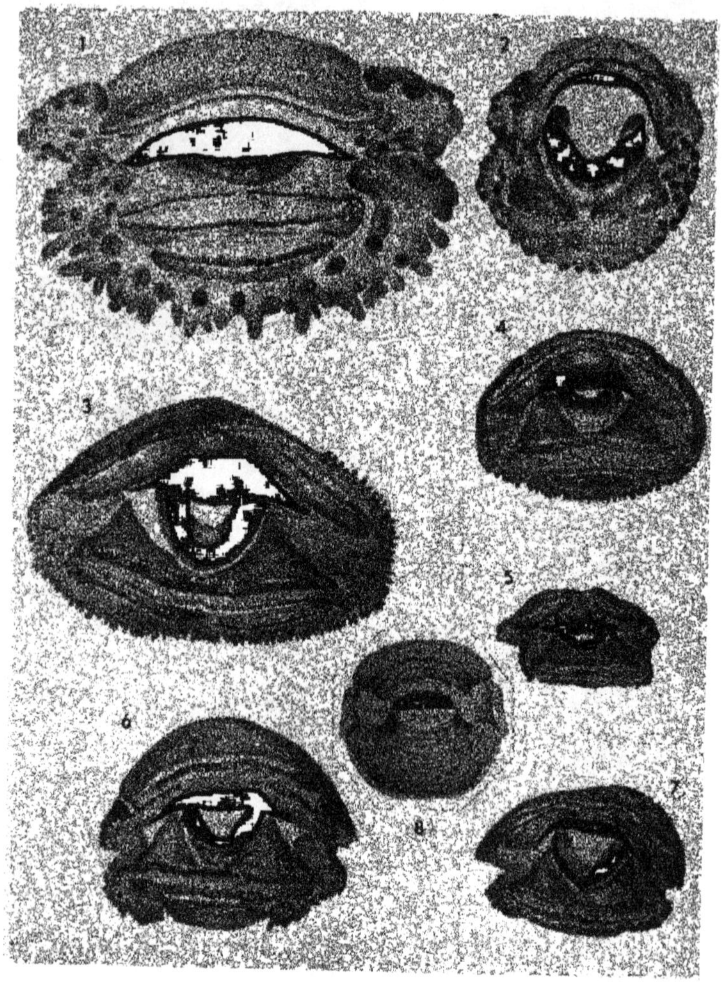


*Plate XIII* Tadpole mouth parts (*Rana, Hyla, Pseudacris, Bufo, Ascaphus*). 1 Sphagnum frog, *R virgatipes* 2. Nevada frog, *R fisheri*. 3. Canyon tree frog, *H arenicolor*. 4 Clarke's chorus frog, *P nigrita clarkii* 5 Spotted toad, *B. punctatus* 6 Spadefoot toad, *B compactilis* 7 Nebulous toad, *B valliceps* (Wright and Wright, MS, 1930) 8 American bell toad, *A. truei*. (After Gaige.)

The frogs have medium-to-large tadpoles, with spiracle on left side, vent on right side of lower tail fin's base. The spiracle is near the body axis; the papillary border is emarginate on the side; the labial teeth are two or three ridges or more above and three or four or more below. Some may have spatulate tails, if high mountain forms, others may have upper tail crest high and far on the body like a tree frog tadpole, but most have the tail crests neither very high nor extending far on the body.

The tree frogs have small or medium tadpoles, often with high dorsal tail crest extending far on the body, the vent on right side of ventral tail crest, and the spiracle on left side near the body axis. The labial teeth have two ridges above and two or three below.

The following synopsis of tadpoles is offered only after considerable debate. We could have put it in the first edition. No one knows the extent of variation in the mouth-part characters. If one attempts to use other workers' results, he encounters personal equational differences in measuring technique. We might find no median space in the second upper lateral tooth row in some *P. n. clarkii* and a median space in others. Dr. Bragg figures his material with no median space, as we at times have found. What is normal for the whole range of a species? This synopsis is presented in the hope that someone will attempt to learn the frog tadpoles of the United States *in the field* and refine our descriptions. Grace L. Orton may

*Plate XIV* Tadpole mouth parts (*Rana, Microhyla, Scaphiopus*). 1. River swamp frog, *R. heckscheri*. 2 Young of (1) 3 Mink frog, *R septentrionalis* 4 Sphagnum frog. *R. virgatipes* 5. Southern bullfrog, *R grylio* 6 Narrow mouth toad, *M carolinensis* 7. Green frog, *R clamitans* 8. Spadefoot, *S holbrookii* (Wright, Gen., 1932, pp 54–55.)

## SYNOPSIS OF UNITED STATES TADPOLES

A. No tadpole stage
*Eleutherodactylus ricordii planirostris* (Plate LXXVIII–5,7,8), *E. latrans; Syrrhophus campi; S gaigeae; S marnockii.*

AA. A tadpole stage in water.

B. Tadpoles unknown.
*Scaphiopus holbrookii albus; Bufo californicus; B hemiophrys, Pseudacris n. nigrita, P occidentalis; P. n. septentrionalis; Hyla baudinii; H v. phaeocrypta, H. avivoca; H versicolor chrysoscelis; Rana a aurora; R. pretiosa; Microhyla areolata; Hypopachus cuneus*—14 in all.

BB Tadpoles seen but not described in detail
*Bufo alvarius, B. b. boreas; B. canorus; B debilis, B. woodhousii fowleri; Pseudacris ornata, Hyla cinerea evittata, H. wrightorum; Rana a areolata; R. sylvatica cantabrigensis, R fisheri*

BBB. Tadpoles in this synopsis.

a. Mouth disk absent, no labial teeth; no papillae, no horny beaks, spiracle median near anus, nostril within edge of mouth fold, eye on a canthus, tadpoles (23–26 4 mm ) small, black or grayish olive tadpoles with a stripe on the middle of the tail musculature
BREVICIPITIDAE

b Tail tip always black, eyes just visible from ventral aspect, black pointed excrescences back of upper labial edge, lower mandibular prolongation gray, coloration citrine-drab or grayish olive, with middorsum dark grayish olive, venter with white or pale pinkish cinnamon spots, sides of body without striking longitudinal light bands, light band at base of tail musculature not prominent (in alcohol) Outer egg envelope not truncate, mass seldom showing distinct outline of each egg envelope in a mosaic fashion. Texas westward to Fort Davis Mountains *Microhyla olivacea*
Plate CXXVI–4,5

bb. Tail, sometimes with black tip, eyes plainly visible from ventral aspect, inner face of upper labial edge with no black pointed excrescences, lower mandibular prolongation light, general coloration black with purplish gray or hair brown dots, venter with white or yellowish bands and large blotches, sides of body with same coloration; light band at base of tail musculature prominent (even in alcohol) Egg with truncate outer envelope, giving mass a mosaic appearance on water's surface. Virginia to Florida to Texas and up Mississippi River to Indiana. *Microhyla carolinensis*
Plates X–14, XIV–6; CXXV–4

aa Mouth disk present; upper and lower labial teeth, labial maxillae; at least the upper horny beak present, nostril free of mouth

b Spiracle median nearer insertion of hind legs than tip of snout, labial teeth 2/7 to 3/10, upper labial teeth at least two rows to a ridge, no lower beak; many rows of papillae on edge of lower labium, mouth large and round; anus median, black or blackish brown tadpoles speckled with black; tail may be of body color or spotted with creamy white, tail tip white or yellowish white, upper tail crest not extending on the body Washington to California

*Ascaphus truei* ASCAPHIDAE
Plates XIII-8, XVI-2

bb Spiracle sinistral, upper labial teeth not with two close rows on each ridge, labial teeth 1/3, 2/2, 2/3, 2/4, 3/3, 3/4, 4/4 to 6/5, upper and lower horny beaks, papillae on lower edge of labium absent or in one or two rows.

c. Anus median, spiracle lateral below the lateral axis (of tail musculature, projecting) sometimes as much ventral as lateral, upper tail crest extends on the body to a vertical nearer hind legs than the spiracle or only halfway, viscera visible (in preserved specimens) through the skin of the belly. Eyes distinctly dorsal.

d Labial teeth 3/4 to 6/6, papillae extending completely around the border of the labium except for a short-toothed median interval above (sometimes absent in one species); papillary border not emarginate on each side, eyes nearer middorsal line than lateral outline, on lateral axis, tadpoles 24 5–65 mm. in length, spiracle a slit, very low on side, about on the level of the mouth, in general very bronzy tadpoles, myotomes of tail musculature well indicated Tail tip usually rounded.

SCAPHIOPODIDAE

e Teeth 6/6, 5/6, 6/5, 5/5, tadpoles small, 21–28 mm., transforming at 8.5–12 0 mm , inner papillae present, spiracle equidistant between eye and base of hind legs or vent, eye 1 4–1 8 nearer tip of snout to the spiracle, av. 1.52, internasal space in interorbital space 1.28–1.83, av 1 56, depth of body 1 75–2 5 in body length, av. 2 04, muscular part of tail in depth of tail 1.45–2.5, av 1 98, last lower row of teeth longer than horny beak Last lower row of teeth 1 5 times in next to lowest row of teeth Egg mass an irregular cylinder, at first bandlike. Massachusetts to Florida to Texas and Arkansas. *Scaphiopus h. holbrookii*
Plates X-12, XIV-8

ee Labial teeth normally 4/5 or 4/4, sometimes 5/4, 3/4, or possibly 2/4, inner papillae generally absent, tadpoles small or large; eye 1.0–1.6 nearer tip of snout than spiracle, last lower row of teeth less than or ½ of the width of horny beak.

f. Tadpole large (65 mm), transforming at 13–24 mm; teeth 4/4, rarely 5/4 or 3/4, upper fringe of papillae broken in middle by a row of teeth; eye 1.1–1.3 nearer tip of snout than to the spiracle, av. 1.2, muscular part of tail 2.25–2.66 in depth of tail, av. 2.43, width of body in its own length 1.55–1.9, av. 1.66, depth of body 1.05–1.15 in body width, av. 1.09, spiracle 1.25–1.6 nearer eye than base of hind legs or vent, av. 1.37, internasal space 2.5–2.75 in interorbital space, av. 2.6, third lower labial row broken in middle, median interval of second lower row broad, last row of teeth 1.75–2.0 times in next to last row of teeth and usually 1.7–2.0 times in mandibles, second upper row usually broken in middle. Egg mass a loose cylinder, many eggs on stalks. Montana to Texas and westward to Pacific Coast States.

*Scaphiopus hammondii*

(g. Upper labial mandible with beak, lower labial mandible with notch. *Scaphiopus h. hammondii*
Plate XVIII-3,5

gg Upper labial mandible without beak, lower labial mandible without notch. *Scaphiopus h. bombifrons*
After Bragg)

[ggg Probably belongs with gg. *Scaphiopus h. intermontanus*]

ff Mature tadpole small (21–27 mm.), transforming at 7.5–12.5 mm., upper fringe of papillae is conspicuously broken in middle by a row of teeth or not so broken and the first row absent, last lower row of teeth 2.2–2.4 in width of mandibles.

g. Teeth usually 4/5, sometimes 3/4, interval between lateral parts of third upper row 2.5–3.0 in either lateral row or 5.0 in width of mandibles, interval between lateral portions of fourth row 5.0 times in width of mandibles, second upper row normally broken. Eggs tandemlike, or *Bufo*-like or lattice work. (Compiled after Bragg.) Oklahoma and Arkansas to Texas. *Scaphiopus h. hurterii*

gg. Teeth usually 4/4, rarely 5/4, 3/4, or possibly 2/4, interval between lateral parts of third upper row equal to or 2/3 either lateral portion of this row or 1.5 times in mandible, interval between lateral portions of fourth upper row 1.3 in width of mandibles; second upper row normally unbroken, eye 1.0–1.6 nearer tip of snout than to the spiracle, average 1.3, muscular part of tail 2.2–3 33 in depth of tail, av. 2.7, width of body in its own length 1 3–1 6, av. 1 4, depth of body 1.25–1.55 in body width, av 1.35; spiracle 1 5–2 2 nearer eye than base of hind legs or vent, av 1.85, internasal space 1 45–2 3 in interorbital space, av 2.0, third lower labial row continuous; median interval of second lower row very narrow Last lower row 2.5–3 0 times in next to lower row of teeth, second upper row not or barely broken in middle, egg mass an irregular cylinder, at first bandlike Texas to California and Mexico *Scaphiopus couchii*

dd Labial teeth 2/3, papillae confined to the sides of the labium (or lower half only in *Bufo punctatus*), upper and lower edges toothed, papillar border on each side emarginate, eyes slightly nearer lateral outline than middorsal line, above lateral axis, spiracle small, a porelike opening.
e. Tadpoles 24–28 mm in length (a few forms 35–56 mm ) BUFONIDAE

f Papillae only on lower half of lateral margin, or a slight marginal row of 4 to 6 papillae on upper half, no inner papillae normally, third lower row of teeth equal to the first row of lower labial teeth, median space between lateral parts of the second row of upper labial teeth 2-3 times in either lateral row, horny beak 1 2–1 5 in third lower labial row, tadpoles to 25 mm One of the blackest *Bufo* tadpoles, tail musculature evenly dotted with black, venter with light grayish vinaceous spots, eggs single or film or scattered mass on bottom, not in files Central Texas to California, Utah, and Lower California. *Bufo punctatus*
Plate XIII-5

ff Papillae on upper and lower halves of lateral labial margin, some inner papillae

g Bicolor tadpoles distinctly lighter below, not black tadpoles, upper tail fin highly arched, horny beak 1 3-1 5 in first or second lower row of teeth.

h. Light grayish olive, dark olive-buff or clay color, the lightest of our toad tadpoles, in life intestine does not show through the skin of the belly (shows in preserved specimens), third lower row of labial teeth short, 1.8–2 4 in first lower row, third lower row 1 5–2 0 times in the horny beak or 1.6–1 8 in longest lower row, median space between lateral parts of the second row of upper labial teeth large, 1.2–2.0 times greater than either lateral part, depth of tail in length of tail 3.0–3.5, horny beak 1.3–1.4 in first or

second row of teeth, lower loop of papillae to end of third lower but not under it, usually not two rows, tail musculature with dark vinaceous drab band to tail tip, below this a pale vinaceous pink band, belly pale vinaceous pink, eggs in files or strings, brown or buffy brown, cream or straw yellow below, no inner tube Texas to Mexico, Arizona. *Bufo compactilis*
Plate XIII–6

(hh Doubtless Bragg's (1936) *Bufo cognatus* belongs in g Dorsal surface mottled brown and gray silvery areas interwoven with black ones. The ventral surface markedly lighter than the dorsal. The viscera (in mature tadpoles) only slightly or not at all visible, lower tail fin, clear or almost so, third lower row of teeth 1.5–1 8 times in horny beak, or 2 5–3 0 in longest lower row, median space in second upper row (none says Bragg, 1 0–1.2 in either lateral part says Smith), depth of tail in length of tail 2.5, eggs in single row sometimes double, an inner gelatinous envelope and an outer tougher envelope or tube, somewhat scalloped in outward appearance. (After A. N. Bragg, Okla , 1936, p 19 ) Minnesota to Texas and southern California. *Bufo cognatus*)

gg Black or blackish tadpoles, in life the intestine shows through the skin of the belly, third lower row of labial teeth long, 1 2–1 6 in first lower row, third lower row 1.0–1.5 in horny beak, median space between lateral parts of the second row of upper labial teeth small, contained 2 0–4.9 times in either lateral half, not greater than lateral half.

h. Papillae very faint, minute, at times hard to see but present, third lower row of labial teeth not equal to first lower row of teeth, but equal to or greater than horny beak, horny beak 1 2–1 5 in upper fringe, 1.3–1.5 in first lower row; median space of second upper row 2 4 times in either lateral part of it, *upper edge of tail musculature with 8–10 black bars with intervening pale olive-buff areas; irregular black or brown band on tail with cartridge buff or tilleul buff below it; tadpoles to 23 mm.* Eggs in files, inner tube present, one or two rows of eggs. Louisiana to Costa Rica. *Bufo valliceps*
Plate XIII–7

hh. Papillae plainly visible

i. Tadpoles of Rockies to eastward. Tadpoles usually less than 30 mm , third lower row of labial teeth 1 2–1 5 in first row.

j. Tadpole to 24 mm ; horny beak in upper fringe 1.75, in first or second lower row 1.5, horny beak equal to or less than the third lower row of teeth, median space between two parts of second upper row 1.4–2.1 in either lateral part; third lower row of teeth in first lower row 1 2–1 4, two or more rows of strong papillae from end of upper fringe to end of third lower row, sometimes 3–5 rows at side of labium; lower loop of papillae far below level of third row and with at least two rows of papillae, mouth in interorbital space 1 0–1.5, av 1.17, mouth larger than internasal space 1.2–1.6, av. 1 36, depth of tail in tail length 2 4–4 5, av. 3 27, eye nearer snout than spiracle 1 0–1.57, av. 1 2, nostril nearer eye than snout 1 1–1.8, av. 1 48. Egg mass long file, inner tube with no partitions. North Carolina to Florida to Louisiana.

*Bufo terrestris*
Plate XII-11

jj. Tadpole to 27 mm ; horny beak in upper fringe 1 2–1.5, in first or second lower row of teeth 1 1–1 2 or 1.2–1 3; horny beak greater than third row of lower labial teeth, median space 1.15–2 0, 1 0–4 0, or 1.3–3.0 in either lateral part, third lower row of teeth 1 3–1 5 or 1.4–1.5 in first lower row, one row of weak papillae from upper fringe to end of third lower row of teeth with a few scattering papillae at the side of the labium, lower loop with only two or three scattering papillae beside the outer row of weak papillae.

k. Mouth in interorbital distance 0 77–1 0, av 0 92, horny beak in upper fringe 1 2–1 4, horny beak in first or second row 1.1–1.2 times, third row in first lower row 1.3–1 5, depth of tail in tail length 1 25–2 7, av. 1 97, spiracle nearer eye than vent 1.04–1 54, av. 1 28; eye nearer snout than spiracle 1 0–1.27, av. 1 16, mouth larger than internasal space 1.4–2 2, av. 1 76, papillae of lower labial loop do not extend under the end of the third row of labial teeth, tail musculature in tail depth 1.26–2 66, av. 2.04, internasal space 1.2–1 8 in interorbital distance, av. 1 6, spiracle 1 05–1 55 nearer eye than vent, av. 1.28. Egg mass long file, partitions, inner tube present. Eastern North America from Hudson Bay southeast. *Bufo a americanus*
Plate XII–10

kk. Mouth in interorbital distance 0.9–1.5, horny beak 1.4–1.9 in first upper fringe of teeth, horny beak in first or second row 1.2–1.4; depth of tail in tail length 2.75–3.8.

l. Mouth in interorbital distance 1 07–1.5, horny beak in upper fringe 1.4–1 5, horny beak in first or second row 1.2–1.3, third lower row 1.3–1 6 in first lower row, depth of tail in tail length 2 88–3 83, av 3.33, spiracle nearer eye than vent 1.25–1 7, av. 1 45, eye nearer snout than spiracle 1 0–1.6, av. 1.16, mouth larger than internasal space 1 1–1.83, av 1 47, papillae of lower labial loop extend slightly or not at all under the end of the third lower row, tail musculature in tail depth 1.6–2.3, av. 1.85, internasal space 1 5–2 16 in inter-

orbital space, av. 1.86; spiracle 1 25–1 7 nearer eye than vent or base of hind legs, av 1 45. Egg mass long file, no inner tube, sometimes two rows of eggs Massachusetts to Missouri on the north and South Carolina to Texas on the south. *Bufo w fowleri*
Plate XII–7

ll. Horny beak in upper fringe 1.8–1 9; in first or second lower row of teeth 1.6; third lower row 1 3–1 4 in first lower row, depth of tail in length of tail 2 75, spiracle nearer eye than vent 1.25; eye nearer snout than spiracle 1.0–1 1 or equidistant, papillae of lower labial loop slightly extends under the ends of the third lower row, tail musculature in tail depth 2.2–2 5, egg mass a long file, no inner tube, sometimes two rows of eggs (After K. A. Youngstrom and H M Smith, Kan., 1936, p 633) Western Iowa south through Texas into Mexico and west to Idaho and Imperial Valley, California. *Bufo w. woodhousii*

ii. Tadpoles of Pacific Coast area. Tadpoles often over 30 mm (maximum 27–56 mm, 27 *canorus*, 33 *exsul*, 29 *nelsoni*, 44 *boreas*, 56 *b halophilus*—*boreas* group) Third lower row of labial teeth 1 4 or 1 5–2 0 in first lower row.

j. Smaller tadpoles (27 mm. *canorus*, 35 mm *exsul*) Median space in second upper row of teeth almost equal to or 1 2 times in either lateral portion of this row, third lower row 1.5–2.0 in first and second lower rows, 1 2–1.5 in first upper fringe

k. Third lower row 1.5 in first lower row, 2 0 in second lower row or 1.2–1.3 in upper fringe. (After Storer) Yosemite region
*Bufo canorus*

kk Third lower row 1 4 in first or second lower row or equal to or 1.5 in first upper fringe. Deep Springs, Calif. *Bufo exsul*

jj Larger tadpoles (29 mm. *nelsoni*, 55 mm *b halophilus*) Median space in second upper row of teeth 2.0–3 7 in either lateral rows, third lower row 1 4–2 0 in first or second lower row.

k. Median space in second upper row 2.0–2.5 times in either lateral portion of this row or 2.5–3 0 in horny beak, third lower row of teeth 2 times in first or second lower row of teeth. Southern Nevada into California *Bufo b. nelsoni*

kk. Median space in second upper row of teeth 3 2–3.7 in either lateral row or 3.8 in horny beak; third lower row 1.4 in first or second lower row or 1.5–1.6 in first upper fringe. (After T. I. Storer.)

Montana and Colorado to northern California and British Columbia, possibly Alaska

*Bufo b. halophilus*

[The characters used for this *boreas* group are trivial and not to be given too much significance.]

ee. Tadpoles 55 or 56 mm (body 23 and tail 33, see Storer for description). *Bufo b. halophilus*

cc. Anus dextral, spiracle distinctly lateral on or near body axis

d. Papillary border on side with an emargination, tadpoles 50–149 mm. in length, papillary fringe on upper labium extends not at all inward beyond the end of the upper fringe of teeth or only 1/8 to 1/16 of the length of the fringe, length of horny beak in upper fringe of teeth 1.0–1 5 times, labial teeth 2/3 or 3/3 or 3/4, rarely to 7/6.

RANIDAE

e. Labial teeth 7/6 to 3/3, not customarily 2/3, tadpoles 47–88 mm

f. Labial teeth 7/6 or 6/6, depth of tail in length often 3 3–4 2. (See T I Storer for description ) Coastal California and Oregon.

*Rana b boylii*

ff Labial teeth 2/4, 3/4, 4/3, or 5/3, not 2/3.

[R. *aurora aurora*, labial teeth 3/4, belongs here, no detailed description on record, probably some *R. a. draytonii* also fall here though some are 2/3 (T. I. Storer).]

g. Labial teeth 5/3 or 4/3, tadpoles large to 88 mm , tadpole tail very prominently spotted and mottled, all three lower labial rows long, median space of second upper row 1 3–1.5 in either lateral section of this row, tail tip pointed or rounded, depth of tail in tail length 3 3–3 4 times, spiracle 1 2–1 3 nearer vent than tip of snout, nostril 1 3–1 8 nearer eye than snout, spiracle 1 8–2.0 nearer eye than vent New Mexico, southern Arizona to central Mexico.

*Rana tarahumarae*
Plate CXXII–2,6

gg Labial teeth 3/4, tadpoles 49–72 mm in length Dorsal crest very high extending to vertical of the spiracle (*Rana sylvatica*) or tail broader nearer its tip than at its body insertion, rounded, spatulate, or elliptical (*R. b sierrae*); upper fringe of teeth about 1.5 times the length of the horny beak.

h Tadpole to 49 mm , dorsal crest very high, extends on the body to vertical of the spiracle; tail tip acuminate, tail musculature begins to taper at once, dorsal crest higher in cephalic half, depth of tail in length of tail 1.9–3 1, av. 2 5, spiracle 1 5–2.0 nearer base of hind legs or vent than tip of snout, av. 1 75, nostril equidistant from snout and eye, internasal space in interorbital space 1 7-2.9, av. 2 5, depth of body 1.08–1.23 in body width, av. 1.14, depth of body 1.66–2 0 in body length, av. 1 78, second upper lateral row about 2/5 of the upper fringe of teeth, the median space between the lateral portions of the second row 0.4–0.8 times either lateral portion, the third upper row is 1/4 to 2/9 of the upper fringe, fourth lower row of teeth is 6/11 to 7/11 of the first lower row; spiracle 1.0–1.47 of the first lower row, spiracle 1.0–1.48 nearer eye (5.0–6.0 mm ) than base of hind legs or vent (4 5–7 6 mm.) Egg mass submerged, globular. Ontario to Nova Scotia, south to South Carolina, west to South Dakota and south to Arkansas. *Rana s. sylvatica*

hh. Tadpole to 72 mm., dorsal crest low extending on body to a vertical twice nearer hind legs than spiracle, tail tip rounded, elliptical, or spatulate, tail musculature for an inch or more does not taper, dorsal crest narrow in cephalic half, depth of tail in length of tail 2.5–5 7, av 4 0, depth of body 1 1–1 8 in body width, av. 1 43, depth of body in body length 2 0–3.0, av. 2.325, spiracle 1.0–1 33 nearer base of hind legs or vent than tip of snout, av 1 17, spiracle 1.45–2 375 nearer eye (4.0–8.0 mm ) than base of hind legs or vent (5 8–12 0), av 2 05; young tadpoles occasionally with teeth 2/4, rarely 3/3, nostril 1 0–1 75 nearer the eye than snout, internasal space 1 3–2 0 in interorbital space, av. 1.5, second upper lateral row 1/4 to 2/9 of the upper fringe; median space between lateral portions of second upper row 1.0–2 3 times either lateral part, the third upper row is 1/9 to 1/12 of the upper fringe, the fourth lower row of teeth is 1/3 to 1/4 of the first lower row. The Sierras, California. *Rana b. sierrae*

ggg Labial teeth 2/4, fourth lower labial row 1/4 of length of other three, median space in second row small (After J R Slater, Wash ) Tadpoles 40–50 mm. Northern Oregon into Central Washington *Rana cascadae*

ee. Labial teeth 2/3, occasionally 3/3, rarely 1/3.

(We have seen no tadpoles of *R pretiosa* or *R. p. luteiventris* in the field; we have seen preserved tadpoles with teeth 3/3. "In *pretiosa* there are four rows of labial teeth, one very short upper row and three lower rows. In *luteiventris* there are five rows, two long upper rows and three lower, as figured by Thompson (1913). The first lower row in *luteiventris* is longer than the analogous one in *pretiosa*" (A. Svihla, Wash., 1935, p 121) ) Tadpoles 74–150 mm. in length, dorsal crest not extending to vertical of the spiracle but usually just ahead of the buds of the hind legs; tail always elliptical not spatulate, upper fringe of teeth equal to or slightly larger than (never 1.5 times) the horny beak.

f. Tadpoles 74–84 mm.; tadpoles usually transform the same season they are born; transformation sizes 18–30 mm., av. 24 mm. (except *R. areolata* group), tadpoles (except in *R. capito* or *areolata* group) not strongly pigmented on belly, viscera plainly or slightly showing through skin (in spirit specimens). Egg mass globular or plinthlike beneath surface of water.

g. Belly strongly pigmented or somewhat pigmented, in spirits looking white and viscera not visible or but slightly visible, tail covered with large prominent dark spots; transformation 25–35 mm.

h. Nostril equidistant eye and snout, av. 1.25; spiracle equidistant vent and snout, nearer eye (1.5) than vent, intestines show through belly but not quite like *R. pipiens;* median space between second upper row of teeth 1.25–1.5 times in length of either lateral part, third lower row 0 40–0.66 of the second lower row; spotting not so prominent as in *R. capito* but heavier than in *R. pipiens* group; inadequate characterization. Southwestern Ohio to Kansas and Oklahoma and northeastern Louisiana. *Rana areolata circulosa*

hh. Nostril 1.0–1.5 nearer eye than snout, av. 1.25, eye 1.0–1.3 nearer spiracle than snout, av. 1.12, median space between the second upper row of labial row 1.0–2.0 times the length of either lateral part of this row, third lower row 0.33-0.66 shorter than the first or second rows, tail covered with large prominent dark spots, belly strongly pigmented (in spirits it looks white), viscera not visible; depth of tail in length of tail 2.6-3 5, av. 3.0. North Carolina to Florida. *Rana capito*
Plates XI-1,2; XV-3–8

gg. Belly not strongly pigmented, in spirits dark, viscera shows through skin, tail in *R. pipiens* group with fine flecks or small spots, or in *R. palustris* heavily washed with purplish or purplish black, transformation sizes averaging smaller, 18–31 or 32 mm. [*Rana aurora draytonii.* Body 1 2–2.2 in length of tail; depth of tail in length of tail 2 5–3.2 in its length. (See T. I. Storer's description.)]

h. Median space in second upper labial row 2–4 times the length of either lateral part; third row of lower labial teeth 0.33–0.66 shorter than the first or second rows, usually at least 0.50, eye nearer the snout than spiracle or equidistant, nostril nearer eye than tip of snout; depth of tail in length of tail 2.3–3.2, av. 2.7, spiracle 1.5–1.8 nearer eye than snout, av. 1.63. Hudson Bay to Texas and eastern states. *Rana palustris*
Plate XI–14

hh. Median space 0.5–1.0 or 1.0–1.5 times either lateral part of the second upper row, third row of labial teeth 0.22 or 0.285–0.33 shorter than the first lower row, depth of tail in length of tail 2.0–2.8 or 2.7–3.4

i. Median space of second upper row 0.5–1.0 times either lateral part, third lower row of teeth 0.285–0.33 shorter than the first lower row, nostril to snout equal to nostril to eye, eye 1.15–1.3 nearer tip of snout than spiracle, av. 1.2, body length in tail length 1.35–1.66, av. 1.5, mouth 0.9–1.6 larger than internasal space, depth of tail in length of tail 2.0–2.88, av. 2.65, tail crest usually with wide prominent dark spots, greatest length of tadpole 74 mm; spiracle 1.1–1.86 nearer eye than snout, av. 1.46. Southeastern states to Texas, Oklahoma, and Indiana.

*Rana pipiens sphenocephala*
Plate XI–9,10

ii. Median space 1.0–1.5 times either lateral part, third lower row 0.22 shorter than the first lower row, nostril 1.1–1.5 nearer the eye than snout, eye nearer spiracle than snout 1.1–1.3; body length in tail length 1.3–2.0, av. 1.7, mouth larger than internasal space, depth of tail in length of tail 2.7–3.4, av. 3.0, tail crest usually translucent with fine spots or pencilings, greatest length of tadpole 84 mm, spiracle 1.4–1.86 nearer eye than snout, av. 1.59. North America east of Sierra Nevada and southward into Mexico

*Rana p. pipiens*
Plate XI–12

ff. Tadpoles 83–142 mm, tadpoles usually winter over at least one season, transformation sizes 28–59 mm. (except *R. virgatipes* 25–35 mm, possibly *R. fisheri*), tadpoles usually with strongly pigmented bellies, viscera not plainly showing through the skin (in spirit specimens)

g. Tadpole with prominent continuous black crest margins and a black musculature band, belly bluish; tadpoles to 95 mm, young tadpoles black with transverse yellowish band on the body, spiracle 0.86–1.2 nearer vent or base of hind legs than snout, average 1.0, spiracle 0.85–1.2 nearer eye than base of hind legs or vent, i.e., usually equidistant, eye equidistant from spiracle and tip of snout, muciferous crypts very distinct, spiracle below lateral axis, tail tip acuminate, second upper labial row in upper fringe 1/3 to 1/4, upper fringe distinctly greater than horny beak, median space between two parts of second upper labial row 1 to 1½ of either lateral part, third lower labial row equal to horny beak, third lower labial row longer than single row of lower papillae, third lower labial row 1/4 to 1/5 shorter than first lower row. Eggs not described. South Carolina to Florida and Louisiana.

*Rana heckscheri*
Plates XI–7,8, XIV–1,2; XCVIII–2,6

gg Tadpole without black crest margins or lateral band, belly white, cartridge buff or yellow to maize yellow, no transverse yellow band in young tadpoles, spiracle nearer vent than snout 1.1–1 8, spiracle to eye rarely less than 1.25 greater than spiracle to vent, eye nearer tip of snout than spiracle 1.0–1.4, second upper labial row to upper fringe 1/4 to 1/15, upper fringe equal to or slightly greater than horny beak, median space in either lateral part 1½ to 11; third lower labial row much less than horny beak, third lower row much shorter than or equal to single row of lower labial papillae.

h. Tadpoles to 140 mm, eye well above lateral axis, muciferous crypts indistinct; spiracle just below lateral axis, spiracle 1.08–1 44 nearer base of hind legs or vent than tip of snout, av. 1.26; depth of tail in length of tail 2.4–3.5, av. 2.8, tail tip obtuse; second upper row in upper fringe 1/4 to 2/7, median space in second upper row 1½ in either lateral part, third lower row in first lower 1/4 to 1/5 shorter; teeth 2/3, rarely 3/3. Transformation size 43–59 mm. Egg mass, surface film North America east of Rockies. *Rana catesbeiana*
Plate XCIV–3

hh. Tadpoles to 83–110 mm, eye on or just above lateral axis, tail tip acute or acuminate (rounded in *R fisheri*), teeth, 2/3, second upper row fringe 1/6 to 1/15, median space in second upper row 2.5–11 in either lateral part, third lower row in first lower row 1/2 to 1/3 shorter

i Depth of tail in length of tail 1.45 1 8, average 1 7, tail tip acuminate, dorsal crest equal to or less than tail musculature, muciferous crypts indistinct, spiracle 1 08–1 44 nearer vent than snout, mouth in interorbital distance 1 5–2 37, av. 1 94, internasal space in interorbital distance 1.8–2.6, av 2 16, second upper row 1/6 to 1/8 of the upper row, median space of the second upper row 2½ to 4½ times either lateral row, third lower row 1 5 less than horny beak, much shorter than single row of lower labial papillae and 1/2 shorter than first lower row of teeth, first row of lower teeth equal to horny beak. Transformation size 32 or 37 to 48 mm., egg mass, a surface film. Georgia to Florida to Louisiana *Rana grylio*
Plates XI–5,6, XIV–5

ii. Depth of tail in length of tail 2 5–4.7, avs 3 1–3 87, tail tip acute, dorsal crest less than tail musculature, muciferous crypts distinct, species 1.07–1.8 nearer vent than snout, mouth in interorbital distance 1 3–1.8, av. 1.5, internasal space in interorbital space 1 25–2.0, avs. 1.6–1.75; second upper row 1/6 to 1/15 of the first upper row; first lower row of teeth equal to or greater than horny beak, spiracle 1.1–1.8 nearer vent than snout.

j. Tadpoles to 99 mm, transformation size to 29–38 mm, depth of tail in length of tail 3.2–4.7, av 3.87, spiracle just touches lateral axis, eye just above lateral axis, spiracle 1 06–1 38 nearer eye than base of hind legs or vent, av 1 24, spiracle 1 25–1.6 nearer eye than vent, 1.45, mouth in interorbital distance 1.3–1.75, av 1 55, width of body in its own length 1.3–2 1, av. 1 55, third lower labial row of teeth 1.25 less than horny beak, about equal to single row of lower labial papillae, 1/2 shorter than first lower row, sometimes a row of inner papillae below the third lower row of teeth, median space in second upper labial row 3 5–4.5 times either lateral portion, second upper row 1/6 to 2/15 of the upper fringe, belly straw yellow, colonial buff, or deep colonial buff, tail with round cartridge buff or pinkish cinnamon spots, no black line in dorsal crest as in *R. grylio* or *R virgatipes*. Eggs in a compact submerged mass Hudson Bay to Minnesota, New York to New England. *Rana septentrionalis*

Plates XI–11; XIV–3

jj. Tadpoles to 92 mm, transformation sizes at 25–38 mm, depth of tail in length of tail 2 5–3 7, spiracle just below lateral axis, eye on lateral axis, third lower labial row of teeth 1 5–1 25 less than horny beak, much shorter than single row of lower labial papillae, almost 1/2 shorter than first lower row, median space of second upper row 6–11 times the length of either lateral portion, second upper row 2/15 to 1/15 of the first upper row.

k Spiracle nearer vent than snout 1.35–1 8, mouth 1.3–1.8 times in interorbital distance, av 1 5, width of body in its own length 1 25–1 7, av 1 47; belly deep cream color, tail green, mottled with brown and covered with fine yellow spots Egg mass, surface film Canada to Louisiana to Florida to New England. *Rana clamitans*

Plates XI–3,4, XIV–7

kk. Spiracle nearer vent than snout 1 07–1 45, av 1 23–1.3, mouth 1 0–1 37 in interorbital distance, av 1.12

l. Teeth 2/3 or 1/3, no inner papillae or few inner papillae from end of the upper row to the end of the lower labial row, no row of finer papillae below third lower row of teeth, spiracle nearer eye than vent 1.1–1.75, av 1 43, nostril nearer eye than snout 1 1–1 9, av. 1 5, tadpoles medium (our material, 42 mm, Stanford University material, 83 mm), width of body in body length 1 6–2 0, av. 1 77, second upper row 1/6 to 1/8 of the first upper row, belly pure white or pale cinnamon pink, tail musculature with black clusters outlining cartridge buff areas, upper tail crest sometimes reticulated with black dots Lower crest except for caudal half free of spots Eggs unknown. Transformation size unknown Nevada.

*Rana fisheri*

Plate XIII–2

ll. Teeth 2/3 or 1/3; four to six rows of inner papillae from end of first upper row to end of lower labial row, a row of heavy inner papillae below the third lower row of teeth, spiracle nearer eye than vent 1.42–1.82, av. 1 62, nostril nearer eye than snout, 1.0–1.42, av. 1.2, width of body in body length 1.45–1.86, av. 1 6, tadpole large (92 mm ), second upper row 2/15 or 1/15 of the first upper row or second upper row absent, belly pale chalcedony yellow, sulphur yellow, vinaceous, pale grayish vinaceous or vinaceous-buff, ***upper tail crest with a black line or row of large black spots, more prominent than in*** R grylio, ***middle of musculature with another black line, tail dark with pale chalcedony yellow spots.*** Transformation size 25–35 mm. Eggs a submerged mass. New Jersey to Okefinokee Swamp, Ga. *Rana virgatipes*

Plates XI-13, XIII 1

dd Papillary border on side of labium without an emargination, tadpoles 23–50 mm length, labial teeth 2/3 or 2/2. HYLIDAE

e. Labial teeth 2/2, tip of tail normally black (sometimes lost), median space of second upper tooth row wide (like *Rana*) and 1 33 greater than either lateral portion, horny beak 1 1–1 35 in first upper row, eye dorsal just inside the lateral outline in dorsal aspect (more like Ranids). Eye 1.0 1.66 (av. 1 22) nearer tip of snout than spiracle; depth of tail in length of tail 3 25–5 0, av 4 0, suborbital region oblique, not vertical, spiracle to eye usually equals distance from spiracle to vent, spiracle plainly showing from dorsum, ***spiracular tube in life stands out at an angle from the body and opening is apart from the body proper;*** papillary border does not end above the end of the upper row (like *Rana*), eggs single, occasionally a mass. *Acris*

Plates X–11, XII-6, XLV 4, XLVI–9

ee Labial teeth usually 2/3, rarely 2/2, tip of tail not normally black, median space (sometimes absent) of second upper tooth row narrow, 1.6-4 0, rarely 4 5–7 0 in either lateral portion, i e , smaller than either lateral part, horny beak or mandible 1 3- 2 3 in first upper row, eye lateral visible from ventral as well as the dorsal aspect, eye 1 0–1 75 nearer spiracle than tip of snout, depth of tail in length of tail 1 6–4 4, av. 2.1–3.55; suborbital region vertical, spiracular tube in life parallel with opening at inner edge closely connected with or near to body proper. HYLIDAE exclusive of *Acris*

f. Labial teeth occasionally, or frequently 2/2; tadpoles 23–33 mm

g *Tail musculature with black-brown lateral band with light area below; tail crests clear* with fine elongate fleckings, single row of papillae on lower labial border below second lower row of teeth, upper fringe somewhat angulate in middle (like *H. femoralis*), spiracle 1 4–1 9 nearer base of hind legs or vent than tip of snout, av 1 42, nostril to eye 1 37–2 0 in nostril to snout, av 1 6, median space between the second upper row of teeth 2½–5 in either lateral portion, ends of second lateral row extending not at all or slightly beyond the end of the upper fringe; horny beak about 1 5–1 6 in upper fringe Eggs an irregular mass.

*Pseudacris nigrita triseriata*

gg. *No black-brown dorsal and white or light lower band on tail musculature;* tail fins clear except where heavily pigmented with *purplish black blotches* on the outer edge of the tail fin; two rows of papillae on lower labial border below second lower row of teeth, upper fringe not perceptibly angulate in the middle, spiracle 2 0–2 6 nearer base of hind legs or vent than tip of snout, av 2.16, nostril to eye 2 0 in nostril to snout; median space between second upper row of teeth 2–3 in either lateral row; ends of second lateral row extending beyond upper fringe for 1/4 to 1/6 of either lateral portion, horny beak 1.75–2.25 in length from one end of second upper lateral row to end of other lateral row. Eggs single. *Hyla crucifer*

Plates X–3, XII–1

ff. Labial teeth 2/3

g Third row of labial teeth short, shorter than horny beak or 0.20–0 40 of the first lower row in length, first upper row very angulate (1 form), somewhat angulate (2 forms), not angulate (3 forms), no flagellum ordinarily present yet some have pointed tails, tadpoles 23–50 mm., light papillary development, lower labial corner not with three or four strong rows of papillae, one or two rows of papillae below third lower row of teeth or none (*H crucifer*), the papillae extend above and beyond the end of the upper fringe for about 0.14–0.285 of the length of the upper fringe.

h. Tadpoles 23–33 mm., eye equidistant between spiracle and tip of snout (0.8–1.3 times), spiracle 1.2–2.6 nearer vent or base of hind legs than tip of snout, spiracle 1 0–3 2 nearer eye than vent, papillae extend above the fringe for 0.16–0 25 of the length of the first upper row.

i. *Musculature with no distinct brown lateral band with light area below;* crests usually heavily pigmented with purplish black blotches on outer rim, nostril to eye in nostril to snout 2 0, spiracle to vent 2 0–2 6 in spiracle to tip of snout, *no papillae below third lower labial row of teeth* thus appearing as a goatee, median space between second upper labial row 2–3 in either lateral portion, horny beak in first upper row 1 75–2 25 Eggs single, submerged. End of second upper row extends beyond end upper fringe 1/4 to 1/6 width of second lateral row, upper fringe not angulate in middle, median space in second upper row 1.4–1.5 in horny beak; third lower row in first or second lower row 3–5 times, second lower row distinctly longer. *Hyla crucifer*

Plates X–3, XII-1

ii. *Musculature with a distinct brown lateral band above with light area below, i e., bicolored;* crests usually clear with fine scattered fleckings, sometimes with fleckings gathered nearer outer rim, one or two rows of papillae below third lower labial row of teeth (rarely absent), spiracle to vent in spiracle to tip of snout once or 1 1-2 0 or 2 1 times, one or two rows of papillae below the third lower labial row of teeth, median space between second upper row 1 6–5 0 times in either lateral portion, horny beak in upper fringe 1.3–2 3, end of second upper lateral row to end of first, slightly or distinctly shorter, or rarely slightly beyond, first upper row very angulate (1 form) somewhat angulate (3 forms), not angulate (2 forms) in middle, median space (absent in 1 form) of second upper row 2 5–3 5 in horny beak, third lower row of teeth from 1 1–4 times in first or second lower row, second and first equal (except one with first considerably shorter and one equal or first 1 1–1 2 shorter). Eggs in a mass except *P ocularis* where single *Pseudacris*

j. Tadpoles 15–23 mm , adults 11 5–17 5 mm , eggs single, dorsal crest to vertical midway between spiracle and eye, spiracle equidistant from eye and vent; median space 3.5 in horny beak, horny beak 2 0 in upper fringe, horny beak 2.0 in first or second lower rows of teeth, third lower row of teeth 3–4 in first or second lower rows, third lower row 4 0 in first upper row, first upper row somewhat angulate in middle, mouth and internasal space equal, spiracle 1 7–2 1 nearer vent than snout, one row of papillae below the third lower row of teeth, *dorsum of body in life with definite scattered black spots,* musculature with three bands, apricot buff (light), chestnut brown (dark), martius yellow (light). *Pseudacris ocularis*

Plates X–8, XII–8

jj. Tadpoles 23–36 mm ; adults 19–48 mm., eggs in a mass, dorsal crest to vertical of spiracle or within 1 or 2 mm. of such vertical; spiracle to eye 1.0–3.0 or 3 2 nearer eye than spiracle to vent (one form sometimes equidistant); median space usually present, 2 5–3 0 in horny beak; horny beak 1.3–2.3 in first upper row; horny beak in first or second row 1 1 2 2, rarely over 2.0 times, third lower row of teeth in first or second lower row 1 1· 2.8, rarely 3.0 3.2 times, third lower row in first upper row 2 6 -3.8 occasionally 4 0. *Pseudacris* (exclusive of *P. ocularis*)

⟨k. Adults 25 -48 mm , first and second lower tooth rows equal and united at their outer ends, median space of first upper tooth row *very angulate;* musculature depth 3.0 in tail depth, median space of second upper row 1 6–1 7 in either lateral part, median space 2 5 in horny beak, horny beak 2.1 2 3 in first upper row, third row 1.3 in horny beak, internasal space 1.6-1.7 in interorbital space, tail depth greater, brown gray dorsally, with median interorbital rectangular darker area and a crescent at rear of each nostril, belly white (After Bragg )⟩ *Pseudacris streckeri*

kk. Adults to 19 36 mm , musculature depth in tail depth 1 2–2 9, median space of upper labial tooth row somewhat angulate or not angulate, median space of second upper row 2 -5 in either lateral portion (absent in 1 form, sometimes absent in another), median space of second upper row in horny beak 3 0 or more, horny beak 1 3–2 0 in first upper row; third row 1 3 3 0 in horny beak, first and second lower rows equal, or first, 1 1 1 2, or considerably shorter, free at ends (in one form almost united), internasal space in interorbital 1 33 2 4, usually 2 0 or more, tail depth in tail length usually 2 2 -4 0, rarely 4 4.

⟨l Tail depth in tail length 2 2 2 5, musculature of tail 2 7 3 0 in tail depth, eye to spiracle 1.5 in eye to tip of snout, internasal space 2 8 in interorbital space, internasal space 2.0 in mouth, nostril equidistant from eye and snout or 1 15 nearer eye than tip of snout, first upper row not angulate in middle, median space of second upper row 2 0– 2 3 in either lateral part or 3.0 in horny beak, horny beak 1 6 -1 8 in first upper row, or 1 6 in first or second lower row, third lower row 1.5 1 6 in horny beak or 2 6 2.8 in first or second row, first and second lower rows equal and almost united on their ends, black-brown above, under parts bronzy black, black along side, body transparent. (After Green )⟩ *Pseudacris brachyphona*

ll. Tail depth 2.4 5.0, seldom under 2 5 in tail length, musculature 1.2– 2 6 in tail depth, eye to spiracle 0.8 1.36 in eye to snout, internasal space 1 3 2.4 in interorbital space, internasal space about equal or 1.1 or 1 2–1 7 in mouth, nostril to eye 1.2–2 0 in nostril to snout.

m. Upper fringe of teeth not angulate, no median space in second upper row or median space 1.8–2.0 in either lateral part or 2.0 in horny beak, horny beak in upper first row of teeth or fringe 1.3– 1.7, first and second rows unequal, first considerably (1.2–1.5) shorter than second row; horny beak 1 2–1.5 in second row and

1.1–1.4 greater than first row, horny beak 1.3–2 0 in upper fringe, third lower row 2.5–3 0 in horny beak, one row of papillae under third lower row, spiracle nearer eye than vent, tail depth in tail length 2.4, musculature of tail 2.6 in tail depth, third lower row 2.0–2.3 in first lower row, 2 3–3 2 in second lower row, gray olive or grayish brown tadpoles. *Pseudacris n. clarkii*

Plate XIII 4, L–5

mm. Upper fringe of teeth somewhat angulate, median space of second upper row 2–7 in either lateral portion of this row (occasionally absent in *P n. feriarum*), or 3 or more in horny beak, first and second lower tooth rows equal or first 1.1–1 2 shorter than second row, third lower row 1.3 1.8 in horny beak, horny beak 1 5 2 0 in upper fringe or 1.3–2 2 in first or second lower rows, spiracle to eye 1.0–1.7 nearer than spiracle to vent, tail depth 2 5 3 15 in tail length, musculature of tail 1.2 2.5 in depth of tail, third lower row 2 0–3.0 in first and second lower row.

n Two rows of papillae under third row of teeth, median space of second upper row sometimes absent, if present 2½ or 3-7 in lateral part, horny beak 2 0–2 2 in first or second lower rows of teeth, third lower row 1 3 -1.4 in horny beak or 3 4 in upper fringe. *Pseudacris n feriarum*

Plate XII 5

nn. One row of papillae under third lower row of teeth; median space of second upper row 2 5 in either lateral row, horny beak 1 3- 1 5 in first or second lower rows of teeth, third lower row 1 8 in horny beak or 3 0 in upper fringe

*Pseudacris n triseriata*

[The key to *Pseudacris* may be worthless, and the characters given here may be extremely variant.]

hh. Tadpoles 35–50 mm , tadpoles not bicolored (brown above and white below) but green, citrine tadpoles or scarlet- or orange-tailed tadpoles, high-crested tadpoles, eye 1.0–1.75 nearer spiracle than snout, spiracle 1 0–1 6 nearer vent than tip of the snout, spiracle 1 25–2 5 nearer eye than vent or base of hind legs, papillae extend above the upper fringe for 0 14–0 285 of the length of the upper fringe.

i. Tadpoles 50 mm. in length, body in tail 2 3–3 25, av. 2 5, depth of body in width of body 0 83–1 0, av. 0 9, depth of tail 10 14 mm , beautiful green tadpoles, young tadpoles with a black saddle spot on the back of the musculature near its base and with a light line from eye to tail, one row of papillae below lower third labial row, papillae extending above first upper row for 0.25–0.285 of the fringe's length,

dorsal crest extending to a vertical halfway between eye and spiracle. Eggs single, submerged North Carolina to Louisiana *Hyla gratiosa*
Plates X–5,6, XII–2, LXIX–5

ii Tadpoles 35–45 mm., body in tail 1 1–2 0, av 1.6, depth of body in width of body 1 0–1 8, depth of tail 5–9 mm., no black saddle spot in young tadpoles.

j Tadpole small (35 mm.), dorsal crest extending to vertical halfway between spiracle and the base of the hind legs, depth of tail in tail length 2.5–3.5, av. 3 0, nostril to eye 1.2–2 1 in nostril to snout, mouth in interorbital space 1.33–2.6, internasal space in interorbital distance 1 33–2.2, eye just touches lateral axis or is below it, beak in first upper row 1.5–1.7, papillae extending beyond the end of the upper row 0.25–0.285 of the length of the upper row, two rows of papillae below third lower labial row, median space between second upper labial row 1.25–2 0 in either lateral portion; third lower labial row 0 20–0 22 of the first lower row, first row of lower labial teeth 1 0–1 5 times the horny beak Eggs strewn in water among sphagnum (Noble and Noble) New Jersey to South Carolina *Hyla andersonii*
Plate X–1, XII–3

jj Tadpole medium (40 and 45 mm ), dorsal crest extends ahead of spiracle or to eye, depth of tail in tail length 1 5–3.2, av. 2.75, nostril to eye 1.0–1.7 in nostril to snout, mouth in interorbital space 1 4–2.0, internasal in interorbital space 1 25–2 0, eye on lateral axis, papillae extending beyond end of first upper row 1.4–2 5 of the length of the first upper row, median space in second upper labial row 3–5 in either lateral portion, third labial row 0.25–0 40 of the first labial lower row, first row of lower labial teeth 1 0–1.3 greater than the horny beak

k. Dorsal crest to the vertical halfway between spiracle and the eye, depth of body in body length 1 7–2 5, musculature of tail in depth of tail 1 75–2 4, av. 1.9, spiracle 1 4 2 3 nearer eye than vent; mouth 1.0–1.4 larger than internasal space, av. 1 25, two rows of papillae below the third lower row of labial teeth, papillae extend beyond the end of the first upper row 0.22–0.25 of the length of this fringe, horny beak in upper row 2 0–2 3; third labial lower row 0.25–0.40 the length of the first lower row. Eggs surface or submerged irregular mass. Eastern Maryland to Florida to Texas to Illinois *Hyla cinerea*
Plates X–2; XII–4

kk. Dorsal crest extending to the vertical of the posterior edge of the eye, depth of body in body width 1.5–2.0, musculature in depth of tail 2.3–2.8, av. 2.5, spiracle 1.6–1.75 nearer eye than snout, mouth 1.0–1.2 larger than internasal space, one row of papillae below the third lower labial row of teeth, papillae extends beyond the end of the first upper row 0.14–0.20 of the length of this upper fringe, horny beak in upper fringe 1.4–1.8, third labial lower row 0.25–0.33 the length of the first lower row. Eggs loose irregular mass. Vancouver to Lower California and east to Utah and Arizona. *Hyla regilla*

gg. Third row of labial teeth long, longer than horny beak, or 0.75–1.00 of the first lower row in length; first upper row very angulate in middle; flagellum on tail, tadpoles 32–50 mm., heavy papillary development, lower labial corner with three or four rows of papillae, two more or less complete rows of papillae below third row of teeth (except in *Hyla arenicolor*), papillae extend above and beyond the end of the upper fringe for about 0.3–0.4 of its length

h. Third lower labial row 0.8–1.0 of the length of the first lower row, dorsal crest extends to the vertical halfway from hind legs to spiracle, to spiracle, or halfway from spiracle to eye, dorsal crest equal to, greater, or less than depth of tail musculature, tadpoles 36–50 mm., red may be present in the tail, tail crest distinctly or more or less clear of spots next to the musculature, tail heavily blotched with dark blotches or spots.

i. Median space between lateral upper rows 5.0–10.0 times in either lateral row, spiracle 1.44–2.5 nearer eye than vent, width of body in its own length 1.6–2.1, eye 1.0–1.7 nearer spiracle than tip of snout, tail sometimes suffused with coral red or coral pink.

j. Median space between lateral upper rows of teeth contained 6.0–10.0 in either lateral row, first and second lower rows of teeth 1.4–1.6 greater than horny beak; mouth equal to internasal space, depth of tail in length of tail 1.6–2.75, av. 2.25, muscular part of tail in depth of tail 1.8–2.3, av. 2.1, depth of body 1.33–2.2 in body length, av. 1.68, dorsal crest usually equal to or greater than musculature depth, center of belly solid sulphur yellow; *tail 3–5-banded,* light lateral band bounded above and below by a brown band, flagellum clear of pigment, body olivaceous black. Eggs a surface film. Virginia to Florida to Texas. *Hyla femoralis*

Plates X–4; XII–13; LXVIII–3

jj. Median space between lateral upper rows contained 5.0–10.0 times in either lateral row, first and second lower rows of teeth 1.5–2.0 greater than horny beak; third lower row of teeth may be equal to or slightly shorter than the first lower row, no or few papillae beneath the third lower row of teeth, surely not a complete row, mouth in internasal space 0.83–1.7, av. 1.3; depth of tail in length of tail, 2.85–5.15, av. 3.75, musculature of tail in depth of tail 1.28–1.76, av. 1.6; depth of body in body length 1.75–2.3, av. 2.0, dorsal crest halfway to, or to, vertical of the spiracle, dorsal crest less than the musculature, flagellum or tail tip spotted, body greenish olive or deep olive; center of belly solid pale cinnamon pink. Eggs single, submerged (Atsatt and Storer). Western Texas (Devil's River, Fort Davis Mountains, etc.), Utah, California, Mexico. *Hyla arenicolor*
Plate LX–6,7

ii Median space between lateral upper rows contained 3.25–5.0 times in either lateral row, spiracle 1.12–1.5 nearer eye than vent, eye about equidistant between spiracle and tip of snout, internasal space in mouth 0.7–1.0, dorsal crest extends to vertical of spiracle or halfway between eye and spiracle, dorsal crest equal to or greater than musculature depth; muscular part of tail in depth of tail 1.72–1.9, av. 1.8; depth of tail in length of tail 3.1–4.0; width of body in its own length 1.3–1.7; *no lateral bands in tail; tail more or less scarlet or orange vermilion with black blotches more prominent near the margins of the crests,* bodies olive-green, belly conspicuously white or very light cream. Eggs a surface film. Minnesota to Texas to Maine to Florida.
*Hyla v. versicolor*
Plates X–9,10; XII–12

hh Third lower labial row 0.75 of the length of the first row, dorsal crest extends to the vertical of the posterior edge of the eye, dorsal crest usually less than depth of the musculature, tadpoles to 32 mm; width of body in its own length 1.7–2.2, av. 1.875; depth of tail in length of tail 2.2–3.3, av. 2.8, third lower row of teeth not equal to first lower row; median space between lateral upper rows contained 3.25–5.0 times in length of either lateral row; papillae extend above and beyond the ends of the upper fringe for 0.3–0.33 of the upper fringe, horny beak in upper fringe 1.8–2.0, no bands or red in tail; tail crest clear, *uniformly sprinkled with distinct black dots;* body greenish (like *H. cinerea* or *H. gratiosa*); belly testaceous or chalcedony yellow. Eggs single, submerged. Texas to Indiana to Florida to Virginia. *Hyla squirella*
Plates X–7; XII–9

**Development and transformation:** Some frogs have limited breeding periods and other species may breed almost any month in the year. The males usually precede the females to the water and croak vigorously during breeding time. The male with its forearms seizes the female. In almost all frogs the eggs are fertilized just at or slightly after the extrusion of the eggs. At first no envelopes about the eggs are apparent, and the egg mass may feel soft and sticky. After a few minutes this substance absorbs water, and each egg is then revealed with its vitelline membrane and one or more jelly envelopes.

The eggs hatch in 3 to 25 days, depending on temperature and other conditions. At hatching the larva has a distinct neck, with a prominent head and body. The tail is very small or absent. On the ventral side of the head is an invagination or depression which is to be the mouth. Behind this comes the ventral adhesive disk or disks, which help the little creature to attach itself to the egg mass or to hang itself upon some plant. In front of the mouth are two deep, dark pits which later become the nostrils. On either side of the head appear swellings which become the external gills. The eyes do not yet appear.

As development goes on, the external gills appear as branched organs, two or three on a side; the eye shows as a ring beneath the skin; and the tail grows and presents a middle muscular portion where the muscle segments clearly show. This middle part supports a thin, waferlike tail fin the parts of which are called the lower

*Plate XV.* Development of the gopher frog, *Rana capito* 1. Egg mass (×⅕). 2 Eggs (×⅘). 3-7. Tadpoles (×⅝) [4. Lateral lines and spiracle, 5, with two legs; 6, with three legs, 7, with four legs.] 8. Transformed frog (×⅝). 9. Adult (×¼).

and upper crests. The nasal pit shifts in position and becomes the nostril, and the vent opens. The mouth appears, and dependence on the yolk of the belly ceases. Soon the external gills begin to disappear, a lateral flap or fold of skin connects the head with the body, and the neck region disappears. Beneath this fold internal gills develop. Usually on the left side but on the middle line in the belly in ribbed frogs and narrow-mouthed toads, the flap does not close completely, but leaves an opening, the spiracle. The water passes into the mouth over the internal gills and out of this hole. On the mouth a membranous, fringed lip, with upper and lower portions (labia) comes into being. At the portal are horny jaws or mandibles. On the upper and lower portions are ridges of horny teeth. The eyes are no longer covered, pigmented rings but are now at the surface. The intestine has become much elongated and coiled and in some can be seen through the skin. The skin of the back and head comes to have a series of sense organs (or lateral line dots).

The buds of the hind limbs begin to appear. The fore limbs start to develop beneath the skin. When the hind limbs have reached considerable size, the left arm comes out through the spiracle, or the skin breaks down and the right arm appears through the skin or the skin weakens for its egress. It is held that the left arm normally comes out first, but often the right arm appears first.

The process of transformation continues. The tail crests decrease in size and the creature begins to live on its tail—that is, to absorb it. The gills vanish, and the lungs begin to serve as the sole respiratory organs, if the skin be not considered. The tadpole appears more and more at the surface or near the shore. The eye assumes eyelids. The tadpole mouth fringe, with its horny jaws and horny teeth, is discarded, and a true frog mouth begins to appear. The long intestine becomes wonderfully shortened, for a carnivorous diet, and the small frog, with a vestige of a tail, is ready to leave the water. This process is termed transformation or metamorphosis.

In the accompanying table of 51 tadpoles, wherein total length, tail length, body length, and range of transformation size appear, we have a surprising correlation in an ascending scale for all four characters. The first criterion of arrangement is the arbitrary choice of total length. Strictly speaking, body length and transformation sizes should have governed the arrangement, but all seem more or less correlated. The most striking point is that the body length of the largest tadpoles for each species falls within the range of transformation size in all except six forms. In two of these the differences are only 2 mm. and 1 mm. In the spadefoot, *Scaphiopus couchii*, the body length of the tadpole is 2 mm. greater than the known size at transformation, and in Hammond's spadefoot, *Scaphiopus hammondii*, it is 5 mm. greater than the known transformation size. In *Scaphiopus holbrookii* no such condition obtains. Is it because these two species are desert species which breed in the most transitory places, and is there consequently a decided shrinking in body, before transformation, to speed development? Many have thought there is considerable shrinkage in the body of the tadpole before transformation. This may be true of some species, but in the following table there is no striking decrease as in the paradoxical toad (*Pseudis paradoxus*). Rather, the uniform parallel in body length of tadpole and of transformed individual is surprising even to the present authors, who have long worked with them.

At least 35 of the 51 tadpoles are less than 50 mm. in total length, and of the 26 species whose tadpoles are unknown or not minutely described at least 12 more will doubtless fall in this group of small or medium tadpoles. In our descriptions we have used ***small, medium,*** and ***large*** for tadpoles. We have called ***small*** 23–35 mm.; ***medium*** 40–50 or 55 mm.; ***large*** 60–140 mm. (***large,*** 60–86; ***quite large,*** 95–100; ***very large,*** 110–145).

In the table at least 32 species have tadpoles with body lengths of 18 mm. or less. Probably in time we will know that 50 of our species fall in this class, or, put in another way, at least two-thirds of our frog species will be found to transform at 18 or 20 mm. or less. Except for the true frogs (Ranidae), Hammond's spadefoot, and a toad or two (*Bufo*), no species grows tadpoles over 2 inches (50 mm.) in length.

We cannot say that the order of maximum length of tadpoles corresponds with the order of maximum length of adults. As would be expected, the smallest swamp cricket frogs and narrow-mouthed toads have small tadpoles, but with them appear most of the toads (*Bufo*) and spadefoots (*Scaphiopus* except *S. hammondii*). Toads and spadefoots are much larger than the tree toads (*Hyla* and *Acris*), which follow with larger tadpoles. Beginning with the tree frogs through the true frogs (Ranidae), the order of tadpole length more or less corresponds to that of adult size.

| *Name* | *Greatest length* | *Greatest tail length* | *Greatest body length* | *Transformation size* |
|---|---|---|---|---|
| | *mm.* | *mm.* | *mm.* | *mm.* |
| *Bufo quercicus* | | | | 7–8 |
| *Bufo debilis* | 22 | | | 8–11 |
| *Pseudacris ocularis* | 23 | 14.2 | 8.8 | 7–9 |
| *Pseudacris nigrita triseriata* | 23 | 14 2 | 8 | 7.5–11 |
| *Pseudacris n. septentrionalis* | | | | 7.5–13 |
| *Bufo valliceps* | 23 | 13 | 10 | 7.5–12 |
| *Bufo terrestris* | 24 | 14.2 | 9 8 | 6.5–10.5 |
| *Scaphiopus couchii* | 24.5 | 11 | 14.5 | 7.5–12.5 |
| *Pseudacris brachyphona* | 25 | | | 8 |
| *Microhyla olivacea* | 25 | 15.4 | 10 | 10–12 |
| *Bufo punctatus* | 26 | 16 | 10 | 9–11 |
| *Microhyla carolinensis* | 26.4 | 16.4 | 10 | 7–12 |
| *Scaphiopus h. hurterii* | 27 | 16 | 12 | 8–10 |
| *Bufo canorus* | 27 | | | 10.5 |
| *Bufo w. fowleri* | 27 | 17 | 10 | |

| Name | Greatest length | Greatest tail length | Greatest body length | Transformation size |
|---|---|---|---|---|
| | mm. | mm. | mm. | mm. |
| *Bufo a. americanus* | 27.8 | 17.6 | 10.2 | 7–12 |
| *Bufo w. woodhousii* | 27 | 17 | 10 | 10–17 |
| *Scaphiopus h. holbrookii* | 28 | 16.4 | 12 | 8.5–12 |
| *Bufo compactilis* | 28 | 16 | 12 | 12 |
| *Bufo cognatus* | 29 | 17 | 12 | |
| *Pseudacris n. clarkii* | 30 | 19 | 11 | 8–13 |
| *Hypopachus cuneus* | 30 | | | 10–12 |
| *Bufo hemiophrys* | | | | 9–13.5 |
| *Hyla squirella* | 32 | 20 | 12 | 11–13 |
| *Pseudacris ornata* | 32 | 18 | 14 | 14–16 |
| *Leptodactylus labialis* | 32 | 15 | 17 | 16 |
| *Pseudacris n. feriarum* | 33 | 22.4 | 10.6 | 8–12 |
| *Hyla crucifer* | 33 | 22 | 11 | 9–14 |
| *Hyla femoralis* | 33 | 22.5 | 10 | 10–15 |
| *Pseudacris streckeri* | 33 | 21 | 12 | |
| *Hyla andersonii* | 35 | 23 | 12 | 11–15 |
| *Bufo exsul* | 35 | 20 | 15 | |
| *Hyla c. cinerea* | 40 | 25 | 15 | 12–17 |
| *Acris g. gryllus* | 42.2 | 29.2 | 13 | 9–15 |
| *Hyla wrightorum* | 43 | 26 | 17 | 11–17 |
| *Bufo b. boreas* | 44 | | | 9.5–12 |
| *Hyla v. versicolor* | 46.6 | 30.8 | 15.8 | 13–20 |
| *Hyla regilla* | 46.6 | 30 | 16 | 11–17 |
| *Acris g. crepitans* | 47 | 32 | 15 | 11–15 |
| *Rana b. boylii* | 47 | 29 | 18 | 23–30 |
| *Hyla gratiosa* | 50 | 31 | 19 | 14–20 |
| *Hyla arenicolor* | 50 | 33 | 15.4 | 14–16 |
| *Rana a. aurora* | 50 | 30 | 20 | 17–21 |
| *Rana s. sylvatica* | 50 | 33 | 17 | 16–22 |
| *Rana s. cantabrigensis* | 50 | 30 | 20 | 14–22 |
| *Ascaphus truei* | 51 | 33 | 18 | 14–18 |
| *Hyla baudinii* | | | | 21 |
| *Scaphiopus hammondii intermontanus* | 52 | 30 | 22 | 20–24 |
| *Bufo b. halophilus* | 56 | 33 | 23 | 12–15 |
| *Bufo b. nelsoni* | | | | 15–18 |
| *Rana p. sphenocephala* | 62.5 | 37.5 | 25 | 18–33 |
| *Scaphiopus h. bombifrons* | 63–95 | | | |
| *Scaphiopus h. hammondii* | 65 | 37 | 28 | 13–23 |
| *Rana p. pretiosa* | 68.5 | 43 | 25.5 | 16–23 |
| *Rana cascadae* | 70 | | 22 | 13–17 |
| *Rana b. muscosa* | 70 | | | 20–24 |

| *Name* | *Greatest length* | *Greatest tail length* | *Greatest body length* | *Transformation size* |
|---|---|---|---|---|
| | *mm.* | *mm.* | *mm.* | *mm.* |
| *Rana b. sierrae* | 72 | 48 | 23.5 | 21–27 |
| *Rana palustris* | 75.8 | 48.8 | 27 | 19–27 |
| *Rana aurora draytonii* | 83 | 55 | 28 | 27 |
| *Rana fisheri* | 83 | | | 28–30 |
| *Rana areolata circulosa* | | | | 30 |
| *Rana capito* | 81 | 53 | 29 | 27–35 |
| *Rana pipiens* | 84 | 56 | 28 | 18–31 |
| *Rana clamitans* | 84.8 | 57 | 27.8 | 28–38 |
| *Rana tarahumarae* | 88 | 56 | 32 | 30–35 |
| *Rana virgatipes* | 92 | 63 | 30 | 23–31 |
| *Rana septentrionalis* | 99 | 67 | 32 | 29–40 |
| *Rana heckscheri* | 95 | 53.5 | 41.5 | 31–49 |
| *Rana grylio* | 110 | 64.4 | 35.6 | 32–49 |
| *Rana catesbeiana* | 142 | 97 | 45 | 43–59 |
| *Bufo alvarius* | | Not described | | |
| *Bufo californicus* | | Not described | | |
| *Bufo insidior* | | Not described | | |
| *Hyla avivoca* | | Not described | | |
| *Hyla septentrionalis* | | Not described | | |
| *Pseudacris brimleyi* | | Not described | | |
| *Pseudacris n. nigrita* | | Not described | | |
| *Pseudacris n. verrucosa* | | Not described | | |
| *Rana a. areolata* | | Not described | | |
| *Rana sevosa* | | Not described | | |
| *Rana onca* | | Not described | | |

**Journal notes:** These are customarily from our field notes. They treat of habitats, general habits, or breeding; sometimes of experiences in collecting the frogs; of their enemies; or of their usefulness and associated ecological features. Occasionally, you will find comparisons with closely related forms. Under topics such as "Voice," excerpts from our field notes are included. In 1925–1934 we worked on Texan forms, and in the first edition of this handbook only summaries of these forms appeared. In the present edition more notes are added on the southwestern and western forms. These are based mainly on a recent (1942) 25,000-mile trip in that region.

**Authorities' corner:** Here are given references to, or quotations from, some of the more important works on the various frogs. We would have liked to publish excerpts from all the authors cited, but space limitations forbade. Papers that have appeared since the completion of the manuscript (1947–1948) have also been listed. These references are in no sense a bibliography of the form.

*Figure 1* American bell toad, Ascaphidae *Ascaphus truei.* 1. Short anal tube of female. 2. Light band across head. 3 Rear of femur 4 Tail of male, extending from ventral side of body. 5. Vent 6 Horny excrescences (secondary breeding characters) of the male.

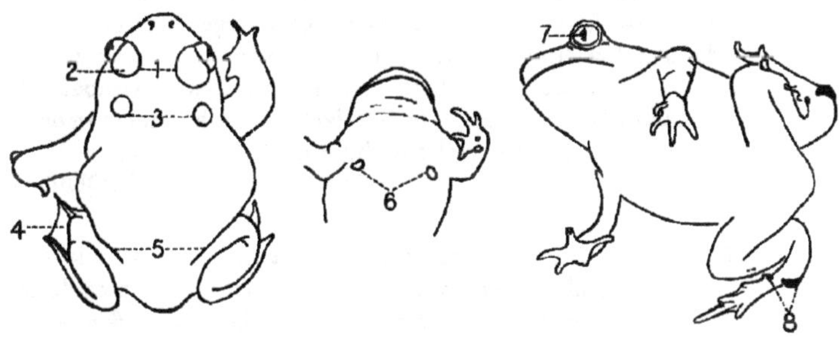


*Figure 2* Spadefoots, Scaphiopodidae: *Scaphiopus* 1 Wide interorbital space. 2. Upper eyelid. 3. Small round parotoids 4. Fleshy webs 5 Broad waist 6 Pectoral glands 7. Vertical pupil. 8. Two metatarsal tubercles, the outer large and with a cutting edge.

# Keys

## FAMILIES

A. Male with taillike process, female with short anal tube, no tympanum, pupil elliptically vertical, upper jaw toothed; short ribs present, internasal space 4.66–8.0 in L., light band across head, size small, 1 1/8–2 in. (28–51 mm.). Ribbed toads, ASCAPHIDAE
Plate XVI

AA. Male without tail; female without short anal tube; ribs absent; internasal space 7.77–21.4 in L.

B. Waist wide, body broad and thick, hind limbs short.

C. With transverse fold of skin across head behind eyes, size small, 3/4–1 5/8 in. (19–41 mm.); no tympanum, no parotoids, snout pointed, head narrow, fingers and toes without webs except slight in *Hypopachus;* eyes small and depressed.
Narrow-mouthed toads, BREVICIPITIDAE
Plates CXXIV–CXXVI

CC. Without transverse fold of skin across head, behind eyes, size medium to large, 1 1/2–8 4/5 in. (37–220 mm.), except *B. debilis* and *B. quercicus* (2/3 in.), tympanum distinct or indistinct; parotoids present except in 2 species of *Scaphiopus;* feet with extensive fleshy webs, snout blunt, eyes large; head broad

D. Pupil vertical (by day), parotoids absent in 2 species, present but rounded and indistinct in 1 species, sole without subarticular tubercles, skin relatively smooth, venter smooth, no cranial crests, males without discolored throats
Spadefoots, SCAPHIOPODIDAE
Plates XVII–XXIII

DD. Pupil not vertical, parotoids present and elevated, sole with subarticular tubercles; skin warty, venter usually granulated; cranial crests present in most species, lacking in *Bufo boreas, B. canorus, B. compactilis, B. debilis, B. exsul, B. insidior, B. punctatus;* males usually with discolored throats
Toads, BUFONIDAE
Plates XXIV–XLIV

BB. Waist narrow, body narrower and thinner, hind limbs long, no parotoid.

C. Disks on digits, neither thumb nor other fingers enlarged in male

D. Disks transverse, venter usually smooth, subarticular tubercles saw-toothed; eggs large, male throat not discolored.
Robber frogs, LEPTODACTYLIDAE
(*Syrrhophus, Eleutherodactylus*)
Plates LXXVII–LXXXIV

DD. Disks round, large or small; pupil elliptically horizontal; subarticular tubercles rounded, venter usually granular or areolate, male throat discolored. Tree frogs, HYLIDAE
Plates XLV–LXXVI

CC. No disks on digits.

D. Extensive webs on toes, thumb of male enlarged at base, venter smooth Frogs, RANIDAE
Plates LXXXV-CXXIII

DD Toes free, males, if different, with strong conical spine on inner side of first digit and another on each side of breast, and forelimb much enlarged.
Robber frogs, LEPTODACTYLIDAE (*Leptodactylus*, etc )
Plates LXXXI, LXXXII

### Spadefoots, SCAPHIOPODIDAE. Scaphiopus

A. Parotoid absent or indistinct, tympanum indistinct, no pectoral gland.

B Hind limb longer (0 78–0 96 in L ); fore limb longer (1 51–2 19 in L ), fourth finger longer (6 28–8 0 in L ), foot with tarsus longer (1.57–1.76 in L ), fourth toe longer (2 66–3 29 in L ); size small, 1 1/2–2 2/5 in (37–61 mm.), back uniform or with light bands.
Hammond's spadefoot, *Scaphiopus hammondii*
Plates XVIII–XX

Limits of range and gradations need to be worked out After Tanner we present this synopsis.

(C. "Interorbital boss present, rounded, not elongate tubercle, fronto-parietal fontanelle present, body smooth or less rugose dorsally than CC, head width narrower" (width of head in L. 2 6–2 95, av. 2.74, eye smaller, 10 1–12 4 in L --A.H.W.).
*Scaphiopus h. bombifrons*
Plate XIX

CC. "No interorbital boss present. In some specimens of *intermontanus* there is a glandular interorbital elevation which resembles the true boss in *bombifrons*." Head wider (width of head in L. 2.22–2 58, av 2 35; eye larger, 7 3–8 6 in L.—A.H.W ).

D. "Body rugose or with many individual prominences or warts."

E "No fronto-parietal fontanelle, interorbital space with prominent fronto-parietal bones forming ridges . or in some specimens the interorbital space is filled with a glandular prominence resembling the *bombifrons* species, confined in the main to the Great Basin area." (Hind toes longer, second toe 4.3–6.2 in L., third toe 3.1–4 0 in L., fourth toe 2.2–2 66 in L.—A.H.W ) *Scaphiopus h. intermontanus*
Plate XX

EE. "A fronto-parietal fontanelle present, interorbital space smooth, size intermediate between *bombifrons* and *intermontanus*; . . . found on Pacific Coast south into Arizona and Texas" (Hind toes shorter, second toe 6 2–7.3 in L, third toe 4.0–4 2 in L, fourth toe 2 6–3.0 in L.—A H W)
*Scaphiopus h. hammondii*
Plate XVIII)

BB. Hind limb shorter (0 89–1 15 in L), fore limb shorter (2.0–2.31 in L), fourth finger shorter (8 0–11 2 in L), foot with tarsus shorter (1.7–2 35 in L); fourth toe shorter (3.02–4.0 in L.); size larger, 1 7/8–3 1/5 in. (48–80 mm.), back greenish, more or less marbled with light. Couch's spadefoot, *Scaphiopus couchii*
Plate XVII

AA Tympanum distinct, parotoid distinct, pectoral glands present, size 2–2 7/8 in (50–72 mm) *Scaphiopus holbrookii*
Plates XXI–XXIII

B Head to angle of mouth smaller (3 14–3 81 in L), width of head smaller (2.58–2 66 in L), snout smaller (5 4–6 3 in L.), tympanum smaller (11 5–16 0 in L)
Hurter's spadefoot, *Scaphiopus holbrookii hurterii*
Plate XXIII

BB. Head to angle of mouth greater (2.93–3.56 in L); width of head greater (2 24–2 75 in L.), snout larger (5.17–6 6 in L), tympanum greater (10 1–12 0 in L); skin relatively smooth with two or more evident light dorsal stripes Spadefoot, *Scaphiopus h. holbrookii*
Plate XXI

(C. "Great amount of white on back, flanks, and upper surface of limbs, vermiculated irregular white bands."
Key West spadefoot, *Scaphiopus holbrookii albus*
Plate XXII)

## Toads, BUFONIDAE **Bufo**

A Gland on leg, fold skin on tarsus, warts at angle of mouth.

B Crests curved around rear of eye, size large, 3 1/5–6 3/5 in. (80–165 mm), skin smooth, head broad (2 2–2 8 in L), color uniform, glands conspicuous on both tibia and femur, tympanum medium (12–15 in L) Colorado River toad, *Bufo alvarius*
Plate XXIV

BB. Crests absent, gland on tibia only, pitted warts on back, tympanum small (14–26 in L).

C Dimorphic, interparotoid interval less than width of gland; parotoid and leg gland obscured by pattern; skin smooth, male uniform green, female spotted, size small, 2–3 in (50–75 mm.)
Yosemite toad, *Bufo canorus*
Plate XXXI

CC. Not dimorphic; parotoids widely separated, interval greater than width of gland, parotoid and leg glands evident, size small, medium or large (42 5–125 mm ) 1 4/5–5 in *Bufo boreas* group

D. Eyelid narrower (11 8–14.6 in L ), eye smaller (9 4–11 7 in L ), head narrower (2 66–3.1 in L ), third toe longer (2.8–3 5 in L ); fourth toe longer (2 0–2 5 in L.). "Spread of hind foot from end of first toe to the fifth toe more than 36% of length" (Camp, 1917b).
Northwestern toad, *Bufo boreas boreas*
Plate XXVII

DD Eyelid wider (7 3–14 in L ), eye larger (7.0–10.5 in L ); head wider (2 4–3 0 in L ), third toe shorter (3 1–4 25 in L ), fourth toe shorter (2 53–3.8 in L.), spread of hind foot less than 36% of the length.

E Dorsum almost entirely black, size small, 1 4/5–2 1/2 in (44–61 5 mm ), eyelid wider (7 3–12 in L ), width of head 2 77–3 0 in L., fourth toe longer (2.53–2.66 in L.), venter heavily spotted with black.
Black toad, *Bufo exsul*
Plate XXXV

EE. Dorsum gray, green, or brown spotted, size medium to large, 1 4/5–5 in. (42 5–125 mm.), eyelid narrower (9.3–14 in L ), fourth toe shorter (2 57–3.8 in L ), venter uniform white or lightly or moderately spotted

F. Size medium to large, 2 2/5–5 in. (60–125 mm.), hind limb longer (0 8–1 0 in L.), head wider (2.4–2.85 in L.), fourth toe shorter (3 3–3 8 in L.), third toe longer (3 2–3 8 in L ).
California toad, *Bufo boreas halophilus*
Plate XXVIII

FF Size small to medium, 1 4/5 to 2 1/2 in. (42.5–61 mm ), hind limb shorter (1 0–1 2 in L ), fore limb shorter (1.86–2 15 in L.), head narrower (2 8–3 1 in L ), fourth toe longer (2 57–2 94), third toe shorter (3 5–4 25 in L.), "elbows and knees not meeting when appressed to the sides of the body" (Stejneger).
Amargosa toad, *Bufo b nelsoni*
Plate XXIX

AA. No gland on leg, no fold of skin on tarsus.

B. Femur almost entirely enclosed in body skin; vocal sac elliptical (sausage), 2 sole (metatarsal) tubercles with cutting edge.

C. Crests prominent, boss on snout, interorbital narrow (11–19 in L.)—less than internasal, middorsal stripe and light-bordered large dark spots (sometimes small spots).

Great Plains toad, *Bufo cognatus*
Plate XXXII

CC. Crests absent, interorbital broad (9.7–11.7 in L.)—greater than internasal; drab with small, dull citrine spots

Spadefoot toad, *Bufo compactilis*
Plate XXXIII

BB. Half or more of femur free from body skin, outer metatarsal tubercle without cutting edge.

C. Parotoids oval to elongate (sometimes triangular in *Bufo quercicus*)

D. Crests absent or obscure, parotoids broadly oval, divergent, interorbital broad (9.4–11.8 in L.), narrowing forward; snout 7.0–8.25 in L.

Southern California toad, *Bufo californicus*
Plate XXX

DD. Crests present.

E. Size small, 3/4–1 1/4 in. (19–32 mm.), vocal sac a sausage; mouth small (4.0–4.6 in L.), tympanum small (14–20 in L.), snout long (5.7–7.0 in L.), yellow stripe down mid-back, many red tubercles

Oak toad, *Bufo quercicus*
Plate XL

EE. Size greater, 1 5/8–4 3/4 in. (40–118 mm.), snout shorter (6.2–9.4 in L.).

F. Mouth small (4.1–4.7 in L.), tympanum small (14–22 in L.), head narrower (2.5–3.1 in L.); head shorter (3.4–3.9 in L.), crests, a boss, from snout to rear of eye, with sides parallel, snout 7.4–9.3 in L.

Canadian toad, *Bufo hemiophrys*
Plate XXXVI

FF. Mouth large (3.3–4.3 in L.), tympanum large (10–18.2 in L.), head wider (2.3 in L.)

G. Crests prominent with knobs in rear, skin finely and evenly roughened with tubercles between larger warts, red, gray, or black, snout 6.8 in L.

Southern toad, *Bufo terrestris*
Plate XLI

GG. Crests low, paired spots of darker color down back, superciliary crests meeting postorbital at right angles, snout 6.2–9.4 in L.

H. Small uniform warts on back, several warts in each dark dorsal spot, dark pectoral spot, no preparotoid longitudinal crests, under parts usually unspotted, back greenish, size smaller, 2–3¼ in. (51–82 mm.), snout 7.7–9.4 in L.
Fowler's toad, *Bufo woodhousii fowleri*
Plate XLIV

HH. Large dorsal warts, one or two warts in each dark dorsal spot, under parts spotted or plain.

I. Many warts spiny, particularly on hind limbs, parotoids parallel, closest together at midpoint, parotoid on dorsolateral line or on dorsum; no boss, preparotoid longitudinal crest present, venter often spotted, middorsal absent or present, snout 6.2–9.1 in L.
American toad, *Bufo a. americanus*
Plate XXV

J. Brilliant coloration, long, narrow parotoids; greater width between parallel cranial crests, hind limbs shorter, ventral granulation smooth.
Hudson Bay toad, *Bufo americanus copei*
Plate XXVI

II. Warts round, smaller, parotoids slightly divergent at rear and on lateral aspect, parotoids usually in contact with postorbital crest, often with boss on nostril with crests extending backward, venter unspotted or with median pectoral spot, middorsal line present, snout 7.0–9.1 in L.
Rocky Mountain toad, *Bufo w. woodhousii*
Plate XLIII

CC. Parotoids round or triangular, sole (metatarsal) tubercles round, small, noncutting, dorsal pattern without the 4–6 paired spots (of the *B. americanus, w. fowleri, terrestris, woodhousii*, etc., group)

D. Crest prominent, size large, 2–8 4/5 in. (50–220 mm.), parotoid subtriangular.

E. Parotoid as large or larger than side of head, divergent, not bicolored, toes 1/2–2/3 webbed, crests not trenchant and top of head not a deep valley, brown with some black, yellow, red, olive, with or without black spots on a light vertebral line, snout 7.3–8.6 in L. Marine toad, *Bufo marinus*
Plate XXXVIII

EE. Parotoid much smaller, not as large as side of head, not divergent, bicolored, row of light conical tubercles on side, body flat, toes 1/3 webbed, crest high trenchant and top of head a deep valley; brown or blackish brown with light olive, buff, or cinnamon area down back and a similar band or stripe on either side, snout 6.6–10.4 in L Nebulous toad, *Bufo valliceps*
Plate XLII

DD Crests absent or obscure, male excrescences on first two fingers not prominent, size small, below 3 in (45 mm.).

E. Parotoids large, low, descending on side, as long as side of head, body rounded; head narrower (2.7–3 15 in L.), snout distinctly pointed and protruding (6 9–9 2 in L.), foot with tarsus short (2 0–2.4 in L ), size small, 1–1 4/5 in (26–46 mm.), green or gray. [Recently subdivided by Taylor into Girard's two forms, *B debilis* and *B. insidior* ]

(F Toes about 1/3 webbed, nostril back from tip of snout; preorbital and suborbital crests smooth, without tubercles, parotoid as large as side of head; anterior edge of tympanum not strongly elevated
Little green toad, *Bufo debilis*
Plate XXXIV

FF. Toes about 1/2 webbed, nostril at extreme tip of snout; parotoid larger than side of head; anterior edge of tympanum elevated *Bufo insidior*
Plate XXXVII

After Smith and Taylor's 1948 checklist.)

EE Parotoids small, raised, rounded, body flat, head broader (2.3-2 6 in L ), snout not distinctly protruding, canthus rostralis prominent, foot with tarsus medium (1 66–1 88 in L ), size medium, 1 3/5–3 in (40–74 mm ), red to gray.
Spotted toad, *Bufo punctatus*
Plate XXXIX

**Tree Frogs,** HYLIDAE· **Acris, Pseudacris, Hyla**

A Alternating dark and light bands on rear of thigh, oblique white stripe from eye to shoulder; vertical dark and light bars on upper jaw, white margined triangle between eyes, hind leg very long (0.55–0.62 in L ); tibia very long (1.5–1 7 in L.). Cricket frog, *Acris gryllus*

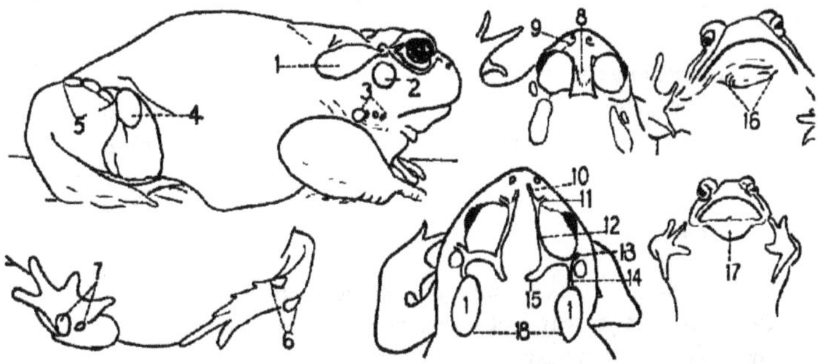


*Figure 3.* Toads, Bufonidae: *Bufo.* 1. Parotoid. 2. Tympanum (ear). 3. Warts at angle of mouth. 4. Gland on femur. 5. Glands on tibia. 6. Two metatarsal (sole) tubercles. 7. Two metacarpal (palmar) tubercles. 8. Crests united forming a prominent raised boss between the eyes. 9. Canthus rostralis. 10. Canthal crest. 11. Preorbital crest. 12. Supraorbital crest. 13 Postorbital crest. 14. Preparotoid crest 15. Parietal crest 16. Folds of skin of lower throat of male, covered at periods of rest by the lappet (17). 17. Lappet or apron at rear of throat of male 18. Interparotoid interval.

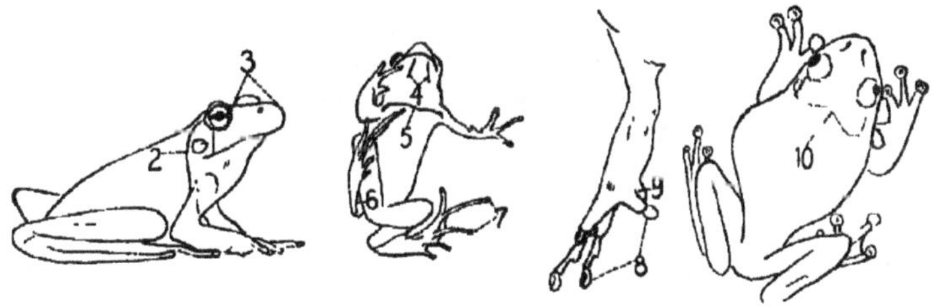


*Figure 4.* Tree frogs, Hylidae: *Acris, Pseudacris,* and *Hyla* 1. Tympanum (ear). 2. Tympanic fold. 3. Snout (muzzle). 4. Plaits on throat of male 5. Pectoral fold across breast. 6. Tarsal fold. 7. Small adhesive disks. 8. Large adhesive disks. 9. Prepollex. 10. Rear of casque (skin fastened to skull) outlines rear of head.

(B. Smaller, less web (3 phalanges of toe 4 free, toe 1 partly free); more rugose; anal warts less prominent, legs longer, heel reaching beyond snout, rear of thigh more definitely striped *Acris g gryllus*
Plate XLV

BB. Larger, more web (2–1½ phalanges of toe 4 free, toe 1 completely webbed); smoother, anal warts more prominent, legs shorter, heel not reaching to snout; rear of thigh less definitely striped.
*Acris g crepitans*
Plate XLVI

After Dunn.)

AA No alternation of dark and light bands on rear of thigh, triangle between eyes, if present, not white-margined, no alternation of dark and light bars on upper jaw.

B. No dark, brown, black, or plum-colored stripe in front of or behind eye

C. Head skin attached to skull, thumb rudiment apparent, rear of femur reticulated; no light jaw spot or dark bar between eyes, disks very large, size large, 2 3/5–5 1/5 in (64–130 mm.).
Giant tree frog, *Hyla septentrionalis*
Plate LXXI

CC Head skin not grown to skull, no thumb rudiment; rear of femur unspotted.

D. Rear of thigh purple; no interorbital bar between eyes; throat with green on either side.

E. Green of female's throat not edged with white, back smooth green; body slender (head's width 3.0–3 6 in L )

F. Yellow or white line along side and on upper jaw, tibia 1.7–1.95 in L., third finger longer (3.4–4 0 in L ).
Green tree frog, *Hyla c cinerea*
Plate LXIV

FF. No yellow or white line along side or on upper jaw, tibia 1.95–2 1 in L., third finger shorter (4.5–5 4 in L ). Miller's tree frog, *Hyla c evittata*
Plate LXV

EE. Green of female's throat edged with white; back usually granular and dark-spotted; body stout (head's width 2.3–2 8 in L.), white stripe from tip of snout along upper jaw backward. Barker, *Hyla gratiosa*
Plate LXIX

DD. Rear of thigh orange or ocher, interocular bar present; throat without green on either side.

E. Light stripe below eye to shoulder, back black, green, or brown, spotted or not; smooth; first finger 7.0–9.3 in L.; first toe 7–14 in L.; interorbital space 8.0–9.3 in L.

Squirrel tree frog, *Hyla squirella*
Plate LXXII

EE. No light stripe on upper jaw or light spot below eye, brown or gray usually spotted; large disks, first finger 5.1–6.5 in L.; first toe 5.5–8.8 in L.; interorbital space 9.0–10.6 in L.

Canyon tree frog, *Hyla arenicolor*
Plates LX, LXI

BB. Dark, brown, black stripe or band in front of or behind eye or both.

C. Rear of thigh spotted

D. White-edged, plum-colored band from eye to groin, back green, unspotted with dark, rear of femur with deep orange spots, no interorbital bar, throat with green on either side, green white-edged in female. Anderson tree frog, *Hyla andersonii*
Plate LIX

DD. No plum-colored band, interocular bar present, back usually with spots.

E. Network of black on yellow sides, broad dark vitta back from eye becoming a vertical shoulder bar, throat with greenish or yellow, rear of thigh netted with greenish yellow and purplish russet, light yellow or green spot below eye; size large, 1 3/4–3 3/5 in. (44–89 mm.).

Mexican tree frog, *Hyla baudinii*
Plate LXIII

EE. No network of black on yellow sides; no black or brown shoulder bar; throat not prominently greenish, medium to small.

F. Rear of thigh brown, no netted pattern.

G. Rear of thigh with distinct round or elliptic orange yellow spots, no light spot below eye, a cross-shaped spot on back. Pine woods tree frog, *Hyla femoralis*
Plate LXVIII

(GG. Rear of thigh specked with yellowish brown and darker brown; three rows of approximated spots on back or cruciform spot, light spot below eye present or absent (After Cope.)

Dusky tree toad, *Hyla versicolor phaeocrypta*)
Plate LXXVI

FF. Rear of thigh netted with black or dark; light spot below eye.

G. Rear of thigh with green in network; groin greenish, cross on back in center or rear of back; back less rough, intertympanic space 2.6–3.2 in L., internasal space 8–10 in L., third finger 2.9–3.2 in L.

Viosca's tree frog, *Hyla avivoca*
Plate LXII

GG. Rear of thigh with orange in network, groin orange; cross on forward half of the back; skin commonly rough, intertympanic space 3.0–3.8 in L., internasal space 9.0–12.5 in L., third finger 3.2–4.8 in L.

Common tree toad, *Hyla versicolor*

H. Dorsal surfaces smooth, "a number of subcircular golden spots in the brown ground on rear of thighs; interspaces [on rear of femur] often reduced to small circular spots." Cope's tree frog, *Hyla v. chrysoscelis*
Plate LXXIV

HH. Dorsal surfaces rough, "brown reticulation on yellow ground of the posterior face of the thighs", "more fully marbled with yellow and brown, even covering the whole inner face of the tibia and the light interspaces more or less angular."

Common tree toad, *Hyla v. versicolor*
Plate LXXIII

CC. Rear of thigh unspotted, usually a transverse bar or triangle or median longitudinal line between eyes.

D. A narrow oblique cross on back, rear of thigh olive ocher or raw sienna, no prominent lateral dark stripe. Peeper, *Hyla crucifer*

(E. Slight and indistinct chest spotting, stripe along margin of upper jaw, coloration less rich, dorsal stripes less broad.

Peeper, *H. c. crucifer*
Plate LXVI

EE. More or less pronounced ventral spotting, dark spots along margin of upper jaw, coloration richer, broader dorsal stripes.

Florida peeper, *H. c. bartramiana* Harper
Plate LXVII

After Harper.)

DD. No oblique cross on back, usually a triangle or spot between eyes or median dark longitudinal line; dorsal and vittal stripes or rows of spots.

E. Size very tiny, 2/5–5/8 in. (11 5–17.5 mm ), three dorsal stripes usually but not always absent; stripe from eye backwards usually present; very long hind limbs (0 53-0 64 in L ), tibia very long (1.5–2.1 in L.).

Little chorus frog, ***Pseudacris ocularis***
Plate LVI

EE Size small, 3/4–1 7/8 in (19–48 mm ), 4 or 5 dark stripes or rows of spots usually present; hind limb 0.62–0 87 in L.

F. Five stripes or rows of spots usually present, size small, disks inconspicuous.

***Pseudacris*** type of coloration (middorsal, dorsolateral, and vittal stripes or rows of spots, 5 in number) more or less evident.

A dark equilateral interocular triangle (sides concave or straight).

Prominent white stripe on upper jaw, extending backward below prominent vittal stripe and more or less along side of body

A dark lateral stripe more or less evident.

No oblique cross on back (occasionally present in ***Pseudacris brachyphona*** and ***P. streckeri***).

Tympanum smaller, usually 11–28 in L.

Winter or early spring breeders (December-May).

(G. Lateral black stripe sharply defined with weak dorsal 3-stripe pattern; tendency for leg markings to be longitudinal; narrow dark line on outer tibial edge; more delicate, smoother skin; yellowish venter. (After Brandt and Walker ))

Brimley's chorus frog, ***Pseudacris brimleyi***
Plate XLVIII

GG. Each lateral stripe and 3 dorsal stripes more or less equally defined; leg markings more or less transverse, small size (adults reaching 30, 32–37 mm , 1.2–1 5 in ), sexually mature at 19–22 mm or more, ***Pseudacris*** type pattern (5 stripes or rows of spots) generally discernible; middorsal stripe or row of spots usually present; disks small, inconspicuous, body slender.

Swamp cricket frog, ***Pseudacris nigrita***, 6 subspecies
Plates XLIX–LIV

H. Hind limb shorter (0 74–0 82 in L , av 0 79), tibia shorter (2 36–2.8 in L., av 2 59), foot with tarsus shorter (1.55–1 75 in L , av. 1.69), fore limb shorter (2 06–2.22 in L., av. 2.14); head shorter (head to tympanum 3 29–3.63 in L., av. 3.40), mouth shorter (head to angle of mouth 3 73–5.71, av 4 39). Minn to B.C., Great Bear Lake, and Hudson Bay.

Northern striped tree frog, ***P n. septentrionalis***
Plate LII

HH. Hind limb longer (0.62–0.75, avs. 0.64–0.72), tibia longer (1.87–2.54, avs. 1.94–2.36); foot with tarsus longer (1.23–1.60 in L., avs. 1.36–1.47), fore limb longer (1.5–2.33, avs. 1.80–1.99), head longer (head to tympanum 2.55–3.29 in L., avs. 2.94–3.24), mouth longer (head to angle of mouth 3.0–4.66, avs. 3.39–3.71).

I. Tibia shorter (2.24–2.54 in L., av. 2.36), head shorter (3.14–3.29 in L., av. 3.24); dorsum finely granular. "All the upper part an inconspicuous dark greenish gray with three longitudinal rows of large elongated spots . . ." (Wied) Middle row "unbroken . . to middle of the back," then "separate spots." N.Y. and Ont. to Idaho and northern Ariz. Striped tree frog, ***Pseudacris n. triseriata***
Plate LIII

II. Tibia longer (1.77–2.26 in L.), head longer (2.55–3.29 in L., av. 2.94–3.04).

J. Head shorter (av. 3.04 in L.), head wider (av. 3.13 in L.) "Above dark or fawn, with three nearly parallel stripes down the back, the central widening but scarcely bifurcate behind . . ." (Baird) Dorsum more or less smooth. N.J. to N.C., possibly S.C.
Eastern chorus frog, ***Pseudacris n. feriarum***
Plate LI

JJ. Head longer (av. 2.94 in L.), head narrower (av. 3.28–3.6 in L.).

K. Snout shorter (5.71–7.0 in L., av. 6.33). "Above grayish brown or ash with distinct large circular blotches" (Baird). Dorsum smooth or only slightly tubercular. Texas to Kansas.
Clarke's chorus frog, ***Pseudacris n. clarkii***
Plate L

KK. Snout longer (4.6–6.66 in L., av. 5.70), dorsum more or less tubercular.

L. "A light line is present along the jaw." "Above, speckled with small white warts, middle of back cinereous, with an interrupted stripe of black" (Le Conte). N.C. to La. Swamp cricket frog, ***Pseudacris n. nigrita***
Plate XLIX

LL. "Upper lip dark plumbeous with a series of . . . white spots" (Cope) or these absent. (Dorsum often tubercular, hind limb light intervals broader than in ***P. n. nigrita.*** Dorsal spots smaller and better separated—Brady and Harper) Florida.
Florida chorus frog, ***Pseudacris n. verrucosa***
Plate LIV

FF. Four stripes or rows of spots.

G. Vittal stripe slender, dorsolateral bands curved, sometimes making a cross or transverse bar on back; hind limbs long (0.60–0.67 in L.), triangle between eyes, disks distinct.

Mountain chorus frog, *Pseudacris brachyphona*
Plate XLVII

GG Vittal mask white-bordered above, vittal stripe darker than other stripes or rows of spots, hind limb 0.62–0 87 in L

H Body broad, toadlike (1.75–2 0 in L ); disks inconspicuous; vitta ends at shoulder, hind limbs shorter (0 73–0 87 in L )

Strecker's ornate chorus frog, *Pseudacris streckeri*
Plate LVIII

HH. Body narrow (1.94 in L.), hind limbs longer (0 62–0 78 in L.).

I Disks inconspicuous, dark mask ending beyond shoulder sometimes to groin, oblique groin spots light-bordered, interorbital space narrow (8 8–14 4 in L.)

Ornate chorus frog, *Pseudacris ornata*
Plate LVII

II Disks distinct, interorbital wide (7.2–10 in L ), no light borders around groin spots if present

J. Vitta may extend some distance along the side, interocular triangle or bar absent, dark spot each eyelid usually present, a pair of dark longitudinal postsacral bars or spots—the conspicuous dorsal marking, tympanum smaller (14.4–20 in L ), first finger shorter (7 20–10 in L ), first toe shorter (7.0–13 3 in L.), anterior edge of tibia with heavy brown spots, lacking white line. Wrights' tree frog, *Hyla wrightorum*
Plate LXXV

JJ. Vitta commonly ends at shoulder, interocular triangle usually present, no very distinct postsacral bars, the dorsal spotting often quite pronounced and varied, tympanum larger (11–14 in L.), first finger longer (5.6–8.0 in L ), first toe longer (5.6–8.8 in L.).

Pacific tree frog, *Hyla regilla*
Plate LXX

**Robber Frogs, LEPTODACTYLIDAE· Leptodactylus, Eleutherodactylus, Syrrhophus**

A. Pupil horizontal, tympanum distinct.

B. Fingers and toes free without distinct terminal disks, toes without

dermal border, size small, 1 2/5–2 in. (25–49 mm.), a lateral fold, white band along jaw to canthus oris and humerus; dorsal color chocolate-brown, limbs dark cross-barred, two small tarsal tubercles, narrow tarsal fold, heel to orbit White-lipped frog, *Leptodactylus labialis*
Plate LXXXII

BB Tips of phalanges T-shaped, toes and fingers free, terminal disks small, no white upper jaw stripe, no dorsolateral or lateral fold.

C. Size large, 1 7/8–3 3/5 in. (48–90 mm.), a ventral disk, voice a resounding bark, head broad (2-2.57 in L.), head wider than head to tympanum; eye small (7.2–9.25 in L.), eye much less than first finger, fingers larger, light stripe down middle of back, intertympanic fold present (in preserved material).

D. Fourth toe longer, fairly closely aggregated black blotches, sides and hinder half of abdomen faintly areolate, skin in adults on dorsum stiff, coarse, areolate. Belly without vermiculations or spots, back covered with large black spots.
Texas cliff frog, *Eleutherodactylus latrans*
Plates LXXIX–LXXX

[DD Fourth toe shorter, upper parts either green or with scattered tubercles, belly with faint spots, broad light transverse band across back just back of fore limbs
Mexican cliff frog, *Eleutherodactylus augusti*
Plate LXXVII]

CC Size small, 3/5-1 3/5 in. (15-39.5 mm), without ventral disk, voice a cricketlike chirp, head narrower (2.66–3.38 in L.), head usually narrower than head to tympanum, eye larger (5-8 in L.), eye greater than first finger, fingers smaller.

D Usually a light stripe from eye backward along dorsolateral region, a light transverse band between eyes, toes longer, fore limb shorter (1.7-2.0 in L.), foot with tarsus longer
Ricord's frog, *Eleutherodactylus ricordii planirostris*
Plate LXXVIII

DD Usually without light dorsolateral stripe from eye backward, usually no transverse band between eyes; toes shorter; fore limb longer (1.45–1.88 in L.).

E. Tympanum smaller (11–13 in L.), hind limb shorter (0.72-0.87 in L.), internasal broader (8-9 in L.), fore limb usually greater than foot with tarsus.
Marnock's frog, *Syrrhophus marnockii*
Plate LXXXIV

F. Vermiculate dorsal pattern, wider head (ratio to L. 0.40), smaller size (21–28 mm.) Chisos Mts.
Gaige's frog, *Syrrhophus gaigeae*

FF. Spotted dorsal pattern, narrower head (ratio of width of head in L 0 36), larger size, 25–35 mm. Central Texas
Marnock's frog, *Syrrhophus marnockii*
Plate LXXXIV

EE. Tympanum larger (8–10 in L), hind limb longer (0 72–0 73 in L), internasal narrower (9–10 in L), fore limb usually less than (rarely equal to) foot with tarsus
Camp's frog, *Syrrhophus campi*
Plate LXXXIII

## Frogs, RANIDAE· Rana

A. Tympanum larger than eye in male, equal in female (rarely smaller in *R virgatipes*), 5 6–12 5 in L, throat of male differently colored, upper jaw unicolor, no black mask, no light jaw stripe, no regular dorsal rows of spots, no pronounced yellow, orange, or red on undersides of hind limbs or on belly or groin, tibia 1 8 2 6 in L

B. Rear of femur with alternations of light and dark horizontal bands, dorsolateral folds absent, edge of jaw uniform

C. Size small 1 5/8–2 5/8 in (41 66 mm), usually a light yellowish dorsolateral stripe extends back from eye, two joints of fourth toe free of web, vocal sacs of male like a marble on either side of head, intertympanic space 3.42- 4 4 in L, foot with tarsus 1 36–1 56 in L.
Sphagnum frog, *Rana virgatipes*
Plate CXXIII

CC. Size large 3 1/4 8 in (82 200 mm), no or only one joint of fourth toe free of web, back uniform in color, no vocal sacs in males on side of head

D. Alternation of color on rear of femur conspicuous, first finger generally less than second finger, intertympanic space narrower (5 0 6 8 in L), foot with tarsus shorter (1 4–1 67 in L)
Southern bullfrog, *Rana grylio*
Plate XCVII

DD Alternation of color on rear of femur not conspicuous, first finger generally equal to second, intertympanic space wider (4 5 -5 2 in L), foot with tarsus greater (1.28–1 53 in L)
Bullfrog, *Rana catesbeiana*
Plate XCIV

BB. Rear of femur without alternation of light and dark horizontal bands, edge of jaw mottled, barred, or uniform

C. Dorsolateral fold absent, size large, 3 1/4–5 1/4 in. (81–131 mm), rear of femur light or white spots on brown, edge of upper jaw

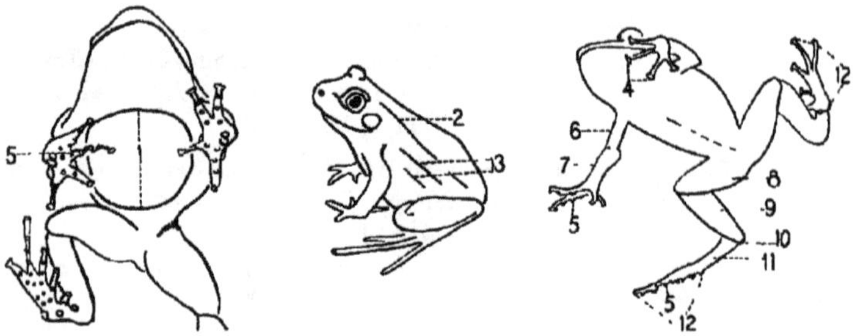


*Figure 5.* Robber frogs, Leptodactylidae: *Leptodactylus, Eleutherodactylus,* and *Syrrophus.* 1. Ventral disk 2 Dorsolateral fold 3 Lateral folds. 4. Transverse (T-shaped) disks 5. Subarticular tubercles sharp and saw-toothed 6. Brachium (upper arm). 7. Antebrachium (forearm) 8. Femur. 9 Tibia 10 Heel. 11. Tarsus. 12. Foot.

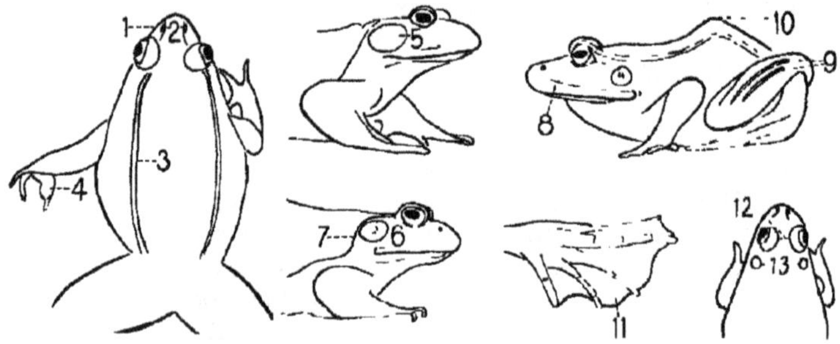


*Figure 6* Frogs, Ranidae· *Rana* 1 Nostril. 2. Internasal space. 3 Costal (dorsolateral) fold 4. Enlarged thumb of male 5 Enlarged tympanum of male. 6. Tympanum of female 7. Tympanic fold 8. Fleshy fold on jaw 9 Glandular folds on tibia. 10. Sacral hump. 11. Full webbing of male bullfrog 12 Narrow interorbital space 13 Intertympanic space.

*Figure 7* Narrow-mouthed toads, Brevicipitidae: *Hypopachus* and *Microhyla.* 1. Broad waist. 2. Femur partly involved in body skin 3. Two metatarsal tubercles. 4. Slight basal web 5. Transverse fold of skin across head. 6. Depressed form of body. 7. Body thick. 8 Legs short

mottled, head to angle of mouth 2.0–2.7 in L.; first finger 6.5–7.3 in L. River-swamp frog, *Rana heckscheri*
Plate XCVIII

CC Dorsolateral fold present, indistinct, or absent; edge of upper jaw uniform or barred, size medium to small, first finger 5.0–6.8 in L.; head to angle of mouth 2.7–3.4 in L.

D. Dorsal folds lacking or interrupted; back and sides mottled or with prominent spots, rear of femur vermiculated in its spotting; males with lateral external vocal sacs somewhat developed, size small, 1 7/8–3 in. (48–76 mm.), third toe 2.5–2.9 in L., interorbital space 19–28 in L.
Mink frog, *Rana septentrionalis*
Plate CXVIII

DD Dorsal fold on cephalic half only, cheek green with mottled jaw below, back uniform or with fine black speckings; rear of femur with fine and scant speckings, males with no lateral external vocal sacs, size medium, 2–4 in. (52–100 mm.), third toe 2.7–3.7 in L.; interorbital space 11–23 in L.
Green frog, *Rana clamitans*
Plate CXV

AA Tympanum of male not enlarged (enlarged in *R. onca*, rarely in *R. areolata* and *R. sphenocephala*), smaller than eye (9–19 in L.), throat not so differently colored in males, upper jaw with light stripe or mottling of light and dark, a vitta or regular spots between dorsolateral folds or with yellow, orange, or red on hind limbs, groin, or belly, tibia 1.4–2.3 in L.

B Dorsolateral folds absent or indistinct, low, broken, under surface of hind limbs yellow, skin rough, no vitta, body odor pronounced.

C Size larger, 2 1/3–4 1/2 in. (58–115 mm.); no outer sole (metatarsal) tubercle, no stripe on upper jaw, throat and lower jaw uniform or cloudy, hind limbs shorter (0.65–0.69 in L.), tibia shorter (1.86–2.0 in L.). Mexican frog, *Rana tarahumarae*
Plate CXXII

CC. Size smaller, 1 3/5–3 3/8 in. (39–84 mm.), outer sole (metatarsal) tubercle, stripe on upper jaw present or obscure, throat and lower jaw spotted, hind limbs longer (0.57–0.66 in L.), tibia longer (1.61–1.88 in L.) Yellow-legged frog, *Rana boylii*
Plates LXXXIX–XCI

("Vomerine teeth rudimentary, on two oblique ridges between the nares . . . ; tympanic region not darker than rest of head;

fold along upper lip colored like rest of body, mottled or dark; red never present in coloration. *Rana boylii* and subspecies"

"2. When hind leg is brought forward along the body, inside angle of bent tarsus and tibia reaches at least to nares and often beyond the end of the snout, tympanum covered with many hispid points.

"3. A light patch on top of head, darker area crossing the posterior half of each upper eyelid merging insensibly into dorsal color behind, body-length under 70 millimeters.

[California yellow-legged frog,] *Rana boylii boylii* Baird"
Plate LXXXIX

"3F No light patch on top of head, darker areas crossing posterior half of each upper eyelid, when present, contrasting with dorsal coloration, body length reaching 81 millimeters.

[Sierra Madre yellow-legged frog,] *Rana boylii muscosa* Camp"
Plate XC

"2. When leg is brought forward, inside angle of bent tarsus seldom reaching beyond nares, tympanum smooth or with but a few hispid points, no light patch on top of head, body length reaching 73 millimeters.

[Sierra Nevada yellow-legged frog,] *Rana boylii sierrae* Camp"
Plate XCI

C. L Camp, Calif., 1917, p. 123 )

BB. Dorsolateral folds distinct full length of body (folds not conspicuous in *R aurora*.), usually with a mask; skin smoother, body odor not pronounced

C. With mask to angle of jaw (sometimes less conspicuous or absent in *R. aurora*), males with no external vocal sacs between ear and shoulder, rear of femur finely dotted and without heavy spots

D No red or yellow on the under parts, mask black or dark brown, size small 1 1/6–3 1/4 in (29–82 mm.), tympanum larger (11-15 in L)

E Dorsal color usually a mid-band of darker color within light dorsolateral folds, middorsal light stripe present or absent, breast more spotted Hind limb short (0 62–0 75 in L.), tibia short (1.93-2 3 in L ), tibia usually equals foot

Northern wood frog, *Rana sylvatica cantabrigensis*
Plates CXX, CXXI

EE Dorsal color between dorsolateral fold usually like dorsum, no middorsal stripe, breast usually without spots, hind limb long (0 53–0 62 in L ); tibia long (1.6–1.88 in L.); tibia longer than foot Wood frog, *Rana s. sylvatica*
Plate CXIX

DD Some red or yellow on under parts, size average larger, 1 4/5–5 in. (45–125 mm ), tympanum larger (11–17 in L.) or smaller (17–22 in L.).

E Angle of tarsus and tibia reaching to eye, not beyond nostril, no mottling in groin, mask absent (if present obscure brown), inky spots on back sometimes light-centered, no prominent white strip from snout or eye to shoulder, tympanum small (16.4–21 in L.), eggs with 2 jelly envelopes, internasal space shorter (11–16.4 in L.).

F Two metatarsal tubercles, palmar tubercles present, back and top of head with inky black spots, tympanum smaller (16 4–21 in L.); interorbital space larger (12–17 6 times in L.), fingers longer, especially first (6.2–6 45 in L ) and second (6.0–6.45 in L.), upper eyelid narrower (14.4–22 in L ).

Western spotted frog, *Rana p pretiosa*
Plate CXVI

FF. One metatarsal tubercle, the outer absent, palmar tubercles small or wanting; few irregular dorsal spots, sometimes considerable spotting, under parts yellow or deep orange, tympanum larger (13–16 times in L ); interorbital space smaller (16 2–29 2 in L ), finger shorter, especially first (5 8–7 8 in L ) and second (5 8–7 8 in L.), upper eyelid wider (11.6–16 in L.).

Nevada spotted frog, *Rana p. luteiventris*
Plate CXVII

EE. Angle of tarsus and tibia reaching nares or beyond end of snout, always or slightly mottled in groin, mask prominent black or dark brown (rarely, absent), prominent stripe from eye or snout to shoulder or shorter, tympanum normally larger (11–17 in L ), eggs with 3 distinct jelly envelopes, internasal space greater (8 6 14.1 in L ).

F. Slight mottling in groin Dorsum greenish brown with many black spots, under parts light yellow or pale salmon orange, third finger shorter (4 08–5 17 in L ), hind limb slightly shorter (0 62–0.73 in L ), fourth toe slightly shorter (1 9–2 45 in L.). Cascades in Washington and northern Oregon 4000 ft. or higher.

Slater's frog, *Rana cascadae*
Plate XCIII

FF. Prominent mottling in groin, dorsum without inky or black spots (some few light-centered) under parts red, third finger longer (3 16–4 71 in L ), hind limb slightly larger (0.50–0 69 in L ), fourth toe slightly longer (1.51–2.15 in L )

*Rana aurora* group
Plates LXXXVII, LXXXVIII

G Skin smooth, dorsolateral folds distinct, dorsum without spots or dotted, head to tympanum in width of head 0 93–

1.03, head narrower (2 5–3 2 in L ), intertympanic space (3.5–5 1 in L.); tibia shorter (1 67–2 53 in L.), first toe (5 4–8.0 in L ) and second toe (3 4–4 85 in L.) shorter; size smaller, 1 3/4–3 1/2 in (44–87 inches)

Oregon red-legged frog, *Rana a aurora*
Plate LXXXVII

GG. Skin rough, dorsolateral folds distinct, dorsum with light-centered spots, head to tympanum in width of head 0.98–1 25, size larger, 2 1/2–5 2/5 in. (58–136 mm.); head wider (2 25–3 0 in L.), intertympanic space wider (3 0–4.45 in L.), tibia longer (1 46–2 06 in L ), first toe (4 5–6.5 in L ) and second toe (2 9–4 4 in L ) longer California and Lower California. Introduced into Nevada.

California red-legged frog, *Rana a draytonii*
Plate LXXXVIII

CC. With no mask, males with external vocal sacs between ear and shoulder.

D Without white line on upper jaw

E Upper jaw uniform or with few dashes, size small, 1 3/4–3 in (44–74 mm ), dorsum unspotted or with more numerous spots than R *pipiens*, with yellow on under parts, males with enlarged tympana, hind limbs shorter than in *Rana onca* (1.1 1.5 in L.)

Nevada frog, *Rana fisheri*
Plates XCVI, CVIII

F "Fewer dorsal spots and much shorter hind legs" (Linsdale). Hind limbs longer than R *fisheri* (1 46–1 8 in L ), no enlarged tympana.

Utah frog, *Rana onca*
Plates XCIX, CIX

[The *Rana fisheri* of Las Vegas region, *Rana onca* of Utah and Nevada, and *Rana pipiens* of Utah, Nevada, Arizona, and Imperial Valley need close examination ]

EE. Upper jaw mottled, size larger, 2¼–4½ in (63–113 mm ), three or four rows of spots between dorsolateral folds, males rarely with enlarged tympana.

F Dorsal spots large, light-centered, round with light borders, throat and chin clear except at sides, three or four crossbars on legs with small intermediates, snout shorter, head to tympanum 2 8 to 3.2 in L ; head to angle of mouth 3 15–3.8 in L., eye small (9.8–12.3 in L ), intertympanic space medium (3.8–4.7 in L ), width of head in L. narrower (2 6 to 2 92 in L ).

(G "Head U-shaped in outline when viewed from above; dorsum often smooth, or nearly so, tibia length less than

40 mm. in adults, posttympanic fold poorly developed, dorsolateral folds narrow or only slightly raised or both.

[Texas gopher frog,] *Rana areolata areolata* Baird"
Plate LXXXV

GG. "Head orbiculate in outline when viewed from above, dorsum rugose, tibia length more than 40 mm in adults; posttympanic fold well developed, dorsolateral folds prominent.

[Northern gopher frog,] *Rana areolata circulosa* Rice and Davis"
Plate LXXXVI

After Goin and Netting, La., 1940, p. 146)

FF Dorsal spots small, irregular slightly or not light-encircled, 5 or 8 uniform bars on hind limbs, snout longer, head to tympanum 2 2-3 0 in L , head to angle of mouth 2 5-3 1 in L , eye large (6 8-10 3 in L ), intertympanic space broad (2 95-3 65 in L.), width of head in L. wider (1 93-2.6 in L.), venter of head heavily spotted.

(G. "Head triangular in outline, dorsolateral folds high and relatively narrow, dorsum with numerous prominent warts; dorsal spots poorly differentiated from gray, brown, or black ground color, venter always spotted at least from chin to midbody, dark bars on hind limbs separated by interspaces that are never wider than the bars

[Dusky gopher frog,] *Rana sevosa* (Goin and Netting)

GG "Head subtriangular in outline, dorsolateral folds low and very broad, dorsum smooth or lightly warty, dorsal spots distinct against pale ground color, chin and throat spotted, belly usually immaculate posteriorly, dark bars on hind limbs separated by light interspaces that are wider than the bars."

Gopher frog, *Rana capito*
Plate XCII

After Goin and Netting, La , 1940, p 146)

DD With white line on upper jaw.

E. No orange on under parts, dorsal spots round with interspaces of same diameter or more.

F. Snout shorter (6 0-6 8 in L ), more lateral spots below dorsolateral fold, tibia shorter (1 73-1.94 in L ), head to tympanum 2.8-3 2 in L., upper eyelid wide (11 2-14 in L ), tympanum normally without light center

Meadow frog, *Rana p. pipiens*
Plate CI
[*R. pipiens* complex. Plates CV-CXV.]

FF Snout longer (5.23–6.3 in L.), fewer lateral spots below dorsolateral fold, tibia longer (1 55–1 82 in L ), head to tympanum 2.38–2.8 in L , upper eyelid medium (9.3–11.7 in L.), tympanum usually with light center.

Southern meadow frog, *Rana p. sphenocephala*
Plate CIV

EE. Orange on under parts; dorsal square spots in regular rows, spots with interspaces less than diameter of spots.

Pickerel frog, *Rana palustris*
Plate C

## Narrow-mouthed Toads, BREVICIPITIDAE Hypopachus, Microhyla

A. Two sole (metatarsal) tubercles, basal webs on feet, snout shorter (9–10 in L ), usually a middorsal yellow line and mid-ventral white line, oblique white band from eye to shoulder

Taylor's toad, *Hypopachus cuneus*
Plate CXXIV

AA. One sole (metatarsal) tubercle, no webs on feet, snout longer (6 6 8.2 in L ), no middorsal or mid-ventral lines nor oblique postorbital band.

B Muzzle shorter; hind foot unusually short, hind limb short, back areolate, the posterior parts even pustular

Mitchell's narrow-mouthed toad, *Microhyla areolata*

BB. Muzzle longer, hind limb longer

C Body depressed (thickness in length 3 0–5 6 in males, 4.0–4 3 in females), tibial width in tibial length 3–4, body width in females 2 46–3 1 in L , upper eyelid 10–18 in L , eye 8 7–12 7 in L ; skin usually smooth, under parts white, dorsum grayish olive.

Texas narrow-mouthed toad, *Microhyla olivacea*
Plate CXXVI

⟨D. Ventrum immaculate or with scattered melanophores.

E A blotch or spots on the femur and tibia which form a bar or continuous line when the limb is folded, dorsum with dark spots. Taylor's Microhyla *mazatlanensis*

EE. Spots rarely present on the femur and tibia, if present usually not forming a distinct bar when the limb is folded, dorsum tan and generally without markings *olivacea*.

After M K. Hecht and B. L. Matalas, Gen., 1946, p 7⟩

CC Body less depressed (2.5–3.35 in males, 2 65–3 4 in females), tibial width in tibial length 2.5–3.0 times, body width in females 1.83–2.3 in L., upper eyelid 18.6–28 in L., eye 10–14 in L , skin smooth, tuberculate, or pustular, under parts gray, or brown speckled and mottled, dorsum black, gray, or brown.

Narrow-mouthed toad, *Microhyla carolinensis*
Plate CXXV

# Accounts of Species

## ORDER SALIENTIA Laurenti

### FAMILY ASCAPHIDAE

#### Genus *ASCAPHUS* Stejneger

Map 4

THE first recognition of this form by Dr. Stejneger and the subsequent studies of it by Dr. Helen Thompson Gaige were two of the outstanding events in North American batrachology in the last forty-five years. This "tailed" frog has relatively the broadest internasal space of all our frogs, 4.66 to 8 into length, whereas all others range from 8 (or 7.77) to 21.4 into length. In hind limb it is relatively longer than robber frogs, narrow-mouths, spadefoots, or toads and comparable to tree frogs and frogs. It has long fore limbs. Possibly both fore and hind limbs are long for climbing. Of the first live ones we had, all except one escaped by crawling up the inner sides of a barrel. It has a large mouth, snout, eye, interorbital space, and upper eyelid.

The relationships of this frog have been much discussed. When Stejneger (1899) with rare courage and fine discrimination described this form, he called it a Discoglossid. Later, VanDenburgh (1912) found it to be not "ecaudate," and followed Stejneger. American authors such as Barbour and Cochran (1932) and most foreign workers like Boulenger (1910), Gadow (1920), Nieden (1923), and Perrier (1925) kept it within the Discoglossidae. From 1924 to 1931 and until his death Noble placed it in the Liopelmidae, and Villiers (1934) and Pusey (1943) are in agreement with this view. In 1923 Fejervary created a special family, the Ascaphidae, and in the third to fifth editions of Stejneger and Barbour's check list (1933, 1939, and 1943) these authors adopt this family name, which we now follow. We have seen considerable material both preserved and alive and are much impressed with its Discoglossid affinities.

### American Bell Toad, American Ribbed Toad

*Ascaphus truei* Stejneger. Plate XVI; Map 4.

**Range:** Washington, Oregon, northern California (south to Dyerville; Myers, 1931, 1943), Emida, Idaho (Ehrhardt, 1946), western Montana (Anderson and Smith, Hazzard, 1932; Donaldson, 1934; Rodgers and Jellison, 1942; Slipp and Carl, 1943), British Columbia (Ricker and Logier, 1935; Slipp and Carl, 1943; Carl, 1945).

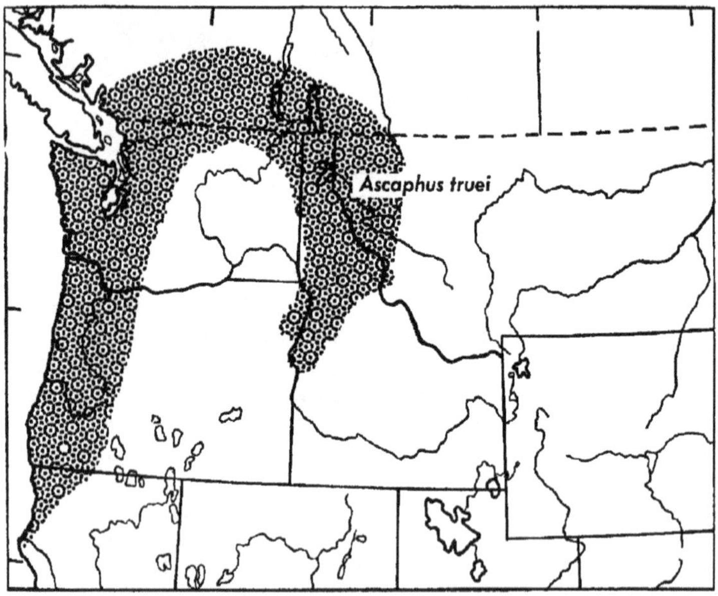


*Map 4*

**Habitat:** These "toads" live in forested sections, under rocks in perennial, usually swift-flowing, small mountain streams of low temperature. After heavy rains several collectors have found them in moist woods, at varying distances from the streams

**Size:** Adults, 1⅛–2 inches. Males, length to tail 29–42 mm., tail 3–10 mm. Females, 28–51 mm.

**General appearance:** This small "toad" is gray, pink, or brown to almost black. Numerous black spots occur on the tops of the legs and on the back. The bar across the head is pale green to pale yellow; the underside of legs rose. The females are usually lighter than the males. The brown parotoid gland is well developed or may be broken into a glandular ridge along the side. The fingers are long and slender, free of webbing; the toes, slightly webbed. The head is flattened, slightly broader than long, the snout obtusely pointed, and with no visible tympanum. The skin is smooth or slightly roughened with granules, wrinkles, warts, and small tubercles. The conspicuous "tail" of the male is level with the ventral side of the body. This is ⅛–⅖ inch (3–10 mm.) long, ⅙–⅕ inch (4–5.5 mm.) broad. The anus is a large swollen orifice just ahead of the constricted tip. The female appears much like a tree toad.

**Color:** Carbon River Valley, Rainier National Park, from J. R. Slater, May 16, 17, 1930. *Female.* Middle of back from eye bar to rump grayish olive or citrine drab. Parotoid wood brown, cinnamon, or mikado brown. From parotoid along side is pecan brown, mikado brown, orange-cinnamon, or sayal's brown. Same wash on upper parts of tibia and an area near anus. Vertical part of snout except central bar (like bar between eyes) black, aniline black, or dull purplish black. Area below eye ageratum violet or vinaceous-purple. Bar from snout to eye and behind eye to shoulder insertion same color as vertical snout. On top of forelegs and hind legs and along side a few larger black spots. Along sides these are more elongate below, defining the browns. Color of hind legs and forelegs same as mid-back. Bar across head at front of eyes glass green or deep seafoam green. Same color on side of face below black nostril, eye, and shoulder insertion bar. This bar bordered above with same color. Top of snout mignonette green or ecru-olive. Underside of body except belly and femur dull citrine, ecru-olive, or barium yellow with interstices of vinaceous, dark anthracene violet or dark maroon purple. Some of belly light orange-yellow with some vinaceous or pinkish vinaceous interspersed. Femur pure deep vinaceous or purplish vinaceous. Iris: bar across top of vertical pupil cream color or pale chalcedony yellow with some reticulum of burnt sienna or hazel. This color in upper part of eye obscures the cream or yellowish. Lower eye auburn, chestnut, or chestnut-brown with little specks of orange-rufous.

*Male.* Back kaiser brown, hazel, tawny, cacao brown, or vinaceous-russet. Top of hind legs and forelegs with numerous black spots, so also back; bar from orbit to orbit pale chalcedony yellow. Top of snout deep olive-buff. Vertical snout bar like eye bar. Male has venter, all except femur, like female described. Two patches on arm and base of finger black or seal brown or warm blackish brown. Iris: see *female.*

**Structure:** The tail is an intromittent organ; lower jaw from below an almost perfect semicircle; second, third, and fourth vertebrae bearing short ribs; tongue attached by broad surface, and cannot be protruded; arms of male conspicuously heavier than in the female, as also are the hind limbs and feet. Breeding males with dark excrescences on the inner edges of the inner fingers and along the inner edge of the forearm, a ball-like excrescence at the base of the thumb, and often dark excrescences on each side of the breast; tubercules much finer on the rear portion of the back and on the hind limbs in the female; eye large with a vertical pupil.

**Voice:** No vocal sac.

**Breeding:** Known dates are in May, June, July, August, and September. The eggs in circular masses of rosarylike strings are attached to the underside of stones in creeks. The eggs are not pigmented, few in number, and very large, ⅓ inch (8 mm.), the yolk ⅕ inch (5 mm.) in diameter. The mature tadpole is medium in size, 1⅝–2³⁄₁₆ inches (42–55 mm.), its body round, its tail long, its crests not conspicuous. The tooth ridges are ³⁄₁₀ (upper ridges with more than one row of teeth). The period of development is probably over winter. They transform during July, August, and September at ⅗–¾ inch (14–18 mm., possibly 20 mm.). Wallace Wood (Calif., 1939, p. 110) found tadpoles in January. Ricker and Logier (B.C., 1935, p. 46) in their five British Columbia streams found one-year tadpoles 29–41 mm. and a second-year tadpole 42 mm.

**Journal notes:** March 16, 1942, Russ Grove, northern Humboldt Co., Calif. Mr. Milne says Klamath River is the line of separation for many forms such as *Ascaphus.*

March 17. Went to south side of Wilson Creek, Del Norte Co., Calif., 8 miles north of Klamath and close to the ocean, according to directions of Wallace F. Wood. With seine and hoe we got plenty of *Ascaphus* tadpoles and larvae of *Rana boylii boylii* and *Dicamptodon ensatus.* There were no adult frogs or salamanders under stones in creek or under outlying ones or boards. When you pick them up, the *Ascaphus* larvae attach themselves to the finger or net. Caught against the side of the can, the yellowish white tip with black crescent band behind it is conspicuous.

March 20. Went up MacKenzie River watershed with Ruth E. Hopson of Springfield, Ore. . . . At last caught one *Ascaphus truei* tadpole.

March 23. With Kenneth Gordon up Santiam River. . . . Sixteen and one-half miles from Foster at mouth of Moose Creek. Storm, Livezey, and I pulled seine in creek for *Ascaphus.* Didn't get any, but they are here. An old student, Dr. A. C. Chandler, secured them in Santiam National Forest 25 years ago.

March 29. Near Lake Cushman dam; couldn't get very close because of war regulations. Made a long loop back to the highway through the lumbered countryside. Oh, the desolation of that Hamma Hamma River country! Dr. H. T. Gaige's historic collecting site is under many feet of water.

March 31. With J. R. Slater. Went in afternoon to Carbon River just outside Rainier Park entrance. In a tumbling hillside cataract we saw little *A. truei* tadpoles attached to rocks; their tails were wagging in the current. Caught no adults. . . . Drove up to ranger cabin but soon came back and tried another little stream which also has *Ascaphus* tadpoles.

**Authorities' corner:** Mrs. H. T. Gaige (Wash., 1920, pp. 2–3), working in the Olympic region of Washington wrote: "It was under the rocks in these little creeks that *Ascaphus* lived. . . . One found them only by working slowly upstream and turning over every movable stone. Usually they either floated down the stream with the debris which was released when the stone under which they were resting was overturned, in which case it took quick action to catch them before they were out of sight, or they made no effort to move, and in the shifting lights and shadows their color so closely resembled a bit of fir bark or the small red stones which were abundant in the streams that they were distinguished with difficulty. Occasionally they were alert and slipped away like a shadow. When placed on land they were awkward and stupid in action and appearance and made little effort to escape. They were solitary; never more than one was found under a single stone and individuals were usually well separated in the stream."

"The temperature of the water at 1 P.M. registered 10° Centigrade Here the tadpoles were very abundant, for as many as seven were seen and collected from an area that could be covered by the palm of one's hand. They were first observed in the clear water attached to the rocks on the bottom of the creek. Efforts made to capture them caused them to release their holds and swim upstream for a few inches and there seek shelter under the rocks. Here they were more difficult to see since their coloration blended nicely with the debris under the rocks, but once one knew where to look and what to look for, they were more obvious" (A. and R. D. Svihla, Wash., 1933, p. 38).

"Trip July 14–15, 1941. The tadpoles were at approximately the same stage of development as those taken on June 22, 1930 (which are now in the U.S. N. M.). They have short hind legs. The black caudal area and milk-white tail-tip are prominent in most of the individuals.

"I watched one tadpole feeding on a stone over which the swiftest current in a riffle was falling. He moved about readily when he desired, a millimeter or two at a time, by a slight 'inching along' movement of the adhesive mouthparts He would turn this way and that, his tail fluttering and flapping downstream in the current, and the slight but constant movement of his mouthparts indicated that he was scraping at the surface of the rock. Although nothing could be seen on the stone, there was probably a growth of minute algae. At times the tadpole was almost half out of water, and again he would browse along till he was nearly on the underside of the stone. All of the tadpoles seen were in the swiftest current available, usually on the side of a stone where a drop of a couple of inches formed a riffle" (G. S. Myers, Calif., 1943, p. 126).

"Herewith are being sent to you specimens of the larvae of *Ascaphus truei* that I collected during the past summer. These specimens were collected July 30, 1946 near Emida, Idaho. They are from Township 43 North, Range 2 West, Section 13, East Fork of Charley Creek.

"This area is mostly in the classification of open reproduction, having been burned several times in the past. The streams have numerous beaver dams. These particular specimens were gathered where the water was free flowing and the stream bed of gravel. They were common lying on the top of the gravel and offered no resistance to capture. I was unable to locate any adults.

". . . The boys in the camps at first enjoyed swimming in one or another of the beaver ponds, but they soon began to complain of the 'leeches' which attached themselves to their legs and toes. I found that these were the same larvae. The ponds accumulated a silt deposit but were still water" (letter from R. P. Ehrhardt, Kenyon College, Ohio, Sept. 6, 1946).

*Plate XVI. Ascaphus truei* (×1). 1,5 Females 2. Tadpole. 3,4. Males

*Plate XVII. Scaphiopus couchii.* 1,6. Males (×⅔). 2 Male (×½). 3. Female (×½) 4. Male croaking (×⅙). 5 Eggs (×½).

## Family SCAPHIOPODIDAE

### Genus *SCAPHIOPUS* Holbrook

Maps 5–7

**Couch's Spadefoot, Southern Spadefoot, Rain Toad, Sonoran Spadefoot, Sonora Spadefoot, Cape St. Lucas Spadefoot**

*Scaphiopus couchii* Baird. Plate XVII; Map 5.

**Range:** Texas to Arizona and Utah, northern Mexico and Lower California.

**Habitat:** These spadefoots live in subterranean burrows, often under logs or similar shelter, and are nocturnal in habit. They breed in temporary pools, coming out only after heavy rains.

**Size:** Adults, 1⅞–3⅕ inches. Males, 48–70 mm. Females, 50–80 mm.

**General appearance:** The short, fat, toadlike body has a greenish back, more or less marbled. The skin is roughly tuberculate, with many light tubercles on the sides. Both the ear and parotoid glands are indistinct The eyes are large and protuberant with vertical pupils. The venter is whitish; the fingers and toes are light; and the rear of the arm and leg has a light band. The outer sole tubercle and sometimes the tips of fingers and toes are dark.

**Color:** *Male.* Beeville, Tex., March 26, 1925. Upper parts yellowish oil green; on sides same, oil yellow mixed with yellowish oil green; tubercles on side, posterior back, and tibia calliste green; tubercles below vent white; rear of legs and groin parrot green; below eye and lower muzzle buffy citrine; tympanum oil yellow or yellowish oil green and a little livid brown. Under parts white except small pectoral patch of Martius yellow or pale greenish yellow, and area from groin to groin across rear of belly where only livid brown or purplish vinaceous exists. Eye: pupil vertical, rim lemon yellow, iris lemon yellow to bright green-yellow reticulated with black.

*Female.* Comfort, Tex., May 19, 1925. Bands on front and rear of upper eyelid citron green or oil yellow; same color on side of upper jaw, above and below tympanum, along sides, on back, on dorsum of hind limbs, in each case interspersed with oil green. These two colors are sharply contrasted in the female, while in the male the color is a more uniform calla green or oil green, with little spotting of lighter color. Black bars on the limbs, and some black on nostril. Another has mignonette green on sides spotted with black and ivy green, tea green, or water green on back. Fingers white on dorsum, toes with some white on dorsum. Outer bands on feet whitish. Under parts white except lower belly and under legs, which are slate violet (2) to vinaceous-lilac. Iris green-yellow or bright green-yellow with black on outside, which is sometimes a horizontal bar in front and behind. From black on outside, black lines run almost to the vertical pupil. In general one can identify females because they are spotted, while males are more uniform.

**Structure:** No pectoral gland; skin on crown of head thin; tongue subcircular, slightly emarginate; hand nearly as long as forearm; toes fully webbed.

**Voice:** The chorus is harsh and noisy, a great caterwauling, and can be heard a considerable distance. The individual call—*wow, me ow,* or *a ow*—is a most unearthly noise like that of someone in pain.

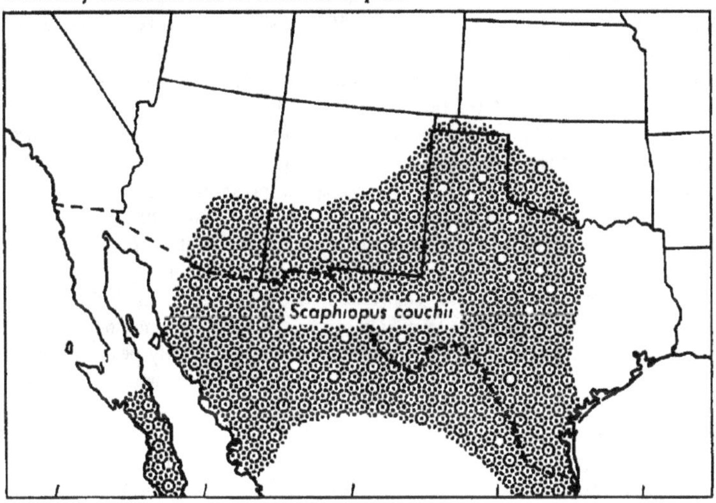


*Map 5*

"The cry of the male is a loud, resonant 'ye-ow' repeated at intervals; that of the female, a short grunting 'ow' uttered several times in shorter intermissions" (J. K. Strecker, Jr., Tex., 1908e, p. 203).

"In the case of *S. couchii* it [the song] is a bleat lasting from 5–6 seconds ordinarily. This can be best described as sounding so much like the bleat of a lamb as to be mistaken for it. The song is given while the male sits upon the mud near the edge of the puddle" (A. I. Ortenburger, Ariz., 1925, p. 19).

**Breeding:** The time is from April to August at periods of heavy rainfall. The eggs are in bands ¼ inch (6 mm.) across or cylindrical masses on plant stems, the jelly is rather firm, the eggs are close together, black above and creamy white below. The vitellus is ⅟₁₈–⅟₁₆ inch (1.4–1.6 mm.). In warm spots they hatch in 1½ days. The "bronzy" tadpole is black, dotted with old gold or fawn, small, 1 inch (24.5 mm.), broad with tail tip rounded. The tooth ridges are 4/4, rarely 5/4, 3/4, 5/5, 2/4. After a period of 15–40 days, the tadpoles transform during the summer months and early fall at 3/10–1/2 inch (7.5–12.5 mm.).

**Journal notes:** May 29, 1925, Comfort, Tex. The spadefoots are calling as they float spread out on the surface. Their sides are swelled out and vibrating. They often seem to curve their backs in their tremendous efforts.

June 4. In Comfort, Tex., in roadside pools where, on May 29, we found Couch's spadefoot breeding, there are now large tadpoles. The rain came May 28. The eggs must have been laid then. How fast!

June 7. At Encinal, Tex., roadside pool alive with spadefoot tads. . . . More spadefoots 2 miles beyond Cactus. Whenever the pools begin to dry up, grackles go there to eat the tads.

June 8 Near Dolores, Tex, we stopped beside a long roadside rain pool. It is a sandy area with scattered bushes, very little herbaceous material, and mesquite rather far apart. All stages were here, even tiny transformed ones leaving the pond. They were hopping out so thickly that they formed a seething mass, several spadefoots deep. They were gathered around small herbs, small bushes, and larger ones, when possible, for shade, and generally just enough in a place to match the shadow of the plant. Many of them crawl out of the pond when they still have very long tails. I wonder if this hastens the shrinking of the tail.

June 11, east of Hebronville, Tex Last night we went out with flashlights. Near a clump of cactus saw a frog. It proved to be Couch's spadefoot. Caught it. The instant we released it, it started for a clump of prickly pear and went down into a pack rat's hole. I verily believe this is one place where they aestivate.

**Authorities' corner:**

J K. Strecker, Jr, Tex., 1908e, p. 203.
A. I. Ortenburger, Ariz., 1925, p. 20.
F W. King, Ariz., 1932, p 175
L. W. Arnold, Ariz., 1943, p. 128.

## Hammond's Spadefoot, Western Spadefoot, Hammond's Spea, Western Spadefoot Toad, New Mexican Spea

*Scaphiopus hammondii hammondii* Baird. Plate XVIII; Map 6.

**Range:** California to Lower California, east through Arizona, southwest Colorado, New Mexico, to Texas and Mexico.

**Habitat:** They live underground in burrows which they dig in soft earth by backing into the ground and digging with their hind feet, which are armed with spades. They rock the body as they dig, and the dirt falls into the burrows on top of the toads. They breed commonly in temporary rain pools or temporary overflow areas.

**Size:** Adults, 1½–2⅖ inches. Males, 37.5–59 mm. Females, 37.5–61 mm.

**General appearance:** The body is stout and toadlike, small in size. The eyes are large and protuberant with vertical pupils. The skin is fine, relatively smooth, dotted with fine roundish tubercles. The back is greenish, the sides yellowish glaucous, light mineral gray, or greenish. There are green spots on the back, top of head, and legs. The forward under parts are white, sometimes

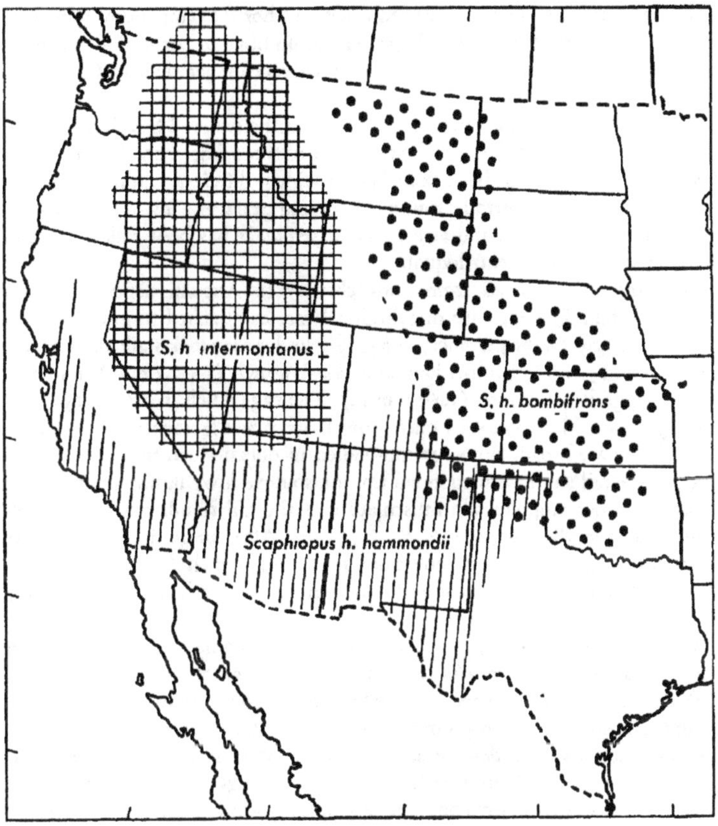


*Map 6*

buffy on the throat; the rear under parts purplish. The males have a wash of grayish green on each side of the throat.

**Color:** "Color (in life) above dark green, with scattered spots of dusky; four (or two) incomplete longitudinal stripes of dull white, inner pair in line with inner margins or orbits, the outer in line with tops of tympanic membranes; tubercles on back and sides tipped with red or orange in young individuals;

ventral surface plain white; throat region (vocal sac) blackish in males, dusky in females. Females lack the conspicuous longitudinal dorsal streaking of white, this being broken and much less extensive" (T. I. Storer, Calif., 1925, p. 149).

**Structure:** Head broader than long, muzzle short and overhanging the lower jaw; epidermis on top of head thick and horny; tympanum indistinct; no parotoid gland; tongue very large, entire; no tibial or pectoral gland; hind limb, tibia, foot, fourth toe, and fingers relatively longer than in Couch's or in Holbrook's spadefoot.

**Voice:** The males call, lying on the surface of the water. The call is a rolling or bubbling one, a croak more like the croak of some frog than Couch's or the hermit spadefoot. It has been described in widely different ways: as the loud purr of a cat with the metallic sound of grinding gears, as a low-toned *trr-r-r-r,* as a loud *crah-crah-iah,* and as a resonant *ye-ow*. It has been called unusual, weird, plaintive, and ventriloqual.

**Breeding:** They breed from mid-February to August, dependent upon heavy rainfall. The eggs are in cylindrical masses attached to grass or plant stems. The eggs on the periphery of a jelly cylinder may look stalked, the stalks 1/5–3/8 inch (5 or 6 to 9 mm.) long and 1/16–1/10 inch (1.4–2.3 mm.) in diameter, the eggs 1/25–1/16 inch (1.0–1.6 mm.). The eggs hatch in 1½–2 days. The dark greenish black tadpoles may grow large, 2 3/5–2 4/5 inches (65–70 mm.) long. They are broad, almost round-bodied in dorsal view, the eyes close together, the tail short with rounded tip, the spiracle low, almost ventral. Like most spadefoot tadpoles, the musculature of the tail stands out very prominently. The tooth ridges are 5/5, 4/4, 3/4, 3/4, 2/4. After 30–40 days the tadpoles transform from May 20 to September 1, at ½–1¼ inch (13–32 mm.). The tadpole is carnivorous in habit and may prey on its own kind, but it is a very effective enemy of the mosquito.

Ortenburger (Ariz., 1925, p. 19) wrote: "(a) Diameter of egg including gelatinous layers—*S. couchii* 2.5–3.5 mm.; *S. hammondii,* 1.5–2.0 mm.; (b) thickness of jelly layers—*S. couchii,* usually more than 1 mm; *S. hammondii,* mostly less than 0.5 mm.; (c) method of attaching the individual eggs to others in mass—*S. couchii* attached with very short stalk and *S. hammondii* by a slender stalk 5–10 mm. in length . . . ; the eggs of *S. hammondii* were arranged on similar objects but arranged spirally around them, thus differing from *S. couchii* in which no spiral arrangement could be easily made out."

Our measurements closely follow those of Ortenburger. The egg masses on stems may be from 6 or 7 to 25 mm. in diameter. Egg stalks may be from 5–9 mm. long and 1.4–2.3 mm. in diameter; vitellus 1.0–1.6 mm.; hatching period 1½–2 days.

**Journal notes:** July 8, 1917. Quite a rain fell near Sierra Blanca, Tex. At 7 o'clock, we heard no notes in the creek, but later from our camp one-half mile away, we heard the chorus plainly and decided it must be spadefoots. We found toads and spadefoots of two species migrating from the mountain side of Sierra Blanca toward the pool and noise. . . . Along the edges of the swift stream now flowing across the flooded area we found *Scaphiopus couchii.* Their cries were catlike. The *S. hammondii* were on the surface of the water and their calls were bubbling. . . . The Hammond's male will float like *S. holbrookii.* When he croaks, the rear half of the back dips beneath the water.

July 9. The stream has disappeared; it is now broken up by intermediate mud flats. The spadefoots and toads have disappeared from last night's rendezvous.

July 27, 1925. Found Hammond's spadefoot eggs, tads, and transformed in ponds by the roadside 16 miles east of Vail, Ariz. In one pond must have been 40–50 masses of eggs on the ends of grass stems. The eggs seemed to be out on periphery of the jelly cylinder. They look to be stalked. This is the same thing we found in Texas Pass 8 years ago, when we suspected it might be *Hyla arenicolor,* but now we know it is *S hammondii.* These eggs were laid last night and are already nearing hatching.

April 20, 1942. With Hadsell and Culbertson to Fresno, Calif, slough. Before we reached White Bridge we came to two or three ponds where we took large light-colored tadpoles (*S. h. hammondii*). Here Culbertson took some that were almost transformed, earlier.

June 13, Mesa, Ariz. Went out last night toward Florence Junction. Heard bullfrogs and Hammond's spadefoot in a pool at Desert Wells.

July 9, Lakeside, Ariz. Tonight, early in the evening heard no frogs. After I went to bed about 10 P.M. heard a few *S. h. hammondii* in one of the ponds above us.

July 10. Tonight, heard a few isolated *S. h. hammondii* again.

**Authorities' corner:**

E. D. Cope, N. Mex., 1884, p 14.
T. I. Storer, Calif., 1925, pp. 156–157.
F. W. King, Ariz, 1932, p. 175.

## Central Plains Spadefoot, Central Plains Spadefoot Toad, Cope's Spea, Western Spadefoot Toad

*Scaphiopus hammondii bombifrons* (Cope). Plate XIX; Map 6.

**Range:** Not fully defined. Stejneger and Barbour apparently consider the form from the Dakotas to Oklahoma, northwestern Texas, New Mexico, and west to Idaho to be *S. h. bombifrons,* but V. M. Tanner (1939) considers those west of Utah's east line, north of northern Arizona, and east of Nevada's west line to be Cope's old form *intermontanus.* H. M. Smith (Kansas, 1934) remarks that the range overlaps with *S. h. hammondii* in Colorado, western

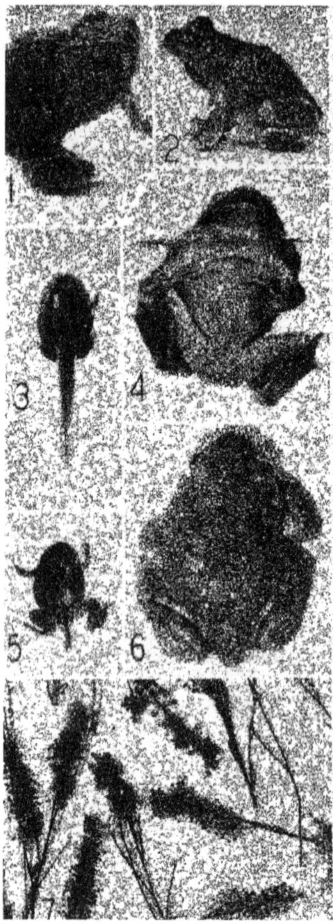

*Plate XVIII. Scaphiopus hammondii hammondii* (×⅔). 1,2,4,6. Males 3. Tadpole. 5. Transformed frog. 7 Eggs.

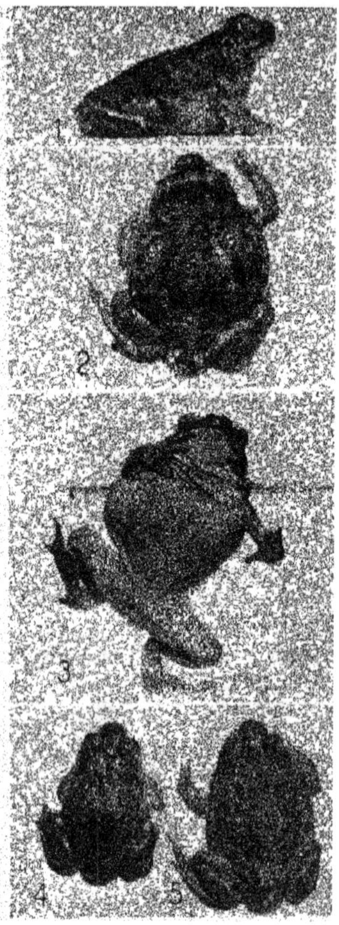

*Plate XIX Scaphiopus hammondii bombifrons* (×⅔). 1,2,3,5. Females. 4 Male.

Oklahoma, and northern and western New Mexico. P. Anderson (Mo., 1945) recently added Missouri to its range.

**Habitat:** "East of Colorado Springs in the low rolling hills is one of these areas. The soil is a mixture of sand, gravel, and loam and generally quite dry. It is here that adult spadefoot toads are found at depths varying from a few inches to several feet. . . . It usually chooses soft ground in which to burrow. With its spade-armed feet it pushes the soil aside, and by a slow rocking movement sinks backwards beneath the surface of the ground. The heavy skin of the head is probably used to keep the burrow open in front or to pack the earth of the walls of the burrow. The descending toad leaves no trace on the surface to indicate its course" (R. J. Gilmore, Colo., 1924, pp. 1–2).

"Along the Powder River near Powderville in Montana, on June 15, 1916, while lying upon my cot, I heard a curious rustling in the dry leaves about our tent. Upon investigation with a flashlight many small spadefoot toads were found. They were hopping about in the dry leaves which were scattered about on the sandy soil. When hunted with a flashlight they endeavored to burrow out of sight and but a few minutes were required for them to entirely conceal themselves. These spadefoots make circular holes in the ground and yet in sandy soil it is very difficult to find the place where they have burrowed down, for in most cases it seems as if they had pulled the hole in after them. After the breeding season is over they take more pains in constructing their burrows, as . . . [the burrows] are well rounded and resemble somewhat an earthen jar with a narrow top. Around this opening there is present some sticky matter which may aid in the ensnaring of insects. I have usually found this toad most plentiful in sandy areas, especially along the banks of streams, though they occur on the elevated plains from Kansas to Montana" (R. Kellogg, Mont., 1932, p 36).

**Size:** Adults (roughly) 1½–2⅛ inches. Males 38–52 mm. Females 40–57 mm.

**General appearance:** Stout; small; vertical pupil; interorbital boss. Grayish, reticulated or uniform; white below except throat of male. Two series of dorsal stripes or these absent. Smoother than *S. hammondii*. Internasal distance 1½ in eye to nares in ***bombifrons***, 1 in ***hammondii***.

**Color:** Colorado Springs, Colo., July, 1928, from R. J. Gilmore. *Female.* Sides yellowish glaucous or light mineral gray or water green; back in general, top of head, and hind legs vetiver green, tea green, or water green. Back of each eye on back is a dull citrine, water green, or yellowish glaucous spot edged with Lincoln green or deep grape green. On hind legs, rear of back, and top of head are spots Lincoln green or dusky olive-green. Some of these spots have light centers which are tubercles (under the lens, dark olive-buff in color). Under parts are white or cartridge buff, particularly on the throat; other parts are congo pink to salmon-buff or light ochraceous buff. There are two tubercles ahead of vent and also beside it that are white to light buff. Iris pale greenish yellow or light green-yellow unbroken around pupil; rest with black lines. Iris may be orange-pink. A spot or transverse bar like dorsal spots occurs on upper eyelid.

*Male.* The males on either side of throat have wash of deep bluish gray-green, or light terre verte, or grayish blue-green. [This from memory of males alive three days ago.] In alcohol the throats of male are very bluish or plumbeous.

**Structure:** Metatarsal tubercle rounded; parotoid gland absent. "A *Scaphiopus* with rounded, not elongated, inner metatarsal tubercles; tip of fifth toe frequently blackened and corneous; anterior interorbital region swollen, convex; parotoid glands indistinct, tympanum also usually; toes nearly fully webbed, fingers very slightly; pupil vertical" (H. M. Smith, Kan., 1934, p. 427).

**Voice:** "The call of this toad is quite weird and unusual and may be likened to the squawk of some animal when severely injured or a resonant *ye-ow*. Once heard this distinct call is not likely to be forgotten" (R. Kellogg, Mont., 1932, p. 36). "After arriving at the ponds the male spadefoot indulges in very vigorous nuptial song, which continues without interruption until the mating has been completed. The effect has been described as 'weird plaintive cries,' 'hoarse and woeful' " (R. J. Gilmore, Colo., 1924, p. 3).

**Breeding:** These frogs breed from May to August in the rainy season. The amplexus is inguinal. "The egg masses vary in size. Large masses contain 200 to 250 eggs, smaller ones 10 to 50 The mass is attached to submerged vegetation, or to any object protruding from the bottom. The mass is elliptical in shape." "The incubation period as observed in the field seems to be less than forty-eight hours." "Two and one-half inches is the maximum length of the majority of adults in any tadpole community." "In 1921, specimens were found completely transformed after thirty-six to forty days" (R. J. Gilmore, Colo., 1924, pp. 4, 5). The tadpole is carnivorous and herbivorous.

From conversations, letters, material, and experience, it is evident that our friends, Gilmore and Kellogg, know this form best. Dr. Gilmore has used this species in classes for a quarter-century and Dr. Kellogg has known it equally long. In recent years A. H. and M. S. Trowbridge and A. N. Bragg of Oklahoma have added the most to our knowledge of this frog.

In 1934 H. M. Smith characterized the tadpole thus: "Upper mandible with a large median beaklike projection, lower mandible with a deep elevated median notch; a black, corneous toothlike projection from roof of mouth; buccal musculature conspicuous and visible through skin as are viscera!" In 1929 we had described the tadpole of *S. hammondii* with no thought of separation into its three forms.

In 1942 A. N. Bragg (Okla.) characterized the tadpole of *S. h. bombifrons* as having "jaws without a beak and notch; jaw muscles not overdeveloped." In 1941 in New Mexico he discovered that "Smith's figure and description are of *S. hammondii,* and R. J. Gilmore (1924) and Wright's (1929) are of *S. bombifrons,* although labeled the reverse of this."

**Authorities' corner:**

J. A Tihen and J. M. Sprague, Kans., 1939, pp. 501–502.
G A. Moore and C. C. Rigney, Okla , 1942, p. 78.

### Great Basin Spadetoot Toad, Western Spadefoot Toad

*Scaphiopus hammondii intermontanus* (Cope). Plate XX; Map 6.

**Range:** Utah, Nevada, northern Arizona, western Colorado, southwestern Wyoming, Idaho except extreme north, southwestern Washington, eastern Oregon—a Great Basin form (after V. M. Tanner). British Columbia

**Habitat:** Canyon pools; desert springs and pools, intermittent and permanent; irrigation ditches; stream edges; rain puddles; water pockets; water depressions made by cattle.

**Size:** Adults 1½–2½ inches (40–63 mm.). Males, 40–59 mm. Females, 45–63 mm.

**General appearance:** "The evolution of the subgenus *Spea* seems to be from *hammondii* through *bombifrons* to *intermontanus.* In these species there is a progressive development of the osseous parts of the cranium with a closure of the fronto-parietal fontanelle in practically all specimens of *intermontanus.*" ". . . Fairly rugose." "*Intermontanus* has a greater internarial distance than either *bombifrons* or *hammondii*" (V. M. Tanner, Gen , 1939, pp. 15, 16).

"They appear to demonstrate that *bombifrons* and *hammondii* are in the same species, for there is obvious intergradation in every character. Moreover, it seems likely that additional material from this intervening area [Nevada]

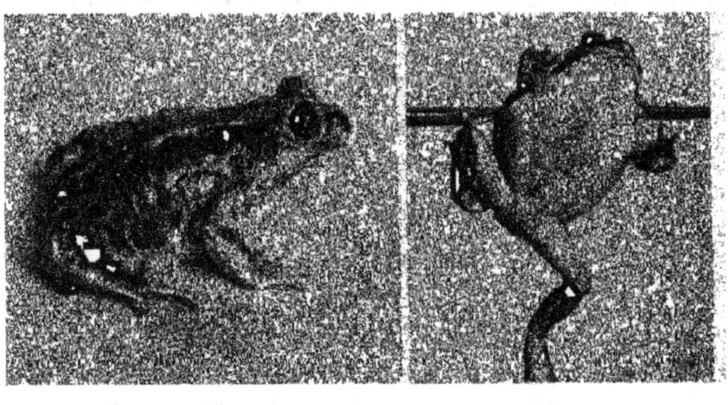

*Plate XX. Scaphiopus hammondii intermontanus* (×⅝). From C L. Patch, Okanagan Landing, B.C. Adults.

would demonstrate the validity of a third race, *intermontanus*." "Compared with *hammondii* this form was supposed to be distinguished by larger size, lighter colors, and the presence of the superior pair of light lines" (J. M. Linsdale, Nev., 1940, p. 200).

**Color:** "Their color was yellowish olive above, spotted with darker olive, belly soiled white, chin darker, sides of front legs and feet gray, the hind legs tinted on the under surface with blood red. The eye was large and very brilliant, the iris brassy with fine black reticulations. The pupil was very sensitive to light. There were two broad, grayish stripes on the back, and one on each side of the body. The glands were usually darker than the surrounding skin, and in some examples scattered glands bore brick red caps, which with darker rings appeared as ocelli. Some specimens were lighter than others, and an occasional one had a strong infusion of pale reddish brown" (J. O. Snyder, Nev., 1920, pp. 83–84).

"The colour in life was grayish green above and more or less mottled: a longitudinal whitish stripe down each side of the back from behind orbits to a little behind knees, and one along each side from behind ear; a short median whitish stripe on posterior part of back (over urostyle); a darkish blotch over orbit passing backward and inward, and a darkish line from eye to nostril; tubercles on back and sides tinged with orange; throat dusky, belly white" (E. B. S. Logier, B.C., 1932, p. 319).

**Structure:** "No interorbital boss present. In some specimens of *intermontanus* there is a glandular interorbital elevation which resembles the true boss found in *bombifrons*. This may be removed and the true nature of the skull revealed. . . . Head width wider 20.9–22.5 mm. Body rugose or with many individual prominences or warts. Color mottled whitish and black above; venter whitish; in preservative the back becomes blackish with some white areas. At times the back is streaked with whitish lines. Venter white. No fronto-parietal fontanelle; interorbital space with prominent fronto-parietal bones forming ridges; . . . in some specimens the interorbital space is filled with a glandular prominence resembling the *bombifrons* species; head width 22.5 mm., whole foot 31.2, confined in the main to the Great Basin area" (V. M. Tanner, Gen., 1939, pp. 11–12).

**Voice:** "Their appearance was at once announced by a loud chorus which differed markedly from that of *Hyla* or *Rana*, being in a lower key, somewhat guttural, and a little rasping. It was entirely different from that of *Bufo*" (J. O. Snyder, Nev., 1920, p. 83).

"I would describe the call as a soft, though very penetrating *kwak*, low-pitched with something of the quality of the vibrating of a heavy rubber band" (W. Wood, Utah, 1935, p. 101).

"A very secretive, wholly nocturnal, but really common species. Its call, a loud crah-crah-rah, repeated at short intervals, was first heard at Bellevue late in April and again, following a cold spell, on May 5. Thereafter it increased in volume nightly until June 1, after which it decreased, stopping about June 15. Rain puddles, overflows from irrigation ditches, in fact every pool of standing water served as breeding places. Drying up of the pools rarely permitted a development beyond the egg or early larval stages" (G. P. Englehardt, Utah, 1918, pp. 77–78).

**Breeding:** Records indicate breeding from April (Hardy), May (Snyder, Carl), June (Snyder, Tanner, Wood), July. Transformations are from late May through June and July to August or September.

"This, the commonest Carbon County amphibian was heard croaking on April 9, 1937; eggs were collected April 22. Numerous; breeding near river at Price, April 27. Also found breeding in puddles of rain water, in stagnant pools, in water, in alkali washes, in city reservoirs and swimming pools, and in sewage near Price River. Eggs deposited in the laboratory hatched after four days. Eggs collected in water containing algae were green due to inclusion of algae in the outer jelly while eggs deposited in muddy water included soil" (R. Hardy, Utah, 1938, p. 99).

"On the evening of June 2, 1911, I happened upon a small pond separated from the water of Pyramid Lake by a narrow bar. The pond was but a few feet in width, and perhaps a hundred feet long. The water was clear and slightly alkaline like that of the lake. In it were hundreds of spadefoots depositing their eggs in masses one layer deep on the upper surface of small rocks. The eggs were not piled up after the manner of frogs, nor were they in strings like those of toads. One mass presented fresh eggs and likewise others in which development was marked, plainly indicating that the mass was made of at least two contributions" (J. O. Snyder, Nev., 1920, p. 84).

Tanner records and describes a 51-mm. tadpole, coppery color in water, bluish black in preservative. He gives labial teeth rows as 2/4. Snyder secured a 60-mm. tadpole with teeth 3/4, 4/4 and transformation sizes of 20–24½ mm.

"From accounts of spadefoots that I have read I judged that the toads come out of their burrows only after a rain, and that a certain amount of moisture was necessary to bring them to the surface. However, the fact that so many hundreds of individuals came out of the ground in Smoky Valley in 1932, when no rain had fallen for a long time, indicates that other circumstances are able to initiate activity in this species." "In 1933, with Compton I worked in this same vicinity from mid-May to mid-June. The pasture was fairly dry this time, but a large proportion of the 1932 brood of spadefoots had survived, and we saw them almost daily. We were surprised to see them day after day foraging on the surface of the ground in daylight hours" (J. M. Linsdale, Nev., 1938, pp. 21, 23).

"On July 4, many small, recently transformed specimens were collected in mud cracks in the bed of a dried-up irrigation ditch near Maggie Creek. It was found that the easiest method of collecting them was to stamp on the ground. The vibration disturbed them and they would thrust their heads out of the cracks. If the jar continued, they came out and hopped about on the ground where they were conspicuous and easily captured, but when the stamping ceased they soon disappeared. A few had completely transformed, but the majority had tails varying in size from mere rudiments to the length of the head and body. Later many half grown specimens were observed coming up out of the ground behind the mowers in a hayfield near Annie Creek" (A. G. Ruthven and H. T. Gaige, Nev., 1915, p. 16).

**Journal notes:** May 20, 1942, Beaver Dam Lodge, Ariz., at bridge. We heard in several directions a few *Scaphiopus hammondii* subspecies. They were mainly concentrated in the big pool at north end of bridge. Two were too far out to collect—only one did we get. Its call is a harsh far-carrying call very different from the trill of *B. woodhousii*.

June 5. Stopped at Jacob's Lake, Ariz. The assistant forester, Harlen Johnson, said about May 1 they heard an awful squawking and he wondered what it was I asked him if they had spadefoots. He said "Yes." He sent droppings of coyotes to the Colorado laboratory and they said there were spadefoot remains in them. I went down to the lake and found two sizes of Hammond's spadefoot tadpoles.

**Authorities' corner:**

E B S. Logier, B C., 1932, p. 319. W F. Wood, Utah, 1935, pp. 101–102

## Spadefoot, Holbrook's Spadefoot, Hermit Spadefoot Toad, Spadefoot Toad, Hermit Toad, Solitary Toad, Solitary Spadefoot, Hermit Spadefoot, Storm Toad

*Scaphiopus holbrookii holbrookii* (Harlan). Plate XXI; Map 7.

**Range:** From West Virginia (Green and Richmond, 1942) and Ohio, down the Ohio River to southeastern Missouri and northeastern Arkansas, across extreme southeastern Texas, and along the Gulf and Atlantic coasts to Massachusetts.

**Habitat:** Shallow burrows in the ground; nocturnal in habit. They breed only after heavy rains, and then usually in temporary rain pools The following note relates several items about their general habits. Dave Mizzell of the Folkston, Ga., region, told of "a frog called 'storm frog' because it appears when there are storms or floods. It hollers *wank!* It folds up so that you can't see its legs. It is larger than the 'hop toad.' One was dug up in a potato field." "Very common at breeding time; seen on warm nights at the mouth of burrows, and hopping about in the woods" (O. C. Van Hyning, Fla., 1933, p. 3).

No other form in this country has had more printed about it than this elusive form Our account, however, will be one of our shortest summaries. No one has nightly visited these creatures in their nonbreeding holes more than Neil Richmond.

**Size:** Adults, 2–2⅞ inches. Males, 54–72 mm. Females, 50–71 mm.

**General appearance:** Like the common toad, it is short and broad in body, and with small round posttympanal glands (parotoids). The skin is relatively smooth but bears scattered warts; is usually brown in color, frequently with two more or less evident light dorsal stripes. The arms and legs are short and thick; the feet, broad. The inner tubercle of the sole is a large dark horny process with which the toad digs its burrows. The eyes are large and protuberant with vertical pupils indicating nocturnal habits. The throat and breast are white; the lower belly is grayish.

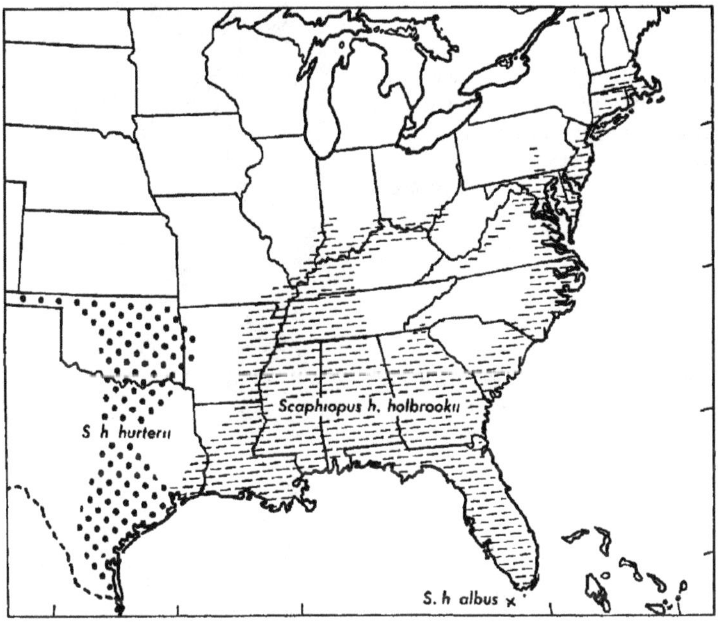


*Map 7*

**Color:** Hilliard, Fla., Aug. 18, 1922. *Male.* Stripe from eye back to vent lemon yellow or greenish yellow; other light colors of the back are same as stripe from eye to vent, so also on the sides. The snout is mummy brown, Prout's brown, sometimes blackish brown, or bone brown. This is also the remaining color of the back, which is sometimes virtually black. Limbs on dorsum, much the same color or slightly washed out greenish yellow of the light back colors; under parts of hind limbs and lower belly light grayish vinaceous. Rest of the under parts are white, especially the white glistening throat, which shows so conspicuously in the "croaking bubble." First three fingers with black excrescences. Spade of hind foot dark-edged, as is also the tip of first toe. Web of foot much darker than the grayish vinaceous web of female. Iris light greenish yellow with black on the outer rim. Pupil vertical.

*Female.* Sometimes uniform warm sepia or bone brown above. Throat and breast white. Underside of fore limbs and hind limbs and lower belly light grayish vinaceous. Sometimes the stripe on females may be sulphur yellow instead of the intense greenish yellow of the male. Almost always each male of a pair had a predominance of yellowish hues and the females inclined to the brownish hues.

**Structure:** Tympanum much smaller than the eye; large, wide hind feet; skin on crown of head, thin; parotoid gland present; male with a subgular vocal sac; males with fingers broader than females.

**Voice:** Hoarse, coarse, monosyllable, ***wank, wank,*** like the calling of young crows Aug. 16, 1922, we heard the congress at a half-mile distance. At this distance, to one it sounded like the calling or snarling or complaining note of a cross baby; to another member of the party, like young crows; or at other times like young herons in a herony. One member characterized it as ***naarh naarh,*** complaining, nasal, not shrill or high-pitched. Near by it sounds somewhat like ***where, where, where, where.***

*Plate XXI Scaphiopus holbrookii holbrookii* 1,4. Males (×⅜) 2,3 Females (×⅔) 5. Egg mass (×½) 6 Forearm of male (×⅔).

When we first approached, the males called on all sides in full daylight, almost at our very feet. The inflated throat by day is a beautiful glistening white golf ball. The male before he calls lies on the water's surface with hind legs partially submerged. When he croaks he dips the hind end of the body and the head is reared to a 45°–75° angle with the water's surface. When at the height of the performance, or slightly before, he closes his eyes. Then the throat deflates and the body inflates. He croaks about once in every two seconds.

A big congress may make as much noise as a steam calliope, though of a different nature. Normally the mated pairs are quiet. It is the calls of free males which are searching a mate or annoying the already mated pairs which make up the chorus.

"The peculiar, harsh croaking of this singular toad must be heard to be appreciated, and can then never be confounded with that of any other species. The only sound we can liken it to is that of a heavily loaded, creaking wagon rolling over hard and uneven ground" (F. W. Putnam, Mass., 1867, p. 109).

"We have found only one reference to a spadefoot singing while underground (A. H. Wright, 1932). We found this to be one of the most striking peculiarities of the animal. In the early part of the evening, between nine and ten o'clock, no toads were visible in the ponds, but from all around the margin came their much muffled calls. It was a most peculiar sensation to be in the midst of the chorus but to have only a barren expanse of sticky clay visible under the flashlight. Excavating with considerable difficulty we found the songsters to be several inches below the surface in apparently quite solidly packed earth. No sign of entrance to the burrows was visible. As the evening wore on one after another pushed out to the surface and entered the pond to float and sing with greater vigor. The chorus reached its height shortly after midnight" (E. G. Driver, Mass., 1936, pp. 67–68).

**Breeding:** On this topic as on voice there are countless observations The spadefoot breeds from March to September at periods of heavy rainfall. The eggs are in irregular bands along grass blades or plant stems, the band 1–2 inches (25–50 mm.) wide and 1–12 inches (25–300 mm.) long, the egg 1/16–1/12 inch (1.4–2 mm ), the envelope 3/16–1/5 inch (4–5.6 mm.). They hatch in 1½–2 days. The bronzy tadpole is small, 1⅛ inches (28 m.) broad, but not deep, its tail short and rounded. After 14–60 days, the tadpoles transform from July to September at ⅓–½ inch (8.5–12 mm.).

**Journal notes:** Aug 16, 1922. We started from Callahan in a hard rain, a little before noon. On a detour two miles south of Hilliard, Fla., we stopped for cars going across a swollen creek. Francis went to look for birds and heard spadefoots calling. We drove through the woods and back on the Dixie Highway and pitched camp, 1 mile south of Hilliard on an oak ridge. An old road filled with water made a shallow pond, and here we saw the males croaking, their white throats looking like shiny white golf balls. Just beyond was a shallow surface pool made by the heavy rains. The ground was covered with herbs: a little *Xyris*, a few sedges, *Rhexia*, a small umbelliferous plant with violet-shaped leaf, wire grass, and *Hypericum*. The spadefoots were calling here, in another similar pool, and in a third deeper pool as well. At a distance the chorus sounded like young crows trying to call The pond was filled with mated pairs.

A few eggs had been laid. The eggs were laid in more or less irregular band form along the grass blades or plant stems. In the third pond where the water was deep, the bands were long. The pair might be floating on the surface. When ready to lay, they went to the bottom of the pond, often the male with his eyes closed and the female with hers partly closed. They moved along slowly on the bottom or rested a minute. When she found a stem to suit her, she seized it with her front feet and pushed with her hind feet. The male clung close to her back, his chin tight against her back. (One we photographed had an abrased chin as if from pressure.) He held his knees against her knees, or sometimes his feet, which are conspicuously broad, were pressed against her feet. She walked or climbed up the grass blade or along it, if it fell to horizontal position, and pressed her vent against the blade as she laid the eggs. He humped his back to press his vent close to hers while she was laying. As they reached the top of the blade, they sometimes moved immediately to a nearby one, or rested a short period. When first laid, the eggs had an irregular band appearance as they were strung along the blade, sometimes being much thicker if more eggs had been emitted at such periods. When first laid, they had a brownish appearance with conspicuous creamy-white vegetative pole. As the jelly swelled and the eggs all turned right side up, they looked very black.

By the next morning some eggs were almost ready to hatch (these must have been the ones we found when we first found the pond). The other clusters were swollen into loose, irregular, elongate bunches attached to the stems which tipped so that many times the bunches lay lengthwise on the water. There seemed to be a tendency for the bunches of eggs to be more or less clustered in areas We noticed many pairs close together that first afternoon, and unattached males trying to get to a female, thus making tangled masses of toads. There was a strong chorus that night and by the next morning the pond was all churned up and muddy. Many, many eggs were there, but no toads. The story was told for the season.

**Authorities' corner:**

A. Nichols, Mass., 1852, pp 113–115.
F. W. Putnam, Mass , 1865, p. 229.
F. Overton, N Y., 1915, p. 17.
N D Richmond, Va , 1947, pp. 53–67.

## Key West Spadefoot

*Scaphiopus holbrookii albus* (Garman). Plate XXII; Map 7.

**Range:** Florida Keys and possibly the extreme southern part of Florida.

**Habitat:** The query that naturally arises is: Do the other species of frogs such as the green tree frog, southern tree toads, toads, or frogs have a similar tendency toward albinism in the Keys? Is it due to salt or a light beach habitat? Or, was this lot of spadefoots an isolated albinistic collection that might possibly occur on the mainland in other portions of the spadefoot's range? One would expect the subterranean spadefoot to tend more toward albinism than almost any other species of the country.

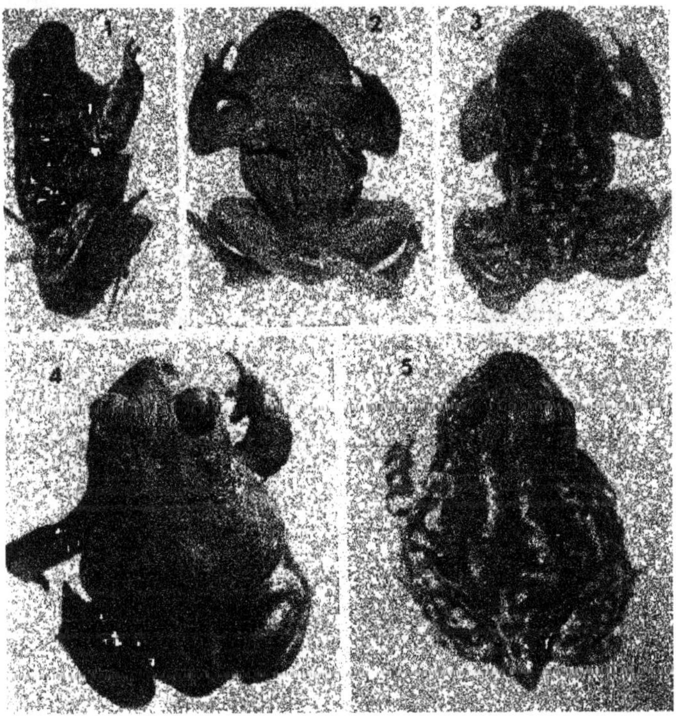

*Plate XXII. Scaphiopus holbrookii albus* (×1) 1,2,3 Males, from USNM. 4 Male, from Gainesville, Fla. 5. Female, from Gainesville, Fla.

**Size:** Adults 2⅛–2¾ inches. The three specimens in the National Museum are males measuring 54, 56, 56 mm. The University of Michigan Museum has a female 56 mm

**General appearance:** This spadefoot is like Holbrook's but with an excessive amount of white in the pattern.

**Color:** "Average size less than that of preceding (*S. h. holbrookii*). Brown of the back lacks the red or chocolate tinge. Readily distinguished by the great amount of white on back, flanks, and upper surface of limbs. The white forms spots or vermiculations which coalesce into bands of irregular shape and extent" (S. Garman, Gen. Check. L., 1884, p. 45). A doubtful subspecies.

**Structure:** Apparently the interorbital distance is narrower in *S. h. albus* than in *S. h. holbrookii*, being in body length 9.3–10 in *S. h. albus* and 6.77–8.5 in *S. h. holbrookii*. Two pectoral glands are present.

| *Scaphiopus h.* | *albus* | | *holbrookii* | |
|---|---|---|---|---|
| | Male | Female | Male | Female |
| Body length | 56 mm. | 56 mm. | 56 mm. | 56 mm. |
| Interorbital space | 6.0 mm. | 5.5 mm. | 8.0 mm. | 8.0 mm. |

**Voice:** Their cries sound like "ow, ow," and "miow," but the latter much deeper in tone than the well-known cat cry. The noise made by a dozen males is deafening when one is near, though the call lacks carrying power (R. F. Deckert, Fla., 1921, p. 22).

"The habits of the two seem to me to be identical, and I can detect no differences in the voices" (A. F. Carr, Jr., Fla., 1940b, p. 54).

**Breeding:** We have seen live specimens from Gainesville which seemed almost as light as the preserved specimens of this subspecies. Pending the determination of the status of *S. h. albus* and whether it extends to the southern tip of Florida, we wish to point out that Richard F. Deckert does not describe the spadefoots of Miami as *S. h. albus*. He calls them *Scaphiopus holbrookii*.

"*Scaphiopus holbrookii* (Harlan). On April 23 (1920) a male specimen was found by the writer, about six inches down, in sandy marl at Brickell Ave. and Broadway, Miami. During a prolonged thunderstorm many of the spadefoot toads were encountered by the writer on the streets south of Miami River, on the afternoon of May 16, and during the night were found breeding at 19th Street and Ave. H., also at 22nd Street and Miami Ave., and great numbers were reported from the low grounds near the 'Alligator farm,' Miami" (R. F. Deckert, Fla., 1921, p. 22).

**Journal notes:** March 18, 1934. Looking for Florida spadefoots, we spent one night at Caribee Colony on Matecumbe Key, and went out in the evening with our flashlights to "shine their eyes." A few were out, but more were in their burrows with the tops now shaken open.

**Authorities' corner:**

C. E. Burt, Gen., 1938, p. 335.
V. M. Tanner, Gen., 1939, p. 3.
A. F. Carr, Jr., Fla., 1940b, pp. 31, 53–54.

## Hurter's Spadefoot, Hurter's Solitary Spadefoot

*Scaphiopus holbrookii hurterii* (Strecker). Plate XXIII; Map 7.

**Range:** Eastern half of Texas. Records exist from Houston and Edna to Cameron County. Smith extends it to western Arkansas.

**Habitat:** Like other spadefoots, these frogs come out of their burrows to breed in temporary pools.

**Size:** Medium. Type 67 mm, from Waco Refugio specimen 63 mm. The range of size of ten breeding adults from Lytle, Texas (collected by A. J. Kirn, June 28, 1931) is 66–78 mm. Adults, 1¾–3⅛ inches. Males, 43–73 mm. Females, 44–82 mm.

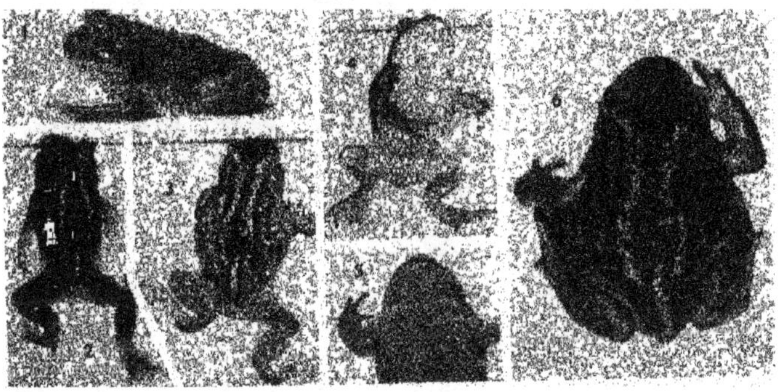

*Plate XXIII. Scaphiopus holbrookii hurterii* (×½). 1,2,3,4,6. From Albert Kirn, Somerset, Tex. 5 From USNM to show pectoral glands.

**General appearance:** "Head short, length about equal to width. (In *holbrookii* the head at angle of mouth is much wider than long.) Snout heavy and blunt, not extending beyond the mouth. Parotoids nearly round, higher and even more conspicuous than in the eastern species. Tympanum distinct but rather smaller than in *holbrookii* (In type hardly more than half the diameter of the parotoid.) Crown distinctly rugose. No black granules in space between and in front of the eyes. Upper surfaces with small, closely set tubercles, very uniform in size and distribution. Many tubercles on sides, buttocks, and posterior portion of the abdomen.

"Color above, pale greenish, with a pale yellowish line from each orbit; these converge again in the coccyx. Upper surface of head and area between the light lines, dark plumbeous, parotoids olive. Sides of head and under surfaces yellowish-white" (J. K. Strecker, Jr., Tex., 1910, pp. 116–117).

**Color:** Somerset, Tex., from Al Kirn, June 20, 1945. *Males.* The dorsal background color is Saccardo's olive, medal bronze to raw umber. A light stripe on either side crosses the rear of the eyelid, outlines the corner of the head boss, the pair becoming parallel for ¾ inch and about ½ inch apart, next bowing outward and then approaching each other toward the groin. These stripes are dull green-yellow or bright chalcedony yellow to buffy citrine. From the vent forward is a short middorsal stripe of the same, which also occurs on outer edge of foot and tarsus and on a few tubercles on the outer edge of tibia and along the sides of the body. There is a patch of the same color above the arm insertions. The tympanic area is buffy citrine to dull green-yellow. The top of head and boss are smooth and unspotted mummy brown. The iris is light cendre green to light ochraceous-buff with a horizontal bar of black, which is seldom complete. The under parts are cream to white, most intense on chin and pectoral region. The rear portions are vinaceous-buff, which color sometimes suffuses the whole under parts. The upper ¾ of first finger and inner and upper half of second bear black excrescences.

*Females.* Females have a tendency to be less green The stripes are more buffy, in one almost white. The lateral tubercles may be almost white and arranged in 5–7 series. The excrescences on fingers are lacking.

**Structure:** The boss on head is large, conspicuous, and much raised at the rear. The axillary breast glands are present.

"Many pustules on upper surface of tibia. Glands on thorax present, conspicuous. Enlargements resembling glands on inferior surface of femur (present in both specimens). Spade-like process of foot narrowly margined with black. Palmar tubercles rather small. Fingers slender. Tibia about equal to that of *S. holbrookii* but femur and foot much shorter" (J. K. Strecker, Jr., Tex., 1910a, pp. 116–117).

Distinguished from *S. h. holbrookii* by "its more compact form, narrow head, blunt muzzle, unusually high parotoids, smaller palmar tubercles, and shorter hind limbs. The sides, buttocks, tibia, and posterior portion of the abdomen are covered with tubercles instead of being almost perfectly smooth. The tubercles on the upper surfaces are more uniform in size" (same, p. 116).

Mr. Kirn's material (June 28–29, 1931), when compared with male *S. h. holbrookii* of the same size, has smaller measurements. The head to angle of mouth, the width of head, the tympanum (equal in one), the snout (greater in one) were less than in *S. h. holbrookii* The hind limbs were equal in the two species.

Mr. Kirn's specimens include 66-, 68-, 68-mm. males. We studied also Strecker's material and that of USNM and Baylor University. Our custom of measuring males and females of every species of frog in the United States at 20, 28, 36, 44, 56, 66, 68, and 82 mm. makes the measurements more readily comparable than random ones of unsexed specimens. The following table is part of the 25 measurements we made for each specimen:

| | *S. h. hurterii* 44 mm. | *S. h. holbrookii* 44 mm. | *S. h. hurterii* 56 mm. | *S. h. holbrookii* 56 mm. |
|---|---|---|---|---|
| Head to angle of mouth | 14 | 15 | 15 | 18 |
| Width of head | 17 | 19 | 21 | 23 |
| Snout | 8 | 8.5 | 9 | 10 |
| Tympanum | 3 | 4.0 | 3.5 | 5.5 |
| Hind limb | 43 | 45 | 53 | 49 |
| Tibia | 14 | 15.5 | 18 | 17.5 |
| Foot with tarsus | 22 | 24 | 28 | 28 |
| Foot without tarsus | 16 | 16.5 | 20.5 | 19 |

**Voice:** "The call is a single note, which, while guttural, has a peculiar soft quality not unpleasing to the human ear, quite different from that of *Scaphiopus bombifrons, S. couchii,* or *S. hammondii,* and different also from descriptions of the cry of *S. h. holbrookii,* which is commonly stated to be very harsh and loud (cf. Ball, 1936). Nevertheless the voice of *hurterii* has a quality characteristic of spadefoot breeding calls; I recognized it at once when first heard as a spadefoot call. The cry is not exceptionally loud, although a large chorus can be heard for at least one-half mile. (I have heard *S. bombifrons* for more than 2 miles on a still prairie night.) The calls of males tend to stimulate other males to call and to attract both females and other males to a given pool.

"Each call is explosively given, and the vocal sac becomes fully distended and then deflated each time. Intervals between calls vary, both with the numbers of individuals present and with numbers calling at any one time. The usual interval in a large, excited congress is from one to two and one-half seconds. There is no tendency for the calls of males to be synchronous" (A. N. Bragg, Okla., 1944, pp 231–232).

**Breeding:** January to December (Kirn).

"All masses of eggs of *S. hurterii* seen were produced near the shore, at and near the water surface, and strung out over vegetation. When in place, they superficially resemble those of *Bufo* rather than those of other spadefoots. Each egg is black at the animal pole, shading to very light grey or white at the vegetal. Each is inclosed in a ball of jelly considerably larger than itself, i.e., in a single thick gelatinous envelope. Individual eggs vary little in size, each being about 2.3 mm. in diameter. The gelatinous capsules also are quite uniform at about 6.7 mm. The gelatinous coats are elastic and quite sticky so that they easily pick up particles from the surrounding water. This tends to conceal them after a few hours. The little gelatinous balls tend to stick together in various patterns. These patterns are quite irregular, but most often the eggs attach tandem-fashion so that an irregular string is produced with some similarity to the eggs of toads. There is no continuous, gelatinous, encasing tube as in *Bufo,* and one egg within its covering can easily be separated from others to which it is joined. Such strings may be very short or several inches long. Individual eggs of one such string commonly attach to others in adjacent strings, forming a network. Several such lattices are sometimes similarly joined to form a three-dimensional pattern. A winding string of eggs, loosely attached to other such strings wherever contact happens to be made between them, is most commonly found.

"The number of eggs in a complete clutch is unknown, but the complement must consist of several hundred at least" (A. N. Bragg, Okla., 1944, pp. 232–233).

**Journal notes:** On Feb. 9, 1932, Mr. A. J. Kirn of Somerset, Tex., sent us ten preserved *Scaphiopus* which Mr. Strecker pronounced *S. h. hurterii*. On Feb. 15, 1932, Mr. Kirn wrote, "They [the spadefoots] are not calling as yet. I found one of them last year, January 27—in the road, during a rainy spell. I will send you some of the *Scaphiopus* when they come out to lay. Do not know when this will be." His field notes for these ten spadefoots are somewhat as follows: "Lytle June 29 (Monday) 1931. Rain Friday 8 P.M. through most of Saturday and again yesterday, early morning and late evening, again early this morning and this afternoon, about three inches altogether. Weather warm. *Scaphiopus hurterii* heard last night at all pools at wells (old slush pits). Collected a dozen at No. 10 and No. 13 (4 pairs in copulation; in all of these the smaller and lighter one was male). Collected between 10 and 11 P.M., June 28. This afternoon, I found eggs already hatched at Nos. 10 and 13 wells. No spadefoots heard before 8:30 P.M. yesterday. Eggs evidently laid last night after midnight. Were hatched at 7 P.M. today and how long before I do not know. The spadefoots collected last night varied from gray and yellowish green to dark, all with two dorsal stripes (widening on middle posterior back). Parotoid glands distinct in all. Had in can all of today. Many eggs laid in the can. Not any spadefoots heard or found tonight, June 29."

We had a group of spadefoots in a laundry tub, in which we had 3 inches of dirt. We fed them mealworms, from a glass dish in the center of the tub. By day no toads were visible, nor was there any evidence of their burrows, but about 9:30 in the evening they began to shake their heads and loose spots appeared here and there, and slowly the toads came out, and quickly snapped up the proffered worms.

We have no personal experience with this form in the field. Our latest lot (1945) of live material came from A. J. Kirn, who knows it best. Some of his notes are:

"2/12. Much rain last 2 nights. Spadefoot toads calling loudly tonight 7:30 on. From water pools. This first heard this spring and winter. Weather mild. 2/12. Very heavy rain last night and nearly as much night before that. Many spadefoot toads calling from all pools. Temperature 57 at 11 P.M. 2/13. Egg clusters of spadefoot toads this A.M. in a pool. Also numbers of tadpoles, various size from small (⅛ inch) to large, hind legs showing beneath skin. Evidently eggs laid some time ago. (January?) See 2/21. 2/17. A few spadefoots in roads tonight. 2/21. Tadpoles, large, of 2/13—have hind legs today. Egg cluster pool of 2/13 has numbers of tadpoles about 6 mm. 2/27. Spadefoot tadpoles of Feb. 12–13 still not as large as the largest seen Feb. 13. Therefore those were from eggs laid in January, possibly about January 21. This is my first and only record of eggs laid during that month, though I always contended that they would lay eggs any month of the year if temperature and conditions were right. Weather colder Feb. 26 and 27. March 1. Milder and foggy.

"7/5. On June 19, I sent you a box with 25 spadefoot frogs, hope that they reached you alive, and that they were enough to suit your needs. We had a four-inch rain the night before and they called until 12:15 noon, then sun came out, they quit until after sundown, when some came out. I went to nearby ponds (tanks) found them scarce, and wild. However I managed to pick up two dozen, then got one in the house-yard. Can get more later on when it rains hard enough, if you need them."

**Authorities' corner:**

H. M Smith, Tex, 1937, pp 104–108.
V. M. Tanner, Gen., 1939, p. 9.
A. N. Bragg, Okla, 1942b, p. 506.

## Family BUFONIDAE

### Genus *BUFO* Laurenti

Maps 8–14

**Colorado River Toad, Giant Toad, Girard's Toad, Colorado Toad**

*Bufo alvarius* Girard. Plate XXIV; Map 8.

**Range:** Imperial Valley, Calif., up the Colorado River almost to Nevada's tip, up the Gila River almost to New Mexico's border, and south into Sonora, Mex.

**Habitat:** Lower Sonoran life zone. Semiaquatic. In the general locality of large permanent streams or the irrigated portions of our southwestern desert regions.

Pima Co., Ariz. "*Bufo alvarius* is much commoner near the Steam Pump than other species of the genus. With a few exceptions it is found only in the wet places around the cattle watering troughs of the ranches in the mesquite association. The only other place where we found it was in a temporary roadside pond formed by a heavy rain where *Scaphiopus couchii* and *S. hammondii* were breeding. These, however, had very probably come from the watering troughs of the ranch only a few hundred yards distant. While *Bufo alvarius* was found in the pond with the breeding *Scaphiopus,* none of the former were breeding. One specimen was found at dusk at the mouth of a canyon on the dry sandy bed, and a few were found at night by the roadside. Practically all were found after dark, but we discovered that their daytime hiding place was in hollows under the watering troughs" (A. I. Ortenburger and R. D. Ortenburger, Ariz., 1927, p. 102).

**Size:** Adults, 3¼–7 inches. Males, 80–156 mm. Females, 87–178 mm.

**General appearance:** This is a very large grayish or brownish-green toad with smooth, leathery skin and a few scattered small, rounded warts. The under parts are light. The head is broad and flat, marked by low, broad, crescent-shaped crests curving around the rear of the eye. These are like fleshy folds. The canthus rostralis is marked by a ridge which turns down in front of the eye as a preorbital. One to four white warts are present back of the angle of the mouth. The parotoids are large, subreniform in shape, spreading downward at the shoulder. There is a large glandular wart on the femur and a long one or several shorter ones on the tibia. These glands are the conspicuous mark of this toad and appear early, being present in a 1¾-inch (44-mm.) individual.

**Color:** *Female.* Bard, Imperial Co., Calif., from L. M. Klauber, May 22, 1930. Color deep olive, dark olive or citrine-drab, or dark greenish olive on back and buffy olive on either side of back. Warts on back not conspicuous, buckthorn brown or Dresden brown. Some of same color on each upper eyelid. This brown scanty on femur, absent on forelegs, tibia, and hind foot. Fore limbs deep grayish olive. Arm insertion olive-gray and some spots of same color each side of pectoral region and edge of throat. Throat same color as venter. Venter white. Back of angle of mouth are two pale ochraceous-buff or shell pink glands. Tympanum like dorsal color. Iris cream-buff below and

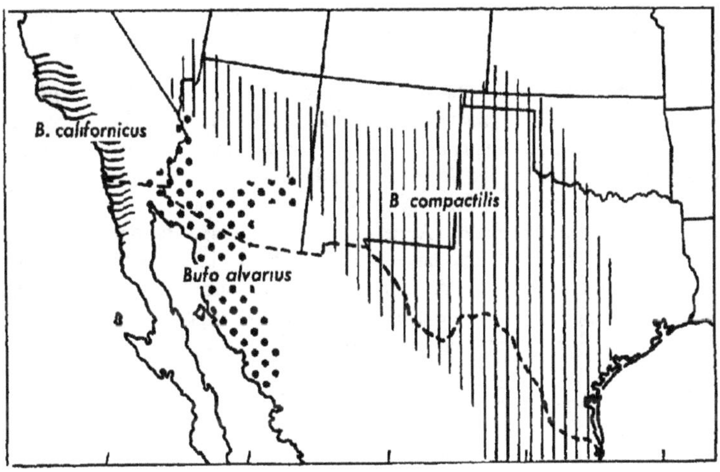


*Map 8*

above, with some tawny or russet streaks. Dark longitudinal bar through eye, brownish olive ahead of and behind eye.

A young specimen (USNM no. 21802, 44 mm.) has a spotted back and at first appearance looks like a *B. punctatus.* The parotoids are oblong, spreading apart, the glands on femur are close to tibia, and those on tibia barely show. Tympanum very distinct, slightly elliptic. Two white warts back of angle of mouth present.

**Structure:** Two metatarsal tubercles; two large palmar tubercles; first finger about equal to second; first finger of female may look very long and slender, that of male much heavier at base; palms and soles tuberculate; interorbital much wider than internasal space; a membranous fold at the inner edge of the tarsus; horny excrescences on fingers of male may be very prominent, starting from back of wrist and extending all along inner side of first finger and covering upper surface as well; second finger has upper surface with excrescence as well as triangular patch from tip backward; slight on third; tympanum may be obliquely vertical and elliptical or almost round and very little oblique.

**Voice:** "When held in the hand, this toad jerks spasmodically, and vibrates the whole body, as if about to explode with wrath. The only sound, however, produced in protest is a gentle chirping note, less loud and emphatic than that of the American toad" (M. C. Dickerson, Gen., 1906, p. 108).

"I assure you there was no lack of noise that day nor night, the croaking being incessant" (A. G. Ruthven, quoting J. J. Thornber, Ariz., 1907, p. 506).

"On the night of July 13th, a chorus of giant toads was heard from a ditch near the Sells-Robles road southwest of Tucson" (C. F. Kauffeld, Ariz., 1943, p. 343).

"Of batrachians, a toad (*Bufo*) and a frog (*Rana virescens brachycephala* Cope) were found at Warsaw Mills; and at Buenos Ayres, at the beginning of the summer rains, Lieutenant Gaillard observed great numbers of a very large froglike toad, named *Bufo alvarius* by Girard. Nothing was seen or heard of them until the advent of the early summer rains, which formed a large shallow lake near Buenos Ayres and about 10 kilometers (6 miles) north of the Boundary Line. These large toads then filled the air with their loud cries, which increased until a deafening roar was produced. Numbers of them were seen hopping about, but their rarity was not suspected by Lieutenant Gaillard, on which account none were collected" (E. A. Mearns, Ariz., 1907, p. 113).

**Breeding:** "Deep brown above and tan below, the eggs are encased in a single long tube of jelly. The envelope is somewhat loose, but quite distinct in outline; the gelatinous material is, for the most part, clear, transparent, and not very adhesive. There are no partitions between the individual eggs, whose arrangement varies from a perfectly linear series of near spheres to a zigzag pattern of broadly wedge-shaped eggs. The number of eggs per inch averages eighteen (range 12 to 28). Vitelline membranes are close to the vitelli and not visible with the unaided eye; at times they are difficult to see even under magnification. Measurements on the eggs are as follows: vitellus 1.4 mm. (range 1.14 to 1.70 mm.); vitelline capsule 1.6 mm. (range 1.25 to 1.70 mm.); envelope 2.2 mm. (range 2.12 to 2.25 mm.). Affinities: Except for the deeper color of the vitelli, the lesser degree of convolution and lack of slight scalloping of the gelatinous tube, eggs of *B. alvarius* are similar to those of *B. compactilis*. Measurements of both average approximately the same in all respects. The total mass of eggs is larger in *B. alvarius* and the crowding within the tube is more intense (12 to 28 per inch for *alvarius* to 14 to 20 for *compactilis*), this difference, however, being barely noticeable. Superficially *B. alvarius* eggs also look like those of *B. terrestris*. But here the lighter color of the eggs and greater degree of convolution of the tube plus the presence of an inner envelope serve to separate eggs of these species immediately." (R. Livezey and A. H. Wright, Gen., 1947, pp. 193, 194, 214).

The eggs we secured July 2–3, 1934, were in long, ropelike strings (400 inches) of 7500–8000 eggs.

"Two of the females collected at Alamos between August 27 and September 2 contain mature eggs in the oviduct" (C. M. Bogert and J. A. Oliver, Gen., 1945, p. 339).

**Journal notes:** July 30, 1917, just southeast of Tempe, Ariz. Made only 49 miles. In a water hole near a culvert Ralph Wheeler and I caught six immense toads (*Bufo alvarius*). All males. Probably tardy ones. Tadpoles (*Bufo*) in the hole probably of this species.

June 25, 1934, Florida Experiment Station, Ariz. Mr. R. R. Humphrey said that at 10 P.M. on the road from Nogales north he saw several *Bufo alvarius* after rain. Mr. Gorsuch said they often gather at the Continental pond, that he once found several pairs of *B. alvarius* which he brought up to the station. They laid long strings of black eggs. Had he known they were not described he would have saved them.

June 29. At Continental we walked around an irrigation pond. Under a tin cover found a large male *B. alvarius.* How he did protestingly chuckle as we carried him off. His body under my hand was clammy with secretions.

July 2, Tucson, Ariz. Rained in many places. Went about 5 to Sabino Canyon. At picnic spot two pools, the upper pool filled with *R. pipiens* When almost dark we went to the lower pool with its dam. At upper end we saw about 12 dead females of *Bufo alvarius.* Several large *B. alvarius* males jumped in. We continued to find males until we came to where Prof. Wehrle's small daughter had spotted a just perceptible gray spot in the shallow water (4–8 inches). This proved to be a pair. There were six or eight pairs here. Brought in three pairs and put them in a tub. How the males did cluck! They sound like contented chickens or chickens when sleepy at night. At 11 P.M. we found they had laid and we fixed some. What immense ropelike masses! They clucked when disturbed.

July 3. This morning many *B. alvarius* eggs in the tub. One pair yet mated. The other pairs are broken. Went to Sabino Canyon. No *B. alvarius* to be found or eggs.

**Authorities' corner:**

J. G. Cooper, Calif., 1869, p. 480.
F. Mocquard, Gen., 1899, p. 168.
E. A. Mearns, Ariz., 1907, p. 113.
A. G. Ruthven, Ariz., 1907, p. 506.
A. I. and R. D. Ortenburger, Ariz., 1927, p. 102.
F. W. King, Ariz., 1932, p. 175.
C F. Kauffeld, Ariz., 1943, p 343.

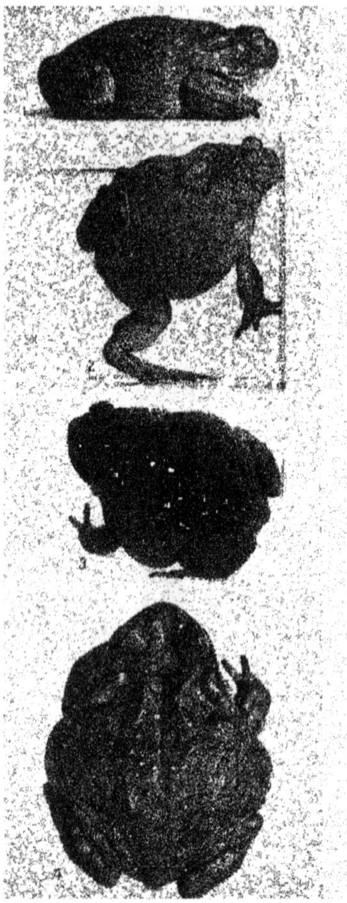

*Plate XXIV. Bufo alvarius.* 1,2,3,4 Females (×⅓).

*Plate XXV. Bufo americanus americanus.* 1,2,3,7. Males (×½) 4 Male trilling while sitting in shallow water (×⅓). 5. Young (×½). 6. Coils of egg strings on bottom of a pond (×¼).

### American Toad, Northern Toad, Hop Toad

*Bufo americanus americanus* Holbrook. Plate XXV; Maps 9, 10.

**Range:** Manitoba eastward on latitude 50° N. to Gaspé and the Maritime Provinces. Minnesota south through Iowa to eastern Kansas and Oklahoma, thence eastward to northern Georgia, along Appalachians to central Virginia, thence to the coast and northward to Nova Scotia. A transition and Canadian zone form. Common throughout its range.

**Habitat:** Common in gardens and cultivated fields, appearing more by night than day. During the sunshiny hours they seek cover beneath piazzas,

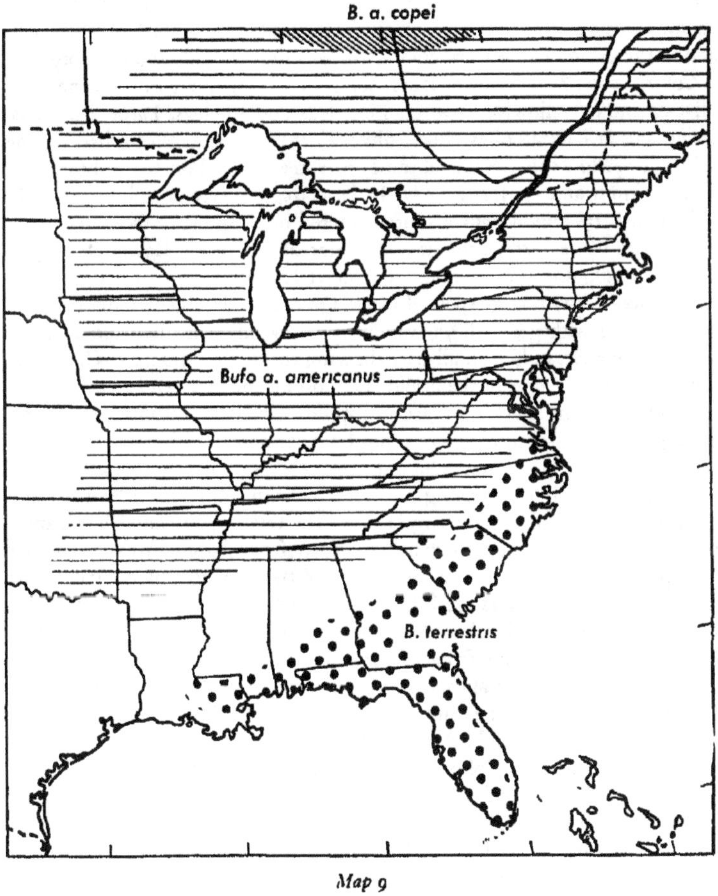


*Map 9*

under board walks, flat stones, boards, logs, wood piles, or other cover. When cold weather comes, the toad digs backwards into its summer quarters or may choose another site for its hibernation.

**Size:** Adults, $2\frac{1}{8}$–$4\frac{1}{4}$ inches. Males, 54–85 mm. Females, 56–110 mm.

**General appearance:** Short and fat in body, it has a short broad head and the snout is broadly circular. The lower surfaces are roughly granular, the back is covered with various-sized warts, some of which are large ones in pairs down the middle of the back. There are three or four pairs of dark spots down the back, each with one large wart. The eyes are prominent. The arms and legs, hands and feet, are warty or roughly tubercular. There are dark spots on the arms and legs, along the sides, and a few on the belly. Some males have yellow throats and considerable yellow on the underside of the base of the legs and in the groin. The general color is olive, with parotoids and crest brown.

**Color:** *Male.* May 7, 1929. Back, sides, and tympanum dull citrine with olive-citrine or yellowish olive on hind legs and forelegs. Parotoids, crests, snout, and face ahead of eye buffy olive. Throat old gold, olive-ocher, aniline yellow, or yellow ocher. Some of same color in axilla and on rear of brachium, also on groin and on lower belly. In latter region may be ochraceous-buff. Whole pectoral region with distinct scattered black spots; in fact these occur over entire venter except throat and center of rear belly. Lower throat oil-yellow or sulphine yellow. Some apricot yellow across arm insertion. Sides heavily spotted with large spots of black. On back is an obscure oblique black bar bordered with greenish yellow on upper eyelid. It is interrupted by the superciliary crest, only a small part showing inside this structure. One buffy olive tubercle in center of the eyelid is almost on the outer end of this bar. A more or less round black spot, greenish-yellow-edged, is just inside front end of long parotoid and just back of postorbital bar and end of superciliary crest, with tubercle in the center. Opposite the rear portion of parotoid are two oblique, posteriorly divaricating narrow bars with tubercles on forward end of each. Just beyond end of parotoids are the two largest round black spots with a large tubercle in each center. Halfway from parotoid to vent another such pair. Back of this pair are suggestions of two or three obscure pairs. The tubercles in the five pairs are buffy olive. Femur and tibia are more or less crossbarred with black. Fore limbs spotted with black and a prominent oblique black spot across front of arm insertion. Rear of femur spotted or vermiculated with black and olive-citrine, old gold, olive-ocher, or primuline yellow. Iris · dark in front of and behind pupil. Pupil rim citron yellow. Above pupil, mustard yellow and ochraceous-buff.

*Female.* July 24, 1929. Color of back, light brownish or buffy olive; parotoids isabella or dark olive-buff; the bigger warts on the back, which are in centers of dark spots, buffy brown; crests also buffy brown; stripe down middle of back, deep olive-buff, yellowish glaucous, or pale vinaceous-fawn, with more or less of the same color on oblique stripe that leads from parotoid to groin, and also along the sides above and below the dark lateral band. The dark lateral band is brownish olive, olive, or deep olive. The tympanum may be buff olive or light grayish olive. The paired spots down the middle of the back are (1) oblique bars on upper eyelids; (2) spots inside the front of parotoid; (3) another pair of about the same size at rear end of parotoid with a spot near the middle line between these two. Back of these and farther from the middle line are (4) two larger, usually two-tubercled, spots sometimes with two small, single-tubercled spots inside each of these and nearer the meson. The next pair (5) are about the middle of the back and close to the meson. These are the most prominent of the back and are from 1- to 4-tubercled. Then back some distance, close to the meson and slightly ahead of the vent, is another pair (6). These spots are black, fuscous black, or clove brown and are surrounded by reed yellow borders Below the eye and tympanum is a black spot with a snuff brown center. The side of the face is clay color or buffy pink. The iris is same as in the male. Under parts are cream buff on the throat, becoming primrose yellow on the belly and honey yellow or deep colonial buff on middle of lower belly and inner portion of buttocks. Among this is some orange-vinaceous or pale grayish vinaceous. In center of breast is a dark spot.

**Structure:** Parotoids large and oblong, connected to the postorbital crest by a longitudinal ridge. Crests on the head form a right angle at the corner of the eye, one branch extending downward in front of the ear; males with dark throats; males with excrescences on inner-upper side of first two fingers and on inner carpal tubercle; many spiny warts, particularly on the hind limbs.

**Voice:** "The note of the toad is long sustained, quite musical, rather high in pitch. Their low variable trills or pipings in chorus are rather pleasing and do not especially annoy, even though continued day and night during the height of their breeding season" (A. H. Wright, N.Y., 1914, p. 27).

"In general it sounds like whistling, and at the same time pronouncing deep in the throat, bu-rr-r-r-r. It will be found that different toads have slightly different voices, and the same one can vary the tone considerably, so that it is not so easy after all to distinguish the many batrachian solos and choruses on a spring or summer evening" (S. H. Gage, N.Y., 1904, p. 186).

"The common toad of the mainland of New York State is called *Bufo americanus*. Its song is a sweet, trilling whistle, and may be imitated by whistling in a low monotone with drops of water held between the lips. Each individual song is prolonged for about thirty seconds. The prolonged song of the American toad is a ready means of distinguishing it from the short song of the common toad (*fowleri*) of Long Island" (F. Overton, N.Y., 1914, p. 27).

**Breeding:** They breed from April 5 to July 25, the crest about April 30. The eggs are in long spiral tubes of jelly, each egg 1/25–1/16 inch (1.0–1.4 mm.) in diameter; the inner tube 1/15–1/12 inch (1.6–2.2 mm.), the outer tube 1/8–1/6 inch (3.4–4.0 mm.). The eggs, 4000–8000 in number, are laid in two strings, and hatch in 3–12 days. The small, dark, almost black tadpole 1 1/12 inches (27 mm.) has an ovoid body broader near the vent than at the eyes. The dorsal crest is low, extending slightly onto the body, the tail short, its tip rounded. The tooth ridges are ⅔. After 50–65 days, the tadpoles transform June 1 to August at ¼–½ inch (7–12 mm.).

**Journal notes:** June 8, 1911. Found at Crossroads Pond, Ithaca, N.Y., numerous *Bufo americanus* transformed and transforming, also several *Rana sylvatica* transformed (at least 12 or 15). At Beebe Lake on south side near the spring are myriads of transformed *Bufo americanus*.

June 9, Beebe, north side. On this side also are countless *Bufo americanus* transformed. John Rich reports them numerous yesterday on Wait Ave. just over Triphammer bridge. Beebe, south side, *Bufo* transformed still numerous.

June 12, Beebe, by the spring. Little toads are crossing the road above. They are not so numerous at water's edge.

April 23, 1912, Crossroads Pond. Found two pairs of *Bufo americanus* laying. Water cold, not much warmer than 40° F. Found hidden males at varying distances from the pond on the hillside below. Many of them were not entirely under cover. They were in little pockets at the surface of the ground, their backs exposed and the skin as dark and dirtlike as the dirt itself.

**Authorities' corner:**

C. C. Abbott, N.J., 1868, p. 805.
A. H. Kirkland, Mass., 1897, p. 24.
H. Garman, Ky., 1901, pp. 60–61.

## Hudson Bay Toad, Hudson Bay American Toad, Cope's Toad

*Bufo americanus copei* Yarrow and Henshaw. Plate XXVI; Maps 9, 10.

**Range:** Hudson Bay, James Bay. Gaige (Ont., 1932, p. 134), who brought it out of synonymy, wrote: "During a vacation trip to the James Bay region in August of this year Mr. Calvin Goodrich kindly collected a series of toads (10 specimens, ranging from 10 mm. to 69 mm. in length) for us at Moose Factory." Rivière des Rapides, Labrador (F. G. Speck, Lab., 1925, pp. 5–6); Quebec.

**Habitat:** "The colony . . . inhabits the abandoned clearing of a lumber operation of some years ago. Three or four decayed log stables and sheds and a surrounding mass of fine succulent meadow grass near the mouth of the river formed the environment. This small race is very active, and I have noticed that the living specimen spends much time buried about an inch deep in the sand . . ." (F. G. Speck, Lab., 1925, pp. 5–6).

**Size:** Adults 1⅗–3 inches (40–75 mm.).

**General appearance:** "The brilliant coloration, the long, narrow parotoid glands, the greater width between the cranial crests and the fact that they are nearly parallel, are the most obvious characters. The smoothness of the ventral granulation, mentioned by Henshaw and Yarrow, is evident, but it may be

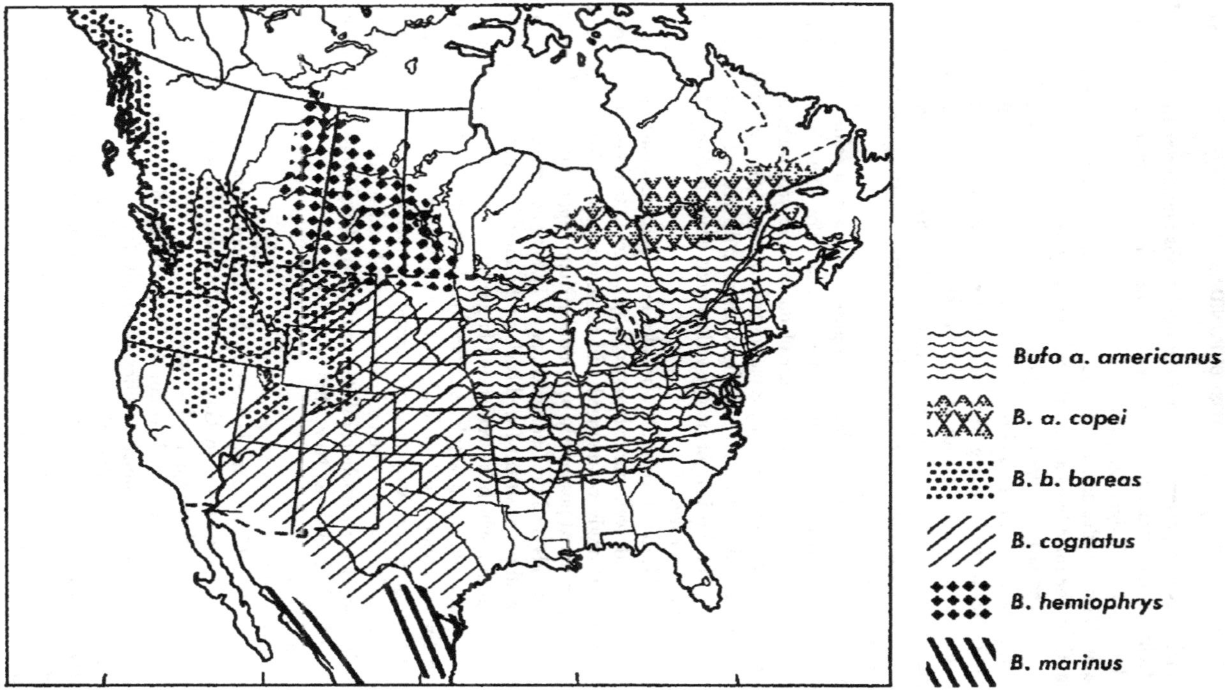
Bufo a. americanus
B. a. copei
B. b. boreas
B. cognatus
B. hemiophrys
B. marinus

Map 10

seasonal or due to preservation, and the hind limbs are shorter than is usual in Michigan specimens of *B. americanus,* the adpressed heel reaching the shoulder" (H. T. Gaige, Ont., 1932, p. 134).

**Color:** Thirty miles east of Moisie, Labrador, from H. W. Jackson, 1937. In captivity the male lived a year, the female two years.

*Female.* The larger, more brightly colored of the two. The groin and rear axilla are brazil red. There is also a wash of the same color on rear under parts. A few dorsal tubercles along mid-back are claret brown or chestnut brown. The snout and parotoid glands are hazel. The middorsal stripe, light lateral stripe, and other light dorsal spots are pale smoke gray. The under surface is cartridge buff with heavy black mottling. The iris has glass green pupil rim and flecks of the same color.

*Male.* The smaller toad is almost completely uniform in color. The snout, crests, parotoid glands, and warts are isabella color. The back is olive-ocher or ecru-olive. The spots on rear of dorsum are yellowish olive, a few near the head are black. The belly is pale olive-buff, heavily spotted with black. The groin, rear of femur, and to a slight extent axilla are apricot orange. In the eye, the pupil rim is light orange-yellow with heavy flecking of the same in upper part of the iris.

**Structure:** "Head subtriangular, broader than long; snout acuminate, protruding; head with well-marked groove, which extends to tip of snout; superciliary ridges strongly pronounced and terminating posteriorly in a slight knob; orbit bordered posteriorly by a similar ridge; upper jaw slightly emarginated; parotoids medium, elongated, twice as long as broad, perforated by numerous small pores, situated well back on the shoulders; not approximated to the tympanum, which is circular and large; limbs long and comparatively slender; palm rugose; a single well-developed tubercle; first, second, and fourth fingers about equal in length, the third longest; hind limbs rather longer than head and body together; tarsus and metatarsus with small and smooth tubercles; body above covered with small and somewhat roughened tubercles; under parts finely papillated; metatarsal shovel large" (H. C. Yarrow and H. W. Henshaw, Nev., 1878, p. 207).

**Voice:** Not of record.

**Breeding:** Not of record.

**Journal notes:** We have made notes on the Clausen, Trapido, and Vladykov material. Several explorers in Gaspé, Labrador, and Hudson Bay have remarked: "What is the bright toad we saw?"

**Authorities' corner:** "Toads common in the valley of the Ste. Anne des Monts River, Gaspé Peninsula, differ strikingly from *Bufo a. americanus.* Comparison at the Canadian National Museum with material of *B. americanus copei* from Moose Factory and from Cape Hope Islands in James Bay demonstrated that our toads were that subspecies. The coloration is much brighter than in *B. a. americanus,* with the black spots of the back fused on the sides to form broken bands and blotches. These markings are usually so arranged that there is a broad light middorsal band, and frequently a light lateral stripe on each side, from the parotoid to the insertion of the hind limb. Our specimens also resemble *B. a. copei* in the pink coloration in the axils of the limbs and in the pink tipped warts over the dorsal body surface, as Cope (1895: 286) noted for a specimen from Moose River, British America, which he assigned to *copei* of Yarrow and Henshaw, although he did not consider that form valid. The parotoids not only are long and narrow, as Gaige (1932) has pointed out, but tend to be constricted towards their middle, while the chest and belly are speckled or in some individuals strongly mottled with black.

"Sexual dimorphism is pronounced in a pair of living specimens which we have examined from Seal River, on the north shore of the St. Lawrence River. The female is brilliantly colored with black and pink dorsally, and with black marbling ventrally, while the male is a drab yellow brown, with the black and pink much less pronounced and the middorsal stripe lacking. The underside of the male is spotted with black, though not so extensively as in the female. The parotoids of both male and female are narrow and long, while the cranial crests are well spaced. Our collection from the Ste. Anne River differ from this pair in that the males are as brilliantly colored as the females" (H. Trapido and R T. Clausen, Que., 1938, p. 120).

"*Bufo americanus americanus* (Holbrook). Common throughout the area and very abundant locally; usually found on land, but a few taken from water. Most of the toads were brilliantly colored, with patches of pink below and many small pink tipped warts on the sides. The dorsal spots were deep black, with several large warts in each. These toads thus tend to resemble *B. americanus copei* Yarrow and Henshaw in coloration but lack the structural peculiarities of that subspecies. Logier (1928) has noted the more brilliant coloration of northern toads. The call was heard occasionally until July 17" (R. Grant, Que., 1941, p. 151).

## Northwestern Toad, Baird's Toad, Mountain Toad, Columbian Toad, Small-spaded Toad, Northern Toad, Western Toad

*Bufo boreas boreas* (Baird and Girard). Plate XXVII; Maps 10, 11.

**Range:** Prince William Sound, southeastern Alaska, southeastward to eastern Montana and northeastern Colorado and southwestern Utah, thence west to California (Mono County to northwestern California).

**Habitat:** Terrestrial except at breeding time. Ruthven and Gaige (1915) stated the situation very well and tersely in their table of habitat distribution in Maggie Basin in northeastern Nevada. *Bufo b. boreas* occur in "general vicinity of larger water courses. Breed in water but can endure rather dry habitats during other times of the year." It was common in "basin floor valleys

*Plate XXVI. Bufo americanus copei* (×½) 1,2,3. Females. 4 Male

*Plate XXVII Bufo boreas boreas.* 1,2. Males (×½). 3 Hind foot of male (×⅔). 4,5. Females (×⅓).

and mountain canyons nearly to highest elevations. . . . Lives in tules about lake shores, along streams, and in mountain meadows" (J. Grinnell and C. L. Camp, Calif., 1917, p. 143).

**Size:** Adults, 2¼–5 inches. Males, 56–108 mm. Females, 60–125 mm.

**General appearance:** This is a large brown, gray, or green toad with a light streak down the speckled back. The head is narrow and pointed in proportion to the fat broad body. There are rounded glands on the middle of the tibia. Lack of a discolored throat makes the males hard to distinguish from the females.

**Color:** Aug. 31, 1929. *Male.* The light middorsal stripe is pale cendre green, pale dull green-yellow, or pale veronese green, or even cartridge buff or sea-foam yellow. The ground color along the back is dark olive or clove brown, becoming about one-half inch from middorsal line pale brownish drab, light drab, or drab-gray. As it approaches the belly it becomes an ecru-drab or pale drab-gray. The belly color is tilleul buff to pale vinaceous-fawn, or pale smoke gray. The throat, clear of spots, may be vinaceous-buff, tilleul buff, olive-buff, or pale smoke gray. Along either side of the middorsal line is an irregular row of warts. The next series outside begin to be conspicuously surrounded by black or black interspersed with citrine-drab areas. On the lower side the conspicuous warts in the middle of the dark areas are lacking, and only the citrine-drab or water green spots are present. Across the belly these large black spots are very much in evidence as also on the inside of the hind legs out to the toes. The underside of the forelegs also have them, but they are localized on the rear and upper margins. On the rear of the belly and the underside of the buttocks the black spots are very fine, interspersed with cream color or light vinaceous-fawn. Here the tubercles are much larger and mainly cartridge buff or pinkish buff. The tubercles on the underside of the fore feet and tips of toes are light vinaceous-cinnamon. The parotoid is buffy olive or buffy brown, as is also the rim of the upper eyelid. The upper jaw and face ahead of the eye are uniform grayish olive. There is a dark oblique area from the lower rear of the eye past the angle of the mouth There is another dark area from the middle of the rear of the eye over the small tympanum and along the lower margin of the parotoid. There is a long longitudinal bar from the shoulder insertion along the front of the forearm. The eye is black or raw umber through the middle. The rim of the pupil is maize yellow. The lower pupil rim is of the same color or warm buff, but it is narrow and broken in its middle point. Above the upper pupil rim is the most conspicuous feature of the eye—a prominent zinc orange or mikado orange longitudinal band. The lower part of iris is dotted with ochraceous-buff or zinc orange.

**Structure:** No cranial crests; rounded gland in middle of tibia; body flat, broad; head narrow and pointed in proportion; no discolored throat in male; spread of hind foot usually more than 36 per cent of total body length. "Warts on back show a tendency to run in longitudinal rows. Tibia with one large and one small parotoidlike wart located respectively in the central and the rear cross bars" (C. L. Patch, B.C., 1922, p. 77).

**Voice:** Cope heard this form in a pond near the shore of Pyramid Lake, Nev. It was associated with a spadefoot (*Scaphiopus intermontanus*) of which Mr. Cope wrote: "Like other allied species, it was very noisy, almost obscuring the voice of the less vociferous *Bufo*" (E. D. Cope, Nev., 1884, p. 18).

Our captive male toads, when held in hand and frequently at other times, give little birdlike chirps, very pleasant in tone.

"At this time the males call with a high-pitched tremulous note, amplified by the vocal sacs distended beneath the chin" (G. C. Carl, B.C., 1943, p. 43).

"The adults were large and tame, they usually walked instead of hopped, and when confined in a bag they scolded much like *B. americanus*" (A. G. Ruthven and H. T. Gaige, Nev., 1915, p. 14).

**Breeding:** They breed from March to July. The eggs are in strings like those of *B. boreas halophilus* of California. Several workers have seen the eggs but none has described them in detail (except Slater in manuscript). Our evidence is not sufficient, but it appears that the eggs are as follows: Two envelopes; no partitions between the individual eggs; eggs largely in a double row within the jelly tube; outer envelope large; 4.8–5.3 mm., some loose and distinct; inner envelope 3.5–3.8, distinct; vitellus 1.5–1.75 mm.

The tadpoles are small, 1 1/12 inches (27–44 mm.) with teeth 2/3. There is no description of them on record. After a tadpole period of 30 to 45 days, they transform from July to September at 3/8–1/2 inch (9.5–12 mm.).

"On the nights of June 11 and 12, 1928, these toads were seen in numbers in a larger pond on the beach at Kaslo [B.C.] The males were calling and greatly outnumbered the females; nearly all the specimens collected or examined at the pond were males. One male was seen on the beach in embrace with a dead female which was much dried and shrivelled. . . .

"A female of 108 mm. taken at Kaslo on June 11, 1928, had apparently finished spawning; two other specimens of 81 and 101 mm. taken at Summerland in July, one on the 17th, were full of eggs. A specimen of 93 mm. taken at Lytton between the 1st and 8th of July, 1925, had evidently spawned.

"On the night of June 12, strings of eggs were found strewn among the grasses in the pond of water six or eight inches deep. The water temperature was 66° F." (E. B. S. Logier, B.C., 1932, p. 321).

"*Bufo boreas* in Alaska: In the winter of 1896, Mr. A. W. Greeley, a student at Leland Stanford Junior University, gave me for examination 2 toads which he had 'taken swimming in a large lake near Prince William's Sound, Alaska, July 15, 1896.' . . . One of these specimens contains eggs which must have been nearly ready for laying" (J. Van Denburgh, Alas., 1898, p. 139).

Several workers in Oregon, Utah, and Washington have found this form breeding. James Slater has sent us some fine tadpole material but we are awaiting his *Amphibia of Washington* before venturing on further allusion to them.

We have found on record no detailed description of the eggs or tadpoles.

**Journal notes:** March 30, 1942. Went with James Slater to Sparaway Lake, Wash. As we approached the lake we saw a *Bufo boreas boreas* male. Caught it.

April 7. East of Ashland and where road crosses creek (junction with Sampson Creek) saw *Bufo boreas boreas* run over.

April 8. Up creek above Trail, Ore. In one pool took a female and a male *Bufo boreas boreas.*

**Authorities' corner:**

E. D. Cope, Ore., 1883, p. 19.
M. M. Ellis and J. Henderson, Colo., 1915, p. 254.
C. E. Burt, Gen., 1933a, p. 351.
C. F. Schonberger, Ore., 1945, p. 121.

### California Toad, Salt-Marsh Frog, Baird's Toad, Common Toad

*Bufo boreas halophilus* (Baird and Girard). Plate XXVIII; Map 11.

**Range:** According to Camp, the seven northern counties of California have *Bufo b. boreas,* while south of Eureka toads are *Bufo b. halophilus.* This species extends the length of the Great Valley and along the coast to northern Lower California. Somewhat east of Los Angeles, avoiding the southeastern deserts, the range cuts diagonally north of Owen's Lake to Lake Tahoe or Pyramid Lake in Nevada.

**Habitat:** Open valleys, rarely wooded areas. In high mountains found in wet meadows and along lake shores.

**Size:** Adults, $2\frac{2}{5}$–$4\frac{5}{8}$ inches. Males, 62–101 mm. Females, 60–116 mm.

**General appearance:** This is a large stocky toad with short limbs, green or greenish brown with a light streak down the back, and the back mottled with irregular dark areas which surround the warts singly or in irregular groups. The warts are rounded and the skin between the warts quite smooth. The white or yellowish under parts are in some individuals blotched with black.

**Color:** April 22, 1928. *Male.* Stripe down the back is light lumière green, or chrysolite green, or glass green. Upper parts mignonette green, light yellowish olive, or yellowish olive, becoming on the sides of the head buffy olive. Yew green or jade green on sides of body with background pale glass green or glass green. Under parts white. Buttocks buffy olive or buffy brown. A few dark spots on under parts. Throat not different from breast. Iris chrysolite green above and below with black; black through the middle of the eye. Iris rim cream-buff.

*Another male.* Sides and upper parts dark olive-buff. Upper parts citrine becoming sulphine yellow, olive lake, or ecru-olive, then reed yellow or prim-

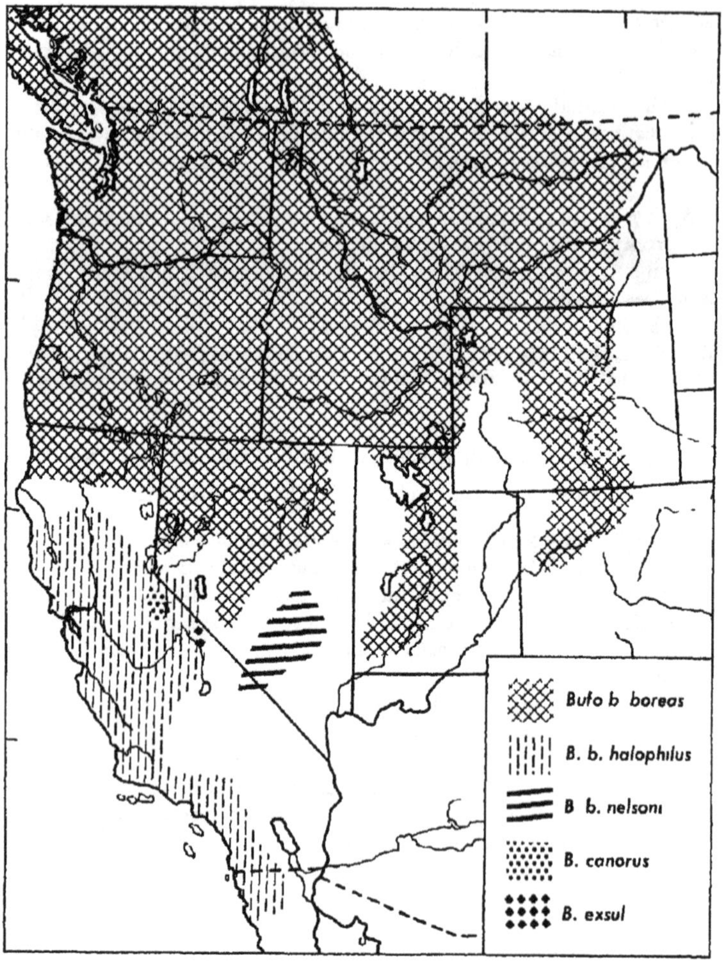


*Map 11*

rose yellow, then cartridge buff on lower side. Some warts with honey yellow on hind legs and sides; browning olive on warts along median line. Median line reed yellow from snout to vent. Under parts pale olive-buff. Throat with wash of cream-buff. Buttocks and lower belly isabella color and purplish. Black areas of upper parts with buckthorn brown centers. A few spots of ochraceous-orange along sides.

*Female.* Grayish olive above; upper parts of fore and hind legs light grayish olive; or olive-buff upper parts; or light mineral gray on all upper parts. Stripe down back chalcedony yellow or citron yellow. Upper parts with numerous black areas; these often with olive-buff centers. Along either side of median line are warts, some with dark olive-buff or picric yellow centers. Throat olive-buff, pectoral region and upper belly pale olive-buff. Under part of femur and lower belly olive-gray or deep olive-gray. Iris, sulphur yellow pupil rim, above which are black reticulations, then sulphur yellow becoming pale yellow-green, then beryl green rim on outside above, but seafoam yellow or ivory yellow behind and in front. Lower part of iris black with a little cream-buff or pinkish buff.

**Structure:** No cranial crests (except occasionally in very large individuals); parotoids elongate, widely separated; two long metatarsal tubercles, inner with a free blunt end; spread of hind foot usually less than 36 per cent of head and body length; glands on tibia present; no external vocal sac apparent in the males; interorbital space only slightly greater than internasal space; first and second fingers equal; not so heavily pigmented as *B. boreas boreas.*

**Voice:** Its song is a slow, deep-toned, prolonged trill.

"The males, while in the water, utter a series of low mellow tremulous notes. In chorus the notes may be compared to the voicings of a brood of young domestic goslings. The call of each male is uttered for a second or two and repeated at short intervals, so that a practically continuous chorus issues from a breeding colony. To human ears the notes lack carrying power and can scarcely be thought to be of use in attracting toads at any great distance from the pools where the males are calling. Occasionally males in their daytime retreats will utter the notes once or twice. This species does not have an enlarged vocal pouch such as is possessed by many species of toads (for example, *americanus, cognatus, woodhousii*), and this lack of a 'resonating pouch' is probably responsible for the small volume of sound uttered. Calling, with *halophilus,* is to be heard in the daytime as well as at night" (T. I. Storer, Calif., 1925, p. 177).

**Breeding:** This species breeds from January to July, according to the climate of location. The eggs are in long strings laid at the margins of ponds or at edges of flowing streams and are occasionally in two or three rows. There are no partitions between the eggs. The vitellus is 1/16 inch (1.7 mm.), the outer tube 1/5 inch (5.0 mm.), the inner tube 1/7 inch (3.6 mm.). The dull blackish medium tadpoles are 2 1/5 inches (55 mm.). The tooth ridges are 2/3. After 28 to 45 days, the tadpoles transform from April to August at 1/2–5/8 inch (12–15 mm.).

**Journal notes:** Feb. 12, 1942. Visited W. M. Ingram. He had a pair of *B. boreas halophilus* mated axillary fashion.

March 6. About 10 A.M. Anna and I went to Stanford artificial lake to look for *A. t. californiense.* Didn't find any. At last found at end of a pond a mated

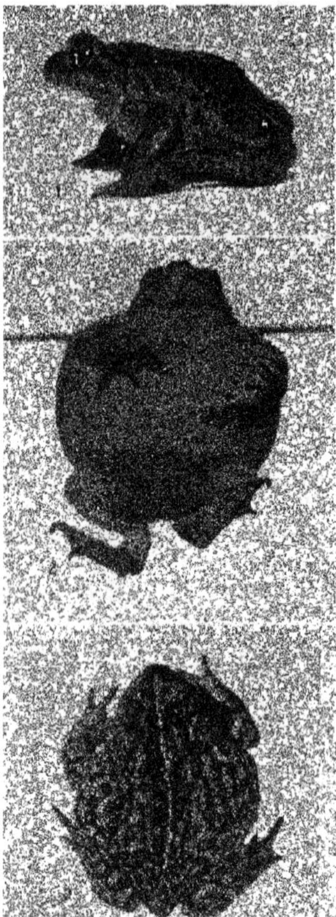

*Plate XXVIII. Bufo boreas halophilus* (×½). 1. Male. 2,3. Females.

*Plate XXIX. Bufo boreas nelsoni* (×½). 1,2,3,6. Males. 4,5. Females.

pair of *Bufo b. halophilus*. The male has a friendly chuckle, which it gives at times while mated. Presently I came to an area in the water near a fallen tree. Here, all about, at least 10 feet out from the bank in water 12 inches to 2 feet deep, were long strings of eggs. The pairs must be very restless. The strings are wound around many tussocks and are often in two bands for a long distance. The spider web is quite different from our usual *Bufo a. americanus* bands, which are in the very shallow muddy edges and very heavily massed. The egg file is a double row of eggs and somewhat like that of *Bufo fowleri* and *Bufo woodhousii*. Later near edge saw a pair "scrunch" down under the edge of a board and beside a tussock. Captured them and another single male.

April 11, around Chico, Calif. In the forenoon went out beyond golf links. Found toad eggs. Later in grass, beside a reservoir took a toad. In edge of a stream saw a toad "scrunched" down in grass. Caught it. In pools around reservoir no end of tadpoles. Some *Bufo* just hatched.

**Authorities' corner:**

H. C. Yarrow, Nev., 1878, p. 208.
J. Grinnell and T. I. Storer, Calif., 1924, pp 655–656.
J. R. Slevin, B.C., 1928, pp. 95–96.

### Amargosa Toad

*Bufo boreas nelsoni* Stejneger. Plate XXIX; Map 11.

**Range:** Southern and eastern Nye County and northern Lincoln County, Nev., to Resting Springs, Morans, and Lone Pine, Owen's Valley, Calif.

**Habitat:** "So far known from three separated localities, but most characteristic population is in the upper part of the Amargosa River. Apparently this toad is more closely restricted to water than even its near relatives which inhabit more humid districts" (J. M. Linsdale, Nev., 1940, p. 204).

**Size:** Adults 1⅝–3⅞ inches. Males 42–68 mm. Females 46–89 mm.

**General appearance:** "Similar to *B boreas* skin between warts smooth; snout protracted, pointed in profile; webs of hind legs very large, soles rather smooth; limbs shorter, elbows and knees not meeting when adpressed to the sides of the body; inner metacarpal tubercle usually very large" (L. Stejneger, Calif. and Nev., 1893, p. 220).

**Color:** Springdale, Nev., May 13, 1942. This is another *boreas* type toad. The general background of back is buffy olive, with the side of face and upper part of hind limbs the same. The stripe down mid-back is primrose yellow to pale olive-buff. The parotoids bear the most prominent color of the back, being tawny-olive to tawny. There are three paired rows of tubercles: one along either side of middorsum, one from parotoid backward, and the third an irregular intermediate one. All these tubercles have centers of cinnamon-brown or mikado brown. Back of the angle of mouth is a patch of ochraceous-tawny or ochraceous-orange, which color extends backward topping a row of very flat tubercles. Below these the black spots become large and prominent, each centered with a light-tipped tubercle. There is a prominent black area below the eye, another from tympanum downward, and sometimes one below the nostril, all three along the upper labial border. The upper eyelid bears some tawny-olive or tawny. The iris is black with a cream color or citron yellow pupil rim, the same colors flecking the whole eye. There is a prominent oblique bar of primrose yellow or marguerite yellow at the front edge of eye. The throat is primrose yellow to marguerite yellow almost clear of spots; the rest of under parts are pale olive with scattered black spots.

Males and females are alike in color, but after being in captivity and after breaking their axillary mating hold the males were very black and the female markedly lighter, this past night. When first brought in all five toads looked quite light. This afternoon they are much the same in color pattern

**Structure:** "The 51 specimens now on hand from Oasis Valley and the Amargosa River near Beatty . . . contrast with toads of the species *Bufo boreas* to the north and west in the following characters. Small size: the largest adult in the lot measures 72.5 mm. in head and body length. This is a little more than half the maximum size of *Bufo b. boreas*. The narrow, wedge-shaped head, especially when viewed from below, is one of the striking peculiarities of this toad. This seems to be correlated with the snout protracted and pointed in profile as mentioned by Stejneger. Limbs so reduced that when adpressed to sides of body elbows and knees do not meet, as was pointed out by Stejneger. Small feet and reduced webbing are especially noticeable and are just the reverse of Stejneger's statement, which may not have been as he intended. Reduced spots below in all the large individuals contrasts with *boreas* and with all small ones from the Amargosa Valley. Possibly the old ones tend to lose ventral spotting. Smooth skin and small weakly developed warts which characterize this lot may be an indication of close restriction of these toads to the water. Inner metacarpal tubercle appears to average large, as Stejneger indicated" (J. M Linsdale, Nev., 1940, p. 204).

**Voice:** Beatty, Nev. The male frequently gives a short cheerful chuckle. We don't know that we can tell this from the chuckle of *B. exul* Both are *boreas* types.

**Breeding:** J. M. Linsdale, D. M. Hatfield, and J. K. Doutt secured transforming toads in May from 15–18 mm. in length.

"Near Beatty, about May 20, 1931, many small young toads were picked up near the stream; large tadpoles were obtained here on May 4, 1936" (J. M. Linsdale, Nev., 1940, p. 204).

**Journal notes:** May 13, 1942. At Springdale, Nev., in the hamlet itself, saw a muddy pool with full-grown tadpoles; looked around but saw no toads. Came to Beatty about 4 P.M., walked 1½ miles north along Amargosa River. No toads. Went to Springdale. In her pool, Mrs. Howard said they had tadpoles. I looked at them. They were about one-third grown. She said the eggs were laid two weeks ago in the water-lily box. "They were in strings with a little egg, then space, then another egg." One man said these toads could be seen almost any night.

Last night after 8 we went from Beatty, Nev., to Springdale. With dogs barking and peacocks calling we thought our mission ruined. We went to our tadpole pool. Across the pool I saw a light toad or frog. Made for it and caught my first *Bufo b. nelsoni,* the Amargosa toad. Soon saw another resting in shallow water. Went to another pond near by and here soon espied two more—a large male and a small female. None are mated. These are shallow pools, mucky, and no more than 2 to 8 inches deep. Returned to the first pool and here another male was suspended in water in the weeds. These are not hard to capture. Where were they in the daytime when I was here? Last night about 5, at the suggestion of Mrs. Howard, we looked up Bobbie Shoshone, an alert Indian boy, and told him what we wanted.

May 14. Bobbie Shoshone went out last night and caught one *Bufo b. nelsoni* and several *Hyla regilla.* This morning he went out again and secured three more toads.

**Authorities' corner:**

L. Stejneger, Calif. and Nev., 1893, pp. 220–221.
J. M. Linsdale, Nev., 1940, p. 204.

## Southern California Toad, Arroyo Toad

*Bufo californicus* (Camp). Plate XXX, Map 8.

**Range:** Coastal region of southern California—San Luis Obispo Co. (Miller and Miller, 1936) through Ventura Co. (Camp, 1915) and San Diego Co. (Klauber, 1928)—to lower California on Rio Santo Domingo (Klauber, 1933; Tevis, 1944).

**Habitat:** Arroyo stream beds; inland valleys and foothills.

"In San Diego County the range seems largely restricted to the sandy washes of the rivers in the Upper Sonoran Zone" (L. M. Klauber, Calif., 1931, p. 141).

"The river bottom has marginal growths of oaks and cottonwoods on sandy beaches with willow and *Baccharis* thickets bordering the stream. The small flow of clear water gave promise of continuing well through the summer. The stream subdivided frequently and at places formed comparatively quiet pools in the gravel as much as 18 inches deep. It was within a few feet of one of these that a trilling animal was watched in the beam of a flashlight as it sat half submerged in a puddle not more than 2 feet across. The fore part of the throat was moderately distended, not to compare with the *Hyla regilla* which were calling on all sides" (L. and A. H. Miller, Calif., 1936, p. 176).

**Size:** Adults, 1⅝–2¾ inches. Males, 44–58 mm Females, 44–68 mm.

**General appearance:** This is like a small Great Plains toad (*Bufo cognatus*) but is more uniform in color on the back. This little toad is very short and thick in body, very short in head, and the arms and legs appear very stolid. The foot is a little longer than in *B. cognatus*. The eyelids and parotoids are tuberculate. Several of the larger warts have spiny tips, in some cases several tips to one wart. In a toad that has recently shed its skin, there is a row of conspicuous light tubercles on the side, bordered above and below by irregular black lines. In the young the light and dark areas of the head and back are strongly contrasted. Since 1930 we have seen most of the *Bufo californicus* specimens in collections. Those who know it best wonder if it should be compared to *Bufo compactilis* rather than *Bufo cognatus*. Somehow we cannot now bring ourselves to place *woodhousii, w. fowleri,* or *californicus* in the *lower throat*-lappet group of *Bufo compactilis* and *Bufo cognatus*.

"A toad with divergent head crests, a nasal boss, short slightly divergent parotoids and with an internal, cutting tubercle on hind foot; femur short as in *Bufo cognatus cognatus,* the Great Plains toad. Size medium; parotoids wide; coloration nearly uniform, without large spots; no vertebral streak; external tubercle on hind foot small and rounded, not provided with a cutting edge" (C. L. Camp, Calif., 1915, p. 331).

**Color:** *Females.* Warner's Hot Springs, San Luis Rey River, Calif., from L M. Klauber, described June 12, 1929. Upper parts olive-brown or dark olive. On top of snout are two parallel black bars to level of front of eye where they connect with transverse bar. From middle of upper eyelid an oblique backward bar of black extends inward but does not meet its fellow. Just inside the front end of parotoid is faint black spot centered with a wood brown or avellaneous wart. Opposite back end of parotoid two narrow black spots meet at an angle pointed forward. Just back of each of these and farther from meson is a larger round spot. About midway from eye to vent is a pair of spots near the meson. Thereafter to vent spots are very small, possibly three or four either side of meson. Ahead of oblique black bar of eyelid is a prominent light band across top of head, olive-buff in young or wood brown to avellaneous in adult. Same color on front third of parotoid, between angle spots and back of next pair of spots to each side of meson midway from vent to eye. On each side an oblique line of olive-buff warts extends to the groin with black line below it and sometimes an avellaneous band above with a black line above that. Sides olive-buff or pale olive-buff. Under parts white. Throat pale olive-buff or tilleul buff. Underside of feet and forefeet vinaceous buff. Underside of hind legs and rear belly light vinaceous fawn or light grayish vinaceous. Two or three olive-buff warts back of angle of mouth. Two black crossbars on forearm, none on brachium. One-half crossband on front of femur and two on rear half of tibia. Each bar has centers or warts of avellaneous or wood brown. Space between tibial crossbars olive-buff or pale olive-buff. Dark spot below eye; oblique olive-buff area in front of eye in young, wood brown in adults. Iris black. Pupil above and below, but not back or front, with prominent rim of light or pale chalcedony yellow and with spots of this color or apricot buff on iris.

*Male.* Glen Lonely, San Diego Co., Calif., from L. M. Klauber and L. Cook, March 28, 1930. The two males in hand have the light band between eyes, deep olive-buff or yellowish citrine. The front third of parotoids is not conspicuously different from the rest of parotoid as in female described. It may have touch of vinaceous buff. The upper parts of these males are dull citrine, grayish olive, or dark grayish olive. The prominent warts are tipped with one to several spines. Sometimes, but not always, these are dark or brownish tipped. The dorsal spots of these males are not so prominent as in females described. The short wood brown or avellaneous band down mid-back is inconspicuous in these males. The lateral oblique line of olive-buff warts is not conspicuous in these males nor in the female in hand. (Another female with freshly shed skin is much brighter in color and this line of light warts appears.) The throat is slightly different from the rest of under parts. The middle and lower throat is vinaceous-buff. On upper jaw below the rear of eye, in both males and females, is a light vertical band of wood brown, avellaneous, or vinaceous-buff. Iris of each male is more spotted and not so black as in the female in hand.

**Structure:** Parotoids wider and longer (width in length 1.75–2.0) than in *B. cognatus* (width in length 1.5–1.8), parotoid interval wide, twice the gland width. Occasionally a postorbital bar present and the posterior end of the cranial valley slightly suggesting embossment. One cutting metatarsal tubercle and one small one; femur short; foot about one-half webbed; hind limbs long; half or more of femur free from body skin.

Description of type: "Size medium; hind legs very short, femur almost entirely enclosed in skin of abdomen; head short and thick; nasal region elevated into a bony protuberance; longitudinal cranial crests more or less united across median region, and slightly divergent; transverse crests divided by width of median groove; parotoids oval, slightly divergent and very broad; inner tubercle of hind foot with a sharp edge; outer tubercle very small, rounded and without cutting edge; eyelids and back evenly tuberculated; tympanum oval, shorter than diameter of eye; a dozen or more large whitish tubercles below and just posterior to the tympanum" (C. L. Camp, Calif., 1915, p. 332).

**Voice:** "Three animals were trilling, spaced about equally along a quarter-mile of stream bed. . . . There is considerable resemblance to the louder, more raucous call of *cognatus,* even granting the difference which Myers emphasizes" (L. and A. H. Miller, Calif., 1936, p. 176).

"The call of *cognatus* is a trilled rattle, with much of the timbre of *Acris* in it. The call of *californicus* is a sweet trill reminding one of *B. americanus* but somewhat lower and less prolonged" (G. S. Myers, Calif., 1930, pp. 74–75).

"The call is a beautiful, penetrating trill with a peculiar ventriloquistic quality which makes it difficult to determine the direction from which it emanates" (L. M. Klauber, Calif., 1934, p. 6).

**Breeding:** May and June.

We need more descriptions of the egg masses, individual eggs, tadpoles, and transformation.

**Journal notes:** March 25, 1930. Our experiences with these toads in life have been entirely with material sent us by L. M. Klauber. At present we have four, two males and two females in our toad garden. During the day they keep themselves buried in the moist soil with just their heads out. They are not always sleeping, however, as they promptly stir if an ant is thrown near them. Toward evening they are more active and hop around. One toad seems to have adopted an evening perch in a pot of herb robert. During the evenings the males sometimes give brief calls, just enough to suggest their little trill.

April 24, 1942, Atascadero, Calif. Went to Salinas River northeast of Santa Margerita for toads, hoping for *Bufo californicus*. No luck!

April 25. Big Pines Area: a public camp just beyond (E.) of Jackson Lake. Came to shallow pool beside the road, shadowed with willows. The outlet was through grassy field and row of willows and shortly fell rapidly into a deep cut While Bert explored the willow tangle outlet, I walked slowly around edge of pond. There were tussocks of grass. I soon came to a shallow corner and there tangled on surfaces of grasses were two toad egg strings. These seemed small and narrow for *Bufo b. halophilus*. Eggs close set and tending to be in a double row, type like *Bufo woodhousii* or *Bufo fowleri*. Are these *Bufo californicus* or *Bufo b. halophilus*? Not the same as *Bufo b. halophilus* we saw at Palo Alto. If they are *Bufo californicus* eggs they are totally unlike *Bufo compactilis* or *Bufo cognatus* eggs.

May 5. Have we arrived at Klauber's "3½ or 4 miles south of Buckman Springs" where he caught *Bufo californicus*, i.e., at the bridge below the confluence of La Posta and Cottonwood Creek? Here is a wide expanse of sand, willow along creek, oaks farther back. We took here three *T. o. hammondii*, two *H. regilla*, and one *R. a. draytonii*. This would be an ideal place to get the toad if it were out. Saw no *Bufo*, *Rana*, or *Hyla regilla* tadpoles.

May 6. Collected at Green Valley Falls Public Camp on Sweetwater River (creek). Just above water crossing, found two fresh complements of *Bufo*. Each is a small complement of a small toad. They are more or less in double arrangement in tube like *Bufo woodhousii*, *Bufo w. fowleri*, *Bufo b. boreas*, and *Bufo b. halophilus*. Two other complements are hatched.

Robert Livezey of Stockton, Calif., has examined these eggs. He concludes that they are different from *Bufo boreas halophilus* and from the *Bufo boreas boreas* he knew at Corvallis, Ore. We both suspect they are *Bufo californicus*, the form we so often sought in vain. Our summary follows: "Files or strings with a continuous gelatinous encasing. One envelope present. Envelope more than 5 mm. in diameter; 5.62–6.12 mm., average 5.77 mm.; distinct and relatively firm. Vitellus 1.25–1.62 mm., average 1.42 mm.; black above and gray below. Average of 42 eggs per inch; several thousand per female. Deposited in tangled strings on bottom of pool among leaves, sticks, gravel, mud, etc. Range, coastal area of southern California from upper Salinas Valley to Lower California on Rio San Domingo. Season May and June. *Bufo californicus.*" We hold that *Bufo cognatus, B. b. boreas,* and *Bufo b. halophilus* have two envelopes in a file. Our identification of these eggs as *B. californicus* is presumptive and circumstantial.

**Authorities' corner:**

C. L. Camp, Calif., 1915, p. 332.
G. S. Myers, Calif., 1930, pp. 75–76.
L. Tevis, Jr., L.C., 1944, p. 6.

### Yosemite Toad, Yosemite Park Toad

*Bufo canorus* Camp. Plate XXXI; Map 11.

**Range:** Yosemite National Park, high central Sierra Nevada, 7,000–11,000 feet altitude. West branch of McGee Creek trail, Mono Co., Calif., at 10,500 feet, Sept. 18, 1939 (O. R. Smith and K Stanton). Two stations in Tuolomne County, 35 miles northwest from Tioga Lake locality (I. L. Wiggins, Calif., 1943, p. 197). Occupies the Canadian and Hudsonian life zones, extending even into Alpine-Arctic (J. Grinnell and C. L. Camp, Calif., 1917, pp. 143–144). (See Map 1, p. 6.)

**Habitat:** Wet mountain meadows, margins of streams and lakes.

**Size:** Adults, 1¾–3 inches. Males, 46–64 mm. Females, 45–75 mm.

**General appearance:** This small toad has a moist skin and the skin is smooth between the few large, low-rounded warts. The large broad parotoids marked with russet pattern or crossed by the pattern of the back and the glands on legs are the conspicuous marks. This species is dimorphic, the female with conspicuous touches of black, yellow, and russet, the male somber olive.

**Color:** *Male.* Described Oct. 12, 1929. The male lacks the striking pattern of the female, being an almost uniform yellowish olive to olivaceous black with a broken thread of yellow down midback. The black-dotted borders of the darker markings and dark areas around warts are evident to greater or less degree as the toad is lighter or darker in color. These may be outlined by broken threads of yellow—a delicate tracery. Along the sides where belly merges into side may be a yellowish band.

*Female.* Yosemite Park, Calif., from C. A. Harwell and Dr. H. C. Bryant. Beginning with upper eyelid there extends along the back either side of the narrow vertebral line a longitudinal band of black. In this there are from time to time warts, dark olive-buff or isabella color. On rest of back are large spots of black with these colored warts in them. On sides, large black spots, but with few or no warts in them. Middorsal stripe may be pale lemon yellow to sulphur yellow or primrose yellow. Background color is lime green, citron green, light chalcedony yellow, sulphine yellow, or olive-lake. Back of angle of mouth

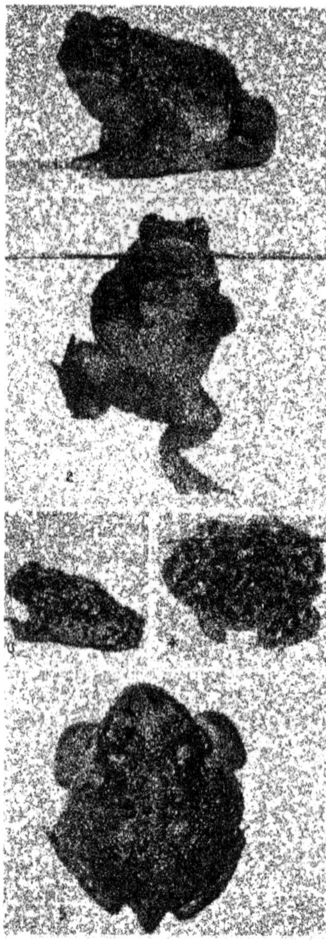

*Plate XXX. Bufo californicus* ($\times \frac{2}{3}$). 1,2. Males. 3,4. Young. 5. Female.

*Plate XXXI. Bufo canorus* ($\times \frac{2}{3}$). 1,2,5. Males. 3,4. Females.

is a xanthine orange wart. Along on sides and base of arm insertion are some mars yellow or xanthine orange spots on ground color. Fore limb heavily spotted with black. Hind limb to tarsus same, also on rear of femur. Edge of upper eyelid and rear part of parotoid xanthine orange or less bright. From upper eyelid across parotoid is a longitudinal band of pale drab gray. The yellows of the background color encircle the black spots and in alcohol or formaldehyde make them appear white encircled. Under parts white or pale smoke gray or pale olive gray. Few spots on side of lower belly, and a very few on rear of buttocks or on ventral side. All in all this specimen is pure color below. Iris with background color plus xanthine orange or mars yellow; this reticulated with black.

*Half-grown specimen.* Oct. 12, 1929. Unlike large female, under parts are ivory yellow or white with spotting from angle of mouth across pectoral region to angle of mouth; also on sides of belly and somewhat on belly proper. Buttocks and lower belly light mouse gray. Back darker; no middorsal stripe or slight. Spots more numerous. Background color drab or light drab except where surrounding black spots, then cartridge buff or sulphur yellow. There is hardly any impression of yellow in upper part as in full-grown female. Parotoid with prominent antique brown or "rusty-like" spot. Same wart back of angle of mouth. Little touch of same color around vent. Sides of head and face spotted, as is back. Iris black with some sulphur yellow, pale brownish vinaceous, or some "rusty," but more black than full-grown adult female.

*Male.* Peregoy Meadows, Yosemite National Park, Calif., from Carl E. Van Deman and G. B. Upton, June, 1930. These males vary greatly in color when kept in tub of dirt and when exposed to sunlight. The back may be olivaceous black or dark olive, becoming deep olive on the sides. The wart at corner of mouth may bear a dash of ochraceous-orange or orange-rufous and the parotoids a wash of Sanford's brown. There is a reed yellow thread down the back, broken and irregular. Lower surfaces are white to seafoam yellow with many black dashes around edge of jaw, in pectoral region, and on belly. The iris bordering pupil is buff-yellow, then a ring crossed with network of black lines gives medal bronze appearance. Along the upper edge is a band of kildare or glass green specks.

Held in hand for this description, the color has grown lighter, the back is yellowish olive, the sides light yellowish olive. The bars on legs appear as dark greenish olive bands with black dots around them forming irregular borders. Some dark greenish olive areas appear on back surrounding some of the warts. Some of the warts have wash of Sanford's brown or amber brown. There is a dash of reed yellow in front of eye. After photographing, the back had become yellowish oil green.

**Structure:** Short, broad, raised parotoids close together; muzzle rounded; cranial crests lacking or slight in some males; legs short; gland on hind leg; interorbital space narrow; internasal space wide; warts few, low, flattened, and rounded; foot with two metatarsal tubercles; skin moist like that of a *Rana*.

This toad has a distinct rounded ridge from the nostril over the outer edge of the eyelid. This gives the canthal region a distinct border above and with the steep snout gives the toad a square-snouted appearance The head is not so short, however, as in *Bufo cognatus*. The nostrils are widely separated. In general shape, the toad reminds us of *Bufo boreas halophilus*. Its color is intermediate between the color of that form and the heavy inky blotches and contrasting light areas of *Bufo cognatus*.

"In profile, lack of head crests, small tympanum, and short legs this toad resembles *Bufo boreas* and its subspecies, but may be distinguished at once from these forms by its smaller size, enormous width of parotoids, slight interval between parotoids, very smooth skin, absence of a broad vertebral stripe, and markedly different color pattern in both sexes. In extent of webbing of hind foot the present species most nearly resembles *B. boreas halophilus*, its near neighbor in the southern Sierra Nevada and the San Joaquin Valley. Specimens of *B. boreas boreas* from Mono County, directly to the east of the range of *canorus*, have the large hind foot characteristic of the more northern subspecies" (C. L. Camp, Calif., 1916a, p. 60).

**Voice:** The song is a sustained, rapid, melodious trill.

"The specific name selected, *canorus*, refers to the long-sustained, melodious trill uttered by this toad. This diurnal singing accompanies the breeding activities, which take place as soon as the snow melts from the Sierran meadows, June 1 to July 15. Many of the females captured at this time contained mature eggs" (same, p. 62).

"The mating song of the Yosemite toad is a sustained series of ten to twenty or more rapidly uttered notes, constituting a 'trill,' and the whole song is repeated at frequent intervals. The notes, though mellow in character, carry well considering the size of the animals, and have a ventriloquial quality which makes it difficult to locate any one animal by sound alone. When a number of males are giving their songs in the same place the songs overlap one another so that the general chorus is continuous. There is some difference in the pitch at which the several members of a group sing, varying perhaps with the size of the individual toad. . . . The notes recall the courting song of the Texas nighthawk" (J. Grinnell and T. I. Storer, 1924, p. 659).

"The toad chorus at different levels may begin at least as early as May 20 and last until July 9; and according to our experience, singing is carried on quite through the daylight hours and into the early evening at least" (J. Grinnell and T. I. Storer, Calif., 1924, p. 660).

**Breeding:** These toads breed during late spring and summer, May 20 to July 16. G. S. Myers at Peregoy Meadows June 20, 1928, secured transformed toads 10½ mm long and tadpoles 27 mm. long with teeth ⅔. [T. I. Storer, Calif., 1925, p. 42, figures teeth ⅔.]

**Journal notes:** "June 5, 1930, Peregoy Meadows. Saw at least two dozen old and young. Majority were young. They were not so abundant as the croaking tree frogs, *Hyla regilla.* Hadn't distinguished sexual dimorphism until I found a mated pair in a very wet grassy meadow, water three or four inches deep when one steps in it. These meadows are surrounded by snow fields. Found no toad eggs. Toads must have just come out" (C. E. Van Deman).

July 24, 1934. Between Tuolomne and Dana Meadows. An intermittent stream went through the meadow leaving many isolated pools. No standing pools over the whole surface, though the water comes almost to the surface in some of the "rat" holes. Our first sight of *Bufo canorus* was of something scuttling along the runway of a "rat" hole at the base of a shrub. We found two small toads here. Near the pools we found many transformed ones, and several adults were in holes or under overhanging turf at the edge of the pool. We found one adult under a stump. Under a shrub were two in water and one on land. Many tadpoles and transforming toads were in one of the rather shallow pools; many transforming ones just under the edge of tussocks in the water.

At Dana Meadows. Occasionally in a pool with sedges or vegetation or in a more marshy pond, *Bufo canorus* adults started to swim out into the water. In a few pools may have seen as many as 20 to 25 *Bufo canorus* tadpoles. The predominant tadpoles are of *Hyla regilla.*

**Authorities' corner:**

C. L. Camp, Calif., 1916a, p. 61.
J. Grinnell and T. I. Storer, Calif., 1924, pp. 658–659.

## Great Plains Toad, Say's Toad, Western Toad, Plains Toad, Texas Toad, Western Plains Toad

*Bufo cognatus* (Say). Plate XXXII; Map 10.

**Range:** Imperial Valley, Calif., up Colorado River to southeast Nevada, through Salt Lake, Wyoming, Montana to Alberta, thence to extreme western Minnesota and Iowa, northwest Missouri, western two-thirds of Kansas and Oklahoma southward to Texas coast; also in Mexico.

**Habitat:** Grazing lands or agricultural lands of the Great Plains, along irrigating ditches, flood plains of streams, and overflow bottom lands.

**Size:** Adults, 1⅞–4 inches. Males, 47–95 mm. Females, 60–99 mm.

**General appearance:** This is a large broad-bodied toad with a general color of brown, gray, or greenish. There is a light middorsal stripe, and the back is marked with dark spots. These spots may be broken up and the light areas or borders become more conspicuous so that the toad appears obliquely streaked with light bars on the sides. The spotted condition seems the more common. Often there are four pairs of bright green spots down the back, the pair at the rump leading diagonally to the groin. There are green spots on the legs, and an oblique row of green spots extending backward from the sharply raised parotoid. There is a green band along the side. These green spots are partially outlined with black on the green and cream on the outer edges. The under parts are light, including the throat. In these males the light throat extends back as a flap over the thin, dark-colored skin of the lower throat, which extends forward when inflated. In another toad the green spots are more broken up, and the green band on the side becomes broken into spots. The hands and feet are light with dark tips.

**Color:** *Male*. Bard, Imperial Co., Calif., from L. M. Klauber, May 15, 1930. Back drab, buffy olive, buffy brown, light drab, or avellaneous. Parotoid same color as back. Fore and hind legs same as back, or lighter, such as ecru-drab. On sides interstices of green spots are pallid brownish drab, pallid vinaceous-drab, or pale drab-gray. Same color on light areas on side of face. Dark dorsal spots citrine-drab, deep grape green, or grayish olive outlined by chrysolite green edges or deep seafoam green. On sides, warts of green spots have rainette green or deep chrysolite green tips and interstices. On dorsum, warts are wood brown or avellaneous. Front and rim of upper eyelid vinaceous-fawn. Round spot on upper eyelid. Elongate pair inside rear end of parotoid and near meson. Another oblique pair in middle of back. Another small pair far back and near meson, and another pair far separated just ahead of horizontal of vent and just at edge of femur. From rear of parotoid a long spot. From eye over tympanum along lower edge of parotoid a spot. This broken but soon resumed as long band from shoulder insertion to groin. Between this and mesal spots are irregular small spots; so also below this spot. Fore limbs and hind limbs with prominent spots, also groin. Dark spot from eye to over angle of mouth. Spot below eye. Faint line from eye to nostril to labial edge; spot oblique below nostril. Under parts white. Belly and underside of femur cream color, warm buff, or colonial buff, becoming pale cinnamon-pink on tibia. Throat same color as venter except lower throat under lappet, which is vivid brown, vinaceous-drab, or black. Iris rim pale cinnamon-pink or shell pink; otherwise black with much spotting of light congo pink.

*Another male*. Back drab gray or light cinnamon-drab. All the spots described in other specimen absent or very small. Face uniform. Toes, fingers, and membranes somewhat onionskin pink or vinaceous-cinnamon. Otherwise like other specimen.

*Female*. Back buffy brown. Spotting much as in male. Throat same color as venter. No throat apron.

**Structure:** Head broad; snout short; sides and front of snout steep; boss conspicuous, ridges divaricating at rear; parotoid glands small, elevated, widely separated, oval in shape extending obliquely downward; two metatarsal tubercles with free cutting dark edge; hind leg approximates body length; hind foot long in proportion to hind limb; interorbital space narrow; internasal space greater than interorbital; snout only equal to or less than eye; toes webbed, webs deeply indented; nostrils set far apart; femur short; horny excrescences on back of first finger of male, and to less extent or lacking on the second finger.

**Voice:** The vocal sac of the male is a large "sausage" extending out and upward. Deflated, the thin discolored skin is closely folded under an apronlike extension of light colored pebbly skin of the throat. It is at the rear of the throat, and the "apron" may hang down over the forebreast as much as 15 mm. The call is made up of harsh, low-pitched notes.

"This form is one of the rarer amphibians of the region. With *Bufo alvarius* it was found almost always in the vicinity of watering troughs. Several were caught during the night of July 7 singing on the bank of a pond where the large series of *Scaphiopus* were taken. . . . The song or trill is exceedingly loud and very harsh and tinny, reminding one very much of a Klaxon auto horn. The interval between songs is rather long, nearly a minute, and as in *Bufo americanus* and *Bufo fowleri* the trill is sustained for a considerable length of time. When singing, the pouch is very pointed and arises under the throat and projects forward and upward when fully distended to a point about level with the anterior part of the lower jaw (A. I. and R. D. Ortenburger, Ariz., 1926, p. 103).

Green River, Emery Co., Utah. "Songs of this species and *B. woodhousii* with which it was associated, could be heard in many parts of this little valley at night" (V. M. Tanner, Utah, 1928, p. 24).

**Breeding:** These toads breed from April to September, dependent upon rainfall; in the northern states of their range, from May to July. Little is known about the eggs and tadpoles. Amplexation pectoral; egg strings single, sometimes double, no inner tubes or partitions seemingly of *Bufo compactilis* type; mature tadpole mottled gray and brown dorsally; light greenish yellow and reddish ventrally; tail fin highly arched, obtuse apex; tooth rows ⅔; transformation size, 21–28 mm.; tadpole period 1½–2½ months (largely after A. N. Bragg).

Bragg's studies (1936, 1937, 1939a) of *Bufo cognatus* were much needed. They mark one of the most significant contributions to anuran life histories, in which the Oklahoma group have recently been leading. Bragg gives the individual egg diameter as 1.18 mm., the egg inner envelope 0.22 mm. beyond the egg, and an outer tube of jelly 2.05 mm. in diameter or 2.66 mm. when eggs are in a double row. He gives an egg complement of 20,000, the eggs with black animal pole and white vegetative pole. The scalloped outer tube places this egg file in the *Bufo compactilis* class.

"At hand are two series of tadpoles of this species; one series was collected July 2, 1938, 1.5 miles east of Meade County State Park, Kansas, and the other lacks data. The second lot contains numerous sizes of tadpoles from 14 mm. to 31 mm., and several transforming specimens which clearly possess the pattern so typical of this species.

"Mouthparts in both series (consisting all told of about 200 specimens) are fairly constant except in the transforming and extremely young specimens. . . . The outer row of teeth of the lower labium is sometimes a little shorter or longer than the figure shows, but the average is about as indicated. The extent of the medial edge of the papillae on the lower labium varies somewhat; in some, the papillae barely reach the level of the ends of the outer row of teeth, while in others they overlap the ends slightly.

"Measurements agree with those given by Bragg, except that appearance of the hind legs occurs at about 15 mm.; the fore legs appear at about 28 mm. A pattern recognizably similar to that of the adult is evident at about 20 mm.

"These tadpoles show such a striking similarity to those referred by Wright to *Bufo compactilis* Wiegmann . . . that their conspecificity is suggested" (H. M. Smith, Kans., 1946, pp. 95–96).

**Journal notes:** July 8, 1917. We found a large stream rushing through Sierra Blanca, Tex. They had not had rain for six months. The flat land was overflowed, and a swift current went under the small bridge. At seven o'clock, while it was still day, we heard no notes in the creek, but later when we were camped one-half mile away, we heard the chorus plainly and decided it must be spadefoots. . . . We found three species of toads and two of spadefoots migrating from the mountain sides of Sierra Blanca downward toward the pool and noise. The boys, at night, captured *B. woodhousii, B cognatus,* and *B. compactilis* on the hillside and in the stream.

May 20, 1942, Beaver Dam Lodge, Ariz. Big pool north end of bridge. From the pool came two very piercing shrill calls. It was *B. cognatus.* We collected the one we heard call and another in the pool. In the closed bag its note is a harsh nasal clack; that of the *woodhousii* is a friendly chuckle.

July 21, El Paso. On road from North Junction toward Smeltertown took one or two *B cognatus* adults and some three or four young.

**Authorities' corner:**

F. A. Hartman, Kans., 1907, p. 228.
J. K. Strecker, Jr., Tex., 1910, pp. 19–21.
H J. Pack, Utah, 1922, p 8.
F W. King, Ariz., 1932, pp. 175–176
A. N. Bragg, Okla., 1937a, p. 283
G. A. Moore and C. C. Rigney, Okla., 1942, p. 78.

## Spade-footed Toad, Spadefoot Toad, Sonoran Toad, Western Toad

*Bufo compactilis* Wiegmann. Plate XXXIII; Map 8.

**Range:** Southern portions of Utah and Nevada, south far into Mexico, and east to southwest Oklahoma and the eastern timber belt of Texas.

**Habitat:** We found this toad breeding in rain pools in open fields near streams, in pools in creek valleys, in irrigation tanks or cattle tanks. It is a desert form that may at times be seen feeding at night under the street lights of desert towns.

**Size:** Adults, 2$\frac{1}{12}$–3$\frac{5}{8}$ inches. Males, 52–78 mm. Females, 54–91 mm.

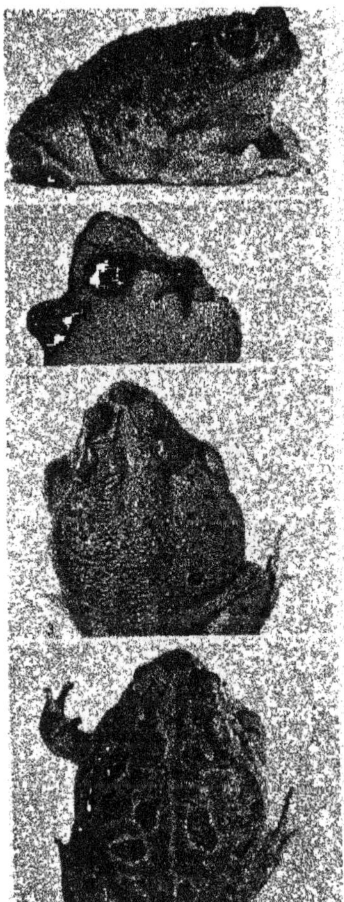

*Plate XXXII. Bufo cognatus* ($\times\frac{5}{8}$). 1,4 Females. 2,3. Males.

*Plate XXXIII Bufo compactilis.* 1,2,5. Males ($\times\frac{2}{8}$). 3. Male croaking ($\times\frac{1}{2}$). 4. Egg files ($\times\frac{1}{2}$).

**General appearance:** This broad, squatty toad of medium size is pinkish drab in color, marked with dull citrine spots. The fingers and toes are light in color. The under parts are light. The back is covered with light-tipped tubercles.

**Color:** Beeville, Tex., March 27, 1925. *Male.* In general color a light drab or cinnamon-drab. Tips of the tubercles (under lens) are xanthine orange but to naked eye flesh pink, this giving some pinkish tone to the upper parts. Spots on back, sides, legs, look dull citrine. Under lens the spots are Prout's brown or some other brown with bases of the tubercles mignonette green and tips of tubercles xanthine orange. Fingers, toes, and tubercles of fore and hind feet pinkish cinnamon. Tip of chin is white, then folded part of throat is pinkish buff with ecru-olive in center. This area is followed by a circular pectoral area of purplish lilac. Pupil of eye distinctly horizontal, with horizontal black bar through the eye at either end of the pupil. Rim cartridge buff or marguerite yellow Iris spotted vinaceous-buff and bright green-yellow with sudan brown vermiculations. Lower eyelid clearly transparent. Tympanum dark gray.

*Female.* White below. Chin with a few light grayish olive spots. Tubercles, fingers, and toes buff-yellow Back is cinnamon-drab. Upper parts not strikingly different from male. Tympanum pale olive-gray.

**Structure:** Parotoid, elongate, sometimes smooth; no sharp-edged ridge from eye to nostril, nostril area smooth; crown without bony ridges, snout short, blunt; interorbital space about equal to upper eyelid; first finger at least equal to second; toes half webbed; sole tubercles large, each with a cutting edge; tympanum much smaller than the eye.

**Voice:** The vocal sac is a large fat oblong "sausage." Deflated, it forms a light apron covering several darker folds in the rear of the throat. J. K. Strecker, Jr. (Tex., 1926f, p. 12), calls it "a loud explosive quack."

May 11, 1925. San Antonio, Tex. At Leon Valley Creek a big chorus of *B. valliceps, B. debilis, B. compactilis,* and *S. couchii* in considerable numbers. . . *B. compactilis* males were calling from the bank. Each one seemed to have a favorite perch, and when scared away from it by our light sometimes would return almost immediately. Their call is loud and shrill and with a big chorus would be deafening.

May 12. No *B. compactilis* calling at Leon Valley Creek tonight.

May 29, Comfort, Tex. A few were calling when we first reached the spadefoot pond. Their call is very shrill. . . . In the pond were many oats half-grown or more with oats on the stems. Beside an oat stem where a clump of oats might be, a male would rest in water in vertical fashion, sausagelike throat extended 1½–2 in., directed outward and upward above his head much like *B. quercicus.* When a pair is picked up, the male gives a call like a pea fowl or hen, clucking much of the time. The water was very shallow where I caught the pair.

June 15. Left Rio Grande City 7:45 A.M. Stopped at Santa Cruz ranch opposite hill with U.S. Geological Survey marker. At top of hill we could clearly hear *B. compactilis* in a pond across the road. These males which are croaking in the daytime are in the dense shade of some overhanging trees.

**Breeding:** These toads breed from May 1 to July 10, with a few stragglers later at the time of the late summer rains. The brown and yellow eggs are in long fine coils; the jelly tube narrow, 1/12 inch (2 mm.); the eggs crowded, 14–20 eggs in 1 1/5 inches (30 mm.); and the vitelli 1/16 inch (1.4 mm.). The eggs hatch in two days. The bicolored tadpole is small, 1–1 1/8 inches (24–28 mm.), light-colored, its back a drab or light grayish olive and its belly pale cinnamon pink; its tail crests are translucent. The tooth ridges are 2/3. After 40 to 60 days, the tadpoles transform, June 1 to August 1, at 1/2 inch (12 mm.).

**Journal notes:** March 22, 1925. Started for Corpus Christi, Tex., at 6 P.M. Captured *B. compactilis*, north of Kansas City. A female crossing the road.

March 25. Tonight took two *Bufo compactilis* males In no place are they breeding so far as we can see. Tonight we picked up what we at first took for a toad of *B. compactilis* build. Not until later did we realize we had a spadefoot.

March 26. Tonight in Beeville, Tex., under electric light saw a female moving along. Caught her.

May 29. Comfort had 3 inches of rain in the afternoon of May 28. We went to San Antonio and at 5:30 P.M. started for Comfort. At Big Joshua Creek evidences of flood but no frogs calling. . . . Left Boerne and arrived at Comfort about 8:30 P.M. The Guadalupe River had been up high but was down at this time. No frogs at all. When we pulled up to Comfort filling station, heard a great chorus south of the filling station. We went down from the main road south toward baseball field, then left toward the creek. It was slippery. We crossed creek and in a cultivated field 1/4–1/3 mile farther on was a great volume of "wows or meows" or catcalling (*S. couchii*). In this pond were many *B. compactilis*. A few were calling near the edge but more in the water. . . . At the far end of the cultivated field the pond extended into a grassy pasture. Here the *B. compactilis* were calling in considerable numbers. A few had standings on the shore, several were out in clumps of grass. They are well called the spadefoot toad. They are usually the associate of the spadefoot (*S. couchii*).

We left this pool and went on to Cypress Creek where there are water lilies. Nothing doing. We went on 2 or 3 miles, then returned. Down a side road heard *S. couchii*. Found pools beside the road. Herein were many *S. couchii* and many *B. compactilis*.

June 7. As we approached Encinal, close to the road in two pools were many small tads—toad tads, but not spadefoots. We had lost our net but found strainers good for catching them. Are the toads *B. compactilis* or *B. debilis*? When the pools begin to dry up, grackles go there to eat up tads.

June 9. At Dolores, Tex., collected many Couch's spadefoots and *B. compactilis* in large concrete-bottomed irrigation tank. Around the edges are a few places where mud has gathered, and in such places *B. compactilis* has dug into the mud—sometimes leaving an opening, sometimes just leaving the earth rough.

June 2, 1942. Beyond Rockville in Virgin River saw countless small *Bufo* tadpoles. Two to three miles from Springdale, Utah, I went after toads in the dark. Had to jump a drainage ditch. In a cultivated field no end of water; one pool. I thought I had *Scaphiopus* but the call was not so harsh—but much harsher than the few *Bufo woodhousii* then calling. Caught five female *B. compactilis*. When I approached, the males stopped; never saw one. We saw a *Bufo compactilis* crossing the road in Rockville.

July 22, 1942. Toyahvale, Tex. Night trip west on highway. Heard one *Bufo*. This proved to be *Bufo compactilis.*

**Authorities' corner:**

J K. Strecker, Jr , Tex , 1908b, p. 82.
J. K. Strecker, Jr., Tex., 1915, p. 52.
G. P. Englehardt, Utah, 1918, pp. 78–79.
J. K. Strecker, Jr., Tex., 1926f, p. 12.
J. K. Strecker, Jr., Tex., 1928b, p. 7.
H. M. Smith, Gen., 1947, pp. 7–13.

In 1940 Linsdale (Nev.) wrote: "It is necessary, in making final taxonomic appraisal of toads, to study the living animals in their natural surroundings. Until further field studies can be made on this group of forms, satisfactory conclusions cannot be reached. However, the preserved material is sufficient to show that some changes in systematic treatment of the group will be required. Present indications are that these toads are all in the same species. The oldest name in the lot is *compactilis*. At least four races seem to deserve recognition, as follows· *Bufo compactilis compactilis* Wiegmann 1833, *Bufo compactilis woodhousii* Girard 1856, *Bufo compactilis fowleri* Hinckley 1882, *Bufo compactilis californicus* Camp 1915."

He may not be far from the right solution but we cannot yet accept this appraisal without more study of the western forms in the field. Should *Bufo californicus* be placed as a *Bufo compactilis* subspecies rather than as a *Bufo cognatus* affiliate? Is Linsdale's *Bufo compactilis* of Nevada the same as the large *Bufo compactilis* of Texas? In 1942 Dr. Klauber remarked that he wished we could solve the *B. compactilis* problem. The Texas *Bufo compactilis* is an old acquaintance, but the western representatives we do not know well in the field.

In a recent paper H. H. Smith (Gen., 1947) divides *B. compactilis* into two forms restricting *B. c. compactilis* to the main Mexican plateau and *B. c. speciosus* for the U.S. form. We are glad he did not set off the Nevada and Arizona form as new. The discontinuous range of his *B. c. speciosus* may not be real. Field work in the interval in Arizona may yet produce this burrower.

### Little Green Toad, Sonoran Toad, Green Toad, Sonora Toad

*Bufo debilis* Girard. Plate XXXIV; Map 12.

**Range:** "Eastern Texas and Tamaulipas" (Taylor, 1936). "In the lower part of the valley of the Rio Bravo (Rio Grande del Norte) and in the province of Tamaulipas" (Girard, 1854; Stejneger and Barbour, 1938).

**Habitat:** On grassy mesquite flats, breeding in temporary rain pools, ditches, or shallow pools in streams of intermittent flow.

**Size:** Adults, 1–1⅘ inches. Males, 26–41 mm. Females, 31.5–46 mm.

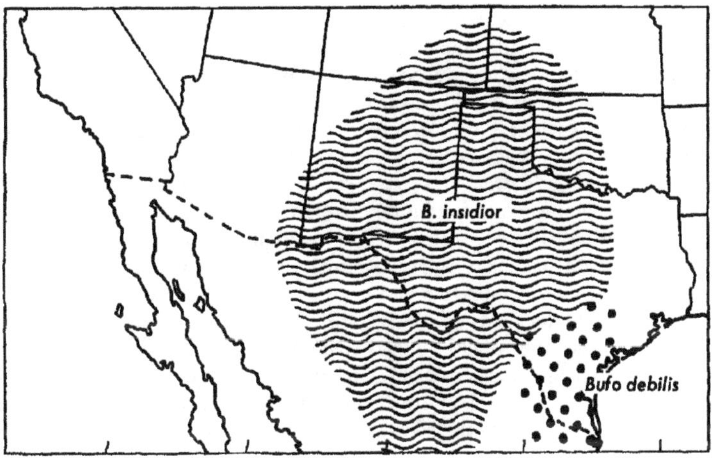


*Map 12*

**General appearance:** This beautiful little green toad has black spots on the back and some gold- or yellow-tipped tubercles on the sides and legs. The legs have a few dark barlike spots with light central areas. The legs are short, the snout pointed, the parotoids large and elongate or triangular, the body narrow and rounded in contour, the head narrow with interorbital space proportionally wide. There is a black bar at the arm insertion and there may be a black line or two or three spots in the middle of the lower breast.

**Color:** *Male.* Alice, Tex., March 31, 1925. Back spinach or cedar green or hellebore green to calliste green or cosse green. Back with black spots and black tubercles on these spots. On the sides, besides green and black, some tubercles are light cadmium, lemon chrome, or maize yellow. These colors also appear on dorsum of hind legs and brachium of fore limb, and on webbing of hind feet and tubercles. The rear of thigh is green, black, and light cadmium color. There is a line of light cadmium where dark colors meet the white under parts. Some of the tubercles on greenish background with light cadmium tips. Light buff or cream-buff along upper jaw to arm insertion. Rim of lower jaw has a white margin followed by dense black, then pale olive-gray to deep olive-gray. There is a black bar on the venter in the pectoral region opposite arm insertion; also black on the brachial insertion. Sometimes there is a black line in the middle of lower breast or two or three black spots. Iris is mainly black with some pale ochraceous-buff.

*Female.* June 15, 1925. In general the same as male, but without the black chin. Under parts are olive-buff or white. In some the two pectoral black spots are absent or not so well developed as in the male.

**Structure:** Crown without bony ridges; snout protruding; first finger shorter than the second; hind limbs usually shorter than body length; tympanum small; toes slightly webbed at base; foot short; no tarsal fold; parotoids sometimes extending downward to the level of the jaw.

In view of Taylor's (1936) concept, the following Strecker quotation is composite, i.e, for both species: "Structure: Girard's original description (May, 1854) of *Bufo debilis* (p. 87) varies so slightly from his *Bufo insidior* (p. 88) that we include it for future clarification of the status of each form. The description is: Upper surface of head without any crest on ridge. Snout rounded. Mouth moderate. Upper jaw emarginated. Tongue small. Tympanum small. Parotoids moderate and elongated. Limbs of moderate development, femur shorter than tibia. First finger longer than the second. A large metacarpal disk. Toes slightly united at the base by a web. Two metatarsal processes. No membranous fold at the inner lower margin of the tarsus. Skin above pustulous; pustules of moderate development; warts beneath very small. Color above brownish yellow, spotted. No dorsal lighter vitta. Beneath of a uniform soiled yellow. Allied to *Bufo speciosus*. . . ."

**Voice:** The vocal pouch is a round ball reaching to the tip of the chin. The call is cricketlike, a low sustained trill.

March 28, 1925. Between San Diego and Alice, Tex., we heard a note absolutely new to us—something like a cricket. When we came to the pond and it appeared light-colored under the flashlight, I knew it must be *Bufo debilis.* It is rightly named "the little green toad." In some ways its note makes me think of Fowler's toad, but it is not nearly so loud or strong. The call is sustained. When I first went down to the pond, I thought I heard only one, but before I got the light on it to see how it croaked, two of them started hopping toward the ditch. In some ways, the toad and its note remind me of *B. quercicus,* but *B. quercicus* is much louder and shriller.

When held in hand the male gave a little batlike click, like marbles hitting together. Over in the mesquite, "devil's elbow," and prickly pear, we went for two or three we heard, and came back with one of them. There was a small ditch or runway there.

In a shallow overflowed mesquite area, several *B. debilis* males were calling.

Oftentimes when you approach, or particularly when you put light on them, they duck flat to the ground. *Bufo debilis* note at times something like the "clucking" one gives to make a horse travel faster.

**Breeding:** This species breeds from the last of March to mid-June. "The eggs are in small strings and are attached to grass and weed stems. . . . The tadpoles are slightly smaller than those of *B. punctatus*" (J. K. Strecker, Jr., Tex., 1926f, p. 10). They transform at ⅓–⅖ inch (8–11 mm.).

Couch at Matamoras, Mexico, took six specimens (USNM no. 2621) which measured respectively 8.0, 8.5, 9.0, 10.5, 11.0, 11.0 mm. This probably represents a close approach to transformation. Doubtless this species transforms at a little larger size than *B. quercicus*, of which the smallest transformed individual recorded is 7 mm.

"Their metamorphosis is accomplished within a very short space of time. This is necessary on account of the extremely temporary character of their breeding places. I returned twenty days later to one pond in which I had found *debilis* breeding and discovered that it was almost perfectly dry, only a few mud holes remaining to indicate moisture. In one of these mud holes were a few belated tadpoles, and in the grass along the banks I found two small toads with tails" (J. K. Strecker, Jr., Tex., 1926f, pp. 10–11).

**Journal notes:** April 3, 1925, Gardendale, Tex. In a shallow pool near the station were some small *Bufo* tadpoles. Returned tonight at 8:30 P.M. Air at least 72°. Heard 3 or 4 *Bufo debilis*.

May 9, San Antonio, Tex. At Leon Creek, several *Microhyla*, and one *Bufo debilis*. This one we photographed. He did not duck under the flashlight. In the next valley bottom—in gravel pit stream—several *B. valliceps*, one *Microhyla*, and one *B. debilis*.

May 11, San Antonio, Tex. Went to Somerset in the afternoon and "spotted" ponds by the roadside. Back to the city for supper; then out Somerset road again. First stop on return 7:45 at roadside pond now swelled by rain. Heard lots of *Pseudacris*, meadow frogs, *Hyla versicolor*, *Bufo valliceps*. *Bufo valliceps* are calling from temporary islands and the banks. Little nearer the city, beside road nothing but *Microhyla*. Next stop—roadside pond—25 male *Bufo debilis*, sometimes 3 or 4 together at edge of plowed ground—3 or 4 Marcy's garters evidently enemies of all of them. Great chorus of *Microhyla* and *Pseudacris*.

Jan. 18, 1942. Visited Al Kirn of Somerset. Showed me his material—plenty of *Bufo debilis*. These he loaned me.

**Authorities' corner:**

J. K. Strecker, Jr., Tex., 1908b, p. 81.
J. K. Strecker, Jr., Tex., 1915, p. 51.
R. Kellogg, Gen., 1932, p. 50.
E. H. Taylor, Kans., 1929, p. 445.
E. H. Taylor, Gen., 1936a, p. 513.

*Plate XXXIV. Bufo debilis.* 1 Female (×1) 2. Male croaking (×⅝). 3. Male (×⅔). 4,5. Females (×¾). 6. Female (×1).

*Plate XXXV Bufo exsul* (×¾). 1. Young 2,7,8. Females. 3,4,5,6. Males.

## Black Toad

*Bufo exsul* Myers. Plate XXXV; Map 11.

**Range and Habitat:** Known only from Deep Springs. "Deep Springs Valley is an isolated depression in the desert mountains of northeastern Inyo County, California. It is elongate in form, trending northeast by southwest, about twelve miles long and five miles broad at its widest part. The lowest part of the valley, at its wide southwestern end, is a flat area of about three by five miles, of almost exactly 5,000 feet elevation, although the rest of the gently rising valley floor is also very level. Surrounding Deep Springs, the White and Inyo Mountains rise to heights of 7,000 to 8,000 feet. Westgard Pass, through which one enters the valley from Owens Valley to the west, reaches 7,276 feet, and the top of the pass into the southern arm of Fish Lake Valley, on the east, is at 6,374 feet. The lowest entrance to the valley appears to be the dry, narrow, and now virtually unused Soldier Pass, from the dry northeastern corner of Deep Springs Valley into Eureka Valley on the southeast; the top of this pass appears to be at approximately 5,400 feet.

"Like other desert valleys to the east of the Sierra Nevada, Deep Springs is exceedingly dry, and on its floor the vegetation consists of sparse low desert brush (*Chrysothamnus*). The surrounding mountains support growths of juniper and piñon.

"The valley has few sources of water Aside from washes carrying water only during infrequent desert rains, I know of only three. Wyman Creek, the course of which leads into the northern end of the valley, contains a little water, at least in its upper reaches, most of the year, and tiny Antelope Spring, on the west side of the valley, appears to be permanent, but neither of these contributes water to the valley floor, except during exceptionally heavy rains. The chief water source is formed by the Buckhorn or Deep Springs which flow from the base of the southeastern valley wall just above the sink. These springs issue from the rocks for a distance of a mile or more, but only a few of them have a strong flow. The flow from the more southerly springs forms a marshy area of several acres, the water finally draining down into a shallow lake of alkaline, sulphurous water that sometimes reaches a diameter of a mile or more. There is also a smaller pond of good water between the springs and the lake. The marshy area and the watercourses through it emit a strong sulphurous odor. Much of this is apparently due to sulphur bacteria, but some of the springs themselves must carry sulphur" (G. S. Myers, Calif., 1942, pp. 1–2).

**Size:** Adults 1¾–2⅖ inches. Males 44–59 mm., average 52 mm., mean 51 mm.; females 46–61.5 mm., average 54 mm. (Measurements of 51 specimens of the Ferris-Wiggans-Myers accession May 1, 1937, and of the C. L. Hubbs family accession Sept. 4, 1934.)

Of 25 adults in our collection from Deep Springs Valley School, May 12,

1942, we have the following sizes: adults 45–56 mm.; males (17) 45–53.5 mm., average 49 mm., mean 48 mm.; females (8) 45(?)–56 mm., average 49 mm., mean 51 mm. There were five questionable as to sex, 39–43.5 mm. The intermediates measured 29–40 mm., except for one 25.5 mm., average 33 mm., mean 34 mm. What is the transformation size?

**General appearance:** "A localized derivative of *Bufo boreas,* closely similar to *B. b. nelsoni* in its small size, narrow head, and smoothness of skin, but sharply distinguished from *nelsoni,* from all forms of *boreas,* and, indeed, from any other North American *Bufo* by its strange color. The dark dorsal markings of *boreas* have enlarged, fused, and darkened until the upper surfaces are almost entirely a shining lacquer black (deep dull blackish brown in alcohol; grayish black in formalin), the remnants of the light interspaces remaining as irregular, whitish, or brownish vermiform markings, and the vertebral line showing as a white or whitish hairline, frequently greatly interrupted, down the middle of the back. The markings of the underside are even more remarkable and diagnostic. The sparse black spots of *boreas boreas* or *boreas nelsoni* have developed into a dense mottling or marbling of black, which appears in life as if made with india ink. Not only are the belly and lower surfaces of the tibiae and tarso-metatarsals heavily marbled, but the throat is usually spotted, and the undersides of the femurs and rump are completely black except for the tubercles, which are white. The tarsal fold is very poorly developed and is almost obsolete in most of the specimens" (G. S. Myers, Calif., 1942, p. 3).

**Color:** Deep Springs, Calif., May 12, 1942. *Young, half grown.* Middorsal stripe is primrose yellow in one and marguerite yellow in another. The parotoid in one bears a prominent patch of isabella color, another of olive ocher. This color extends down the back between tubercles and becomes lighter, sometimes deep seafoam green. The general background of back is light brownish olive with about three irregular rows of warts, one on either side of middorsum, one back from parotoid, and an intermediate one. Bordering this light brownish olive area is a broken irregular thread of marguerite yellow, below which is a band of almost clear black along the sides. The black of the lower sides is broken into mottling by marguerite yellow. Marguerite yellow or ivory yellow is the dominant ventral color, very heavily spotted with black—so heavily spotted on rear of belly and across thighs that the nickname "black pants" was used in the laboratory. On the face is an oblique band of ivory yellow or marguerite yellow extending backward from the eye, sometimes forming a half moon and reaching the angle of the mouth. There is a black band from eye to arm insertion, bordered behind by a longitudinal stripe of marguerite yellow or a broken row of spots of the same. The iris is black with prominent speckings of glass green and with a wash of cinnamon in the upper portion; the pupil rim is of reed yellow. The young are very suggestive of the females of *B. canorus.*

*Female.* The female has very low tubercles, smooth and flattened, the mid-dorsal stripe of the young, and a few flecks of marguerite yellow along the sides (otherwise the dorsum is entirely black). These toads have the most prominent marguerite yellow and black markings on the upper surfaces of fore and hind limbs, particularly on the underside of tibia and dorsum of foot. The underside of the foot is black, except for the articular tubercles which are light yellowish olive. The throat is more heavily spotted than in the young. Iris as in the young. The face marking has the oblique light line, then black area from eye down, then irregular light longitudinal stripe back of angle of mouth.

*Male.* No striking difference from female. The inner palmar tubercle is very prominent.

This lack of sexual dimorphism makes these toads different from *B. canorus,* but in general appearance they seem like a smaller black *B. canorus.*

Some random notes on the Ferris, Wiggans, and Myers material follow: All except one male have thin light stripe full length of body. One female has line absent in rear half and broken in the front half. One female has line broken in many places. The young have a prominent stripe. The first young to have uniform black back is 40 mm. long (no. 2553); those 36 mm. and 38 mm. are spotted on either side of middorsum. Even some of smallest have black on sides. One of striking things in this form is the thin light line going through interorbital area and the oblique bar crossing from one eyelid to the other. In many this cross thread is absent and there is a light longitudinal spot on parotoid, but this is absent in some. The venter is heavily mottled with black from pectoral to pelvic region; the groin and underside of femur and pelvic region are black with white pebbling. On forward half of venter the white and black are about equally divided. The throats are lighter, are creamy, but with black dots in most cases. Six of the small ones have scant spotting on throat region and four with heavy dotting. All ten of these have prominent black pectoral spot. Some of females look ripe.

**Structure:** "Description of Holotype. Head rather narrow, its width approximately three times in length to vent, with a weak canthal angle. Snout moderately rounded when viewed from above, the eyes projecting somewhat beyond the line of the upper lip. In profile the snout is bluntly rounded but sloping and not vertically truncated, the upper lip being the most anterior point. Nostrils slightly nearer to eye than to tip of upper lip, the distance from the eye equal to internarial space and to interocular space, which is flat. No cranial crests. Loreal region somewhat inclined, slightly concave. Depth of subocular area equals half length of exposed part of eye. Distance from nares to tip of upper lip equals length of exposed part of eye. Tympanum indistinct, its upper posterior border partly obliterated, vertically oval in form, its depth equal to distance from nares to eye, or not quite two-thirds horizontal diameter of orbit. Tympanum close to eye, its distance from latter scarcely equal to the narrower (horizontal) diameter of tympanum. Distance of tympanum from the corner of the mouth (directly below it) equals slightly more than (vertical) depth of tympanum. Parotoid glands moderate, oval to triangular, wider and more distinct posteriorly than anteriorly, where they fade out just before reaching eyes, their length approximately equal to distance from eye to tip of upper lip (snout tip); the glands are much farther apart than their own width and do not descend to the sides appreciably behind the tympanum.

"Arms moderately stout, the fingers entirely free of web. Third finger longest; second and fourth approximately equal, reaching base of penultimate phalanx of third. First finger equal to or barely surpassing second. Subarticular tubercles single, well developed only at base of each finger. Several small, scattered tubercles on each palm. Two distinct, enlarged palmar tubercles, the outer large and rounded, its highest point toward its distal end, the inner about half the size of the outer and somewhat more convex.

"Legs stout and relatively short, the tarso-metatarsal joint reaching middle of tympanum when leg is brought forward, the heels not quite touching when femur and folded tibia are brought to right angles with body. Toes more than half webbed, the web reaching as far as the base of the antepenultimate phalanx of the fourth toe and the penultimate phalanges of the other toes; the webs are not greatly excised. Inner metatarsal tubercle moderate, elongate oval in form, its end only slightly free and without cutting edge; the tarsal fold running proximally from the tubercle is nearly obsolete and only barely visible. Outer metatarsal tubercle smaller, rather conical and rounded. Subarticular tubercles of toes single but weak" (G. S. Myers, Calif., 1942, pp 4–5).

Comparison of comparable *Bufo canorus* and *Bufo exsul,* each at 44 and 56 mm., shows head wider, eye and interorbital space slightly larger, tympanum much larger, fore limb longer in *B. canorus,* and third toe slightly longer in *B. exsul.* One must remember that the *Bufo canorus* is hardly mature at 44 mm. and reaches 75 mm. in extreme size, whereas *B. exsul* is mature at 44 and reaches only 61.5 mm. in extreme size.

**Breeding:** On May 12, 1942, two different sizes of tadpoles were with the adults: many tadpoles were 19 or 20 mm in length, and a mature tadpole set were 29–35 mm., with body lengths such as 12 5, 13.0, 13.5, 13.5, 14.0, and 15.0 mm. for six we measured. The tooth formulae are ⅔. The tail tip is very rounded.

**Journal notes:** May 12, 1942. Went to Deep Springs. At 12:30 arrived at Springs, 5000 feet elevation 7½ miles south of Deep Springs School and above Deep Springs Lake. Just below the first spring, in the water runways between tussocks, began to see *Bufo exsul.* The bottoms are mud, water 2 to 4 inches deep. These areas more or less shaded by tussocks. Soil dark and mucky. Depressions between tussocks 8 inches to 1½ feet deep. The toads often dashed into holes in tussocks or into shaded runways. The first three running springs unite into one clear stream. In the stony clear sources no toads; just above confluence of three springs, where streams are not so fast, among some rushes and muck, several of the biggest ones were found. One ran into a hole under a tussock. Along this stream 4 feet wide and nowhere more than 2 feet deep, usually 1 foot or less, were many toads. Every so often toads would swim out from bank and stay poised on top. Often they would swim downward and hide in vegetation. Occasionally they would rush into the mud but seldom completely out of sight. Sometimes one could see in one area as many as 3 or 4 toads on bottom or poised in water below surface. Often a shaded spot or place with no shade would have 2, 3, 4, or even 6 toads in one localized area. Are they approaching breeding? No mated pairs. In this area one also could see toads in the vegetation at surface or see one or two poised on a mat of algae at the surface. The farthest from the stream we took toads was 6 feet. Even near stream they made for stream and escaped in it.

In the stream were three different sizes of tadpoles. Some seemed mature but no transformation sizes were available. The warm sulphur spring beyond had just as many toads. Some of the largest ones are blacker, some of the smaller ones were somewhat yellowish. Mr. Dieffenderfer said he and another found 2800 of them frozen in the water of Antelope Spring west of Deep Springs Valley Lake. Did the big tadpoles come from breeding in March this year?

May 13. Started about 8.30 from Deep Springs Snow all about.

Dr. Myers showed us his and the Hubbs material from Deep Springs previous to the publication of his new form (September, 1942)

**Authorities' corner:**

G. S. Myers, Calif., 1942, pp. 8–9.

## Canadian Toad, Winnipeg Toad, Manitoba Toad

*Bufo hemiophrys* Cope. Plate XXXVI; Map 10.

**Range:** North Dakota, Manitoba, Alberta to northwest provinces. In country tributary to Lake Winnipeg in Canada. Some range discussions include Minnesota, South Dakota, Montana, and Mackenzie.

**Habitat:** Stream valleys, lakes, and Turtle Mountain region.

**Size:** Adults, 2¼–3⅕ inches. Males, 56–68 mm Females, 56–80 mm.

**General appearance:** These are brownish or greenish toads of medium size and with short snouts. The most marked characteristic is the boss on the head. This is a narrow raised horny structure extending from the rear of the upper eyelids to the snout. Frequently the rear end of this boss forms quite a prominence. It makes one think of a frontal plate of the upper mandible of some rail and cootlike birds. Their backs are covered with many fine, rounded warts, generally two to five to a dark area. There are many spiny warts on the femur. There is a light stripe down the middle of the back and a conspicuous dark band along the side, bordered above by a light line. The under parts are cream or buffy with numerous small black spots, a prominent one in the middle of lower throat. The throat of the male is dark. The broad upper eyelids with closely set tubercles are in sharp contrast with the narrow interorbital. This makes the eyes stand out.

**Color:** Walhalla, N.D., Sept. 1, 1930. *Male.* The stripe down the middle of the back is white or ivory yellow, edged on either side with reed yellow. From eye backward over lower edge of parotoid and along side to groin extends a cream-buff line, becoming chamois on lower edge of parotoid and in vertical bar that extends down to the arm. Below the dark lateral band, the interstices among the dark spots are the same color. The color of the back in its lighter portions is ecru-olive; in darker portions, it is yellowish olive or dark greenish olive. The dark bar on either upper eyelid, the area just inside the inner tip of parotoid, and the succeeding paired spots along median line are dark greenish olive or olive with brownish olive warts. The band on side of body is also dark greenish olive or dark olive. The dark oblique bar, below eye, and big bar on shoulder insertion are the same color. The tympanum and interstices between these bars are malachite green. The arms and legs are barred with the dark color of the dorsal spots, with interstices the color of back and cream color. The rear of femur has the dorsal background color with strontian yellow or wax yellow spots. This color comes into the color of the lower belly and underside of femur. The belly is cream-buff, heavily marked with light grayish olive. In middle of pectoral region and on lower throat is long bar spot of the same. The throat is suffused with light grayish olive. Upper portion of parotoid is drab. The boss is argus brown. The inner metatarsal tubercle is mummy brown. The upper surfaces of first two fingers are covered with excrescences of same color or of chestnut-brown. The eye is olivaceous black or dark ivy green with prominent lemon yellow iris ring; upper part of iris is heavily spotted with same color, lower slightly spotted, and upper and lower parts slightly spotted with russet-vinaceous.

*Female, young.* The spots on belly are larger; the throat is clear of spots except for pectoral spot. Throat is cream-colored. First two fingers without excrescences. Otherwise marked as in the male. The outer circle of the iris bears a deep bluish glaucous ring.

(From preserved material in USNM.) Back brown with a median light band. A broad brown lateral band starts back of the arm insertion extending backward to the groin and forward as a broken band to the eye, above the tympanum. This is bordered above by a light margin, which sends a series of more or less vertical lines to the arm insertion, the main branch going forward involving the parotoid. This dark band borders the light color of the belly, which is strongly mottled with dark along the sides. The median line is bordered on either side by a dark area more or less continuous to the vent. In some of the older frogs this breaks up into detached spots about some of the collections of warts. The warts are lighter colored. Between the dorsal series of brown spots and the lateral band are two rows of spots, the more regular one being above the light margin of the dark lateral band. There is a brown area back of the eye and below the tympanum, a brown suborbital spot, and a bar from nostril downward; between this bar and suborbital spot is another bar. Therefore the upper lip is an alternation of light snout, nasal bar, light interval, dark bar, light interval, suborbital dark spot, light interval, and subtympanic spot. There is a light line from below the tympanum or near angle of the mouth, backward over the arm insertion; it, with the vertical bar from the light side band, extends to the dorsum of the arm. The upper eyelid has a prominent brown transverse band, margined in front and below by a conspicuous light gray margin. This eyelid coloration stands out in sharp contrast to the boss of the head. Breast and belly spotted with dark. The hind legs have dark cross bands with reddish tubercles in the center of cross bands. Dark reticulations prominent on back of femur.

**Structure:** Boss on head from snout to rear of interorbital space; slight furrow down the middle and outer ridges forming boss are parallel; these ridges connected by a bar at rear and with slight extension toward the eye; broad upper eyelid with closely set tubercles, in sharp contrast with narrow interorbital; snout short, vertical in profile; tympanum elliptical and vertical; two cutting metatarsal tubercles, inner large and spadelike; ventro-basal portion of femur discolored; fore throat of male discolored.

**Voice:** "Its spring note is a soft trilling, uttered about twice a minute and lasting about three seconds" (E. T. Seton, Man., 1918, p. 83).

**Breeding:** This species breeds from May onward, in shallow edges of lakes or ponds or other water. There are no descriptions of the tadpole on record They transform at ⅜–½ inch (9.0–13.5 mm.).

**Journal notes:** August 30, 1930. At 11 o'clock we started northward from Grand Forks. At Ardock we found a stream dried up except for isolated pools. Around one in the cow-punched and cracked mud, we took some seven or eight young of *Bufo hemiophrys*. They were of two sets: 36 mm., 33 mm., 26 mm., 23 mm., 22 mm., and 18 mm. All of these young specimens have a suggestion of the dark pectoral spot, and only the two larger ones begin to show cranial ridges.

August 31, 1930. It rained in the afternoon. We went through Neche to Walhalla, N.D., at the edge of Pembina Mountains. We arrived about 5:30 P.M. It was still raining. We began to get desperate in our desire for live adults of *Bufo hemiophrys*. Before dark we took an excursion around town looking for possible covers for toads. The evening was cold, the rain had stopped, and it was doubtful if toads were abroad feeding. This has been a summer of remarkable drought. We used one of the best expedients of a collector. We engaged a bright-eyed young boy (Audrey Miller) to search the town. Inside of half an hour he appeared with an adult male. He and another lad started promptly again with a flashlight and returned twice, each time with an adult

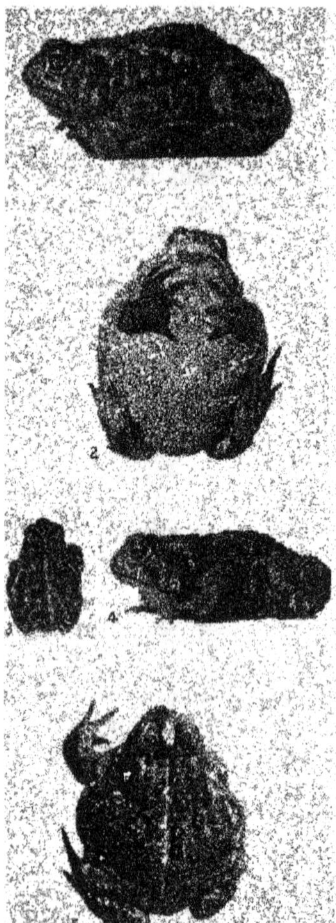

*Plate XXXVI. Bufo hemiophrys* 1. Male (×4/5). 2,4,5. Males (×3/5). 3. Young (×3/5)

*Plate XXXVII Bufo insidior* (×3/4). Males, from Toyahvale, Tex.

toad. We asked where they got them and he said in the gutters, and later he said he got them in the sewers.

Sept. 1, 1930. We went out with the boys to a place where they had a toad located, but had missed him last night. We wondered why they carried a flashlight and a pail on a long rope. We soon found out. The town has drainage manholes. The boys took off the cover and with flashlight searched the surface of the water and the walls of the hole. They pointed out a toad floating at surface. They let down their pail and drew it up under the toad and so caught it. They brought up two toads instead of one, but one was dead. Quite likely the toads were caught here as in a trap, but at this long period of drought it was our best chance of getting material.

These males have a throat of the *Bufo americanus* class, but close examination of one which half inflated its throat revealed that the lower throat region expanded first, and there also seemed to be a secondary swelling at the ventral base of each arm. The throat seems to have a slight fold across the lower throat on the pectoral region. Its boss, this slight indication of a lower throat pouch, and two cutting metatarsal tubercles suggest relationship with *B. cognatus*.

**Authorities' corner:**

E. T. Seton, Man., 1918, p. 83.

## Sonoran Toad

*Bufo insidior* Girard Plate XXXVII; Map 12.

**Range:** Colorado and Kansas south through New Mexico, Arizona, and Texas into northern Mexico.

**Habitat and Size:** Since Dr. Taylor's (1936) resurrection of this Girard species from the synonymy of *Bufo debilis* and since the inclusion of it in the check lists (Stejneger and Barbour), little material has appeared to add to our understanding of it.

**General appearance:** From our limited experience with this form in Trans-Pecos, Tex., we would call it more bleached than are southern Texan little green toads.

"The absence of cranial crests, or the presence of very narrow ones closely approximated to orbits, coupled with the broad, elongate parotoid gland and greenish coloration is very distinctive of this Kansas toad" (H. M. Smith, Kans., 1934, p. 443).

**Color:** July 22, 1942, Toyahvale, Tex. This toad has a flat head, pointed snout, and very large, elongate, and broad parotoids. The back of one is courge green, with the top of the head clear yellow-green. Another has a biscay green back with top of snout and upper eyelids touched with old gold. The back and limbs bear tubercles encircled with mustard yellow and tipped with mummy brown. The back and top of head are also flecked with black, each spot with its black central tubercle. Some spots are dumbbells in shape. A prominent oblique black bar crosses the eyelid. The hind limbs have two or three bars on femur, two on tibia, and one on metatarsus. On the sides the tubercles, encircled with chartreuse yellow and tipped with black or mummy brown, are on a mummy brown background, which forms a broken line across the rear of parotoid and along the side. The groin, underside of thighs, and sides of belly are pale brownish vinaceous; the center of the belly is light glaucous-blue, one immaculate, another with several spots. The throat of the female is white, that of the male discolored, the forward part deep purplish vinaceous, the rear a pale vinaceous-lilac, the middle deep medici blue. The underside of hand and of toes is vinaceous-cinnamon, toes and fingers tipped with cinnamon-brown. The two metatarsal tubercles and the palmar tubercle are russet. The black eye has a citron yellow pupil rim broken in four places, and the iris is heavily flecked with ochraceous-buff.

**Structure:** The original description (C. Girard, Gen., 1856, p. 88) is as follows: "Upper surface of head plane and smooth. Snout subacute, protruding. Mouth moderate, upper jaw slightly emarginated. Tongue elongated tapering towards both ends. Tympanum inconspicuous. Parotoids large and elongated, situated obliquely upon the shoulder. Limbs moderate. First finger equal to the second in length. A metacarpal disk, and a tubercle. Toes slightly webbed at base. Two metatarsal tubercles. Skin papillous above, warty beneath."

**Voice:** "This species is rather abundant throughout the region traversed (eastern border of the Staked Plain of Texas). It is frequently found in the grass, where its green color aids in concealing it. When in the water, its cry is like that of *B. lentiginosus americanus,* but is more feeble, and very nasal" (E. D. Cope, Tex., 1893, p. 332).

**Breeding:** Like *B. debilis,* it doubtless breeds from mid-March to August. Ripe females have been secured to mid-July.

**Journal notes:** Since the re-establishment of *Bufo insidior,* we have had no opportunity to examine the collections of *Bufo debilis* and *Bufo insidior* to outline their contrasting characters or to determine their actual distinctness. The instant we saw Taylor's range of *Bufo insidior* we thought of the time, July 10, 1925, near Fort Davis, Tex., when we heard narrow-mouthed toads and green toads; and also of the time in 1934 when we heard these same little toads at Alpine, Tex. On our 1942 trip we secured the toad near Balmorhea State Park.

July 22, 1942, Toyahvale. Night trip west on highway. . . . In this pond heard one lone *Microhyla olivacea.* Farther on heard plenty of *Microhyla.* Then I began to question whether they were all *Microhyla.* There was a call halfway between that of a *Microhyla* and a *Bufo.* A little toad under my feet put into the pond. I didn't see it well. Then I realized that it must be old *Bufo debilis.* Now that we were in the range of Taylor's *Bufo insidior,* might it be that form? Caught three males (36, 38, and 43 mm.). As we came back heard many more, and where we heard it most, there on edge of road, saw a female just hit but yet alive.

When we compared three Toyahvale specimens of *B. insidior* with three of our southern Texas *B. debilis* we seemingly had these differences:

| | *B. insidior* | *B. debilis* |
|---|---|---|
| Snout | 6.9–7.8 in L. | 8.0–9.2 in L. |
| Upper eyelid | 9.5–10.0 in L. | 11.5–12.5 in L. |
| 1st finger | 7.6–8.6 in L. | 8.8–11.5 in L. |
| 3rd finger | 4.4–4.5 in L. | 5.2–6.5 in L. |
| 4th finger | 5.06–5.5 in L. | 6.5–8.0 in L. |
| Foot with tarsus | 1.7–1.8 in L. | 2.0–2.15 in L. |

Whether these measurements will obtain with a large series we dare not assert. They point to bigger snout, upper eyelid, first, second, and fourth fingers, and longer foot with tarsus in *B. insidior*.

**Authorities' corner:** "In September, 1886, coming down the valley of the Cimarron river from New Mexico, I first noticed the little Sonoran toad, *Bufo debilis*, Girard, near the Z H ranch in the Public Lands (now Beaver county, Oklahoma), at a point thirty-five or forty miles west of the southwest corner of Kansas. The species was observed a few days later in great abundance and activity (during rainy weather) in Morton county, Kansas, and in the southern part of Hamilton county. I have collected a single specimen in the western part of Barber county, Kansas, also" (F. W. Cragin, Kans., 1894, p. 39).

"Two specimens (U.S.N.M. no. 2622) from Chihuahua, collected by Dr. Thomas H. Webb, are designated in the museum catalogue as the cotypes of Girard's *Bufo insidior*. The preservation of these specimens is fair, but both are very much bleached" (R. Kellogg, Gen., 1932, p 52).

When Dr. E. H. Taylor described a new species from a locality near Mazatlan, he said that this small toad, *Bufo kelloggi* (named in honor of Dr. Remington Kellogg) "is most closely related to *Bufo debilis* and *Bufo insidior* Girard." "From *Bufo insidior* Girard (Kansas, Texas, New Mexico, Chihuahua, Durango, and Zacatecas) it differs in the presence of the cranial crests (lacking or with only an occasional faint trace of crests in *insidior*), in having shorter hind legs, a shorter snout, larger eye, narrower head, and narrower interorbital width, a differently shaped parotoid and a totally different dorsal color pattern. It has very much larger and more numerous spiny tubercles on dorsal and lateral surfaces; the inner palmar tubercle is less developed, as are the metatarsal tubercles; the webbing between the toes is slightly more extensive. The color pattern is entirely different" (E. H. Taylor, Gen., 1936a, p. 513). We have seen two *B. kelloggi* and hold them distinctly different.

"*Bufo insidior* Girard. The little green toad, although common in Texas and known from Kansas, has apparently not been recorded previously from

Oklahoma. Charles C. Smith and I found it to be fairly common in the southwestern part of Oklahoma where it was breeding with *B. compactilis* Whereas *B. compactilis* was also found in great numbers on roadways, *B. insidior* was seen only in breeding pools. We collected specimens in Cotton, Jackson, southern Kiowa, and Tillman counties. In addition, Mr. Kuntz has furnished one specimen taken on a street during an evening shower in Lawton, Comanche County; and the University of Oklahoma Museum of Zoology has a single specimen from extreme northern Garvin County" (A. N. Bragg, Okla., 1941a, pp. 51–52).

"Under the name *Bufo debilis,* Campbell [Ariz., 1934, p. 3] recorded this species from the Huachuca Mountains in Arizona, and more recently Kauffeld . . . has reported a specimen from the vicinity of Tombstone (30 miles south of Cochise). In view of the fact that Taylor . . . has reported specimens from Zacatecas, it is reasonable to suppose that the species occurs in northeastern Sonora.

"The specimen collected by Kauffeld is now A.M.N.H. No. 50914 in the collection of the American Museum of Natural History. This specimen, an adult female with mature eggs in the oviducts, compares favorably in coloration and pattern with Zacatecan specimens depicted by Taylor . . . , particularly the individual depicted by him as figure 9 of plate 45. Taylor states that *B. debilis,* with which Kellogg (1932) synonymized *insidior,* inhabits Eastern Texas and Tamaulipas, whereas *insidior* occupies an extensive range from Kansas and New Mexico southward through Texas and the adjoining states in Mexico to Durango and Zacatecas. We have compared the Arizonan specimen with individuals from Archer, Presidio, McLennan, and Bexar counties, Texas. Presumably some of these specimens would be referable to *debilis,* if Taylor's views are correct. Obviously there are differences in pattern and postulation, but there is no conspicuous difference aside from these between the Arizonan and Texan specimens. The specimens from Archer County in northern Texas are certainly the same species as that from the other Texan counties, including Bexar, which lies immediately north of Atascosa County, where the toads depicted as *debilis* in figures 5 and 6 of Taylor's plate 45 were taken. If *insidior* can be removed from the synonymy of *debilis,* we strongly suspect that it represents a subspecies of the latter. Furthermore, if our specimen from Bexar County is properly assigned to *debilis* it is obvious that the form has a wider range than Taylor's statement implies, probably including Oklahoma and Kansas, to judge only by a photograph of a Kansan specimen, and the proximity of Archer County to Oklahoma. San Diego County, Texas, where the toad in figure 4 of Taylor's plate was reputedly taken, seems to be non-existent; possibly the specimen came from San Diego, in Duval County.

"Unless the type or other specimens from Chihuahua more closely resemble the Arizonan and Zacatecan individuals than Texan specimens, the applicability of the name *insidior* to the former is open to considerable question.

Taylor does not compare *debilis* with *insidior,* but compares each separately with *kelloggi* from Mazatlan. The latter evidently is a valid form inhabiting the coastal plain from Mazatlan at least as far south as Acaponeta in Nayarit where the specimens (A.M.N.H. Nos. 43877–43878) were secured by one of us in November, 1939" (C. M. Bogert and J. A. Oliver, Gen., 1945, pp. 409–410). See page 87 for Taylor and Smith's recent (1948) comparisons.

### Marine Toad, Giant Toad

*Bufo marinus* (Linné). Plate XXXVIII; Map 10.

**Range:** From southern Sonora to Tamaulipas in Mexico to Patagonia. Introduced into Puerto Rico, Jamaica, and several smaller West Indian islands, some of which may possibly have had it originally native. Some distance north of William Lloyd's collection of it in Hidalgo, Tamaulipas, E. H. Taylor and J. S. Wright took it near Zapata, Tex. They wrote: "While collecting along the highway between Zapata and Arroyo Loma Blanca, in southern Texas, on the night of August 20, 1931, encountered a number of toads in a temporary pool, which on examination proved to be the widespread *Bufo marinus* (Linn.), the largest known species of *Bufo*."

**Habitat:** In 1891 Ives found it in the courtyard of a house In 1901 Waite in Bermuda reported them around houses, in gardens, and in water tanks. In 1917 in Bermuda P. H Pope stated that they were "abundant about roadsides, gardens and edge of mangrove swamps. A street light halfway between 'Grasmere' and Hamilton was a favorite place for them, and two or three were usually seen under it, picking up the insects that were attracted by the light. . . . In the day-time they hide under stones or boards or burrow in the soft earth. I have sometimes seen them in little burrows in the side of a bank, where they had dug themselves in just enough to be out of the sun." In 1932, R. Kellogg declared that "these large toads are nocturnal in their habits and hide under fallen tree trunks, matted leaves, and stones, or burrow into loose soil."

**Size:** One synonym, *Bufo gigas* Walbaum, suggests its size. It is the giant of toads. Gunther in 1858 (Gen.) remarked on the very large specimens and in 1885–1902 he noted that "Central-American specimens, at least those of the more temperate districts, do not appear to grow to the enormous size to which the species attains in Brazil and Guiana." His measured specimen is 166 mm. P. H. Pope (1917) in Bermuda wrote, "An average female measured 145 mm. from snout to vent and Waite describes one 155 mm. in length." "The male is smaller, usually about 13 mm. shorter, and more active than the female." Schmidt in 1928 had a 103-mm. female and a 95-mm. female from Puerto Rico. Kellogg (1932), among the 104 specimens he examined, mentioned individuals measuring 110 mm., 125 mm., and 167 mm. Taylor and Wright (1932) took several measuring from 66–168 mm., but the record seems to be that of

Miranda-Ribero, who reports a body length of 22 cm. (220 mm.) or 8.6 inches.

**General appearance:** This is an enormous toad with an immense triangular pitted parotoid. The forward side of this triangular gland is just back of the tympanum, the base starts just back of the angle of the jaw and slants slightly upward to meet the very oblique or slanting upper side at a point well back on the side of the body. From this point a row or fold of large, blunt, rounded, brown-tipped warts extends ⅝ to ¾ of the way to the groin. From *Bufo valliceps* it may be distinguished by its very large parotoids; larger outer sole (metatarsal) tubercle; its coarser, less even, and less pointed tubercles; blunter and lower cranial crests; the usual absence or indistinctness of the parietal ridge; and less distinct color pattern.

**Color:** We have seen none alive in recent years and consequently use Dr. Kellogg's (Gen., 1932) summary: "In general, the coloration of *Bufo marinus* is quite variable, ranging through various shades of brown, including yellowish, reddish, and even blackish, and occasionally greenish olive; upper parts with or without large insuliform spots, which when present are usually edged with pale yellow; a light vertebral line occasionally visible; arms and legs of immature individuals usually banded with dark brown; underparts dingy white or yellow."

**Structure:** Interorbital region smooth, decidedly concave, shallower in front than behind; crests pronounced—the canthus rostralis is a prominent crest beginning ahead of and above the nostrils and ending at the anterior corner of the eye, where it forks into two ridges, a broad preorbital and a well-defined supraciliary crest which curves around the eye, sending off a prominent supratympanic ridge to the parotoid and a very short postorbital; parietal crests absent, indistinct, or poorly developed; large broad head, box-snouted; parotoids huge, as long as head or bigger, ⅘ to 1⅛ times the head; parotoids widely divergent behind; toes ½ to ⅔ webbed; free inner metatarsal tubercle; outer metatarsal tubercle large and flat; a thin edged tarsal fold from inner metatarsal tubercle backward; prominent palmar pads at base of first and second fingers; eyelid finely tuberculate; two rows of large fleshy warts, one down each side of middorsum to vent, more prominent in male. Back of angle of mouth the skin is divided into two or more vertical folds so that at times it might be thought a postrictal gland. However, it is not like the white wart of *Bufo alvarius*

**Voice:** Taylor and Wright heard these toads at Zapata, Tex., but did not describe their call Pope in Bermuda has stated that they have a more resonant and louder call than *Bufo americanus*—"a deep booming trill."

**Breeding:** In Bermuda February to July is the breeding season, April being the optimum month. In Trinidad they breed from August to October; in Demerara, from mid-April to September, possibly also from November to January. The eggs are in strings. Dr. E. L. Mark had some hatch in 68 hours. The black tadpole transforms after 45 days or less. The tops of the first two fingers of the males have excrescences, and there are excrescences on the inner side of third finger and the inner palmar tubercle. Some males have brown and spiny-tipped warts and tubercles.

Clark has a note that this species lays twice a year, but Pope is sure that in Bermuda an individual breeds but once a year. In Bermuda in 1903 Mark made the following observations:

"In the spring of 1903 . . . we visited 'Spanish Rock' near midday, April 22. Before reaching the Rock we found, on the slope facing away from the ocean and toward Spittal Pond, a small pool of rainwater (there had been a heavy shower the night before), and in this pool there were large numbers of the huge toads *Bufo aqua*—in pairs. The females were engaged in spawning, and the numerous strings of spawn were stretched across the pool in almost every conceivable direction. The pool, some fifteen or twenty feet in diameter and only a few inches deep, was of so temporary a character that its bottom consisted throughout of turf, not unlike the land immediately surrounding it, which was not submerged."

Ruthven (1916) "recorded that on the Demerara River, about thirty-five miles south of Georgetown in 1914, tadpoles were abundant in July and August. . . ." Pope (1917) thought that development might be more rapid than Ruthven's 45 days from egg to adult. Mark (1903) observed this species from eggs April 22 to free-swimming larvae April 27. In describing some tadpoles collected by L. J. Cole in Bermuda Pope wrote: "The tadpoles are black in color and resemble those of *B. americanus*. They measure from 8.5 to 10.9 mm. in length. They have the typical early tadpole form. The buds of the hind limbs are present, but hardly visible to the naked eye."

Transformation must be over as extended a period as is the egg laying. Ruthven records it on August 16 about 45 or 46 days after egg laying. No other notes apparently exist on transformation.

**Journal notes:** We present none. Our experiences consist in seeing a few captive specimens in aquaria or zoos.

**Authorities' corner:** Taylor and Wright (Tex., 1932, pp. 247–249) found their specimens had been feeding on "tenebrionid and carabid beetles, the bulk of the food being of the genera *Eleodes* and *Pasimachus*." Pope (1917) says that when the residents of Bermuda found that these toads ate cockroaches, they no longer called them after their introducer "Captain Vesey's nuisances." In 1918 Noble found that the *Bufo marinus* he had from Nicaragua fed principally on cockroaches. Our friends, Drs. M. L. Leonard and Stuart Danforth, years ago (1930 or earlier) told us how some of their colaborers in Puerto Rico had successfully shipped them to Hawaii to control insects, and today plenty of reports appear on their role in Hawaii.

Regarding the poison Verrill says: "This toad is believed . . . to have a very poisonous secretion from its parotoid and dorsal glands. It is said that dogs that mouth them invariably die within a few hours. The secretion of the glands, when injected into the circulation of dogs, birds, and other animals, causes convulsions and death, even when in small doses. Mr. A. H. Verrill . . . on one occasion saw the venom ejected as a fine spray, from the parotoid glands of a large toad, when it was much irritated."

On this topic the observations of C. T. Dodds seem pertinent: "During the summer of 1922 I spent some time at Los Mochis, in Northern Sinaloa, Mexico. It was very interesting each evening to note the appearance of large toads under the electric lights. One evening, about the end of July while one of these toads was occupied in catching insects, a small terrier dog started to tease the amphibian. At first the toad only hopped in an effort to escape the barking dog, which did not attempt to bite. Soon the toad became tired and its hops were less frequent and not so long. The dog was urged on by the bystanders and finally snapped the toad while the latter was in mid-air, catching it just back of the foreleg. Although the dog's mouth was not in contact with the toad for more than an instant, he immediately lost all interest in the animal. Spitting and shaking his head, he gave all indications of having received something very distasteful in his mouth. He was offered some water but refused to drink and in about a minute's time showed signs of weakening and general paralysis. He sank to the ground with his legs spread out, writhing and whining with pain, and unable to recognize his master. During this time he was able to push himself along the ground, gradually becoming weaker and very rigid, with eyes greatly protruding and respiration and heart action exceedingly rapid. After twenty minutes he was somewhat quieter as if he was going to die. It was suggested that castor oil be given him in the hope that it might save his life. Accordingly his mouth was pried open, for every muscle was rigid, and about 50 cc. of oil was poured down his throat. Ten minutes later he showed signs of improvement, although I do not know that the oil had anything to do with the change. Within another 15 minutes he was able to get upon his feet but was very feeble and his hind quarters were still somewhat paralyzed. Presently he recognized his master and within an hour from the time he took his distasteful nip he was apparently quite normal again."

E. H. Taylor and H. M. Smith recently expressed the following opinion: "We are convinced that *Bufo marinus* Linnaeus, as generally accepted, comprises species or/and subspecies and is in fact of almost generic significance. However, certain difficulties are involved in properly delineating and naming these forms. In the first place the type localities of *Bufo marinus* and *B. aqua* are unknown except that they are from the Western Hemisphere. *Bufo maculiventris* and *B. lazarus* of Spix are Brazilian, but lack exact localities; *B. ictericus* Spix, however, is cited with Rio de Janeiro as type locality. *B. humeralis* Daudin 'existe dans diverses countries meridional du nouveau continent.' He mentions one in the Musée d'Histoire naturelle from Cayenne (French Guiana). This may be presumed to be the type locality for this species.

"A second difficulty is that seldom are good series of these great toads collected; and the age, sex, and environmental variations are known for only a few localities.

"Wiegmann described *Bufo horribilis* from a series of cotypes from the State of Vera Cruz, and we are reviving this designation for most of the toads of this group in Mexico, aware that there are probably variant populations even here, that may warrant subspecific designations" (Gen., 1945, pp. 551–552).

"The third series of eggs was at the yolk plug stage when placed in 15 and 10% sea water and in tap water. Mortality appeared to be slightly less in the dilute sea water, and development in the early stages, at least, somewhat accelerated.

"Twenty-seven days after laying, the first completely metamorphosed animal was taken from the 15% sea water and 2 days later metamorphosis was occurring in the other solutions. Thereafter, over a period of 9 days, metamorphosed animals were taken from all solutions.

"In general, these preliminary experiments seem to show that low concentrations of sea water constitute a favorable environment for the development of *Bufo marinus* larvae" (C. A. Ely, Gen., 1945, p. 256).

"In the latter part of November, 1939, the senior author secured several specimens of *Bufo marinus* under boulders along the river at Culiacán in Sinaloa. This was during the dry season and apparently the toads were hibernating. While these specimens were being collected a native boy watched with interest as the toads were placed in the sack and finally commented, 'Echan leche' (they throw milk), in reference to the whitish venom secreted by the parotoid glands. This secretion is readily ejected a distance of a foot or so if the glands are squeezed. However, the toads have not been observed to expel the poison such a distance voluntarily.

"It has been noted on several occasions that *B. marinus,* when killed by being placed in formalin or alcohol, commonly secretes quantities of viscous, whitish liquid from the parotoid glands" (C. M. Bogert and J. A. Oliver, Gen., 1945, pp. 340–341).

### Spotted Toad, Belding's Toad, Canyon Toad, Red-spotted Toad

*Bufo punctatus* Baird and Girard. Plate XXXIX; Map 13.

**Range:** South-central Texas west to Nevada, southern California, Sonora, and Lower California.

**Habitat:** Desert canyons, breeding in rock-bottomed pools of intermittent streams.

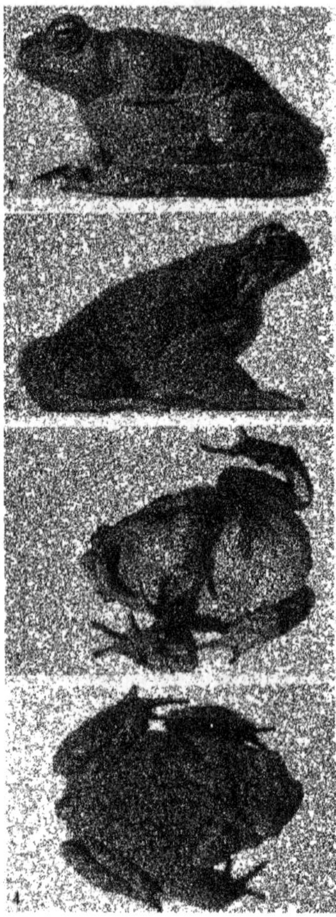

*Plate XXXVIII Bufo marinus.* 1,2. Male (×⅓) 3,4. Male (×¼).

*Plate XXXIX. Bufo punctatus.* 1. Male croaking (×⅗) 2,3,5. Males (×⅘). 4. Female (×½).

"Lower California, Aguaito Springs, 15 miles E. Rosario, 1300 ft. lat. 30°4′; 37244; June 9. 2 miles NNW Cataviña, 1950 feet, lat. 29°47′; 37245–37248; June 11.

"The red-spotted toad from Aguaito Springs was the only individual of this species seen at that locality—a series of spring-fed pools in an arid terrain. Of the four from near Cataviña, two were hopping at night on the dry, sandy floor of an arroyo at least 100 feet from water, and two were squatting in a pool" (L. Tevis, Jr , L.C., 1944, p. 6).

**Size:** Adults, 1⅗–3 inches. Males, 40–68 mm. Females, 42–64 mm., or even 74 mm. in Lower California.

**General appearance:** This is a small, delicately formed, alert, attractive toad of grayish, greenish tan, taupe, drab, or even red color, with a flattened body and a broad flat back evenly covered with scattered tubercles of small size The tubercles on the back, sides, and legs may be reddish, orange-cinnamon, or light vinaceous-cinnamon. There may be black rings or partial rings at the bases of the tubercles. The under parts are buff or white and may be spotted with black in the smaller toads The legs may be barred or spotted with black. The conspicuous marks of this toad are the small, round parotoids, the broad interorbital area, and the sharp-edged, often pebbly, canthus rostralis that gives the nostril a "boxed" appearance The eyelids also are so tubercular as to appear pebbly. It is a fine little toad of very neat, compact appearance. It frequently gives a pleasant birdlike chirp in captivity. We picked up one and turned it over. It lay in the shallow water with legs drawn up as if to "possum"; we never saw any *Bufo* feign this lifeless attitude more than this individual.

**Color:** *Female*. Helotes, Tex., March 13, 1925. Upper parts light brownish olive, buffy olive, or buffy brown on parotoids and interparotoid area (The next day the upper parts in general were drab.) Upper part of hind legs dull citrine sharply marked from light under parts by wax yellow or primuline yellow This color or cream color on underside of thighs Tubercles on top, lateral, and ventral surfaces of thighs and on underside of fore and hind feet are orange-cinnamon or vinaceous-cinnamon to light vinaceous-cinnamon. Under parts cartridge buff, the area ahead of hind legs olive-gray. The iris has cream or pale chalcedony yellow rim around the pupil. It is black heavily spotted with tilleul buff, vinaceous-buff, and light vinaceous-fawn.

*Male*. Grand Canyon, Oct. 12, 1929. Back buffy citrine or olive-lake, buffy olive, citrine-drab, or light grayish olive. Legs fore and hind olive-buff. Over back are scattered little spots of flame scarlet, rufous, or apricot orange On sides are several spots of black, some without and some with rufous or apricot orange centers. On back each spot has such a center. Black or grayish around snout to eye, more or less around tympanum, slightly on upper eyelid, and somewhat on parotoid. Forelegs spotted with black but these spots with centers of ground color. Femur, tibia, tarsus, and outer toe with bars of black. Upper labial margin olive-buff. Undersides of hands and feet and more or less of fore limb and hind limb cinnamon or cinnamon-buff. Throat honey yellow, old gold, or tawny-olive. Lower throat with gnaphalium green, tea green, dark bluish glaucous, or greenish glaucous-blue. Lower belly and most of buttocks light brownish drab, army brown, or deep brownish vinaceous. Eyelids above and canthus heavily tubercled with rufous or apricot orange. Iris rim broken above and below, behind and in front viridine green; iris black, heavily dotted and splashed with ochraceous-salmon, ochraceous-buff, or antimony yellow. Under parts white dotted with small black dots.

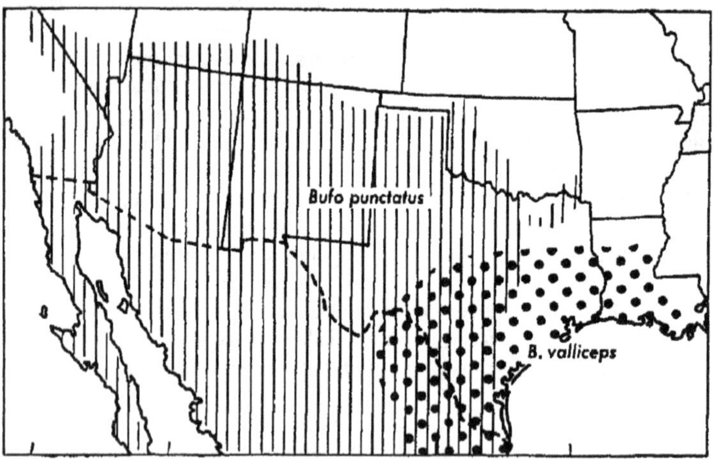


*Map 13*

Another male has no spots underneath. A third has them on forward chin and rear pectoral region, those on chin white-centered; a fourth has them faint on pectoral region. One is light drab, another cinnamon; the drab one is avellaneous or wood brown, uniform on back except for reddish tubercles.

Specimen collected by V. Bailey, at the bottom of the Grand Canyon, Sept. 13, 1889. "I took the following color description from one of the fresh specimens (No. 16185). Above 'malachite-green' densely speckled with small dots of bright vermilion; limbs paler, dotted with vermilion and also with minute black specks which likewise occur on the flanks; region surrounding nostrils black; upper lips and whole under surface bluish white, irregularly speckled with black; posterior part of belly and underside of thighs dark brownish flesh color; soles, dull orange" (L. Stejneger, Ariz., 1890, p. 117).

**Structure:** No cranial crests, or crests obscure; parotoids small and round;

interorbital area broad; ridge from nostril to eye sharp and often pebbly, giving the nostril a "boxed" appearance; finger excrescences of males not prominent; throat of male somewhat discolored

**Voice:** The vocal sac of the male is a round subgular pouch. The call is birdlike. It is a high-pitched, yet very pleasing, trill, lasting while one counts to 15 or 25.

"Cape Region of Lower California. While collecting with a light early in the evening forty-six specimens were taken around the public square in the little village of San Antonio. They were heard calling late in the evening. A specimen captured was observed to make a shrill whistling noise of four or five seconds duration, at intervals of about the same length" (J. R. Slevin, B.C., 1928, pp. 101–102).

"A long continued clear trill, resembling that of a hearth cricket but with more volume" (J. Grinnell, MS; and T. I. Storer, Calif., 1925, p. 197).

**Breeding:** They breed from April to September, May being the most common month. The eggs are single, with very sticky jelly, and sometimes the eggs are stuck together loosely as a small film on the bottom. The envelope is single ⅛ inch (3.2–3.6 mm.), the black and white vitellus 1/25–1/20 inch (1.0–1.3 mm.). The eggs hatch in 3 days or less. The small tadpole, 1 inch (24–25 mm.), has a very black body and a whitish tail with many evenly spaced black dots. The tooth ridges are ⅔. After 40 to 60 days, the tadpoles transform from June to August, at ⅖ inch (9–11 mm.).

**Journal notes:** July 19, 1917, from 5–7 P.M. at Texas Pass, Ariz. We heard plenty of toads but could not find them. At last P. A. Munz and I dug a croaking male from beneath a rock. They croak in the crevices and underneath rocks. In the pools are plenty of tadpoles large and small. In the evening we picked up a female *B. punctatus.* In the canyon were no end of males in the water and along the banks, males seizing each other. As yet there are few females.

Aug. 2. We started down Bright Angel Trail at Grand Canyon. At Indian Gardens, in a flat shallow area, water 6 inches deep, we found two egg complements of *B. punctatus* on the muddy bottom. They were near the west edge in shallow water and not under overhanging willows nor in the water cress. The eggs were more or less agglutinated on the bottom about one egg deep, in a few places more Later, we found many complements in all stages and took three or four transformed stages of *Bufo punctatus* here.

May 6, 1925, Helotes, Tex. Where I found the female *B. punctatus* and two males, there are strewn over the bottom eggs, black and white. Some are single; some touch in masses but not strings or masses which would stay as masses if above the bottom. These occupy a foot square or 1 by 1½ feet. These are nearly hatched. On the rocky bottom they look like the black-fly masses we get in swift water in the Northeast. Water here is 1 inch deep. Nothing but *B. punctatus* was calling here last night or the night before. We discovered these at 11:30 A.M. We photographed them at 1 P.M. Just now under some near-by stone a *B. punctatus* male can be heard.

June 3, 1942, St. George, Utah. Went up on Red Hill near Dixie sign. In a ditch Anna saw tads and some eggs. She found a dead *B. punctatus* in ditch. Under a stone I took a *Bufo punctatus*.

**Authorities' corner:**

G. P. Englehardt, Ariz., 1917, p. 6.
N N. Dodge, Ariz., 1938, p. 12.
R. R. Miller, Calif, 1944, p. 123.

## Oak Toad, Oak Frog, Dwarf Toad

*Bufo quercicus* Holbrook. Plate XL; Map 14.

**Range:** North Carolina to Florida west to Louisiana.

**Habitat:** Abundant in the pine barrens, seeking shelter in little burrows shielded by vegetation or under boards or logs. Many breed in shallow cypress ponds or in temporary surface rain pools or ditches.

**Size:** Adults, 3/4–1 1/4 inches. Males, 19–30 mm. Females, 20.5–32 mm.

**General appearance:** This pigmy toad has a light stripe down the back and four or five pairs of unconnected spots along the middle of back, from the first pair between the eyes to the last, which are merely two pinpoints just ahead of vent They may be light brown or almost black so that the spots barely show. The skin is finely roughened with tubercles, many of which are red. This brightly colored little fellow looks like a bit of velvet or tapestry. The arms and legs are barred with black. The vocal sac of the male is conspicuous when deflated, and is a triangular apron with the base on the gular line and the point extending backward over the pectoral region. Under parts grayish or buffy.

**Color:** June 8, 1921. *Adult.* Dorsal stripe white, pale orange-yellow, maize yellow, sulphur yellow, or cream-buff. The four or five pairs of dorsal spots are black. Upper parts with some gull gray, pearl, or pale olive-gray. Stripe from lower part of tympanum almost to groin of the above grays; also patch of the same back of angle of mouth, below tympanum, above arm insertion, in front of femur, and on back part of upper eyelid. All these lighter dorsal portions are with burnt sienna tubercles, which are especially prominent along either side of dorsal stripe from hump backward, on oblique lateral stripe, and on posterior part of eyelid. The tubercles on black areas look black but many are really burnt sienna. Parotoid with fine and thickly studded burnt sienna tubercles. Tubercles on palmar and solar surfaces, posterior surface of thighs (partially), groin (a little), pectoral region (a few tubercles) vinaceous-rufous, Hay's russet, or mars orange. Ventral parts smoke gray, grayish white, pale olive-buff, or cream color. Each tubercle stands out: on venter, close together and black between; on sides and underside of limbs, wider apart and intervening black more apparent. Iris cream color; rim around pupil and eye naphthalene yellow; rest largely black with cartridge buff or ivory yellow.

**Structure:** Head to angle of mouth short; snout pointed; body short; flat; hind limbs shorter than body length; first finger less than or equal to second; cranial crests divergent, ends connected by transverse series of raised warts, giving the cranial hollow a parapet behind; parotoids finely spinose; excrescences on fingers of male not prominent; interorbital region broad.

**Voice:** The vocal sac of the male is an oblong "sausage." When deflated it is made up of folds of skin on the lower throat covered by a conspicuous apron or lappet. The call is very birdlike, not froglike. It is a very high-pitched whistle. The chorus is deafening and can be heard ⅛ mile or more.

May 16, 1921. The oak toad male was calling before we approached. He piped only low. After we had worked him around for a photo, he suddenly, to our surprise, backed into a hole at the base of a saw palmetto. The hole was ¾ of an inch in diameter and not deep. The note of this toad is birdlike. One will hear three or four calls sounding like those of piping chickens. Sometimes the note is repeated three or four times. Then this process is repeated after a short interval. Once its note was likened to that of a swallow-tailed kite. Truly the most unfroglike note I ever heard. It sometimes sounds like some animal in distress. There are several calling in the piney woods. One calling from a tangle of chokeberries (*Aronia*), *Osmunda cinnamomea*, Bamboo brier (*Smilax*), and sweet bays. Couldn't find it. Are the toads moving pondward? Later in the evening we heard none.

1922. A combined chorus of *Hyla gratiosa*, *Hyla femoralis*, *Hyla squirella*, *Chorophilus*, *Acris*, and *Bufo quercicus* left our ears ringing for a long time after we left the pond. By half closing our ears, we shut out *Hyla femoralis* and heard the others more distinctly. The whole was a terrible din.

In 1912 and 1921 some of the residents who were almost invariably accurate assured me that the black snake had a whistle and that this note of the oak toad was the call in question. The timed calls ranged from 32 calls in 16 seconds to 10 calls in 26 seconds.

In inflation of the throat these toads are like *Bufo compactilis* and *Bufo cognatus*. The lower throat is the principal part involved in the process; it is thrown out into an elliptical bag or sausagelike balloon. One can tell when a toad is going to trill after a rest because the body will inflate to a large size and then the ludicrous sac projects in the throat region. The tip of the sac when not really inflated comes close to the tip of the chin. Otherwise it appears as a little, loose, vibrating sac ½ cm. out from the lower part of the throat. When the sac is deflated, the body inflates. When the body is compressed or deflated, the sac inflates.

**Breeding:** They breed from April 1 to September 5. It takes a heavy warm rain to start these little toads calling vigorously. The eggs are in bars of 2, 3, 4, 5, or 6, and the bars are from 1/12–¼ inch (2–7 mm.) long and 1/20 inch (1.3

mm.) wide. The eggs, black and white, $\frac{1}{25}$ inch (1 mm.) in diameter, are laid on the bottom of shallow pools. The small tadpole is grayish with six or seven black saddles on the musculature, and with heavily marked upper tail crest, and the venter is one mass of pale purplish vinaceous. They transform July 13 to August 16, at $\frac{1}{4}$–$\frac{5}{16}$ inch (7–8 mm.).

**Journal notes:** May 26, 1921, Billy's Island, Okefinokee Swamp. In pipewort, sedge, and grassy places at 10 A.M. found a female *Bufo quercicus*. We hear males in the woods. The calls are more lively and insistent. Is *B. quercicus* going to the ponds soon? We have taken four or five toads this morning. Females are about more since last night's thunderstorm. In a burnt-over area it seemed as if more were present. Possibly they are easier to find in this area. We found three males and three females. The males are not in holes.

June 4, Billy's Island, Okefinokee Swamp. About two inches of rain dropped, and the island seemed teeming with oak toads They bred almost everywhere. All about the cleared fields, in piney woods, in hammocks, and in numerous other places, we found oak toads that day. On July 3 the species was abroad in great numbers. Every transient shallow pool filled by the rain had them calling. We took three or four pairs and 30 to 40 males in short order.

On July 27, 1922, in a shallow pond, we heard so many oak toads we looked for eggs. We found single bars of two to six or eight eggs rarely attached to sticks at the surface, usually attached to grass blades 0.5 to 1 or 2 inches below the surface of the water, the water 1 to 3 inches deep. Other bars were attached to pine needles. Once in a while two bars extended out from a common focus Normally they were close together.

**Authorities' corner:**

J. E. Holbrook, Gen , 1842, p. 14.
E Loennberg, Fla., 1895, p. 338.
H. W. Fowler, Fla., 1906, p. 109
P. Viosca, Jr., La., 1923a, p. 37.
A. F. Carr, Fla., 1940b, p 54.

### Southern Toad, Carolina Toad, Gray Toad, Land-Frog (Bartram), Land-Toad (Catesby), Latreille's Toad, Charming Toad, Hop Toad

*Bufo terrestris* (Bonnaterre). Plate XLI; Map 9.

**Range:** North Carolina to Florida, west to the Mississippi River. We rather incline to the limitation of this form to the coast below the fall line. Are the isolated records (one, western South Carolina; one, northern Georgia; one, northern Mississippi; one, northern Louisiana; several, extreme western Louisiana) misidentifications or intermediates? S. N. Rhoads in southeastern and middle-central Tennessee calls his specimens intermediate.

**Habitat:** Abundant throughout its range, particularly common in cultivated fields. It occurs throughout the pine barrens and hammocks, in fact in any land habitat. When breeding, it is usually in shallow water from the tiny

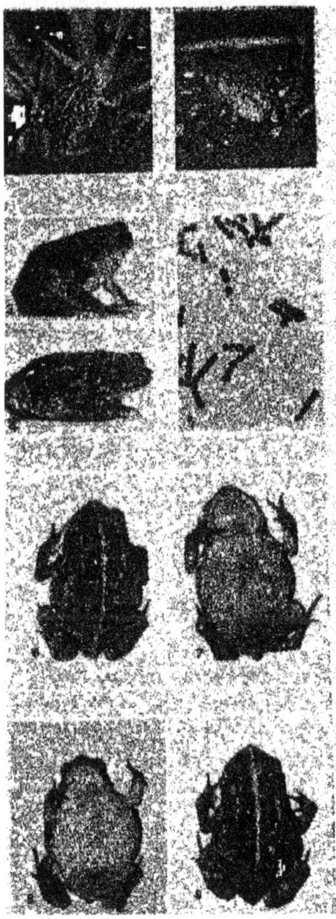

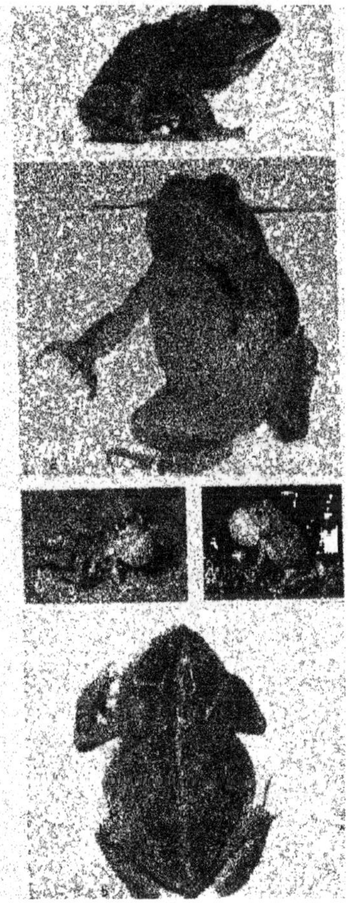

*Plate XL. Bufo quercicus.* 1,2. Males croaking (×¾) 3,8. Males (×1). 4,6,7,9. Females (×1). 5. Egg bars (×⅔).

*Plate XLI. Bufo terrestris.* 1. Mal (×⅗). 2. Male (×¾). 3,4. Males croak ing (×¼). 5. Female (×¾).

pool to the edges of lakes. Frequently these toads are in pools so transient that they can last but a few hours, as in the furrows in fields or in temporarily overflowed grassy areas. On one occasion their eggs were so plentiful in impermanent pools that we wrote (June 4): What a frightful waste of frog life in transient pools!

**Size:** Adults, 1⅝–3⅝ inches. Males, 42–82 mm. Females, 44–92 mm.

**General appearance:** These toads vary in color from red or gray to black. The crests on the head are prominently raised at the rear into clublike prominences or knobs. The skin between the larger warts is finely and uniformly roughened with tubercles all over, including the eyelids and parotoids.

**Color:** June 9, 1921, Okefinokee Swamp, Ga. *Male.* Line from front line of eyes almost to vent pale gull gray or mineral gray. Black spots along dorsum: one pair near cephalic edge of eye; one pair from upper eyelid connected across the meson; one in the middorsum between tympana; a pair either side of middle between the rear ends of tympana; a pair of small spots; a pair of large spots where hump comes; a pair of small spots; a pair just ahead of vent —all black spots of dorsum thinly encircled with chalcedony yellow. More or less broken pale gull gray or mineral gray line from tympanum to groin; below this a prominent black area. Tubercles of back black or deep brown tipped. Lighter areas on rear of hind legs sulphur yellow. Either side of vent a few orange tubercles Under parts pale smoke gray. Pectoral region, under parts of hind legs, and sides with black spots. Lower jaw rim like belly color. Throat deep mouse gray or dark mouse gray with widely spaced white dots, giving throat discolored appearance. Light area of dorsum of hind foot same color as the rear of thighs. Very little rusty on front of thighs and groin. Top of first two fingers with excrescences and slight line of such on edge of third finger. Color of excrescences chocolate, or better, Hay's maroon or maroon.

*Female* Lighter, larger. Practically no spots on pectoral region. None on throat. Throat same color as belly. Practically no rusty spots. Ground color of the dorsum more greenish olive Sometimes at breeding season males and females may be alike in color, e.g., on April 24, 1921, several were thus, several pairs reddish, one pair gray. Most of the pairs, however, were diverse.

**Structure:** Prominent knoblike crests; backs of thumb and second finger of male with excrescences, which are also on inner edge of the third finger; female throat usually light; male throat usually dark; pectoral region may be heavily spotted, sometimes only a median spot.

**Voice:** The note sounds much like our droning *Bufo americanus* of the North, not like the scream of *Bufo w. fowleri*. The trill is perhaps shorter than that of *B. americanus*. The trill lasts 7–9 seconds, with intervals of 4–60 seconds. It is musical in character. It has been described as a high trill, a drone, or even a bass roar, for when many are calling close to the observer, the sound is deafening. The choruses can be heard some distance away. Like other species, they may give weak notes; individuals may be freakish, hesitant, shrill, or even, rarely, open the mouth to scream, or with half-inflated throat give puzzling notes. Usually when croaking, the throat is distended to its full capacity with the body compressed. Then the body is distended and the throat collapsed.

The calling toads in cypress ponds and bays may be perched on a log, on a cypress knee, stub, or stump, at the base of a cypress or gum tree, on the moss, or resting on aquatic plant stems, leaves, or dead twigs, usually in shallow water or at the edge of a pond. In overflow pools they may be anywhere in shallow places. Rarely if ever do they float when croaking. This toad is truly an alert, pert animal.

**Breeding:** These toads breed from March 1, or earlier, to September. The eggs are in long coils of jelly, the egg 1/25–1/16 inch (1–1.4 mm.), the outer tube 1/10–3/16 inch (2.6–4.6 mm.), the inner tube 1/12–1/8 inch (2.2–3.4 mm.). The eggs, separated in the tube and with no partition apparent between them, number 2500–3000, and hatch in 2–4 days. In the small tadpole, 1 inch (26 mm.), the body is broader toward the rear, the tail crests are narrow, the tail is short and rounded, and the eyes are dorsal, close together; it is black in color. The tooth ridges are 2/3. After 30–55 days, the tadpoles transform from April to October, at 1/4–1/2 inch (6.5–11 mm.).

**Journal notes:** April 24, 1921, Okefinokee Swamp, Ga. At 9:15 A.M. *Bufo terrestris* were calling. Water 66°. Sun very bright. There were 15 pairs in an area 6 feet square. One pair, both male and female reddish. Male about 3/5 size of female. Male embraces female in axillary fashion, the last two fingers not dug into axil but resting on arm insertion of the female. When the pair are not laying, the male has the hind legs free and floating, but when the female ovulates several inches of egg string, the male brings his knees into the groin of the female and heels almost touch, the upper surface of hind feet against the underside of femur and near cloacal opening. Female with hind legs stretched back sometimes heels touching, sometimes not. The eggs rest in the cup made by heels and feet of male. The pair may remain in emission attitude 4 or 5 minutes or less. Then the female crawls 1 foot or more. A minute may elapse before another emission. By 11:30 A.M. surface of water was 81°.

May 2. One of the boys called this toad "charming toad," because "it charms you, turns your eyes right green."

June 8, 1930, 2 miles north of Mandeville, La. In the pine-barren parishes of eastern Louisiana, Viosca finds *Bufo terrestris;* the first one I espied in a mixed magnolia thicket was as intense a reddish brown as I have ever seen in a toad.

**Authorities' corner:**

J. E. Holbrook, Gen., 1842, 5, 9.
R. F. Deckert, Fla., 1914, p. 2.

## Nebulous Toad, Wiegmann's Toad, Mexican Toad

*Bufo valliceps* Wiegmann. Plate XLII; Map 13.

**Range:** Louisiana, eastern and south-central Texas to Mexico and Costa Rica.

**Habitat:** Lowlands in the West Gulf Coastal Plain of Louisiana, in the hills in northwestern Louisiana, in the pine lands of eastern Texas, and in open stretches of streams in central and southern Texas. Frequently found in railroad ditches or roadside pools.

**Size:** Adults, 2⅛–5 inches. Males, 53–98 mm. Females, 54–125 mm.

**General appearance:** This is a large brown toad, with a light streak down the middle of back from snout to vent, a light area over each parotoid extending diagonally backward to the groin. This light lateral area is bordered below with a fringe of white conical tubercles. The skin of back and venter is closely set with tubercles. There is a light line on the upper lip, continued beyond the rear of the angle of mouth by another row of light tubercles. The throat of the male is discolored—a citrine drab or water green.

**Color:** *Male.* Beeville, Tex., March 12, 1925. Parotoid and interparotoid area wood brown, fawn color, or cinnamon, changing to drab or buffy olive on interorbital and upper eyelid, face, and nasal area. Stripe down middle of back deep olive-buff, vinaceous-buff, or pale pinkish cinnamon. Stripes on either side the same color. Stripe on upper jaw tilleul buff or cartridge buff. Light spots on lower side the same color. Belly cartridge buff becoming from pectoral region rearward cream-buff, spotted with black. Dark bands on side and back brownish olive. The dark lateral band may be clove brown on side and olive-brown above. Two pairs of black spots on each side of dorsal stripe. Hind legs and forearms banded with deep olive, the interspaces wood brown or avellaneous. Front of chin cream-buff. Pectoral region pale vinaceous-fawn, rear chin discolored citrine-drab or water green. Iris pupil rim ivory yellow or pale green-yellow with a warm sepia line above it; iris largely tawny, ochraceous-orange, or lemon chrome; lower eyelid transparent with spinach or calla green rim; rest of lower eyelid with scattered spots of this green.

*Female.* The female has dorsal stripe and light areas pale olive-buff, while two males have them dark olive-buff. Top of head and parotoids grayish olive or light grayish olive. Upper parts olive or deep olive with little of brownish shades as in males. Under parts including throat deep olive-buff, cleaner on throat than on abdomen, where it is rather dirty in appearance.

April 2, 1925, Nueces River, Tex. Found a young *B. valliceps* under a log. It has about a dozen scattered, prominent, buff, yellow, or light cadmium spots on the back Very spotted under parts and particularly in midpectoral region

**Structure:** High projecting crests on crown of broad head; these are canthal, preorbital, supraorbital, postorbital, parietal, and orbitotympanic ridges; parotoids rather small, round, or triangular; snout obtuse; toes ½ webbed; interorbital space wide; internasal space narrow; upper eyelid much less than interorbital space; male with a subgular vocal sac not revealed by wrinkles on the throat; body flat; mouth large; excrescences on two fingers of male prominent.

**Voice:** The vocal sac is a large, round, subgular pouch. The call is louder, harsher, and lower in pitch than that of *Bufo americanus*. The croak lasts 3–4 seconds. Often the males take stands several feet up from the pond's edge.

March 24–26, Beeville. *Bufo valliceps* calling vigorously along roadside ditches, in streams and around tanks near windmills. Found no females or mated pairs. Night of March 25. *Bufo valliceps* males are hard to photograph at night. After all is set up, they usually move when the flashlight is taken off preparatory to the gun flash. What a time between the moving toads and the frequent cars! This was a roadside pool.

March 28, San Diego-Alice, Tex. By railroad and creek bridge heard *Bufo valliceps*. At first thought it was a toad much like our *B. americanus*. It sounded something like it at a distance, and not harsh as it is when near by.

**Breeding:** This species breeds from March to August. The eggs are often in double rows in long strings of jelly with the wall of the inner tube close to the outer. This jelly grows looser with age, so that there may be a double row of 25 to 27 eggs in 1⅕ inches (3 cm.) or a single row of 7 to 10 eggs in 1⅕ inches (3 cm.). The outer tube is ⅛ inch (3 mm.), the inner tube ⅒ inch (2.6 mm.), and the vitellus ⁄20 inch (1.2 mm.). The eggs are purplish black and hatch in 1½–2 days. The small blackish tadpole has 8–10 black bars with intervening pale buff areas on the dorsum of the tail musculature. The tooth ridges are ⅔. After 20–30 days, the tadpoles transform, April to September, at 5⁄16–½ inch (7.5–12 mm.). The season varies with the periods of heavy local rainfall from March–August. Pope found a female ready to spawn as late as August 25 in Houston, Tex.

May 10, 1925, Helotes, Tex. Captive pair laid eggs. Egg strings. Some of the eggs seem to be in double rows in string; other parts of same string may be with single rows. There are many single eggs or eggs without string effect.

May 13, Helotes. Went to Marnock's Second Crossing. Found *B. valliceps* egg strings widely spread out. These were long strings in midwater and buoyant in midplane They were more above the bottom than eggs of any toad I have seen. One bow of two strings, 3 feet long, was attached only at ends. These eggs covered an area of 6 or 4½ feet square. They seem to be the complement of one female.

June 16, 1930, San Benito, Tex. Among the *Hypopachus cuneus* disgorged from *Thamnophis sauritus proximus* were several transformed *Bufo valliceps*, 9, 10, 10, 10, 10.5, 11, 11, 11.5, 12 mm. Around edges of pond were many more but most were away from edges as were some larger ones (16, 19, 19 mm.).

**Journal notes:** April 2, 1925, Cotulla Free Camp Ground. Here in an over-

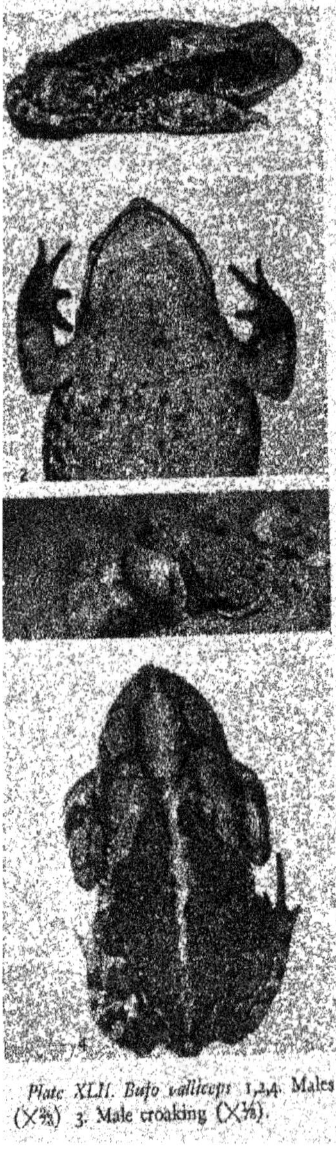

*Plate XLII. Bufo valliceps* 1,2,4. Males (×⅔) 3. Male croaking (×⅓).

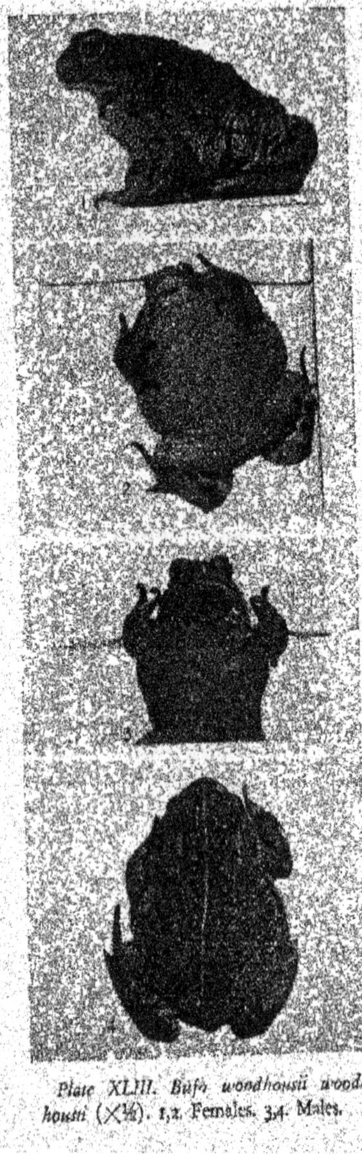

*Plate XLIII. Bufo woodhousii woodhousii* (×½). 1,2. Females. 3,4. Males.

flow cove of Nueces River where water purslane grew were several male *Bufo valliceps*. Saw a female near the shore but was going away when we saw her. Possibly our light was responsible. Some 10 or 15 males were calling vigorously.

April 22, San Benito, Tex. Pond in a mesquite region. On the east side of this beautiful blue water-lily pond we found *B. valliceps* on the moist earth, transforming. Soon after transformation the toads show the light line of tubercles on the side and the white spot below the eye. They do not show the furrowed interorbital at this small size.

May 6, Helotes, Tex. Tonight at 9 P.M., as we approached the pond, we espied a small head of *Thamnophis proxima*. A few moments later two larger water snakes were close together. They were after a near-by croaking toad. A little farther on we heard two male *B. valliceps*. Presently we saw something rolling over and over in the water. It was a water snake. In the semidarkness I scooped up the snake and all. The snake dropped a toad. The toad hopped limply away. Farther on we found a young *Natrix rhombifera* beside another pair.

June 16–20, 1930, Brownsville. All along the river in its high state heard *B. valliceps* at night. It is the amphibian note of the river, as is *S. campi* of the dooryards.

**Authorities' corner:**

P. H. Pope, Tex., 1919, pp. 94–95.

### Rocky Mountain Toad, Woodhouse's Toad, American Toad

*Bufo woodhousii woodhousii* Girard. Plate XLIII; Map 14.

**Range:** Southeastern Oregon through Idaho, Montana, South Dakota, to western Iowa and western Missouri, south through Kansas, Oklahoma, and Texas to Mexico, west to Imperial Valley and up Colorado Valley to southeast Nevada and through Utah to Idaho.

**Habitat:** This toad lives in canyons in mountains and on plains along irrigating ditches. It is also found along rivers and in swamps. In fact its habitat is very diverse, being any place where sufficient moisture obtains.

"The habitat of *Bufo woodhousii* is by no means restricted to mountainous regions, but includes surroundings as diverse as the sagebrush flats of eastern Montana, the prairie fields among the chalk cliffs of western Kansas, the Hudsonian Zone mountain sides of eastern Colorado, the irrigation ditches that traverse the mesquite plains of New Mexico, and the bottomlands along the Colorado River near Yuma, Arizona. During May and June, according to locality, adults of this species may be found breeding in shallow sluggish creeks, in irrigation ditches, or in freshwater pools in the canyons" (R. Kellogg, Gen., 1932, p. 74).

**Size:** Adults, 2¼–4¾ inches. Males, 56–99 mm. Females, 58.5–118 mm.

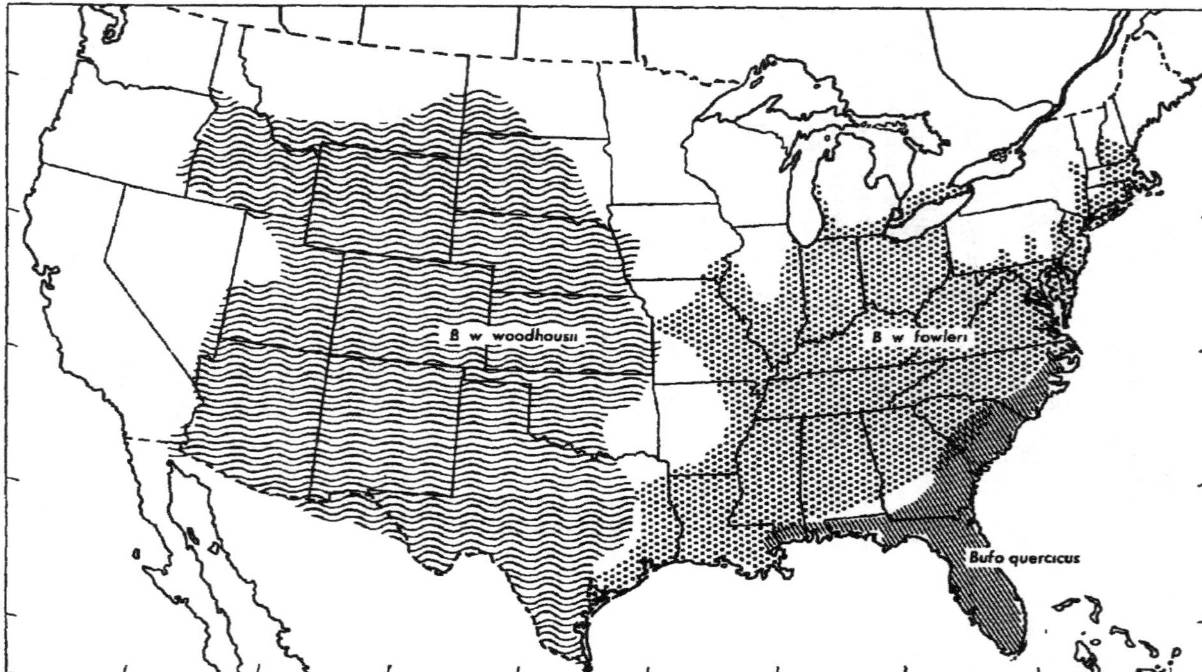


*Map 14*

**General appearance:** This toad looks much like our eastern *Bufo a americanus* but is larger. The general color is grayish drab on the back, with several large brownish warts that are usually surrounded by a slightly larger blackish area. There is a narrow, light middorsal stripe. The sides are marked with several black spots. The crests on the head are dark in color, but not particularly conspicuous. The tubercles and tips of fingers and toes are reddish brown. The head is short and thick.

H. M. Smith (Kans., 1934, p. 450), who has given us our best account of this species, contrasts this form with *Bufo a. americanus.*

| *a. americanus* | *w. woodhousii* |
|---|---|
| 1. Warts on body larger, less numerous. | 1. Warts on body smaller, more numerous. |
| 2. Usually but one or two warts to a dark color spot. | 2. Some of dorsal spots including many warts (eastern specimens), or but one or two (western specimens). |
| 3. Skin on median anterior surface of tarsi and metatarsi with blackish spines. | 3. Skin on median anterior surface of tarsi and metatarsi without blackish spines. |
| 4. Parotoids broad and closely approximated, not separated by more than their own length. | 4 Parotoids narrow, although not so long, and separated frequently by more than their own length. |
| 5. Cranial crests never swollen to form a "plateau." | 5. Cranial crests frequently swollen forming a "plateau." |
| 6. Snouts of males in lateral profile pointed to some extent. | 6. Snouts of both males and females sharply truncate in lateral profile |
| 7. Belly usually profusely spotted. | 7. Belly usually immaculate or with a single median dark breast spot. |
| 8. Song a high trill of long duration —20–30 seconds or so. | 8. Song a low trill of 3–4 seconds or so. |
| 9. Eggs laid single file, enclosed in a double tubular membrane, with a partition between each egg. | 9. No partitions between eggs; but a single tubular membrane. |
| 10. A median dorsal light line rarely present; when present very irregular. | 10. A median dorsal light line always present. |
| 11. Parotoids usually separated from postorbital ridge; the latter, either directly or by a secondary arm, in contact with the tympanum. | 11. Parotoids usually in contact with the postorbital ridge, the tympanum separated distinctly from the latter. |
| 12. Second subarticular tubercle of fourth toe frequently divided; first but seldom not divided. | 12. Second subarticular tubercle apparently never divided; first but seldom. |

**Color:** *Female.* Ephraim, Utah, Aug. 19, 1929. Back light grayish olive becoming on sides and fore and hind legs tea green. Tympanum pea green, parotoid vetiver green or light grayish olive. Crests clove brown or fuscous. Spots on upper parts are fuscous, becoming on sides dark ivy green or dull greenish black. No very regular spots on either side of back. Each fuscous spot on dorsum wart centered, the wart being drab or hair brown. On sides spotting more pronounced. Forearm with at least two oblique crossbars. Tibia with two or three indistinct crossbars. Under parts deep olive-buff or cream-buff. Underside of hind legs pinkish cinnamon. Iris fuscous spotted with vinaceous-cinnamon or pinkish cinnamon and sulphur yellow or marguerite yellow; pupil rim broken behind and in front, marguerite yellow.

Ephraim, Utah, Sept. 6, 1929. *Female.* Throat cream color or pale chalcedony yellow becoming warm buff on breast, cinnamon-buff on belly, and clay color on lower side of femur and lower belly. Underside of hind legs reed yellow. Underside of forelegs like breast. Upper parts mineral gray or smoke gray becoming on fore limbs, side of face, and hind legs tea green or light grayish olive to grayish olive. Spots on sides most prominent with grayish olive or vetiver green dots in them. Spots on dorsum small and warts not large. Line down back faint, white for front half. Eye black; pupil rim sulphur yellow or light vinaceous-fawn, upper eye with prominent band of vinaceous-buff. Inner metatarsal black or clove brown.

"San Francisco Mts. From fresh specimens: Above pale olive-green with a somewhat lighter stripe down the middle of the back; tip of tubercles pale red surrounded by black rings; lower surface olive-white" (L. Stejneger, Ariz., 1890, p. 116).

**Structure:** Cranial crests, prominent, forming right angle back of orbit; longitudinal ridges almost parallel; supratympanic or preparotoid ridge absent; parotoid glands long, slender, divergent; interparotoid space more than twice the interorbital space; two metatarsal tubercles, one very large, one very small; throat of male black from line of angle of mouth forward; first finger slightly longer than second; large warts on back, each with several pits; this toad is larger than *B. americanus.*

**Voice:** The vocal sac is a rounded throat pouch. The call is a vibrating note of high pitch, sweet and musical.

**Breeding:** This toad breeds from March to July. "The eggs . . . very closely resemble those of *fowleri.* The inner membrane is absent, there being but a single tube, about 3.5 mm. in diameter. The egg complement of a single female which laid in captivity was 25,644 by actual count" (H. M. Smith, Kans., 1934, p. 452). They transform March 25 to September at $\frac{2}{5}$–$\frac{3}{5}$ inch (10–13.5 mm.).

On May 19, 1942, at Beaver Dam Lodge, Ariz., we took about 6 adults and about 23 transformed and transforming specimens. These last varied from 13.5–17 mm. in length, with a mean and also average of 15 mm.

**Journal notes:** July 24, 1925. At Duncan, Ariz., the engineer at the electric light plant told me of several "big" toads at the plant. We went over. They were all female *Bufo woodhousii*. He said they would hop up on the doorsill and wait for insects to drop from the wall below the light. Why are they all females? Have the males gone to ponds since the recent rains? All these females are ripe, not spent.

May 20, Beaver Dam Lodge, Littlefield, Ariz. Went down to the creek. Everywhere toad tadpoles of one sort. Never saw so many. Thousands. In the ditches and in the stream countless tadpoles, large for toad tadpoles. At first I thought I had *Rana* or *Scaphiopus* tads. Many of these tads were transforming or transformed. They would take to the stream, and the toadlets had a hard time stemming the current. We would go along the bank and cause them to jump in, and then we scooped them with the net The tadpoles were in the clear drainage ditches, in the big pond in the creek. Here on the algae, not quite emergent, the tadpoles assembled in great numbers. On the algae mats that were solid the toadlets could leap along in fine shape. Went out in fields next to the creek and caught ten *Bufo woodhousii*. Tonight at 9 o'clock went to the bridge and could hear plenty of *Bufo woodhousii*. It is a light trill, not feeble but sweet, of the quality of the *Bufo americanus* call. They are not in chorus. Individual calls not far-carrying. In the closed bag the note of *woodhousii* is a friendly chuckle.

July 2. Went up Ramsay Canyon, Ariz. Went to Newmans. Here we saw *B. woodhousii* leaping along in the bright sun of midday. It was a scrawny individual.

July 16, below Albuquerque. Last night at camp a *Bufo woodhousii* feeding around our car.

**Authorities' corner:**

W. P. Taylor, Nev., 1912, pp. 344–345.
J. M. Linsdale, Kans., 1927, pp. 75–76.
G. A Moore and C. C. Rigney, Okla., 1942, p. 78.
J. C. Marr, Gen., 1944, p. 480.

## Fowler's Toad, Danver's Toad

*Bufo woodhousii fowleri* (Hinckley). Plate XLIV; Map 14.

**Range:** New Hampshire to eastern Texas, eastern Arkansas, Missouri, southeastern Iowa, eastward in Michigan through Ohio, West Virginia to coast. Extensions up Hudson, Delaware, Susquehanna, Ohio, and other rivers. Many such Pennsylvania and New York records. Often where *B. a. americanus* and *B. w. fowleri* are co-existent *B. w. fowleri* is of the river, stream banks, or lake beaches; *B. a. americanus* of the hilly or mountainous regions near by. Except for the Northeast our range closely accords with Blair's range. Intermediates or misidentifications with *B. a. americanus, B. terrestris,* and *B. w. woodhousii* make its range difficult to determine at this date.

**Habitat:** Beaches, coasts, lake shores, or river banks, which are the more sandy and warmer places throughout its range, are the usual choice. It is common along roadsides, about homes, in fields, pastures, and gardens, in sand dunes and pine barrens. It breeds in the shallow water of permanent ponds, in flooded low ground or roadside ditches, or along river shores.

**Size:** Adults, 2–3¼ inches. Males, 51–74.5 mm. Females, 56–82 mm.

**General appearance:** These toads generally have a greenish cast with a yellowish or buff middorsal stripe. The back is marked by distinct black-edged dark spots. In a pair, the male *Bufo fowleri* is usually darker than the female. Live toads sent us from Virginia we described as follows: These are small toads with low crests. One is dull greenish in color and one reddish brown, each with a light middorsal line. The warts are small and rounded, with several grouped in each dark spot of the dorsal pattern. The parotoids are elliptic and nearest together at their midpoints. The ventral surfaces are buffy. The throats of the male are greenish black. One toad has the black pectoral spot, another one lacks it. Both toads have dark bands along the sides. One has much yellow in groin, on rear of the femur, and on tibia and tarsus.

**Color:** Lakewood, N.J., from W. H. Caulwell, May 9, 1930. *Male.* General appearance "dark greenish." Dorsal color citrine drab, parotoids buffy brown, drab, or wood brown. Top of hind legs and forelegs like dorsum or deep olive. Rear of femur, lower half, dark olive or black Rear of unexposed femur with pinard yellow or straw yellow. Spots larger and most conspicuous on rear edge of tibia between bars. Groin with some barium yellow or deeper yellow spots. Oblique bar on upper eyelids meeting or not on meson. Spot just inside of forward end of parotoid, pair of spots midway near meson, larger pair near rear end. Last two pairs sometimes united on either side. Pair of big spots near meson in middle of back. Other pairs frequently present. These spots, two bars on tibia and one on femur, and bars on arm are olive or dark olive. Several warts to each spot drab or light grayish olive. Dark spot on lower rear of parotoid connected or not with irregular lateral band of dark grayish olive or olive. Oblique dark spot from over tympanum to arm insertion. Side spotted or with dark lateral band mentioned above. Area above band and dorsal streaks cartridge buff, ecru-olive, olive-buff, cream-buff, or picric yellow. Eye to angle of jaw spot like dorsal ones. Under parts white. Pectoral spot of olive or black. Throat deep grayish olive or dark grayish olive Iris rim reed yellow or straw yellow, iris black spotted with light ochraceous-salmon, or rufous.

*Female.* Dorsal color light grayish olive. Parotoids drab. Bars on eyelids and dorsal spots olivaceous black (1) with warts fawn color, army brown, or orange-cinnamon ("reddish"). Dorsal streak cartridge buff or pale pinkish buff. Light area along side cream-buff or cartridge buff. Warts on hind legs reddish in this individual. Belly cream-buff. Black pectoral spot. Throat like rest of under parts.

**Structure:** Crests variable, at times forming a boss; adults never reaching the greater size of *B. a. americanus;* warts on back small and uniform; no preparotoid ridge from parotoid to postorbital.

**Voice:** "The usual note of Fowler's toad is a brief, penetrating, droning scream. Only once have I heard a decided departure from this. I heard this note late in April in Gwinnett Co., in upper Georgia. A single individual of a noisy congregation of males had the unmistakable trill of the common toad, but short and decisive like the Fowler's song. It was a perfect combination of the notes of both" (H. A. Allard, Ga., 1908, pp. 655–656).

"While we do not agree with Mr. Allard in calling the song of Fowler's toad a 'scream' or 'wail,' it certainly has much less music to it than the trill of the American toad. The notes are more closely connected, so that a sort of buzzing is produced" (W. DeW. Miller and J Chapin, N.J., 1910, p. 316).

"A male toad is a persistent singer during its stay in the water. Its song is a combination of a low whistle and a moan, and the two sounds do not melt into a chord. The combined sound is discordant and decidedly unpleasant to a musical ear, but at a distance the sound is more pleasant, for the moan is not apparent and only the whistle is heard. The sound lasts from two to three seconds, and may be repeated at intervals of about ten seconds. In 1911 many sang in the daytime, but in 1912 and 1913 very few were heard except at night" (F. Overton, N.Y., 1914, p. 27).

"One of the most striking differences between the two species lies in their voices. While that of the Common Toad is high-pitched and musical, the note of Fowler's Toad is nasal, and lower in pitch. Like the voice of the Common Toad, it carries well and may be heard at a considerable distance" (K. P. Schmidt, Ill., 1929, p. 9).

**Breeding:** This form breeds from April 15 or earlier to mid-August. In a given locality it breeds later than the American toad. The eggs are in long files, crowded at first in a double row, and numbering as many as 8000. The egg is 1/25–1/16 inch (1.0–1.4 mm.), the outer tube 1/10–3/16 inch (2.6–4.6 mm.), the inner tube absent. The tadpole is small, 1 1/12 inches (27 mm.), its greatest width toward the rear of the body. The tail crests are low, the tooth ridges 2/3. After 40 to 60 days, the tadpoles transform from mid-June to August or later at 5/16–1/2 inch (7.5–11.5 mm.).

"The egg strings, which resemble those of the American toad except that the gelatinous tube shows no distinct inner layer nor partitions separating the eggs, have been noted in Ohio as early as May and as late as June 24" (C. F. Walker, Ohio, 1946, p. 35).

Notes by S. C. Bishop and Walter Schoonmaker: "The eggs of the Fowler's toad, *Bufo fowleri* (Garman), are laid later than the American toad, *Bufo americanus* (Holbrook). We collected some of the eggs of the Fowler's toad on the 13th of May, 1924, at Raft's Pond, near Albany, New York. From these we made the following observations. The eggs of the Fowler's toad, unlike the American toad, are sometimes laid in the double string.

"May 14. The eggs were segmented. Later they became elongated.

"May 15. Hatched. The tadpoles were hanging on by their suckerlike mouth parts, tails down.

"May 16. Grown considerably larger.

"May 17. Length 7 mm. Gills present.

"May 18, 11:30 A.M. Actual length 8.5 mm. Gills larger.

"May 19, 9:55 A.M. Length 10.5 mm. Gills gone from both sides. Mouth parts developed.

"May 20 Length 11.5 mm.

"May 21. Length 12.5 mm.

"May 26. Length 14 mm.

"June 12. Length 20.5 mm. Hind legs present.

"June 16. Length 21 mm. Hind legs very well developed

"June 20. Length 21 mm.

"June 24. Length 21 mm. Hind legs well developed. Front legs also developed. Shape of body changed greatly, also smaller. Tail beginning to shorten.

"June 28. Tail nearly gone in some specimens and in others the tail is entirely gone. Some specimens grow faster than others. The young now look like the adult.

"On May 19, 1924, at the pond more eggs were laid, embryos elongated May 21st, and hatching May 22nd, and July 1–2, little toads leaving ponds. Males began calling May 13, heard May 19, noted calling at intervals until July 2."

The pair brought to the authors were near the maximum sizes for the species, the male being 70 mm. and the female 80 mm. in body length.

**Journal notes:** June 1, 1917. About 6 miles beyond Dinwiddie, Va., near the road, found several files of toad's eggs. In one case the string was strung out in a file 8 or 10 feet long in the current. In another case, in a backwater, the mass was tangled around sticks. In most cases the file seems to contain a double row of eggs. The note we questioned yesterday evening was *Bufo fowleri*. It is quite different from the sweet droning note of *Bufo americanus*. Went out at night with a flashlight and captured many *B. fowleri* and a few mated pairs. One pair laid in the fish can overnight. The embrace is axillary.

April 15, 1921. Air temperature 68°F. Tonight at 9 o'clock, Drs. Vernon and Julia Haber took me out to the Oakwood Cemetery, East Raleigh, N.C., and to St. Augustine grounds. Just beyond, we heard a chorus of what I at first mistook for the "bleat" of *Microhyla carolinensis*. It surely is not the note of our northern *Bufo americanus*, which is a sweeter drone than that of *B. fowleri*. In shallow water along a little drain were plenty of them. The call is a striking nasal whir-r-r-r. The Habers say "like a lamb."

April 15, Raleigh, N.C. Fowler's toads were still in chorus and strongly breeding, though started much earlier. The male of the mated pair has the first two fingers doubled back and dug into the axils of the female. Often the other two fingers may not be doubled back but lie next to the belly of the female, or sometimes these two fingers will rest on the shoulder insertion with only the first two in the axil proper. The pairs brought in were not laying at 3 A.M. but at 6:45 A.M. they were well along in oviposition. Water temperature at which they were laying is 67°F.

April 16, St. Augustine grounds, Raleigh, N.C. In the stream near the edge found Fowler's toad eggs wrapped around plants. They were in shallow turbid areas, cattle-punched, and in water 2 to 4 inches deep; many were laid last night. They were among speedwell, chickweed, smartweed, marshy St.-John's-wort, and other plants, hardly any of which were more than 3 or 4 inches high at this season.

June 11, 1930, Tickfaw River country, La. At night found *Bufo valliceps* and *Bufo fowleri* in same woods. Found and heard *B. fowleri* in ditches. This form is *Bufo fowleri* in voice and structural characters; in some ways not typical in color. Viosca says that *Bufo valliceps* and *Bufo fowleri* may possibly interbreed in Louisiana.

**Authorities' corner:** Much printer's ink has been employed on the differences between *B. w. fowleri* and *Bufo a. americanus.* No one has known the form more intimately than W. DeWitt Miller. Two authors who helped clarify the differential characters are G. S. Myers (Ind., 1927, pp. 50–53) and M. G. Netting (Gen., 1930, pp. 437–443). At the same time, 1927–1930, we independently assembled these characters in manuscript (15 pp.). We regret that space necessitates the elimination of this material, but we include references on the points of discussion.

## READING REFERENCES TO 1930

1. Voice
   a. S. Garman, Check List, 1884, p. 42.
   b. F. Overton, N.Y., 1914, p. 27.
   c. M. Brady, Va., 1927, p. 27.
   d. Almost every author on the species.
2. Crests
   a. S. Garman, C.L., 1884, p. 42.
   b. E. D. Cope, Gen., 1889, pp. 278, 279.
   c. M. C. Dickerson, Gen., 1906, p. 97.
   d. R. F. Deckert, Gen., 1917, p. 114.
   e. E. R. Dunn, N.C., 1917, p. 621.
   f. M. G. Netting, Gen., 1930, p. 439.
3. Size
   a. S. Garman, see above.
   b. O. P. Hay, Ind., 1892, p. 458.
   c. W. DeW. Miller and J. Chapin, N.J., 1910, p. 458.
   d. E. R. Dunn, N.C., 1917, p. 621.
   e. M. Brady, Va., 1927, p. 27.
4. Head
   a. E. D. Cope, Gen., 1889, p. 278.
   b. A. G. Ruthven, Mich., 1917, p. 4.
5. Length of leg
   a. O. P. Hay, Ind., 1892, pp. 458–459.
   b. R. F. Deckert, Gen., 1917, p. 114.
   c. A. G. Ruthven, see above.
   d. W. DeW. Miller and J. Chapin, N.J., 1910, p. 316.

e. M G. Netting, Gen , 1930, p. 438.

6. Color
   a. O. P Hay, Ind , 1892, p. 458.
   b. M. C. Dickerson, Gen., 1906, p. 96
   c. W. DeW. Miller and J Chapin, N.J., 1910, p. 316.
   d. R. F. Deckert, Gen., 1917, pp. 113, 114
   e. E. B. S Logier, Ont., 1925, p. 94.
   f. G. I. Myers, Ind , 1927b, pp. 51, 52.
   g. K. P. Schmidt, Ill., 1929, pp 8–9
   h. Many more writers.
7 Vertebral line
   a. O P. Hay, Ind., 1892, p. 458.
   b M G. Netting, 1930, p. 441.
8. Dorsal pattern
   a. M. C. Dickerson, Gen., 1906, p. 96
   b. G. S. Myers, Ind., 1927b, pp. 51–52.
9. Under parts
   a. M. C Dickerson, Gen., 1906, p 96.
   b. H A. Allard, Ga , 1907, p. 381
   c. W. DeW. Miller and J Chapin, N.J , 1910, p. 316.
   d. E. R Dunn, N C , 1917, p 622.
   e. G S Myers, Ind., 1927b, p 52.
   f. M. G. Netting, Gen , 1930, p. 441.
10 Iris
   a. W. DeW. Miller and J Chapin, N.J., 1910, p. 316.
   b A. G. Ruthven, Mich , 1917, p. 4.
   c. G. S. Myers, Ind., 1927b, pp. 51–52.
11. Warts
   a. M. C. Dickerson, Gen., 1906, p 97.
   b. H. A. Allard, Ga., 1907, p. 304.
   c. W DeW. Miller and J Chapin, N.J., 1910, p. 317
   d. E. R. Dunn, N.C., 1917, p. 621.
   e. R. F. Deckert, Gen , 1917, p. 114.
   f. G. S. Myers, Ind , 1927b, p. 51.
   g. K. P. Schmidt, Ill., 1929, p. 9.

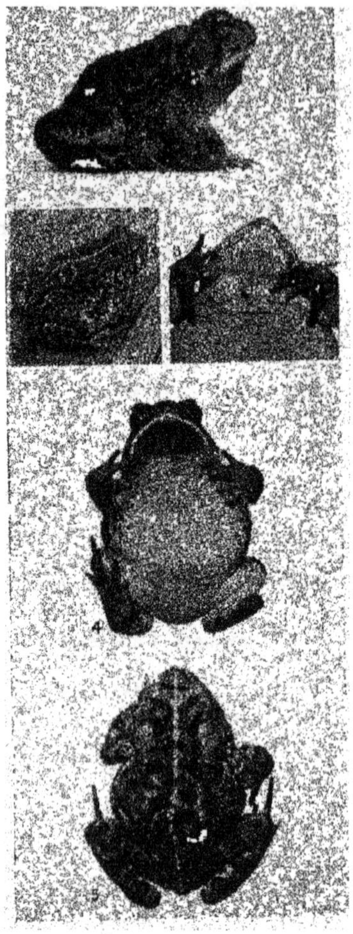

*Plate XLIV. Bufo woodhousii fowleri.* 1,4,5 Males (×⅔). 2. Adult (×⅓) 3. Female (×⅝).

h. M. G. Netting, Gen., 1930, p. 440.

12. Muzzle
    a. M. C. Dickerson, Gen., 1906, p. 96.
    b. R. F. Deckert, Gen., 1917, p 114.
    c. E. R. Dunn, N.C., 1917, p. 621.
    d. M. G. Netting, Gen., 1930, p. 440.
13. Parotoids
    a. M. C. Dickerson, Gen , 1906, pp. 96, 97.
    b. A. G. Ruthven, Mich., 1917, p. 1.
    c. E. R. Dunn, N C., 1917, p. 621.
    d. K. P. Schmidt, Ill., 1929, p. 9.
14. Shape
    a. H. A. Allard, Ga., 1907, p. 384.
15. Odor
    a. W DeW. Miller and J. Chapin, N J., 1910, p. 316.
16. Breeding season
    a. All authors agree the breeding season is 2–4 weeks later than in *Bufo a. americanus.*
17. Eggs
18. Palettes
    a. M. G. Netting, Gen., 1930, pp. 439, 440.
19. Range
    a. K. P. Schmidt, La., 1920, p. 85.
    b. G. S. Myers, Ind., 1927b, pp. 51, 52.
    c. Many more writers.
20. Bars on hind legs
    a. M. G. Netting, Gen , 1930, p. 441.
21. Supra-anal warts
    a. M. G. Netting, Gen., 1930, p. 441.
22. Hybridization
    a. W. DeW. Miller and J. Chapin, N.J., 1910, p. 317.
    b. C. L. Hubbs, Ill., 1918, p. 43.
    c. A. L. Pickens, S.C., 1927a, pp. 25, 26.
    d. A. L. Pickens, S.C., 1927b, p. 109.
    e. M. G. Netting, Gen., 1930, p 442.

For five recent papers on *B. w. fowleri,* see A. P. Blair (Gen., 1943a), M. G. Netting and C. J. Goin (Fla., 1945), C. F. Walker (Ohio, 1946), R. A. Littleford (Md. 1946), and A. P. Blair (N.J., 1947).

## FAMILY HYLIDAE

### Genus *ACRIS* Duméril and Bibron

Map 15

**Cricket Frog, Savannah Cricket, Cricket Hylodes, Peeper, Southeastern Cricket Frog, Cricket Hyla, Sphagnum Cricket Frog, Coastal Cricket Frog**

*Acris gryllus gryllus* (Le Conte). Plate XLV; Map 15.

**Range:** Dunn (Gen., 1939, pp. 153–154) gives southeastern Virginia (Norfolk) to Florida to parishes of Louisiana.

**Habitat:** Terrestrial, shade-loving frog. In meadows or about creeks or ponds in the open vegetation mats or wooded edges.

"All in the region of coastal sphagnum swamps" (C. S. Brimley, N.C., 1940, p. 15).

"The most abundant amphibian of the region and the only one which could be taken during every month of the year. Each roadside pool or ditch contained numerous individuals and the swamps and marshes literally swarmed with them. In the short winter season, here lasting from about the middle of December till the first week or two in February, Cricket Frogs were much less in evidence than at other times, and as collecting is then at its easiest it is clear that the majority hibernate. But even on the coldest winter days no difficulty attends the capture of a plentiful supply, which thus provides a dependable source of food for many of the snakes kept in laboratory cages throughout the year. Sporadically met with in the piedmont" (J. D. Corrington, S.C., 1929, p. 65).

"Almost any aquatic situation; commonest in marshes and ditches with shallow margins choked with hydrophytes" (A. F. Carr, Jr., Fla., 1940b, p. 55).

**Size:** Adults, ⅝–1⅓ inches. Males, 15–29 mm. Females, 16–33 mm.

**General appearance:** This is a small tree frog, but it looks like a small true frog (*Rana*). It varies in color, black, dark brown, reddish brown, light brown, green, or gray; or the markings may be reddish on a green ground. Between the eyes there is usually a dark triangle, white-bordered behind. This species possesses rear femoral stripes, oblique bars on the sides, light spots on the jaw, and an oblique white stripe from the eye to the arm. The skin is more or less tubercular.

"Much like the preceding [*A. g. crepitans*], but the head is longer and more pointed, the dark triangle between the eyes is longer and more acute behind; the edge of the upper jaw is dark with three or four light vertical bars or spots on each side and the dark stripe on the back of the thigh is darker and more constant. Slightly smaller and slimmer than the common cricket frog. This species averages darker and smaller than the preceding, the darker color probably owing to the darker soil of the region it inhabits, and I have seen but few wholly green specimens. In habits it is similar, being quite as

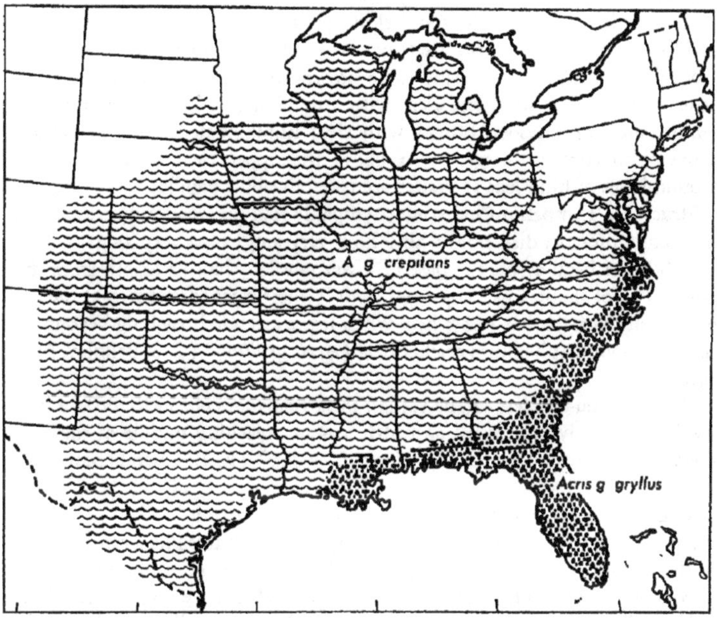


*Map 15*

active if not more so. Both species occur in both shady and sunny situations. By Cope this was considered a more Southern race of the preceding, but most authors have recognized it as merely an individual variation. Dr. Percy Viosca, Jr., however, seems to have shown fairly conclusively that they are two distinct species and I agree with him. Dunn (1939) says the difference in the amount of the webbing on the hind feet is the best criterion by which to separate the two, and I find in looking over some fifty specimens in the State Museum, about evenly divided between the two forms, that a glance at the first or shortest toe is usually sufficient to distinguish either; if the webbing extends to the tip, the frog is *crepitans,* if the last joint is free from web it is *gryllus*" (C. S. Brimley, N.C., 1940, p. 15).

**Color:** On one day, April 23, 1921, in Georgia, I saw black, dark brown, reddish brown, light brown, green, and gray specimens of *Acris*.

Okefinokee Swamp, Ga., June 25, 1921. *Male*. Stripe down back and around triangle dark olive-buff. Throat raw sienna. All over the throat are collections of dark dots, sometimes arranged in a reticulate fashion. Iris pale vinaceous-drab on black, light orange-yellow pupil rim.

*Female*. Clove brown above; triangular spot between eyes obscured by this dark color; throat, breast, and belly pale olive-buff; more or less of same color on underside of forelegs, the spot below eye, along the upper and lower jaw, and the line from eye to arm insertion; area back of arm insertion pallid vinaceous-drab; oblique bar on side clove brown with pale olive-buff and olive-ocher; underside of hind legs clear with little pigment; long stripe on rear of femur, snuff or Dresden brown with clear unpigmented stripe below and above; also another brown stripe above the upper clear area; from vent around bases of hind legs to venter are pale olive-buff papillae.

**Structure:** Tympanum indistinct; tympanic fold present; fold across breast frequently present; disk small; hind limb very long; tibia very long.

"Width of head across the base of lower jaw less than its length from that point to tip of snout, legs longer and hind feet less webbed, the web of the first toe absent from the last joint; heel when leg is extended reaching beyond the tip of the snout. Sphagnum cricket frog (*Acris gryllus*)" (C. S. Brimley, N.C., 1940, p. 15).

"Webbing on toes less extensive; last three phalanges of fourth toe free from webbing; usually with third and fifth toes not reaching middle of the third phalanx from tip of fourth toe. *Acris g. gryllus*" (E. B. Chamberlain, S.C., 1939, p. 12).

**Voice:** Characterizations of the *Acris* call are numerous.

April 16, 1921, at Raleigh, N.C. *Acris gryllus* call sounds like a rattle or some of the metal clickers, *gick, gick, gick*, or *kick, kick, kick*, in rapid succession. Frequently one finds the males with inflated vocal sacs even when not calling. When calling, the throat is never fully deflated. After a call it may be swollen to three-quarters its full capacity. Then when the call is given, the body sides are compressed and the vocal sac is extended to its limit.

Holbrook (Gen., 1842, IV, 132) wrote, "This is a merry little frog, constantly chirping like a cricket, even in confinement. . . ." Of his captives he said, "Their chirp, at times, was incessant and sprinkling them with water never failed to render them more lively and noisy."

"Call an irregular series of iiks; comparable to sound made by scratching teeth of a comb; somewhat cricket-like; ik-ik, ii-ik, ii-ik" (A. F. Carr, Jr., Fla., 1934, p. 21).

**Breeding:** This species breeds from February to October. The single eggs are few (250), are brownish and white, and are attached to stems of grass in shallow water or are strewn on the bottom. The egg, 1/25 inch (0.9–1.0 mm.), has a single envelope 1/10–1/8 inch (2.4–3.6 mm.). The dark olive tadpole is medium, 1 11/16 inches (42 mm.), full and deep-bodied, its tail long with acuminate tip and with a black flagellum. The tooth ridges are 2/2. After 50 to 90 days or longer, the tadpoles transform from April to October at 2/5–3/5 inch (9–15 mm.).

June 1, 1917, at Dinwiddie, Va., we found this species breeding. They had chosen a shallow grassy meadow pool 1 to 4 inches deep. The eggs were attached singly to sedge stems or were strewn singly on the bottom. In one or two cases, three or four eggs were close together. Many of the eggs were in water not more than an inch deep. The eggs are firm. We found no more than ten eggs.

"Calling was earliest heard on January 22. This increased to the proportions of a chorus by March 17. Clasping was first observed on April 19 while the first eggs were procured on April 25" (B. B. Brandt, N.C., 1936a, p. 217).

"They may breed during any month of the year. The eggs are laid in very shallow water, often among semiaquatic or terrestrial vegetation which has been temporarily inundated" (A. F. Carr, Jr., Fla., 1940, p. 55).

**Journal notes:** The Cornell party of Dec. 22, 1913–Jan. 1, 1914, found this species active and took several specimens. Doubtless this species is more or less active throughout the year in the Okefinokee Swamp.

April 23, 1921, Okefinokee Swamp. *Acris*—captured a lot of them. Sometimes black on a black soil and hard to see except when they jump. Some brown all over back (except for dark marks) when on brown pine needles. Sometimes green all over except for the dark marks. Sometimes gray over drier sand. Among some of the light brown needles *Acris* reddish brown even on back of fore limbs and hind limbs.

A few of our notes on the jumping records of *Acris* follow:

April 23, 1921. *Acris* usually jumps for several leaps before it disappears. April 25. *Acris* males jump 3 feet at a time on the water's surface. May 17. *Acris* can leap at least my own pace. May 21. *Acris* has been hopping around on the ground and into small bushes from the ground and down to the ground again.

**Authorities' corner:**

W. Bartram, Gen., 1791, p. 278.
P. Fountain, Ga., 1901, p. 63.
R. F. Deckert, Fla., 1915a, p. 22.
A. F. Carr, Jr., Fla., 1940, p. 55.
C. J. Goin, Fla., 1943, p. 148.
P. Viosca, Jr., La., 1944, p. 55.
G. L. Orton, La., 1947, pp. 377–378.

## Cricket Frog, Western Cricket Frog, Valley Cricket Frog, Western Cricket, Peeper, Savanna Cricket Frog, Rattler

*Acris gryllus crepitans* Baird. Plate XLVI; Map 15.

**Range:** Dunn (Gen., 1939, pp. 153–154) gives Connecticut, s(
New York, New Jersey, Pennsylvania, Maryland, Delaware, northwest to

*Plate XLV. Acris gryllus gryllus* (×1). 1,3. Females. 2. Male. 4. Tadpole.

*Plate XLVI. Acris gryllus crepitans* (×4/5). 1,2,5,6,7. Females 3,4 Males. 8,9. Tadpoles.

Canada, west to Utah and New Mexico, and south through Virginia to Georgia and western Texas. Sea level to 2000 feet.

**Habitat:** Swales, lake margins, stream edges, springs, pasture pools.

"This tiny frog is distributed all over the State wherever there are lakes, ponds, springs, or streams. I have found it even in the heart of well populated cities in little pools formed by rains. While allied to the true tree frogs, this species never climbs trees but lives among water plants and in the vegetation along shore. When alarmed it retreats to the water after the manner of a true water frog" (J. K. Strecker, Jr, Tex., 1915, p. 49).

"This is one of the commonest forms found in the Wichita National Forest and if an effort were made large numbers could be taken. Several dozen were preserved on this trip and some hundreds are in the collections as the result of many short collecting trips which have been taken to this forest. They are found almost anywhere that water was available and in this region were plentiful along most parts of the streams and particularly around the edge of Lost Lake and other slow-flowing water areas. Their abundance along West Cache Creek in spite of numerous campers was very noticeable" (A. I. Ortenburger and B. Freeman, Okla., 1930, p. 177).

"It is generally abundant wherever permanent waters are to be found, where it may be taken as early as the middle of February and as late as November" (D. A. Boyer and A. A. Heinze, Mo., 1934, p. 189).

Viosca stated that *Acris gryllus* abounded along the creeks of his Pine and Hardwood Uplands division or "Shortleaf Pine Hills." "Fresh Water Marshes: *Acris crepitans,* although a lowlands species generally, is especially abundant here . . " (P. Viosca, Jr., La., 1923a, pp. 36, 39).

W. S. Blatchley (Ind., 1891, p. 27) calls this species "the most abundant tailless batrachian in the country. Hundreds are to be seen along any small stream in spring and autumn. They appear less common in summer."

"This species was the most abundant amphibian within the limits of this area. It was found most abundantly at the edges of bodies of water in all parts of the area in spring although some were found on the shores of the lake through summer and until late in the fall. On February 2, 1924, several were found in the creek above the bridge. They were in the water above some old ice and below a top layer of new ice. All the frogs were stiff and floating and apparently they were dead. In the warm water of the springs and just below the springs a few frogs of this species were found throughout the winter" (J. M. Linsdale, Kans., 1927, p. 76).

**Size:** We have made no study of this segregated group. A tentative summation is: adults, ⅝–1⅜ inches; males, 17 or 18–30 mm.; females, 20–35 mm. Did Fowler's (1907) 2¼ inches mean 1¼ inches?

We measured 20 males and 20 females from Texas and Mississippi Valley with these results: males, 17.5–29.0 mm., average 21 mm., mean 23 mm.; females, 19–28 mm., average 24 mm., mean 23 mm. In one lot a 19-mm. male was debatable; in another lot three individual specimens, 17, 18, 18 mm., were hard to sex; in another lot we had some males 17.5 and 18.5 mm.

**General appearance:** In 1923 Viosca (La., 1923a, p. 43) said: "The puzzling status of *Acris*, as far as Louisiana is concerned, has been positively cleared by these studies. There are two distinct species in Louisiana, the upland species being, tentatively, *Acris gryllus*, and that of the lowlands, *Acris crepitans*. Wherever their ranges overlap, they are found side by side without interbreeding, each with its characteristic chorus and habits." Dunn (Gen., 1939, pp. 153–154) confirmed Viosca's opinion that two distinct species are involved and the distinguishing characters are those he mentioned: " 'The best character for distinguishing the two species is the amount of webbing of the toes, *crepitans* having much more web.'

| "*gryllus* | *crepitans* |
|---|---|
| Smaller | Larger |
| Less web (3 phalanges of toe 4 free, toe 1 partly free) | More web (2 to 1½ phalanges of toe 4 free, toe 1 completely webbed) |
| More rugose | Smoother |
| Anal warts less prominent | Anal warts more prominent |
| Legs longer, heel beyond snout | Legs shorter, heel not to snout |
| Thigh more definitely striped | Thigh less definitely striped." |

"If this form actually exists, as Viosca (1923, 1931) maintains, it certainly does not exist in Kansas. The specimens examined are too uniform in character to permit of more than one species, and the extent of variation is well within that of *gryllus*" (H. M. Smith, Kans., 1934, p. 461).

"Dunn (Gen., 1939, p. 154) lists six criteria for use in distinguishing *crepitans* from *gryllus*. Four of these, (1) larger size, (2) more extensively webbed feet, (3) shorter legs, and (4) less definitely striped thighs, are evident in our specimens when they are compared with topotypes of *gryllus* from Riceboro, Georgia. The two other diagnostic characters used by Dunn do not hold in our specimens; they seem, therefore, to merit further discussion. First he characterizes *gryllus* as 'more rugose' than *crepitans;* the contrary is true in the Rockingham County specimens which are definitely more rugose than are *gryllus* topotypes. Wide variation in the amount of rugosity occurs in both species and we feel that this character is the least useful of those used by Dunn. Secondly, Dunn states that the anal warts of *gryllus* are less prominent than those of *crepitans*. This statement is ambiguous because it fails to indicate whether the warts are prominent by reason of their color, size, or number. The startlingly white color of the subanal warts of some specimens of *Acris* is a result of preservation in formalin, as the senior author has determined experimentally; specimens preserved in alcohol show less color change and the subanal warts do not fade to an ivory white. It is quite evident however that rugosity of the central thigh area is more characteristic of *crepitans* than of *gryllus;* the Virginia specimens and many examples of *crepitans* from elsewhere exhibit a greater number of subanal warts than do topotypes of *gryllus,* but brilliant white warts are present in some specimens of each species. In addition to the characters mentioned by Dunn, *crepitans* has a shorter head and a more obtuse snout than *gryllus*" (M. G. Netting and L. W. Wilson, W. Va., 1940, p. 6).

**Color:** "Color above, some shade of gray, brown, or olive-green, often with a median longitudinal diffuse band of red or green, and with several black spots, of which a triangular one between the eyes is constant and characteristic. Beneath pale. Upper jaw black or dark brown, with four vertical pale lines on each side. A narrow pale line extends from the lower posterior part of the eye to the base of the fore leg. Above this line lies an elongate black spot which extends from the eye towards, but does not quite reach, the fore leg. Behind the insertion of the fore leg, on the side, is a large oblique black spot margined with white. Another similar but smaller spot lies in advance of, and above, the insertion of the hind leg. The triangular spot between the eyes is narrowly margined with white, its apex pointing backward. The middle of the back is often occupied by a longitudinal red or green band, and immediately on each side of the latter are several obscure black spots. Color beneath pale, sometimes tinged with yellow on the throat. Throat more or less speckled with dusky or brown. Lower jaw pale, or with a few dark specks at the symphysis, becoming darker towards the angle of the mouth, from which point a dark dash passes to and upon the base of the fore leg. Legs and digits dark above, with round dark spots; pale and unmarked below. A black spot may often be visible over the vent, and generally a dark bar passes from this region along the posterior surface of the thigh" (H. Garman, Ill., 1892, p. 341).

"*Acris gryllus.* Cricket frogs are common along the shores of all bodies of water. Some of them were very large. All were dark in color and most of them showed either a red or green streak down the center of the back" (K. P. Schmidt, Ill., 1923, p. 49).

**Structure:** (See *A gryllus gryllus* for differences in the two forms.)

"Width of head across base of lower jaw about equal to distance from that point forward to tip of snout; legs shorter and hind feet more fully webbed, the web on the first (shortest) toe reaching its tip; heel when leg is extended not reaching tip of snout—Common Cricket" (C. S. Brimley, N.C., 1940, p. 15).

"Webbing on toes more extensive; last two phalanges of fourth toe free from webbing; usually with third and fifth toes reaching beyond middle of the third phalanx from tip of fourth toe. *A. g. crepitans*" (E. B. Chamberlain, S.C., 1939, p. 12).

"None of this questionable species was found in Beaufort County although Brimley (1926) gives the range in North Carolina as 'central and part of eastern districts.' The writer has seen individuals commonly in Durham County which are referable to this species. Viosca (1923) has taken considerable interest in the genus, as a result of field observations maintaining that in Louisiana there are two distinct species of *Acris*. The writer is inclined to the view that more field and experimental study is needed to solve the problem. It was observed that in Chase's Lake, Brooksville, Mississippi, only typical *gryllus* forms occur while at Cryme's Pond both forms occur with calls which are recognizably different. The former locality is in a Lafayette Red Clay area while the latter, less than four miles distant, is in a Selma Chalk area" (B. B. Brandt, N.C., 1936a, p. 217).

**Voice:** Feb. 24, 1925, Helotes, Tex. Tonight air 64° at 8.30 P.M. Heard at "Ornate Fork" quite a chorus of *Acris, gick, gick, gick*—or *kick, kick, kick*.

March 8–12, Helotes, Tex. Evenings—in great chorus for several days. Creek is filled with them.

"Besides their rattling call a squeaky sound was heard occasionally, though only during the breeding season. . . .

"It may be stated that in my experience their call appears to be variable. The usual note is not heard at a great distance, and is described by one writer as exactly imitated by striking two marbles together, first slowly, then faster and faster, for a succession of about 20 to 30 beats. Perhaps the rattling of castanets would be a better suggestion" (H. W. Fowler, N.J., 1907, pp. 102–103).

"The name Cricket Frog was given to it, on account of its song, which bears a strong resemblance to the chirping of the black cricket. These tiny frogs sing in chorus in spring. The sound can be imitated by striking together two pebbles or two marbles, beginning slowly and continuing more rapidly for thirty or forty strokes. The male frog is the singer and in doing so inflates his yellow throat enormously. . . . The first warm days in early spring bring them out. Feb. 14, 20; Mar. 5; May 1; Sept. 7; Oct. 16" (J. Hurter, Mo., 1911, p. 102).

"Feb. 8, 1918. Buffalo Bayou. They are fairly abundant all along the banks and are calling vigorously. The call is a soft trill resembling the tree cricket or the mole cricket" (P. H. Pope, Tex., 1919, p. 97).

"The cricket-like chirping of these abundant little frogs is a familiar sound about the marshy borders of streams and ponds from April to July. The singer is often hard to locate due to the carrying capacity of the sound and a more or less ventriloqual effect" (G. E. Hudson, Neb., 1942, p. 25).

"The voice of a cricket frog is a combination of a rattle and a musical clink, but it is only about half as loud as that of a spring peeper. A chorus heard at a distance sounds like the jingling of small sleigh bells, for the musical element of its call travels farther than the rattle. A chorus heard close by sounds like the rattle of small pebbles poured upon a cement pavement.

"An individual frog sings for from thirty to forty-five seconds at a time. Its call has three phases. The first phase lasts for about five seconds and sounds like the clicks of a boy's marble dropped upon a cement pavement, once or twice a second from a height of about six inches. The second phase sounds like the galloping of a small pony on a brick pavement, or like the clicks of a boy's marble dropped upon a pavement from a height of only an inch or two, and allowed to bounce each time. The third phase sounds like the regular cree-cree-creeing of a tree cricket, or like the rattle of a boy's marble that bounces rapidly when it is dropped at frequent intervals from a height of only half an inch. The time and rhythm of the sounds are about the same as that of the following syllables pronounced with the speed of ordinary reading: click, click, click, click . . . click-e-ty, click-e-ty, click-e-ty, click-e-ty, click-e-ty . . . cree, cree, cree, cree. . . .

"The cricket frog inflates a vocal sac under its chin during its call. It often sits quietly with its sac distended for many minutes between its calls. The violent efforts of its body in producing its sound make the frog resemble a small boy on his hands and knees blowing a fire with all his might. The vocal sac is bright yellow, and when it is seen distended in the day time, it is so conspicuous that it reveals many a singer that otherwise would be almost invisible on a lily pad" (F. Overton, N.Y., 1914, p. 31).

**Breeding:** Early April–July. (See *A. g. gryllus.*) H. M. Smith (Kans., 1934, p. 389) gives the egg as having a single envelope 2.3 mm. or more. Dr. Katherine Van Winkle (Mrs. E. L.) Palmer who worked over our *Acris* collections and our 1917 transcontinental material found that in an Ames, Iowa, congress of *Acris* June 12, 1926, some eggs tended to be in bunches or masses. We measured her Ames material and found males 21–29 mm. in length and females 27–29 mm. Most of the records indicate transformation from 13–15 mm., but we were quizzical and, on testing out our Texas material, found they ran mainly from 11–12 mm., sometimes 10 or 10.5 and 12.5 or 13 mm. An inclusive range of 10–15 mm. is, therefore, better for transformation sizes. In the same way, few tadpoles reach 45 or 46 mm.; most run from 30 to 36 mm., with the body of the tadpole usually 11.5–14.0 mm.

Miss Dickerson believed their chorus was loudest in late April and early May when they attached their eggs to grass blades or leaves in the water. She stated: "The development of this frog is less rapid than that of the Common Tree Frog, the Eastern Wood Frog, or the American Toad. The tadpoles may be found in the water as late as August. The final transformation takes place in September. The young tree frogs, as well as the older ones, seek shelter from the cold under stones and leaves at the margins of their brook or marsh."

"[Eggs are] not deposited in large groups, and not concealed under objects; outer envelope usually not over 7.5 cm. Envelope single. Envelope 2.3 mm. or more—*Acris gryllus* (Le Conte)" (H. M. Smith, Kans., 1934, p. 389).

"Although individuals are sometimes collected throughout the winter, and are rather abundant in March, their breeding activities do not begin until early April. . . . Near Lawrence clasping pairs have been collected as late as May 9 (1933); they probably breed much later, as their songs are frequently heard as late as July, and Gloyd (personal notes) has heard them singing about Manhattan as late as July 15. Eggs have been laid in the laboratory on May 10, from females collected the preceding night (1933). The breeding sites chosen are varied. In regions where the species is found in abundance, permanent lakes, streams and springs always have their quota. Frequently they breed in and sing from temporary pools in pastures or at road-sides" (same, p. 459).

"On July 17, 1932, metamorphosis was occurring in these frogs at Isle Du Bois Creek, where, it was estimated, many thousands of these small frogs occurred, and where specimens in almost all stages of development were present. Some juveniles without fully absorbed tails had bright green dorsal patterns, while tailed specimens approaching transformation possessed the typical triangular dorsal marking, but no such larvae were observed to have the black tail tip characteristic of the tadpoles occurring in a woodland pond at Danby, about two miles distant A transforming specimen upon emergence from the water on August 9 possessed a body length of 14.4 mm., tail 14.9. Two hours and forty minutes later the tail measurement was 10.75, an absorption of 4.15 during this period. Another larva, measured at 9·15 P.M., had a body length of 15.1, tail 31.7, of which 9 mm. possessed dark pigmentation; the mouth was transformed, the dorsal pattern distinct. By 7:30 P.M. August 10 the body length was 14.4, tail, 24, dark tip, 3.5 and by 2 P.M August 11 the body length was 14, tail, 1.5. In this period of 40¾ hours the reduction in body length was 1 1 mm , tail 30 2. By September 18 the transformation period was nearing its end and few larvae could be taken by seining at this time. On this date, however, a ribbon snake, *Thamnophis sauritus proximus* was lying on a mat of aquatic vegetation at a pond near Danby, and when captured it disgorged three cricket frogs, one a transforming specimen" (D. A. Boyer and A. A. Heinze, Mo , 1934, p. 189).

"The eggs were laid singly or in small masses One female had 248 . . ." (G. E. Hudson, Neb., 1942, p. 25).

**Journal notes:** We have seen it from New Jersey to Georgia, Louisiana, Texas, and Iowa, but like most workers we have neglected this most ubiquitous tree frog. Everyone remarks their choruses. We will forbear except to give the scanty notes of two seasons in Texas.

Feb. 8, 1925, Rio Cibola River, Tex. A few *Acris* called.

Feb. 8–Feb. 21, Helotes. Once in a while hear a few *Acris* calling. Not a loud full-throated *Acris* call yet.

Feb. 21 Heard them calling, air and water 70°F., 9–10 P.M

Feb. 24 to March 8–12. [See "Voice."]

March 13. In great chorus last night and tonight. In our fork it is very common.

March 16. Last night no *Acris* calling.

April 1. Heard cricket frogs at Sabinal, at Nueces River, and at Uvalde.

April 2, Cotulla. Heard in Nueces River or extension many, many *Acris.*

May 5, Helotes. On talus slope we turned over a flat stone and saw a greenish frog. Another jumped and my eye followed it. It impressed me as *Acris.* I let the stone down. Later looked under the stone, and behold a Marnock's frog—a red-letter day. Later we went to the spot where the other frog jumped and it proved to be an *Acris*. It must have finished breeding to be here.

May 9, San Antonio, 8:30 P.M. *Acris* calling strongly near St. Mary's College and in Bandera.

May 14, Boerne. Heard a few *Acris*.

May 24, Helotes. Went to Lee's Branch to get *Acris crepitans* series. Many *Acris* transformed.

June 6, Devine. Found *Acris* tadpoles with black-tipped tails.

Jan. 17, 1942. With Quillins to Classen Ranch. In clear Fork of Cibola . . . Roy dug under roots of a tree and brought out a *Bufo valliceps*. In the creek saw plenty of *Acris crepitans*, tadpoles minute to almost mature of *R. pipiens*. Saw an immense *R. catesbeiana* male in mass of vegetation.

July 22, Toyahvale, Tex. Tonight at 9:30 drove to where Cherry Canyon goes across the highway and several miles beyond. At first we heard a note I thought was a rattle in rear of our auto, but Anna persisted, and then I got it: full *Acris crepitans*. Got plenty of them for first 2 or 3 miles west of Toyahvale.

July 23. Trip to Phantom Lake with Alex Izzard of Balmorhea State Park. Saw several *Acris* here and caught them. Water about 70°F. A fine spring.

August 2. Beyond Carrizo Springs, Tex. At Sycamore Cr. boundary line of two counties took one transformed *Acris*.

In Texas in 1925 we began trips about February 8, when *Acris* appeared if nothing else. For many entries we merely say, "No end of *Acris*," "*Acris* in all creeks of whatever size." Always merely "*Acris*." Not until May 24–26, when they were transforming and transformed, did we courageously enter *A. crepitans*. At present we are almost willing to grant *crepitans* and *gryllus*, but are there one to three or more forms of *Acris* yet undescribed? This omnipresent species may prove more involved than *Rana pipiens*.

**Authorities' corner:**

H. Garman, Ill., 1892, p. 342.
J. Hurter, Mo., 1911, p. 101.
T. L. Hankinson, Ill., 1917, p. 324.
B. W. Evermann and H. W. Clark, Ind., 1920, p. 634.
C. S. Brimley, N.C., 1940, p. 15.
G. A. Moore and C. C. Rigney, Okla., 1942, p. 78.
G. L. Orton, La., 1947, pp. 375–377.

In a recent paper (May 10, 1947) F. Harper (Gen., 1947) restricts *Acris g. crepitans* to the eastern portion of its credited range, i.e., from Connecticut to New York to eastern Texas, and establishes a new form, *A. g. blanchardi* for the cricket frogs from southwestern Michigan to southwestern Missouri to southwestern Texas and westward to Utah and Arizona. The new form "is distinguished . . . by slightly greater linear measurements, by decidedly greater bulk, by somewhat more extensive dusky area on the posterior face of the femora in the vicinity of the vent." Our preceding discussion of *Acris g. crepitans* is therefore composite if this interpretation proves the correct one.

## Genus *PSEUDACRIS* Fitzinger[1]

Maps 16–18

### Mountain Chorus Frog, Chorus Frog, Ohio Chorus Frog

*Pseudacris brachyphona* (Cope). Plate XLVII, Map 16.

**Range:** Southwestern Pennsylvania, western Maryland, southeastern Ohio, eastern Kentucky, West Virginia, northern Alabama (Viosca), northern Mississippi. Must be in Tennessee.

**Habitat:** Springy hillsides, grassy pools, ditches, sources, and along upper courses of upland rivulets—more hilly than lowland habitats.

**Size:** Adults, 1–1⅜ inches. Males, 24–32 mm. Females, 27–34 mm.

**General appearance:** These are small frogs, gray or brown in color, medium in size for *Pseudacris,* with the most distinct digital disks of this genus. They are more stocky in body and broader in head than *P. n. triseriata* and *P. n. feriarum*. The usual middorsal stripe or row of spots is lacking. They often have a light middorsal area somewhat after the pattern of the cricket frog (*Acris gryllus*). The interorbital triangle is not white-edged behind. The dorsolateral bands curve from the eye to midback to groin, making two crescents. They often meet in midback to form a cross or transverse bar. Sometimes the pattern consists of a cross or a bar alone.

**Color:** (See "General appearance," "Structure," and "Authorities' corner.") In general color these frogs range from the sorghum brown, deep brownish drab, or mars brown of *Hyla femoralis* to some of the grays found in *Acris* or *Hyla femoralis* or to the blackish olive of *Pseudacris n triseriata.*

**Structure:** The original description—"A specimen of nearly the size and form of *Hyla femoralis* was taken in western Pennsylvania, near the Kiskiminitas River. In proportions it does not differ from the *Feriarum,* but the toes are fringed, the dilations larger and the coloration different. Above blackish-ash, abruptly defined on the sides. Lateral band not extending beyond tympanum. No median dorsal band, but two black dorso-laterals of double ordinary width converge from each tympanum and extend to end of urostyle inclosing with the interorbital triangle a narrow, anteriorly bifurcate dorsal band of ground color" (E. D. Cope, Gen., 1889, p. 341).

Compared to *P. ornata, P. n. feriarum, P. n. triseriata,* it has a wider head

[1] The two workers who in the last ten to fifteen years have added most to clarification of this genus are C. Walker and F. Harper.

and a longer hind limb, tibia, and foot with tarsus. In most ways it falls into the *Pseudacris ornata* group; in some with the *Pseudacris nigrita* group, e.g., as shown in the statistics (number of times in length) below:

| | *P. ornata* | *P. brachyphona* | *P. n. feriarum* | *P. n. triseriata* |
|---|---|---|---|---|
| Width of head | 2.86–3.4 | 2.5–3.1 | 3.0–3.33 | 3.25–3.5 |
| Hind limb | 0.68–0.75 | 0.60–0.67 | 0.65–0.74 | 0.71–0.75 |
| Tibia | 2.06–2.28 | 1.82–1.93 | 2.0–2.26 | 2.24–2.54 |
| Foot with tarsus | 1.33–1.56 | 1.26–1.42 | 1.23–1.60 | 1.37–1.57 |

These measurements distinguish it from *P. n. triseriata*, but not so clearly from *P. n. feriarum*. The proportions for *P. brachyphona* are in three parts very close

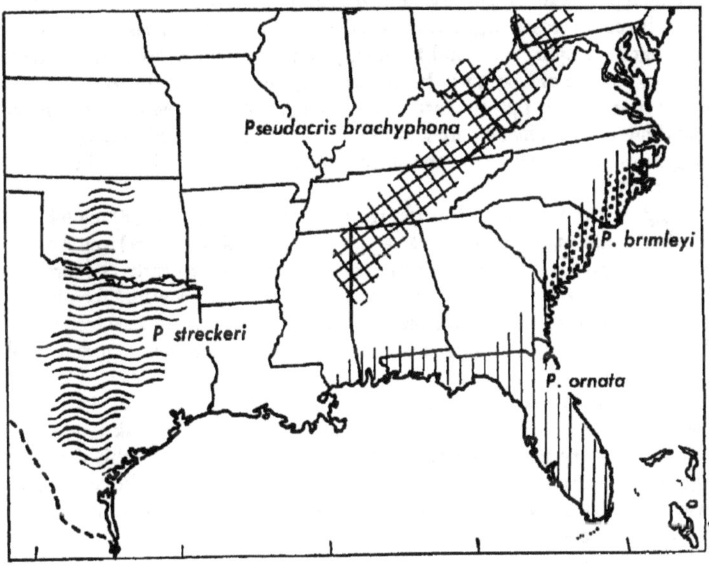


*Map 16*

to those of *P. n. nigrita*. Although we have put this species in the *P. ornata* group in the key, nevertheless there are some respects in which it is not clearly divorced from the *P. nigrita* six subspecies.

**Voice:** "The note of this species is quite different from that of the *C. triseriatus*, not being continuous, but in sets of crepitations repeated in time and at intervals" (E. D. Cope, Gen., 1889, p. 341). When *P. n. triseriata* and *P. brachyphona* are calling they are different; the latter has a faster, higher note, yet its call belongs distinctly in quality and form with the *P. nigrita* group.

"The voices of the two (*triseriatus* and *brachyphona*) are much alike but the call of *brachyphona* is given more quickly, with a higher pitch and a different quality so that the effect of a chorus is quite distinctive" (C. F. Walker, Ohio, 1932, p. 383).

"Their notes are repeated at the rate of about 50 to 70 times a minute and may be continued for several minutes although they usually stop in fifteen to twenty seconds. The call is strong and rapid and on a clear night a chorus may carry a quarter of a mile" (N. B. Green, W. Va., 1938, pp. 79–80).

**Breeding:** March–July. Amplexation axillary. Eggs in masses, 10–50, attached to vegetation or trash. Egg complement 300–1500; vitellus 1.6 mm.; envelope 6.0–8.5 mm. Tadpole period 50–60 days. Tadpole 25 mm. Labial tooth rows 2/3. Transformation size 8.0 mm. (after Green, Walker, Welter, Carr, Barbour, and Sollberger, the last four of whom have sent us many a puzzling specimen of this species, of *Hyla crucifer*, and of *Acris*).

"Its breeding season begins somewhat later than that of *triseriata* and is more prolonged. Clasping pairs and fresh eggs have been found as early as March 20th and as late as May 12th. In the same region our dates for *triseriata* eggs range from March 14th to April 16th. The eggs of *brachyphona* are so much like those of *triseriata* and are laid in similar masses, attached to twigs, leaves, or grasses, often well below the surface of the water" (C. F. Walker, Ohio, 1932, p. 383).

"Egg masses were found in the region under observation (Randolph and Tucker counties, West Virginia, at an elevation of 2000 feet) on April 5. Walker (1932) states that fresh eggs have been found as early as March 20, presumably in southern Ohio. Pairs in amplexus and eggs were taken at Porterwood, Tucker County, on June 10, 1936, at an elevation of 2200 feet and on Point Mt., Randolph County, on June 7, 1937, at an elevation of 3500 feet following a rainy spell of several days. Freshly laid eggs were collected by C. J. Goin at Camp Woodbine, Nicholas County, on July 2, 1936, at an elevation of 2000 feet. His notes for this date read, 'Small pool visited at dusk following a rain. A long dry spell had preceded this rain. One clutch of freshly deposited eggs was observed. . . .' On April 13, 1937, five females were collected on their way to the pools. In the laboratory each female was put in a separate jar with a male in an effort to determine the number of eggs an individual laid. They laid respectively 1479, 383, 318, and 406 eggs" (N. B. Green, W. Va., 1938, p. 80).

"Egg masses were collected from a conical hole about two feet deep in the vicinity of Reightown on April 22, 1939. On the evening of June 30, 1939 a single specimen was collected in a ditch in a field adjacent to the highway between Homer and Ruggles Gap" (H. D. Yoder, Pa., 1940, p. 92).

"A very common spring frog. Breeding begins as early as February 12 when the marshes ring with the songs of this species and of *Hyla crucifer*. It is as abundant as *H. crucifer* and is usually found with it" (W. A. Welter and K. Carr, Ky., 1939, p. 129).

**Journal notes:** July 18, 1931, Beckley, W. Va., Fair Grounds woods. The botanists found a queer *Pseudacris feriarum* near a sawdust pile.

July 19, Beckley, W. Va., Fair Grounds. Tonight after a heavy rain, in a puddle beside the grandstand and in pools beside the track heard several *Hyla versicolor,* and in the distance several *Hyla crucifer,* but the notes which drew us to the spot were new—surely a *Pseudacris* in character of voice, not a *Hyla crucifer* nor an *Acris.* It was different from *Pseudacris n. triseriata* and *Pseudacris n. feriarum.* When we first caught it, its long legs reminded us of an *Acris,* and we looked for the rear femoral stripes. They were not present. It seems like a *Pseudacris,* but has too large disks for a normal *Pseudacris* species. Must look up Cope's *P. f. brachyphona.*

July 21. Prof. P. C. Bibbee, of State College at Athens, Mercer Co., brought us a jar of preserved swamp cricket frogs. They have such queer coloration (more like an *Acris* type) and such spindling legs. Are they a *Hyla, Pseudacris,* or *Acris?* They must be *Pseudacris.* Bibbee let me take a few for our collection and said they collect them in the spring. Surely someone will have to collect *Pseudacris* across southern Pennsylvania from Carlisle (type locality of *P. feriarum*) to southwestern Pennsylvania and West Virginia to see where this form, if *P. f. brachyphona,* meets *P. feriarum feriarum,* in mid-Maryland or mid-Pennsylvania.

July 24. Visited R K. Brown's laboratory at Bluefield, W. Va. He had a jar with several puzzling *Pseudacris.*

C. F. Walker was the first author to redescribe Cope's *Chorophilus feriarum brachyphonus,* and it is interesting that four groups at about the same time independently concluded to revive Cope's description; Walker on Ohio material, Netting on west Pennsylvania and northern West Virginia material, Dunn on west Maryland and Pennsylvania specimens, and we on southern West Virginia material. But the question is not entirely settled yet. Is this form in eastern Tennessee? Even as early as 1931 or 1933 when this form was revived, we had seen material from northern Mississippi and northern Alabama to cause us to credit it to those states. Viosca (Ala., 1938, p. 201) furnished a very fortunate record.

A former student supplies the following: "The surprise of the trip was a voice heard for the first time near Moundville. The origin of the strange 'Qurack,' suggestive of the voice of *Hyla squirella,* eluded us for about two hours before the first specimen was located; then the next six, all males were taken in about 15 minutes. This locality, in the foothills at the extreme southwestern limits of the Appalachian Highlands, extends the range of this species [*P. brachyphona*] some 500 miles southwestward" (letter). "To determine the number of eggs laid by each female, ten average-sized individuals were dissected. The largest number of eggs found in any one of these was 1202 and the smallest number was 983. The average number found in ten females was 1092 eggs. The eggs were deposited in masses attached to a stem or leaf.

*Plate XLVII Pseudacris* ***brachyphona*** (×1). 1–7. Males.

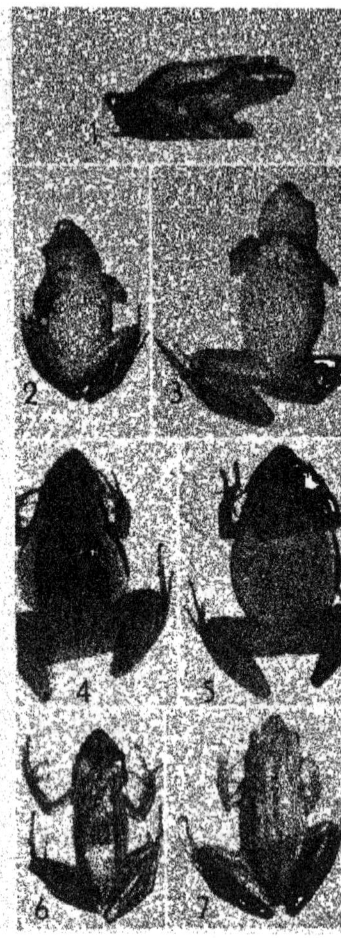


*Plate XLVIII. Pseudacris* ***brimleyi*** (×1). 1,2,4,5,6. Males 3,7. Females.

The number of eggs found in each of eleven masses was counted, and the number found to vary from 28 to 40, the average being 34 per mass. In the laboratory at temperatures varying from 18 to 22 degrees [C], hatching occurred from 72 to 96 hours after the eggs were laid In the pools, however, where the temperature ranged from 2 to 13 degrees, hatching did not occur for a week or ten days. Several tadpoles kept in a large aquarium in the laboratory at room temperature metamorphosed from forty to fifty days after hatching. Tadpoles in outdoor pools metamorphosed in forty-five to fifty-five days" (R. W. Barbour and E. P. Walters, Ky., 1941, p. 116).

**Authorities' corner:**

C. F Walker, Ohio, 1932, pp 380–381.
P. Viosca, Jr., Ala., 1938, p. 201.
N. B. Green, W. Va., 1938, p. 79.

## Brimley's Chorus Frog

*Pseudacris brimleyi* Brandt and Walker. Plate XLVIII; Map 16.

**Range:** Dismal Swamp, Va., south in the Coastal Plain to Bryan Co., Ga. In North Carolina, Brandt has taken *brimleyi* in Beaufort, Greene, Pitt, and Wilson counties, and has voice records from Craven and Edgecomb counties. Newbern, N.C. Type locality—Washington, N.C. (after Brandt and Walker, N.C., 1933, p. 5). Charleston, S.C. (E. B. Chamberlain, S.C., 1939, p. 17).

**Habitat:** Heavily wooded flood-plain pools. Swampy areas. Brandt (N.C., 1936b, p. 500) called it a "palustrine species. . . . This chorus frog was selected as the representative of an arboreal form which has reverted to terrestrial life." "It is of especial interest in comparison with its more arboreal relative of similar size, *Hyla crucifer*. About four months are spent at the breeding pools; the remainder of the year this species usually spends along swampy shores."

**Size:** Adults, 1–1¼ inches. Males, 24–28 mm. Females, 27.0–32.5 mm.

**General appearance:** "A dark middorsal stripe from tip of snout to vent. On each side of this a similar stripe extending from eyelid to posterior end of trunk. A darker, sharply defined line from snout through eye, and along side to groin Dorsal surfaces of legs with several large dark spots, the long axes of which are longitudinal, and many smaller dark spots. A distinct dark line along outer edge of tibia and on under side of foot. A light line along upper jaw continuing back to shoulder. Edge of jaw dark. An irregular, more or less discontinuous, dark line along posterior side of arm. Under surface light in color with dark spots on chest. Smaller but similar spots on under surface of legs" (B. B. Brandt and C. F. Walker, N.C., 1933, p. 3).

"A medium-sized *Pseudacris* with long legs and a *triseriate* dorsal pattern, closely related to the *nigrita-feriarum-triseriata-brachyphona* series, but differing in having a more delicate, smoother, skin; a sharply defined black lateral stripe combined with a rather weak dorsal pattern; a pronounced tendency towards longitudinal rather than transverse leg markings; a narrow dark line along outer edge of tibia; well defined dark spots on chest in most individuals; and in life, a distinctly yellowish venter" (same, pp. 2–3).

**Color:** "Dorsal color brown (yellowish to reddish shade); dark mid-dorsal stripe from snout to vent, and on each side of this a similar stripe from eyelid to posterior end of trunk. A darker, sharply defined lateral line from snout through eye to groin. (In light phases the dorsal stripes are usually obscure, but the lateral stripes remain black and sharply defined.) Under surface yellowish with small dark spots" (E. B. Chamberlain, S.C., 1939, p. 17).

"Living specimens show considerable variation in the ground color of the upper parts, but are apparently restricted to yellowish and reddish shades of brown, ranging from a pale buffy brown to a very dark shade near Light Seal Brown (Ridgeway). The dorsal stripes and the peculiarly shaped leg spots are usually obscure in the lighter phases, the lateral stripes remain black and sharply defined. The color of the venter also varies but seems always to be yellower than that of *nigrita*. The iridescent surface makes an accurate description of this color difficult. In the paler individuals it approaches Cream-buff, and in more richly colored examples it is near Buff-yellow or Pale Orange-yellow. The light cheek stripe below the vitta is similarly colored. Frequently there is a deeper yellow spot in the groin. The undersurface of the legs is grayish The scattered dusky pigment of the gular sac is underlain with greenish yellow. There is an obscure dark bar through the eye. The iris shows gold and reddish flecks, the latter restricted to the lower half" (B. B. Brandt and C. F. Walker, N.C. and Ga., 1933, p. 4)

"The more distinctive marks are the black lateral stripe which extends through the eye almost to the groin, the longitudinal not transverse markings on the hind legs, and the spotted under parts" (C. S. Brimley, N C., 1940, p. 18).

**Structure:** Smoother than *P. n. nigrita*. Venter coarsely granulated; heel to anterior eye; disks slightly dilated; muzzle rounded and projecting; tympanum distinct, smaller than eye.

Brimley (p. 15) gives these characters: "Upper parts with small warts at least on the side; snout longer than width across lower jaw at base; snout rounded when viewed from above; breast spotted."

"The leg markings of *brimleyi* and *ocularis* remain quite different. An approach to the longitudinal spots of *brimleyi* is seen occasionally in *brachyphona,* and the voice also resembles that of *brachyphona,* which is a very different frog in head shape, pattern, and skin texture" (B. B. Brandt and C. L. Walker, N.C. and Ga., 1933, p. 6).

**Voice:** "Walker, who heard the species in northern Georgia, considers the call very similar to that of *Pseudacris brachyphona.* To the writer the call sounds like a rasping trill, 'Kr-r-r-ak,' somewhat less than a second in duration. The note is suggestive of that of *Hyla squirella* but is more strongly accented at the end, and the intervals between the individual calls are shorter. Calling has been heard in rare instances as early as November" (B. B. Brandt, N.C., 1936a, p. 218).

"The type locality is Washington, N.C., where it is the earliest breeding species of the genus, mated pairs having been taken by Brandt and his friends of the Washington Field Museum from February 19 to April 17, 1933" (C. S. Brimley, N.C., 1940, p. 18).

We still need detailed descriptions of the egg masses, individual eggs, tadpoles, and transformation stages.

**Journal notes:** Feb 22, 1934. We have visited the Bughouse at Washington, N.C., and George Ross has shown us some of the live adults and tadpoles of *P. brimleyi*. There are yet no detailed descriptions of the eggs and tadpoles, but they do not depart markedly from the *Pseudacris* type.

Feb. 23, 1934. Left Kinston, N.C., southward on No. 11 at 2.30 P.M. Farther along in a cattail and roadside ditch heard a few isolated *Pseudacris*. Are they Brandt's *P. brimleyi* or what?

**Authorities' corner:**

B. B. Brandt and C. F. Walker, N C. and Ga., 1933, p. 5.
B. B. Brandt, N.C., 1936a, p. 218.
B. B. Brandt, N.C., 1936b, p. 525.
E. B. Chamberlain, S.C , 1939, p. 17.

## Swamp Cricket Frog, Swamp Chorus Frog, Swamp Tree Frog, Swamp Tree Toad, Striped Tree Frog, Rough Chorus Frog, Le Conte's Chorus Frog, Black Chorus Frog

*Pseudacris nigrita nigrita* (Le Conte). Plate XLIX; Map 17.

**Range:** North Carolina to northern Florida. Mississippi, possibly into Louisiana. The western limits are not very clearly defined.

**Habitat:** Breeds in ditches, ponds, or bayous, and later moves to dryer hammocks and ridges of the pine barrens.

**Size:** Adults, $\frac{4}{5}$–$1\frac{1}{5}$ inches. Males, 21–28 mm. Females, 22–30 mm.

**General appearance:** This small frog has a slender body and pointed snout, prominent eyes, and long legs The skin is finely granulated This form has the most numerous small dorsal spots of any *Pseudacris* It is gray or olive to black in color, with three irregular rows of dark spots on the back and darkly mottled sides. The dark spots are outlined with white dots. The row of dark spots down mid-back divides into two rows toward the rear. A light line is present along the jaw with a dark area extending from the snout through the eye and beyond the tympanum. There is a light speck back of the tympanum. The legs are barred with black spots. There is no triangle or crossbar between the eyes. The male has a dark greenish yellow throat with longitudinal folds in the middle.

**Color:** *Female*. Okefinokee Swamp, Ga., June 15, 1922. Back dark gray, smoke gray, drab, or grayish olive. From snout down middle of back is one

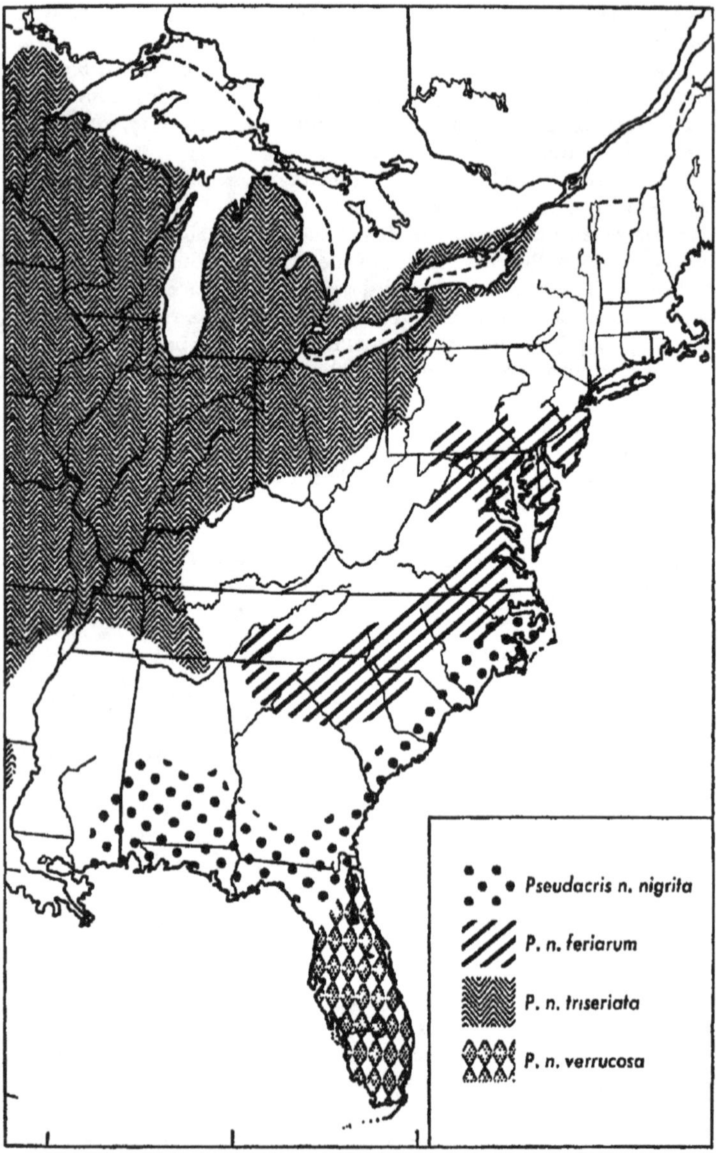
Pseudacris n. nigrita
P. n. feriarum
P. n. triseriata
P. n. verrucosa

Map 17

row of more or less connected dusky drab or deep brownish drab to black spots. Stripe along jaw pale rose purple, pale salmon color, or cartridge buff with some seafoam green.

The row of spots continuous down the back becomes at halfway point two rows of separate spots. On each side is one more row of separate spots. Dark area from snout through eye, back of eye, and extending along the side to groin. Crossbars of legs are same color as spots of back, and light thin bars between the spots of legs are like the background of the back. Under parts white. Iris black with brownish vinaceous dots. At times, iris has considerable glass green. (See A. H. Wright, Gen., 1932, pp. 199–200 for various color characterizations.) Sometimes the frogs are blackish olive, and white or creamy below. The maxillary stripe may be white, greenish, or a little yellow.

**Structure:** Slight webs at bases of second, third, and fourth toes; slight disks at tips of fingers and toes; hind legs long; in many ways this is the most distinctive of all six subspecies of *P. nigrita.*

The original description—"Above black speckled with small white warts; middle of back cinereous with an interrupted stripe of black, upper lips with a white line; beneath granulate whitish; irides golden; legs barred with whitish, hind part of thighs brown; hind legs very long" (J. Le Conte, Gen., 1825, p. 282).

**Voice:** "Its call is similar to that of the Cricket 'frog,' but much louder, and the crepitations are slower" (R. F. Deckert, Fla., 1915, p. 23).

In 1921 at Fargo, Ga., F. Harper noted in his journal: "During downpours on the afternoon of August 5 . . . began to hear several frogs calling in a field grown with grasses and sedges and flooded with rain. The notes consisted of a shrill metallic staccato trill, frequently repeated i-i-i-ik, i-i-i-ik, i-i-i-ik. They were indistinguishable from those of representatives of this genus in the Athabaska region (*septentrionalis*) and in the District of Columbia (*feriarum*)."

**Breeding:** Breed from December to April. Larval period 40–60 days. Transformation April 1–June 1 or July. Size about 9–15 mm.

Several naturalists in the South have made notes on the breeding of this early species. At Biloxi, M. J. Allen (Miss., 1932, p. 7) wrote: "Several pairs were taken in copulation on Dec. 15, 1929 and forty-two breeding pairs and some clumps of eggs in daylight on January 20, 1931."

Carr recorded: "Breeding: Jan. 16 to April 2, in temporary flatwoods ponds and ditches and in the shallow margins of cypress ponds. January and February choruses almost always in company with those of *P. ornata.* The young emerge in April and May. They often remain for several weeks about the ponds from which they emerged" (A. F. Carr, Jr., Fla., 1940, p. 56).

**Journal notes:** June 15, 1922, Folkston, Ga. Near Chesser Schoolhouse under chips, small boards, and logs found three *Pseudacris* in dry pine barrens, associated with *Bufo quercicus.* Area beneath boards and cover more or less dry.

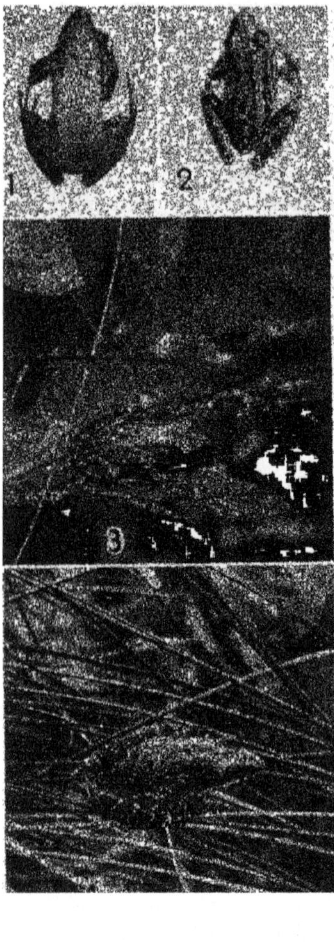

*Plate XLIX. Pseudacris nigrita nigrita* (×1). 1–4. Adults.

*Plate L. Pseudacris nigrita clarkii* (×1). 1,3,7. Females 2,6. Males. 4. Eggs attached to small twig. 5. Tadpole.

July 15, Folkston, Ga. On high sandy ridge south of Spanish Creek, *Quercus catesbaei, Quercus cinerea, Gaylussacia dumosa* and a very much serrated poison ivy (*Rhus*) were growing. Miles and I were looking at the *Rhus* carefully and gingerly. He saw something jump among it. Thought it a grasshopper but he soon found it to be a frog. It was *Pseudacris n. nigrita.* We took its picture right there. Other plants there were persimmon, *Baptisia,* brake, and croton. The frog was first on a dead twig of a fallen branch. It would leap among dead leaves, among wire grasses, and among the ivy.

Aug. 16. In making a detour on the Dixie Highway about a mile south of Hilliard, Fla., we came to the road opposite a wet pine woods. In one little temporary pond in a tussock of grass beside the small pool was a *Pseudacris n. nigrita* calling. To me this form which was finally captured sounded like our New York *Pseudacris.* To F. Harper it sounded like a metallic staccato trill, five notes, *ic, ic, ic, ic, ic.* All our records in July and August are clearly sporadic croakings long after breeding and only after heavy rainfall.

**Authorities' corner:**

R. F. Deckert, Fla., 1915, p. 23. E. B. Chamberlain, S.C., 1939, p. 15.
C. S. Brimley, N.C., 1940, p. 18.

### Clarke's Chorus Frog, Clarke's Striped Tree Frog, Striped Tree Frog, Striped Chorus Frog

*Pseudacris nigrita clarkii* (Baird). Plate L; Map 18.

**Range:** Texas to Kansas. "The extension of the range of the species northward has been a gradual and a continuous one, with the proper interpretation of the recorded species, so that the discovery of the species in Kansas is not so surprising. Cope extended its range to northern Texas (Dallas) in 1880, and into Oklahoma in 1894, shortly after recording it from the panhandle of Texas (1893). Ortenburger then (1926) reported *nigrita* (almost certainly *clarkii,* by this interpretation) from Creek county, Oklahoma, a record verified by a specimen from the same locality in the K. U. Museum, collected by Dr. Taylor. Burt (1932) found it in Kay county, Oklahoma, and subsequent collecting and examination of the K. U. material has revealed its existence far northward into central Kansas, in essentially the same ecological relations as exist where it is found in central Oklahoma" (H. M. Smith, Kans., 1934, p. 465).

**Habitat:** Abundant in vicinity of marshes. Breeds in roadside ditches, shallow water-lily ponds, shallow mesquite ponds, grassy ponds, or other transient pools.

"*Chorophilus triseriatus* Wied. . . . Baird's types of *Helocoetes clarkii* were from Indianola. In East-Central Texas, during the breeding season, this species fairly swarms in the roadside ditches and in shallow pools on the grassy flats" (J. K. Strecker, Jr., Tex., 1915, p. 48).

"*Chorophilus triseriatus clarkii.* Baird and Girard. . . . An abundant species, especially so in the vicinity of marshes" (J. K. Strecker, Jr., Tex., 1902, p. 7).

"Abundant and noisy in pools near the Cimmaron River, at Tucker, Oklahoma. Similar to the individuals reported by me from Clarendon, Texas" (E. D. Cope, Okla., 1894, p. 386).

"The specimens found in Oklahoma were in wooded areas. They seemed to avoid the deeper, muddier, less protected pasture pools where *Scaphiopus* and *Bufo* were numerous. Some were found, however, hopping about in the grassy fields, not far distant from pools. The specimens from Sedgwick county, Kansas, were found in a habitat essentially similar to the above, except that the pool in which they were found was permanent, while the other apparently was not" (H. M. Smith, Kans., 1934, p. 464).

**Size:** Adults, ¾–1¼ inches. Males, 20–29 mm. Females, 25–31 mm.

**General appearance:** This is a small grayish or olive frog with dark longitudinal spots, or these spots may be arranged in three stripes. A dark lateral banding extends to the nostril. There is a light stripe on the upper jaw. The legs are barred above and white or pale buff beneath. Venters are white or ivory yellow with the throat of the male a dark olive buff. They are protectively colored little things in the grassy edges of the ditches where they call and breed.

**Color:** *Four males.* Brownsville, Tex., Feb., 1923. Upper parts light grayish olive, pale olive-gray, grayish olive, or tea green. Spots on back and triangular spot and bars on legs yellowish oil green, oil green, or courge green. Bar from snout through nostril, through eye and tympanum, and onto sides black. Sometimes back of shoulder it has the greenish color of dorsal spots. Triangular area between eyes equilateral in one, long-caudally prolonged in another, divided into three spots, the two forward angles each making a spot and the caudal angle prolonged backward. Area in another not a triangle but with prolongation backward at one end like a figure seven. Two of these four have a spot ahead of the triangle. Above lateral vitta, through eye, over shoulder is a parallel series of dorsal spots, usually two, the caudal one longer, or the cephalic one larger, or all one or occasionally more than two. If there are other dorsal spots, they are in the posterior half of the back. There is no distinct middorsal line of spots or line. Belly and under parts white except for throat, which is olive-ocher, orange-citrine, olive-yellow, or lemon chrome.

Detailed color descriptions of a pair taken at Beeville, Tex., March 26, 1925, follow:

*Female.* Back deep olive-gray; on sides pale olive-gray above lateral stripe. Spots on back hellebore green surrounded by black. Stripe through eye and along side dark grayish olive. Bars and spots on fore limb like lateral stripe. Stripe on upper jaw cartridge buff with marguerite yellow or primrose yellow in it. Tympanum brownish olive or light brownish olive. Venter white, pale olive-buff, or ivory yellow. Underside of hind legs light grayish vinaceous or light brownish drab. Iris—upper part of rim marguerite yellow or primrose yellow, rest dotted black, primrose yellow, and cinnamon drab.

*Male.* Background pale smoke gray, also areas of tea green. Spots vetiver green, surrounded by black. Lateral stripe bone brown. Tympanum army brown. White or primrose yellow spots on tubercles below vent and on basal insertion of thighs. Throat discolored dark olive-buff or more yellowish. Two longitudinal plaits in middle of throat Iris of this male has also some avellaneous in it and a tendency to a dark horizontal bar through it to complete nasal and lateral stripe.

March 25, 1925. In the two pairs which laid, the females were more spotted, the males more striped. Is this a natural tendency or an individual variation? The male of a third pair is very much striped. Another male we captured is very much spotted.

**Structure:** Snout acute, projecting beyond lower jaw; toes slightly dilated at tips; male throat with one to three longitudinal folds. The hind limb, tibia, snout, and head are longer than in *P. n. triseriata.*

The original description—"*Helocoetes clarkii* Baird. Snout acute, projecting. Extremities somewhat dilated. Tibia half the distance between eye and anus. Foot but little longer, not nearly half the length of body. Above grayish brown or ash, with distinct large circular blotches A dark band from snout through eye and tympanum down the sides, and a whitish line on the side of jaw. Size about one inch long. *Hab.* Galveston and Indianola, Texas" (S. F. Baird, Gen., 1854, p. 60).

**Voice:** The call is a grinding note, more measured, and not so shrill as the call of *Acris.* It is raucous and grating, *it-it/it-it/it-it,* sometimes 60 times without a stop, sometimes uniform, sometimes double speed. They call from under the grass edges. Sometimes there is a synchronized chorus of sawing notes.

March 24, 1925, Beeville, Tex. Air is resounding with *Pseudacris.* 8.30 P.M., air 74°. Croaked 24 times, stopped instant, then began again 25 to 30 times, hardly catch a breath then start again, another 29 in 30 seconds. They are hidden under the grass edges like *Microhyla,* which is calling at the same time in the same roadside ditches. It is the dominating note over *Microhyla* and *Bufo valliceps* just now.

"Sometimes in later afternoon or early dusk, preceding a heavy chorus during the night, *P. clarkii* males call as they approach a breeding pool after the manner of *Hyla v. versicolor.* These calls, however, are enough different from the typical breeding cry that when I first heard them I was not sure of the species responsible till I had run down and captured a specimen. Such calls are not so loud nor so frequent as the typical breeding call. They have an indescribable quality which for want of a better term, I call 'pensive' or 'pleading.' Because of these differences I suspect (but have not proved) that this pensive call functions to attract other males to appropriate breeding pools that have been sensed by males nearer to them. At least, such calls in my experience have been limited to a circle of some four hundred feet in diameter whose center is covered by water appropriate for breeding activities. How the first males find a pool in this (and other) species is almost entirely unknown" (A. N. Bragg, Okla., 1943c, pp. 131–132).

**Breeding:** The species breeds with the spring rains, March 5–May 20, occasionally in summer to mid-August. The citrine drab and ivory yellow eggs are in a loose irregular mass attached to plant stems, their number few, 150 to 175 eggs in groups of 3 to 50. The egg is 1/32–1/25 inch (0.65–0.9 mm.), the outer envelope 1/12–1/10 inch (2.2–2.4 mm.) or more loose and irregular, the inner envelope 1/16 inch (1.4–1.8 mm.). The grayish olive tadpole is small, 7/8–1 1/5 inch (23–30 mm.), its crests nearly transparent, the tooth ridges 2/3. After 30 to 45 days, the tadpoles transform, April 1 to June 20, at 5/16–1/2 inch (8–13 mm.). H. M. Smith's (Kans., 1934, p. 464) specimens were slightly larger, 13.5–17.0 mm. in length.

One pair in captivity laid 154 eggs in several small masses arranged about one inch to one and a half inches apart on the stem. These masses were 17, 27, 30, 37, 16, 13, and 14 eggs, respectively. The last mass rested on the debris in the bottom of the jar. There is a very loose outer envelope, at times irregular.

We found the tadpoles transforming in extreme southern Texas on April 22 From the region of San Antonio we have the following note: May 29, 1925. Some *Pseudacris* are approaching the fully developed two-legged stage. Size, 8–13 mm.

"Found breeding in temporary pools from early May to mid-June. Common" (G. A. Moore and C. C. Rigney, Okla., 1942 [1941], p. 78).

"Feb. 25, 1944. Heard *Pseudacris nigrita clarkii* frogs at Duck Pond about 2½ miles north of my station. These are first near here. Formerly nearest were near Lytle (9 miles)" (A. J. Kirn, Tex.).

**Journal notes:** March 25, 1925, Beeville, Tex The pair we caught last night broke and one was lost. Captured an extra female. Put in photographic jar, two females and one male This morning when I arose, they were mated, but had not laid. The female of this pair was not the female of the original pair captured. They laid in one-half hour or less. The first pair captured had been resting at the grassy edge of a roadside ditch. The female was larger than the male. The embrace was axillary.

April 7, 1925. The eggs laid in Beeville, March 25, are developing nicely.

April 22, San Benito, Tex. In sedges around a pond one mile south of San Benito, these little transforming frogs were swimming in shallow water. They often duck. Hard to collect without killing them, they are such delicate little creatures. Skinned hind legs of two in their capture. They can turn heads like some other *Pseudacris*. Found only a very few tadpoles in the pond. The species must be through metamorphosis in this pond. This is a beautiful water-lily pond with *Marsilea* and *Castalia elegans.*

**Authorities' corner:**

E. D. Cope, Tex., 1893, p. 333.
J. K. Strecker, Jr., Tex., 1910c, p. 80.
A. N. Bragg, Okla., 1941, p. 52.

"The comparison of these two tadpoles [*triseriata* and *clarkii*] reveals an interesting situation. They are so nearly alike that those who believe them of separate species (e.g., Smith 1934; Bragg 1943) can take little comfort from the data. However, those who call them subspecies or varieties of one species (Burt, 1932; Wright and Wright, 1933, 1943; Stejneger and Barbour, 1939) must explain the proportional differences reported. It would seem, therefore, that either (1) one of these forms has fairly recently been derived from the other, or (2) both have been derived in recent geological times from a single ancestral form. The latter seems the more probable in view of lack of intergrading specimens where their ranges meet" (A. N. Bragg, Okla., 1943c, p. 138).

Having seen most of the tadpoles of the United States, even though we have not described them all minutely, we smile at "take little comfort from the data." We would have faith today in no one who pretended he could distinguish the tadpoles of all *Pseudacris* or all *Bufo* species. Bragg, than whom no one has been more active recently in life histories, must have enjoyed writing the paragraph above. *P. n. clarkii* and *P. n. triseriata* are close. When we find several times in the field (not in alcohol) pairs of *P. n. clarkii* with the males striped and the females spotted, or when we find males longer-legged and females shorter-legged in some *P. n. septentrionalis* specimens, it means that herpetologists do not know the species; or original descriptions alone do not solve; or that the *Pseudacris nigrita* complex is difficult to explain by any classificatory schema conceived long ago.

## Eastern Chorus Frog, Eastern Swamp Cricket Frog, Swamp Tree Toad, Swamp Tree Frog, Chorus Frog, Striped Tree Frog, Common Chorus Frog

*Pseudacris nigrita feriarum* (Baird). Plate LI; Map 17.

**Range:** New Jersey, Pennsylvania to North Carolina, and possibly into South Carolina.

**Habitat:** Breed in marshy stretches or shallow ponds, or at edges of ponds where there is matted vegetation, sedgy clumps, or moss.

"Between the railroad station at Annadale and Seguine's pond [Staten Island], there are several marshy places and one little artificial pond. For several years we have heard in these lowlands, from the middle of March to the first week in May, the song of what we considered to be the swamp tree frog, *Chorophilus triseriatus* (Wied)" (W. T. Davis, N.Y., 1912, p. 66).

"This species I have found abundant on the sides of pools and ponds in the neighborhood of Gloucester, N.J., in the spring and early part of summer. It delights in those small and often temporary pieces of water which are inclosed in the densest thickets of spiny *Smilax* and *Rubus,* with scrub oaks, and surrounded by the water loving *Cephalanthus,* where no shade interrupts the full glow of sunlight" (E. D. Cope, Gen., 1889, p. 344).

"As the pools in which they stay are usually full of grass, low rushes and other vegetation, they are not easy to catch although patience and perseverance will secure specimens without too much trouble. . . . Outside the breeding season these frogs are not often seen, but may be sometimes found hopping about in damp places or in cool, shady woods. On the ground they are not much more active than toads" (C. S. Brimley, N.C., 1940, p. 18).

**Size:** Adults, ⅘–1⅓ inches. Males, 21–30 mm. Females, 22–33 mm.

**General appearance:** These are small frogs with pointed heads, extremely long fourth toes, very little or no webbing between the toes, and with small disks on their toes. They are grayish olive or brown. There is a dark triangle between the eyes that extends backward as a dorsal stripe, with another stripe on either side. A dark stripe extends through the nostril and eye to the shoulder. This is bordered below with a light stripe on the upper jaw. The throats of the males are usually dark but not always so. The under parts are a buffy cream color.

**Color:** Carlisle, Pa. *Male.* Back deep grayish olive, drab, or drab-gray. Triangle between eyes going back as dorsal stripe with a stripe on either side. Each of these may be light-centered with body color. These dorsal stripes may be black, grayish olive, light grayish olive, or deep olive. Undersides of hind legs are brownish drab or benzo brown. Belly cartridge buff, cream-buff, or cream color. Throat buckthorn brown near tip to yellow ocher in posterior part. Band from snout to halfway along sides mummy brown or black. Iris same, with little burnt sienna in upper half. Stripe along upper jaw almost to shoulder, warm buff, cream-buff, or chamois.

*Female.* Upper part of head, back, forelegs, and hind legs, russet, hazel, verona brown, or warm sepia. Underside of hind legs benzo brown, drab-gray, or brownish drab. Under parts of body cream color, becoming slightly massicot yellow or naphthalene yellow on throat Stripe down middle of back, stripe either side of median stripe, and faint spots on sides are black, chestnut brown, mummy brown, or sepia. Stripe through nostril and eye to shoulder and beyond warm sepia or Vandyke brown. Band around upper jaw extending backward beyond shoulder below the dark stripe is warm buff, cream buff, or chamois. Iris same color as vitta through eye but dotted with mars orange or burnt sienna. These predominate in the upper half, giving the iris a "reddish" or "coppery red" appearance.

**Structure:** The original description—"*Helocoetes feriarum,* Baird. Body stout, squat. Head broad. Femur and tibia and hind foot about equal, and half the length of the body. Above dark or fawn, with three nearly parallel stripes down the back, the central widening, but scarcely bifurcate behind, and commencing behind a triangular spot between the eyes. A similar dark vitta on sides of head and body, with a white line along edge of the jaw. Body about one inch long. Hab. Carlisle, Penna." (S. F. Baird, Gen., 1854, p. 60).

**Voice:** A penetrating and grating *it-it/ it-it* is given many times without a stop. "Its note resembles that of *Acris* in being crepitant, and differs from the toned cry or whistle of the Hylae. It is not so loud as the former and is deeper pitched; it may be imitated by drawing a point strongly across a coarse comb, commencing at the bottom of a jar and bringing it rapidly to the mouth; or better, by restraining the voice to the separate vibrations of the vocal cords, and uttering a bar of a dozen or twenty vibrations, beginning with the mouth closed and ending with it well opened" (E. D. Cope, Gen., 1889, p. 345).

"This species is rarely seen except during its breeding season, when it is quite common. Its cry consists of two or three clear whistlelike chirps, like those of a young turkey, and after one has learned to distinguish it from that of *H. pickeringi,* serves to betray its presence at once. In the spring of 1896 I collected thirty specimens in less than an hour from the gutters along the Conduit Road near Cabin John's Bridge" (W. P. Hay, D.C., 1902, p. 129).

"The earliest of our frogs to breed at Raleigh, and its lazy chorus may be heard any warm day in February and March and even in December and January, though the very early songsters are usually only single individuals. The cry is a sort of grating rattle rising at the end, and is uttered by the male frogs lying at the surface of some shallow pool. They are very shy and sensitive and one always stops singing before an observer gets near enough to perceive the author of the noise, while others further away keep up the chorus" (C. S. Brimley, N.C., 1940, p. 18).

April 15, 1921, Raleigh, N.C. Temperature of air 68°F. Tonight at 9, Vernon and Julia Haber took me out to the Oakwood Cemetery at East Raleigh and to St. Augustine Grounds. Up in the woodland, where we couldn't find it, was a *Pseudacris feriarum* which sounded much like our northern swamp cricket frog. In the ponds were tadpoles of the cricket frog in all stages of transformation. If anything, these transform at a little larger size than those farther north. In order of activity the meadow frog and *Acris gryllus* are practically through breeding, though in the ponds the swamp crickets have left for uplands. Fowler's toads are still in chorus and strongly breeding though started much earlier, and *Hyla versicolor* is just coming to the pond.

"I have heard the swamps of the barrens and thickets of Southwestern New Jersey resound with them as early as the twentieth of March, when a skim of ice covered part of the water. I have also heard it in other level parts of the same State later in the season, and in the lower part of Chester County, Pa." (E. D. Cope, 1889, p. 345).

**Breeding:** They breed from February to May 10. The black and cream eggs are in irregular loose jelly masses attached to the stems of matted vegetation. The egg is 1/25 inch (0.9–1.1 mm.), the single envelope 1/8–1/6 inch (3.2–4.0 mm.). The vitelline membrane is close to the vitellus. The envelope in the mass becomes larger and irregular. The small tadpole, 1–1 5/16 inches (25–33 mm.), has the tail medium, with tip acute or acuminate, and is blackish or olive in color with bronzy belly. The tooth ridges are 2/3. After 50 to 60 days the tadpoles transform until mid-June, at 5/16–1/2 inch (8–12 mm.).

April 6, 1929, North Mountain, Carlisle, Pa. There were many egg masses attached to the stems in this vegetation mat. The jelly was loose and indeterminate in shape. It stuck to the stems in irregular fashion and to get a mass a little chunk of vegetation had to be pulled out.

"The distribution of *Pseudacris* is limited to an area in extreme southern Berks County from Gerger's Mill almost to Hopewell [N.J.] and south to Elverson. They were found laying eggs at Cold Run, May 4, 1937, by Earl L. Poole. Earliest record: calling, Mar. 15, 1939. Full chorus at 45°, intermittent, scattered calls at 34°; an occasional short call at 31°; silent at 30°F" (C. E. Mohr, Pa., 1939, p. 78).

"The eggs are laid in small masses surrounded by a very weak and watery gelatinous envelope and are attached to the stems of plants or other supports just below the surface of the water in which they are laid. The tadpoles develop very rapidly and I have found them as early as April 16 with the hind legs sufficiently developed for them to be able to hop although they had not yet lost their tails" (C. S. Brimley, N.C., 1940, p. 18).

**Journal notes:** April 3, 1929. On to Carlisle, through Harrisburg. Just south of Harrisburg is a fine grassy shallow pond but no *Pseudacris* were calling there by day. Drove around Carlisle that afternoon to spy out ponds suitable for *Pseudacris.* We heard some out the Mt. Holly Rd. in a punched tussock and swampy area in a field. Other ponds between Mt. Holly and Dillsburg had many peepers but no *Pseudacris*. Went out the Chambersburg Rd. (April 4) and on the way back found a surface pond at the edge of town, in fact in a vacant lot near a big building. Heard just three *Pseudacris* here and caught them all. We hated to give up with only three real Carlisle *Pseudacris,* but the next night brought out no more.

April 6, started up North Mountain. Just before Indian Springs, well up on the mountain, we heard a great chorus of *Pseudacris feriarum*. On the hillside, beside the road in an open field was a springy area. Finally we saw two little fellows with their amber throats so distended that they showed from the rear. They were sitting in the mat of vegetation, a little ways from a tussock, with their heads held up vertically, above the water. We went down to catch them and found the stream area fairly deep but filled with this mat of grassy vegetation. We rolled this back a bit at a time and caught an occasional frog in the tangle. One was a female, ripe, and strange to say she looked slender, as did the males from the Carlisle Pond, while the males from this Mountain Spring area were fat and squatty. We caught six or seven males and one female there.

June 10, 1929. Over the hills from Scranton to Harrisburg, leaving the main road at Clark's Ferry, and over the mountain toward Carlisle, back to the spot, Indian Springs Garden, where we caught *Pseudacris n. feriarum* at Easter time. Our springy hillside is almost dried up but is still spongy and water stands where you step, but no *Pseudacris* visible. Looked for little transformed ones but found none. Bert has gone down to the pond in the meadow below; yellow sweet clover, red clover, daisies, wild roses are in bloom. No luck at all. On toward Carlisle with crestfallen faces. A pond by the roadside—many tadpoles, but not the right ones. Came to a small stream with culvert in the road, a deep-cut stream with 6-foot banks. Above one bank was a springy inlet with masses of sensitive fern, grassy tussocks, touch-me-not, smartweed, and a little sedge. To the left in quiet water pockets sometimes no more than 4 to 6 inches deep, among grassy tussocks and a little sedge and fern was our big game. Tadpoles in general quite dark. As they approach transformation the triangle between the eyes becomes quite prominent. It curves in on each side, and the rear point extends as a line down the back to the sacral region. On either side of middorsal stripe appears a dorsolateral one of the same length. As the tads rest in the water, the tail region seems to be more or less speckled or to have an alternation of light and dark. We were impressed with long tail and bronzy belly. Some tadpoles were only half grown.

**Authorities' corner:**

R. Sutcliff, Gen., 1812, pp. 213–214.
W. T. Davis, N.Y., 1912, pp. 66–67.

*Queries and comments:* 1. Good authorities have identified specimens from eastern Tennessee, Arkansas, and Illinois as *P. n. feriarum,* and Del-Mar-Va specimens as *P. n. triseriata.* Are *P. n. feriarum* and *P. n. triseriata* one?

2. In 1921, we became acquainted with *P. n. feriarum* at Raleigh, N.C., and in 1934 we saw in Washington, N.C., live tadpoles and material of *P. brimleyi* Much remains to be done on these two forms.

3. Our Carlisle, Pa. (type locality), material did not correspond too exactly with Baird's description.

4. For 30 to 40 years our students from Philadelphia and New York City have from time to time queried whether there were two different forms in New Jersey.

5. Is *P. n. feriarum* coastal in the northern and Piedmont portions and inland in the southern portion of its range?

6. Does *P. n. feriarum* really reach northwestern Florida? The Tampa Bay record must be a mistake.

*Plate LI. Pseudacris nigrita feriarum* (×1). 1,2,6. Females 3,5,7. Males 4. Eggs.

*Plate LII. Pseudacris nigrita septentrionalis.* 1,3,4. Females (×1) 2. Male (×1). 5. Female (×1⅛).

### Northern Striped Tree Frog, Northern Chorophilus, Northern Pseudacris, Spotted Tree Frog, Northern Spring Peeper, Peeper Frog, Swamp Whistler

*Pseudacris nigrita septentrionalis* (Boulenger). Plate LII; Map 18.

**Range:** Minnesota to Hudson Bay, to upper British Columbia and Mackenzie through Montana, Saskatchewan, and Alberta; Canadian Northwest. Edward A. Preble found it from Lake Winnipeg to York Factory on Hudson Bay and from Edmonton, Alberta, to Ft. Norman west of Great Bear Lake. Some authors and collectors have felt inclined to assign some of the swamp cricket frogs of our northwest border states from Minnesota to Montana to this form, and surely some of the specimens we collected in the Red River of the North were short-legged enough to fall within this subspecies. G. C. Carl (B.C., 1943) reports it for Peace River district.

**Habitat:** Swampy borders of rivers, lakes, ponds, and meadows.

**Size:** Adults, ¾–1⅖ inches. Males, 19–32 mm. Females, 19–35 mm.

**General appearance:** Pembina, N.D. This is a small, long-bodied, short-legged tree frog. The snout is pointed. The color may vary from a gray to tawny or buff. The most prominent marks are the dark brown lateral stripe from snout to groin, and the light creamy stripe on the jaw below the eye. Certainly when seen at rest, you are impressed with the very short hind legs in sharp contrast with the long body. It has five darker stripes down the body. The median dorsal one may be broken into dots, the two laterodorsal stripes are more constant and the lateral ones most prominent. The male has a greenish yellow throat, the female, a light throat. The legs of the female are short and stout, those of the male longer and thinner. The under parts are greenish white.

**Color:** "The following brief description of the color was taken from a live specimen from Oxford House: Body light green above, greenish white beneath; body stripes bronzy lavender; tympanum brownish; hind legs light green above, flesh color beneath" (E. A. Preble, Keew, 1902, p. 134).

*Females.* Pembina, N.D., Aug. 30, 1930. *First female.* The color of top of head, top of arms and legs, and back between the three dorsal stripes is drab. The color between outer dorsal stripe and lateral band is a smoke gray or pale drab-gray. The band extending from snout through eye and over tympanum to near groin is olive-brown or brownish olive. This color is solid to the arm insertion, then goes over a pebbly surface, the interstices of which are smoke gray or pale drab-gray, like the color above the band. The median and two laterodorsal stripes are buffy brown outlined with dotted lines of olive-brown. On top of head are a few specks of olive-brown. The femur and tibia also have spots of olive-brown, and on front of tibia and rear of foot and tarsus are half bars of the same color. On the upper jaw there is a prominent line of olive-buff or chartreuse yellow bordered below, broadly on upper jaw and narrowly on lower jaw, by a finely punctate band of buffy olive or drab. Under surfaces are pale dull green-yellow, except for underside of hind legs, which is light grayish vinaceous. All five stripes are continuous. The eye is olive-brown, except for the upper rim of pupil, which is clear yellow-green; the iris is dotted all over with clear yellow-green and mars orange spots; the front, back, and lower margin of pupil rim is a succession of clear yellow-green dots.

*Second female.* In middle of back the dorsal stripe breaks into two irregular rows of small spots.

*Third female.* The back is tawny-olive to ochraceous-buff. The dorsal stripes are indistinct but nevertheless indicated. The lateral stripe is most prominent.

*Male.* Walhalla, N.D., Sept. 1, 1930. The area between lateral band and laterodorsal stripe is pale olivine or pale fluorite green. The top of back is mignonette green. The three dorsal stripes are Kronberg's green surrounded by broken lines of olive-brown. The same color extends from snout through eye and halfway along the side. The stripe below the eye is glass green. The eye is like the lateral stripe in color and has the same dots as the female's, except that the upper iris rim is primuline yellow. Under parts are pale niagara green. The throat is citrine, old gold, or olive lake.

**Structure:** Hind legs short. The original description—"*Chorophilus septentrionalis. . . . Pseudacris nigrita,* part 1, *Gunth. Cat.* p. 97. Tongue oval, slightly nicked. Vomerine teeth in two small groups behind the level of the choanae. Head longer than broad; snout subacuminate, prominent, twice as long as the diameter of the eye; latter very small, canthus rostralis rather indistinct; interorbital space a little broader than the upper eyelid; tympanum nearly as large as the eye. Fingers and toes moderately slender, latter with a slight rudiment of web; first finger shorter than second; an indistinct outer metatarsal tubercle. The hind limb being carried forwards along the body, the tibio-tarsal articulation reaches hardly the tympanum. Skin granulate above and beneath. Yellowish olive above, with five longitudinal dark bands—the median bifurcating on the sacral region, the outermost extending from the tip of the snout through the eye to the middle of the side; beneath whitish, immaculate. From snout to vent 25 millim. . . . a. ♀ Great Bear Lake. Well distinguished from *C. triseriatus* by its shorter hind limbs" (G. A. Boulenger, Gen., 1882, pp. 335–336).

Boulenger's key separates this form from *nigrita* and *triseriata* by its rough dorsal region.

**Voice:** Its call is like those of the more southern forms.

"This little frog, whose trilling notes are exactly similar to those of the more southern forms of the genus, is fairly common nearly throughout the region [Athabaska-Mackenzie Region]. . . . At Fort Simpson I first heard its notes on May 3, 1904, but failed to take specimens. I heard it also on the Mackenzie above Fort Norman early in June" (E. A. Preble, Athab., 1908, p. 502).

"Though its piercing '*prreep prreep,*' from the chilly pond, in early springtime is familiar to all, very few have seen the originator of the noise or know that it is a tiny frog that makes this small steam-whistle. While uttering it, his throat is blown out like a transparent bladder, and is nearly as big as himself. At Shoal Lake, in 1901, I found them still singing in the first week of July. The note is more rattled than that of *H. crucifer*" (E. T. Seton, Man., 1918, p. 83).

"Northern Frog. *Pseudacris*—1924: June 18, heard at One Four; Milk River July 21, one and again on Aug. 4. Common about McGrath from middle to end of August" (M. Y. Williams, Alta. and Sask., 1946, p. 49).

Harper (Athab., 1931, pp. 68–70) heard them trilling from May 11 to Oct. 21.

**Breeding:** This species breeds from May to early June. The eggs are in an irregular jelly mass attached to vegetation. The eggs are ½₀–⅟₁₆ inch (1.2–1.4 mm.). The tadpoles transform at about ⁵⁄₁₀–½ inch (7.5–13 mm.).

In Manitoba E. T. Seton has taken several immature specimens between 14.5 and 17.0 mm. R. Kennicott at Ft. Resolution, Canada, secured immatures as small as 16.5–19.0 mm. In Minnesota, in the valley of the Red River of the North, the same collector secured immatures 15.0 and 15.5 mm. Young of the latter size were secured by J. P. Jensen, September, 1908, at Eagle Bend, Minnesota. In Montana at the Crow Agency M. A. Hanna secured a similar set 16–18 mm. on July 11, 1916. All these must be well beyond transformation size, for three out of the five *nigrita* subspecies we know transform at 7.5–13 mm.

**Journal notes:** Aug. 31, 1930, Red River of the North, Pembina, N.D. Started out about 8 A.M. to beat the vegetation along the river bank, expecting to find more northern wood frogs. Along the shore is a mud flat, baked and broken into squares. The cracks are deep and fairly wide. There are deeper holes punched by cows and horses. Many crickets and spiders were running over the flats, and clouds of small insects come out of the more moist footprints. We walked along the shore, more or less abreast; Bert was in the vegetation and I walked on the flats at the edge of the vegetation. I beat the bordering vegetation with a cane and searched particularly along the mud at the edge, expecting at any moment to see a wood frog. Suddenly my eye spied a small frog sitting at the edge of one of the clumps. As I looked at it, it jumped into a crevice. As I looked closely, imagine my surprise to find that it was a *Pseudacris n. septentrionalis*. We have been looking for suitable places for the search of this species for some days. Soon after, I saw a second clinging to the edge of another crevice. As we came close to catch it, it cocked its head to one side as some other *Pseudacris* do at times. A little later, a third appeared clinging to a close-grown grassy edge covering clumps bordering the mud flats. All three are females. They certainly have short hind legs. In no case did we get the impression of the frog leaping. They must have moved to have caught my eye, but it was not a leap like that of a wood frog or meadow frog. The last one acted as if crawling up the grass. In captivity they leap from 2 to 8 inches. There are a few meadow frogs along the shore and we caught several northern wood frogs.

Sept. 1, 1930, Walhalla, N.D. The boys in searching the manholes of drainage sewers saw a midget on the side wall of one hole and with searchlight climbed down the ladder after it. It proved to be the much-desired game, a male *Pseudacris n. septentrionalis*. It is smaller than the females from Pembina and the hind legs look longer and slimmer.

**Authorities' corner:**

L. Agassiz, Ont., 1850, p. 379.
E. T. Seton, Man., 1918, pp. 82–83.
I. McT Cowan, B.C, 1939, p. 92.
G. C. Carl, B.C, 1943, p. 46.
W. J. Breckenridge, Minn., 1944, p. 67.

## Striped Tree Frog, Three-striped Tree Frog, Swamp Cricket Frog, Striped Bush Frog, Three-lined Tree Frog, Swamp Tree Frog, Peeper, Spring Peeper, Western Striped Frog, Western Marsh Toad

*Pseudacris nigrita triseriata* (Wied). Plate LIII; Maps 17, 18.

**Range:** Along the shores of Lake Ontario westward through Ontario, Michigan, Wisconsin, Minnesota, North Dakota, Montana, to Idaho southward to northern Arizona and northern New Mexico. No records in western Nebraska and Kansas. Eastern Kansas southeastward through Oklahoma to Arkansas and eastern Texas, possibly to northern Louisiana, thence through Tennessee and Kentucky (few records) to Ohio and western Pennsylvania.

**Habitat:** Low bushes and plants, and on the ground. Breeds in ditches, swamps, or temporary ponds.

"This species, though called a tree-frog, probably never climbs trees. They seem to live on the ground among the fallen forest leaves and in the grass" (O. P. Hay, Ind., 1892, p. 471).

"This is one of the nicest marked of the small frogs, found generally in early spring in the ditches along the country roads, Wet Prairie, Madison County, Ill., and near Bluff Lake, St. Clair County, Ill. It is often seen during harvesting season and for that reason farmers call it the 'Hay Frog' " (J. Hurter, Ill., 1893, p. 254).

"This species is almost always found on the ground, where it hides away under loose stones or fallen timber" (M. M. Ellis and J. Henderson, Colo., 1913, p. 58).

"It is to be found in swamps on low herbage or on the ground" (M. Morse, Ohio, 1904, p. 119).

**Size:** Adults, ⅘–1½ inches. Males, 21–32 mm. Females, 20.0–37.5 mm.

**General appearance:** These are small, slender frogs with pointed heads, extremely long fourth toes, and small disks on their toes They are brown, olive, or grayish with a dark brown triangle, spot, or stripe between the eyes The most prominent stripe is one from the nostril through the eye, over the arm, and extending along the side halfway to the groin. There are three dark stripes down the back, continuous or more or less broken up, and dark spots on the legs. There is a prominent light cream or silvery line along the upper jaw. They are light cream or white beneath. Their skin is finely granular.

April, 1928, Hilton, N.Y. At night it looks mud-colored. Seldom did the stripes or spots appear much revealed. Pointed head, long legs, small and delicate in form. When perched on a stick or floating mass, sometimes reminds me of *P. ocularis*.

**Color:** Ann Arbor, Mich., from Mrs. H. T. Gaige, April 7–8, 1929. *Female*. Sayal brown, tawny-olive, or wood brown on back and upper part of fore and hind legs and tip of head. Stripes and spots bone brown, black, or chestnut brown. The marks are: a triangle at the eyes extending backward as a median stripe, which may be interrupted and resumed and subdivided on rear back into two parallel lines; another band along dorsolateral region from above shoulder to groin; and a stripe from snout through nostril, eye, and tympanum halfway to groin. Tympanum snuff brown or mikado brown. Stripe on upper jaw warm buff or cream-buff with upper part light pinkish cinnamon below dark stripe through nostril and eye. Dark edge below this light stripe is on labial border. Iris same color as stripe along head, with dottings of mars orange or burnt sienna; over pupil rim is light yellow-green. Under parts as in *P. n. ferarium* from Carlisle, Pa., are cream color, becoming slightly massicot yellow or naphthaline yellow on throat.

*Male*. Black above (only under lens are any stripes revealed, except stripe from snout through eye halfway to groin, which is black). Light stripe on upper jaw as in female. Throat yellow ocher or old gold. Venter white. Underside of hind legs as in female. While in hand the upper parts changed to buffy olive or grayish olive.

**Structure:** Vocal pouch round and subgular.

"On the forefoot the second toe (counting from the outside) is much longer than the others, which are short; on the hind foot, very much longer still; webs of the hind feet take up not quite half the room between the toes; iris golden colored; a dark brown stripe runs from the nose through the eye up to the hind leg; the edge of the upper jaw white; all the upper part an inconspicuous, dark greenish gray, with three longitudinal rows of large, elongated spots of the same hue (only somewhat darker) on the back, . . . belly white; throat and chin brownish-olive colored; under side of the hind legs reddish gray. . . . Length 1½'; length with hind legs extended 2'9"; length of the longest foretoe 2¼"; length of the longest hind toe 4½"" (M. zu Wied, Gen., 1839, I, 249–250).

**Voice:** The call is a vibrating chirp.

"During the last weeks of March *Chorophilus* (*Pseudacris*) appears in considerable numbers about the outskirts of Buffalo. The male chorus, which is easily distinguished from that of *Hyla pickeringii*, rises from most of the swamps and temporary ponds, even within the city. The singers themselves, however, are not easily seen, for, upon approach, they become silent and further disturbance causes them to disappear into the vegetation at the bottom of the pond where they remain until some time after the disturbance has ceased. Then, from some remote corner the chorus is gradually taken up until the whole pond resounds with the ringing notes. In taking up the chorus, the assurance evidenced by the single voice is extremely contagious. This fact makes it possible to overcome some of the difficulties which ordinarily present themselves in collecting this species. One has but to place the first captures in a bag or other close receptacle and carry it on one's person. The prisoners chirp up and sing as boldly as though undisturbed in their natural haunt. Their voices elicit an almost immediate response from those in the pond. Indeed, at such a time, with a little practice one can wade about, while they sing on all sides and dip up as many as one desires. In this way after spending several hours in capturing the first two, 30 specimens, 25 males and 5 females, were taken in less than an hour" (A. H. Wright and A. A. Allen, N.Y., 1908, pp. 39–40).

"It has a note somewhat similar to the preceding species (*Acris gryllus crepitans*), but the pitch is higher and the rattle is less definite. The note is seldom heard in daylight hours except on dark days. The writer has never heard it, as Cope says, in the hottest hours" (M. Morse, Ohio, 1904, p. 119).

"With the first mild spring days, often before all the snow and ice of winter have disappeared, the loud trill of this small species may be heard from pools and ditches. The note is so resonant that on quiet evenings it may be heard a half mile or more and is commonly attributed to the larger frogs of the genus *Rana*. When the note is uttered the vocal sac is extended to its utmost and is larger than the head" (H. Garman, Ill., 1892, p. 345).

"The swamp tree frog is found in marshes and damp places throughout the summer and fall. During this time it is solitary and its call is rarely heard. It is also seldom seen because of its small size and protective coloration. When disturbed it disappears in the water, but it is a very poor swimmer and soon comes back to land. . . . It comes from hibernation early. The song is very loud. When croaking, the male sits upright in the water, supporting himself with grass, leaves or twigs, and sings with the head and vocal pouch out of the water. When disturbed, he sits perfectly still and does not resume his song until the source of the alarm has passed" (A. G. Ruthven, C. Thompson, and H. Thompson, Mich., 1912, pp. 47–48).

**Breeding:** This species breeds from March 20 to May 20. The egg mass is a loose irregular cluster, the mass small, less than 1 inch in diameter, 20–100 eggs in the mass, 500–1500 eggs in the complement. The brown or black and white egg is $\frac{1}{25}$–$\frac{1}{20}$ inch (0.9–1.2 mm.), the single envelope $\frac{1}{5}$–$\frac{5}{16}$ inch (5.0–7.8 mm.). The tadpole is small, $\frac{15}{16}$ inch (23 mm.), deep-bodied with a long tipped tail, quite black with bronze on the belly and sides, and the tooth ridges are $\frac{2}{2}$. After 40 to 90 days, the tadpoles transform in June at $\frac{5}{16}$–$\frac{7}{16}$ inch (7.5–11 mm.).

"While travelling along the state highway in the southern part of Logan, Utah, on the 15th of May, 1919, I heard great numbers of the swamp tree frog, *Pseudacris triseriata,* uttering their characteristic songs. I found this amphibian very common in small ponds at the roadside, and there were scores of egg masses, attached in most cases to blades of grass. No tadpoles had yet appeared. So numerous were the egg masses that I collected a representative lot of them. The number of eggs in the twenty-two egg masses taken were as follows: 66, 45, 53, 33, 65, 46, 88, 38, 40, 67, 32, 50, 64, 87, 77, 15, 65, 51, 73, 45, 130, and 190. The number of eggs here found is much greater than that typical of the species as given by Dickerson in The Frog Book, i.e., 5–20 (page 159). The masses containing 130 and 190 eggs respectively seem extreme. There is a possibility that two egg masses became fused in these cases, but except for the fact that the numbers of eggs are unusually high there is no reason for believing so, as the gelatinous material remained in one compact body, and gave no evidence of a multiple origin" (H. J. Pack, Utah, 1920, p. 7).

"Eggs and adults of this little frog were taken in temporary pools formed by the melting snow along a railroad right-of-way near Boulder, during the first ten days of May, 1914. On May 9 eggs were collected in the four-celled stage and kept out of doors in water from the pool in which they were found. The development of these eggs was very rapid, a fact which may be correlated with the use of temporary pools as the spawning grounds by this species. On the 11th all the eggs were in the elongated stage preceding hatching, and during the 12th most of the eggs hatched. The tadpoles of *Chorophilus triseriatus* immediately after leaving the eggs were very black and about 8 mm. in length, resembling the tadpoles of the common toad in outline" (M. M. Ellis and J. Henderson, Colo., 1915, p. 257).

"May 17, 1919, Fort Sheridan, Ill. Found *Pseudacris feriarum* [*triseriata*] breeding in trenches on the Rifle Range and collected a couple of egg clusters. The eggs are attached to grass stems arranged in a layer one or two eggs thick all around the stem, forming a mass about two inches long and less than half an inch in diameter. . . . June 22. Tadpoles of this species are metamorphosing in the same pools on the Rifle Range where eggs were found on May 17. They were in all stages of development, from tadpoles two-thirds grown, with short hind legs, to young frogs with tails nearly absorbed. The measurements of several specimens follow: Two full-grown tadpoles with short hind legs measured 26 and 26.5 mm. Four with large hind legs and fore-legs almost ready to burst out; 25.5, 27, 27.5, and 28 mm. Four young frogs with all four legs well developed and tails in different stages of absorption measured 10, 10, 10, and 11 mm. in body length" (P. H. Pope, Ill., 1919, pp. 83–84).

"Its eggs were found in a small pool on the 22d of March. They were attached to twigs in small and large bunches. Each egg was one-third inch in diameter, including the usual coating of jelly. . . . The tadpoles were set free on April 5. They are slenderer than the larvae of the Leopard Frog, and not so dark in color. They are dark gray rather than black. . . . The rudiments of the hinder limbs appear about the 20th of April. At the same time two rows of horny teeth appear on each lip, and a few days later an additional row on the lower lip. These teeth are minutely denticulated at their tips, and they form an admirable apparatus for scraping off the layer of nutritious slime that covers all objects in the water. There are from 55–95 of these teeth in each row. . . . By April 20 the length has become one-half inch and by May 4 about three quarters. The body is of a dark color, adorned with numerous blotches of gold. The belly is nearly covered with a shimmer of gold and coppery. When three-fourths inch long the young were observed to come to the surface and take in air. By the 20th of May the young have attained the total length of a little over an inch. By the 26th of May the tadpoles had attained a length, in some cases, of 28 mm., 16 of which is tail" (O. P. Hay, Ind., 1889, p. 773).

"Many of them about this time succeed in releasing their forelegs from the skin which has held them down. Now the tadpoles grow smaller instead of larger. This is largely due to the shortening of the intestine at this period of transformation. These four-legged tadpoles are very lively and very timid. They show a great inclination to get out of the water and to hop about. They soon lose their skill in swimming, and if confined to the water too long will drown. The disks are seen on their fore feet as soon as these feet appear. The tails are rapidly absorbed, and by the 12th of June all have become little frogs like the adults, except in size. At the time of transformation the length of the head and body is less than one-half inch" (same, p 471)

"In Kansas the eggs are more numerous in their respective masses than these previous accounts would indicate, numbers varying from 110–300, the mode being about 140. Wright and Wright [Gen., 1924, p. 381] give 500–800 as the egg complement One female observed by the writer laid 1,459 eggs during a single night in the aquarium in which she was isolated. The membranes of the eggs from females near Lawrence differ somewhat from the type figured by Wright and Wright [Gen., 1924, pl. 1, fig. 7]. The outer envelope is typically about 3.0 mm.; there was, in several bunches of eggs, a second membrane about 2.1 mm. in diameter; the vitellus is as given by Wright and Wright (0.9 to 1.2 mm.). . . . There is always a vitelline membrane closely applied to the vitellus" (H. M. Smith, Kans., 1934, pp. 467, 468).

In 1936 K. A. Youngstrom and H. M. Smith (Kans., 1936, pp. 629–630) described the tadpoles of this species. The distinctive thing they showed is lower labial tooth rows 3 instead of 2. This is a fact that like many others we discovered soon after our 1929 paper.

**Journal notes:** Ithaca, N.Y. Frogs from Buffalo, N.Y. On the morning of April 2, 1907, the 25 males were placed with the 5 females. At 9:50 A.M. the first pair was recorded and within 20 minutes the female began laying. With one exception, she chose a different perch for each egg-laying period, thus giving a bunch to each period of sexual activity. In one instance she sought the same perch three successive times. This pair consumed 2½ hours in laying a complement of 500–600 eggs. The process required about 90 fertilizations and emissions. Each time from two to ten eggs were voided, being emitted in small strings, a condition readily seen when occasionally the eggs were unattached and hung down from the vent of the female. All the eggs were laid in water 66°F.

April 4, 1928, Hilton Beach, Hilton, N.Y. The common name, "Chorus frog," is very appropriate. Only a few toads, meadow frogs, and peepers were speaking. It was a very deafening chorus, not like *Hyla femoralis* and some larger Hylas but very pronounced. This Swamp Cricket Frog may be in swampy places where there is brush, but it can hardly be kept down in note to a cricket when in chorus.

In New York I had never heard it except at Hilton, Hilton Beach, Buffalo, and Hamburg. By its chorus, we found it in Greece, April 4, at Hilton and Hilton Beach April 4 and 5, and at Buttonwood Creek at Parma and Greece town line. On April 5 heard it near Rochester, near Webster, Williamson, near Westbury, 3 miles north of Auburn on the Auburn Weedsport road.

April, 1928, Hilton, N.Y. West of Mt. Reed Church, Greece, we found it in a pond in an orchard where several small trees and bushes were, and also brush. The frogs seemed to be in a grassy field, but mostly along a fence-row pond with trees and brush. Along Parma and Greece town line, they were in overflow pools of Buttonwood Creek. Not brushy there. They were also in pools in grassy fields toward Braddock's Bay.

May 30, 1942. With Wilmer Webster Tanner went 1 mile west of Provo, Utah, to a spring. Here heard a great chorus of *P n. triseriata*. Anna caught a female.

June 8, Flagstaff, Ariz. Went to Museum of Northern Arizona Met E. D. McKee, H. S. Colton, Major Brady. At museum saw *Pseudacris n triseriatus* from Apache County. . . . Tonight went to Mary's Lake, 7 miles long. At upper end a great chorus of *P. n. triseriatus*. When we returned, in a stream back of the motel heard several *P. n. triseriata*.

**Authorities' corner:**

F. W. Cragin, Kans., 1876–81, p 121.
B. W Evermann and H W. Clark, Ind., 1920, pp. 635–636.
A. R. Cahn, Ill., 1926, pp. 107–108.
F. G. Evenden, Jr, Ida., 1946, p. 257.

## Florida Chorus Frog, Florida Winter Frog

*Pseudacris nigrita verrucosa* (Cope) Plate LIV; Map 17.

**Range:** "Peninsular Florida. Known from the following counties: Alachua, Duval, Volusia, Marion, Putnam, Sumter, Lake, Hernando, Pinellas, Polk, St. Lucie, Charlotte, Lee, Collier, Broward and Dade" (Carr, Fla., 1940, p 56).

**Habitat:** Flatwoods, prairie lands, glade depressions, and ponds. "Swamps

*Plate LIII. Pseudacris nigrita triseriata* (×1). 1,3,5,6 Females. 2 Male 4. Eggs.

*Plate LIV. Pseudacris nigrita verrucosa* (×1). 1–6. Males.

and grassy ponds and ditches; moderately common" (O. C. Van Hyning, Fla., 1933, p. 4).

**Size:** Adults ⅘–1⅕ inches (22–30 mm. or more).

**General appearance and structure:** "The length of the head to the posterior margin of the membranum tympani enters the total length to the vent three and one-sixth times. The head itself is narrow and acuminate, the muzzle projecting acutely beyond the labial margin. The external nares mark two-fifths the distance from the end of the muzzle to the orbital border. The membranum tympani is only one-fourth the diameter of the orbit. The canthus rostralis is distinct, but obtusely rounded. The vomerine fasciculi are approximated, and near the line of the posterior border of the nares, which are larger than the minute *ostia pharyngea.* The tongue is large and wide behind and faintly emarginate.

"The heel of the extended hind limb extends to between the orbit and nostril: the femur is short, while the tarsus is long, a little exceeding half the length of the tibia, and exceeding the length of the remainder of the foot, minus the longest toe. The skin of the gular and sternal region is smooth; of the abdomen, areolate. That of the dorsal region is tubercular, smooth warts of large and small size being irregularly crowded over its entire surface, and not at all resembling the areolate surface of the belly.

"Color above leaden, with three longitudinal rows of darker, light-edged spots, extending, one on each side, and one on the median line. They are each composed of a series of spots joined end to end. Femur and tibia cross-barred. Upper lip dark plumbeous, with a series of five white spots; a similar spot below the tympanum Inferior surfaces yellowish. . . .

"From Volusia, Florida; Mrs. A. D. Lungren. 'This *Chorophilus* is similar in proportions to the *C. triseriatus,* but is well distinguished by the characters of the skin, and the coloration. The tubercular upper surface is quite peculiar, and the smooth gular region is equally wanting to the Northern Frog The dorsal skin is somewhat like that of *Acris gryllus*' " (E. D. Cope, Fla., 1877, pp. 87–88).

"Cope is clearly in error in stating [Gen., 1889, p. 338] that *verrucosus* differs from *C. nigritus* (Le Conte) in the somewhat longer tarsus, and from *C. feriarum* (Baird) in the longer hind leg. He records the tarsus of *nigritus* as 9 4 mm, and the 'hind leg' of *feriarum* as 1.77 in. (45 mm.), as compared with a 'hind limb' of 26 mm. in *verrucosus.* The type of *verrucosus* is unquestionably immature" (M. K. Brady and F. Harper, Fla., 1935, p. 108).

These authors emphasize "the maxillary stripe broken to form a series of irregular dots and bars or lacking" (A. F. Carr, Jr., Fla., 1934, p. 32).

**Voice:** "During the night of January 20, 1932, R. F. Deckert and I were collecting in the Royal Palm Hammock, on Paradise Key. In this tropical setting we were surprised to hear the trilling of *Pseudacris* coming from the 'glade' on the west side of the hammock. The call, though possibly a little higher in pitch, was remarkably similar to that of *P. n. feriarum* as heard in the vicinity of Washington, D.C. The chorus was very small and localized. After considerable difficulty we managed to approach the position of the calls and found them coming from depressions and 'potholes' among the limestone rocks and 'glade' vegetation. These depressions contained shallow ponds that were choked with *Isnardia.* Once we had gotten into their immediate vicinity, the frogs became silent, but by running a finger along the teeth of a pocket comb, we were able to imitate the voice sufficiently to induce them to call again. We thus located the males, which occupied well-separated stations and were sitting on projections of the limestone above the water line of the little ponds" (M. K. Brady and F. Harper, Fla., 1935, p. 109).

"The call is similar to that of *nigrita,* but the individual crepitations come much faster—perhaps twice as fast—and to some extent suggest the song of *feriarum*" (A. F. Carr, Jr., Fla., 1940, p. 56).

**Breeding and Journal notes:** "Flatwoods; prairie lands of the south-central peninsula. Not common Habits apparently similar to those of *nigrita* Breeding February to August 15, in cypress ponds, flooded meadows, drainage ditches in the muck land around Lake Okeechobee, and in 'pot-holes' and ditches in the South Florida limestone" (A. F. Carr, Jr., Fla , 1940, p. 56).

On Feb. 7, 1932, O. C. Van Hyning of Gainesville, Fla., wrote as follows: "I went out into the middle of the Prairie a few nights ago, where there was a little water, and caught eight males and one female of *P nigrita;* the female and one male I watched from the time they were about a foot apart, until they mated, and would have stayed on another hour or so, but the mosquitoes had just about eaten me up, so I caught them. They have so far failed to mate again although two males were together once. The amplexation was axillary. I am going out to the same place as soon as I finish this letter, and see if I can get any additional females and see the eggs deposited."

The following week, on Feb. 15, he wrote: "I have . . . two pairs mated, one of a male and a female, one of a female and two males, and one case of two males [in the laboratory]. I have one bunch of eggs laid in the laboratory, but they were pretty well walked over before I rescued them. I didn't know whether they were fertile or not and have preserved them."

Brady at Royal Palm Hammock wrote: "In addition to a series of six calling males, we took a pair in amplexus. The female deposited 160 eggs, a few separately, but the majority in a loose mass not differing from the egg mass of *feriarum.* The brown and white eggs resembled those of *feriarum,* but seemed somewhat smaller, the vitellus measuring less than 0.5 mm. The single envelope measured 1.5–2 mm. Development was very rapid and hatching took place within 60 hours" (M. K. Brady and F. Harper, Fla., 1935, p. 109).

On Feb. 4, 1933, at Gainesville, Fla., Messrs. A. F. Carr and H. K. Wallace found this species breeding at the same time as *P. ocularis* and *P. ornata*. The eggs they sent us were brown and cream or white, the vitellus 1/25 inch (0.9–1.0 mm.), the single envelope 1/10–1/9 inch (2.6–2.8 mm.).

Cope emphasized the warty upper surface. We have seen very warty ones in the southern half of the peninsula, and W. J. Hamilton, Jr., at Ft. Myers March 11, 1940, took very tubercular specimens.

**Authorities' corner:**

A. F. Carr, Jr., Fla., 1940, p. 55.

## Western Chorus Frog

*Pseudacris occidentalis* (Baird and Girard). Plate LV.

This frog probably does not exist.

If Cope (1889) was unwarranted in assigning *Chorophilus occidentalis* (B & G) (1853) to the eastern *Rana ornata* Holbrook (1836) or *Cystignathus ornatus* Holbrook (1842), what then is this *Litoria occidentalis* which Baird and Girard described in a paper entitled "A List of Reptiles Collected in California by Dr. John L. Le Conte . . ."? We prefer to believe it was collected in *California*. All the other batrachians of the report were strictly western forms. Baird and Girard report *Hyla regilla* in this same paper (Calif., 1853, p. 301), first describe it in another place of this same volume (p. 174), and Hallowell also describes *Hyla regilla* in the same volume (p. 183) as *Hyla scapularis*. Nevertheless the *Litoria occidentalis* of this report might well be another variant specimen of the very variable *Hyla regilla* At that period we have Hallowell in the one paper (Calif., 1856, pp. 96–97) describing *Hyla regilla* three times as *Hyla scapularis*, *Hyla nebulosa*, and *Hyla scapularis* var. *hypochondriaca*. We therefore suspect *Litoria occidentalis* of being a synonym of a western *Hyla*, presumably *Hyla regilla*. A glance at the plate of *Hyla regilla* (Plate LXX) will show at once how many resemblances this species has to *Pseudacris*.

In 1889 Cope (Gen., p. 337) speaks of *C. occidentalis* (which we now term *P. ornata*) as ranging "to the Wichita River, in north central Texas. Specimens were sent me from the latter locality by that excellent naturalist, Jacob Boll, of Dallas. . . . It does not occur in California as supposed when first described." What are these Texan forms?

The records of three friends, C. S. Brimley, J. Hurter, and J. K. Strecker, are yet to be discussed. Brimley (Ala., 1910, p. 11) secured "*Chorophilus occidentalis* from Bay St. Louis, Mississippi, February and April 1898, 5" and *Chorophilus ornatus* "Hastings, Florida, June, 1901, 1; Green Cove Springs, Florida, July, 1898, 5." Doubtless a specimen in U.S. National Museum, no. 29189, labeled *C. occidentalis* Hastings, Fla. H. H. & C. S. Brimley, is the one specimen Brimley rightly called *C. ornatus* above. He is the only person to receive each from the Southeast and the only one in that period to call the Floridan form *C. ornatus*. But what was the *Chorophilus occidentalis* of Bay St. Louis, Miss.?

In the *Amphibians and Reptiles of Arkansas,* Hurter and Strecker record *Chorophilus occidentalis* from "Hot Springs (Combs)." Strecker knows *Pseudacris streckeri* (*ornata* of Cope, 1889) and has contributed as much as or more than anyone living to its habits, but the *Pseudacris occidentalis* is the puzzle.

Since the paragraph above was written, there have come to hand Strecker's records of *Pseudacris ornata* (*streckeri*) and *Pseudacris occidentalis.* In recent times only two people have collected *Pseudacris occidentalis* in life to recognize it. Richard F. Deckert secured it in Jacksonville along with *P. n. nigrita* and *P. ocularis.* This author does not record *P. ornata* and his descriptions of *P. occidentalis* are those of *P. ornata,* but the records of the other author who has recently seen this species cannot be so readily allocated to *P. ornata* (*occidentalis* of Cope and Deckert), or *P. streckeri* (*ornata* of Cope and Strecker). The only collector in America who has taken *P. occidentalis* and the Texan *P. ornata* (now called *P. streckeri*) in the same region, alive, is J. K. Strecker.

On Sept. 1, 1929, he wrote of the capture of specimens of each species in the Fort Worth region:

"Western Chorus Frog (*Pseudacris occidentalis* (Baird and Girard)). I captured two specimens. One, a junior, was caught four miles beyond Benbrook, in grass under the edge of a rock along a roadside; the second example, an adult, was caught among grass growing along a creek bank. Ornate Chorus Frog (*Pseudacris ornata* Holbrook). North and east of Fort Worth, I caught three adults among grass growing on the banks of small creeks" (J. K. Strecker, Jr., Tex., 1929, p. 11).

In one museum some little *P. ocularis* were termed *P. occidentalis.* Of several different museum accessions considered *P. occidentalis,* we have made the positive note: "This is *P. streckeri.* Possibly some of the Texan representatives may prove *P. n. clarkii.*"

In 1930 we visited Dr. J. K. Strecker, Jr., and received many kindnesses from him. While we were in the field for *P streckeri* (*ornata* of Strecker), he remarked that what he had recorded as *P. occidentalis* appeared different from *P. streckeri* (*ornata*) and had different habits. He kindly loaned us what specimens he had of *P. occidentalis.* At first they puzzled us, but the more we examined them the more we inclined to interpret them as the spotted individuals of the so-called *P. n. clarkii.* Taking his Nos. 4501 and 4502 (Baylor Museum) of Fort Worth and Bluff Creek, McLennan Co., and comparing them with his 3507 *P. nigrita,* we call all three *P. n. clarkii.* Another specimen, *P. occidentalis,* from Gayle, La. (Frierson), may be a large female *P. nigrita* (*triseriata*).

Before we saw these specimens (4501, 4502) we wondered if they might be like *P. streckeri,* but in longer head-to-tympanum, wider head, smaller eye, wider internasal, shorter hind limb, shorter first, second, third, fourth, and fifth toes, *P. streckeri* does not overlap the relative measurements (number of times in length) of these two *P. occidentalis* specimens.

| | 4501, 4502 | *P. streckeri* |
|---|---|---|
| Head to tympanum | 3.16– 3.29 | 2.38 – 3.0 |
| Width of head | 3.11– 3.47 | 2.4 – 2.88 |
| Internasal sp. | 11.2 –11.8 | 8.0 –10.2 |
| Eye | 8.44– 9.33 | 9.33 –12.0 |
| Hind limb | 0.66– 0.72 | 0.734– 0.87 |
| First toe | 5.45– 5.6 | 6.22 – 9.0 |
| Second toe | 4.3 – 4.52 | 4.66 – 5.53 |
| Third toe | 2.8 – 2.95 | 3.11 – 3.6 |
| Fourth toe | 2.0 – 2.18 | 2.15 – 2.57 |
| Fifth toe | 2.66– 2.68 | 2.8 – 3.5 |

The relative measurements of Nos. 4501 and 4502 fall within the relative measurements of *P. n. clarkii* in almost every respect except head length and intertympanic and internasal widths. Most of the measurements of No. 1378, the specimen from Gayle, La., fall within those of *P. n. triseriata.*

All in all our conclusions are that these *P. occidentalis* specimens may be forms of *P. nigrita* and are not *P. streckeri* (*ornata* of Strecker and Cope). Frogs called *P. occidentalis* in Georgia and Florida are *P. ornata* (Holbrook)

### Little Chorus Frog, Swamp Tree Frog, Swamp Cricket Frog, Tree Frog, Savanna Cricket (Bartram), Least Swamp Frog

*Pseudacris ocularis* (Holbrook). Plate LVI; Map 18.

**Range:** North Carolina to southern Florida.

**Habitat:** Sphagnum edge of cypress pond. Grassy or sedgy area of pond or wet edge of pine barrens.

May 18, 1921, *Pseudacris ocularis* may start up from sphagnum edge of cypress pond or may start up from the ground. They will leap 1–1½ feet at times. These specimens sat on *Eriocaulon*, small *Sarracenia minor*, sedge, and saw palmetto. We took a dozen of them. On June 25, we found them common in one pond, many in bamboo (smilax) vines, on bushes some 4–5 feet up, others on level of water. July 15, we found them abundant in outer edges of cypress ponds, margins of cypress bays. Most of them we caught in the grass near the edge of ponds. June 17, 1922, we found them in grassy and sedgy areas on wet edge of pine barrens or outer edge of cypress bay or branch.

"Wet grassy places, especially in the pine flatwoods, common" (O. C. Van Hyning, Fla., 1933, p. 4).

**Size:** Adults, ⅖–⅝ inch. Males, 11.5–15.5 mm. Females, 12.0–17.5 mm.

**General appearance:** These are the brownies of frogdom in the United States. They may be uniform gray, brown, greenish, or reddish on the back with a dark vitta from the eye backward as a stripe of variable length. This is set off by a light area below the eye extending backward to the shoulder. There may be a dark triangle between the eyes with a stripe extending down the

*Plate LV* *Pseudacris occidentalis* (×⅔). 1–7. Males. 8. Female.

*Plate LVI.* *Pseudacris ocularis* 1,4,5,7,8. Adults (×1¼). 2,6 Males (×1¼) 3 Male croaking (×1).

mid-back and a stripe on either side of this. These little frogs are so tiny, so delicate, that it does not seem possible that they are adult frogs. Their form is slender, their legs long, their eyes bright and beadlike, their snouts very pointed and extending beyond the lower jaw. The nostrils are on the sides of the pointed snout. These little midgets can turn their heads or tip them upward or sideways without turning the body.

**Color:** On May 17, 1921, Okefinokee Swamp, Ga., we had diverse colorings in a lot of 16 in one pan. Some were tawny, hazel, or amber brown on upper surfaces; others buckthorn brown; one a light grayish olive or light olive-gray; another deep olive-gray. The stripe on the upper jaw was almost cream, chalcedony yellow, or glass green. Belly chamois or cream-buff. Iris cinnamon.

On Aug. 18, 1922, at Hilliard, Fla., found a little *Pseudacris ocularis* which is cinnamon or ochraceous-tawny in color. It is an adult male with a plaited throat. The ten specimens vary in color from gray, greenish, light yellowish olive or dull citrine through to chestnut or bay; four specimens were of the yellowish olive or gray group, four of the chestnut or bay group, and two intermediate. The most distinctive, yet not always constant, mark is a line of dark color which runs from the snout or nostril through the eye and tympanum to or beyond the arm insertion. In three specimens it runs halfway to the hind limbs. In two more it just passes the arm insertion, as Holbrook figures it. In two this dark stripe is absent. In the striped individuals the limbs bear crossbars. In all material, the entire upper surfaces have a very fine speckling of close-set dark dots. The under parts are whitish or yellowish white with the fine speckled dots of the upper parts all over the ventral side. In some the underside of limbs is almost as dark as the upper parts.

When four specimens arrived May 7, 1929, from Gainesville, Fla., from O. C. Van Hyning, in sphagnum, all were different: one was uniform carnelian red above with no stripes except vitta on side; another dark olive; one deep olive-buff with three stripes on back; and one avellaneous. Later the carnelian red was entirely changed.

**Structure:** Midgets in size; snout pointed and projecting beyond the lower jaw; nostrils on sides of snout; slender in form, hind legs very long; eyes bright and beadlike; disks on fingers and toes small but distinct; skin of back covered with very fine warts.

"*H. ocularis. H. ocularis* Daudin, 1 c. p. 32. *Hylodes ocularis* Holbrook, pl. 35. Above brown or bronzed or silvery grey, very finely speckled with dusky or darker, a tolerably wide band of black proceeds from the tip of the nose to the middle or beyond the middle of the sides, this is bordered beneath with white. Chin and underside of the thighs speckled with black. Legs speckled like the back and more or less spotted and barred with dusky, fingers and toes all furnished with small disks. Length .6. Inhabits Georgia. The smallest of all known Ranina. From the small size of this and the preceding species, the web between the third and fourth toes is not very perceptible" (J. Le Conte, Gen., 1855, p. 429).

**Voice:** The call is a high, shrill, cricketlike chirp or trill. Vocal sac of the male even when collapsed sometimes appears to cover almost half of the venter

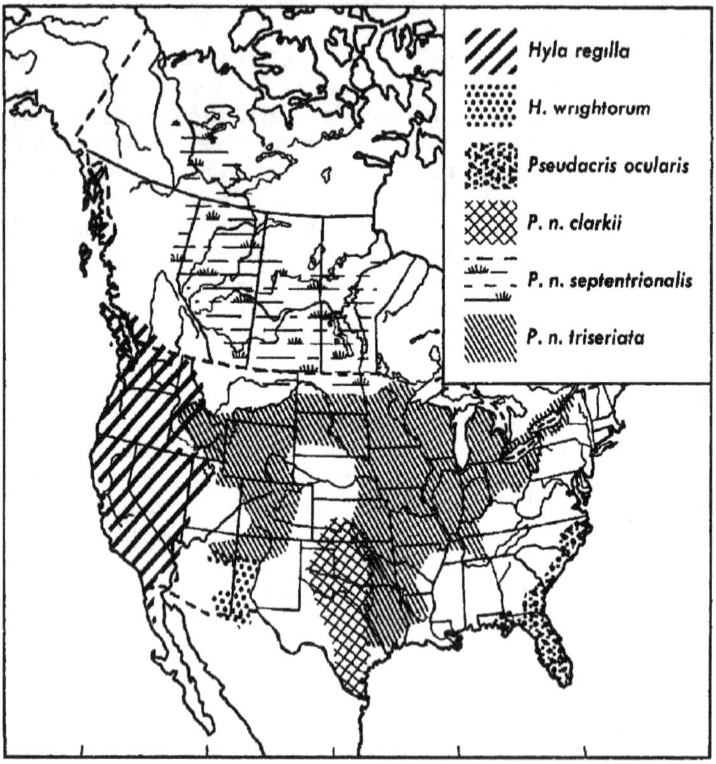


*Map 18*

of the body. The rear of it may reach caudad to the pectoral region, to the line connecting one arm insertion with the other. Our first acquaintance with a chorus came the evening of May 20, 1921, in Okefinokee Swamp, Ga. Went down to the pond east of the Negro quarters and it sounded as if bedlam had broken loose. I heard a cricketlike note everywhere. It was *Pseudacris ocularis*. One frog was on a grassy mat, one on a log, another calling from pine brush at the edge of the water, another on the bole of a tree. They do not like the electric spotlight. One on pine brush worked up into the leaves. We flashed one on the side of a black gum. Its throat pouch was transparent and we could see through it and discern the bark behind. The croaks were given 30–65 per minute. The note is high-pitched, penetrating, can be heard 150–200 feet away. Whether characterized as chirp, trill, cheep, squeak, or high shrill insect call, it surely is a loud piercing call for so little a mite of frog flesh. It is an amusing little creature as it squeezes its slender body and throws out its large sac one-half the size of the body.

**Breeding:** It breeds from January to September. The brown and cream eggs are single, laid on the bottom of ponds and in vegetation in shallow water, about 100 in number. The egg is 1/40–1/30 inch (0.6–0.8 mm.), the single envelope 1/20–1/12 inch (1.2–2.0 mm.). The greenish tadpole is small, 15/16 inch (23 mm.), its tail long. Its tooth ridges are 2/3. After 45 to 70 days the tadpoles transform, June 30 to August 18, at 5/16–3/8 inch (7–9 mm.).

**Journal notes:** In 1921, on July 3, we took a handcar trip to Honey and Black Jack Islands. It was a misty day at first, then sunny a while; it rained all the afternoon, however. The temperature was from 71°–76°. On the sphagnaceous strand of Honey Island heard these creatures near Black Jack Island; in mid-afternoon on Honey Island, in Cypress Bay between the Pocket and Jones Island, and all over the prairie, in sphagnum of wet thickets especially. Also all along the trestle between Jones Island and Billy's Island. Never heard such a frog din.

On July 29, 1921, we were caught in a downpour on Black Jack Island. We were encamped in the moist pine barrens. All about was the strongest chorus of *Pseudacris ocularis* we ever heard. Temperature about 73°.

In 1922, we secured them on Chesser Island, near old Suwannee canal, along the road to Folkston, in ponds near Trader's Hill, near an overgrown sphagnum bog outside the swamp, and along the road from Folkston, Ga., to Jacksonville, Fla.

**Authorities' corner:**

W. Bartram, Gen., 1791, p. 278.
F. M. Daudin, Gen., 1801–1803, VIII, 68–69.
J. E. Holbrook, Gen., 1842, p. 138.
G. K. Noble, Gen., 1923, pp. 1–5
F. Harper, Ga., 1939, p. 148.

## Ornate Chorus Frog, Ornate Tree Frog, Ornate Swamp Frog, Swamp Cricket Frog, Ornate Winter Frog, Holbrook Chorus Frog

*Pseudacris ornata* (Holbrook). Plate LVII; Map 16.

**Range:** North Carolina (B. B. Brandt, 1933) to Georgia, Florida, and possibly west along the Gulf to Louisiana. Alabama (Viosca).

**Habitat:** Holbrook wrote of its habits: "I have always found it on land and in dry places, and frequently in cornfields after light summer showers. It is very lively and active, making immense leaps when pursued, and consequently is taken with great difficulty." "The structure of this species indicates terrestrial, possibly subterraneous habits. I have dug specimens out of the sweet potato hills in my garden" (R. F. Deckert, Fla., 1915). M. J. Allen found it breeding in grass-land pools. "Grassy ditches and ponds; moderately common" (O. C. Van Hyning, Fla., 1933, p. 4).

**Size:** Adults, 1–1⅖ inches. Males, 25–35 mm. Females, 28–36 mm.

**General appearance:** This is a large *Pseudacris,* looking almost like a small *Rana sylvatica.* The general color of this frog is chestnut brown with two indistinct darker dorsal bars and an indistinct darker spot between the eyes. There is a prominent dark, almost black, vitta from tip of snout through eye over tympanum, usually beyond the arm insertion, often extending halfway to the groin. Two frogs with more prominent stripes have, between the eyes, Y-shaped triangles, which in the other four do not show. The groin spots are inclined to be almost black oblique bars, with light outlines. In fact, the spots on groin are on a yellow background. The tiniest rim of the upper jaw is dark, but above this is a conspicuous light line extending to the arm insertion and broadest under the eye. On the front of the upper arm is a dark bar. The eyes are very prominent with the upper part of the iris a bright gold band. The throat of the male is dark olive, with a central longitudinal plait. The throat of the female is light. The legs are barred.

Cope characterized it well enough but added to the confusion by calling it *Chorophilus occidentalis* B & G.

"Muzzle rounded in profile, projecting. Skin of upper surface smooth. . . . More slender [than *C. ornatus*]; width of head entering length 3 to 3.5 times; nostril nearer end of muzzle than orbit; posterior foot longer, not webbed, and without subarticular tubercles; heel reaching middle of orbit" (E. D. Cope, Gen., 1889, p. 332).

G. A. Boulenger, who called it *Chorophilus copii,* wrote "Vomerine teeth behind the level of the choanae; tibio-tarsal articulation not reaching the eye; back immaculate" (Gen., 1882, p. 332).

"*Chorophilus copii.* Tongue circular, entire vomerine teeth in two slightly oblique oval groups behind the level of the choanae Head slightly longer than broad; snout rounded, as long as the diameter of the orbit; canthus rostralis rather indistinct; interorbital space as broad as the upper eyelid; tympanum somewhat more than half the diameter of the eye. Fingers and toes moderate, the tips very indistinctly dilated; first finger shorter than second; toes with a slight rudiment of web; subarticular tubercles small; no outer metatarsal tubercle. The hind limb being carried forwards along the body, the tibio-tarsal articulation marks the tympanum. Skin smooth above, granulate on the belly. Olive above; sides with three black spots, viz, a streak from the eye to the shoulder, an oval spot in the middle of the side, and one or two smaller ones on the loan. Georgia. A ♀ Georgia.

"Mr. Cope considers this frog specifically distinct from *C. ornatus* and identifies it with *Hyla ocularis* of Daudin. The latter opinion I cannot share, as nothing in the French author's description and figure indicates the least analogy with this form. The toes are represented as half-webbed in *H. ocularis* and the digital expansions of *C. copii* are so slight that they would certainly have escaped Daudin's observation. Moreover the colour is quite different" (same, p. 334).

**Color:** Gainesville, Fla., from O. C. Van Hyning, March 24, 1932. *First male.* The background color of the back and top of head is sayal brown or tawny-olive, becoming on top of fore limb and eyelids and top of head cinnamon or orange-cinnamon. The hind legs may be verona brown. The band on either side of middle of back is indistinct and is snuff brown or Saccardo's umber. The stripe from snout obliquely upward to nostril, thence through eye over tympanum, shoulder insertion, two-thirds of way to groin, may be black or sepia in front and warm sepia at the caudal end. The one or two groin spots may be warm sepia, chocolate, or walnut brown. The three bars on femur are the same color. The interstices of groin spots are light cadmium to lemon yellow. There are also flecks of the same on the front of the upper half of the femur. The front of the femur is partly dark vinaceous-brown. The rear of femur has punctulations of vinaceous-brown or dark vinaceous-brown. Lower end of rear of femur has a few spots of lemon yellow or lemon chrome. The side of body is vinaceous-buff, at times becoming on top of hind legs and side light drab or pale drab-gray. The light band on upper edge of upper jaw is pale dull green-yellow, becoming at angle of mouth and under the tympanum white. The dark vitta from eye backwards on its upper margin has a thin outline of seafoam yellow to white; the groin spot or spots have a suggestion of the same thing. The upper jaw rim is a thin line of buffy brown. The eye color in the lower half partakes of color of the vitta, wherein the upper half is the color of top of head. There is a prominent natal brown or vinaceous-brown band from the lateral vitta down across the arm insertion extending even onto the forearm to make its first crossbar. On forearm, there is a prominent bar of same color at base of hand. The underside of fore and hind limbs is brownish vinaceous. The belly is a dirty white with considerable spotting in the rear pectoral region of drab or olive-brown. The throat is pronouncedly discolored, its rear sharply outlined by a fold; the caudal half is olive-ocher or old gold, the cephalic portion is Saccardo's olive, the two central plaits becoming olive-citrine. The edge of the lower jaw is spotted with white or pale dull green-yellow. After we had finished describing it, the dorsal color came to be uniform with no suggestion of long dorsal stripes.

*Second male.* A uniform mahogany red, chestnut, or bay on the back.

*Female.* Charleston, S.C., from E. B. Chamberlain, Nov. 4, 1932. The background color of the back and top of head is Hay's russet, becoming on side orange-cinnamon or sayal brown. The two parallel dorsal bands are liver brown or carob brown, so also are the bars on the femur and tibia. Those on tarsus and foot merge into black. Snout stripe, eye vitta, lateral and groin spots are light cadmium or lemon yellow. The rear of the femur much as in the male. The light band along the upper jaw is very narrow and whitish. The upper jaw rim is bone brown. The eye is like that of the male. The venter is more or less like that of the male, except that the throat is white without discolor.

**Structure:** Form more slender than *Pseudacris streckeri;* head narrower than *P. streckeri;* arms and legs longer and more slender than *P. streckeri;* fingers and toes long and slender, with mere trace of web at base of toes; snout pointed; nostril equidistant between snout and eye; vomerine teeth between nares.

"The head is small, with a broad, indistinct, triangular spot between the orbits, the apex of which is directed backwards. A black line extends from the snout to the orbit of the eye, including the nostrils; below this black line is a yellowish blotch, covering most of the upper jaw. The lower jaw is cinereous above and white below. The mouth is small, and the palate is armed with two groups of exceedingly minute teeth between the posterior nares. The nostrils are placed on a slight prominence. The eyes are large and projecting, the pupil very dark, the iris of a golden colour. The tympanum is small, very dark colored, and placed in a dark vitta, or blotch, which extends behind the orbit to within a short distance of the shoulder. The body is short, of a delicate dove-colour above, with two or more oblong spots of dark brown, margined with yellow, on each side of the vertebral line; below these, and on each flank, are three smaller spots, likewise margined with bright yellow, the anterior one being the largest; these, with a smaller one above the vent, form a triangle on each flank. . . . The toes are five in number, not palmated, the two outer ones only are united at the base. Dimensions. Length of body from the snout to the vent, 1¼ inches; of the thighs, ½ an inch; of the leg, ½ an inch; of the tarsus and toes, nearly ⅞ of an inch" (J. E. Holbrook, Gen., 1842, pp. 103–104).

**Voice:** "This call is very loud, similar in pitch to that of *Hyla pickeringi,* but much shorter, and at a distance sounds like the ring of a steel chisel, when struck by a hammer . . ." (R. F. Deckert, Fla., 1915).

Norman Davis of Gainesville, Fla., says, "The call reminds me of *Hyla crucifer* but is without the trill."

"I have timed *ornata* and found the calls to be repeated from 65–80 times a minute. I have never actually timed *crucifer,* but its calls are a good deal slower, probably 40–50 per minute. *Ornata's* call is a single sharply terminated note, while *crucifer's* is a more deliberate slur from a lower to a higher" (letter from A. F. Carr, Feb. 5, 1933).

**Breeding:** Winter months. November, December, January to March depending upon the rains. H. K. Wallace and A. F. Carr, Jr., at Gainesville, Fla., secured eggs laid Feb. 5, 1933. They are brown and cream or white, and measure: the vitellus 1/25 inch (0.9–1.0 mm.), the single loose envelope 1/7–1/6 inch (3.6–4.2 mm.). They transform at ⅝ inch (14–16 mm.). Tadpole reddish brown, 23–25 mm.

Our evidence on transformation comes from two lots of material (USNM and AMNH). The first accessions (USNM nos. 71030–3) were collected at Gainesville, Fla., by Gerrit S. Miller, Jr., and C. R. Ashemeier. They measure respectively 14, 15.5, 15, 14 mm. These specimens reveal none of the characteristic spots of the adult except the bars on the fore and hind legs. All four have an indication of the dark band from eye to shoulder.

The other notes were taken on 19 "*Pseudacris copii*" specimens collected by T. Hallinan in Florida (AMNH nos. 15155–8, 15234–47, 15976–7). My notes designate them as transformed specimens, but evidently some of them are slightly or well past transformation.

They range from 14–19 mm. in length. Of two we write: No. 15157—18 mm., tail 9 mm., musculature light below, dark above. No. 15158—16 mm., tail 16 mm., very spotty musculature, dorsal and ventral crests.

The measurements of all were: 14, 15.5, 15.5, 16, 16, 16, 16.5, 16.5, 17, 17.5, 18, 18, 18, 19, 19, 19, 19, 19, 19 mm. In 1922 Hallinan also took at Arlington, Fla., a transformed specimen (AMNH no. 215360). It is just transformed and 17 mm. long.

Finally three specimens (Fla. State Mus. no. 47679) taken 6 miles southwest of Gainesville, Fla., May 7, 1930, by O. C. Van Hyning and Norman W. Davis measure 16, 18, and 20 mm., respectively. The first is just transformed and the others, though past, still show signs of transformation. The transformed one of 16 mm. has a dark bar from eye to shoulder and a spot halfway from fore limb to hind limb. The 20-mm. specimen has the vitta from snout through eye and onto sides, also oblique groin spot and oblique pair of spots on back from anus forward.

We still need detailed descriptions of the egg mass, individual eggs, and tadpoles.

**Authorities' corner:**

F. Harper, Ga., 1937, pp. 260–272.
A. F. Carr, Fla., 1940b, pp. 57–58.

[Note: See comparison with *P. streckeri* in the account of that species.]

## Strecker's Ornate Chorus Frog, Texas Ornate Chorus Frog

*Pseudacris streckeri* Wright and Wright. Plate LVIII; Map 16.

**Range:** Texas, Oklahoma, southeastern Arkansas. The Mississippi record may have been a mistake. Was it *P. brachyphona* or *P. ornata?* Bragg (1942) records it from 19 or 21 counties in Oklahoma, and we have seen it from Beeville to Waco in Texas.

**Habitat:** Moist shady woods, grassy pastures, among grain stalks, or in cotton fields. We found it breeding in a semiswampy, springy fork of a rocky branch of Helotes Creek in Texas. From our first experience with it and Strecker's site (1910) we concluded it preferred rocky ravines or deep gulches, but the males are not choosy at all.

*Plate LVII. Pseudacris ornata* (×1). 1–4. Females.

*Plate LVIII. Pseudacris streckeri.* 1,3,4,5,6. Males (×1). 2. Male (×¾).

Strecker writes (Tex., 1926e, p. 11): "These frogs inhabit all kinds of situations. We found them in moist shady woods, in weed clumps and among grain stalks along the edges of corn, wheat, oat, and cotton fields, among weeds along the sides of dry, dusty roads, in grassy pasture land near lagoons and streams, and among sparse vegetation on the crests of low rocky bluffs. They were lively and seemed perfectly comfortable under the hot rays of the sun. Several specimens flushed by us sprang into small bushes and clung to their branches."

**Size:** Adults, 1–1⅞ inches. Males, 25–41 mm. Females, 32–46 mm., possibly ripening as early as 27 or 28 mm. In Strecker's collection there is not much evidence of ripening at 28 mm.

**General appearance:** The head is short and wide; the body, short and squatty. The fingers of the hand are chubby, forming a toadlike hand. The toes are very slightly webbed, the disks slight. The frog varies in color from pale drab-gray or pale smoke gray to hazel, brownish olive, or pea green. Usually there are dorsal spots and frequently a triangle between the eyes. A dark line extends from the snout through the nostril and eye, over the tympanum to the arm insertion; it is sometimes continued as spots along the side. Dark crossbands are on the legs. The groin and the front and rear of the femur in males may be yellow or green or olive-buff. The throat of the male is dark. The tympanum is very small.

**Color:** *Male*. Helotes, Tex., Feb. 16, 1925 Back drab-gray; triangular spot between eye and spots on arms, legs, and back grayish olive; line on nostril, spot below eye, vitta back of eye, shoulder spot, and spots in a row along the side, black, and tympanum included in this color; crossbands on femur grayish olive behind, blackish in front; a black spot at the insertion of arm; grape green or dark olive-buff in groin and on front of femur; throat very discolored, dark olive-buff at its caudal edge shading forward into deep olive; under parts white; underside of thighs slightly dark olive-buff and buffy olive. Iris vinaceous-fawn or light cinnamon-drab with "bronzy cast." There is a tendency for a horizontal line of black across the iris to connect the nostril line with the spot back of the eye. Another specimen brownish olive above with no dorsal spots. Another one with dorsal spots of calla or parrot green. In one, the spots through nostril, back of eye, over shoulder, and back of shoulder seal brown. In this specimen, groin, front and rear of femur, and tibia are lemon, chrome, or aniline yellow Light color on upper jaw and rim of lower jaw back to under tympanum is olive-buff.

Strecker (1926e) says, "The following are the three principal types of permanent marking:

"A. Large and distinct black-brown dorsal markings in regular pattern. (Mostly males.)

B. Distinct markings along both sides of the dorsal area, but absent from the middle of the back. (Mostly females.)

C. Markings of the dorsal region broken up into spots and flecks. A very distinct and uncommon type, confined to a few female specimens."

Of a series of 20 males and 12 females, Strecker (Tex., 1926d, p. 9) found a range of color thus: Light dove gray, dark gray, light plumbeous wood-brown, purplish brown, chestnut, bronze-buff, dull green, pea green, suffused with green above. He specifies the markings in each case.

**Structure:** Tongue rounded behind. Vomerine teeth behind nares. Very little webbing on feet. When wiping off one male for photographing, I sensed that it had considerable secretion. Very pebbly or granular on femur and venter to pectoral fold. Two metatarsal tubercles.

In preserved specimens a median plait on throat, or two plaits, or as many as six or more. Each side of throat often pebbled. The male sometimes, like the female, may have a transverse fold across the pectoral region. Some females may also have one across the base of the throat (in preserved specimens).

E. D. Cope's first description of present *P. streckeri* follows: "*Chorophilus ocularis* Daudin, Cope. This species resembles the eastern *C. ocularis*, but some specimens differ in the tuberculate character of the skin of the superior surfaces, and in the rudimental web of the hind foot. The head is rather short, and the anterior outline is a narrow oval. The extremity of the muzzle projects beyond the mouth, and the lores are slightly oblique and a little concave. The nostril is but little nearer the extremity of the muzzle than the orbit. The vertical diameter of the tympanum a little exceeds the transverse, which is one-half the long diameter of the eye-slit. The pupil, as in the other species of this genus, is horizontal. The tongue is wide, discoid, and entire behind. The *ostia pharyngea* are smaller than the small choanae. The vomerine patches are short and transverse; they are entirely within the lines of the inner borders of the choanae and behind the line of the posterior borders of the same.

"The tubercles of the superior surfaces are small and rather closely placed; they are largest on sides of the back. There is a faint areolation of the gular region. The limbs are short and stout. The humerus is half or more inclosed in the skin. The palm reaches nearly to the end of the muzzle. The fingers are short and stout, and have neither dilations nor borders. The first is shorter than the second, which equals the fourth. The palmar tubercles are not distinct. The heel of the appressed hind foot in thin specimens marks the middle of the tympanic disc or posterior border of orbit, and the end of the muzzle the extremity of the tarsus. The hind foot beyond the tarsus is only as long as the tibia. The toes have no dilatations, but possess dermal margins, and a short but distinct basal web. There is but one solar tubercle, a small cuneiform prominence. Total length, m., .035; of head, to line of posterior borders of *membranum tympani*, .011; width of head at the latter, .014; length of hind leg, .045; of femur, .013; of hind foot, .022; of tarsus, .009.

"The color above is olive-gray, and below, uniform straw-color. A black band passes from the end of the muzzle on each side, through the eye, and expanding over the ear-drum, terminates in front of the humerus. One or two dark spots above and behind the axilla may unite to form part of a lateral band. There may or may not be blackish spots above the groin and on the coccygeal region and anterior part of the back. The limbs have a few dark-brown cross-bands; the femur is yellowish and unspotted behind.

"There is some difference between the Texas specimens and those from Georgia. Specimens from the latter State are very smooth, and the limbs, especially the feet, are slender. The heel reaches to the orbit, or at least to the front of the tympanic membrane, and the end of the tarsus extends to or well beyond the end of the muzzle. The web and digital dermal borders are much less marked. Two specimens were obtained by Mr. Boll near Dallas, and three at Helotes by Mr. Marnock. All the latter have large brown dorsal spots" (E. D. Cope, Tex., 1880a, pp. 27–28).

Cope compared this Texas form with *P. ornata,* which he called both *C. ocularis* and *C. occidentalis.* Workers now have a simple time in comparison with our struggles when we tried 30 to 40 years ago to identify *Chorophilus* now *Pseudacris.* From 1900 to 1915 everyone was hopelessly confused in terminology and records. Field experience, of which we yet need much more, was the main factor in clarification.

**Voice:** This call is rather shrill, somewhat like that of the common tree toad.

"The calling habits of *P. streckeri* are distinctive. The voice is clear and bell-like and has considerable carrying power. The breeding cry is a single note but, when heard in a chorus, the sound resembles the squeak of an ungreased wooden wheel. This effect results from a lack of synchrony of individual calls. Males call from various positions. I have found them hanging to vegetation by their hands in water two feet deep, in vegetation above the water, and on the banks of pools, sometimes as far as five or six feet from water. One was found sitting on a floating board in a deep ditch calling lustily. In the more than fifty cases that I have observed, *P. streckeri* did not stand 'on tip-toe' while calling as does its close relative, *P. ornata.* . . .

"The call of an individual of this species stimulates other males to call also. I have often approached a pool when no males were calling. Within a few minutes, when one call was heard, a whole chorus would break out and continue lustily for ten minutes or more. Then all lapsed into silence again. After an interval of five to fifteen minutes this process would be repeated. This phenomenon is more prevalent during daylight than at night. Usually after darkness has fallen, especially after heavy rains within the breeding season, calling is continuous on through the night" (A. N. Bragg, Okla., 1942h, p. 49).

**Breeding:** These frogs breed from December to late May. Our Texas friends. Mr. Kirn and Mr. and Mrs. R. D. Quillin, hold that they are more or less active and breed through the winter from December to late February. Mr. Garni at Boerne, Tex., says, "They are heard throughout the winter, especially after rains."

"The eggs, like those of *Pseudacris triseriata* (Wied) are in small bunches, usually from ten to twenty-five. In the ditches leading to Belle Mead (Dry Pond), they are attached to weeds and water grasses, occasionally to twigs and water-logged branches" (J. K. Strecker, Jr., Tex., 1926e, p. 11).

One egg mass in Strecker's collection is very large. There are approximately 200 or 250 eggs in one loose mass. Each egg is brown above and cream below. Apparently, according to a superficial examination, there is one envelope, which is about 2½ or 3 times the diameter of the vitellus, which is roughly 2 mm. or less. Detailed measurements of these eggs reveal the following:

The egg mass is rather milky in its formaldehyde preservation and has some precipitate on it. There seems to be only one envelope, though at times appearances indicate a second inner one; but of this we are not certain. Our impression is one envelope, which measures from 3.0 through 3.6, 3.8 to 4.4 or 5.0 mm. in diameter. The vitelline diameter is from 1.2–1.8 mm., average 1.4, mode 1.4 mm.

"The tadpoles are small, blackish-brown creatures similar to those of *triseriata,* but are rather shorter and more robust. . . . About sixty days are required for them to go through with their complete transformation after leaving the egg" (J. K. Strecker, Jr., Tex., 1926e, p. 11).

"The young specimens captured at Dry Pond near Waco, and at San Marcos, were about twelve millimeters in length, and must have been out of the water for several days, for the dorsal pattern was clear and distinct. When they first come to land, they are dark gray with hardly any trace of markings" (same).

We have examined the Baylor material on which the previous statement is partially based. There are frogs, apparently just beyond transformation, measuring from 12 mm. (Baylor Mus. no. 3512) through 13 (3509) to 13.5 (3228) mm. The body of the largest tadpole Strecker has is 12 mm. in length.

The most precise information on the eggs and tadpoles comes from A. N. Bragg (Okla., 1942h, pp. 50–59), who has written:

"The eggs are attached to vegetation in masses of from ten to about one hundred, just under the surface of the water. The usual number in a mass is from twenty to fifty and adjacent masses are often loosely joined by thin sheets of jelly. . . . The egg complement is of medium size. Three females produced the following numbers of eggs in the laboratory: 708, 695, and 401 and counts of several sets of adjacent masses of eggs collected in the field and presumably coming in each case from one female gave comparable values. More superficial observation of about fifty sets offered evidence that the above numbers represent fairly closely the usual yearly egg capacity of one female. . . .

"The eggs may be described as follows. color, brownish gray at the animal pole, the pigment extending downward to beyond the equator, then fading rapidly through shades of lighter gray to cream or nearly pure white at the vegetal pole. The animal pole is really quite dark and the color is only slightly less intense at the equator. The sizes of the eggs are nearly uniform and there are no differences observable to the naked eye as one sees them *en masse* in culture dishes. Measurements of twenty live eggs by means of an ocular micrometer were as follows: 13 measured 1.23 mm. each; 4, 1.29 mm.; 2, 1.26 mm.; and 1, 1.17 mm. . . .

"The jelly is very sticky, almost absolutely hyaline, soft, and very elastic. Even in clear water, tiny particles of soil and algae catch easily upon it and serve to protect the eggs from detection. In a muddy pool, the jelly collects a complete coating of particles within a half hour so that its color becomes exactly that of the surrounding water.

"The sizes of the individual masses of jelly of course vary with the number of eggs contained in each. The portion of jelly between each two adjacent eggs is also variable in amount but the distance separating each egg from the nearest one adjacent is usually between 5.58 and 7.25 mm. Staining of the jelly for one hour and forty-five minutes in Schneider's aceto-carmine revealed that (1) only one jelly envelope occurs about each egg; (2) this envelope is finely laminated, the jelly apparently laid upon the egg in concentric spheres, the wall of each of which is thin; and (3) there is a very thin, nongelatinous membrane surrounding a *very* small cavity in which the egg actually lies."

**Journal notes:** Feb. 16, 1925, Helotes, Tex. Anna says this is a fat squatty *Hyla*, not a *Pseudacris*. It is not in a class with *Pseudacris ocularis* or *Pseudacris n. clarkii*.

Feb. 16. Rather shrill call. At once it appealed as a note new to me. A note somewhat like *H. versicolor*. Soon found three males calling. One was on a bank, another among vegetation in water 3 or 4 inches deep, and another hanging to a branch at the water. Put these in a bag, and they began to croak; had three or four diverse notes in the bag. These "bag frogs" made others croak. Caught five or six in all. Do not believe the species is at its height. Air 31° at 7:30 P.M. when these were calling, water about the same. This afternoon was very humid.

Feb. 19, Helotes, Tex. During the night, one or two captive males called in the can. Temperature close to 32°F. This morning air in the can is 41°. Most of the frogs are rather inactive.

Feb. 21. At 9 P.M. air 70°, didn't hear them. When I returned, air about same; heard one, then later two at once, but they soon stopped.

Feb. 23. Tonight at 8:30 P.M. when air was 56°F., two ornate chorus frogs were calling at the east end of the "ornate area," and one above it at west end. Could not find them. Water was 5° or 10° warmer.

Feb. 24. When air was 64°, 8:30 P.M., about three *P. streckeri* were calling. They generally are almost wholly out of the water. The one I watched was wholly so. Even when not croaking, the throat is overmuch swollen. This one was quite brown, with hardly a dorsal spot showing.

March 24, Beeville, Tex. Air is resounding with *Pseudacris n. clarkii*. When we came to little creek, we heard peculiar note, went up one road and started across soft field, but gave it up, followed up another road, and found the one peculiar beast to be a male *Pseudacris streckeri*. It was in the middle of the road. We drove on. Coming back, we heard another in the same place and later a lone voice near our camp. Is it a land call?

Feb. 9, 1932. We received 13 live *Pseudacris streckeri* males from our friend Albert J. Kirn, of Somerset, Tex. In a subsequent letter (Feb. 15) he spoke of them as follows: "I sent by express thirteen of the *Pseudacris* (*ornata*) *streckeri*—two of them reddish (1 cinnamon and smooth, the other warty) two green and the remainder normal colored. So you will find that at least color and smoothness of skin have nothing to do with the stability of the subspecies. The frogs quit calling the last night I got them, or at least I have heard very few since then. They can be heard clearly for a distance of more than half mile.

"I had on hand three specimens of *Pseudacris* in pickle (one small). I included them with ten *Scaphiopus hurterii* that I mailed a few days ago."

Notes on these three are: (1) A female 35 mm. long, practically devoid of dorsal and lateral spots or leg bars and with no vitta; taken at Lytle, Tex., Nov. 30, 1931, by A. J. Kirn. (2) A well-spotted spent female, 34 mm. long. Mr. Kirn's notes are: "Lytle, Texas, May 31, 1931. Dug into sandy soil about 1⅛ inches to its back. Found by our seeing the sand pushed up. Silent since January. Call all winter." Mr. Kirn unhesitatingly identifies these two as *Pseudacris* (*ornata*) *streckeri*. (3) A small, much-spotted, slim-legged specimen 26.5 mm. in length, taken 1931 in Pleasanton, Tex., by L. Clayton Foster for A. J. Kirn. The latter merely identifies this specimen as *Pseudacris*. Were it not for the numerous dorsal spots, we might put it with the *Pseudacris ornata* of Florida, whose fingers are less chubby than those of the adult *P. streckeri*, but this character, like the slender, prominently barred hind legs, may be an indication of its immaturity. We provisionally call it *P. streckeri*.

At last, March 24, 1932, we have in hand at the same time live frogs of the so-called form *Pseudacris occidentalis* from Florida, and live frogs of the so-called form *Pseudacris ornata* from Texas. They are different forms. There is no doubt that the form from Florida is the *Pseudacris ornata* of Holbrook and the form from Texas is no longer *P. ornata* We call it *Pseudacris streckeri*. Several live frogs of each form put side by side reveal the following from superficial examination:

*Pseudacris ornata* from Florida is the more slender form: the snout is pointed; the arms and legs are longer and more slender; the fingers and toes are long and slender, with a mere trace of web at base of toes. The indistinct darker marks on the back are bars. The nostril is equidistant between snout and eye; the dark bar on the arm is long.

*Pseudacris streckeri* from Texas is a short, fat, squatty form: the snout is shorter and broader at the tip; the arms and legs are short and broad; the fingers are short and fat, giving the frog a toadlike hand. The dark vitta on the face usually ends in front of the arm insertion. The dark rim of the upper jaw is conspicuous. The light area is broad at the nostril and again back of the eye. The dark pattern on the back is made of irregular, spotlike bars, these frequently having a fork at the upper end. The marks on the legs are only partial bars; the spots are inclined to be lighter in the center and darker at the rim even when indistinctly outlined with light. The bar between the eyes may be a conspicuous V. The dark spot is at the base of the arm only, or slightly on the upper arm.

**Authorities' corner:**

J. K. Strecker, Jr., Tex., 1915, p. 48.

G. A. Moore and C. C. Rigney, Okla., 1942, p. 78.

"Dec. 4th. A few Chorus frogs heard late P.M. yesterday and today late P.M. Heard late last night also. A few heard Nov. 18. Rainy at these times.

"Dec. 6th. Chorus frogs calling last night when I went to bed. Temperature 43, calling again tonight 10 P.M. 45°.

"12/26. Chorus frogs calling every night. Heard at 10 A.M. and 5 P.M. yesterday. Weather cloudy, misty.

"Jan. 19. Chorus frogs heard calling at noon, and all morning not so many but heard. Weather clear and mild. Rain day before and Thursday night.

"1/27. Chorus frogs, a few calling now and then all day today. Weather cloudy, mild.

"2/2. Many chorus frogs calling this evening and night. Weather milder. Temperature in evening, 48–53, misty weather for 3 days.

"2/12. Chorus frogs also calling and today and Feb. 6, also Feb. 2, heard striped treefrogs (*P. n. clarkii*) calling from water pools in south part of San Antonio.

"2/19. Foggy all day; milder after 9 P.M. yesterday. Chorus frogs—a few tonight.

"2/24. Weather in afternoon a little cooler. Chorus frogs tonight and last night, not many" (notes, A. J. Kirn, Somerset, Tex., 1944).

We named this species after Dr. John K. Strecker, Jr., for many reasons: (1) Dr. Strecker was a pioneer herpetological student in Texas life histories; (2) he did many personal favors for us and for other workers; and (3) he first described this form in his paper "Studies in North American Batrachology: Notes on the Robber Frog (*Lithodytes latrans* Cope)" (*Trans. Acad. Sci. St. Louis,* June 14, 1910, XIX[3], 73–82).

[In 1910 few knew *Pseudacris* forms, and Strecker's statement that *Lithodytes latrans* laid egg masses in water and had tadpoles in water seems, in season and description, to apply to *P. streckeri*. Doubtless Dr. Julius Hurter, his early herpetological mentor, helped him identify the frog, for the paper appeared in the St. Louis Academy of Science *Transactions*. He (Hurter) too must have been confused because in the USNM Hurter collection (USNM no. 57706) we found *P. streckeri* labeled *Lithodytes latrans.* We have examined all the Baylor University material, and by 1915, certainly by 1926, Strecker knew the *Pseudacris* well and the fog over names was clearing.]

## Genus *HYLA* Laurenti

Maps 18–24

### Anderson Tree Frog, Anderson Frog, Anderson's Hyla, Anderson Tree Toad, Green and Yellow Tree Toad

*Hyla andersonii* Baird. Plate LIX; Map 19.

**Range:** Central New Jersey (Middlesex Co.) to South Carolina.

"About eight years ago James Chapin and I found this beautiful Tree Frog at the Runyon Pond two miles south of Sayreville, Middlesex Co. [N.J.]. Since that time I have found it at several other localities in the same region—one mile south of Old Bridge, about one mile southeast of Browntown and at Freneau near Matawan. These localities are all in the sandy pine barren 'island' north of the Pine Barrens proper. Thus this species extends northward to within three miles or less of the lower Raritan River, its range coinciding at this point with that of the Carolina Chickadee" (W. DeW. Miller, N.J., 1916, p. 68).

"Considerable doubt has been cast on the type locality record by later workers. Thus, the Anderson record 'has always bothered' Wright (1932), who remarks: 'Anderson is twice as far from the coast as Southern Pines, N.C. (where he also took specimens) or Cheraw, S.C. is from the coast. Possibly the species extends that far inland along the Savannah River. . . . Anderson's tree frog is a Lower Austral (Austroriparian, Upper Coastal, etc.) form and Anderson, S.C. is in Upper Astral (Carolinian, Piedmont, etc.) country.'

"Pickens (letter, 1938) points out that at the time the type specimen was collected most of the travel to the 'Up Country' was inland from the coast. Miss Charlotte Paine (later Mrs. M. E. Daniels), originally from Maine and an inveterate collector, sent many specimens of amphibia, etc., to the Smithsonian Institution and she has generally been credited with taking the type of *andersonii*. If this was the case, Pickens goes on to suggest, she may have picked up the specimen in question at some junction point, as Charleston, Columbia, or Augusta.

"Although I believe that *andersonii* may occur in the Savannah River swamp well above the Fall line, the question can be satisfactorily settled only by the taking of another specimen reasonably close to Anderson" (E. B. Chamberlain, S.C., 1939, p. 21).

**Habitat:** White cedar swamps. We found larvae in several pools, grassy, sedgy, sphagnaceous, along a dense woody border below one of the lakes at Lakehurst, N.J.

"The exact positions of ten individuals were located, of which seven were captured. High-bush Blueberry tangles festooned with Green Briars made further investigations in this line impossible. The individuals are here referred to by number.

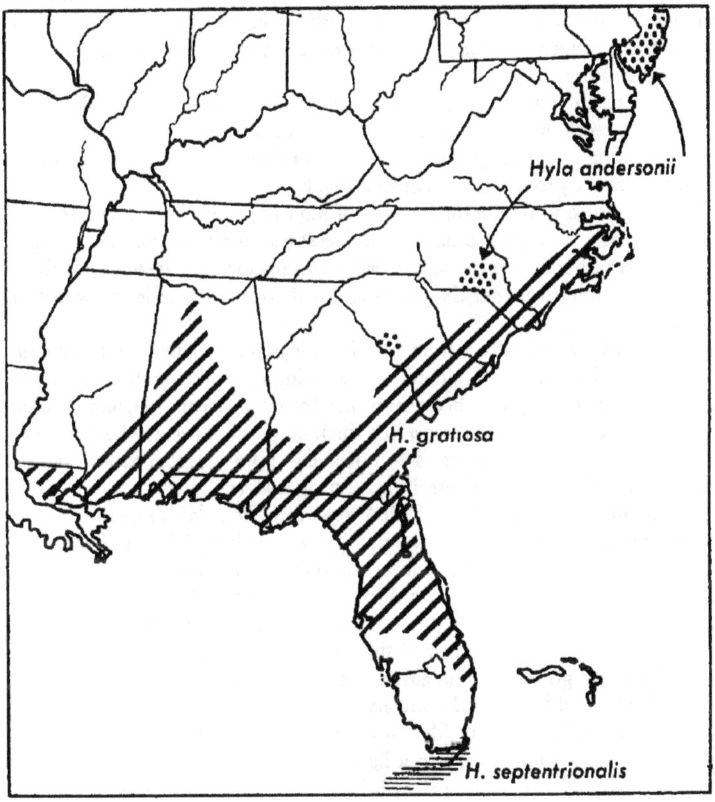


*Map 19*

"Numbers 1, 2, 3, 4 and 5 were in one group, within 50 feet of the main 'pike' from May's Landing to Hammonton. The ground was covered quite evenly with Blueberry bushes from a foot to 18 inches high. Scattered Pitch Pines up to 12 inches in diameter stood from 10 to 30 feet apart. The ground was at most damp, and the only water nearby was a shallow pool about 30 feet away which probably dries up in the summer. Near the bases of the pines stood taller Blueberry bushes, up to three feet in height. No. 1 was sitting on the main stem of a small Blueberry bush, 18 inches from the ground and six inches from the tip of the bush. A Pine stood 1½ feet away. No. 2 was on the leaf of a blueberry bush, 2½ feet from the ground and 1½ feet from a Pine trunk. No. 3 was on a little twiglet growing out from the trunk of a pine 3½ feet from the ground. No. 4 was on the ground at the base of a Pine. No. 5 was one foot from the ground, where the twig of a Blueberry bush lay against the trunk of a Pine. All of the specimens in this group showed a strong preference for the near vicinity of a Pine.

"Nos 6, 7, and 8 were in a thicket of small Red Maples and high Blueberry bushes in a creek 'bottom.' No. 6 was on the main stem of a Blueberry bush about four feet from the ground. No. 7 was similarly located. No. 8 was about six feet from the ground in a small Red Maple.

"Nos. 9 and 10 were in a thick tangle of high Blueberry bushes and *Smilax.* Both were near the tops of Blueberry bushes at least nine feet from the ground. For fifty feet around none of the vegetation was any lower, so it seems that these individuals climbed higher than is usual for the species in order to be out in the open.

"Not all of the individuals were as tame as is generally noted for *andersonii.* A number of individuals would not continue singing when the observer turned the light on them or approached nearer than fifteen or twenty feet, and so could not be located. A silent *andersonii* in a thick tangle of Blueberry bushes could give points on hiding to a very small needle in a very large haystack. No females were taken" (A. B. Klots, N.J., 1930, pp. 108–111).

**Size:** Adults, 1⅕–1⅞ inches. Males, 30–41 mm. Females, 38–47 mm.

**General appearance:** This is a small green tree frog. The light-bordered, plum-colored band along the side of the body, with its yellow spots below, gives this beautiful little frog its distinctive character. This band marks its green dorsal color very sharply from its white ventral parts. It has orange in axilla and groin and on the rear of the femur. The throat of the female has a white-bordered green patch on either side. In its stout body it differs from the more slender and larger *Hyla cinerea.*

**Color:** *Male.* Upper parts (dorsum, upper lip, angle of mouth, and dorsal surfaces of limbs) cress green to a light cress green, on sides lighter to deep chrysolite green. Stripe along side, behind vent, along limbs and upper jaw cartridge buff, ivory yellow, marguerite yellow, or seafoam yellow. Area back of eyes, along side to vent vinaceous-drab or purple-drab, becoming over tympanum dark purplish drab. A little of the same color scattered on throat. Tops of forefeet and hind feet deep brownish drab except for first two digits, which have the cadmium yellow spots on the top. Fore part of underside of antebrachium and under part of brachium with cadmium yellow, deep chrome, or orange spots; the same color also in axilla, groin and most of fore and hind parts of femur, whole undersides of tibia, and inner side of foot. All these orange or deep chrome spots are on a raw sienna or mars yellow background.

*Plate LIX Hyla andersonii* (×1¼). 1–3 Males.

Iris more or less vinaceous-drab or purple-drab with vinaceous-tawny spots. Under parts white except for dark purplish drab of throat.

*Female.* Throat white, grayish, or with slight purplish drab tinge. Green patch below angle of mouth usually white-edged, this usually absent in males.

**Structure:** Form stout, head broad and flat; skin smooth; posterior surface of femur spotted; vocal sacs subgular

**Voice:** This frog calls *aquack-aquack-aquack,* many times, perhaps twenty, at infrequent and irregular intervals.

Dr. C. C. Abbott (N.J., 1890, p. 189) says, "The *andersonii* utters a single note, better described by the syllable 'keck,' which it usually repeats three or four times. It is not a frog-like note at all, but much resembles the call of the Virginia rail (*Rallus virginianus*)."

"June 16–28, 1928. To the writer the call seemed a nasal 'quack,' almost verging on a 'quank' but without the strong 'n' sound of the latter. The call was never disyllabic.

"The note is repeated at about half-second intervals for sometimes fully 30 seconds. When the frogs are in full song an interval of about two minutes intervenes between outbursts. We had no difficulty in starting the frogs calling again at distances of from fifty to three feet, after they had been silent for a minute or so. One individual was recorded as having called 74 times in one period of song

"The frogs definitely associate together for singing, whether because of the presence of females or for companionship The latter probably plays a considerable share in the performance, as is evidenced by the quick response to an imitation of the call. Five such singing groups were definitely located. Of these the first contained seven individuals, the second contained three, the third contained eight, the fourth contained three and the fifth, which was just across an uncrossable creek, contained at least six. Only once was a single individual noted in song alone, and that was a frog which called three times in a spot a half-mile distant from any others and was never heard from again.

"The locations of the groups were fixed, and during our stay did not change a particle. Night after night a group would be in exactly the same area, though the individuals composing it shifted position a bit.

"The time of singing was remarkably constant. On every night but one [June 16–28, 1928] the chorus started between ten and fifteen minutes before sundown. On the one exception, a clear dry night with a bright moon, the first songs were not heard until twenty minutes after sundown.

"The carrying power of the song was excellent. A chorus was plainly heard as an entity over 800 paces away, with two patches of woods and a brushy swamp intervening. The wind was negligible. Individual voices were distinguishable 754 paces away down a straight road, with a light wind blowing from the observers toward the frogs" (A. B. Klots, N.J., 1930, pp. 108–111).

"At dusk we have usually taken our supper, and then waited for darkness to come on and for the Hylas to begin to sing; we have had good luck taking Hylas by the following method: One of us with an electric flashlight would start for the nearest singing Hyla, while the other waited some distance away. As soon as the Hyla stopped singing, the person who was not trying to approach would imitate the call of the frog, and this would start it singing again vigorously, and while it was singing the collector bearing the light would approach as quickly as possible, standing still as soon as the singing ceased. This process was kept up until finally the light flashed on the vibrating white throat of the singing Hyla, and its capture then became a perfectly simple matter, as they stared stupidly at the brilliant light. . . . This year, however, we did not get down to Lakehurst until the 8th of July, when we found the Hylas singing in goodly numbers in the white cedars about the lake. After capturing a number of singing males (I had never taken a female before), my light flashed by merest chance upon a pair of Hylas sitting well up in a pine tree, in embrace. This, and another taken in a similar situation, were the only females secured, although we took several males from the low oak shrub about a small fresh water pool in the pine barrens" (T. Barbour, N.J., 1916, pp. 6–7).

**Breeding:** This species breeds from May 1 to July 20. The eggs are single, attached to sphagnum or on the bottom. The egg is 1/20–1/18 inch (1.2–1.4 mm.), the inner envelope 1/12 inch (1.9–2.0 mm.), the outer 1/8–1/6 inch (3.5–4.0 mm.). The olive tadpole is small, 1 2/5 inches (35 mm.), its tail medium long with tip acuminate. The tooth ridges are 2/3. After 50 to 75 days, the tadpoles transform from the end of June to September 1 at 7/16–3/5 inch (11–15 mm.).

Noble and Noble (N.J., 1923) say that the eggs are single, scattered among waterweeds, attached to sphagnum, or free on the bottom, in small, nonstagnant pools or in slow-moving streams of the pine barrens. Color, dark brown and creamy white. Egg 1.2–1.4 mm. Inner envelope 1.9–2 mm. Outer envelope 3.5–4.0 mm. Complement 800–1000.

"When the tail is nearly absorbed and they leave the water, they are about 25 mm. long and of a dull olive green. They grow lighter, that is, brighter green in hue with the disappearance of the tail, until the little frogs, which in length of body are 15 mm., resemble the mature individuals. The white that margins the green of the back and extremities is not so conspicuous as in the adults, and the saffron of the underparts is wanting in those that I have examined" (W. T. Davis, N.J., 1907, p. 50).

**Journal notes:** On June 8, 1922, on our way to Okefinokee Swamp, we camped in the evening on the north side of Everett's Pond, N.C., near the S. Car.-N. Car. line. The instant it became dark we heard plenty of *Acris gryllus, Bufo fowleri,* and *Rana catesbeiana,* a few *Rana clamitans* and *Hyla cinerea* in chorus, and *Hyla versicolor.* . . . Later heard *Hyla andersonii.* These *H. andersonii* were in a stream or branch with sweet gum, tangle of oaks, bamboo briars (*Smilax*), *Magnolia glauca,* maples, black gum. Later in the evening Miles Pirnie heard one opposite our camp. All the frogs heard were in or near the lake. Harper speaks of the calling of these Hylas thus: "I heard the note of *H. andersonii* at a distance of 200 yards and suspected almost at once what it was. Trailed it and after a long wait located it in some tall bushes in the edge of a branch swamp. Its note bears a general resemblance to that of *H. cinerea* but goes about twice as rapidly, is about half as loud and sounds more like quak, quak than quonk It carries fairly well at 200 yards and about 300 yards would probably be the limit. . . . Did not see it croak. Its periods are infrequent and irregular, 2 minutes' interval. Perhaps 15 or 20 or 25 notes given in one period."

On June 28, 1929, we heard these *Hyla andersonii* in the wooded edge of Mr. P. H. Emilie's lake at Lakehurst, N.J. The males were among magnolias, maples, huckleberries, azaleas, *Ilex glabra, Viburnum.*

**Authorities' corner:**

W. T. Davis, N J, 1905, p 795.
W. T. Davis, N.J., 1907, p. 49.
G. K. and R. C. Noble, N J., 1923, pp. 419 ff.
C. S. Brimley, N.C., 1940, p. 22.
L. R. Aronson, N.J., 1943, pp. 246–249

*H. andersonii* is a handsome species and it has been superbly illustrated. From the time of Miss Dickerson's beautifully colored plate in her fine *Frog Book* (Chapin's specimens 1906–1908), and L. A. Fuertes' painting of them to the days of our private preparatory tips to Dr. Noble's well-illustrated, first (1923) outdoor life history of *H. andersonii,* we have been interested in this form. Several students, Mr. and Mrs. A. B. Klots, W. H. Caulwell, and others, have brought us specimens, particularly in the period since 1923.

### Canyon Tree Frog, Canyon Tree Toad, Desert Tree Toad, Cope's Hyla, Arizona Tree Frog, Sonoran Tree Toad

*Hyla arenicolor* Cope. Plates LX, LXI; Map 20.

**Range:** Southwestern United States: western Texas through extreme southern Colorado and Utah to the region of the Colorado River in Nevada, down it to Lower California and up southern Californian coast to Ventura County. In Mexico to Guadajuata, Guadalajaca, and Toluca.

**Habitat:** Rocky canyons From Fern Canyon in Ft. Davis Mts., Tex., to Tahquitz Canyon, Calif Invariably we found them in rocky, clear streams. They have been reported by others from mountain springs, irrigation ditches, and "rapidly flowing streams."

"Throughout this region [Southern California], its habitat appears to be confined to streams and mountain springs between 1000 and 5000 feet elevation. Here the writer has found it associated with such trees as *Alnus rhombifolia, Platanus racemosa,* and *Acer macrophyllum* and in this state at least it may be regarded as an inhabitant of canyons within the upper sonoran zone.

"It is apparently more strictly aquatic than the smaller *Hyla regilla* Baird and Girard, whose range in Southern California is, in part, co-extensive with it. The former species has never been found far away from the vicinity of water, while the latter has often been seen under vegetation a considerable distance from it" (C. H. Richardson, Jr., Gen., 1912, p. 607).

"Occupies chiefly the Upper Sonoran life-zone, extending locally into Lower Sonoran. Lives on boulders and exposed rock faces close to cañon streams" (J. Grinnell and C. L. Camp, Calif., 1917, p. 145).

"Fairly common around shady moist places in the Canyon and occasionally up to South Rim. Lower Sonoran and Upper Sonoran Zones" (E. D McKee and C M Bogert, Ariz, 1934, p. 178).

"Common in the pine-fir and chaparral-woodlands zones but uncommon in the semidesert. Calling individuals and clasping pairs were common in water at a dam in the pine-fir forest on May 19, 1936. After a mating season adults are found occasionally about buildings" (E. S. Little, Jr., Ariz., 1940, p. 262).

"This species is confined to the High Plateaus-Colorado River region of Utah. They are common in Zion National Park and St. George. . . . This species is commonly found on the rocks and banks of the small streams and pools of the Colorado River drainage of this state. It is seldom if ever found farther than a few feet removed from running water" (V. M Tanner, Utah, 1931, pp. 186–187).

**Size:** Adults, 1⅙–2⅙ inches. Males, 29–53 mm. Females, 30–54 mm.

**General appearance:** This tree toad averages smaller in size and duller in color than our common tree toad (*Hyla versicolor*). When sitting quietly it (a specimen from Grand Canyon, Ariz.) looks surprisingly like the little spotted canyon toad (*Bufo punctatus*), but when it climbs, its conspicuously long legs and large disks on fingers and toes immediately show it to be a tree toad. It easily clings to a vertical surface and climbs up even a sheet of glass. The back is brown or grayish in color with dark dots scattered over it. The legs are barred with dark areas. There is much yellow or orange on the rear of the legs, in the groin, and in the axilla. It is light beneath. The skin is slightly rough, becoming more so as it becomes dry. Unlike the Pacific tree frog (*Hyla regilla*), this species has no stripe through the eye and along the side of the body. The skin is roughened in *H. arenicolor,* smooth in *H. regilla.* This frog has slight webs between the fingers.

"Size small, head-and-body length 50 mm. (2 inches) or less; fingers and toes with expanded adhesive disks; no webs between fingers; dorsal skin rough-surfaced, with many small papillae; side of head concolor with rest of head and body; coloration light or dark gray. . . . Distinguished from other Salientia of California by expanded disks on fingers and toes and by small size of adults; from *Hyla regilla* by average larger size (especially of females), by larger discs on digits, by rougher skin on dorsal surface of body, and by lack of dark stripe on side of head through eye" (T. I. Storer, Calif., 1925, p 204).

**Color:** Sentenac Canyon, Calif., from L. M. Klauber, March 31, 1928. *Male.* Upper parts olive-buff, drab, light grayish olive or deep olive-buff. Snout ahead of eyes avellaneous or wood brown, some of larger warty spots with touch of same color or pale cinnamon-pink to vinaceous-cinnamon. Bar between eyes, line in front of eye and from eye through ear, four or five larger spots on back, three crossbars on femur, four on tibia, four on hind foot, and two on forearm are from deep olive-buff to citrine-drab. These spots are outlined with broken black and filled in with body color giving the deep olive-buff or citrine-drab combination. Interspaces between bars on legs and arms vinaceous-buff or avellaneous. Groin, olive-ocher, yellow ocher, lemon chrome, becoming aniline yellow or raw sienna on front and rear of femur. Dorsal color on femur very narrow. Dorsal color extends around vent; with tilleul buff or pale olive-buff on each tubercle. Ventral view of legs and arms vinaceous-fawn or light russet-vinaceous or light grayish vinaceous. Venter white or cartridge buff. Vocal sac when inflated light buff except near chin where spot below eye is light pinkish cinnamon or sulphine yellow. Iris with benzo brown, cinnamon-drab, or brownish drab band in front and back of pupil, this finely dotted with olive-buff; iris below and above pupil largely olive-buff with wavy, more or less vertical lines of brownish drab; pupil rim above dull green-yellow or chalcedony yellow, light below; pupil rim below with vertical slit of black. Another male has back pale olive-buff or pale drab gray.

*Another male.* Dorsal color pale olive-gray or pale smoke gray to light grayish olive with light vinaceous-cinnamon on snout and forelegs Belly not white but dark olive-buff.

*Female.* Underparts white or pale olive-buff, middle of belly or rear belly olive-buff. Groin with very little lemon chrome.

*Plate LX. Hyla arenicolor.* (×1). Part 1. 1–5. From Grand Canyon, Ariz. 6,7. Transformed and tadpole, from Fern Canyon, Davis Mts., Tex.

*Plate LXI Hyla arenicolor.* (×1). Part 2. From California.

*Another female.* Fern Canyon, Tex., July 9, 1925. Spots on back, body, legs, head mouse gray to dark olive-gray; back deep grayish or olive becoming pale smoke gray on the sides next to belly color, on labial margin, snout, and vent region. In axilla, side of lower belly, front and rear of thigh, rear of tibia and inner face of foot, rear of humerus, somewhat on inner face of forearm olive-ocher or aniline yellow or sulphine yellow, becoming on the edges green-yellow. Breast white. Throat white spotted with mouse gray or dark olive gray, especially around edge of lower jaw. Tympanum with some orange rufous or tawny in lower half.

"The color phases run from light gray to brownish black, with numerous roundish spots irregularly distributed and not forming well-marked patterns, except on the hind legs, which appear banded. In the light and dark color phases the spots become obscure" (G. P. Engelhardt, Utah, 1918, p. 79).

**Structure:** Long arms and legs with large disks on tips of fingers and toes; slight webs between the fingers; skin somewhat roughened; more or less uniform in color; tympanum small; prominent fold across breast; prominent fold on tarsus.

A. A. W. has long held it likely that there is more than one race of *Hyla arenicolor*. The following observations are some of her notations: In general, the frogs from California have longer legs and a black bar across the head, a lighter gray background with inky spots, and a more pebbly skin. The frogs from Grand Canyon, Ariz., are smoother, have shorter legs, are reddish in color, spotted rather indistinctly, and bear no marked triangle on the head. Those from Rainbow Bridge collected by Eaton are like the Canyon ones. Those from the White Mountains are rather pebbly, and the one from New Mexico is pebbly. The Canyon frogs had larger disks on the toes, larger eyes, and less distinct spots. In life they sat with body parallel to finger when held, in contrast with the more erect, toadlike posture of the California frogs.

"*Hyla affinis,* Baird—Body rough. Tympanum two-thirds the size of eye. Tibia not quite half the length of the body, but reaching more than halfway from anus to center of eyes. Color ash gray or green, with numerous rounded dorsal blotches. Three transverse bands on each thigh and leg. No vermiculation on anterior and posterior faces of hind legs, nor on lower part of sides. A light spot under the eye. Web of hand extending only to the third joint of the second finger. Arm from elbow less than tibia, but longer than hind foot. About 1½ inches long. Hab. Northern Sonora" (S. F. Baird, Gen., 1854, p. 61).

"General aspect of *H. versicolor,* having the same squat appearance, the granulated skin above and below, the ash-color back with darker mottlings, the white spot under the eye, etc. The most conspicuous distinctive features are the absence of webs of the fingers, the greater length of the hind legs, and the blotches on the back being in round spots, not cuneiform. The legs with three bars not two, and without the reticulate markings behind and below" (E. D. Cope, Gen., 1889, p. 369).

**Voice:** This call has been described as the "quack of a duck" by Storer, and as "the bleat of a goat" by Dugès. To us the note sounded lower, much weaker, and less blatant than that of *Hyla versicolor* and not so persistent. "It was like a hoarse sheep's 'Ba-a-a' when they were in the open, but more like a roar when they were under the rocks" (T. H. Eaton, Ariz., 1935b, p. 7).

"The frogs are most vociferous in the late afternoon and rarely are heard at night" (G. P. Engelhardt, Utah, 1918, p. 79).

"The song of this tree toad is one of the most melodious of all our species" (V. M. Tanner, Utah, 1931, p. 187).

"The note differs markedly from that of our common western treetoad (*Hyla regilla*) in being lower in pitch, somewhat weaker in volume, and without any tendency toward a two-syllable sound such as is heard often from *regilla*. On two occasions, in San Diego County, the two species were heard side by side and there was not the slightest difficulty in distinguishing them. Two separate individuals of *arenicolor* which were timed by the watch were croaking at one-second intervals. With all the males noted on Tahquitz Creek (fully 25 were located) only one female was seen. The chorus began about 4 P.M., soon after the sun had disappeared behind the San Jacinto Range, was strongest just after dark, from about 7:30 to 8:30 P.M., and continued on into the night at least until 2 A.M. On other occasions males of *Hyla arenicolor* were heard croaking up to about 6 A.M., but only a few notes were given as late as that hour in the morning. The duration of the 'song' season is unknown; on the morning of June 21, 1919, Cañon Tree-toads were heard croaking in cañons near the Mount Wilson trail" (T. I. Storer, Calif., 1925, p. 208).

"Tree toads of this species were found in White House Canyon, in the Santa Rita Mountains, August 3. Males were heard calling just before dark from branches of oak trees, about fifteen feet from the ground. The call was an even, strong trill" (F. W. King, Ariz., 1932, p. 176).

**Breeding:** This species breeds from March 1 to July 1. The eggs are single, floating near the surface or on the bottom of the pool usually attached to leaves (Atsatt and Storer). The tadpole is medium in size, 2 inches (50 mm.) long, dark olive in color with some tail crests suffused with reddish, orange-pink to coral red. The tooth ridges are 2/3. After a period of 40 to 75 days, the tadpoles transform from June 1 to August 15, at 3/5 inch (14–17 mm.). We have seen mature tadpoles collected in April from Fern Canyon, Ft. Davis Mts., Tex., and neither in 1917 nor in 1925 did we hear the choruses after July 1, and rarely single voices. C. H. Richardson, Jr. (Gen., 1912, p. 607), indicates "that the breeding season . . . extends from late spring until fall." The extension of the breeding season to fall is apparently based on one female taken Sept. 4, 1906, and containing large eggs.

"White House Canyon, in the Santa Rita Mountains. . . . Tadpoles of *H. arenicolor* were found in pools nearby with some of the larvae transforming at 18 mm. body length" (F. W. King, Ariz., 1932, p. 176).

"I have found it to be fairly common at the Water Cress Spring in St. George in February and on August 28, 1919 I found newly hatched as well as matured tadpoles in the 'Stadium pool' in Zion National Park. The tadpoles are black when small becoming grayish when older" (V. M. Tanner, Utah, 1931, pp. 186–187).

"Ova were observed in the form of small clusters deposited along the margin of pools. The tadpoles, at first black, later become mottled gray when they resort to deeper water" (G. P. Engelhardt, Utah, 1918, p. 79).

**Journal notes:** July 16, 1917, Pinaleno Mts., Ariz. On the rocks over the water, Anna put her hand accidentally on a *Hyla arenicolor* and Ray Shannon found another on a tree trunk about 4 feet up. Paul Needham found another on a boulder just above the water. They do not seem at home in the swifter water.

July 5, 1925, Fern Canyon (near Alpine, Tex.). In the ravine just after a drenching rain, we found four transformed *Hyla arenicolor* on the boulders some 25 or more feet above the level of the creek. The creek was full of them before the rain. Today, July 6, the creek is down and clear. Near the falls we often found one or two *Hyla arenicolor* tadpoles amongst the boulders in shallow water or swimming at the surface. We secured today only one mature tadpole. The rest were small tadpoles. At the pool below the falls were many of them. . . . Also some above the falls.

July 7, Ranger Canyon. About 6:45–7 P.M., we arrived at the big pool or falls of east Ranger Canyon. Mr. L. T. Murray espied a frog in amongst the rocks in our very midst. It was an adult female *Hyla arenicolor.*

July 11, Toyahvale. We drove to Madera Canyon for a night camp. . . . In the canyon caught a recently transformed *Hyla arenicolor,* and just about dark heard several males calling.

June 18–21, 1934, Pena Blanca Spring, Ariz. Found two *Hyla arenicolor* in the overflow area around the spring.

April 26, 1942. In Santa Anita Canyon (see *R. b. muscosa*), Calif., beside the river we caught two *Hyla arenicolor.* The first one I spied was on gravel beside stream and hopped in. It was very light in color—much granitic rock here, light gray in color. Almost no sediment in stream.

April 30. At mouth Strawberry Creek, Calif., above bridge there leaped in from a boulder a female *H. arenicolor.*

May 2. North of Rincon at about 2000 feet in a little stream beside the road, shaded by live oaks, found perched on a boulder, 3 inches from each other, a male and female *H. arenicolor*. They were in full sunlight.

May 6, Buckman Spring, Calif., to bridge 3½–4 miles south. During the evening rode north toward Buckman Springs, hearing several isolated calls which took me some time to locate. Usually they would quit when I approached. One was in a bush. Finally on a boulder upside of stream current saw one with bubble throat inflated. *Hyla arenicolor.* Must have been ten

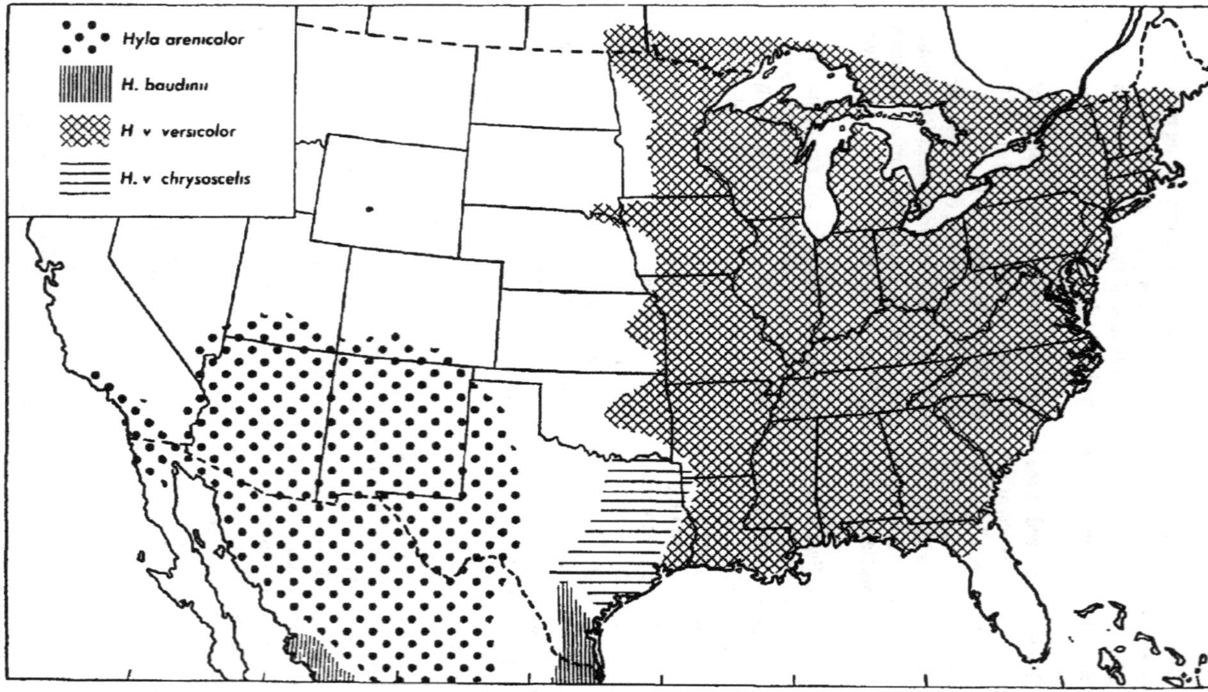


*Map 20*

males scattered along the creek. Their call is not long, not so grating as that of *H. regilla,* neither loud nor strident. No such voluminous call as *Hyla versicolor.*

**Authorities' corner:**

G. P. Englehardt, Ariz., 1917, pp 5–6.
S. R. Atsatt in T. I. Storer, Calif., 1925, p. 209.
J. R. Slevin, B.C, 1928, p. 112.
L. T. Murray, Tex, 1939, p. 5.

**Viosca's Tree Frog, Whistling Tree Frog, Whistling Frog, Bird-voiced Hyla, Bird-voiced Tree Frog**

*Hyla avivoca* Viosca. Plate LXII; Map 21.

**Range:** Southeast Louisiana (Florida parishes of Louisiana) to Florida (O. C. Van Hyning); Georgia (F. Harper); Henderson, Tenn. (Endsley); Kentucky (Parker).

**Habitat:** Tupelo swamps in the valleys of rivers and smaller streams on tupelo or cypress trees and on buttonbush (adapted from Viosca, 1928).

"The Apalachicola drainage. Known from Jackson and Liberty counties. Habitat—Tupelo, titi and cypress swamps. Not rare, but infrequently seen because of the nature of its habitat" (A. F. Carr, Jr., Fla., 1940b, p. 58).

**Size:** Adults, 1⅛–1¾ inches. Males, 28–39 mm. Females, 32–49 mm.

**General appearance:** These frogs are a small edition of our common tree toad, *Hyla v. versicolor.* They may be brown, green, or gray, light or dark. The arms and legs are distinctly barred. There is the characteristic light yellow or white spot below the eye. The color in the groin and on the rear of the legs is a pale yellowish green, instead of orange as in *Hyla v versicolor* males. The throats of these males are more or less darkened with black specks. The dark pattern on the back consists of a bar across the head and the eyelids and an irregular area on the back, the bulk of the pattern being near the rump. The skin is moderately smooth, in some being very finely granular. In appearance they are more slender than *H. versicolor,* and when dark brown, as we first saw them, they reminded us strongly of *Hyla femoralis.*

**Color:** *Male.* Top of head rainette green, courge green, or Scheele's green, with same color on upper eyelid and back to mid-back spot, and on either side of this spot. Interspaces of hind legs night green, courge green, or rainette green. The mid-dorsal spot appears dark olive or deep olive. Under the lens its background is black, spotted with apple green. An oblique bar of similar color extends from upper eyelid toward meson but does not meet its fellow. The color just above the vent may be clear yellow-green. One band across middle of femur is chamois or vinaceous-buff. A line of mummy brown separates dorsal color of hind leg from ventral color. Outer half of rear of femur and rear half of dorsum is spotted with light lumiere green. Bars on tibia green like back of body. Bars on tarsus and foot with cream-buff. Spot below eye is pale glass green. Back of eye is a broad black vitta extending to shoulder. It surrounds the tympanum. From this vitta to groin is a row of black spots separating dorsum from venter. Tympanum is more or less the same color as femur bar or interspaces on top of arms and hands, which are almost old gold. Suborbital spot is margined with mummy brown or black. The forward part of chin is marked with black dots below the lower labial border. Forward throat

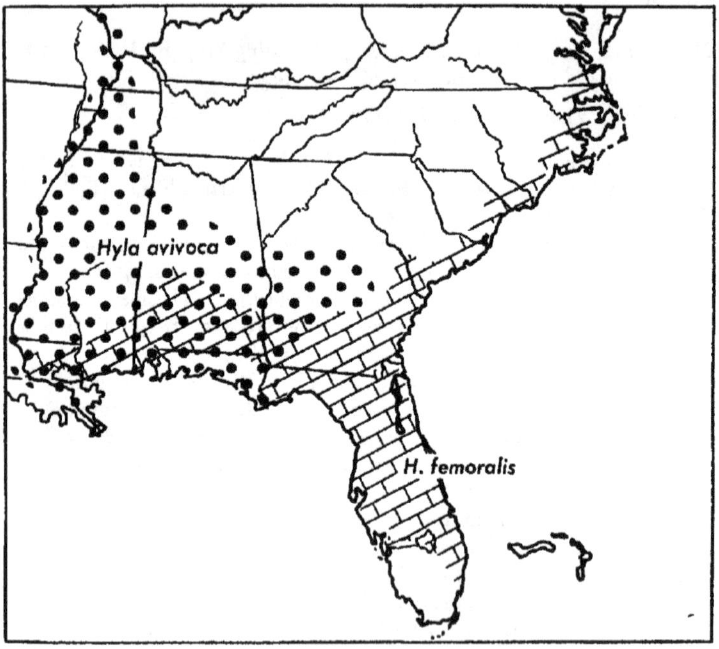


*Map 21*

is white with a wash of marguerite yellow. Lower throat is pale flesh to venetian pink. Lower belly and lower surface of femur are the same. Rear of femur below vent and rear of tarsus are marked with white on pebbly surface. Lower belly and groin have wash of viridine green or other yellow-green. Underside of fore limb is like fore part of venter, lichen green or light gull gray. Pupil rim of eye citron yellow or strontian yellow; iris black, heavily spotted with these yellows

*Female,* Mariana, Fla., from O. C. Van Hyning, Jan. 3, 1933. Top of head drab, buffy brown and the same color on forward part of dorsum. The bar from eye to eye, the forward dorsal spot, and the rear dorsal spot olive-brown. The side of body has background pale olive-buff to pale vinaceous-fawn, the groin olive-buff or pale glass green. The light interspace color on rear of femur may be glass green, pale glass green, or pale olivine. The transverse bars on tibia, interspace color on rear of femur, and spots on groin are bister or raw umber. The pale spot below the eye is clear, prominent, pale olive-buff or marguerite yellow. The whole chin is white with very few black dots near lower labial border. The under parts in general are white or pale olive-buff, with scarcely any suggestion of the wash of greenish present in the male. The pupil rim is encircled by a carnelian red or vinaceous-tawny ring; the iris proper is black dotted with testaceous or terra cotta spots.

**Structure:** More slender than *Hyla versicolor;* muzzle truncate; webs large, but leaving the last two joints of fourth toe free, except for web margin; back almost smooth; ventral surface with distinct granulations; usually with narrow waist; male with folds on rear of throat almost to pectoral region.

**Voice:** "The voice is birdlike, being a plaintive whistle repeated in quick succession, much as in the redbellied woodpecker. This call is sometimes preceded by a few notes of a slower call much like the voice of *Hyla crucifer.*

"The pitch and tone of the voice of *avivoca* is nearer to that of *crucifer* than to any other eastern American *Hyla* although its rate is far more rapid than that of *crucifer*" (P. Viosca, Jr., La., 1928, pp. 90–91).

"The males call from bushes in or near the water and from cypress, tupelo, and black-gum boles" (A. F. Carr, Jr., Fla., 1940b, p. 58).

See F. Harper, Gen., 1935, pp. 290–293, for characteristics of its call.

**Breeding:** This species breeds from June to mid-August. The eggs and tadpoles are not described. "*Hyla avivoca* is more clearly related to *Hyla versicolor* than to any other North American *Hyla*. . . ."

"I located a small chorus in Sweetwater Creek Swamp, Liberty County, April 19, 1935, where *H. crucifer, H. v. versicolor, Pseudacris feriarum,* and *Rana clamitans* were also calling. I have never seen a female" (A. F. Carr, Jr., Fla., 1940b, p. 58).

**Journal notes:** June 8, 1930, New Orleans, Sunday. Went to Mandeville and Lewisburg by myself to search out Viosca's type locality. Didn't succeed.

June 9, New Orleans. Went to Viosca's house. Heard *H. c. cinerea.* While there Chase from office called up that by dint of hard work he had taken four *Hyla avivoca* at Lewisburg, Covington, and in a swamp just south of Mandeville. They are males. They surely are a different frog.

June 10, New Orleans. Started at noon for the north country, Pearl River, and pine barren parishes of Louisiana, with Percy Viosca, Jr., and H. B. Chase. Went to Pearl River. Didn't hear *H. avivoca* in the gum and cypress edges, a haunt of the species. Presently we heard a Flycatcher, which I remarked was like a crested Flycatcher. Then Chase got excited over a note in the tupelo swamp either side of the bridge. Instantly the setting and note made me say, "It is a Pileated Woodpecker." A day or so before Viosca and Chase had said

*Plate LXII. Hyla avivoca* (×1¼). 1–4. Males.

*Plate LXIII. Hyla baudinii* (×⅔). 1. Female. 2–7. Males.

this frog's note was like a Pileated Woodpecker at a distance. Naturally they both laughed at me. Worth it. Would I have guessed it to be a frog, much less a Hyla? Fear not. Heard a few of them in the gums of Tick Faw River where we will go tomorrow night.

June 11. Tick Faw River, La. (near Ferry). In Tick Faw River we heard a few *H. avivoca.* Finally Chase called me to hurry and started off on the run. I followed. We were soon in a tupelo swamp. Near the edge we heard them Chase found his first one crosswise of leaves of buttonbush (*Cephalanthus occidentalis*). My first was on the bole of a gum. Many of Chase's captures were head down on upright branch of buttonbush. Mine were head up. Chase and I followed voices. We got five frogs between us. Viosca with a lamp on his head shone their eyes. He didn't follow voices so much. He got more in this way than either of us. One frog was pure green with no markings. Viosca found several on small gums near the tupelo edge while Chase's and my captures were farther in the swamp On the trees was some poison ivy. On clumps or tree bases in the swamp and at the edge of the swamp were sensitive fern (*Onoclea sensibilis*), royal fern (*Osmunda regalis*), *Utricularia* (purple), a marsh St.-John's-wort, sphagnum, water penny (*Hydrocotyle*), lizard's-tail (*Saururus*), *Nyssa aquatica,* and buttonbushes with mayhaws. Most of the frogs were 3 or 4 feet above the water. Finally Chase found a female on a log, in the water. Sometimes they go higher in trees. Usually they are down at 3–4 feet or less. Their call is birdlike. It is a fine, delicate little species. Viosca did right to call it a new form, *H. avivoca.*

June 11. Tick Faw River, La. Throat in croaking is somewhat swollen, vibrates for 6–10 or 12 calls. These are more or less the same, repeated. Sometimes raises rear end with calling. Chase also noticed the vibration or varied swelling at each call.

**Authorities' corner:**

P. Viosca, Jr., La , 1928, p. 91.
J. R. Endsley, Tenn., 1937, p 70.

### Mexican Tree Frog, Van Vliet's Frog

*Hyla baudinii* (Duméril and Bibron). Plate LXIII; Map 20.

**Range:** South-central and southern Texas through Central America.

"This Mexican species has been found by Mr. Marnock in the low country southwest of San Antonio, commencing with San Miguel Creek, a tributary of the Medina. This is its most eastern known range, that previously given by Professor Baird being Brownsville (as *Hyla vanvlietii*)" (E. D. Cope, Tex., 1880a, p. 29).

**Habitat:** June 18, 1930. At 10 P.M, two miles west of Brownsville, in a resaca, found these frogs in small bushes, in weedy clumps, and even in grassy tangles in overflowed tomato field adjoining the overflowed resaca. Later, along the

Rio Grande in Brownsville, found them in a pond. Mr. Blanchard tells me he saw Mr. Camp take them along the river (Rio Grande) in palms just above Mr. Rebb's palm grove.

June 19. Heard several in the palm grove which is completely flooded by high river. Beyond grove, and along river, a large chorus is calling.

**Size:** Adults, 1¾–3⅗ inches. Males, 44–71 mm. Females, 44–89 mm.

**General appearance:** This large tree frog has a black patch over the arm insertion and a white line encircling the arm insertion. Its color ranges from nearly black to light yellow green, gray, or fawn. It has a transverse bar between the eyes. Various irregular lateral spots of black form a reticulation on a yellow or olivine side area. There are transverse bars on the legs, a light greenish spot under the eye, a light line above the dark-edged upper jaw, and a dark line from eye to shoulder ending in a prominent black patch. The breast and throat may be spotted with dark. The sides are yellow posteriorly. In the female, the under parts of the throat and upper breast are white, the lower breast and belly white suffused with pale green. In the male, under parts are cream buff with lateral throat sacs, a pale brownish drab. The rear of the femur is yellow and russet.

**Color:** *Male*. Brownsville, Tex., June 19, 1930. Back sulphine yellow and aniline yellow on side or olive lake on back becoming old gold on sides (no dorsal marks; last night this frog was brown with prominent marks on dorsum). The back may be chamois to primrose yellow with olive-yellow or some green interspersed. Cream buff line along jaw to beyond angle of mouth and under tympanum. Tympanum pinkish cinnamon or light vinaceous-cinnamon or vinaceous-buff. From eye over tympanum irregular black line ending in a large vertical curl of black above arm insertion. Along side and a little below level of black arm insertion spot are several prominent black spots to the groin. This black spotting is more or less reticulated with lemon yellow. Top of fore limbs warm buff, pinkish buff, or chamois. From eye almost to black shoulder spot is a wood brown band. Chin sulphur yellow or light green-yellow. Each lateral sac with oil yellow to ecru-drab or pale brownish drab. Under parts cream buff except a narrow pectoral area and extension between two sacs. This little area is white. Hind legs more or less color of forelegs. Rear of femur with some viridine yellow or bright green-yellow with vinaceous-russet; under side of hind legs onion-skin pink with every tubercle crowned with sulphur yellow. All of venter very pebbly Iris very bronzy; below heavily spotted with buff-pink, above it is chartreuse yellow; pupil rim pale greenish yellow, broken in front and behind; outside iris is ring of lichen green or Niagara green.

*Other males*. One greenish yellow on back except for top of head and top of hind legs and forelegs, which are viridine yellow. Another bright green-yellow on back. From eye of each extends a horizontal black line ending in a vertical black curve back of axil. Below this is a clay color or cinnamon band outlined by black above, and below by light line from upper jaw edge almost to base of vertical black bar. Tympanum may be vinaceous-cinnamon or cinnamon. Along side where green of back ends and before greenish yellow of reticulated or spotted side begins is cinnamon-buff. In one, no black spots and little yellow. Iris, upper part cinnamon-buff.

*Female.* Brownsville, Tex., from H. C. Blanchard, July 23, 1930. The forward part of head, upper eyelid, face, and arms are vinaceous-buff. The background of back and legs is deep olive-buff or olive-buff. The bars of tibia, femur, and arm, the dark spots on back, and the large spot from each eyelid on fore back are grayish olive or vetiver green. Particularly in the groin and slightly on sides are black spots on pale olivine ground. The reticulation of the sides is less prominent than in the male, and restricted almost entirely to the groin. The black U-shaped spot on shoulder has the opening toward the tympanum. The tympanum is wood brown. The iris is somewhat duller than in the male; lower iris wood brown, the upper avellaneous. The under parts of hands are light vinaceous-fawn. The under parts of feet, femur, and tibia are light russet-vinaceous. The under parts of throat and upper breast are white; the lower breast and belly are white with a suffusion of pale turtle green. After the frog had been in a moist jar for a few hours, the back became darker, Prout's brown, and the reticulation along the sides became more marked.

Aug. 13, the female still continues with the rich brown coloration. She remains under the wet moss. The two males come up in the glass jar, one is a bright green and the other old gold or citrine. Female 54 mm.

**Structure:** Skin, smooth above, set with fine tubercles; under parts granular; tympanum nearly as large as eye; fold of skin from eye to shoulder; prominent fold across breast; disks large, fingers slightly webbed, toes webbed; a distinct tarsal fold.

"*Hyla vanvlietii* Baird—Nearly smooth above. Tympanum nearly as large as the eye. Tibia half as long as the body, longer than arm from elbow, which in turn exceeds the foot. Ash gray or olive, with an irregular cruciform dorsal blotch. Thigh and leg with three transverse bands each. Their inner surfaces when flexed scarcely reticulated, but spotted with white upon a darker ground. Inside of tibia uncolored. Body two inches. Hab. Brownsville, Texas" (S. F. Baird, Gen., 1856, p. 61).

**Voice:** The vocal sac is better developed on either side of throat than in its middle. This is especially noticeable in the live frog.

June 18, 1930, Brownsville, Tex. The first time I heard them I guessed they must be H. *baudinii*. Heard their chorus at ½ mile. The note was a blurred *heck* or *keck* (not high like *Acris*). This may be repeated 5 to 8 or even 10 or 12 times. Then comes an interesting chuckle, or no chuckle at all, or no *keck* and all chuckle. Never heard anything like it. The first call (not chuckle) in some ways reminds me of *Hyla cinerea*, but yet it is much unlike the call of the cowbell tree frog. Does the full dilation of the sac on either side cause the queer note (unlike most Hylas)?

In Mr. F. Rebb's palm grove heard a few *H. baudinii*. They are too far out in an overflow to reach them. To the east of his house and near the river heard a chorus of these frogs. Their repeated *kecks* or *hecks* last about 2 or 3 seconds, then as much interval, whereas *B. valliceps* has a longer call, sometimes to 5 seconds.

**Breeding:** The only record on transformation is of one specimen transformed, or just past, from Panama, ⅞ inch (21 mm.) in length, which was caught Feb. 19, 1911. They were in full chorus in Brownsville, Tex., June 19, 1930. In southern Vera Cruz, A. G. Ruthven found this species common. He observed them breeding on July 17. In 1908, near Cordoba, Vera Cruz, Dr. H. Gadow found a spawning congress of 45,000 frogs. His account is very vivid.

"Whilst rambling along the edge of the forest we became conscious of a noise, at first resembling the mutter of a distant sawmill; but on our reaching the other side of a cluster of trees this sound grew into a roar, like that of steam escaping from many engines, mingled with the sharp and piercing scream of saws. It came from a meadow containing a shallow pool of rain-water. In the wet grass, on its stalks, and on the ground, hopped about hundreds of large green tree-frogs; nearer the pool they were to be seen in thousands, and in the water itself there were tens of thousands. Hopping, jumping, crawling, sliding, getting hold of each other, or sitting still. Most of them were *in amplexus,* and these couples were quiet, but the solitary males sat on their haunches and barked solemnly, with their resounding vocal bags protruding. Every now and then one was making for a mate, and often there were three or four hanging on to each other and rolling over. The din was so great that it was with difficulty that we caught the remarks that we shouted, although we were standing only a few feet apart. Each sweep of a butterfly net caught at least half-a-dozen frogs.

"Now the grassy pool, where the frogs were closest, was about 30 yards square (900 square yards), rather more than the area of a tennis lawn, and each square yard held from 50 to 100 frogs—many square yards certainly held several hundreds each. At the very lowest computation this gives 45,000 frogs; and there was, besides, an outer ring of some five hundred square yards where frogs were fairly numerous, say from 5 to 10 to the square yard, mostly spent females, but these few thousands we may leave out of the reckoning, to understate rather than overestimate the number. Supposing there were only 20,000 females, each spawning from 5,000 to 10,000 eggs—say only 5,000—the total would amount to just 100,000,000 eggs. The spawn literally covered both ground and water thickly. But the greatest surprise awaited us on the following morning, when we went to photograph the scene. There was not a single frog left; the water had all evaporated, and the whole place was glazed over with dried-up spawn! The prospective chance of millions of little frogs was gone, their expectant parents having been deceived in calculating their day of incarnation. That was on the 4th of July, several weeks after the beginning of the rather fitful rainy season" (H. Gadow, Gen., 1908, pp. 75–76).

"We found *H. baudinii* common at Cuatotolapam. Most of the specimens were taken during night rains on the banana trees at San Juan. At these times they were very noisy. During the day we found them secreted under boards, in the bases of such large leaved plants as the 'elephant ears,' bananas, etc. They were observed breeding in a pond near La Laja Creek on July 17" (A. G. Ruthven, Gen., 1912, pp. 310–311).

On the basis of some material from Mr. Sumichrast (taken at Tehuantepec, Mexico) Cope (Gen., 1880b, p. 267) wrote: "Abundant, but only seen in the rainy season, when it comes to pools, lagoons, etc. to breed."

On Dec. 31, 1932, Prof. H. J. Swanson of Edinburg, Tex., sent us three specimens, 30, 32, and 32 mm., respectively. They had the reticulated sides, dark spot below eye, bar on shoulder insertion, and white stripe across vent with black spot below.

**Journal notes:** June 18, 1930, Brownsville, Tex. That night, went out the Military Road 2 or 3 miles where the road comes opposite a resaca which is ½–¾ mile from the road. From road heard a chorus new to me. My guess was *H. baudinii*. Pell-mell I started. The resaca looked very foul and dirty because of ripe, overripe, and green tomatoes afloat. On little bushes or among tomato vines heard these new frogs. The note was a heavy *keck* given 5–10 times with an interesting chuckle following. The first frog heard I never could locate, though I was almost on it, in such a tangle of grass and vines. Finally located one in a bush where water was waist-deep. It was on a branch 1 foot above water. This one was yellow-green. Then followed another. It was brown in color and on the ground where the water was shallow. Tried for several more. Whenever I approached, they stopped. Did my white shirt or something else give me away? For some time raced back and forth between two *Hyla baudinii* and three narrow-mouthed toads. Didn't get the two Baudin's frogs. After 1½ hours' effort turned back for fear taximan had gone or thought me lost. By pointers (stars) worked my way back. Came out by the car. In a pond beside the river heard another *H. baudinii*. It was deep green on back. Only the brown specimen had markings on back. The yellowish green and deep green specimens were all green on the back. The last one was found on the surface of the water among a clump of weeds.

August 22, 1930. Went over to Mrs. Olive Wiley's museum in the Minneapolis Public Library. She had a beautiful *Hyla baudinii* from Central America. It came on a bunch of bananas to a local merchant.

**Authorities' corner:**

A. Gunther, Gen., 1885–1902, pp. 271–272.
J. K. Strecker, Jr., Tex., 1915, p. 50.
R. Kellogg, Gen., 1932, p. 161.
W. G. Lynn, Gen., 1944, p. 189.

## Green Tree Frog, Carolina Tree Frog, Marsh Tree Frog, Cinereous Frog, Bell Frog, Fried Bacon Frog, Cowbell Frog, Bull Frog

*Hyla cinerea cinerea* (Schneider). Plate LXIV; Map 22.

**Range:** Virginia to Texas, up the Mississippi River to Illinois and Missouri.

**Habitat:** Swampy edges of watercourses; on the taller water plants in ditches or pools; on lily pads, trees, bushes, or vines not far from water. Prof. E. A. Andrews in 1928 reported finding them in pitcher-plant trumpets.

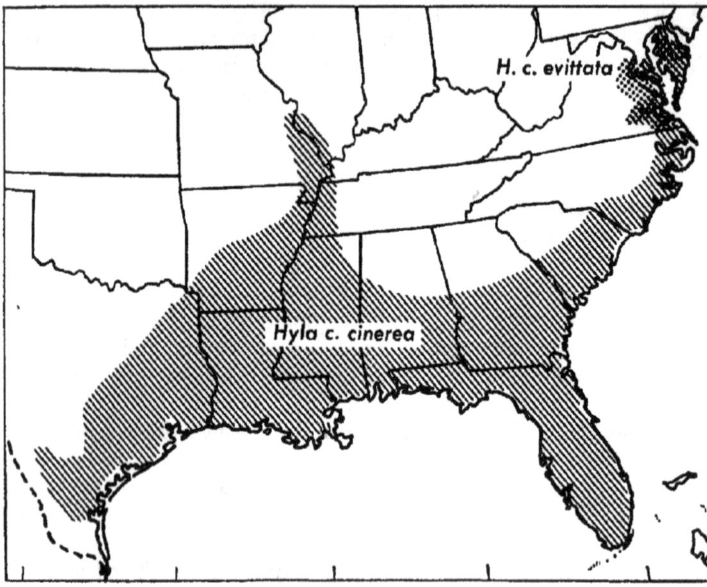


*Map 22*

The frogs may be on the bushes and stems above the water, but more frequently are at the water's level During the day they rest mainly on the stems above the water. They may be hidden in clumps of Spanish moss or under flakes of bark on trees. June 27, 1922, at Camp Pinckney, we took *Hyla cinerea* in Pond No. 2, on a vertical wild rice stem, the frog some 3 feet above the water. July 5, at Pond No. 3, on the wide-leaved grasslike plants were some 7 or 8 *Hyla cinerea* perched 1–3 feet above the water. On August 11, found 3 males, 2 feet above the water.

"The green tree frog has been found climbing out on the emergent portions of water hyacinths on several occasions. Concerning this species, Kilby (MS 1938) says: 'By far the greatest concentration of individuals is found among lake and pond shore vegetation and on the floating rafts of water hyacinths that are common in Florida Lakes.' My own records are for January, February, and October" (C. J. Goin, Fla., 1943, pp. 148–149).

"This is the most beautiful tree-frog of our fauna. It lives on the leaves of plants, frequenting especially lily pads and other aquatic vegetation at the edges of lakes. It occurs also, at times, in fields of corn. Its food consists of insects, the common fly being, it is said, preferred. Its note resembles the tone of a cow bell heard at a distance. Where abundant about water, the frogs are very noisy just before dusk, the chorus being broken, however, by longer or shorter intervals of silence. A single note is first heard, and as if that were a signal, it is taken up and repeated by a dozen noisy throats till the air is resonant with the sound. After a time it ceases as suddenly as it began, to be again resumed after a period of quiet" (H. Garman, Ill., 1892, pp. 347–348).

**Size:** Adults, 1½–2½ inches. Males, 37–59 mm. Females, 41–63 mm.

**General appearance:** This is a very slim, smooth, bright green tree frog with a light side stripe, pointed head, and shallow face. It is relatively the longest-legged *Hyla* of the East. Often there are small gold or yellow spots on the back. The under surfaces are white or yellowish white.

Deckert (Fla., 1915, p. 3) described it as "an aristocratic looking tree toad, with its long, slender figure of the brightest green, edged on each side with a band of pale gold or silvery white."

"This is a larger species than *Hyla lateralis*, the length of which according to Daudin, is 'un pouce et demi au plus.' Dr. Holbrook's specimen, however, measured 1¾ inches. The largest specimen in the collection of the Academy measures 1½ inches (Fr.) It is a much more slender animal than *semifasciata*. In *lateralis* (*viridis*, Holl.) the lateral stripe extends as far as the anus, and there is a white band running the whole length of the tibia, both anteriorly and posteriorly. The anterior band is absent in *semifasciata*" (E. Hallowell, Tex., 1857b, pp. 307–308).

**Color:** Okefinokee Swamp, Ga., April 26, 1921. *Male.* In dark olive-green males there are twenty orange spots scattered over the back. The frog is lighter green on sides below lateral stripe, which is cream-colored and extends almost to hind legs. Obscure on snout ahead of eye. Cream colored or white stripe on back of forearm. Same on back of lower leg and along hind end of foot. Throat from angle of mouth to slightly back of chin green. Chin proper yellowish cream. Back of these two areas, yellowish cream and green, is the wrinkled pink area of the throat proper. One light-colored male has stripe straw-colored and extending only an inch behind insertion of arm area. There is black above and below the stripe. (Non-Ridgway.)

*Another male.* Back may be apple green, dark olive-green, greenish olive, or deep slaty olive to almost black, the stripe on side light dull green-yellow or clear dull yellow. In one male, stripe not beyond tympanum and suggestive of *H. evittata*. The vent, forearm stripe, foot stripe, and heel are white. One dark male had the foot stripe fainter. Iris russet-vinaceous.

*Female*. Has no pink chin, and green extends in on sides of throat for slight distance. Straw-colored stripe to insertion of hind legs prominent, also stripe under eye. Under parts from groin to chin the same cream color. (Non-Ridgway.)

**Structure:** Slender, flat in body; skin smooth or minutely granular; breast fold present; vocal sac a round subgular pouch; a tympanic fold from tympanum to base of arm.

**Voice:** The voice is loud and at a distance sounds like a cowbell. The individual call is *quonk, quonk, quonk, quank*. To some ears, *fried bacon, fried bacon*. To Deckert, *grab, grab, grabit, grabit*. This is easily one of the most characteristic anuran voices of the South. It is one of the rain signals for the residents, who call it the "rain frog." In the daytime when the weather is sultry or especially in the evenings of late May or early June, some of the immense choruses are not easily to be forgotten. Sometimes a chorus starts suddenly, quickly reaches its crest, and ends abruptly, to be resumed later after a shorter or longer sharply defined interval. Along some of the water-courses like Billy's Lake one lone frog near by will begin, then stop, but before he has finished, another just ahead of the speeding boat has taken up the task. Thus the chorus may travel along the margin of a lake for considerable distances.

At Flatwood, Ala., 1917, after 6.30 P.M. in a drying-up, swampy pond, we heard a chorus which sounded to one member of the party like an exhaust running into an oil-well pipe. We took one frog with the aid of a flashlight. It was on some bushes. Its sides and throat looked like a pink ball.

The calls may be given about 75 to the minute. The frog may redouble its speed and at the same time add a rolling quality to the note: *crronk—crronk—crronk*. Two individuals calling together but not in unison produce *bo babe, bo babe, bo, babe*.

J. Le Conte (Gen., 1856, p. 428) said it was commonly known as the bell frog, its notes resembling the sound of small bells.

J. E. Holbrook (Gen., 1842, IV, 120–121) wrote: "Their noise proceeds from a single note, which at a little distance is not unlike the sound of a small bell; and there seems in general to be one leader of their orchestra, and when he raises his note, hundreds take it up from all parts of the corn field, and when he stops, the concert is at an end, until he again begins."

**Breeding:** This species breeds from April 15 to August 15. The black or brownish and white or cream eggs are in small packets or films at or near the surface, attached to floating vegetation. The outer envelope is poorly defined, becoming part of the mass. The egg is $\frac{1}{30}$–$\frac{1}{16}$ inch (0.8–1.6 mm.), the inner envelope $\frac{1}{12}$–$\frac{1}{8}$ inch (2.2–3.4 mm.), the outer envelope $\frac{1}{8}$–$\frac{1}{6}$ inch (3.6–4.0

mm.). The tadpole is medium, 1⅗ inches (40 mm.), its tail long and acuminate, its body green with a sulphur or ivory stripe on the side of the head from snout to eye. The tooth ridges are ⅔. After 55 to 63 days, the tadpoles transform from July 2 to October, at ½–¹¹⁄₁₆ inch (12–17 mm.).

"The breeding season extends from late spring to late summer. . . . The condition of the weather is a controlling factor in determining when, within this period, breeding actually occurs" (J. D. Kilby, Fla., 1945, p. 82).

**Journal notes:** The same conditions do not always produce the same coloration. In one case, we had many *Hyla cinerea* in a botany drum. All were light green except three, one of which was almost black, another olive green or dark green, and the third yellowish green. One noon in 1917 we stopped in a low woods near one of the bays between Pass Christian and Bay St. Louis, Miss. On the saw palmetto leaves we found no end of *Hyla cinerea* and *Hyla squirella* in all color phases. These creatures were on the leaves or in the bases between two stems. In one place found two specimens, one a brown phase and one a green phase. Some have a yellowish or orange color on the posterior faces of thighs, others have purplish. Some have yellowish line on lip and a few besides have faint yellowish line on side. May have a purplish area from nostril to femur along the side. In one clump one yellowish green on back, another dark greenish, and a third purplish brown. There were unspotted *H. evittata; Hyla cinerea,* olive, green, or brownish with or without lateral bands, with or without dark borders to band.

May 10, 1921. This evening at 8 P.M. (temperature 72°) went to new pond. . . . Heard a *Hyla cinerea* near by. Began to search. It stopped. Later thought I saw it. Seized it and it proved a ripe female, not croaker. This female was in a cypress 4 feet above the water. Went away. Later the croaker started again. On the flat side of an iris leaf 3 feet from the captured female was the male.

At night many individuals are seen to be fairly covered with certain tiny insects that are common in the ground vegetation. Some that were collected proved to be harmless flies (*Oscinia longipes*). Their perching on the frogs is probably accidental.

June 14, 1930, Beeville, Tex. All of a sudden several *Hyla cinerea* began croaking around the pond. They were on near-by mesquite bushes or on small dead plants above the water.

June 15, Beeville, Tex., at night. *Acris* began first, soon to be joined by *R. pipiens,* then came *H. cinerea,* and finally one or two *Microhyla olivacea.* . . . We caught several *H. cinerea.* In one mesquite or papilionaceous plant found two males facing each other, and caught each by putting the light between my legs, and grabbing with each hand. *H. cinerea* were about 1 or 2 feet above the water. A beautiful brown garter snake (*Thamnophis eques*) was coursing around the pond, ostensibly for frogs.

June 17–21, Brownsville-San Benito, Tex. In various resacas were several choruses of *H. cinerea.*

*Plate LXIV. Hyla cinerea cinerea* (×⅞). 3. Females. 2. Male.

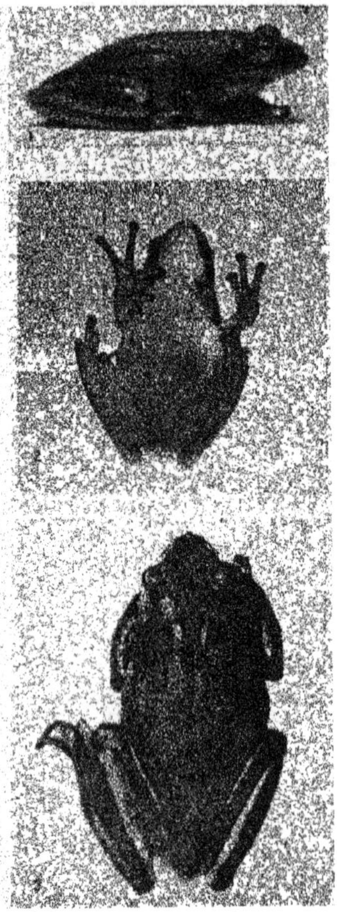

*Plate LXV. Hyla cinerea evittata.* 1,3. Males (×1¼). 2. Female (×1).

**Authorities' corner:**

W. Bartram, Gen., 1791, p. 277.
P. H. Pope, Tex., 1919, pp. 95–96.
V. R. Haber, Gen., 1924, pp. 1–32.
E. A. Andrews, N.C., 1928, pp. 269–270.
J. D. Kilby, Fla., 1945, pp. 81–82.
G. L. Orton, La., 1947, pp. 364–369.

## Miller's Tree Frog, Green Tree Frog

*Hyla cinerea evittata* (Miller). Plate LXV; Map 22.

**Range:** Virginia to Maryland.

"The series *evittata* in the American Museum differ from these *cinerea* in having a more vertical, less sloping profile to the snout. The former race is also said to differ from *cinerea* in its broader head but our series of *cinerea* exhibits a great variation in width and no constant difference can be found here. It thus appears that typical *cinerea* has a more northern range than Wright and Wright (1933) have *assumed*. It follows that *evittata* has a more restricted range for we found only *cinerea* in the Cove Point-Solomon's Island area. It would be interesting to know if all green frogs north of the Washington area are not referable to *cinerea*" (G. K. Noble and W. G. Hassler, Md., 1936, p. 63).

Since 1912 we have been seeing evittate, semifasciate, and striped *cinerea* from Virginia to Bay St. Louis, Miss., and did not *assume* as intimated above. We merely by our action provisionally called the northern population (variable though it is even at Mt. Vernon where we have collected it) *evittata*. Collectors from West Virginia to Florida to Louisiana have recorded or collected evittate *cinerea*. It is interesting to see that E. R. Dunn (Va., 1937, p. 10) so views the northern collection of material:

"To sum up: 81 per cent in the upper tidewater Potomac area have no stripe or a short stripe; 41 per cent in other parts of Maryland and Virginia have no stripe or a short one. Carolina material available to me is not very extensive, but it would seem that there only 25 per cent have no stripe or a short stripe, whereas 75 per cent have a long stripe. Reports from further south indicate that 100 per cent long stripe occurs in the far south, especially on the Gulf Coast.

"We are, therefore, faced with two opposed populations, obviously different. One occurs in the upper tidewater Potomac; the other occurs in the far south. An intermediate population occurs over a wide area. Unfortunately a somewhat intermediate population, that of the Carolinas, was named first. This seems to be nearer that of the far south, so that *Hyla cinerea cinerea* may be properly applied to specimens of *Hyla cinerea* from the Carolinas south. The name *Hyla cinerea evittata* may be *properly* applied to the upper tidewater Potomac population. The rest of the Maryland and Virginia populations are, and should be considered, intermediate between *cinerea* and *evittata*.

"The most northern locality yet known is the western end of the Chesapeake-Delaware canal in Cecil Co., Md., reported to me by Mr. Joseph Cadbury. It is unknown from Delaware or from the eastern side of the Del-Mar-Va peninsula."

**Habitat:** These frogs live in lily pools and reed beds of tidal marshes. At other times, they are found on bushes and small trees near the water.

"Very little is known about the habits of *Hyla evittata*. In June and July the animals are to be found in the rank vegetation of the tide marshes. Here they remain quiet during the day, but as evening approaches they become active and noisy. Their food at this time consists chiefly of a small beetle that is found on the leaves of the pond-lilies. . . . Later in the season the frogs leave the low marsh vegetation. As they are then perfectly silent they are difficult to find, though occasionally one may be seen in a bush or small tree, but never far from water" (G. S. Miller, Jr., D.C., 1899, p. 78).

Recently (Va., 1944, p. 187) Dr. P. Bartsch wrote: "I have been rather interested in the habits of *Hyla evittata* Miller, as observed on our farm, which joins Pohick Bay, a tributary of the Potomac River, some 21 miles south of Washington. Our house is approximately two-fifths of a mile from the water at an elevation of 155 feet.

"In the late summer when the young hylas have reached a little more than half their adult size they leave the lily pads and bonnets of the bay and move inland. At this time the frogs come to our upland level, where we find them particularly partial to okra plants. I have found as many as six attached to the stems of a short row of this vegetable; they blend beautifully into the okra color scheme.

"All the specimens caught on our place are *evittata*, that is, they lack the band characteristic of *H. cinerea*. On the north side of the Potomac River at Foxes Ferry I have found the striped form predominant and the *evittata* color scheme only slightly represented."

**Size:** Adults, 1¼–1⅞ inches. Males, 36–47 mm. Females, 32–47 mm.

**General appearance:** This slim, smooth, green frog is like *Hyla cinerea*, but without the light stripe on the sides and legs. The under parts are white, ivory yellow, or marguerite yellow, with purple-vinaceous to brownish vinaceous on the front of the forearms, femur, the rear of the tibia, and more or less on the underside of the legs. The rear of arms, legs, and hind feet are margined with white to marguerite yellow. Sometimes there are fine yellow spots on the back.

**Color:** *Male*. Upper parts cosse green or lettuce green; sides and legs javel green or dull green-yellow; sides of under jaw from angle almost to tip narrowly bordered with apple green or dull green-yellow; rear of arms, legs, and hind feet margined with white to marguerite yellow; front of legs, feet, axilla, and somewhat on underside of forearm purple-vinaceous, livid brown, or deep brownish vinaceous; under parts including throat white, ivory yellow, or marguerite yellow. This individual had faint line on upper jaw tip to angle of mouth primrose yellow.

*Female.* This one has the faintest line on upper jaw. Upper parts oil green; oil green on sides of under jaw as prominent as in male; under parts white or cartridge buff; front of forearms, femur, rear of tibia, underside of tarsus and foot deep brownish vinaceous. Another female has entire under parts of legs and most of pectoral region purplish vinaceous; line on upper jaw white; fine lemon yellow or light cadmium spots on the back.

**Structure:** Broader head and deeper face than *Hyla cinerea.*

"*Hyla evittata* sp. nov. *Type* adult ♂ (in alcohol) No. 26,291 U.S.N.M., collected at Four Mile Run, Alexandria County, Virginia, July 15, 1898, by Gerrit S. Miller, Jr., and Edward A. Preble. Zonal position.—This frog is probably confined to the Upper Austral zone. Geographic distribution.—While the animal is at present known from the marshes of the Potomac River near Washington only, it is to be looked for near the coast from Chesapeake Bay to Long Island Sound. General characters.—Like *Hyla cinerea* (Daudin) but with broader, deeper muzzle and normally unstriped body and legs. Color.—Entire dorsal surface varying from olivaceous brown through deep myrtle-green to pale yellowish grass-green: ventral surface white, irregularly tinged with yellow, especially on chin and throat; colors of back and belly fading rather abruptly into each other on lower part of sides; skin of under surface of limbs unpigmented, transparent; legs and jaws slightly paler on sides than above; eye very bright and iridescent, the pupil black, the iris golden greenish yellow, thickly dotted with black, back with a few—usually less than half a dozen—inconspicuous minute, yellowish dots. Measurements. —Type: head and body, 48; hind leg, 69; femur, 20; tibia, 21; tarsus, 11; hind foot, 17; humerus, 8; forearm, 8; front foot, 10; greatest width of head, 14; eye to nostril, 3.5; distance between nostrils, 3.5. An adult ♂ from the type locality: head and body, 50; hind leg, 70; femur, 21; tibia, 21; tarsus, 11; hind foot, 17; humerus, 8; forearm, 8; front foot, 10; greatest width of head, 14; eye to nostril, 4; distance between nostrils, 3" (G. S. Miller, Jr., D.C. and Va., 1899, p. 76).

**Voice:** The call is very like that of *Hyla cinerea.*

"The note is like that of *Hyla pickeringii* in form, but in quality it is comparatively harsh and reedy, with a suggestion of distant guinea-fowl chatter, and scarcely a trace of the peculiar freshness so characteristic of the song of the smaller species. The song period continues through June and July" (G. S. Miller, Jr., Va., 1899, p. 78).

**Breeding:** Similar to *H. cinerea.* Smallest specimens in National Museum February, 1928, were two young taken by A. S. Miller at Quantico, Va., Oct. 13, 1901. They were 22–24 mm. Another of 26 mm. was taken September, 1923, at New Alexandria, Va., by Dr. E. T. Wherry. These are 5–15 mm. larger than the 11–17 mm. transformees of *H. cinerea cinerea.*

**Journal notes:** In 1917, on May 29, while encamped on the Alexandria (Henshaw Sparrow) Heights, we heard *Hyla evittata* toward the river. In 1922, in June, we heard them again from Alexandria. One member of the party who knew and had collected *H. c. evittata* thus identified them. The calls impressed the authors as *Hyla cinerea.* On June 3, 1928, Mr. and Mrs. Morris Brady took us to one of the best collecting grounds of *Hyla c. evittata.* We walked along the railroad track and picked up one or two specimens of *Hyla evittata* on the ties, as well as a few toads. On the right-hand side of the track, Brady took me to the water's edge where we heard a few calling. It certainly sounded like *Hyla c. cinerea.* Captured one more. Luckily for me, both sexes are represented. These specimens are evittate, but it would not be hard to conceive of some of them developing a complete stripe or a semifasciate condition. In fact, Mr. Brady informs me that individual frogs may take on these different liveries. The life history of this form, according to what he told me, is very similar to that of *Hyla c. cinerea.* We await with expectancy his account of this species.

**Authorities' corner:**

G. S. Miller, D.C. and Va., 1899, pp. 75–78.
W. P Hay, D.C., 1902, p. 199
H W. Fowler, Md., 1915, pp. 38–39.
G. S Myers, N.C, 1924, p. 60.
O. C. Van Hyning, Fla, 1933, p. 4.
N. D. Richmond and C. J. Goin, Va, 1938, p. 303.

"The material at hand indicates that the population of this frog inhabiting the Del-Mar-Va Peninsula is intermediate between the two subspecies, *Hyla cinerea cinerea* (Schneider) and *Hyla cinerea evittata* Miller" (R. Conant, Del., 1945, p. 4).

### Peeper, Spring Peeper, Pickering's Tree Frog, Pickering's Tree Toad, Pickering's Hylodes, Pickering's Hyla, Peeping Frog, Castanet Tree Frog

*Hyla crucifer crucifer* Wied. Plate LXVI; Map 23.

**Range:** Gaspé Peninsula to Manitoba and Minnesota south to northeastern Kansas, Arkansas, Louisiana, Texas, Mississippi, Alabama, Piedmont Georgia, South Carolina to New Brunswick.

**Habitat:** These frogs live in open lowland marshes, swamps at sources of streams whether wooded or open, sphagnous or cattail, in fact any pool, ditch, or shallow pond transient or permanent, grassy or muddy.

**Size:** Adults, ¾–1¼ inches. Males, 18–29 mm. Females, 20–33 mm.

**General appearance:** This is a small frog with an oblique cross on the back. A male when first captured in early spring may be liver brown or bay to claret brown. The females are usually lighter in color. Both have obscure bands across the fore and hind limbs. The male has yellow on the groin; its throat is olive. The under parts are light vinaceous-cinnamon to pale yellow.

**Color:** *Male.* Upper parts deep olive buff or isabella color with light brownish olive on back and obscure bands across fore and hind limbs; primrose yellow on groin; seafoam green or glass green laterad of vent; below vent, natal brown or clove brown spot; throat olive-ocher, or aniline yellow in rear and citrine near lower jaw rim; pectoral region sulphur yellow or pale chalcedony

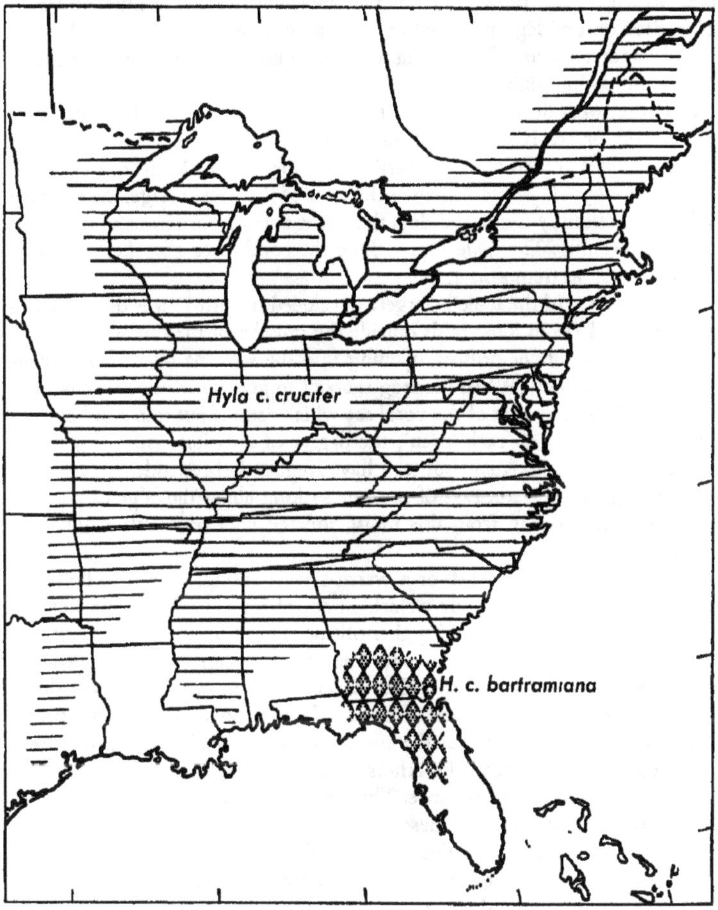


*Map 23*

yellow; rest of under parts light vinaceous-cinnamon; upper jaw cinnamon-buff; bister stripe in front of eye. A male when first captured out in the sun in early spring may be liver brown, chestnut brown, bay, claret brown, or mars brown.

*Female.* Upper parts warm buff, cinnamon-buff, cream-buff, chamois. Bar between the eyes, cross on fore part of back, oblique bar back of it on left and also right, bar on back near vent, bars on forearms and also on tibia buffy brown or drab. Stripe in front of eye and across tympanum and spot on vent olive brown or hair brown. Venter pale olive-buff, cartridge buff, or cream color. Rear of hind legs and front of thigh aniline yellow, olive-ocher. Underside of femur vinaceous-fawn to light grayish vinaceous. Iris vinaceous-cinnamon or onion-skin pink with some dark spots.

**Structure:** Muzzle pointed, projecting considerably beyond the lower jaw; skin smooth or nearly so; fingers not webbed.

**Voice:** Notes are variable, but shrill, clear, high pitched, and can be heard at a distance of half a mile. When at the crest of the chorus stage, the din may be heard incessantly night and day, though it is most vociferous in the afternoon and evening. The male approaching the pond gives a weaker note with a more querulous tremor in it.

"The vocal sac of the male is largely developed in spring; it is of a greenish grey color and lies in loose folds outside the muscles of the throat. Inside the mouth are two slits or orifices, opening into the sac, one on each side near the angle of the jaws. When the frog is about to give voice the whole body is inflated, followed by that of the vocal sac which rounds out into a bubble and does not collapse with each 'peep'; the degree of inflation evidently governs the volume of sound. About sunset I have frequently been aided in discovering the frogs by the level rays of the sun striking along the edge of pond or meadow and reflecting from this moist, inflated vocal sac with a glittering light.

"Unless the day is overcast, or a warm rain is falling, little is to be heard from the frogs till about four o'clock in the afternoon when their concerts begin, to be continued in mild nights till morning. Considering the size, the volume of sound possible from one frog is surprising. As you approach a locality where they are in full voice the air seems to grow gradually dense with this ear-deafening, all-pervading sound; occasionally the voices fall into a regular measure of time, but the effect is usually a medley of shrill sounds, a few voices audible above the others by reason of some peculiarity in key, or lack of smoothness in utterance. The piping of each individual is long continued; the interval between these musical efforts appears to depend on the mood of the musician. One does not note the pause of individual voices in the general effect, but, however loud and earnest the piping may be, the introduction of any unusual sound or appearance, even the low quick flight of a bird over the water, is almost sure to give alarm and still them for a while; the frogs along the edge of the shore commonly settling away out of sight for safety among the dead leaves under water, while those having a position on the low bushes or reeds merely cling more closely, flattening the body against the object on which they are resting. The interval of silence is brief; soon a frog rises and gives a shrill 'peep,' which is immediately answered by dozens of voices. The sounds may appear to come from about your feet, but for the reasons given, the chances are against seeing the frogs till some movement in the water as they rise from their hiding places, arrests the eye, which on perceiving one, usually discovers more" (M H. Hinckley, Mass., 1883, pp. 314–315).

**Breeding:** They breed from April 1 to June 15. The eggs, singly laid, are submerged among fine grass or other plants in matted vegetation, usually near the bottom of the pond, and are 800–1000 in number. They are white or creamy and black or brownish in color, the jelly firm with well-defined outline; the egg 1/25 inch (0.9–1.1 mm.), the envelope 1/20–1/12 inch (1.2–2.0 mm.). The small tadpole, 1⅓ inches (33 mm.), has tooth ridges 2/2 or 2/3. After 90 to 100 days the tadpoles transform from July 1 to Aug. 1, at 3/8–9/16 inch (9–14 mm.).

**Journal notes:** It is interesting to observe how suddenly a chorus will end at one's approach, only to be resumed if the intruder remains quiet. At this time, the frogs may be among the grassy hummocks along the sides of the ponds, or in the shallow pools within the surface film of dead leaves and algae. Not infrequently when disturbed, they may be seen leaping on this matted carpet before disappearance. In one instance we discovered one in the spathe of the skunk cabbage.

March 29, 1910. On the 10 A.M. trip, noticed a pair of peepers come to the surface. Watched them return to the bottom. The male, as always before, was almost as dark as the darkest dead leaf of spring (in the pond); the female was much lighter, about as light as both males and females are at night. The female would lay an egg, then walk or drag along 3 or 4 steps, then stop for another fertilization and emission; and so they went on some time through weeds and matted vegetation without rising to the surface during my observations. Probably they came up occasionally, as when I first discovered them. Put them in a wet handkerchief and then in a glass jar where the sun's rays could not affect them; took them to a crossroads pond. When I planted the jar, they were both lighter in color than when captured, the male considerably so. As I put the jar in the pond, they broke embrace but resumed later and laid eggs later in the day.

April 7, 1929. Went to Ringwood (Ithaca, N.Y.) for peepers and wood frogs. Went about 6 o'clock As it grew dusky, the din grew louder. Peepers seemed all around us, in ponds and on land, on the ground and on bushes. The calls were everywhere, but to find one and see him call was a real job. We both looked for some time without success. Then we both concentrated on one small pond near the road that had cattails in it, also a fence post, a fallen log or rail, and a few bushes around the edge. It was largely made up of tussocks of grass or sedge standing in water. The field grass at one edge was wet and "oozy." We knew we must be looking directly at several, but there was so much noise it was hard to single out one note and locate it. Finally I saw one. It was down in the water, just at the surface, standing almost erect, sunken into the edge of a tussock, his back toward the water, the throat bubble toward the grass stems. He looked dark greenish brown or almost black, like the dirty bases of the grass stems. If his bubble hadn't been vibrating, I never would have seen him. At the same instant, Bert caught one. Then we found a pair, the female looking much lighter. These were at a central tussock. We found another pair at the edge in the "sopping" field grass. Then several feet away from the pond, three feet up on a weed stem, was a male calling lustily. Then we went over to the ponds in the woods. Here were peepers everywhere in ponds and on land. One little fellow was clinging to a stem a foot or so from the ground, clinging rather diagonally so that his bubble went to one side of the stem. We counted his call. It seemed to be about one a second, fifteen calls or so, and then a pause. He sat for periods with his throat extended. On a log extending into the water, Bert saw six peepers calling, but he slipped from the log and they stopped.

July 14, 1929. Went to Ringwood for adult wood frogs. Along the wood road in a fairly open spot where berry bushes and grass are creeping in found many transformed peepers. Some were on the ground in an area covered sparsely with a fine, soft grass. Many were sitting on the leaves of the berry bushes 2 or 3 feet above the ground, others were hopping over the dead leaves in the woods. In the pond, along with the numerous newt adults and larvae, countless larvae of the spotted salamander, a few transforming pickerel frogs, and a very few transforming wood frogs, were many peepers in various stages of transformation.

August 2, 1929. In the same woods, many transformed and a few adult peepers were on the forest floor. In the pond, we found no mature peeper tadpoles, and only three or four transforming ones

**Authorities' corner:**

J. A. Allen, Mass., 1868, p. 190.
M. H. Hinckley, Mass., 1883, pp. 313-317
W. I. Sherwood, Conn , 1898, p. 19.

## Florida Peeper, Southern Peeper, Bartramian Peeper, Southern Spring Peeper, Sabalian Peeper, Coastal Peeper

*Hyla crucifer bartramiana* Harper. Plate LXVII; Map 23.

**Range:** Coastal Plain of southern Georgia and northern Florida. Doubtless some of the coastal records of Alabama and Mississippi are of this form.

**Habitat:** Similar to that of *H. c. crucifer*. "Ponds and ditches in and near woods; moderately common Begins to call in December and January, on warm nights" (O. C. Van Hyning, Fla., 1933, p. 4).

"The six specimens from Alachua County, Florida, listed by Harper . . .

*Plate LXVI. Hyla crucifer crucifer.* 1,2,3. Males (×1). 4. Eggs (×1¼). 5. Female (×1¼).

*Plate LXVII Hyla crucifer bartramiana* (×1).

in the original description of this form, were taken in a small woods pond which is nearly completely covered with hyacinths. The greatest number of individuals I have seen at any one time in northern Florida was in the above mentioned pond, where I collected eighteen on the evening of December 31, 1940" (C. J. Goin, Fla., 1943, p. 149).

"Northern Florida except in the western portion of the Panhandle. Known from the following counties: Jackson, Liberty, Baker, Alachua, Citrus and Lake. Habitat.—Mesophytic and low hammock, swamp borders, the more open bay-heads, and tangles along the smaller streams. Abundance.—Moderately common during breeding season; difficult to collect in numbers during summer and fall. Habits.—They hibernate and aestivate under logs and bark and in knot-holes. In Alachua County they occupy essentially the same habitats as the much rarer *H. v. versicolor*" (A. F. Carr, Jr., Fla., 1940, p. 59).

**Size:** Harper's type, a male, is 28 mm.; the female topotypes are 31.0 and 33.5 mm.

**General appearance:** "Six specimens of *bartramiana* from Alachua County, Florida, generously presented by Coleman J. Goin, exhibit a still more distinct spotting of the under parts than specimens from southern Georgia and probably represent the extreme in subspecific characters" (F. Harper, Ga., 1939b, p. 2).

"Aside from the average difference in spotting, the Coastal Plain specimens were noticeably larger than those of the Piedmont" (F. Harper, Ga., 1939b, p. 3).

**Color:** Gainesville, Fla., from Coleman J. Goin, Feb. 16, 1946. Descriptions of several widely varying patterns follow:

1. Back orange-cinnamon with bars on the back of snuff brown. Of the bars, there are 2 prongs of the cross toward eyes and 2 down sides back of mid-body; between lateral bars of cross there may be intermediate series connected or not; in front of insertion of hind legs is an oblique bar extending up onto the back; also a bar between eyes going onto eyelid; the same color goes from nostril through eye and halfway along side. Color of groin, front and rear of femur, and lower side of tibia is yellow ocher to buckthorn brown; rear of femur heavily spotted amber brown. Upper side of fore and hind legs orange-cinnamon with prominent transverse bars on femur and tibia, line on tarsus and foot of claret brown bordered above by thread of capucine buff. Venter, capucine orange to light ochraceous salmon heavily spotted on breast with amber brown; throat light orange-yellow in mid-portion with rim of lower jaw black. Iris, lower part snuff brown like vitta, upper part mikado orange.

2. Back xanthine orange, groin cadmium yellow or raw sienna. No black on throat.

3. Back cinnamon.

4. Back buffy brown, groin bar goes completely across the back. Rear of

femur extensively spotted and bars of tibia extend onto orange area. Center of throat olive lake, shading to black on margin of lower jaw.

5. Back pinkish cinnamon, bars buffy olive. Venter amber yellow, groin and rear of femur capucine yellow.

6. Back isabella color with face mask and bars of buffy olive; line along tarsus madder brown; throat Saccardo's olive with madder brown flecks.

7. Back mummy brown, no bars showing; bars on legs black; dorsum of legs buckthorn brown; orange groin and both sides of femur; line along tarsus claret brown; throat Saccardo's olive to black on margin of jaw; belly cinnamon-buff.

8. Back ochraceous-tawny with Saccardo's olive bars.

9. Back kaiser brown with markings of carob brown.

Remarks: March 29, 1946. Live material from Gainesville, Fla., and Ithaca, N.Y., compared. Differences most apparent are. the Florida frogs are deeper orange on the belly, with more dark specks on under parts and with the back of the pecan brown order, whereas those of Ithaca are tawny-olive. When we first glanced at the Florida forms we concluded that there were more accessory arms to the dorsal cross than in northern forms, i.e., 6 or 7 arms instead of 4, but some northern ones have the accessory branches also. In general, the cross and bars of the Florida form are somewhat broader and more conspicuous, the bars on legs of some northern forms being very narrow. The belly of northern ones is vinaceous, whereas Florida frogs are nearer honey yellow, a color strikingly apparent on concealed surfaces of hind legs and underside of femur. Furthermore the rear of femur in most of the Florida frogs has many fine black specks that are lacking in our Ithaca ones.

**Structure:** "Length (snout to vent), 28 mm.; tibia, 14; whole hind foot, 19.5; elbow to tip of third finger, 13; interolecranal extent (distance between elbows when humeri are extended in the same line at right angles to longitudinal axis of body), 17.5; intergenual extent (distance between knees when femora are extended in the same line at right angles to longitudinal axis of body), 26" (F. Harper, Ga., 1939b, pp. 1–2).

**Voice:** "The males sing in buttonbush, briars, willows, *Decodon*, etc, at the water's edge in small ponds, ditches and flooded meadows" (A. F. Carr, Jr., Fla., 1940, pp. 59–60).

(See *Pseudacris ornata* for Carr's 1933 comparisons of calls of *P. ornata* and *H. c. bartramiana*.)

**Breeding:** "In Charlton County, Georgia, for example, the breeding season, as far as may be judged by vigorous choruses, extends from late November more or less continuously to early March. Eggs were collected December 9. . . . All (tadpoles) lack the purplish black blotches along the outer edge of the tail crests which Wright records . . ." (F. Harper, Ga., 1939, p. 3).

"January 1 to March 24. Apparently the season is much earlier in Florida than farther north, where it is April 1 to June 15 according to Wright. . . . I have found them breeding when the temperature was 35° F. *P. ornata* is the only other Florida frog which breeds during such cold weather" (A. F. Carr, Fla., 1940, pp. 59–60).

"In the Gainesville region the peepers usually enter the ponds and marshes in late December, and continue to call spasmodically until early spring. My only collection records are for February and December" (C. J. Goin, Fla., 1943, p. 149).

**Journal notes:** We have had no experience with this form in the field.

**Authorities' corner:**

A. F. Carr, Jr., Fla., 1940, p. 59.

## Pine Woods Tree Frog, Pine Woods Tree Toad, Pine Tree Toad, Pine Tree Frog, Scraper Frog, Femoral Hyla

*Hyla femoralis* Latreille. Plate LXVIII; Map 21.

**Range:** Coastal region of Maryland to Florida to Louisiana. We rather question trans-Mississippian records to Dallas, Tex.; they are possible but doubtful. Like *Hyla gratiosa,* at times *H. femoralis* betakes itself into the high pines and is hard to get, and, also like *H. gratiosa,* it is a decidedly Sabalian or Gulf Strip species.

**Habitat:** Trees and shrubs of pine barrens. It breeds in grassy transient pools at the roadside or in the woods, in cypress ponds or bays or in lily-covered swamp prairies.

"High pine, high hammock, and all types of flatwoods, occasionally (at least) climbing to the tops of the tallest long-leaf pines. . . . I have found them hibernating in rotten pine logs; one was disinterred at a depth of two feet in nearly dry sand, Charlotte County, Dec. 16, 1934" (A. F. Carr, Jr., Fla., 1940b, p 60).

"This species is said to stay high up in pine trees but the only two I have personally taken were respectively seven feet up in a small deciduous tree, quite likely a sweet gum, near a stream in the first case, and among rank vegetation in the pine barrens in the second case" (C. S. Brimley, N.C., 1940, p. 22).

R. F. Deckert in 1915 (Fla., p. 3) said: "*Hyla femoralis* Latreille is called the Pine Tree toad, from its habit of frequenting the tops of pine trees almost exclusively during the summer months."

"In 1925 Viosca in discussing the Florida Parishes or uplands of Louisiana comments that 'To the east of the Shortleaf Pine area are the Longleaf Pine Hills with gentle slopes, and intertwined by winding creeks. Here we have a limited representation of practically all species found in the uplands generally and in addition, some species which may be said to be characteristic. *Hyla femoralis* is the typical tree frog of this section.'

"At Leroy, Ala., June 12, 1917, Dr. H. H. Knight while sweeping bushes and lower branches of trees with an insect net for *Capsids* caught two young *Hyla femoralis*" (A. H. Wright, Ga., 1931, p. 275).

**Size:** Adults, 1–1⅗ inches. Males, 24–37 mm. Females, 23–40 mm.

**General appearance:** This frog is commonly a deep reddish brown in color, but may be gray or greenish gray. It resembles a small common tree toad but is more slender and the black markings do not form a regular cross. There are orange or grayish white spots on the rear of the thighs. The under parts are white. The throat may be dark. The upper surface has occasional granulations, the under parts are areolate, granulate on the throat.

"Cope (1889, p. 371) writes: 'Body short, rather broad, and the entire appearance as to pattern of color and shape not very dissimilar from *Hyla versicolor,* from which, however, it is readily distinguishable by the femoral yellow spots; the dark postocular vitta, the absence of light spots under the eyes.'

"Brimley (1907, p. 158) characterizes it as follows: 'Back . . . markings do not form an X-shaped mark. Back of thigh with yellow spots or variegations. No light spot below eye. No yellow spots on sides.'

"Deckert (1915, p. 3) who has studied southeastern frogs more intimately than most observers says this species 'resembles our own gray tree frog, with its rough skin and star-shaped dark patch on the back, but is smaller and more slender.'

"We would consider this species a small species. Cope considers 35 mm. above the average size and his largest is 39 mm. Le Conte a century ago gave 1½–1¾ inches as the adult range and it has been repeated for this little understood form. It may reach 45 mm., as he says, but of the 140 specimens from 20 mm. upwards we have none over 40 mm., the average, 30 mm." (A. H. Wright, Ga., 1931, p. 273).

"The young newly transformed frogs are often green and both in this color phase and when brown are liable to be mistaken for *Hyla squirella* from which species they can always be distinguished by the yellow spots on the back of the thighs" (C. S. Brimley, N.C., 1940, pp. 22–23).

**Color:** June 5, 1921. *Male.* Cephalic half of pectoral fold pale vinaceous-drab to darkish grayish brown; posterior half like the belly. Throat darker than the belly.

*Female.* General color sorghum brown, deep brownish drab, or mars brown on back. Black spot between eyes. Another with four points, two behind and two ahead, the cephalic ends above tympanum. Two on either side of the middle of the back and one over the crupper. Narrow black or deep brown line from snout through nostril to eye, and through tympanum to groin, where it breaks up into spots. Another of the same color on back of forefoot, forearm, front of foreleg, and over vent. Below white line of the vent is a black one. Spots on rear of thighs orange to orange chrome or light cadmium. One female with grayish white instead of orange spots. Under parts white

Pectoral fold pure white to angle of the mouth. Chin white with fine black spots. Iris ecru-drab, drab-gray, or pale vinaceous-drab with reticulation of black.

**Structure:** Upper surface with occasional scattered granulations; belly, under surface of thigh, and breast strongly areolate; throat granulate; pectoral fold smooth or slightly granulate. Tympanic fold usually present. Muzzle rounded.

Holbrook (Gen., 1842, IV, 128) alluded to Duméril and Bibron's mistake as follows: "Duméril and Bibron consider this animal as identical with the *Hyla squirella,* from which it is, however, perfectly distinct."

In 1856 John Le Conte (Gen., 1856, p. 428) referred to the same matter. "It is wrong in Duméril and Bibron to say that this species is a variety of *Hyla squirella.* In shape and size the difference is not considerable. The latter animal during the warm season is always to be met with about the houses, the *Hyla femoralis* never. Besides, their notes are entirely different." As late as 1882 Duméril and Bibron's mistake somewhat influenced Boulenger (Gen., 1882, p. 398) in his statement, "Appears to be specifically distinct from *H. squirella*"

**Voice:** A peculiar cicada note in chorus, the chorus one continuous stridulating din going down the piny woods like a wave. When high in the trees, this frog calls *kek* at intervals When rain brings the frogs close to the water and the evening congress is on, the calls are speeded up. There may be as many as 6–7 a second, with 60–70 calls in rapid succession without deflation of the throat.

"Le Conte, 1856, seems to be the first to note that it differed from *H. squirella* in voice. No one since has remarked about its voice until Deckert (Fla., 1915, pp. 3–4) wrote, 'The noise resulting from the calls of the males on these occasions, is deafening. This call cannot be reproduced on paper, being a rapid succession of harsh, rattling notes higher in pitch than the call of *H. squirella,* and kept up all night. During the dry season this tree toad occasionally calls from the tops of the pine trees, one answering the other.'

"In 1921 the first general calling of *Hyla femoralis* came May 14. Then the author went to Billy's Lake Landing and worked eastward. Heard plenty of *Hyla femoralis* in trees. They are approaching or are on the edge of cypress ponds. Some are yet high in the trees. They are calling at intervals all over the piny woods, particularly near the edges of cypress bays. One call, an interval, one very faint call, interval.

"On May 16, when a threatening storm passed over, *Hyla femoralis* from the trees were almost in chorus. Around cypress ponds several calling. One was on a projecting piece of pine bark on the tree and within reach, about six feet from the ground. Harper saw it croak. Afterwards the throat pulsated all the time. Harper notes that it 'let me come up in plain sight, within a couple of yards and croaked for me on its bark slab-perch. Throat kept distended while its sides, or rather whole body, vibrated. *Kek, kek,* about 20 times, usually ending in *krak, krak.*' Later in the evening we visited this croaker but it was gone. Soon we understood. In two or three trees low down we heard *Hyla femoralis*. Their notes are speeded up, more extended and continuous than when high in the pines. One we found on the moss. The instant we entered another pond we heard a queer note and it was from the trunk of a bay tree right near us. It proved to be a male *Hyla femoralis*. All around us they were calling. One was in a bush three feet above ground. Another on moist ground at edge of pond in amongst six-foot sedges. When a male croaks it is the lower throat which swells out; the chin region does not. Brought back three. . . .

"During a congress when several species are breeding in the same pond the machine-gun calls of *Hyla femoralis* make it difficult to hear or time other calls. Once when we were timing the intervals in *Microhyla's* calls, *Hyla femoralis* calls broke in frequently. In 1921 and 1922 we recorded several instances where their calls drowned out those of *Hyla gratiosa, Hyla squirella, Bufo quercicus,* and *Pseudacris ocularis*. We tried the experiment of half closing our ears to shut out the *Hyla femoralis* calls. The other sounds came out very distinctly in the attempt" (A. H. Wright, Ga., 1932, pp. 277–278).

**Breeding:** This species breeds from April 20 to Sept. 1. The eggs are in groups of small films on the surface or just below it attached to grass blades of floating roots. The jelly is loose and sticky, the eggs are brown and yellowish, their size 1/30–1/25 inch (0.8–0.9 mm.), the inner envelope 1/16–1/12 inch (1.4–2.0 mm.), the outer envelope not distinct, 1/6–1/3 inch (4–6 or 8 mm.). The eggs hatch in 3 days. The tadpole is small, 1 1/3 inches (33 mm.), its tail tip acuminate and free of spots, the lower musculature with a light stripe. Many have bright red in their tails. The tooth ridges are 2/3. After 50 to 75 days, the tadpoles transform from June 16 to October, at 1/2 inch (13 mm.).

"We found breeding congresses in grassy transient pools near the roads in the piny woods, in open ponds in cutover roads, in pools or ditches beside the railroad and roads, in cypress ponds and in cypress bays. We found mated pairs in overflowed grassy fields, shallow transient depressions, in temporary overflows or drenched cultivated fields, swamps or dreens in the cypress bays. Tadpoles were taken in pools beside Indian mounds, railroads, roads, in cypress ponds and sometimes on the prairies, in diverse ponds on the east mainland or in bays outside the swamp" (A. H. Wright, Ga., 1932, p. 284).

"Dangers. This species lays in any pine barrens pool. Many a shallow grassy pool will have packets of their eggs. Many are caught by hatching; certainly many of the tadpoles never mature. There must be a great loss in this species. On July 3, 1921, they were laying in the flooded furrows of cane, corn and sweet potato fields. There all were lost. On June 4, 1921, we made the notes 'Tonight the frogs of several species (*Hyla femoralis* included) are laying in all sorts of transient places' " (same, p. 287).

**Journal notes:** May 19, 1921, Okefinokee Swamp, Ga. On my way back from a trip to Crosby Pond, at 6 P.M. near the remains of an old cypress pond in piny woods saw a female *Hyla femoralis* hopping along into saw palmetto. It was as whitish gray as any *Hyla versicolor* I ever saw. The spot in middle of back showed beautifully, also spot between the eyes. . . . This female I took out to look at. It leaped away onto the gray sand. Had a hard time seeing it because it matched the gray sand so well. In one minute since its capture, it had darkened considerably.

In denser cover 9 inches high with small saw palmetto and small bushes found a half-grown *Hyla femoralis*. It was green on its back (very suggestive of *H. squirella*, which strangely enough we don't get here).

May 21, in the compartment of *Hyla femoralis*, most of the specimens that were green when captured, in fact all (including one little half-grown one), are now Vandyke brown or moss brown. Adults are not often green, but their life at transformation frequently starts in a green livery.

A captive female in a jar, June 19, is pale light mouse gray on back with no markings.

On April 23, 1921, the boys found two on a rail fence at 2:30 P.M. The next day they brought three more from the same fence. On April 26, the boys found some more *Hyla femoralis* in the rain barrels along the railroad and near the lumber company's woodpile. In a pine near camp about 15 or 20 feet up on the end fork of a large branch is a *Hyla femoralis* male. It doubtless is the one we have heard ever since we have been here.

May 18, their calls made a perfect din in cypress bays and north edge of Long Pond. Some were in bushes, others in bay trunks, and others were hopping in moss edges or grassy edges of the pond or among the lizard's-tail. Another congress June 4, 1921. On one palmetto within 2 or 3 feet of each other were five male *H. femoralis* calling.

July 11, 1922, 7:30–11 P.M. We heard no end of *Hyla femoralis* in every crossing and cypress pond. . . . They were especially centered about a clump of saw palmettos. Here Miles Pirnie found one pair and I another. Later, on one blade were two more pairs and one male. In this clump were possibly 20–30 males calling. This breeding came after a hard rain. The females doubtless do not enter the ponds until about ready to lay.

July 6. Mrs. Chesser hoed out another female in the open field. There has been a chorus of them in the pond near by. Probably the female was resting here during the day.

**Authorities' corner:**

J. E. Holbrook, Gen., 1842, IV, 128.
R. Deckert, Fla., 1915, p. 3.
A. H. Wright, Ga., 1932, pp. 293–294.

One of the least known forms of the Coastal Plain is *Hyla femoralis*, which we have always associated with cypress ponds, bays, and thickets. A very significant extension of its range comes in its recorded occurrence by J. A. Fowler and Grace Orton (Md., 1947, p. 6) at Battle Creek, Maryland.

**Barker, Barking Frog, Coat Bet, Florida Tree Frog, Georgia Tree Frog, Florida Hyla, Bell Frog, Giant Tree Frog**

*Hyla gratiosa* Le Conte. Plate LXIX; Map 19.

**Range:** North Carolina (B. B. Brandt) to Florida to Louisiana. Hartselle, northern Alabama (Cahn).

**Habitat:** Trees of hammocks, pine barrens, and bays. Breeds in pine barren ponds and cypress ponds.

"High pine, high hammock, and dry flatwoods, in the upper branches of long-leaf and slash pine and of live-oak. . . . Uncommon locally and generally. Wright (1933) describes the rain-song; this odd call may be heard rarely from the treetops in high pine. On April 11, 1933, H. K. Wallace and I dug two adults and a yearling out of slightly moist sand more than four feet deep in an Indian mound, in cutover pineland in Lake County. On November 24, 1933, I found another in the same mound at about the same depth. This winter-burrowing may be of significance in explaining the fact that *gratiosa* is almost never seen except during warm weather" (A. F. Carr, Jr., Fla., 1940f, p. 60).

**Size:** Adults, 2–2¾ inches. Males, 49–68 mm. Females, 50–68 mm.

**General appearance:** This is our largest native tree frog. It is ashen gray, purplish, or green in color. The skin is evenly granular, the back evenly covered with elliptical or round spots darker than the general color and encircled with black. These spots may be absent in some of the color phases this frog assumes. A light stripe extends along the sides, bordered below by a purplish brown one. There is some yellow on the sides in axilla of arm and in the groin. The under parts are creamy or pinkish white. The throat of the male is green or yellow with dark spots just back of the chin, while that of the female has the center throat light, and the sides of throat and pectoral region sulphur yellow. The colored area of throat is encircled with white on the inner side. The spots on the side, chin, and rim of jaw are reddish brown.

**Color:** "*Male*. June 5, 1921. Lettuce green on hind legs and fore legs, oil green or cerro green on the back. The encircled spots of the back have a ring of mars brown or bone brown or other browns with green ground color within. There are occasional spots as big as pin heads or twice so of bright green-yellow or greenish yellow or green-yellow. This color is in the groin extending to just back of arm insertion where for one half an inch is a clear whitish area. The greenish yellow from groin forward demarcates side color from pinkish white or creamy belly color. From tip of snout along upper jaw under tympanum and along side to within 1 inch or ½ inch of leg insertion is a pinkish white stripe. Below it is a line of mars violet or taupe brown (pur-

*Plate LXVIII. Hyla femoralis.* 1,2. Males calling (×½) 3. Tadpole (×1⅛). 4. Egg cluster (×1). 5. Male (×1¼). 6. Female (×1). 7. Female (×1¼).

*Plate LXIX. Hyla gratiosa.* 1,7. Males (×⅔) 2. Male croaking (×¼). 3. Male in a cornfield at night (×¼). 4 Female (×½). 5. Transforming frog (×⅞). 6. Eggs (×⅔).

plish brown) which expands behind the angle of the mouth into a large area on the side. Same color back of pinkish white or white area back of brachium and antebrachium onto the last finger. Same white line around vent with mars violet below. Same combination on the knee. Two or three white patches on foot with mars violet between and behind them. Back of femur or thigh dull Indian purple. No spots. Below the expanded mars violet area of the side is a small whitish line ½–1 inch long, then comes greenish yellow and finally the belly color. Just back of the chin is grayish white speckled with taupe brown; then lettuce green or oil green from angle of mouth around to angle of mouth, the band ½ inch wide when not inflated; the wrinkled part light orange yellow or deep chrome. This color extends to pectoral fold of skin from forearm to forearm. Iris spotted purplish black and bronzy or vinaceous.

"*Males,* . . . in botany drum. Upon opening the can one was all green with a few yellowish spots but not the regular circles, the stripe along the jaw and on the side reminding one of the same in *Hyla cinerea.* Hardly any white or purplish shows anywhere. Another was a vinaceous gray with the rings. Another dark green and the others still different.

"*Female* Belly and under side of legs white, a few picric yellow spots on side below band, also rear end of white line on side becomes picric yellow in the groin. Picric yellow in the axilla and on either side of light central throat and chin region which is white or sulphur yellow with a few spots. Pectoral region sulphur yellow. Stripe around snout along upper jaw to groin white except for rear and not interrupted as in the male. Spots on back black encircled. Color of side and chin, spots, rim of jaw, bands on arms hays maroon, chocolate, warm sepia or bone brown Upper parts calliste green, cosse green or apple green" (A. H. Wright, Ga., 1932, p. 302).

**Structure:** A large tree frog of heavy build; head broad and short; fingers webbed; large disks on fingers and toes; skin has marked secretion giving strong persistent odor. Upper parts except arms and legs strongly granulate; under surface of hind limbs granulate only on posterior half of thigh, otherwise smooth; under surface of arm, prominent breast fold, and lower throat smooth or slightly granulate; chin granulate; webbing of hind feet extends to the disks which are very large, 3 mm., or 0.5 of tympanum; disks of forefeet, 4 mm., or 0.66 of the tympanum; a dermal fold over the ear to the shoulder and continued often as a loose fold along the side of the body halfway to the groin; a tarsal fold; vomerine teeth between inner nares; head ahead of eye short, obtuse; vocal sac well developed.

"During the last spring, whilst I was residing in the lower country of Georgia, it was my good fortune to meet with three specimens of the animal described below. One of them was taken in the water of a pine barren pond, another was found in a cavity of a sand pit, and the third upon a tree in the forest.

"This Hyla is remarkable for its size, approaching in this respect to those found in tropical regions. Two of them were of a greenish dusky; the second, who had concealed himself in a hole in the sand, was of a bright pea green, but in the space of half an hour he changed to the color of the others, thus showing a complete possession of the faculty of changing color at will, so remarkable in many of the Batrachia.

"There yet remains undiscovered and undescribed in Georgia three species of this genus, which have as yet eluded my search. The notes of these are remarkably distinct from those of others; I may hereafter be fortunate enough to obtain them.

"Coarsely granulate both above and beneath. Color above varying at the will of the animal from bright green to cinereous and to greenish dusky, with roundish spots or irregular blotches of darker, or speckled with variously shaped dots of the same, all of them with some few small yellow irregularly disposed spots on the back and sides. Beneath whitish, more or less inclining to yellow or orange. Upper lip white, or white varied with green or dusky; lower lips sometimes whitish, in others of the color of the back; in some a white line extends from the upper lip along the side to the insertion of the hind leg, in others the sides are more with rounded spots of darker and no line visible. Irides black varied with golden; tympanum copper-colored, a considerable depression between the nostrils and the eyes. Chin varied with dusky or green, with a slight fold at the bottom; transverse space between the arms smooth, without any granulations. Arms and legs barred, with darker, yellowish or reddish on the under side, the former smooth beneath, the latter granulate on the posterior half; the under side of the posterior half of the thighs is smooth. Disks of the toes very large.

"Length of head and body 2.5 inches; humerus .6; antebrachium .6; hand .75; femur 1.2; tibia 1.15; foot 1.6" (J. Le Conte, Ga., 1856, p. 146).

**Voice:** The call is woody, deep, a curious *tonk, tonk*, like someone pounding on a hollow, heavy barrel or hogshead. The call in the ponds is *coat bet*. The call from trees as it approaches water is a bark. The vocal sac is a large subgular vocal pouch.

The first time we heard this species to know it as such was on June 5, 1921. After a period of heavy rainfall, we visited in the evening an oak toad pool near the cultivated fields of Billy's Island, Ga., and heard this curious call. It seemed at first somewhat like the call of *Rana clamitans* only too many times separated, and actually the resemblance is fleeting and slight. There are 55-60 calls a minute, the throat often remaining partly inflated between calls.

**Breeding:** This species breeds from March to August. The eggs are laid singly on the bottom of the pond. The single envelope, 1/10-1/5 inch (2.3-5.0 mm.), is loose, glutinous, and indefinite in outline. The vitelline membrane appears as an inner envelope, 1/16-1/10 inch (1.6-2.5 mm.) in diameter, the egg 1/25-1/16 inch (1.0-1.8 mm.). The greenish tadpole is medium, 2 inches (50 mm.) long, and is the largest Hylid tadpole of the eastern United States.

The tail is long, its tip acuminate with a flagellum, and the tooth ridges are ⅔. The tadpole period is 40 to 70 days. The tadpoles transform from July to October, at 9/16–⅘ inch (14–20 mm.).

"Choruses of more than twenty or twenty-five males are not often seen. They call from deep water in small permanent ponds, from March 3 to August 14. In Gainesville the first choruses have always gathered in the power plant water aerator, where the water is abnormally warm; here I have also seen them feeding on insects at the lighted entrance" (A. F. Carr, Jr., Fla., 1940b, p. 61).

**Journal notes:** While we were in the Okefinokee Swamp, Ga., we usually recorded this species as Barker, Barking Frog, or Coat Bets. The last refers to the normal note in the breeding pools, the others to a puzzle that perplexed us for two seasons.

On July 15, 1921, on Chesser Island we heard of Coat Bet frogs, so named from the sound of their breeding call. On July 16, during the morning, we heard a barking frog in the trees south of camp. That night in a near-by pond was an immense chorus of Coat Bets. In 1922 the barkers perplexed us even more.

Not until July 26 did we solve the puzzle. About three miles along the road from Chesser Island to Folkston we heard in the evening in a cypress pond to the right of the road some *Hyla gratiosa,* and beyond them, a barker or two. We went after the barker, and found one in a small gum 4–5 feet, possibly 6 feet up. It is *Hyla gratiosa!* I saw him do it. There were two more barkers besides the one I caught. Several *Hyla gratiosa* were in the water calling normally. Coat Bets and barkers are one.

June 5, 1921, Okefinokee Swamp. Later we found other croakers. One was on the raised ridge of land beside a cornstalk. It was green with the spots usually figured. Another male was lying flat in the water at the edge of a weedy ridge. It was absolutely flat and spread out. It was without the spots and uniform dull brownish green, like the color of the water Another was in a furrow between two rows of corn. It was spotted and alert. The first one rested on ground more or less horizontally; the second in water horizontally. And the third more or less diagonally upright. The call can be heard at a long distance. Usually the heels are widely separated at croaking and the lower part of the body dips somewhat. Found a male *Hyla gratiosa* beside a grassy bank. He was as big and round as the can top of a mason jar. How his throat would puff out!

**Authorities' corner:**

R. F. Deckert, Fla., 1915, pp. 4–5.
C. J. Goin, Fla., 1938, p. 48.
A. R. Cahn, Ala., 1939, pp. 52–53.

**Pacific Tree Frog, Pacific Tree Toad, Pacific Hyla, Wood Frog** (Cooper), **Pacific Coast Tree Toad**

*Hyla regilla* Baird and Girard. Plate LXX; Map 18.

**Range:** Vancouver Island and British Columbia to Lower California; east to western Montana (Rodgers and Jellison), Idaho, Utah, Nevada, and Flagstaff, Ariz.

**Habitat:** On the ground, especially about streams, springs, ponds, swamps, and other moist places; irrigation ditches.

"Extends to timber-line in the Sierra Nevada; occurs in all zones below Alpine-Arctic. Inhabits damp recesses among rocks and logs; the ground in the vicinity of springs, streams and lakes; rank growth of vegetation, especially in marshy places, trees in damp forests; and in open country, burrows of various animals" (J. Grinnell and C. L. Camp, Calif., 1917, p. 145).

"This tree-toad is probably the most abundant batrachian in California, where it ranges from sea-level to 11,600 feet. It may be found abundantly in marsh-lands, lakes, springs, under the bark of trees and in almost any other place where there is continued moisture. It does not appear to congregate in such large compact masses as does *Hyla arenicolor,* but may be found in large colonies during the breeding season" (J. R. Slevin, B.C., 1928, p 115).

"Rio Santo Domingo at the Hamilton Ranch, 300 ft, lat. 30°45'; 37249–37250; June 2. Aguaito Springs, 15 miles E. Rosario, 1300 ft., lat. 30°4'; 37251–37256; June 9. On the night of June 2 multitudes of Pacific tree toads were strung along the sand bars and along the sandy banks of the shallow, widely spread, slow-moving Santo Domingo River. Their croaking was the dominant night sound. When the toads were alarmed, they would swim to and try to hide in the masses of slimy, thread-like green algae attached to fallen willow branches and other debris. The species was also abundant at night in and around the isolated pools at Aguaito Springs. Individuals beside but not actually in the water, if disturbed, hopped uphill to dry brush cover rather than down into the water" (L. Tevis, Jr., L C. 1944, p 7).

**Size:** Adults, 1–1⅞ inches. Males, 25.5–48.0 mm. Females, 25–47 mm. On the whole, the mature females are larger than the males, except occasional unusually large males.

**General appearance:** This small, delicate tree toad is somewhat smaller and more slender than the canyon tree toad (*Hyla arenicolor*), which like this form has the rear of the thighs uniform, not spotted. This species reminds the authors of species of *Pseudacris.* The disks on the fingers and toes are larger, however. It is very variable in color, usually with stripes on the back and a triangle between the eyes, and also with a stripe along the side of the head.

One male is light brown in color with a dark brown **V** between the eyes and two rows of large dark spots on the back. It has a conspicuous greenish black line from the nostril to the eye and from the eye through and beyond the tympanum. Then there is a broken line of spots to the groin. There is orange or yellow in the groin and on the rear of femur and on the foot. The arms, legs, and feet are indistinctly barred with dark. The upper jaw is a beautiful light pinkish cream color. The throat of this male is dark in color, greenish. In the middle of the light belly is a broad, longitudinal bluish area.

Another male is bright green, with an indistinct triangle between the eyes and round dark spots on the back. The dark mask is bordered above by a light pinkish cream line and below by the light jaw. The throat is olive, with some orange on the center rear portion. Orange-yellow is conspicuous in the groin and on the rear of the femur.

"None of the thirty-one specimens from the vicinity of Lake Como has a color pattern that approaches the uniform bold pattern of the *Hyla regilla* from the Great Basin. Most of them more nearly resemble specimens from Washington, Oregon and California. This evidence tends to confirm what might be expected, namely, that the population of the Bitterroot Valley is related to that of the Pacific Coast through past or present connection along the Columbia River drainage. Fifteen of the specimens have a color pattern that seems to be peculiar to the Bitterroot Valley in that it is broken up into many small units. One specimen, the most extreme in this respect, has 88 small dark gray spots of irregular shape on the back. The heavy Y-shaped mark between the eyes that is so characteristic of *Hyla regilla* is represented on some of these specimens only by a narrow branched line. The markings on the legs are also broken into many more small units than is typical for the species. Since there were more than a thousand specimens in the collection from the Pacific Coast area with which our specimens were compared, it seems reasonable to assume that all of the major color patterns that might appear in individuals from the Pacific Coast were represented, and from this it might follow that the population around Lake Como is unique in having this finely speckled color phase" (T. L. Rodgers and W. J. Jellison, Mont., 1942, pp. 10–11).

**Color:** *Male.* Pullman, Wash., from Dana J. Leffingwell, March 28, 1928. Upper parts some variation of dark grayish olive, olive-buff, isabella color, old gold, chamois, sulphine yellow, oil yellow, oil green, green, cinnamon-buff, or clay color Sometimes with brown band through the eye alone, usually with bandlike spots of Saccardo's umber, sepia, or brownish olive on the back forming a median stripe and one on either side, also with triangle between the eyes, and also stripe in front of eye. Some of small spots on sides are at times almost black. Stripe from below nostril along upper lip to shoulder insertion is primrose yellow. Outside the long dorsolateral spot, back is honey yellow becoming cream-buff or cartridge buff on sides. Upper parts of fore limbs chamois or old gold, with light brownish olive crossbars. Underside of arms olive-ocher, dark olive-buff. A buff-olive line along outer edge of forearm. Groin aniline yellow as also on front and underside of femur and to some extent on underside of tibia and hind foot. Lower part of rear of femur aniline yellow with upper edge of medal bronze. There is also a dark edge to front of tibia. Belly either side of meson vinaceous-cinnamon or pinkish buff; wash of same on underside of fore and hind limbs. Vocal sac when inflated is old gold or olive-ocher; deflated it is buffy olive or olive in front and olive-ocher behind. Iris: pupil rim behind and in front broken by black; above the rim, lemon yellow; rest of iris, raw sienna or antique brown.

*Female.* San Diego, Calif., from L. M. Klauber, March 28, 1928. May be like male, but with little yellow on the groin. Front of femur and underside of tibia olive-ocher or aniline yellow Entire under parts including throat may be cartridge buff, or throat may be light with indistinct dots of olive. Under parts of hind legs avellaneous or wood brown like males.

*Another specimen.* Las Vegas, Nev., Aug. 22, 1925. One half-grown frog was light paris green on upper parts; no dark spots except vitta; a little of clay color or cinnamon buff in middle of back; the fore and hind legs mainly light pinkish cinnamon.

**Structure:** Upper parts smooth, not warty as is the usual condition of *H. arenicolor,* prominent breast fold; tympanum round.

Original descriptions under different names· *"Hyla regilla,* B. & G. This is a species of medium size; the largest individual observed measuring one inch and a half from the nose to the posterior extremity of the body, the head itself occupying about half of this length. The hind legs are long and slender, the web extending only to half the length of the longest toe; fingers comparatively long. The general color is green above, turning to orange yellow along the sides of the head, abdomen and legs. Two oblong, brownish black spots exist on the occiput, from which two vittae (one pair) of the same black color extend along the dorsal region; a similar band passes from the tip of the nose, across the eye and tympanum, and along the abdomen, when it is interrupted and forms a series of black and irregular small spots. In the immature state, green is the prevailing color; a few black spots being present along the whitish abdomen. Specimens of this species were collected on Sacramento River, in Oregon and Puget Sound Drawings from life were made on the spot by Mr. Drayton" (S. F. Baird and C. Girard, Orc., 1854, p. 174).

*"Litoria occidentalis,* B. and G.—Throat smooth. Abdomen, sides of body and lower surface of thighs granulated. Tympanum very small. Fingers almost or entirely free; toes slightly webbed at the base; extremities of both not dilated. Color above pale chestnut, with obscure or obsolete blotches of darker. Beneath white. A few crossbands on the outside of the legs. A dark chestnut line beginning at the nostril, passes back through the eye, behind which it widens so as to include the tympanum, stopping just above the insertion of

the arm. One or two oblique blotches of dark chestnut on each side. Body 1 1/16 inches long; hind leg extended 1 ½ inch. Hab. San Francisco" (S. F. Baird and C. Girard, Calif., 1853, p. 301).

"*Hyla regilla,* B. and G., Proc. Acad. Nat. Sc., Philad., VI. 1852, 174. Syn. *Hyla scapularis,* Hallow., Proc. Acad. Nat. Sc. Philad., VI. 1852, 183" (S. F. Baird and C. Girard, Calif., 1853, p. 301).

"*Hyla scapularis.* Sp. char. Head small; body small and slender, olive green above, with numerous bluish blotches; a bluish vitta running from the eye over the shoulder; total length one and a half inches (Fr.). Description. The head is short and small, depressed; the snout somewhat rounded; the nostrils are small and circular, looking upward and outward, about a line apart, situated immediately below the ridge running from the extremity of the snout to the anterior canthus of the eye; they are nearer the extremity of the snout than the eye; mouth quite large; the tongue is heart-shaped, quite free behind, notched upon its posterior border; there are two series of palatine teeth between the nostrils, and separated from each other by a narrow intermediate space; the eyes are round and project considerably; the tympanum is small and circular; the body is flattened, rather slender, much contracted posteriorly; extremities slender; the upper surface of the body and extremities present numerous small granulations; abdomen and under surface of extremities much granulated; the granulations upon the abdomen vary in size, and are closely in juxtaposition; chin and throat granulated. Color Ground color above greenish olive, presenting numerous irregular bluish blotches upon the surface; several deeper colored blotches upon the sides; a bluish vitta, about two-thirds of a line in breadth, extends from the posterior part of the eye along the sides of the neck over the shoulder, a short distance beyond which it terminates; upper surface of extremities marked with bluish spots. Dimensions. Length of head 5 lines; greatest breadth 5 lines; length of body 1 inch; length of humerus 4 lines; of forearm 3½ lines; of hand to extremity of longest finger 5 lines; length of thigh 7 lines; of leg 8 lines; of foot to extremity of longest toe 7½ lines; total length 1 inch 5 lines. Habitat Oregon Territory. Presented to the Academy by Dr. Shumard" (E. Hallowell, Ore., 1854, p. 183).

**Voice:** The call is *kreck-ek* in rapid sequence.

"This is the common frog of the coastal areas, whose loud croaking is to be heard nightly in the spring about every puddle, pond, and creek. The noise made is surprising for so small a creature. It has the capacity to change its color considerably and may be bright green, gray or brown in almost any shade" (L. M. Klauber, Calif., 1934, p. 7).

"In the spawning season, or more properly, as long as there is any likelihood of spawning, the 'chorus note,' the note which serves to bring the scattered individuals together for breeding purposes, is uttered. This, to human ears, sounds like kreck-ek and is uttered over and over again in rapid sequence. . . . At any season of the year this hyla may be heard to utter a single prolonged note, kr-r-r-eck, lower in pitch than the song note. This note may be used, as indicated above, at the ending of a 'chorus'; but it is also uttered in other seasons of the year when the individuals are hidden in their daytime retreats, and when no 'songs' are to be heard" (T. I. Storer, Calif., 1925, pp. 221–222).

**Breeding:** This frog breeds from early January to mid-May. (See "Journal Notes" for 1942.) The brown and yellowish eggs, in small, loose, irregular masses (10–70 eggs) are laid in quiet water beneath or sometimes at the surface, attached to vegetation. They remind one of *Pseudacris* masses. The egg is 1/20 inch (1.3 mm.), the inner envelope (firm) 1/12 inch (2 mm.), the outer envelope (loose, sticky) 3/16–1/4 inch (4.7–6.7 mm.). The tadpole is medium, 1 7/8 inches (46.6 mm.), full and deep-bodied, its tail tip acute or obtuse without a flagellum. It is dark brownish in color and the tooth ridges are 2/3. After 50 to 80 days the tadpoles transform from May 15 to September 1, at 7/16–11/16 inch (11–17 mm.). Mrs. Katherine Van Winkle Palmer took ten transforming *Hyla regilla* at Oakville, Washington, July, 1923. They ranged from 12 to 15 mm. Our series of 36 from Alta Meadows, Sequoia National Park, Calif., Aug. 22–27, 1917, ranged from 11.5–17.0 mm.; mode 13.5, average 14.5 mm.

"The egg clusters of this *hyla* contain a varying number of eggs. In laboratory aquaria and occasionally in the field single eggs are laid. Some masses total over 60 eggs. Probably the number in a mass reflects in a general way the degree of solitude experienced by a pair when eggs are deposited. Where only one female is laying a few large clumps are to be found. Where many *hylas* have been spawning in one place the egg masses are small.

"At times very large numbers of eggs are laid in a relatively small area. In a small pool near the main Thornhill pond I found, on Jan. 25, 1913, 59 masses in an area approximately 10 × 15 feet. Additional masses were laid in this same area on subsequent nights. Other areas in this same pond which seemed to be of exactly the same character were not utilized by the species.

"The total number of eggs deposited by a single female has been ascertained in two cases. A mated pair was taken from the Thornhill pond on January 31, 1914, and confined in an aquarium. Next morning a total of 730 eggs was found. The average number of eggs in a clump was 18. Another captive which began laying on the night of Mar. 7, 1922, and continued up until 4 P.M. of the day following deposited a total of 1250 eggs, the average of the 58 masses laid was between 21 and 22. The largest mass contained 60 eggs and there were two with the minimum of 9" (T. I. Storer, Calif., 1925, pp. 224–225).

"Insemination occurs at the moment of egg extrusion. The male brings his cloacal aperture close to that of the female, discharges a quantity of transparent semen, and with a quick, firm extension slides his feet posteriorly over the sides and hips of the female, then deftly retracts to his normal position. Simultaneous with this foot action, the female extrudes a clutch of eggs into the cloud of sperm about her cloaca. Some time before releasing an egg mass the female often scratches at the surface of the substratum on which the eggs are to be deposited. As the eggs are extruded the cloaca is brought into close contact with this surface and attachment is thus effected. The female removes any eggs which may partially adhere to the cloaca during extrusion by a precise flexor-extension reflex of the hind legs. In this the tarsi are applied directly to the adhering eggs and a slow extension effects the removal.

"Deposition of an egg mass is usually followed by a quiet moment during which the bodies of the pair become slightly more inflated than normally. The intervals between egg deposition, ranging from 2 to 10 minutes or longer, are spent in bursts of vigorous activity, mainly on the part of the female. What function this may serve, if any, is conjectural, but it apparently takes place under natural as well as artificial conditions. In the laboratory such periods are followed by a rest and then further oviposition. Shortly after laying is complete, the pair becomes separated. The entire time in amplexus has been observed to range from 8 to 40 hours or more.

"The total number of eggs deposited was found to range from 500 to 750; however, Storer reports an instance of 1250 eggs being laid. The number of eggs per clutch is usually about 16, but varies from 5 to 60" (R. E. Smith, Calif., 1940, pp. 379–380).

"Several of these frogs were found at Big Lake, together with the northwestern toads. Egg clusters in the litter on the bottom, near the edge of the lake, were in jelly-like masses a little more than one inch in diameter. The egg diameter might be from 1/32 to 1/16 inch" (F. G. Evenden, Jr., Ore., 1943, p. 252).

"*Hyla regilla* also spawns abundantly in the pool on Alpine Road, the onset of breeding seeming to coincide closely with that of *A. t. californiense*" (V. C. Twitty, Calif., 1941, p. 2).

"One male, *Scaphiopus h. intermontanus* (amplexus inguinal) when collected was clasping a female *Hyla regilla* which died soon after, apparently from rupture of the abdominal wall" (G. C. Carl, B.C., 1942, p 129).

**Journal notes:** Aug. 12, 1917. We camped at Jacumba, Calif., beside the Mexican border. . . . In a little side stream of the creek we found a series of *H. regilla* from tadpole to transformation. In the same place among the weeds of the moist area we took six to ten adults very variable in color.

Aug. 25. In Alta Meadows, we found no end of transformed *Hyla regilla*. In the bog-terraced pools were plenty of tadpoles and advanced stages. On the trail, R. C. Shannon found a full-grown frog and the boys reported a large one from Alta Peak. The transformed frogs were in the meadow land.

Aug. 20–22, 1925, Las Vegas, Nev., Tonapah Road. We followed one tiny stream back into the field and returned with the trophies of the search: 6 *Rana fisheri*, 4 *Hyla regilla*, 1 *Bufo compactilis*. In a broad springy area sedgy and shady, we picked up a *H. regilla.* In one very small sedgy area, we caught four, three of which had triangles between the eyes and some dorsal stripes. A half grown one was green with no triangle and only the vitta back of the eyes. Later at the big springs, we caught one that looked very yellow with very indistinct pattern. We caught several tadpoles.

Starting in January, 1942, we traveled northward west of the mountains from southern California to Washington and southward east of the mountains, arriving in Nevada in mid-May. The Journal notes of that period give a specimen cross section of the activities of this widespread species.

Jan. 31, 1942. Stayed at Julian, Calif., for night. Last night heard a chorus of *Hyla regilla.* The early season and the chorus each make me think of *Pseudacris* choruses in early spring. It is so unlike most true *Hyla* barks of the U.S.A.

Feb. 1. Went to Cuyamaca. In Julian region where I heard the choruses last night took about seven or eight male *H. regilla.* One female and one very small one. Tonight the male is mated axillary fashion. Tonight heard a large chorus of *H. regilla* but no others.

Feb. 7. Five miles out of Monterey at 12:30 P.M., 70°F., sunlight. We heard chorus of *H. regilla* in an overflow grassy area near base of pine hill.

Feb. 8. Salinas to Castroville, Calif. Could find no *Hyla regilla* eggs. Do they lay them in dense vegetation at the edge of water like *P. feriarum* of Carlisle, Pa.?

Feb. 12. Visited W. M. Ingram. He had two *Hyla regilla* masses of eggs ready to hatch.

Feb. 14. Trip to Rancho del Oso—Prof. Theodore S. Hoover owner. Found *H. regilla* in swampy area. Up the creek to sawmill. Here in a little pool found very young *H. regilla* tadpoles. Rodgers took a large *H. regilla* with reddish down middle of back.

March 8. Stanford artificial lake. Found in an overflow shallow some eight fresh masses of *H. regilla* eggs. The yellowish underside is evident. Mass an inch or less in diameter. Sometimes two masses on one grass blade. One or two masses hatching. Found some tadpoles ½ inch long.

March 17. Later went north of Crescent City on Route 101 about 5 miles. In a pond, countless tads of *H. regilla* and a few egg masses almost hatching.

March 18. Took *Hyla regilla* tads Carpenterville, Ore. *H. regilla* calling at midday.

March 20. Up McKenzie River watershed with Miss Ruth E. Hopson of Springfield, Ore. In a pond with fallen logs, no end of *H. regilla* migrating to the pond, mostly females. 1800–1900 elevation.

March 26. Started from Aberdeen at 9 A.M. Foggy. At Springfield School Dist. No. 12 saw, beside road, ponds with pussy willows in them. Here were *Hyla regilla* masses, some just hatching. At Humptulips River crossing, in pools, caught a *Hyla regilla.* Two miles farther took a female.

March 27. Hoh to Borachiel rivers. In meadow heard one lone *H. regilla.* Saw here an egg mass of *H. regilla.*

March 28. Went to Olympic Park headquarters. Mr. Macy gave me a permit and a map. In their pond saw several fresh egg masses and some about to hatch (*H. regilla*). Just as we turned on to Elwah road, in one meadow pond saw some 500–800 egg masses of *H. regilla* hatching and fresh. Anna caught a pair.

April 4. Just out of Maupin, Ore., to the south of town in a gravel-pit pool saw some six or eight *H. regilla* masses. One *H. regilla* jumped in.

April 5. Lapine, Ore., roadside ditch. The *H. regilla* are calling loudly but could find no egg masses. Flatland, open, some cultivated, some meadows, trees.

April 10. From Medford to Project City, in rather barren stream took some almost full-grown *H. regilla* tadpoles.

April 11. Chico, Calif., in a spring watering trough were large *H. regilla* tadpoles.

April 12. Out with Tracy and Ruth Storer. Between Michigan Bar and Consumne spotted beside road a possible *A. t. californiense* pond. *H. regilla* tads mature. White egret here feeding.

April 21. Below Tollhouse, Calif., in one pond we took two *H. regilla* but no *R. b. sierrae.*

April 23. Turned toward the coast again to Atascadero, Calif. Heard no end of *H. regilla* last night.

May 1. In French Valley, Calif., in drying pool took *H. regilla* tads, one adult. At a culvert took *H. regilla* tads mature and one transforming. No end of Brewers black birds around this pool of tadpoles and aquatic insects.

May 5. Three and a half to four miles south of Buckman Springs, Calif., at bridge below confluence La Posta and Cottonwood Cr., took two *H. regilla.* Saw no *H. regilla* tads.

May 14, Springdale, Nev. Bobbie Shoshone went out last night and caught one *Bufo b. nelsoni* and several *Hyla regilla* (3).

May 15, Las Vegas, Nev. Went out Tonopah road 25 miles and returned after dark. Near trailer camp was a large pond with bullfrogs in it and near by a big chorus of *Hyla regilla.*

**Authorities' corner:**

F. C. Test, Gen., 1899, 21, 481
W. P. Taylor, Nev., 1912, p. 343.
J. Van Denburgh and J. R. Slevin, L.C., 1914, p. 135.
A. G. Ruthven and Helen T. Gaige, Nev., 1915, p. 15.
J Grinnell, J. Dixon, J. M. Linsdale, Calif, 1930, p. 141.
A. and R. D. Svihla, Wash., 1933, p. 127.
S. G. Jewett, Jr., Ore., 1936, p. 71.

*Plate LXX. Hyla regilla.* 1,2,6. Females (×1). 3,4 Males (×¾). 5. Female (×¾).

***Plate LXXI. Hyla septentrionalis*** **(×¾).** 1–3 Females.

## Giant Tree Frog

*Hyla septentrionalis* Boulenger. Plate LXXI; Map 19.

**Range:** On Oct. 30, 1931 (Fla., p. 140), Dr. T. Barbour placed it as established at Key West, Fla. In 1914 (p. 347) he had it from New Providence, Andros Island, Rum Cay, Cuba, and Grand Cayman. Matecumbe, Fla., and farther northward.

**Habitat:** Cisterns, wells, outbuildings, drain pipes; banana trees, large leaf axils.

"Old cisterns and damp out-buildings; in the axils of palm and Caladium leaves; banana trees; Barbour (1931) records it from drain pipes. Abundance: Locally common; I have seen twenty-five or thirty clinging to the walls of a single cistern in Key West. Habits: Chiefly nocturnal, but often calling and foraging during the day in the dilapidated cisterns which abounded on the island before 'New Deal' improvements. During humid weather they may be found in trees and shrubs some distance from water. I have discussed *septentrionalis* with some of Key West's most venerable citizens and have found none who can recall a time when the blatant choruses of the 'bull frogs' were not to be heard after summer rains. Feeding: They often congregate around street lights at night; I have watched them feeding on cockroaches and on lepidopterous larvae; they are batracophagous and cannibalistic in captivity" (A. F. Carr, Jr., Fla., 1940b, p. 62).

**Size:** Adults, 2⅗–5⅕ inches (64–130 mm.). "There is a great size disparity in the breeding males; individuals that I have measured varied between 40 and 73 mm." (A. F. Carr, Jr., Fla., 1940, p. 62).

In our Matecumbe Key series (March 18, 1934) we took males 48, 48, 49, 49, 50, 50, 51, 52, 52 5, 57, 58, 59, 60, and 61 mm. in length, fourteen in all, and one small female, 52.5 mm. In 1940 at Key West, Mr. and Mrs. R. H. McCauley, May 5, secured two males, 46 and 48 mm., and one large female, 82 mm.; on April 10, 1940, they secured on Stock Island, Monroe Co., Fla., two females 75.5 and 77 mm. in length. The largest we have is from Key West, taken by M. K. Brady and O. C. Van Hyning. It is a female, 92 mm. in length. We have seen large specimens but recall none over 4 inches. With our limited series we can only approximate the sex sizes as follows: males, 46–75 mm.; females, 52.5–130.0 mm.

**General appearance:** This is a large tree toad. The head is broad; the outline of the skull evident, as the skin is united to the skull; canthus rostralis and nostrils very prominent. The top of the head is smooth; the eyelids and back are roughened with large and fine tubercles. The most conspicuous characters are the very large disks on fingers and toes, those on the fingers being fully as large as the tympanum. The eyes are large and prominent, the iris with brilliant orange tints. The color, when the frog has been under cover, becomes a dull olive-green, but in the light becomes citrine, turtle green, or oil yellow, with indistinct dorsal spots of dull citrine or grayish olive. The legs are barred with the same. The rear of the femur is reticulated with the same. The throat is pale, buffy, and slightly granular; the rest of the venter is conspicuously and roughly granular and dull yellow in color, with the underside of the femur a deeper yellow, and the axilla bright yellow with a wash of the same color along the sides. The tubercles under the joints of feet and hands are prominent and pointed.

"Male with two external vocal vesicles, each being situated near the angle of the mouth; during the breeding-season the inner side of the first finger covered with blackish rugosities. From snout to vent 75 millim." (G. A. Boulenger, Gen., 1882, pp. 368–369).

**Color:** *Female.* Key West, Fla., from M. K. Brady and O. C. Van Hyning, May 5, 1932. Trough of casque and concave loreal region sulphur yellow, ecru-olive, or buffy citrine. Postorbital horns of casque pale turtle green or oil yellow. Wash of this color 1 inch or more wide down middle of back. Area below and behind eye to below tympanum, upper parts of fore limbs, and throat light buff or pale ochraceous-buff. The sides of body with slight wash of the same color. From axilla along either side of belly to groin is a wash of wax yellow or primuline yellow in axil Two bars on thighs ceasing halfway as they meet reticulations on rear of thigh. Tibia with two complete bars. Bars and obscure spots on the rear half of back are dull citrine, grayish olive, or buffy citrine The dark reticulations of the thighs are colored like bars of thighs with the interspaces green yellow. There is a little of same color on front of femur and in groin. The top of the foot has decided wash of same color as top of fore limbs. The digits are turtle green. The center of tympanum like back surrounded by ring of mars brown The iris is capucine yellow or ochraceous-buff finely dotted with black. Sometimes the iris has considerable of the color of the back or of dorsum of fore limbs. Undersides of fingers and toes are cinnamon-drab.

**Structure:** Tongue subcircular; head broader than long in adults; casque emarginate behind; snout rounded, contained two times in head to tympanum; pollex rudiment not free projecting; disks conspicuous; no interocular bar; upper eyelid small; tympanum distinct, ½–¾ diameter of eye. Dunn in 1937 (Copeia, p. 166) placed *H. septentrionalis* in the *Hyla brunnea* group.

"Fingers slightly webbed; no projecting rudiment of pollex; toes two-thirds webbed; disks of fingers nearly as large as the tympanum, of toes smaller; subarticular tubercles well developed; a slight fold along the inner edge of the tarsus. The hind limb being carried forwards along the body, the tibiotarsal articulation reaches between the eye and the tip of the snout . . ." (G. A. Boulenger, Gen., 1882, pp. 368–369).

**Voice:** "This sound is like the jerky pulling of a rope through an unoiled pulley and is very characteristic" (T Barbour, Fla., 1931, p. 140).

"The choruses are unique in their heterogeneity of pitch and timbre. The call is a rasping snarl somewhat comparable to that of *Scaphiopus holbrookii.* The pitch of non-musical sound is difficult to determine, but I would judge that the individual notes vary through at least one octave" (A. F. Carr, Jr., Fla., 1940b, pp. 62–63).

We were first attracted to them at Upper Matecumbe Key by a huge chorus near our cabin. In the circle of bushes around a small very deep pond were these giant tree frogs. We neglected to characterize their call, to photograph them, or to describe them. Doubtless there were eggs, but *Elaphe rosacea* was our chief interest at the moment.

**Breeding:** "June 14 to September 16 (this period corresponds suspiciously with the academic summer-vacation season; however I looked for them in vain during the week of December 18–23, 1932). The eggs are laid in temporary drainage ditches, in the flooded basements of wrecked buildings, and in cisterns. The young emerge at 15.5–16.5 mm. Before the tail is absorbed, the back becomes granular and warty as in the adult; the immature differs strikingly from the adult in the possession of a dorso-lateral white stripe extending from the hind margin of the orbit to the groin. E. Lowe Pierce and I found all stages, from newly hatched larvae to breeding adults, in an old cistern, June 16, 1934. We found a tremendous number (300–400) of recently emerged individuals perched on the twigs of a small thorny bush in a vacant lot, the night of June 14, 1934" (A F. Carr, Jr., Fla., 1940b, p. 62).

March 18, 1934, Matecumbe Key, Fla. Males have enlarged thumbs; on some smaller males the horny, sharp-edged ridge is not so black. In general, it is a dark, horny excrescence on inner side and upper side of the the thumb; it is semilunar, extending from base of thumb to base of last segment of thumb. Outer edge acute and making a sharp acute edge, apparent from ventral side of thumb. It's an expanded addition or prepollex on side of the thumb (pollex).

Some of these males are almost uniform, some streaked in groin like *H. baudinii,* some very mottled on back; almost all with leg bands, some narrow, some wider. Several with two prominent stripes extending backward from eyes.

May 5, 1940. Dr. and Mrs. R. H. McCauley took one specimen just beyond transformation, 40 mm. in length (with 24-mm. body and remnant of tail 16 mm.). This specimen has the tail crests and musculature heavily mottled with black. They also took the following interesting series: at transformation —21 mm.; past transformation—25, 26, 28, 30, 30, 32, 33, 36, 37 mm ; male with black on thumb—46, 48 mm.

Key West, Fla. "The largest of fourteen specimens collected was a female measuring 92 mm. in length of body, and 210 mm. stretched out. Eggs, tadpoles, and recently transformed frogs were also collected" (E. R. Allen and R. Slatten, Fla., 1945, p. 25).

**Journal notes:** March 18, 1934, Upper Matecumbe Key, Fla. Came to Caribee Colony. At night heard a great chorus near the water tank. There were countless small and half-grown *Hyla septentrionalis* in the pond. No end of *Hyla squirella* calling. Are *H. squirella* the prey of the giant tree frog? From limbs higher than my head big tree frogs would leap into the middle of the pond with a pronounced *kerplunk* (like a toad). In looking for the frogs Anna espied in the bushes a fine *Elaphe rosacea*. Does it feed on the frogs?

**Authorities' corner:**

G. A. Boulenger, Gen., 1882, pp. 368–369.
L. Stejneger, Fla., 1905, p. 330.
T. Barbour, Fla., 1914, p. 238.
T. Barbour, Fla., 1931, p. 140.
C. S. Brimley, N.C., 1940, p. 23.

## Squirrel Tree Frog, Southern Tree Frog, Southern Tree Toad, Scraper Frog, Rain Frog, Squirrel Tree Toad, Squirrel Hyla

*Hyla squirella* Latreille. Plate LXXII; Map 24.

**Range:** Virginia to Texas, and north up the Mississippi basin to Indiana. Near Columbia, S.C., Corrington (S.C., 1929, p. 66) "found them on the fall line but never in good typical piedmont territory."

**Habitat:** In and around buildings; about wells; in bushes, trees, or vines; in fields and gardens. It breeds in open ponds in the pine barrens, or in shallow roadside pools.

"This species was found on the ground about shady hammock-land on Boca Chica Key. I also saw one on a Gumbo Limbo tree on Vaca Key" (H. W. Fowler, Fla., 1906, p. 109).

"Common when breeding; frequents gardens and is often seen in crannies about porches of houses" (O. C. Van Hyning, Fla., 1933, p. 4).

"Shows little discrimination in major habitat selection. It exhibits some preference for the more open wooded areas such as high pine and mixed hammock and for edificarian situations. Abundance.—The commonest Florida *Hyla*" (A. F. Carr, Jr., Fla., 1940b, p. 61).

**Size:** Adults, ⅞–1½ inches. Males, 23–36 mm. Females, 23–37 mm.

**General appearance:** This species is small, delicate, and with smooth skin. The head is short, eyes prominent with black pupil and bronzy iris. The back is green or brownish in color with at least a partial transverse bar between the eyes and with white on the upper lip. Frequently there are rounded spots on the back. The rear of femur is not spotted. There is a light line below the eye and over the shoulder. There may be a light, irregular line along the side just above the belly.

"The colours of this animal are even more changeable than in any species with which I am acquainted. I have seen it pass in a few moments from a light green, unspotted and as intense almost as that of *Hyla lateralis,* to ash colour, and to a dull brown with darker spots; the spots also at times taking on different tints from the general surface The markings, too, vary exceedingly in different individuals, the white line on the upper lip and the band between the orbits alone are constant" (J. E. Holbrook, Gen., 1842, p. 124).

See M. C. Dickerson, Gen., 1906, pp. 149–150 for a discussion of the wonderful change of color in this form. For variability of color in *Hyla squirella* and *Hyla cinerea,* see our "Journal notes" from Pass Christian and Bay St. Louis under *Hyla cinerea.* We have not seen Bryan P. Glass's (Tex., 1946, pp. 101–103) specimens of "A New Hyla from South Texas" but suspect he has *Hyla*

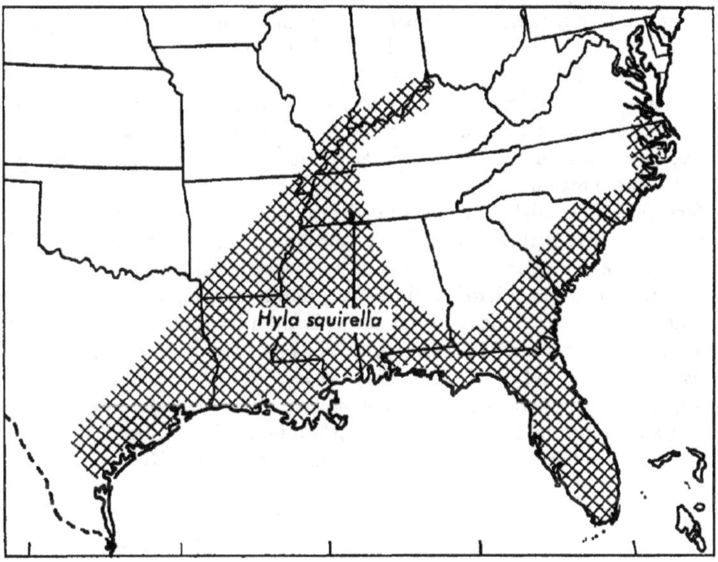


*Map 24*

*squirella* in one of its variable disguises in his new *Hyla flavigula.* Of course examination of specimens alone can confirm this impression. *Hyla squirella* adult males and females range as low as 23 mm. and as high as 37 mm. Glass's specimens may be about the mean of the squirrel tree frog. This species has been recorded four times inland from Aransas country and north of the Nueces River, Tex. P. H. Pope (Tex., 1919) found *H. squirella* the most abundant *Hyla* of the Houston area.

**Color:** *Males.* June 22, 1922. Back citrine or buffy citrine in one; on another ecru-olive or light yellowish olive; rear back and top of hind legs chrysolite green to lime green. Under parts of hand, also hind foot, orange-rufous, xanthine orange, to orange chrome; hind limb posterior and anterior faces and throat raw sienna or mars yellow; throat of another aniline yellow; in another hind leg parts raw sienna. Stripe on upper jaw to body greenish yellow or lemon yellow. Belly cream color or ivory yellow. Tympanum hazel or russet. Iris spotted black and army brown—fawn in one, deep chrome and antique brown in another. Greenish on either side of throat but not clearly defined or definite as in *Hyla andersonii* and *Hyla cinerea* males. One male held in the hand in good light became courge green and another oil green. A small last year's *H. squirella* was light dull green-yellow above, and upper jaw stripe light chalcedony yellow or pale chalcedony yellow. Sometimes those in water may be greenish, while those on edges or on land may be brownish.

*Females.* July 3, 1922. Four females of four different pairs had under parts white, with no discolored throats. Throat slightly primrose yellow, reed yellow, or white. Fore limbs, groin, hind limbs before and aft, tibia, and hind feet reed yellow to olive-yellow. In one, yellow ocher fore and rear part of femur, underside of tibia, and foot and fore foot. The females, unless very large, have none of the bright orange-rufous, xanthine orange, or orange chrome of the males.

**Structure:** Form delicate; skin smooth; canthus rostralis well marked, but not sharply edged; throat of male raw sienna or yellow with light area of greenish on either side; vocal sac a large hyaline subgular pouch.

**Voice:** This call is a harsh trill, regular, mostly continuous, 15 calls in 10 seconds, but not very loud. It could not be heard a few rods away. One gave 67 pumps in 45 seconds. "Call rasping, but not very coarsely so, rather ventriloquistic; flat; short to Italian *a; aaaa* or *waaaaak*" (A. F. Carr, Fla., 1934, p. 22).

Another great chorus came Aug. 16 and 17 after a half-day's rain when about 2 inches of rain fell, maxima 82–91°, minima 65–74°. Spadefoots and *Rana capito,* subterranean species, came out to breed and *Hyla squirella* as well.

In general this species calls even by day in rain or before an imminent rain (July 9). After a downpour of a warm rain 1–5 inches they became very active. As every observer has remarked, heavy warm rains bring them out in midsummer. Our latest record of calling came September 17.

R. F. Deckert (Fla., 1915, p. 3) at Jacksonville, Fla., described its cry as follows· "The cry is rather coarse, sounding like 'cra, cra, cra,' etc. with a second's interval between each note." The same author (Fla., 1921, p. 22) in Dade County, Florida, wrote, "Their rasping calls were heard in May and June at 19th Street, Miami, at Donn's Nursery and at 22nd Street in company. . . ."

**Breeding:** This species breeds from April to August. The eggs, single on the bottom of shallow pools, are brown above and cream below, with outline distinct and jelly firm. The egg is $\frac{1}{30}$–$\frac{1}{25}$ inch (0.8–1.0 mm.), the inner envelope $\frac{1}{20}$–$\frac{1}{15}$ inch (1.2–1.6 mm.), the outer $\frac{1}{16}$–$\frac{1}{12}$ inch (1.4–2.0 mm.). The egg complement is 950. The citrine drab tadpole is small, 1¼ inches (32 mm.), its tail long, the tail tip acuminate with a flagellum. The tooth ridges are ⅔. After 40 to 50 days, the tadpoles transform from June to September at $\frac{7}{16}$ inch (11–13 mm.).

"I have records from April 2 to August 20. Full choruses come with July electric storms. The males usually sing in water from half an inch to an inch deep at the edges of temporary pools or ditches or of temporarily inundated portions of pond margins. The choruses are large. Wright (1933) says that the call is not very loud; it has little carrying power, but at close range a large chorus assaults the ear-drums mercilessly" (A. F. Carr, Jr., Fla., 1940b, p. 61).

**Journal notes:** We found these frogs on porches, in chinaberry trees, oaks, and other trees, as well as in vines around the houses, in fields and gardens around buildings, in open ponds, in pine barrens, in pine and oak groves, along roads, and in shallow roadside and pine barren pools. On June 22, 1922, a boy at Camp Pinckney, Ga., brought me a Scraper taken in his own house.

July 3, 1922. Along the Folkston road, Ga., in temporary pools and ditches with *Bufo terrestris* were plenty of *Hyla squirella*. There is more vibration in the call of *Hyla femoralis*. I could not hear the *Hyla squirella* a few rods away. The calls of *Hyla femoralis* and *Bufo quercicus* drown it out. *Hyla squirella* does sometimes croak from the water surface when sprawled on the water.

Okefinokee Swamp, Ga. On July 3, 1922, about 11:55 P.M., we were at Anna's pond. We heard the *Hyla squirella* at a distance between two distant houses. In the saw palmettos and the grass stools were many scrapers. We found one pair in the grass near the edge. Others were found in saw palmettos about the border of the pool. The same night, near Trader's Hill, we came to a grassy overflow pond. In a clump of bushes and saw palmetto were several *Hyla squirella*. In grassy stools in shallow water were others.

On August 11, 1922, at Camp Pinckney, Ga., 2–3 P.M., we heard several. At 8:30 we returned to Camp Pinckney. There were countless *Hyla squirella* males on the ground in a road filled with temporary pools, in water 1–3 inches deep. The vocal sac is hyaline, more or less inflated for some time. The call is not so fast as that of *Hyla femoralis*, but swift nevertheless. Those in water were greenish, those at the edges of the pool, brownish. . . . We could find no females. Some males, though quite small, were croaking.

**Authorities' corner:**

W. Bartram, Gen., 1791, p. 278.
P. H. Pope, Tex., 1919, pp. 96–97.
A. H. Wright, Ga., 1932, p. 312.
A. F. Carr, Jr., Fla., 1940b, p. 61.
G. L. Orton, La., 1947, pp. 369–375.

## Common Tree Toad, Common Tree Frog, Tree Toad, Northern Tree Toad, Changeable Tree Toad, Chameleon Hyla, Varying Tree Toad

*Hyla versicolor versicolor* (Le Conte). Plate LXXIII; Map 20.

**Range:** Maine, southern Canada, west to Manitoba, Minnesota, South Dakota, south through Kansas, Oklahoma, to the Gulf States and northern Florida (Texas and Arkansas in part only).

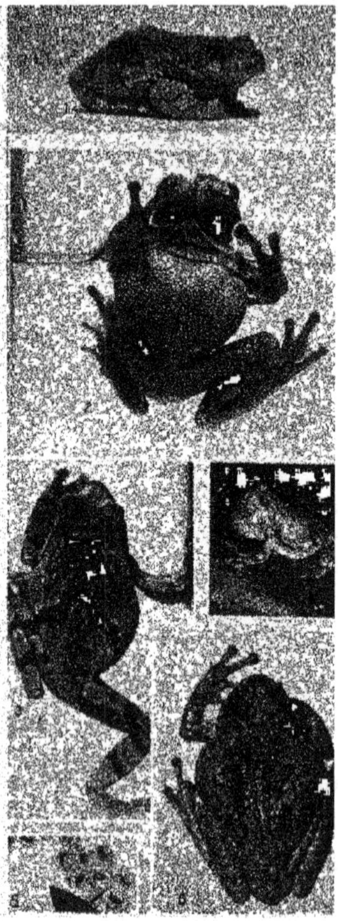

*Plate LXXII. Hyla squirella* (×1). 1. Male croaking 2,3,5. Males 4 Female.

*Plate LXXIII. Hyla versicolor versicolor.* 1,2,6. Males (×4/5). 3. Female (×4/5). 4. Males croaking (×1/2). 5. Eggs (×8/4).

**Habitat:** Trees, mossy or lichen-covered stone fences, decaying fruit trees.

**Size:** Adults, 1¼–2⅖ inches. Males, 32–51 mm. Females, 33–60 mm.

**General appearance:** This frog varies in color from pale brown to ashy gray, to green; it has a granular skin, dark irregular star on upper part of the back, a black bar on the upper eyelid, black-bordered green bars on the legs, a black-bordered light spot below each eye. It might easily be taken for a stone or bit of bark with lichen on it. The rear of the femur has dark reticulations on orange. The groin, axilla, and under parts of hind limbs are orange.

**Color:** *Male.* Belly and lower breast white or cartridge buff. Breast between fore limbs, which is the vocal sac, pale flesh color. Middle of throat dull citrine or ecru-olive with black spots. Chin like belly with blackish spots. Underside fore limbs like belly. Underside of hind legs and rear of thigh bright orange or orange-rufous. The spots on the back, one of which is an irregular star on upper back, are citrine-drab or deep olive with black borders.

*Female.* Raleigh, N.C., from A. P Chippey, May 12, 1930. Under parts including throat white becoming almost hyaline on underside of femur. Front of femur, groin, inner side of tibia, tarsus and first toe, and axilla cadmium yellow, deep chrome, or in places mars yellow. Rear of femur raw sienna, with numerous spots of cadmium yellow or light cadmium. Back of forelegs and hind legs and sides pale olive gray, pearl gray, or light mineral gray, becoming on back tea green or grayish olive or deep olive-buff. Star or spot in middle of upper back is vetiver green or grayish olive with dark grayish olive border. Two bars on femur, tibia, and forearm olive gray to mineral gray with dark borders. Oblique bar across eyelid of each eye but not meeting on meson is same color as star spot of back. Tympanum drab or cinnamon-drab. Spot below eye not so prominent as in male described, is olive-buff. Iris black with ecru-drab or light vinaceous-fawn spots. Iris rim avellaneous or vinaceous fawn; iris rim broken in front, below, and somewhat behind.

**Structure:** Skin rough, warty; conspicuous disks on fingers and toes.

**Voice:** The call is a loud, resonant trill, ending abruptly, 10 or 11 calls in half a minute. About the middle of May, at Ithaca, they are in the chorus stage. In the evening, all over the University hill and the hills near by, along the wooded ravines, in the thickety edges and woods of our marshes, we may stumble upon the noisy tree toads slowly approaching the nearest breeding place. In one instance their resort is a pond at the end of a long hedge. Here, at the breeding season, every evening and sometimes after a thundershower by day, the males can be heard all along its length, slowly bound for the one objective, the pool, where some have already arrived.

**Breeding:** These tree toads breed from the end of April to Aug. 11. The brown and cream or yellow eggs are laid in small scattered masses or packets of not more than 30 to 40 eggs on the surface of quiet pools, the packets loosely attached to vegetation. The egg is 1/25–1/20 inch (1.1–1.2 mm.), the outer envelope indistinct, 1/6–1/3 inch (4–8 mm.), merging in the jelly mass, the inne envelope $\frac{1}{18}$–$\frac{1}{12}$ inch (1.4–2.0 mm.). The eggs hatch in 4 to 5 days. The tadpole is medium up to 2 inches (50 mm.), tail long, scarlet or orange vermilion with black blotches around the edges of the crests, and with a long tip. The tooth ridges are $\frac{2}{3}$. After 45 to 65 days the tadpoles transform from June 27 to August at $\frac{1}{2}$–$\frac{4}{5}$ inch (13–20 mm.).

**Journal notes:** June 19, 1907, Ithaca, N.Y. Ever since Sunday, June 16, the tree toads have been in chorus. Every day this week we have heard occasional tree toads and at night they were deafening when near their ponds. After each thundershower they liven up perceptibly. This evening at 8:45 P.M., I reached the Veterinary College pond. Frogs were in chorus. In 15 minutes I had captured 20 individuals (including a mated pair). Found them also in grass near by, migrating to the pond, one in the road just west. Toads were singing here also. Went out to cross roads. Here they were just as common. The log in southwest corner had four perched on it. To show how tame and how dazed they are by the light, I stroked a croaking male with the lighted end of my flashlight 91 times without his stirring. He croaked just the same. I could have repeated the operation. In a tree on the north edge of the pond were four males, two on one limb facing each other.

June 21, Cross Roads Pond, 11 A.M. All around the pond were tree toad eggs. I staked out about six or seven areas of them. The packets or single emissions of eggs maybe 6–12 inches apart or only an inch or less. Sometimes from groups of eggs at more or less definite intervals one can determine the path of the pair. The eggs are almost invariably at the surface. Those beneath I believe were laid before some of our rainstorms raised the water in the pond. They may be attached to grass leaves, plant leaves, or sometimes algae. The packets are from 15–35 eggs. Some of the first tree toad eggs laid here are now hatching. The wood frog tadpoles are beginning to develop good-sized legs.

June 13, Cross Roads Pond. Today at 1:30 found several fresh packets of *Hyla versicolor* eggs, attached to grass at edge or to *Potamogeton* leaves in mid-pond. Four to ten eggs in a packet. They were all at the surface. Water surface 74°, water bottom 72°.

**Authorities' corner:**

G. H. Loskiel, Gen., 1794, p. 891.
M. H. Hinckley, Mass., 1880, pp. 104–107.
J C. Geikie, Gen., 1882(?), pp. 217–218.
G. M. Allen, N.H., 1899, p. 72.
F. Overton, N.Y., 1914, p. 32.
H. Sweetman, Mass., 1944, pp. 499–501.
R. L. Hoffman, Va., 1946, pp. 141–142.

## Cope's Tree Frog, Western Tree Frog, Chameleon Tree Frog

*Hyla versicolor chrysoscelis* (Cope). Plate LXXIV; Map 20.

**Range:** Southern Arkansas to east-central and southern Texas.

"The two forms of *Hyla versicolor*, the pustulous (typical ***versicolor***) and

*Plate LXXIV. Hyla versicolor chrysoscelis* 1. Female (×1). 2,3. Males (×1⅛).

*Plate LXXV Hyla wrightorum* (×¾). 1,3. Male with throat partly inflated. 2. Female in water. 4. Male in water.

the smooth (variety *chrysoscelis*) are distributed over most of eastern Texas, but the present form seems to be confined principally to the extreme northeastern counties and the Trinity and Brazos valleys" (J. K. Strecker, Jr., and W. J. Williams, Tex., 1928, p. 11).

**Habitat:** Wooded stretches along creeks and rivers.

"In Bowie County [Texas], under slabs of wood lying along the margins of sloughs, Mr. Williams found three specimens of *chrysoscelis*" (J. K. Strecker, Jr., and W. J. Williams, Tex., 1928, p. 11).

**Size:** Adults, 1⅖–1⅞ inches. Males, 36–43 mm. Females, 35–49 mm.

**General appearance:** These frogs are a smooth-skinned version of our common tree toad, *Hyla v. versicolor*. Of a pair in hand, each has a light spot below the eye, legs barred, and the irregular cross on the back. The male at present is a light grayish tan with the pattern in green outlined with black. The female is gray with the pattern in dark olive and black. Both have the characteristic orange on the groin and concealed portions of the legs. In these two there is no black reticulation on the orange rear of the femur. Often the rear of the femur is marked with very fine spots. The dark mottling on the sides is very distinct. The pattern of the back is rather less massive than in the average *Hyla versicolor*. The male seems a little smaller than the average *Hyla versicolor* male. Sometimes the backs are green.

**Color:** *Male* Beeville, Tex., March 27, 1925 Orange or cadmium orange on side of groin and front of thigh, merging into mars yellow or xanthine orange on rear of thighs and on the tibia. Spots on back, calla green. Background kildare green or mignonette green.

*Another male*. Mud Creek, 9 miles north of San Antonio, Tex, taken by R. D. Quillin and A. H. Wright, June 24, 1930. Dorsum along sides pale olive-gray or pale smoke gray becoming on back olive-buff or seafoam green near edges of large dorsal spot. Dorsal spot in center half brown becoming near edge dark greenish olive or dark ivy green. One forward lateral wing of spot dark ivy green. Another oblique wing from rear of spot to each groin, dark ivy green. Rear and front of femur xanthine orange. As front of femur joins body color it becomes cadmium yellow or light cadmium, and this extends along groin. Axil with touch of this color or lemon yellow. Rear of femur spotted with finely sized lemon yellow spots. A few or a line of these along rear tibial edge. Area around vent and along rear of femur a short distance silvery white and black. Two bars like dorsal spot across antebrachium, one across base of third and fourth fingers, one faint one across brachium. Two such prominent spots on femur, two on tibia, one on tarsus, and four or five on foot. In front of vent from first femur bar to other first femur bar seafoam green. Underside of femur, hind foot, some of belly russet-vinaceous or light russet-vinaceous. Black bar from nostril to eye. Dark area from eye through tympanum. Then an imperfect row of large dark spots to groin with smaller spots below it. Spot below eye white, ivory yellow, or seafoam green.

Iris rim deep seafoam green; iris mainly spotted vinaceous-russet with some chocolate or burnt umber reticulations.

*Female.* Same locality. Dorsum smoke gray. Dorsal spots and wings cephalic and caudal separate, each ivy green or lincoln green. Black stripe from snout to eye. Black vitta from eye around tympanum halfway to groin. Below this a light drab band from tympanum almost to groin. Black line above in groin breaks into black spots with light cadmium below it. Spot below eye white. Other colors more or less as in male. Throat, belly, and underside of fore limbs white.

**Structure:** Cope's original description (*Hyla femoralis chrysoscelis*) is as follows: "*Hyla femoralis* Daudin. A specimen larger than the largest individuals I have previously seen; differs also in the greater extent of the palmation of the fingers, and in the coloration of the concealed surface of the femur. In eastern specimens the posterior face of the femur is brown, with rather small yellow spots; in this form it is yellow with a blackish coarse reticulation, which only extends to the lower surface of the proximal half of the thigh. The sides have a double row of small black spots, which enclose a yellow band. This is probably a subspecies and may be distinguished by the name of *chrysoscelis*. One specimen as large as a large *Hyla versicolor* was taken by Mr. Boll near Dallas" (E. D. Cope, Tex., 1880, p. 29).

"Five specimens from Helotes were in the Marnock collection. These specimens are perfectly smooth above and resemble in every particular typical specimens of *chrysoscelis* from the type locality. This is the common *Hyla* of middle and northern Texas" (J. K. Strecker, Jr., Tex., 1922, p. 15).

**Voice:** It is a loud resonant trill.

"This species is fairly abundant near Houston and I have the following notes on it: February 13, 1918. Have heard several in the past few days calling from trees in camp, but have not seen any yet. April 15. Collected one specimen, a male that was calling from the branch of a pine tree. April 24. Found one calling in rain pool where *H. squirella* was breeding. I heard them frequently on warm evenings, answering each other from trees in the woods near camp. After the first of May they became silent and I heard and saw no more of them for the season. If they laid eggs in any of the pools near camp they made no such noise about it as they do in the North" (P. H. Pope, Tex., 1919, p. 95).

"2/17. Heard *Hyla v. chrysoscelis* calling tonight—evening. 1st this spring.

"Feb. 18. Cold. No frogs or toads.

"Specimen 1948. *H. v. chrysoscelis*. 7/15/44 from damp ground under water spigot at house 3″ deep.

"Somerset, Tex. 7½ mi. S.W. 1944. Sept. 2.

"Specimen 1951–1956 inc. *Hyla v. chrysoscelis*.

"I have been hearing a strange frog or (toad) note since Aug. 27, from the Geo. Foster tank or pond about ⅖ mi. S.E. of our house. There had been much rain from Aug. 22 to Aug. 28, clear since 8/28. Tonight I went to the tank and heard a few of these calls. After searching I found them to come from trees and bushes and a tree fallen in the water. I caught two that I thought were the croakers. *Hylas,* somewhat small. Finally I was watching two *Hylas,* one was croaking the other about 6" away. Female was silent, suddenly the croaking male began calling the strange notes: uttered fully twice as quick as the ordinary notes and an altogether different tone, clear, shriller, 2 to 4 notes; ('qui qui qui') sometimes there was a low gurgling preceding the call notes; most times the notes were low but now and then they could be heard a long distance, clearly at our house, ⅔ mile away. This satisfied me that the strange notes were made by the male *H. v. chrysoscelis* during mating times. All the males (6) heard that I saw were near females. On a horizontal limb (3" diameter) 6 feet up were 5 hylas, 2 females, 3 males. They were close together, all five within 10 inches. One male uttered these calls. It was alongside of a female, 'nudged' the female a few times. This pair collected, as was the pair first watched and 2 other single females (?) caught near where these calls heard. I have heard these strange notes a few times before" (notes, A. J. Kirn, Somerset, Tex., 1944).

**Breeding:** They breed from middle March to July. The tadpoles transform at ⅝ inch (16 mm.).

"This spring I found this tree-toad breeding in small rock-bound pools in a gravel pit. The tadpoles were light yellow. Specimens collected April 21st had the hindlimbs well developed" (J. K. Strecker, Jr., Tex., 1910a, p. 118).

**Journal notes:** March 24, 1925, Beeville, Tex. The air is resounding with *Pseudacris.* We heard a few scattering *Hyla versicolor* along the roadside ditches or in the distance and captured three males, but later lost one. They are along these roadside ditches but not in them. They look quite green at night. We captured one on the bole of a mesquite near the pond. Meadow frogs are croaking loudly in these ditches and narrow-mouthed toads are common.

June 14, 1930, Beeville, Tex., at night. We were about to leave the pond when we heard a *H. versicolor.* We started for it when we heard two more at a distance. One we caught. It has spotting on the rear of the femur, very fine spots down the outer half of the femur. When we reached the house we lost the *H. versicolor.*

June 22. We went out with R. D. Quillin. At Mud Creek, 9 miles north of San Antonio, we heard many *Microhyla olivacea, Rana pipiens,* a few *Bufo valliceps,* and several *Hyla versicolor chrysoscelis.* We sought the tree toads. The first one was too high in the oaks. The next one we picked up on mud near the water. Then we heard a croaker near the spot but the one on the mud proved a ripe female. In another oak tree we found a male, 3 feet up. This we put with the female. When we returned to the house they were mated axillary fashion.

June 26, Waco, Tex. I saw some of Strecker's *H. v. chrysoscelis.* He pronounced my San Antonio live *Hyla versicolor, H. v. chrysoscelis.* These are smooth and quite greenish. In three *H. v. chrysoscelis* in the Baylor collection the suborbital spot is obscure or absent or present on one side and absent on the other. The femoral reticulation is more pronounced than in my *H. v. chrysoscelis* from San Antonio.

**Authorities' corner:**

J. K. Strecker, Jr., Tex, 1910a, pp. 117–118.

"In the southern and western specimens there is a tendency to the replacing of the brown reticulation on the yellow ground of the posterior face of the thighs by a number of subcircular golden spots in the brown ground, as in the *Hyla femoralis,* although northern specimens sometimes show traces of it. This is very evident in specimens from Prairie Mer Rouge and Tangipahoa River, Louisiana, and Dallas, Texas. As a general rule, too, the portions of the limbs concealed or in contact with each other when flexed, are in northern specimens more fully marbled with yellow, even covering the whole inner surface of the tibia and the light interspaces more or less angular, while in the *Smilisca baudinii* and the southern and western specimens of *H. versicolor* the amount of marbling is less, and the interspaces are often reduced to small circular spots. I have, however, been unable to characterize them as more than a variety, to which I give the name of *H. v. chrysoscelis*" (E. D. Cope, Gen., 1889, pp. 374–375).

"It is easy to be confused in trying to solve Cope's original *Hyla versicolor chrysoscelis, H. v versicolor,* and *Hyla v phaeocrypta.* Viosca positively asserts that *H. v. phaeocrypta* type is *H. v. versicolor.* Stejneger early pointed out that *H. v. chrysoscelis* could not be *H. femoralis.*

"When after *H avivoca* with Viosca and Chase on June 11, 1930 in Tickfaw and Tangipahoa Country, 'we took in road ditches several *H. v. versicolor.* Are they *H. v. chrysoscelis*? Quite smooth. The female is very large in contrast to the males captured Started for *H. avivoca* nearby. It is not the *H. versicolor* of Louisiana, but is quite different and different in ecological habits. Yet if I read Cope's recharacterization (1889) of *H. v. chrysoscelis* (1880) (partially from Louisiana, Tangipahoa River—this very country I am in) one might suspect Cope might have had some *H. avivoca.* If so his Tangipahoa River, La, and Dallas, Texas, description is of a composite form. Cope (1880) put his form in *H. femoralis,* but *Hyla avivoca* never was *H. femoralis* in habit. It is found in tupelo gums, *H. femoralis* in pine woods. Each of these and *H. versicolor* are in this region of Louisiana. . . .' Strecker redescribes *H. v. chrysoscelis.* He calls it a smooth-skinned frog with a yellow suborbital spot. He also alludes to Cope's character of fine femoral spots. I have taken *H. versicolor* from Beeville to north of San Antonio. I believe that it is the form Strecker has interpreted as *H. v. chrysoscelis.* I showed him some live specimens from Mud Creek 9 miles north of San Antonio, Texas. These seemed much like Waco, Texas, specimens he showed me. Both lots (mine and his) are smooth-skinned but some have no suborbital spot, or occasionally they have a line from nostril to eye and backward. The Louisiana material needs to be restudied. At present we will hold to the Dallas (Boll) material as the center of its (*H. versicolor chrysoscelis*) eastern Texas to Arkansas range" (A. H Wright, MS, 1930).

Recently H. M. Smith and Bryce C. Brown assigned the *Hyla versicolor* of the "Lower Mississippi Valley west through eastern Texas to about Leon and Austin counties" to *H. versicolor chrysoscelis*. This they diagnose as follows: "Like *H. v. versicolor* except rear surface of thigh more extensively dark marked, leaving only isolated, circular light areas of moderate size." This seemingly is in agreement with Cope's saying he had it from Dallas, Tex., and Tangipahoa River, La. The new form, *H. versicolor sandersi*, after our friends Mr. and Mrs. Ottys Sanders, they restrict as follows: "The Balcones escarpment and its vicinity in central Texas, south at least to Atascosa County, east to Bastrop County, north to Travis County and no doubt to McLellan County." "The Texan subspecies may be diagnosed as follows: rear of thigh light (orange in life), with fine white flecks, entirely lacking dark marks except at extreme medial border; fingers not or only barely perceptibly webbed; skin smooth; maximum snout-vent length lesser, 43 mm. in males, 48 mm. in females. . . ."

## Dusky Tree Toad

*Hyla versicolor phaeocrypta* (Cope). Plate LXXVI.

**Range:** Specimens from Nashville, Tenn., Olive Branch, Ill., Mt. Carmel, Ill., Olney, Ill., Gull Lake, Brainerd, Minn., and Springfield, S.D., have been assigned to this form.

**Habitat:** River valley and lake shore.

**Size:** Adults, 1⅓–1⅖ inches. Males, as large as 33 mm. Females, as large as 36 mm.

**General appearance:** This is another of Cope's *H. versicolor-H. femoralis* puzzles based on preserved material. It is as yet unsolved; however, it is probably not a good form. Cope's original description follows:

"A single specimen of a strongly marked variety of this species was sent to the National Museum from Mt. Carmel, Ill., by Lucien M. Turner (No. 12074). It is smaller, having the average dimensions of *H. femoralis*. The color is a dark brown, with three rows of large approximated darker brown spots. The groin and concealed faces of the thigh are yellowish brown, with a very scanty speckling of darker brown, very different from the usual coarse netted pattern. At first sight one suspects this to be a specimen of *Hyla femoralis*, but it possesses all the essential characters of the integument and feet of the

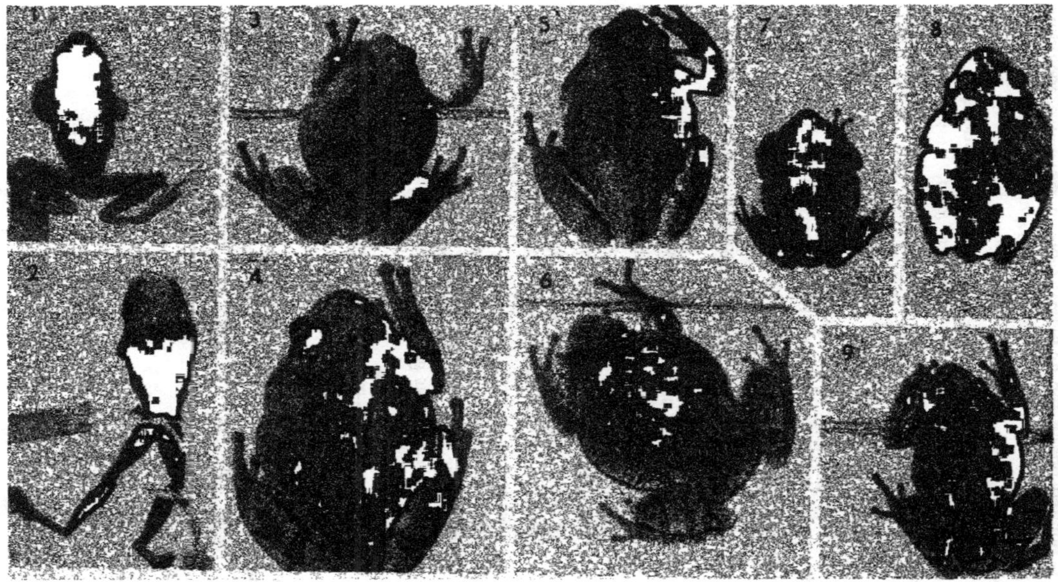

*Plate LXXVI Hyla versicolor phaeocrypta.* 1 Collected by Ridgway, 10 miles northeast of Olney, Ill. In USNM. 2. Male, from Uhler, Gull Lake, Minn. In USNM. 3,4 From Itasca Park, Minn. 5,6. From Walhalla, N D 7. From Fredericks, Minn. 8,9. From Carolyn Weber, Mantawish, Vilas Co, Wis.

*H. versicolor,* as pointed out in the analytical table of the genus, including also the light spot under the eye. It may be called *H. v. phaeocrypta*" (Cope, Gen., 1889, p. 375).

In hurried visits to three of its localities, we have met questionable forms. *Live material from Wabash Valley is our greatest need.* Viosca now pronounces the type of *Hyla phaeocrypta* a poorly preserved *Hyla versicolor*. What is this form? In the last fifteen years little has appeared to add to the solution.

From Itasca Park, Minn. This is a smooth-skinned tree toad, gray with prominent crossbars on legs and varying types of spots on the back. In some these spots assume a cruciform pattern or are arranged in three or four rows. There is a white or olivine spot below the eye. From the eye backward extends an oblique band of gray or vinaceous bordered above with black. There is much cadmium orange or cadmium yellow on rear and front of femur, on underside of foot, in groin, and in axil. From Walhalla, N.D. In darkness and moisture, this frog was dark grayish olive and very little dorsal pattern showed. Brought into the light, he is rapidly becoming lighter and the dorsal pattern is coming out. He lacks the cruciform patch of typical *versicolor* There are about four rows of irregular spots on the back.

These and the Kansas, South Dakota, and Wisconsin records are likely to prove variant *H. v. versicolor.*

**Structure:** For those who wish to follow the relative measurements of *Hyla avivoca, Hyla v. versicolor,* and *Hyla v. phaeocrypta* (Illinois northwestward), the following table of 1930 is given:

| | *H. a.* | *H. p.* | *H. v.* | *H. a.* | *H. p.* | *H. v.* |
|---|---|---|---|---|---|---|
| No USNM | 75026 | 70644 | C U. | 75018 | 70643 | 3636 |
| Sex | Male | | | Female? | Female | Female |
| Length | 28 | 28 | 28 | 36 | 36 | 36 |
| Head-tympanum | 10 | 9 | 10 | 11 | 12 | 12.5 |
| Head-angle of mouth | 9.5 | 7 | 9 | 10 | 10 | 11.5 |
| Width head | 11 | 10 | 12 | 12 | 13.5 | 14 |
| Snout | 5 | 4.5 | 5.5 | 5.5 | 6 | 6 |
| Eye | 3 | 3 | 4 | 4.5 | 3.5 | 4 |
| Interorbital space | 3.5 | 3.5 | 2.5 | 5 | 4 | 5 |
| Upper eyelid | 3.5 | 2.5 | 2.5 | 4 | 3.5 | 4 |
| Tympanum | 2 | 2 | 3 | 3 | 2.5 | 2.5 |
| Intertympanic space | 10.5 | 8.5 | 9 | 11 | 11.5 | 11.5 |
| Internasal space | 3.5 | 3 | 3 | 3.5 | 3 | 4 |
| Fore limb | 18 | 14 | 20 | 20 | 17 | 24 |
| 1st finger | 4.5 | 4 | 3.5 | 5.5 | 4.5 | 6 |
| 2nd finger | 6 | 4.5 | 5 | 7.5 | 5 | 8.5 |
| 3rd finger | 9.5 | 6 | 8 | 10 | 7 | 11 |
| 4th finger | 7.5 | 5 | 6 | 8.5 | 6 | 9 |
| Hind limb | 42 | 35 | 44 | 55 | 53 | 54 |

| | *H. a.* | *H. p.* | *H. v.* | *H. a.* | *H. p.* | *H. v.* |
|---|---|---|---|---|---|---|
| Tibia | 15 | 15 | 16 | 18.5 | | 19 |
| Foot with tarsus | 19.5 | 16 | | 24.5 | 24 | 27 |
| Foot without tarsus | 14 | 9 | 14 | 14.5 | 14 | 15.5 |
| 1st toe | 4.5 | 4 | 3 | 5 | 6 | 7 |
| 2nd toe | 7 | 6 | 4.5 | 8 | 8 | 10 |
| 3rd toe | 10.5 | 8 | 8 | 12.5 | 10 | 12 |
| 4th toe | 14 | 9 | 11 | 14.5 | 12 | 15.5 |
| 5th toe | 11 | 8 | 8 | 12 | 9.5 | 12 |

**Remarks:** The material which comes into this consideration is:
USNM no. 12074, ad. Mt. Carmel, Ill. L. M. Turner (type).
USNM no. 70642, 34 mm. ♂ Gull Lake, 10 mi. n. Brainerd, Minn.
USNM no. 70643, 36 mm. ♀ Gull Lake, 10 mi. n. Brainerd, F. H. Uhler.
USNM no. 70644, 28 mm. yg. Gull Lake, 10 mi. n. Brainerd, F. H. Uhler.
USNM no. 71588, 10 mi. ne. Olney, Richland, Ill., Robt. Ridgway.
USNM no. 68719, 28 mm. yg. or ♀ Springfield, S.D., E. C. O'Roke.

Mittleman kindly showed us his manuscript. It is a good paper and he may be right. In the preceding table we compared one 28-mm. and one 36-mm. specimen of each form, six examples in all. We still retain *H. v. phaeocrypta* in this book for someone to catch the Wabash frog in the act and then for the same person the same season to familiarize himself with the song of *H. avivoca.*

Some of Mittleman's statements and our comments follow:

1. "In addition I have heard the call of this species (*H. phaeocrypta,* i.e., *avivoca*) in the gum trees of the mud flats along the Wabash River on the outskirts of Terre Haute, Indiana" (p. 34). Quite likely he did hear it. Why compare this memory with an old preserved specimen?

2. "The highly distinctive voice of *phaeocrypta* (*avivoca*) need be confused with no other North American hylid save possibly *H. crucifer*" (p. 35). Too comprehensive a statement. Authors speak of "breeding song," "rain song," "chorus note," and other notes for one species. One or two species may vary an octave.

3. "*Phaeocrypta.* Call, a piping, bird whistle. *Versicolor.* Call, a toad-like trill" (p. 36). To DeKay *versicolor* had a ventriloqual quality, to Cope a resonant trill, to Fowler a jerking cry, to Dickerson a cat purr or lamb bleat, to Overton a musical trill like a low-pitched whistle (trill and whistle combined) and a turkey call, to Harper (1921) a vigorous high-pitched trill, and so on. Did Turner actually catch a birdlike *Hyla* at Mt. Carmel? What is birdlike—Overton's turkey root, Viosca's and Wright's woodpecker call for *avivoca,* or somebody's musical thrushlike notes? What birds do we choose?

4. "If Harper's specimen is truly referable to *phaeocrypta* it probably indicates a significant trend in Atlantal coastal populations. It seems much more likely that it is simply a *versicolor*" (p. 34). Harper at Louisville, Ga., took

female *avivoca* of 49 mm., 5 mm. longer than what we reported in 1933, or 6 or 7 mm. more than Mittleman's specimens. Why not? We have been in the field many times with the four veterans who know *H. avivoca* best, P. Viosca, Jr., O. C. Van Hyning, A. F. Carr, Jr., and F. Harper. They know the southeast frogs alive, in alcohol, and theoretically.

**Color:** *Male*. Itasca Park, Minn., Aug. 26, 1930. The spots of back are deep olive-gray with dark margins. These spots consist of four irregular dorsal rows, and a bar from each eyelid extending obliquely backward and inward but not meeting its fellow. The background of the back is smoke gray with black line from snout to eye, resumed back of eye, and extending over tympanum and arm insertion and along side. The area below it and involving the tympanum is drab-gray or light purplish gray. This area on its lower portion is separated from the light cadmium of the axil by oblique black border. The spot below the eye is white. Transverse area above vent is white, bordered below by black. Below this is a pale flesh area. Rear of femur has prominent cadmium orange spots with amber brown interspaces. Underside of tibia is amber brown with a few orange spots. So also is the inside of tibia and foot. The groin is mainly cadmium yellow. The eye is spotted with congo pink. The throat is light grayish olive with rest of venter white.

*Another male*. Walhalla, N D. Sept. 1, 1930. The general dorsal color is dark olive-gray, becoming olivine on top of foreleg, on top of femur and tibia, and on sides above the dark edge of lateral band. The spot below the eye is of the same color. Band from eye through tympanum and over arm insertion is light drab. The tympanum is grayish olive. This lateral band is bordered by black. Just above groin is a prominent black-edged spot; its center is olivine. There is a slight touch of clear orange or cadmium yellow in axil, groin, and front of femur. The rear of femur is finely spotted with cadmium yellow, on a xanthine orange or amber brown background; same on underside of tibia and inner side of foot. The femur is slightly barred, the tibia more so. There is a **V** from one eyelid to the other. The spots of back are black or with citrine centers. The underside of lower jaw is olivine with some dark dashes. The lower throat is deep grayish olive. The rest of under parts are white except for undersurfaces of hind limb, which are pale flesh color. Just above anus is a light lumiere green area bordered below by black, and this in turn by pale grayish vinaceous, below that a silvery pebbling, some of which appears also on tarsus. The iris is black, heavily spotted with vinaceous-tawny; pupil rim broken above, below, behind, and in front; pupil rim is light greenish yellow above.

*Female*. Itasca Park, Aug. 26, 1930 The spots on back are light olive-gray or tea green outlined with dotted lines of black. The bars on femur, tibia, and antebrachium are the same color. The general background of back is pale drab-gray. From the eye there extends backward along the side, an ecru-drab or pale brownish drab band bordered above by black-dotted line. The spot below the eye is white or marguerite yellow. The tympanum is light cinnamon-drab. The front of femur, underside of tibia, and rear lower half of femur is cadmium yellow with same color in groin and to slight extent in axil. This cadmium yellow forms fine spots on rear of femur and slightly on rear and forward edge of tibia, with interstices of sudan brown or antique brown. The iris is heavily spotted with japan rose. Ventral surfaces are white. With this frog, the spots on the back were a large irregularly cruciform one on the forward part of the back and two smaller ones to the rear and laterad.

(These three specimens, two from Itasca Park, Minn., and one from Walhalla, N.D., may eventually, of course, be referred to *H. v. versicolor*.)

**Voice:** "As it is impossible to revive the voice of Cope's type specimen, some one must hear and collect its descendants in or near the type locality. Fortunately, this has virtually been done through the kindness of Mr. Karl P. Schmidt, of the Field Museum, who has called my attention to a series of specimens from Olive Branch, Illinois, in that museum, and these seem to be the same as Cope's *phaeocrypta*. The field notes of Mr. C. M. Barber which were submitted by Mr. Schmidt are especially interesting, as they may supply the missing evidence:

" 'Whilst collecting *Hyla cinerea* with a light in a boat, on Horseshoe Lake, May 23, 1907 with Dr. Chatham, my attention was called to a bird-like cry coming from trees and bushes overhead. At first I thought it resembled the rattle of *Acris*, but it has a bird-like quality quite peculiar. Several searches were unsuccessful, but finally we were able to find the sober-colored little frog when he uttered his cry, fearlessly, within a few feet, and with the light fully on him. Their note is strong and penetrating and more pleasing than any *Hyla* that I know. I had previously taken one in the grass near the lake, but mistook it for a juvenile *versicolor*' " (P. Viosca, Jr., La., 1923b, pp. 97–98).

In 1924 Robert Ridgway (Ill., p. 39) writing under the title, "Additional Notes on *Hyla phaeocrypta* (?)," reminisced as follows:

"Mr. Viosca's observations on *Hyla phaeocrypta* Cope in *Copeia 122* recall to my memory an experience of many years ago in the bottom-lands of the Wabash and tributary streams near Mt. Carmel, Ill. The bird-like notes described by Mr. Viosca were frequently heard by me in the woods, so distinctly bird-like that I was constantly looking for the unknown bird; in fact, there was a "standing reward" offered to my boy friends for a specimen never discovered. Some years later, when my father moved to a farm near Wheatland, Ind., I learned from him that it was a tree-frog. Whether *Hyla phaeocrypta* or not, the species is so abundant in the bottom-land woods that at certain seasons (if my memory is not at fault, in late summer or autumn) its clear, loud piping notes—as different as possible from the croak of *H. versicolor*—were the dominant and often the only sound to be heard" (R. Ridgway, Ill., 1924, p. 39).

**Breeding:** Nothing of record.

**Journal notes:** Sept. 13, 1929, Calhoun, Ill. While collecting in the northern gopher frog areas which Lee Ackert showed us, we came to a pond. When about to leave, we heard a *Hyla versicolor*. It was in a bush in the deep water of the pond, and so distinctly *H. v. versicolor* that we passed it by in our search for *R. areolata circulosa*. Later we wondered if it might not have been Ridgway's *H. phaeocrypta*.

Sept. 14. Went to Mt. Carmel, Ill., and New Harmony, Ind., for a day but heard nothing like the reputed *H. v. phaeocrypta*.

Aug. 26, 1930, Gull Lake, Minn. Wanted to take some of the queer hylas F. M. Uhler secured here, but found instead almost every other species of the region.

Sept. 7, 1930. Drove around the country at Mt. Carmel and listened at night and by day, but discovered no queer *Hyla* notes such as those of *H. v. phaeocrypta* are reputed to be.

Oct. 7, 1929 A small male tree toad from northern Wisconsin (from Carolyn Weber), we provisionally placed in this group. Our general notes on it are: This is a small specimen of tree toad. It is brownish gray on the back with irregular black markings, forming an irregular and imperfect cross. A dark band extends from eye downward across the tympanum and along the side. The top of this band is marked with a broken black line bordered above by light. The sides are speckled brown. The legs are barred, the throat is dark. There is orange on rear of hind legs, in groin, and in axilla

Not until we have several of these frogs alive from Mt. Carmel, Olive Branch, and Gull Lake, will we feel satisfied or competent to weigh the position of this species. Is it a separate form or *H. versicolor versicolor, H. v. chrysoscelis, H. avivoca,* or *Pseudacris brachyphona?*

**Authorities' corner:** In 1923 while provisionally placing his later *H. avivoca* under *H. phaeocrypta,* Viosca wrote: "As virtually all the distinguishing characters of my new frog were lost in the preservative, its general resemblance to *Hyla versicolor* made comparison with museum material difficult, especially since *versicolor* is such a variable species. Except for the smaller size, which could easily have been due to age, there is nothing in Cope's description of *phaeocrypta* that would suggest my specimens Dr. Stejneger has compared specimens of my species with Cope's type of *phaeocrypta* with the result that structurally at least he could not tell them apart, yet this in itself was not conclusive, as my specimens also exhibit a structural resemblance to small specimens of *Hyla versicolor chrysoscelis. . . . Hyla phaeocrypta . . . should however be rediscovered in the type locality and the voice noted.* Although there are apparent differences in the specimens at hand, between the *phaeocrypta* of Illinois and the bird-voiced *Hyla* of Southeast Louisiana, it is difficult to pass an opinion with the limited material available These also must be considered the same until both forms can be compared in life, or better, be heard by the same person" (P. Viosca, Jr., La., 1923b, pp. 97–98).

In describing his Louisiana *Hyla* as *Hyla avivoca* not *Hyla phaeocrypta*

Viosca said in 1928: "The species described herein had been called tentatively *Hyla phaeocrypta* Cope pending its comparison by the writer with Cope's type of *phaeocrypta*, as well as with other North American *Hyla* types in the National Museum. I have had an opportunity recently to make such a study in the National Museum and found the Louisiana form to be a species distinct from any North American *Hyla* heretofore described. Further, I found the type of *Hyla versicolor phaeocrypta* Cope, U.S.N.M. No. 12074, to be a fairly typical specimen of *Hyla versicolor*, poorly preserved as to texture and color, but well within the range of individual variations normally exhibited by that species. The typical cruciform pattern of *versicolor*, though faint, is readily discernible, and the structural characters pointed out by Cope place it unquestionably with that species" (P. Viosca, Jr., La., 1928, p. 89).

Note on W. T. Neill's (1948) significant paper on an eastern race, *Hyla phaeocrypta ogechiensis* for Georgia and Carolina specimens: Having visited the type locality of *Hyla phaeocrypta without success*, we want evidence from someone *with success in Mt. Carmel and the lower Wabash country*. Northern specimens are doubtless *versicolor* but *avivoca-phaeocrypta* is not yet proved. *Avivoca's* range may extend in the Upper Coastal area to North Carolina.

## Sonora Tree Frog, Wrights' Tree Frog, Sonora Hyla

*Hyla wrightorum* Taylor. Plate LXXV; Map 18.

**Range:** North-central Arizona, New Mexico, Chihuahua possibly to Texas.

"To date the author has found this frog only on the southern forested edge of the Colorado Plateau from the vicinity of Williams east to McNary. The full range extends east into Texas and south into Mexico.

"The Colorado Plateau extends roughly east and west through central Arizona into New Mexico. The altitude is approximately 7000 feet above sea level. In general the southern part is in the transition zone and is covered by typical vegetation including a broad belt of ponderosa pine with small areas of Douglas fir, white fir, Mexican white pine, and other trees. . . . No specimens of *Hyla wrightorum* were found in the isolated Pinal Mountains, south of Globe, although they reach from upper Sonoran through the transition zones, ranging from 4000 to 8000 feet in elevation. No frogs were found in the large springs at Pinetop, whose waters have a temperature of about 50° F. The waters of open ponds are warmed during the day, and remain at a higher temperature.

"The lower limit of the distribution of the species in this region seems to be defined by the rim of the Colorado Plateau, with an elevation of 5000 feet. The 1936 season was spent at Indian Gardens, 22 miles east of Payson, in an area directly beneath the rim of the plateau (here called the Mogollon or Tonto Rim). No specimens were found in this well forested area, though frogs were found on the plateau above on several trips. *Hyla eximia* was not listed for the Grand Canyon National Park. . . .

"Judging from the small number of specimens found, Williams is probably the western edge of this frog's range. Although the summer rains were few in 1937, they were heavy enough to have brought out all individuals, but very few were found. Many suitable ponds were completely barren. Continuing east numerous specimens were found along the rim. At Hart Canyon, which is 50 miles south of Winslow, and at Pinetop and McNary the numbers in the summer ponds were very great" (W. L. Chapel, Ariz., 1939, p. 225).

**Habitat:** "Before and after the breeding season the frogs are found occasionally throughout the forest. Clever camouflage and ventriloquism aid them in escaping detection. They are found on the ground in damp places and in the trees. Twice the author found several which had been jarred loose when a tree was felled. In one of these instances, a frog fell from the top of a tree about 75 feet high. On sultry days they were heard calling from the trees" (same, pp. 225–226).

For breeding they seek large, shallow, grassy, rain-water pools, permanent ponds, new ponds, brooks, even wells.

"It is a species apparently adapted to semidesert conditions" (E. H. Taylor, Ariz., 1938, p. 439).

**Size:** Adults, 1–1⅞ inches. Males, 24–44 mm. Females, 24–48 mm.

**General appearance and Color:** At first glance, these frogs look like Anderson's tree frogs (*Hyla andersonii*), green Pacific tree frogs (*Hyla regilla*), or large chorus frogs (*Pseudacris*). They are bright green with a dark purple or black line from the snout through the eye, broadening over the tympanum and extending halfway along the sides. This vittal stripe may be broken into groin spots, is slightly margined above with white, on the sides is irregular in outline, and may be lighter and bronzy in the center. There are two conspicuous linear black spots extending backward from the rump, occasionally paired dark spots on the forward part of the back, but no marks between the eyes. The groin is conspicuously greenish orange or old gold, as is the rear of the femur, which is unspotted. There are irregular spots or bars on the tops of the arms and legs. There are irregular dark borders on the upper and lower jaws ending in a dark spot at the shoulder. The throat of the male is dull greenish tan, that of the female white.

"This species is related more closely to *H. regilla* and *H. lafrentzi* than to the typical *H. eximia*. From the former it differs in having a smooth rather than pustular skin, and in having a longer leg, the tibiotarsal joint reaching the tip of the snout or beyond, instead of to the region of the eye. The webbing of the toes is somewhat less and the diameter of the tympanum is greater than half the diameter of the eye; the toes and fingers are wider with somewhat wider pads.

"From *H. lafrentzi* it differs in having the webbing between the toes somewhat less with narrower fingers and toes, larger choanae, a shorter, blunter snout, somewhat deeper in front of nostrils. The front edge of the tibia is heavily-spotted with brown, instead of having it blackish with a cream-white or silver line which is continued to foot" (E. H. Taylor, Ariz., 1938, p. 439).

**Structure:** Skin smooth above, granular below; a fold of skin across chest; a fold across the base of the throat in the female; fingers and toes with well-developed disks; the fourth toe very long; fingers slightly webbed at the base; toes ⅓ to ½ webbed; tympanum half the diameter of the eye; tibia half the length of the body; a tarsal fold present; inner metatarsal tubercle present, but outer metatarsal tubercle present, inconspicuous, or absent.

"Description of the type. A medium-sized member of the *Hyla eximia* group. The snout is rather truncate or bluntly conical, with the canthi more or less distinct but rounded; the line between eye and nostril somewhat concave, sloping obliquely from canthus to edge of lip; diameter of eye somewhat greater than distance of eye to nostril, and equal to distance of nostril to middle of upper labial border; nostrils below edge of canthus, the distance between them about equal to their distance from eye; the area about nostril slightly elevated, and a slight, shallow groove present between nostrils; diameter of the tympanum is contained in the diameter of the eye slightly more than 1.5 times; the distance between the tympanum and eye about .65 of diameter of tympanum.

"Tongue broadly cordiform or subcircular with a very slight median emargination posteriorly; free posteriorly for two fifths of its length. In males the openings of the single vocal sac are lateral to the tongue and much elongate; tongue papillae not prominent; the raised prominences bearing the vomerine teeth are large, placed slightly diagonally and closer to each other than to choanae; they arise near anterior level of the choanae, but do not reach their posterior level. The openings of the mucous glands form a continuous groove anterior to choanae; latter proportionally large.

"A vestige of a web between first three fingers, but practically obsolete between outer fingers; disks on the fingers moderate, only a little wider than the toes, the widest one on outer fingers equal in width to a little more than half the diameter of tympanum; first finger reaching to a point halfway between the distal subarticular tubercle and the terminal disk of the second; the distal subarticular tubercles large, that on outer finger very slightly bifid on right side (probably abnormally); a slight dermal fringe on the lateral edges of fingers; fourth finger longer than second.

"Legs elongate, the limb laid forward, the tibiotarsal articulation reaches to the tip of the snout or beyond slightly; when limbs are folded at right angles to body the heels overlap about two millimeters; terminal disks on toes not wider than digits, distinctly smaller than finger disks; a well-defined tarsal fold; a prominent, salient, inner metatarsal tubercle, its length in the first finger length about two and one-half times; outer metatarsal tubercle distinct, flattened, lying behind the anterior level of the inner tubercle; inner toes webbed at base, the depth of web from one fourth to one third the length of the outer toes; the web between the three outer toes incised to a point one third the distance between the two proximal subarticular tubercles of the fourth toe; supernumerary tubercles on palm and foot more or less distinct. (In males the large tubercle at the inner part of the base of first finger is covered with a corneous callosity, usually very light brown in color.) Anal flap rather wide, not especially modified; no axillary web; skin on body relatively smooth, under magnification one observes minute corrugations, more evident above eyes; a strong skin-fold across the breast; ventral surface granulate, the granules on the anterior part of abdomen largest, less distinct on throat and chin; granulations prominent on median ventral, and to some extent, posterior part of thighs; a rather thick but relatively indistinct fold above tympanum" (E. H. Taylor, Ariz., 1938, pp. 437–438).

**Voice:** The call is a low-pitched, harsh, metallic clack, with no trill, and consists of two to ten, twelve, or more notes given in succession. These may be speeded up toward the end of the call. The vocal vesicle is very large, single, and transparent, with less yellow or green in it than is found in most tree toads.

"Fresh rains bring out a renewed chorus. A chorus usually lasts two or three nights and then quickly thins out to a few disconsolate males for two to four more nights. A chorus continues all night, with the greatest volume before midnight. Probably new individuals make up most of each new chorus" (W. L. Chapel, Ariz., 1939, p. 226).

**Breeding:** July 9, 1942. These tadpoles range from 28–40 mm. in length (average 32 mm.) with body lengths of 11–17 mm. (average 13.5 mm.) and tail lengths of 17–23 mm. (average 19 mm.).

Tadpole. Hart Canyon, CCC Camp, Winslow, Ariz., July 16–24, 1933. Body dark olive or deep olive dotted with closely set mignonette green, light yellowish olive or dull citrine dots; the snout is almost the color of these dots with no olive. The deep olive of the back extends along as a rim margin on the upper edge of the musculature. There is a tendency for a similar rim on the lower edge of musculature. The middle portion of the musculature is olive lake, olive-ocher, or old gold. The hind legs as they begin to develop have much the same color. The throat also is this color. The sides of the belly have a flesh color or light vinaceous-cinnamon cast. The middle of the belly is white. The tail crest is finely dotted on the back with some tendency toward reticulation of the dots. The lower crest to the naked eye may look to be almost transparent but is actually covered all over with very fine deep olive dots. Pupil rim of eye is salmon colored, succeeded by black iris flecked with light viridine yellow and flesh color. Two transformed at 15 and 13.5 mm. They were green at transformation and had a suggestion of a dark indefinite area or band ahead of the eye.

"The breeding season is from June to August, but in any year the dates vary. The determining factor is the heavy summer rains common on the Colorado Plateau in July and August. These storms delimit the breeding season. The seasons noted were: 1933 Pinetop and Hart Canyon, 7000 feet, July 2–Aug. 9, heavy rains; 1935 Pinetop, 7000 feet, July 7–July 28, normal rains; 1937 Williams, 7000 feet, July 2–July 14, subnormal rains. Breeding is intermittent within this period" (W. L. Chapel, Ariz., 1939, p. 226).

Two ripe females 37.5 and 42 mm. were taken at Santa Fe, New Mexico, June 18, 1874, by H. W. Henshaw.

"The migration of frogs toward fresh rain-water pools begins as soon as the summer rains start. . . . The numbers of specimens present indicate that large, grassy, shallow ponds are quite common in the typical open parks in the ponderosa pine forests in central Arizona. The grass provides resting places for the frogs. In open water a few may swim about, but the majority remain along the edge, resting on the bottom. . . .

"The duration of the egg and tadpole stages is unknown. Some eggs were tagged near Pinetop, but the author was transferred the next day. No eggs have been found elsewhere. Some tadpoles were coralled several times, but subsequent freshets removed the broods. Many choruses and many tadpoles have been found in rapidly flowing brooks but no eggs have been found. Probably the egg masses either are laid in quiet back-washes or are washed into them to hatch. The frequent freshets cause high mortality, and after the rainy season as the brooks dry up many tadpoles are isolated in pools and are dried up with the water.

"Frequently in small pools the water is nearly black with the swimming tadpoles. The tadpoles gather in very shallow, warm side-pools full of decaying vegetable matter. They also gather in great numbers around fresh cow manure and apparently feed on the dissolved and softened material. In areas where this species is abundant, in later summer, when the tadpoles transform, the ground around the ponds is covered with out-going froglets. These vary in length from 10 to 13 mm. Many leave the water still carrying stubby tails" (W. L. Chapel, Ariz., 1939, p. 226).

Nov. 27, 1945. Again Bill Chapel arrives in the "nick-o-time," to tell us that those eggs he tagged near Pinetop were in small loose masses—possibly the size of a small teacup—loosely attached to grass stems just below the surface of the water.

**Journal notes:** On June 10 or 12, 1933, as Mr. W. L. Chapel was starting for Arizona, we showed him illustrations of *Hyla wrightorum*. On July 6, he wrote from Winslow, Ariz., somewhat as follows: "At present I am at Los Burros CCC Camp near McNary. The last few days we have had considerable rain. Toads are quite numerous about camp. Today we were working at Los Burros, which is about six miles from Winslow. In a swampy place, I heard quite a chorus. I found endless numbers of green frogs. No other species could I find. I am sending these, eight of them. . . ." On arrival, they proved to be four males and four females of *Hyla wrightorum*.

July 9, 1942. Put up at Lake-O-Woods Lodge, Ariz. Went down to swampy area below the swimming pool dam. Presently in water 2–4 or 6 inches deep and among grass found tadpoles of *Hyla wrightorum*. The tails are quite spotted with blackish specks and in general they are rather attractive tadpoles; some with two legs, one or two about to have forelegs break through. When did they breed?

July 11, Lake-O-Woods Lodge. Today Anna and I went along a drainage ditch west of the lower pond and down to a swamplike area below a swimming pool. Took a lot more tadpoles of *Hyla wrightorum*.

**Authorities' corner:**

R. Kellogg, Gen., 1932, p. 168.
F. W. King, Ariz., 1932, p. 99.
E. H Taylor, Kans., 1938, p. 439.
W. L. Chapel, Ariz., 1939, pp. 225–227.

# Family LEPTODACTYLIDAE

## Genus *ELEUTHERODACTYLUS* Duméril and Bibron

Map 25

### Mexican Cliff Frog, Robber Frog, Barking Frog

*Eleutherodactylus augusti* (Dugès). Plate LXXVII.

**Range:** Guanajuato. Probably not in the United States. In 1933 we gave its range as Jalisco to southern Arizona on the basis of the following quotation: "A frog of the genus *Eleutherodactylus* has been received from Mr. Sam Davidson, of Fort Worth, Texas. This specimen collected by Mr Davidson, October 1, 1927, in Madera Canyon, Santa Rita Mountains, Arizona. Miss Doris Cochran, of the United States National Museum, to whom this specimen was sent for examination and comparison, very kindly allowed Dr. Remington Kellogg to examine it, and it was referred by him, on account of the peculiar dorsal spotting, to *Eleutherodactylus augusti,* a Mexican species living in the state of Guanajuato, Mexico, rather than to *Eleutherodactylus latrans,* known only from the state of Texas" (J. R. Slevin, Ariz., 1931, p. 140).

In 1942 Mr. Slevin showed us this specimen and we concluded that superficially it appeared to be *E. latrans.* After we saw Mulaik's material of young with light crossbands from Kerrville, Tex., we more than ever held this view Koster's (Carlsbad, N. Mex.) and our (Boerne, Tex.) material also show the light transverse band. (Plate LXXX.)

**Habitat:** (See "Authorities' corner.")

**Size:** Adults, 2⅗–3 inches. 64.5–75.0 mm. (Kellogg)

**General appearance:** "Mocquard concluded that *E. augusti* was identical with Cope's *E. latrans* from central Texas. Direct comparison of Mexican specimens with the cotypes of *E. latrans* does not entirely confirm this assumption. Though there are no constant structural features that will distinguish specimens from these two areas, it was observed that in *E. latrans* the fourth toe is relatively longer, the color pattern consists of fairly closely aggregated large black blotches, the sides and hinder half of the abdomen are faintly areolate, and the skin on the upper parts of old adults is stiff, coarse, and areolate. These two forms are unquestionably rather closely related. An immature individual from Jalisco and an adult individual (with a body length of 75 mm.) collected by Ruthling, which unfortunately is without any definite locality, were used in these direct comparisons. The skin on the upper parts of the immature individual from Jalisco is much more tubercular and warty than that on the Texas specimens. Juvenile characters, such as vestigial postcephalic intratympanic dermal fold and vomerine teeth in minute clusters, are not unusual, but the presence of an abdominal disk seems rather remarkable for so young an individual" (R. Kellogg, Gen., 1932, p. 101).

"*Hylodes Augusti*, A. Dugès, notes manuscript. Aspect heavy. The head is so large that the body is very short; the eyes large and prominent. The tympanum is conspicuously smaller than the eye. The tongue is a little longer than broad with a slight notch in the rear. Vomerine teeth in 2 oblique groups in the rear of internal nares. The body is finely roughened on back, smooth on lower surface. Coloration: The upper parts are a very clear yellow, inferior parts white; the lower side of the throat is marbled with pale brown, the sides and the arms are bordered with brown. The top of head and shoulders are brown black, lined with pale yellow. One sees across the back a clearly defined band spotted with brown. This hylodes is considered very rare. M. Dugès discovered it at Guanajuato, Mexico . . ." (Brocchi 'P.,' Gen., 1879, pp. 19–24).

**Journal notes:** June 23, 1934. In the afternoon after a rain, Anna and I went to Madera Canyon, Ariz. Here, Mrs. Dusenberry said Mr. Sam Davidson of Fort Worth, Tex., stayed with her most of one summer. A woman came from California Academy of Science to collect. (Miss McLellan, whom he later married.) They collected the frog about October 1. It is the specimen now in Calif. Acad. Sci.

June 26, Madera Canyon. Started for old Baldy about 7:30 A.M. Arrived at the lookout about 1:30. L. N. Sprung of Sonoita, Arizona, is the fire watchman. He was here in 1925 with his cousin, Kenneth Putnam, also of Sonoita. Last July, just below the watch station, Mr. Sprung one afternoon espied a queer frog on a rock face. He showed it to two boys who bothered it to see it hop. It was "more round than any other shape," and after hopping on the rock face, it went into a crevice. It was probably the robber frog.

In 1942 we measured the California Academy of Science specimen from Arizona. The measurements (in mm.) of this female are: length 83, head (angle to mouth) 22, width of head 37, snout 15, eye 14.5, interorbital space 5.5, upper eyelid 8, tympanum 6, intertympanic space 25.5, internasal space 7, fore limb 46, first finger 15, second finger 15, third finger 23, fourth finger 21, hind limb from axil 106, tibia 38.5, foot with tarsus 50, foot without tarsus 32, first toe 9.5, second toe 15, third toe 21.5, fourth toe 32, fifth toe 21.5, hind limb from vent 114. Forearm much developed, brachium diameter 6, antebrachium 9; suggestion of a disk on venter; has fold of skin across head from tympanum and one on side of body from rear of tympanum to groin, there bending inward to the vent. It is *E. latrans*

**Authorities' corner:**

P. Brocchi, Gen., 1879, p. 53.
F. Mocquard, Gen., 1899, pp. 160–163.
R. Kellogg, Gen., 1932, p. 101.

In 1938 Taylor (Gen., 1938, pp. 391–394) described a new form, *E. cactorum*, and contrasted it with *E. latrans*, *E. augusti*, and *E. laticeps*. He had a key difference: "Tympanum ⅔ to ⅘ diameter of eye; dorsal surface smooth; Texas; 90 mm. . . . *E. latrans* Cope. Tympanum scarcely more than one half diameter of eye; Guanajuata; 75 mm. *augusti* Dugès." In addition he gave a table of measurements for the three species.

### Texan Cliff Frog, Barking Frog, Robber Frog, Rock Frog

*Eleutherodactylus latrans* (Cope). Plates LXXIX, LXXX; Map 25.

**Range:** Waco to Helotes to Del Rio, Tex., into Coahuila (Schmidt and Smith, 1944) through New Mexico to Santa Rita Mountains, Ariz. We had reports of it at Devil's River, Mertzon, Hondo, and Frio, Tex. R. D. Quillin reported it from Segovia, Medina Canyon, Boerne, Bracken, San Marcos, Concan, and Leakey, Tex.

"Eight specimens from Sacaton, five miles south of Cuatro Cunegas. All were caught in mouse traps. Mr. Marsh states that search for specimens by day and night failed to discover them. They apparently got into his traps just before dawn" (K. Schmidt and D. W. Owens, Tex., 1944, p. 100).

W. Chapel tells us (1945) that he caught a good-sized frog with a prominent ventral disk which he thought must be *E. latrans*. Alas, he lost it. He found it in Parker Canyon, northeast of Roosevelt Reservoir in central Arizona. It is worthy of note that there are limestone outcrops in that region.

**Habitat:** Limestone ledges of the cliffs that front the Edwards Plateau. They have also been reported in caves, under stones and other cover, in rock walls of canyons, rock masses in mountains, or rocky hillsides.

Charles T. Vorhies wrote us of his experience in Madera Canyon, Arizona, "I am still sure of one thing and that is that I have never heard such notes from any other species of frog or toad. However, the specimen I captured was not on a cliff but merely on a steep rocky hillside and was sitting under a jutting rock."

**Size:** Adults, 1⅞–3⅗ inches; 48–90 mm.

**General appearance:** This is a large, short-bodied, squat frog with extremely powerful forearms and long outer fingers. Its fingers and toes have expanded tips and prominent tubercles on the under surfaces. The loreal region is oblique. The skin is smooth. The back may be light drab to greenish.

The young and half-grown may be greenish on the back and have a light fawn, unspotted, transverse band across the middle back.

**Color:** *Male*. Helotes, Tex., Feb. 21, 1925. Background of back light drab shading into pale drab-gray. Light area down middle of back is pale drab-gray or pale smoke gray. Spots on back and upper parts of arms and legs are natal brown or army brown; sides and sides of belly vinaceous-buff; legs and arms, hands, and toes with light vinaceous-fawn or pale vinaceous-fawn; tym-

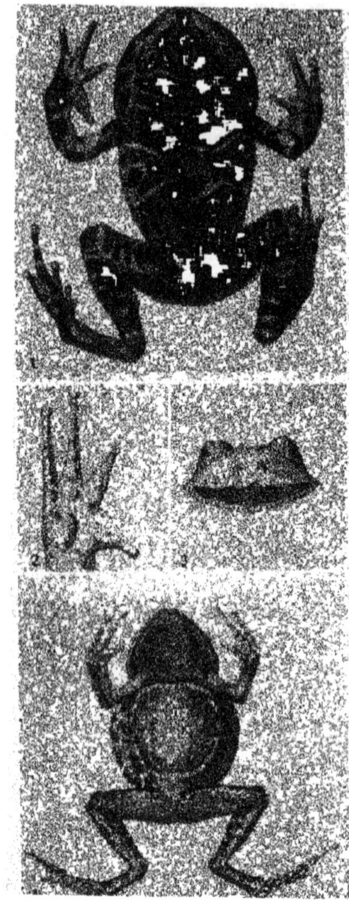

*Plate LXXVII. Eleutherodactylus augusti* 1,3 After Brocchi (×⅔). 2. After Brocchi (×1). 4 After Mocquard (×½).

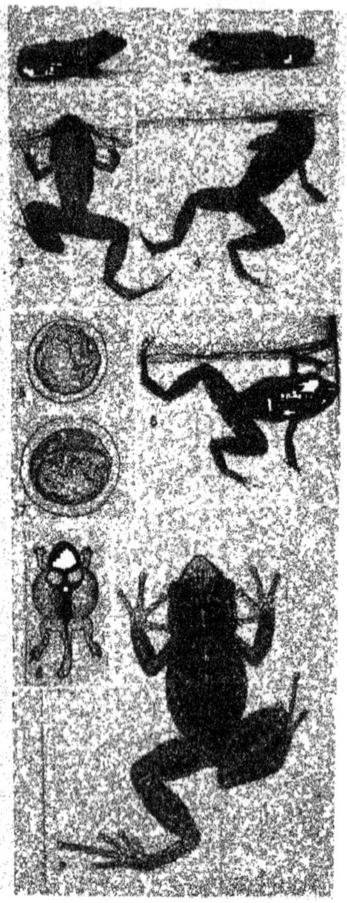

*Plate LXXVIII. Eleutherodactylus ricordii planirostris* 1–4,6. Adults (×1) 5,7. Embryo developing within the egg (×5). [No free tadpole] 8 Larva freed from gelatinous envelope, 3 days older than fig. 7 9 Female (×1¼). (5,7–9. Paintings by R. F. Deckert).

panum vinaceous-slate with a ventral spot from center up of pale smoke gray or pale drab-gray; color on rear of thigh unicolor and is the color of background. Middle of throat and ventral parts are pale pinkish buff. Eyelid is Varley's gray; iris light yellowish olive with a bronzy cast.

In G. W. Marnock's collection, Baylor University, no. 2022 has a prominent transverse band across dorsum from arm insertion to arm insertion. Back of it comes a broad transverse area of olive-buff outlined behind by two dark spots, one either side of the meson. This prominent light band has a median light dorsal stripe extending forward on meson to between the eyes. USNM no. 13633 (G. W. Marnock, Helotes, Tex.), which measures 48 mm., has an indication of this median line between the eyes, and possesses a rather spotted back.

*Half-grown frog.* Cave Without a Name, Boerne, Tex., from V. L. Cockrell, Aug. 14, 1942. General color of snout region, area across shoulders, and rear of back is deep mouse gray heavily spotted with large spots of dark quaker drab. The area between the eyes is vinaceous-fawn with 3 or 4 prominent black spots. *Across the middle back is a light area of fawn with no spots.* The tympanum is natal brown. The femur has 3 bands, tibia 3, metatarsus 2, antebrachium 1 of army brown, the interspaces being avellaneous. The forward half of the venter is pure white with solid pigments; the lower belly, underside of femur and tibia, and inner side of metatarsus have no pigment and the flesh showing through gives appearance of light vinaceous-lilac. In the eye is a thin pupil rim of mars orange, the base a deep mouse gray almost obscured by dots of buff-yellow.

**Structure:** Male with forearm best developed, brachium little developed; two solar, two palmar tubercles; head wide and flat; muzzle projects beyond lower jaw; vomerine teeth in two short raised patches between the inner nostrils; tympanum slightly deeper than wide; tongue slightly nicked behind; fold of skin from eye over tympanum almost to arm insertion; central abdomen surrounded by a circular fold of skin; disks transverse.

The enlarged forearm may come with age. Strecker's no. 2022 (36 mm.) has the forearm not so proportionally larger than brachium as it is in 74-mm. and 77-mm. specimens. This same specimen has not the ventral disk.

In some alcoholic specimens there seems to be a fold of skin across top of head between the tympani. The fold bows slightly forward.

**Voice:** At a distance the call was certainly a bark, but as we climbed the hill and came near, it was more of a throaty *whurr*. It is ventriloquial, and the location of the calling frog back under the ledge doubtless increases the volume of sound.

"Roy [R. D. Quillin] returned Sunday [April 23, 1933] from a trip in the Frio Canyon [Tex.], and the barking frogs do bark. Mr. Fisher on the ranch said that the frogs made so much barking four weeks ago that he was awakened nights. We hear them every evening when we sit on the front porch of the ranch house" (letter from Mrs. Ellen Schulz Quillin).

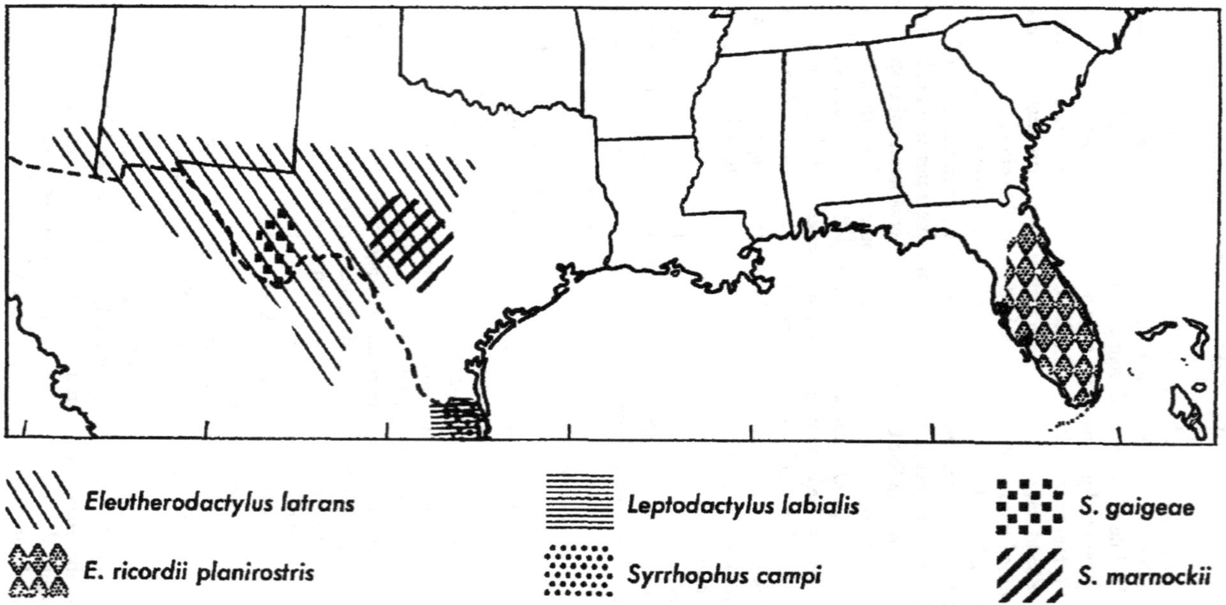
Eleutherodactylus latrans
E. ricordii planirostris
Leptodactylus labialis
Syrrhophus campi
S. gaigeae
S. marnockii

Map 25

Mr. Marnock told Mr. Cope, "During the winter the adults are very noisy, the rocks resounding in the evening with their dog-like bark. The noise is supposed by the country people to be made by lizards, especially the *Gerrhonotus infernalis* which occurs in the same region" (E. D. Cope, Tex., 1878, p. 186).

In 1925 this last notion was still the prevalent one in Helotes, for we were assured that it was the "barking lizard" that made that noise. And though we caught the frog that was "barking" and showed it to the doubters, we judge many are "of the same opinion still," for since our return we have received a newspaper clipping with a picture and a note about the "barking lizard."

Feb. 20, 1925. Heard "barking" near the store at Helotes. Mr. Fuller, who keeps the store, said that for the last week they have been calling but very little and slightly before that. Tonight, we went to *Pseudacris ornata* fork. Air at camp 7.45 P.M. 71°; no ornate chorus frogs calling; in fact, few meadow frogs calling. Went on to Helotes. At the flat crossing right near Helotes hamlet heard a "barking lizard" or "frog." Started north along the creek, soon discovered the frog was way up on the hill though it sounded nearer at first Went across open field back of the store, across fence, and up the hill among cedars, rhus, agerita, prickly pear, and yucca. After we thought we were near, we discovered it farther on. It is not startlingly ventriloquial. We began to suspect it was going to be in a shrubby thicket. When we neared it, it did not croak 5–15 times in succession but only once or twice at a time with longer intervals between croaking. At last we thought we had found the ledge. I determined to come from the left and Anna from the right of a small clump. I halted suddenly. Four or five feet ahead was a nice diamondback rattler asleep or coiled. I was searching frogs. I went around to the other side. Then a long interval. Then Anna thought she heard it below. Then I went above where I thought it was. Finally it croaked between us. We converged only to hear it in another direction. At last we determined it must be under or near a rock I was on. Anna below tried to see it, and I from above. We were about to give up, when I used the flashlight on it—and saw it about a foot under a thick, overhanging rock. Could see only its pulsating throat. Anna put flashlight on one side to prevent its escape and with ruler poked it out far enough for me to get a hold on a leg. Then the game was ours. It truly is a "robber-frog."

A card from A. V. Rutherford of Garner State Park north of Uvalde, Tex., written March 22, 1947 states: "A man here has caught them barking high up on the hills under ledges of rock. He heard the first barking this year, March 15."

**Breeding:** Probably they breed during any rainy period from February to May. It is likely that the large eggs are laid in moist or rain-filled cracks or crevices or even caves in the rocky cliffs and ledges where they live.

In Sept., 1930, we saw a large female (USNM no. 10058) which was collected by G. W. Marnock at Helotes, Tex. Dr. Kellogg had discovered that it was a gravid female. It measures 92 mm. in body length. The egg complement we roughly estimate at 50 eggs. These eggs have the largest vitelli of any frog eggs of the United States. Measurements of four vitelli are 6.0, 7.0, 7.0, and 7.5 mm. (¼–5⁄16 inch).

It seems probable to us that development is in the egg as with *E. ricordii*, yet it is possible that this large *Eleutherodactylus* may have a method diverse from that small form. We were in Texas in a very dry winter and spring, but if the calling frogs bred, we could not find their tadpoles in the creeks, nor could we find pools of water near the ledges that might harbor them.

The likelihood of their laying their eggs in a stream is about as remote as it is with Camp's, Marnock's, and Ricord's frogs. (See *P. streckeri*, "Authorities' corner," p. 280)

**Journal notes:** So few field experiences are described in the records of this frog that we are here quoting our notes at length:

Feb. 20, 1925. Helotes, Tex. The instant I had it in hand it swelled up taut. When I reached the store I realized I was sweating; started to brush sweat out of my left eye, it smarted afterwards. Some cuts on hands also did. It affected mucus of mouth slightly. It certainly has a secretion. It can bloat out bladder-like more than any other form I have ever encountered, as much so or more than *Hyla gratiosa* or some *Scaphiopus* species.

Feb. 21. Heard about 4 30 P.M., air temp. 71°, one robber frog. It was in a crevice of limestone on Helotes Hill. Was near it, too. Just back of the first locality of last night is a Spanish bayonet. These frogs are in the limestone ridges. At 9 P.M., heard none. Air 70°. Breezy but not humid.

Feb. 22. In photographing male *E. latrans*, it would wedge itself in the cell and climb right out of the jar When I had it in hand, it bent the last joint of the two outer digits. These have expanded tips. With these bent digits, it can pull readily and strongly. It must use these for pulling itself along or to prevent animals from pulling it out.

March 18. Tonight about 9 P.M., temp. 70°, heard one calling on Helotes Hill, near where we heard one on Feb. 21. Why the long interval?

March 20. Tonight about 9 P.M. heard one. Temp. about 65°F.

March 21. Tonight after a small shower, didn't hear a robber frog on the hills, but at 9.30 P.M. our captive spoke up for the first time since he was a captive. Why?

May 4. Last night back of camp we heard several calling until midnight. Air 64°. John Barrara (Mexican ranch hand) said they called vigorously at 5 P.M. We heard several north of Lee's, also east of Lee's. We heard none on Marnock's hill about 8 P.M. We rode almost to Babcock Road, but heard few beyond the area already mentioned. We heard one on hill north of our camp.

May 5. On hill to east heard robber frog a few times. On Marnock's hill, heard two or three, then they ceased calling. Not so vigorous tonight as last night. John Barrara says they get down to the creek. The one on our hill we thought was perhaps moving to the creek.

May 9. On half moon of rocks and hills east of us we heard many robber frogs, after the rain, about 1 P.M. Air temp. was 67°F. This morning at 9, I went on hill. Worked around top, saw a *Holbrookia*. Then came back at top of limestone ledge, and then back at base of limestone ledge, then down the canyon in the half moon. I did not see a water pocket of any permanence.

July 4. Storekeeper at Sheffield, Tex., says there are no "barking lizards" here. About 85 miles northeast at Mertzon, they occur. Another man at store said they are also near Hondo. This accords well with information from man at Barton Springs Park. We were told of their being at Leakey, Tex., in the Frio River canyon.

June 22, 1930, San Antonio, Tex. At night Roy Quillin and I went to John Classen's ranch to listen for barking frogs where he and Ellen Schulz Quillin hear them often. Apparently too late in year or else not rainy enough.

June 23, Helotes, Tex. Stopped at Mr. Fuller's store. He informs me he heard many on the hill in the spring but not lately.

Feb. 26, 1942. Went to California Academy; met J. R. Slevin. Glanced at *Eleutherodactylus augusti*. It's *E. latrans*.

Aug. 5. Went south of Kerrville, ideal country for robber frogs, especially about a mile or less north of Raven Ranch where Stanley Mulaik got a few small ones.

These young are very interesting as the light transverse band is conspicuous, and their gray color in preservative is suggestive of green in life.

Later in day went to Cave Without a Name, Mr. Cockrell guide. His wife said, "Surely there are salamanders and frogs in the cave. When they first opened it there were many black salamanders on the walls near the entrance, probably our cats have gotten most of them." When Mr. Cockrell came up, we went in. He said he saw one or two frogs on his last trip, that at times there were three or four near the entrance. In the morning near the entrance he found one of them in a water pail.

We started down and soon in a round pocket in the wall (pocket 6–7 inches deep) was a beautiful *E. latrans* headed outward. What a fine sight and how nicely niched for its life! Caught it. This one has a suggestion of the light band across the back.

**Authorities' corner:**

J. K. Strecker, Jr., Tex., 1908c, p. 59.

J. K. Strecker, Jr., Tex., 1922, p. 15.

"Enclosed is a photo of a frog I collected about 12 miles northwest of Carlsbad, N.M. I can't find any description in our library that fits it really well. For one thing the coloration is quite different. It comes closest to the *Eleutherodactylus latrans* collected by Marnock which you describe on pp. 161–163 of

*Plate LXXIX. Eleutherodactylus latrans.* 1. Male (×½). 2 Male (×⅔). 3. Male (×⅛).

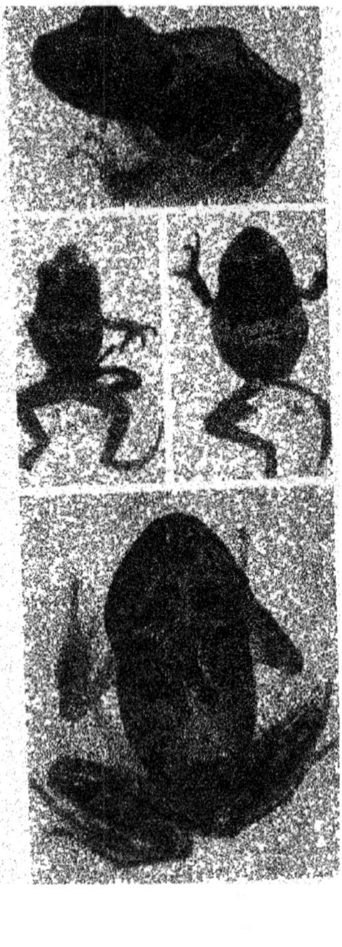

*Plate LXXX Eleutherodactylus latrans. Upper.* 1 Young adult, from W. J. Koster, near Carlsbad, N M. *Center* 2,3 Young, from Stanley Mulaik, near Kerrville, Tex. *Lower.* 4. Adult from Cave, Boerne, Tex.

your Handbook. The following is a description that I made after the specimen had been in formalin for two days:

"Most of the dorsum greenish, darkest on head and neck, venter plain white. Upper jaw whitish with vertical green bars. A double whitish line extends across the anterior part of the interorbital region. An irregular whitish line extends most of the distance between the interorbital line and the interscapular region. Body with numerous dark green spots, the more posterior ones faintly outlined with whitish. Band across back between arm insertions and forelimbs, ivory. Forelimbs with a bar on the wrist, forearm and a faint one on the upper arm. Hind limbs lighter green than the back, with darker green bars, these more or less outlined with lighter.

"The colors were not greatly changed from the condition in life except for intensity. It was strikingly green and ivory or white when first captured. . . .

"The specimen had an eventful history. It was taken from under our tent where it and a *Cnemidophorus* apparently sought shelter from a very heavy and violent rainstorm (3.48 inches at El Paso and the storm was still continuing when we broke camp) which lasted all night and through the morning. I heard short barks which I now suspect were these frogs but which I then thought were dogs. I brought it back alive and when I recovered I tried to identify the beast. I kept it in a deep pan of water to keep it from jumping whilst I was looking at the books and the darn thing nearly drowned. As a matter of fact it passed out and I gave it artificial respiration. It died during the night. After it was preserved, I set the jar on my work table next to the wall. A janitor moved the table for the first time in three years, broke the jar and threw everything into the basket. When I returned to the office I found the specimen in the basket with purple "Ditto" ink spots on it. It has since recovered. You see why I did not send the specimen right off" (letter of W. J. Koster, Albuquerque, N. Mex., Dec. 29, 1944). See condensed account by W. J. Koster, N. Mex., 1946, p. 173.

"Though it's too long for a letter, I'll tell you my story of what I have for several years supposed to have been *Eleutherodactylus*. In 1918, while engaged in much field work on the Santa Rita Experimental Range, I had my family in a cabin well up on the east side of Madera (White House) Canyon, whence I came down to the range below each day. This was the last week in June. The summer rains began in the canyon that week, with an afternoon sprinkle, next day an afternoon light shower, and next day with a rather heavy but brief late-afternoon rain. About dusk a loud, raucous calling broke out in the canyon. I was quite new to this country, especially to summer conditions, and a suggestion that it was 'toads' found no favor with me. I was mystified. I went down into the canyon, only to find the sounds came from the opposite side; climbing up, all the noise hushed up. I seated myself about where I judged the sounds to have come from. After several fruitless minutes of waiting, I was startled by a sudden 'bark' directly behind me. Creeping toward an overhanging rock, there was just enough light left for me to see a strange 'toad,' as I then thought it was. I captured it, but had no preservative, and I lost the specimen by escape or spoilage, I do not know which. Years later, when I first noted a report of ***Eleutherodactylus*** in Madera Canyon, I guessed I had seen and heard one. I still believe it was, and have hoped to run across it again. But I have never since been in Madera under similar circumstances, nor have I ever heard the same thing under other conditions when up there.

"Last summer, having some field work out that way, I made a point of being up there on a late June day when both clouds and calendar indicated a possible first shower, but no luck. Again, after the rains had begun, I explored pools along the creek in the same section of canyon without result. I'll get 'em yet.

"The most I have seen of the Sierra Ancha has been in late fall—no time to find these frogs. But the conditions would seem to be as good as in the Santa Ritas, barring its being further north. In fact, there are better-watered, more precipitous canyons there than in the Santa Ritas. Do you think I had *Eleutherodactylus*" (letter of C. T. Vorhies, Jan., 1946)?

### Ricord's Frog, Cricket Toad, Bahaman Tree Frog, Pink-snouted Frog

*Eleutherodactylus ricordii planirostris* (Cope). Plate LXXVIII; Map 25.

**Range:** Bahama Islands, Cuba, and Florida, north to Duval County. In the USNM is a lot of two specimens (nos. 59419–20) taken at Auburndale, Fla., by Wm. Palmer. In recent years it has been taken as far north as Gainesville, Fla., by O. C. Van Hyning. Each of these records reminds one of Dr. Barbour's statement "It has been taken in Florida and seems to be spreading northward" (Fla., p. 100). In 1931 Dr. H. A. Pilsbry, while collecting pulmonate gastropod *Liguus* on or about Long Pine Key, collected several (F. Harper, Gen., 1935). In 1940 W. G. Lynn and in 1943 Lynn and J. N. Dent spoke of its introduction into Jamaica, where it is now widespread. In 1939 G. A. Skermer of Tampa, Fla., published some of his experiences with the frog. In 1944 C. J. Goin had specimens from Jacksonville.

**Habitat:** Leaf piles in hammocks; rock piles; fern boxes; under walks, logs, debris, trash piles; limestone heaps; wells; irrigation banks. Dr. H. A. Pilsbry (1931) found them under loose bark in the hammocks.

**Size:** Adults, ⅗–1⅕ inches (15–30 mm ).

**General appearance:** It is small, elongate, similar to *Syrrhophus marnockii* but possesses two long transverse curved series of vomerine teeth, behind the internal nares. These are delicate little frogs with the head as broad as any part of the body. The eyes are prominent, beadlike, bronzy, and black. The snout is prominent, truncate, extending slightly beyond the lower jaw. The legs are long and slender. The fingers and toes are very slender with terminal disks and prominent palettes at the joints of fingers and toes, giving a saw-tooth appearance in lateral aspect. The color pattern varies, but in each the coral pink snout is prominent.

**Color:** *Adult.* Top of snout, stripe from eye to hind leg insertion along dorsolateral region, interspaces of hind legs and forelegs, and the tubercles along the side and top of back are light coral red to dragon's-blood red or terra cotta. On top of snout is a dark area which joins with the dark area of the dorsum, which normally starts about on level with a line drawn from middle of one eye to middle of other. This dorsal color is brownish olive, snuff brown. Indistinct bars of the same color on femur, tibia, and forearm or these bars and the markings on the toes may be black. The upper jaw and also the lower jaw are spotted with alternating black or carob brown or warm blackish brown spots. A line of the same color over tympanum to arm insertion. This line sometimes continuing from arm insertion along side as more or less broken dark line. Sometimes from axilla to groin there is an irregular line or row of dark spots parallel with the upper line just described. Front of femur with two or three prominent black spots and several such spots on the front of femorotibial articulation. A horizontal line of same color from arm insertion halfway down the brachium. The under parts are white and heavily punctate with fine brownish olive dots. A mid-ventral blood vessel plainly shows through the skin of the belly. The alternating areas on upper and lower jaws are white. The tympanum may be almost white or with a wash of coral red. In front of, below, and behind eye, below tympanum, and along sides are spots of greenish yellow. Iris is principally coral red to dragon's-blood red with vermiculations of darker color. The iris rim is almost scarlet or scarlet-red.

*Young.* The conspicuous thing about the young one seems to be the light coral red triangular snout patch ahead of the eye, the same color on fore and hind legs and a patch of same along either side. In most of the young there seems to be an appearance of triangular spot between the eyes, the base of the triangle extends between the eyes, and may be truncate, marginate, or concave. The rear portion of the triangle oftentimes and generally merges with the dorsal band, which may be scalloped along its sides. It is a beautiful little creature with its alternation of dark and light spots on upper and lower jaw and with its big bronzy eye. The legs appear barred. There is a slight ridge of skin down the middle back—from near tip of snout to vent. The skin of upper surface is roughened and is areolate on belly and hind legs.

**Structure:** Subgular vocal sac; tympanum ½ size of eye; tongue elongate oval, slightly nicked; heel reaches orbit or even snout; lower jaw with a median tubercle fitting into a median notch in upper jaw; two metacarpal and two metatarsal tubercles.

"Head as wide or wider than the body, longer than broad; the lateral outlines curved; the end of the muzzle abruptly truncated. Ostia pharyngea oval.

Vomerine teeth in two long curved series, which commence behind and opposite to the external border of inner nares, they are separated by a considerable space medially. Tongue elongate oval, slightly nicked. A subgular vocal sack. Tympanum half the size of the eye. Skin smooth above and below; sides rugose. Heel reaching the orbit. Digital palettes small. Two metacarpal, two metatarsal tubercles. Brachium longer than or equal to antebrachium. . . . A single specimen from Key West, Florida, is in the National Museum. Its proper habitat is Cuba" (E. D. Cope, Gen., 1889, p. 318).

**Voice:** "Its twittering call can be heard from hammocks as well as dry pine land, after showers during April, May, June, July, and August" (R. F. Deckert, Fla., 1921, p. 22). "Their call, which they gave at night from the terrarium was a faint 'put put' " (E. R. Dunn, Fla., 1926, p. 155). "Their chirping notes are a common sound after dark and on cloudy days" (O. C. Van Hyning, Fla., 1933, p. 4). "Some five years ago my attention was attracted by a trilling sound which seemed to come from a cluster of ferns around a palm. At first I thought it was some new cricket or grasshopper, but very careful search and watching did not solve the problem. Although I have lived in south Florida for forty years, I had not heard this trill before" (G A. Skermer, Fla., 1939, p. 107).

**Breeding:** This species breeds from April to August. Development goes on within the egg to adult form, there being no tadpole stage. The newly hatched young are ⅜–½ inch (9.0–11.5 mm.) in size.

"Ricord's Frog does not go to the rain-pools in numbers, as do the other Salientia. Pairing seems to take place on land during rainy weather, in dark places. The writer has so far failed to find specimens in copula, but on May 16 two batches of eggs, containing a dozen each, were found in a depression filled with dead leaves and leaf-mold in a 'hammock' " (R. F. Deckert, Fla., 1921, p. 23).

"*Ricordii* lays 19–25 eggs in vegetable debris in woods, . . . yolk being about 2 mm. in diameter, and the outer envelope eventually reaches 4 mm. No trace of external gills could be made out in either species. . . . The night of July 28 a batch of 25 eggs was laid. I left Soledad on July 30 and returned on August 2 and found that a second batch of 19 eggs had been laid in my absence.

"The eggs of the 28th began to hatch August 7, making a period of eleven days. By August 11 all were out, making a period of ten days from the 2nd.

"On August 11, 1925, I found 21 eggs in a fallen Bromeliad. These hatched six days after (August 16) and as soon as the yolk was fully absorbed and the adult coloration assumed they were seen to be *ricordii*" (E. R. Dunn, Fla., 1926, p. 155).

"Presuming that this frog, like others, laid its eggs in a lily pond near its habitat, I did not give thought to the life cycle. While looking over some orchids which I had banked with sphagnum I found a cluster of what appeared to be frog or toad eggs. I had not seen eggs laid in this way before. In order to see what had laid them I lifted the cluster, together with the sphagnum on which they were deposited, and placed them in a glass bowl and covered the bowl with a sheet of glass.

"It was easy to see that the eggs were normal, for the embryo could be seen moving in them. In about seven days the eggs had hatched, the jelly-like cases lying flattened out on the sphagnum. After very close inspection of the sphagnum through the glass I saw a tiny frog not as large as a house fly seated on the moss. Its appearance was exactly that of the mature frog I had previously found so I knew that it was the young of that frog. I have found many nests since then, all made on the ground or close to it in damp shady places" (G. A. Skermer, Fla., 1939, pp. 107–108).

"Mrs. A. N. Dow [of Jacksonville, Fla.] found eight 'small white eggs' in a flower pot in her yard and kept them until they hatched. The baby frogs were sent to me for identification, and proved to be *ricordii*.

"The eight individuals vary in length from 4.5 to 5.5 mm. From subadults from Gainesville they differ only in having the tympanum slightly less distinct, the head relatively broader, and the vomerine teeth less well developed. The eight specimens are now catalogued as number 22557 in the collection of the Carnegie Museum.

"Mrs. Dow informs me that the locality where these frogs were found is in a residential section about 3 miles from the business center of the city. She found the eggs in a flower pot which had been left undisturbed in a flower bed in the yard for several months. The eggs were deposited on the surface of the soil and when Mrs. Dow first discovered them she placed them and the accompanying soil in a jar where they remained until they hatched about a week later. She sent them to me on August 2, 1943, when the frogs were 'three or four days old.' In answer to my query about adults, she stated that she had not noticed them about, but that a neighbor had seen frogs of this description behind the houses in the neighborhood" (C. J. Goin, Fla., 1944, p. 192).

Apparent newly hatched young have been taken in the months of June, July, and August. The two following records are of young apparently not long after hatching: one specimen (USNM no. 36851) taken by Prof. C. H. Eigenmann on July 3, 1905, at Santiago de las Vegas, Cuba, measures 9 mm. and others (USNM nos. 29823, 29825, 29838) taken by Wm Palmer, June 30, 1902, at Baracoa, Cuba, measure 11.5, 11, and 11.5 mm., respectively. In the same lot were some specimens 15–20 mm. in length, and others 27–30 mm. in length.

We have seen another lot (UMZ 64267) from Limestone Ridge, Soledad Cienfuegas, Cuba, 7, 7.5, 9, 11, and 19 mm. in length. The 7 and 7.5 specimens must be near hatching size.

**Journal notes:** (We have been shown the actual boards, rocks, and vegetal cover under which they lived and the actual flower pots in which their eggs have been taken, yet we have very few journal notes worthy of mention.)

**Authorities' corner:** "In the pine country [in Dade Co., Fla.] the writer has found it under heaps of limestone. No matter how dry the surrounding land may be, in the center of these rock-heaps there is always quite some moisture, and all kinds of creatures find hiding places there. Many specimens of Ricord's Frog were secured in rock pits under quite small stones. They are difficult to capture as they leap with lightning rapidity the instant they are uncovered" (R. F. Deckert, Fla., 1921, pp. 22–23).

"*E. ricordii* is frequently found [in Cuba] along with *cuneatus,* never, however, jumping into the water. It is also found at considerable distances from the water.

On July 25, 1924, I caught seven from a colony of about a dozen, which was under two large stones and the fallen leaves of a royal palm, and was some fifty yards from a stream. I kept five of these alive in a jar with some vegetable debris" (E. R. Dunn, Fla., 1926, p. 155).

"*Eleutherodactylus ricordii* is a Cuban species which, it has been assumed (Lynn, 1940), has been introduced accidentally into Jamaica at a relatively recent date It was first recorded from Jamaica by Lynn (1937) who took it at Montego Bay. Later, E. A. Chapin found the species at Hope Gardens in Kingston and it was supposed (Lynn, 1940) that this indicated two separate points of introduction. The present collections however, show that the species is wide-spread in the island and it may be that it has been in Jamaica for a long time. We took specimens at Sandy Bay, Hanover, at Highgate, St. Mary; near Port Antonio, Portland at Chapelton, Clarendon and Mr. L. V. Burns has recently taken the species at Hector's River on the border between Portland and St. Thomas" (W G Lynn and J. N. Dent, Gen., 1943, p. 239).

"Since *Eleutherodactylus ricordii* was first reported in southern Florida by Cope (Bull. U.S. Nat. Mus., (1), 1875 31) it has steadily extended its range northward. Carr (Univ. Fla. Biol. Sci. Ser., III, (1), 1940: 63) gives its range as continuous in south Florida northward to the region of Melbourne on the east coast and Clearwater on the west coast with a separate population at Gainesville. I do not know how rapidly the southern Florida population is spreading northward, but the Gainesville population is certainly expanding steadily and the species is now quite common several miles from the city in localities where it was not known to occur a few years ago" (C. J. Goin, Fla., 1944, p. 192).

Shreve's revision (Fla, 1945) suggests *E. planirostris* for this introduced frog.

"I therefore restrict the name *ricordii* to the form from the highlands of Oriente, Cuba, which has a spotted dorsum. The color is: Above, ground color whitish or brownish white, heavily spotted with dark brown, the spots rounded and frequently coalescing, those on limbs in general smaller. In some, the spots coalesce to such an extent as to give the impression of marbling. . . .

"For the form widespread in Cuba and the Bahamas hitherto called *ricordii,* the name *Eleutherodactylus planirostris* (Cope) is available. Its type locality is New Providence Island, Bahamas. It is *planirostris* therefore, that is now present in Florida as an introduction. On account of the nature of the differences existing between *ricordii* and *planirostris* (as used here), it seems better to use the two names in subspecific relationship, although in the material at hand there is no real evidence of intergradation or hybridization. This may be shown to occur eventually as there is some evidence of hybridization between *planirostris* and the species *casparii*, of the Trinidad Mts. in Cuba, where their ranges meet, a seemingly parallel situation" (B. Shreve, Fla., 1945, p. 117).

Coleman J. Goin (Fla., 1947, pp. 1–66) has just issued his excellent comprehensive monograph, "Studies on the Life History of *Eleutherodactylus ricordii planirostris* (Cope) in Florida." It emphasizes particularly habits, breeding, development, color pattern, and distribution.

## Genus *LEPTODACTYLUS* Fitzinger

Map 25

### White-lipped Frog, White-jawed Frog, White-jawed Robber Frog

*Leptodactylus labialis* (Cope). Plate LXXXII; Map 25.

**Range:** Mexico to extreme southern Texas in Starr and Hidalgo counties. First found in United States by Dr. E. H. Taylor and J. S. Wright in 1931 (Taylor, Tex., 1932). In 1933 and 1934 it was held to be *Leptodactylus albilabris* (Gunther) (Plate LXXXI) and much was made of its occurrence in Puerto Rico and on the mainland. Dr. Noble in 1918 pointed out three characters of difference between the mainland and insular forms but frankly admitted that no criterion is constant. K. P. Schmidt in 1928 called the mainland and insular forms very close but was not able to state that they are identical.

**Habitat:** Moist meadows; irrigated fields; drains; gutters in towns; beneath stones and logs. Near streams; irrigation ditches; roadside ditches; in burrows in sandbanks and fields.

"The specimen was taken late at night hopping about on the table-like top of one of the row of hills just north of the Los Olmos bridge, near Rio Grande City, Tex. The earth was dry, and no rain had fallen for a period of forty-eight hours. The species probably shelters itself in the crevices of the rocky ledge which surrounds the top of the hill" (E. H. Taylor, Tex., 1932, p. 244).

**Size:** Adults, 1⅖–2 inches (35–49 mm.).

**General appearance:** This is a small dark-colored frog with a flattened pointed head, a low narrow lateral fold and a cream-colored labial line. "Among the collections made in Texas during the summer of 1931 by J. S. Wright and myself is a small leptodactilid toad, which offers something of a problem in the way of identification. Through the kindness of Mrs. Helen T. Gaige, Museum of Zoology, Ann Arbor, the specimen was examined and dissected, and found to belong to the genus *Leptodactylus*. She also forwarded for comparison specimens of the species *L. albilabris* Gunther from Vera Cruz, and St. Croix Island, which seem to approach this form in many characters.

"From these two forms, which differ considerably from each other, I note that the Texas specimen differs in the absence of a distinct dorsolateral fold, the very much larger choanae (nearly twice the area of those in the compared specimens), the presence of larger triangular bony prominences, on which the vomerine teeth occur, and their separation by a much greater distance (more than a half of their transverse length); the very narrow lateral fold is not continuous with the small supratympanic fold. There is a small forward extension of the snout to form a 'nose.' The dorsal coloration in life is ash gray to clay without black spots, while the compared forms are dark blackish brown with well-defined large black spots.

"From the specimen from St. Croix (the type locality of *Leptodactylus albilabris* Gunther) I note that the tips of the digits are distinctly less widened, in fact not at all dilated; that the head is longer, more pointed; the eye relatively smaller; and that the ventral brown spotting is lacking.

"From the Vera Cruz specimens it differs in having a flatter, more pointed head; a different coloration. It also differs in the points mentioned above. It agrees with both forms in the presence of a well-defined cream-colored labial line, and the presence of a discoidal disk formed by a skin fold on the abdomen.

"Cope has described a species, *L. labialis,* which has small choanae, and a paucity of dermal folds, and *L. gracilis* with a projecting muzzle and having dermal folds.

"Brocchi has described *L. fragilis* with the vomerine teeth in arched series, with the tympanum nearly twice as large as the eye.

"Remington Kellogg, who is reviewing the Amphibians of Mexico, proposes to place *labialis* Cope, and *fragilis* Brocchi all under the synonymy of *L. albilabris* Gunther.

"So for the present it seems that this Texas specimen must rest as *Leptodactylus albilabris* Gunther until a sufficient series of specimens are available to determine whether the separable characters, apparent in the specimen, are typical or due to individual variation" (E. H. Taylor, Tex., 1932, pp. 243–244).

**Color:** "Above rather lead gray with a few irregularly scattered, slightly dark, grayish blotches; a dark vitta from snout through nostril to eye, continued behind to the tympanum; another irregular black line begins above tympanum and follows the supratympanic fold; below this a narrow, well-defined cream line, bordered below on lip by an irregular, less intense, dark line continued to angle of jaw; a few black spots on posterior part of lower jaw; arm with a few small dark spots, and a few also in axillary region; anterior side of femur with a dark horizontal line and small spots; upper and posterior surface of limb spotted; an indistinct cream horizontal line borders the granular edge of the under part of the femur, below which are a few small dark spots; under surface of chin through abdomen and limbs uniformly cream; a dark broad line from heel across foot. The measurements are, head and body, 25 mm.; foreleg, 13 mm.; hindleg, 40 mm." (E. H. Taylor, Tex., 1932, p. 245).

**Structure:** Cope's description of this form follows: "Vomerine teeth in

*Plate LXXXI. Leptodactylus albilabris.* 1. After Brocchi (×¾). 2. After Boulenger (×¾). 3,4. After Schmidt (×⅔).

*Plate LXXXII. Leptodactylus labialis* (×⅔). Adults, from Stanley Mulaik, Edinburg, Tex.

transverse series behind the posterior border of the internal nares; toes without dermal border; no abdominal discoidal fold; posterior limbs short; end of metatarsus just reaching muzzle; muzzle short, not projecting; teeth behind choanae; one dermal fold on each side; skin rough; below white. . . . This small species belongs to that division of the genus, in which the toes do not possess dermal margin, and there is no discoidal fold of the abdominal integument. Among these it is distinguished by the shortness of series of vomerine teeth and the paucity of dermal plicae. The muzzle is acuminate and rather narrow, but not projecting as in *C. gracilis;* the canthus is not distinct. The tongue is oval and a little notched behind; the choanae are small. The diameter of the tympanic disc is one half that of the orbit. The heel only reaches the orbit. The toes are not very long; there are two small tarsal tubercles and a narrow tarsal fold. . . . Color chocolate brown, the limbs darker cross-barred. A brilliant white band extends from the anterior part of the upper lip, and describing a curve upwards, bounds the orbit below and descends to the canthus oris, from which point it continues in a straight line to the humerus, and ceases. Inferior surfaces pure white. Length of head and body, .020; of head, .007; of hind limbs, 0.28; of hind foot, .013" (E. D. Cope, Gen., 1877, p. 90).

Taylor states: "The snout oval, the outline broken by a slight pointed projection of the 'nose'; the head measures, length 11.5 mm. to angle of the jaw; the width at same point is 9.7 mm.; canthus rostralis rounded, the ridge continued downward in front of eye; between this ridge and the nostril the loreal region is distinctly concave; eye moderate; length of orbit 3.7 mm., the distance from the nostril 2.8 mm. and its distance from the tip of the snout 4.2 mm., tympanum very distinct, rounded, 1.7 mm. long by 1.5 mm. high, separated from eye by half its greatest diameter; a slight supratympanic fold from eye, involving upper edge of the tympanum but bending down some distance behind the posterior edge of tympanum, labial fold distinct posteriorly, becomes very indistinct anteriorly and terminates below nostril, in lateral profile the snout extends beyond the mouth; the angle of mouth reaches directly below tympanum; the distance between orbits 2.4 mm.; of upper eyelid width 1.8 mm.

"Skin on head smooth, showing microscopic corrugation; the dorsolateral fold wanting, represented by a few low rounded or somewhat elongate pustules; a sharply defined, very narrow lateral fold extends from above arm to groin; above this a few elongate or rounded pustules low and indistinct; below this fold the skin on chin, breast, abdomen and limbs smooth except for a strongly granular distinctly limited area on ventral femoral region; two prominent granules below anus; a transverse fold across the breast between insertion of arms more or less connected with a lateral abdominal fold, which curves across the posterior abdomen, forming a disk; a small diagonal fold running back from edge of disk to pubic region; limbs not especially long, the tibia 12.5 mm. is distinctly longer than the femur 10.1 mm.; from heel to tip of longest toe 19 mm.; an elongate sharply defined inner metatarsal tubercle, and a smaller rounded outer; subarticular tubercles strongly defined save under the last distal joint; heel tubercular with a distinct fold; rows of small tubercles below the metatarsals; tips of digits not dilated, the terminal phalanx (bone) pointed, somewhat clawlike; no webs present or only vestiges; two large palmar tubercles; an elongate inner at base of thumb, and a larger rounded basal tubercle with an anterior extension; first row of subarticular tubercles strongly defined; the first finger longer than second by the length of the last phalanx. . . . The measurements are, head and body, 25 mm.; foreleg, 13 mm., hindleg, 40 mm.

"The openings of the choanae are well back from tip of snout—2.5 mm.—their entire outline plainly visible; vomerine teeth on two triangular raised patches, separated by slightly more than half their greatest width; they are between and almost wholly behind choanae and border the raised eye sockets" (E. H. Taylor, Tex., 1932, pp. 244–245).

**Voice:** "The call of the male was repeated at about one second intervals at the height of rapidity, and resembled the plunk-plunk of a drop of water falling from a cave roof into a quiet pool below" (S. Mulaik, Tex., 1937, p 73).

**Breeding:** "The finding of tadpoles, transforming young and a frothy egg mass on June 8, 1935, immediately following heavy rains ten miles northwest of Edinburg, Texas, closed some gaps in the knowledge of the life history of this amphibian. The egg mass containing 86 yellow eggs was found in a rounded excavation about 4 cm. in diameter and 3 cm. deep at the base of a grass hummock a foot from the water edge and several inches higher than the water level.

"These eggs, around which no hyaline sheath could be discerned, measured 1.5 mm. in diameter. Within 40 hours after the eggs were laid, the young hatched. And were practically invisible except for two dark eye spots and the yellow yolk sack. Several hours later light brown pigmentation appeared. The emerging tadpoles measured (in mm.) 6.6 in total length, 2.3 in body length and 1 5 in width. Their external gills remained approximately 20 hours after emergence. They were apparently two branches arising near the same spot; the anterior branch was the larger, measuring about 1 mm. in length.

"The newly hatched young rested much on their sides or even on their backs on the bottom of the aquaria and every few minutes indulged in violent squirmings which brought them toward the water surface. Twenty-four hours after hatching, the tadpoles measured 8.1 mm. in total length, and more pigmentation was noted On the second day the young were observed to feed apparently on algae and diatoms, and their measurements were as follows (in mm.): total length 9.3; body length 3.3; body width 2.

"On the third day measurements of 11 mm. in total length were recorded and in general the growth appeared rapid. The intestinal coil was now clearly visible through the transparent abdominal wall. The animal food provided was not accepted before the eighth day at which time the tadpoles began to feed upon termites offered. Later on, as they developed, the tadpoles readily fed upon other insects and crushed snails.

"On July 9 the front legs of one of the tadpoles emerged. The total length of this specimen was 32 mm. or 6 to 8 mm. less than the same measurement for field specimens taken at this stage. The tail decreased rapidly from this date and was gone by July 11, making the tadpole stage about thirty days. These transforming young averaged 16.1 mm. from snout to vent; rear leg 25.1 mm.; hind foot 12.6 mm.; rear leg adflexed brings heel to rear edge of eye; heel to tip of first toe 6.6 mm.; snout to angle of mouth 4.8 mm.; tympanum 2½ times into eye.

"Since numerous transforming young were also found on June 7, and since the first previous heavy rain for many months was about May 2, the tadpole period for the field specimens was judged to be about 30 to 35 days, about the same as for the aquarium raised specimens. These young were hopping about in the grass at the edge of the roadside ditch and were difficult to catch because of their agility. Though adults seemed quite common, they were more difficult to take. Males when calling from their cavities beneath hummocks of grass, left upon discovery and quickly sought shelter elsewhere. It is believed that the males constructed these cavities to be used by the females for the deposition of the eggs" (S. Mulaik, Tex., 1937, pp. 72–73).

**Journal notes:** May 1, 1934, Edinburg, Tex. Mulaik showed me two frogs which are queer. These he said he found northwest of Edinburg. They were under trash and mud. By digging under it they found the frog. In the grass near by they found a female. They sounded like sea lions.

May 3. Trip with Stanley and Dorothy Mulaik northwest of Edinburg, Tex. We stopped beside the road near a ditch or pit where there were many grass clumps. Here earlier, when there was some water in the pit, they had heard the "sea lion" call of *Leptodactylus*. In one clump they had found the male. Today we dug vigorously but it was too dry and no frogs appeared.

**Authorities' corner:**

K. P. Schmidt, Gen., 1928, pp. 38–39.
S. Mulaik, Tex., 1937, pp. 72–73.

## Genus *SYRRHOPHUS* Cope

Map 25

### Camp's Frog

*Syrrhophus campi* Stejneger. Plate LXXXIII; Map 25.

**Range:** Brownsville, Tex. Lower Rio Grande Valley.

**Habitat:** In moist earth under board pile, brick pile, stones, or similar shelter.

**Size:** Adults, $\frac{5}{8}$–1 inch (15.0–25.5 mm.).

The largest we have seen is a ripe female 25.5 mm. A collection of 13 adults taken April 28, 1925, in Mr. Camp's board-pile station range from 15–24 mm., the average 19 mm., the mode 19 mm. A series of 9 taken by Mr. Camp (USNM nos. 52372-80) range from 16–23 mm. Another series of 10 specimens taken by Mr. Camp (MCZ nos. 10277-86) range from 15–25 mm.

TABLE OF MEASUREMENTS (MM.)

| | *Syrrhophus campi* | | | *Syrrhophus marnockii* | |
|---|---|---|---|---|---|
| | USNM | C.U. | C.U. | C.U. | C.U. |
| No. | 52291 | 1277 | 1379 | 1271 | 1382 |
| Sex | | | Ripe ♀ | ♂ | |
| Length | 20.0 | 22.5 | 25.5 | 22.5 | 26.0 |
| Head to tympanum | 8.0 | 8.0 | 9.0 | 9.5 | 10.5 |
| Head to angle of mouth | 7.5 | 6.5 | 7.0 | 8.0 | 8.0 |
| Width of head | 7.5 | 7.5 | 9.5 | 8.0 | 9.0 |
| Snout | 4.0 | 3.5 | 4.0 | 4.5 | 5.0 |
| Eye | 4.0 | 4.0 | 4.0 | 4.5 | 3.5 |
| Interorbital space | 3.0 | 3.0 | 3.5 | 3.5 | 3.5 |
| Upper eyelid | 2.0 | 2.0 | 2.0 | 2.5 | 2.5 |
| Tympanum | 2.5 | 2.5 | 2.5 | 2.0 | 2.0 |
| Intertympanic space | 7.0 | 6.5 | 7.5 | 7.5 | 7.5 |
| Internasal space | 2.0 | 2.5 | 2.5 | 2.5 | 3.0 |
| Forelimb | 13.0 | 13.5 | 13.5 | 15.5 | 17.0 |
| 1st finger | 2.5 | 3.0 | 3.0 | 3.0 | 3.5 |
| 2nd finger | 2.5 | 3.5 | 3.5 | 3.5 | 4.0 |
| 3rd finger | 4.0 | 5.0 | 5.5 | 6.0 | 6.0 |
| 4th finger | 2.5 | 4.5 | 4.5 | 4.5 | 5.0 |
| Hind limb | 27.5 | 31.0 | 31.0 | 31.0 | 34.0 |

| | *Syrrhophus campi* | | | *Syrrhophus marnockii* | |
|---|---|---|---|---|---|
| | USNM | C.U. | C.U. | C.U. | C.U. |
| Tibia | 10.0 | 10.0 | 11.5 | 12.0 | 12.5 |
| Foot with tarsus | 14.0 | 13.0 | 16.0 | 15.0 | 14.5 |
| Foot without tarsus | 9.5 | 9.0 | 10.0 | 8.5 | 7.5 |
| 1st toe | 3.0 | 2.5 | 3.0 | 2.5 | 2.5 |
| 2nd toe | 4.5 | 4.0 | 4.5 | 4.0 | 4.0 |
| 3rd toe | 6.0 | 6.0 | 7.5 | 6.0 | 7.0 |
| 4th toe | 9.5 | 9.0 | 10.0 | 8.5 | 7.5 |
| 5th toe | 5.5 | 5.5 | 6.0 | 5.0 | 6.0 * |

* Hind foot in rather poor shape.

**General appearance:** This form is very similar to *Syrrhophus marnockii*, and belongs to a Mexican genus. It is a grayish olive frog, with scattered dark spots on the back, with a dark band from the nostril through the eye, and with dark crossbars on the legs. The skin is finely granular. The nose is pointed.

**Color:** Brownsville, Tex., April 28, 1925. Upper parts grayish olive; pale smoke gray from eye to eye; hair brown or benzo brown, fuscous, or black vitta in front of eye meeting fellow on snout. This line goes through the eye, over the tympanum, above the shoulder insertion onto body, or may be broken at tympanum's rear edge and continue backward as broken spots. These spots may go almost to groin or stop in middle of side. Sometimes on back where a lateral fold normally would be is a broken longitudinal black line. On the back are scattered fuscous black or hair brown spots. Femur with one or two obscure spots on front. In rear, uniform light grayish olive; tibia with two or three rather prominent crossbars, interspace vetiver green. On sides of body are elliptic flecks of white or pallid brownish drab, which continue to below eye or farther forward; one or two of these spots are just below and behind tympanum and sometimes some on side of face are light yellow-green. Another specimen has, starting from near vent, a row of black spots or one line on side of back halfway to shoulder. Hind legs barred and spotted on femur and tibia with black and isabella color, which become white or pallid brownish drab spots on foot and toes. Under parts of breast back of arm insertion and forward part of belly are solid pale yellow-green. Blood vessel shows through its very middle. Lower belly and rest of under parts are pale purplish vinaceous to light purplish vinaceous. Forearm is spotted with white spots, brachium with prominent light greenish yellow and dark spots or the light green-yellow may become, in some, dark olive-buff or deep olive-buff. A female has few if any dark spots on the back. Iris is light greenish yellow above and deep chrome, with one vermiculated line of brownish through it; in the rear it is solid black below and in front it is black with light greenish yellow specks; pupil elliptical.

Plate LXXXIII. *Syrrhophus campi* (×1⅛). 1–8. Adults.

Plate LXXXIV. *Syrrhophus marnockii* (×1). 1–6. Adults.

**Structure:** Small, delicate, flat in body; a blood vessel visible down the middle of the belly; fingers and toes long and slender with prominent tubercles, which viewed from the side appear saw-toothed; forearms well developed; tips of fingers expanded and truncate; toes less so; at least one light-colored tubercle just back of angle of mouth, and near the lower rear margin of the tympanum; often a collection of tubercles in this region or an oblique row to the arm insertion. Wrist extends to tip of muzzle. In alcohol, the sides and upper parts of hind and fore limbs seem to be covered with little round white spots amongst the punctae.

**Voice:** This frog gives a brief cricketlike chirp, but with a whistle. It is not a continued call, but often consists of only one or two notes which can be heard a few yards away.

April 28, 1925. Early in the morning went to the board pile station. Heard one chirp over in the west shed, one or two more chirping in a crack in the brick wall near the ground. Heard several in the board pile.

June 17, 1930, Brownsville, Tex. They are a dooryard, front-porch, or garden friend, cheerful as a cricket. The note may be one *tick* or two or three *ticks,* these well measured. Or the two may be rapid and close together. Sometimes after these comes a cricketlike call.

**Breeding:** This species breeds from April to May. The eggs are few, 6–12, and very large, the egg yolks about 1/8 inch (3.0–3.5 mm.). Larval development is probably within the egg. The smallest frogs we have seen in collections range 1/5–5/16 inch (5.0–8.5 mm.).

April 28, 1925, at Brownsville, Tex. We secured a good series of these little frogs. One female contained very large eggs.

May 5, Helotes, Tex. This evening about 5:30 P.M. I looked at the Brownsville *Syrrhophus campi* to compare with our lone *S. marnockii.* Lo and behold, a male was holding a female in inguinal amplexation. The fists met. One finger reached across the thigh and the other across the lower belly. The male is more spotted; the female almost without spots.

May 6. Tonight we had company. When I showed them the *S. campi* specimens, there were three in one embrace, one above another. Each of the upper two had an inguinal embrace.

A ripe female taken April 28, 1925, has six or seven very large ovarian eggs well advanced. These egg yolks range from 3.0–3.5 mm. in diameter, most of them about 3 mm.

The very few large yolked eggs and the very small frogs seem to confirm the opinion of Drs. Stejneger and Barbour and Messrs. R. D. Camp and A. C. Weed that the larval development is carried through in the egg.

A lot of 10 small frogs sent to Dr. Stejneger by Mr. Camp measured 6.5, 7.5, 7.5, 9, 9.5, 9.5, 10, 10, 11.5 mm. Others equally small were seen in Mr. Camp's collection. The American Museum has 3 specimens (7.5–9.0 mm.). The Museum of Comparative Zoology has 18 small specimens: one 5 mm., one 6 mm., six 6.5 mm., seven 7 mm., one 7.5 mm., one 8 mm., and one 8.5 mm. (5–8.5 mm.).

**Journal notes:** April 27, 1925. Mr. Camp of Brownsville, Tex., took me to the type locality. It was in a small back yard of a private residence in the center of the city. In the rear of the house was a laundry, the floor of which was close to the ground. Against the rear of the house were two small piles of brick, each of which was no more than 2–3 feet across and 1½–2 ft. high. The ground was moderately moist there. Mr. Camp said, "Move these bricks and you will find them." He warned me to grab quickly but I was not quick enough for the first one. I had turned over two or three small piles of bricks and become quite discouraged when I espied another under the shade of a little fig tree. Presently I caught my first one. The associates of these creatures are sow bugs, ants, snails, and spiders. Something jumped in a hole; all I got was the impression of the jump. In another case there was a jump under a board which was under the brick pile. Saw 12 or 15, but all I captured were four adults—17 mm., 20 mm., 24 mm., 24 mm.—and a half-grown one 12 mm. in length. Only a keen collector would have discovered this new species.

April 28. It certainly seems as if they come out to the edge of the board pile at dusk or in the evening. Under one square board 1 ft. or 1½ ft. found four at the edge of the pile. Do they feed at night? Someone said they did not want to lose them all because they fed when mosquitoes do and fed on mosquitoes.

April 29. Went to the board pile at 9:30 A.M.—mighty hot. Once or twice while we were moving the pile, we heard the chirp of this species. Beneath this pile is an old cistern, now partially filled with bricks and dirt. It is very moist in this cistern, but no water. We saw two or three frogs in amongst the bricks. We moved about two-thirds of the pile, secured eight or nine frogs. We saw no signs of eggs. One we caught rather harshly gave up a lot of cockroach eggs. These he wouldn't need to feed on at night. We didn't find any of the very little ones, either in the board pile or the yard. These frogs were very quick, leaping the instant they are exposed. They are very flat and, like the robber frog, have the forearm well developed. When under board or cover, they often crawl along.

June 16, 1930. Walked around Brownsville about 11–12 P.M. Was sure the cheerful chirp I heard in many yards was *Syrrhophus campi.*

June 17. About 5 P.M. went over to the board pile station. The board pile which Camp, Weed, and we have successively moved and put back again is gone, but Mr. O. P. Hacker who owns it (corner Washington and 15th Street, Brownsville, Tex.) said there are frogs in the same old place. Mr. A. Holm tells me this area was General Zachary Taylor's old stables. Went into a shed near the old place. Began turning over debris, sticks, wet papers, iron pieces, and clothes. Under these the little frogs were revealed. The first two I lost. Some appeared quite "yellowish green" or old gold with spots. They can crawl rapidly. Most of the specimens were quite dark. In various places while at the task I heard their pleasant notes. They are quick to find a crack in the wall or other cover. Where the old board pile was, now bricks are in a pile. These I didn't move but in the pile were frogs chirping. Took several small frogs. One very tiny.

June 19. Mr. Rebb's palm grove. Arrived at 7. Palm grove flooded In palm grove are plenty of *S. campi* near its unflooded edge. Others sound as if in deeply flooded parts. Are they temporarily on boles of trees, on large palm fans, or in a litter of palm leaves at the surface? Surely this species is not scarce. It is common.

May 2, 1934, Harlingen, Tex. Mr. and Mrs. L. Irby Davis say they have plenty of small frogs under their plant boxes. They are *S. campi*. Saw several of them at the edge of their rear lawn.

**Authorities' corner:**

L. Stejneger, Tex., 1915, p. 132.

## Gaige's Frog

*Syrrhophus gaigeae*. Map 25.

**Range:** "Type from the Basin, Chisos Mountains, Brewster County, Texas No. 27361 Field Museum of Natural History Collected July 24, 1937, by Walter L. Necker . .

"The sixteen paratypes agree well with the additional specimens which were taken in the Basin and one from Pulham Canyon by the junior author. Ten additional specimens from Juniper Canyon were collected by Mrs Helen T. Gaige . . " (Schmidt and Smith, Tex., 1944, p. 80).

**Habitat:** After our examination of the Gaige material of the University of Michigan some 15 years ago we wrote: "The Gaiges [Dr. F. K. and Mrs. Helen Thompson] became very familiar with this species while they were collecting in the Chisos Mountains, Texas. They came to know its nocturnal habits and its notes and collected a good series of adults." How appropriate that in 1944 the authors Schmidt and Smith "named [this frog] for Mrs. Helen T. Gaige, in order to associate her name with the herpetological exploration of the Chisos Mountains, in which she had a pioneer part."

**Size:** Adults 21–28 mm. Mrs. Gaige's ten, collected 15 years earlier, we made 21–31 mm, i.e., slightly lower than our and Schmidt and Smith's range for *S. marnockii*.

**General appearance:** "Closely allied to *Syrrhopus marnockii*, from which it is distinguished by smaller size, wider head, and vermiculate instead of spotted dorsal pattern. . . . These range in length from 21 to 28 mm, compared to 25 to 35 mm. in *marnockii;* the ratio of width of head to body length is 0.40 in seventeen *gaigeae* and 0.36 in twenty *marnockii*. The paratypes agree with the type in vermiculation and diffuseness of the dorsal pattern" (K. P. Schmidt and T. F. Smith, Tex, 1944, p. 80).

**Color:** "Pale brown above, with dark brown reticulation; under surfaces uniform very pale yellow; limb with broad dark crossbars" (same).

**Structure:** "*Syrrhopus gaigeae* sp. nov. . . . Description of type.—Habitus of *Syrrhopus marnockii*, head wider than body, its width equal to the distance from snout to posterior border of tympanum; snout long, the nostril close to the tip; canthus rounded; length of eye much less than its distance from the nostril, about equal to the diameter of the tympanum, which is very distinct; heels overlapping; heel reaching midway between eye and tip of snout; disks of two outer fingers much wider than those of inner fingers; disks of toes small; first finger about equal to second; metacarpal, metatarsal, and subdigital tubercles distinct; skin of back slightly tuberculated; a rounded gland above the insertion of the arm; no glandular fold over tympanum" (same).

**Journal notes:** We have no actual specimens. Once in the Davis Mountains we were sure we saw a *Syrrhophus* disappear under a huge stone and in the same way we were unsuccessful in Devil's River. Is there a wide gap of 250 miles in *Syrrhophus* range or a wide gap in our knowledge? Again, Edwards Plateau to Trans-Pecos needs attention.

**Authorities' corner:** In the account of this species we have used Schmidt and Smith's account almost exclusively for there is little else of record. They write (p. 80):

"The new form is admittedly distinguished from *marnockii* by only trivial characters; it is believed, however, that the differences noted characterize a well isolated population, separated by some 250 miles from the range of *marnockii*, and that these differences indicate that a distinct form is in the process of evolution."

About 1930 we measured two of the University of Michigan specimens, each 28 mm. in length, and compared them with two *S. marnockii* of 28 mm. For the 25 measurements we then made, we found the Tran-Pecos specimens fell within the range of the 25 *S. marnockii* measurements.

We have measured mature *S. marnockii* from 22.55 mm. to 33 mm. and two 28 mm. *S. gaigeae*. We find our measurements are recorded thus: Width of head in body length 2.66–2.8 in the two *S. gaigeae* specimens within the whole range of 2.66–3.29 in our *S. marnockii* specimens. Or put as the describer does (ratio of width of head to body length) it would be 0.357–0.375 for *S. gaigeae* and 0.30–0.375 for *S. marnockii*. The actual measurements for the width of head in the two *S. gaigeae* are 10.5 mm. and 10 mm.

## Marnock's Frog

*Syrrhophus marnockii* Cope. Plate LXXXIV; Map 25.

**Range:** Helotes near San Antonio, San Marcos, and Austin, to San Angelo, Tex., and Sonora.

**Habitat:** Cracks, crevices, caves in limestone ledges of the hills and ravines.

We made our captures under large flat stones near limestone ledges, one above the wall of a ravine.

**Size:** Adults, 7/8–1 3/5 inches (22.0–39.5 mm.).

Our two specimens were 22.5, 26 mm. (See *S. campi* for detailed measurements.)

The American Museum has one (no. 22664) collected by Byron C. Marshall at Ezell's Cave, San Marcos, Tex., May 12, 1928, which is 24 mm.

The Museum of Comparative Zoology has two specimens (nos. 18527, 18527a) from Helotes, Tex. They measure 22 and 25 mm.

The Baylor University Museum has G. W. Marnock's collection, some adults of which vary from 23–33 mm., and others taken by W. J. Williams in 1927 and 1928. One of these is 31 mm.

**General appearance:** This small, flattened frog has a long flat head, with a broad space between the eyes, which are large and prominent, indicating nocturnal activity. In general color, the back is greenish, spotted with brown, the under parts light-brownish vinaceous, the legs crossbarred. The nostril is far in front of the eyes, which are as far apart as the breadth of the hump. The skin is smooth. There are one or two white or deep colonial buff tubercles below and behind the tympanum.

**Color:** Helotes, Tex., May 5, 1925. General color greenish or olive lake; top of head from forward part of upper eyelid mignonette green or grape green or light yellowish olive, the upper eyelid rainette green and unspotted. In fact whole top of head from upper eyelid forward is unspotted and sharply marked off by the vertical purplish loreal area. The dorsum from upper eyelids backward becomes ecru-olive and the upper parts of forelimbs are the same or lighter, a deep colonial buff. On the upper surface of hind limbs this color changes to olive-ocher, yellow-ocher, old gold, or yellower than any of these three. Spots on back, black, sorghum brown, or vinaceous-brown. The tympanum and across shoulder insertion is light purplish vinaceous. The groin is purplish vinaceous. Underside of hind legs, forelegs, and across breast are light brownish vinaceous. Throat pale grayish vinaceous; sides light brownish vinaceous or pale grayish vinaceous; back of eye, some of tympanum, canthus extending around snout, labial rims, sorghum brown; chin specked with sorghum brown. On sides of body are some white or pallid brownish drab or pale russian blue spots; one or two white or deep colonial buff or chamois tubercles below and behind the tympanum. Belly, pale yellow-green or pale fluorite green; a purplish vinaceous blood vessel down middle of belly divides the color into two parts. Iris dull green-yellow above and below with sorghum brown vermiculations or spots on it, or upper part with one wavy longitudinal line and then small spots; front and rear of pupil dark vinaceous-brown, thus from snout to rear of eye one continuous vitta.

In some alcoholic specimens, the upper parts from head to vent are very finely spotted; and in some of the smaller specimens, the following transverse bars on the hind legs may be indicated, two on the tarsus, two on the tibia, one just below the knee, and two on the femur. On the tibia and femur, one of the two bars may be light-centered.

**Structure:** Small flattened body; eyes prominent, widely separated by broad flat space; fingers and toes long and slender with prominent tubercles, which if viewed from the side give the digits a prominent saw-toothed appearance; tips of fingers are expanded and truncate, toes less so. Wrist of forelimb extends beyond extremity of muzzle. Foot 10–11 mm. Tarsus 6.5 mm. No vomerine teeth.

In several we have seen white tubercles on right and left sides of lower belly, also on rear of femur. Are they natural or parasites?

**Voice:** This is a cricketlike chirp of one or two notes of an instant's duration, possibly followed by a trill of two or three notes.

May 6, 1925, Helotes, Tex. While I was describing this specimen it chirped on three different occasions, and reminded me of the chirping *S. campi* of a week or more ago at Brownsville, Texas.

We searched with flashlights more than once along the muddy bank of Helotes Creek at the flat crossing near Marnock's home for the source of a similar chirp. We thought it might belong to a frog, but search as we would, we could not find the musician. It was back a little from the edge of the water, where the mud was soft, punched by cows, and more or less covered with grassy tussocks. Similarly we searched in Brownsville on Camp Brown grounds for a chirp on the side of a grassy ditch. We had no success.

May 10, Helotes, Tex. On our hill, we went walking at 6 P.M. Nighthawks booming; a few robber frogs calling. Below limestone ledge heard a cricketlike call frequently followed by a trill of two-three notes. A froglike note, *Acris*-like only shorter. Is it Marnock's, in among rocks and oaks?

**Breeding:** Development is probably within the egg and during April and May.

A few of the larger specimens in collections taken in May look to be ripe, and almost all the specimens captured have been secured in that month. We suspect that the month of May is an important part of the breeding period. Eggs not described.

It seems likely that these frogs hatch fully developed from the egg, just as Dr. Stejneger and Dr. Thomas Barbour suggest likely for *S. campi*.

There is probably no free-swimming tadpole and no transformation in that sense. There is no record of a specimen of the small size (5 or 6 mm.) of *S. campi*. The smallest we have seen are two taken by W. J. Williams. They are: Baylor University Museum no. 2185 taken at San Marcos, March 3, 1927, and another, no. 3853, taken at San Marcos, June 1928. Each is 17 mm. in length of body.

**Journal notes:** May 5, 1925, Helotes, Tex. In Helotes Creek Canyon above camp . . . where a side ravine comes in, we were searching for a poinsett's lizard we had seen. . . . About 3–4 feet farther up the side of the canyon was a large, flat, loose stone on a stony slope. I lifted it and a small frog hopped out. I got the impression of a greenish frog. I dropped the stone quickly to see where the leaping frog went but lost it. Then I lifted the stone again, and at first my eye did not espy the second frog. Had it been a Camp's frog it would have leaped. Presently my eye saw a *Syrrhophus*. It is Marnock's frog. It is bigger than Camp's, but much like it.

Our second frog was caught May 10 on Marnock's hill, back of the store at 4 P.M. In the morning it rained hard until 1 P.M.; then we went to Marnock's hill. East of the store one-half mile, found on top of the hill a pebbly place with a few flat stones. A banded gecko and Marnock's frog were under a stone. It was moist, black dirt beneath the stone, and it was in a more or less open place with dwarf oaks about.

June 23, 1930, San Antonio. I left at 8 o'clock for Helotes with Gable and his son, Hugh. They parked their car at a crossing above G. W. Marnock's house. They started up a horseshoe hill I never was on in 1917 or 1925. I suspect this was Marnock's special hill for collecting. His house is in the opening of the horseshoe. After we reached the top, we went down toward a glen where there had been seepage earlier. In this place they had found two Marnock's frogs, which they gave to Mr. Parks to send to General Biological Supply. One of these very frogs we received this spring. Their habitat was much the same as that of those found by us.

**Authorities' corner:**

W. J. Williams, Tex., 1927, p. 7.
J. C. Marr, Gen., 1944, p. 480.

# Family RANIDAE

## Genus *RANA* Linné

Maps 26–36

### Texas Gopher Frog, Southern Crayfish Frog, Southern Gopher Frog

*Rana areolata areolata* Baird and Girard. Plate LXXXV; Map 26.

**Range:** Matagorda Co., Tex., north to McCurtain Co., Oklahoma, and Lafayette Co., Ark.; probably also in extreme northwestern Louisiana (L. Stejneger and T. Barbour, Check List, 1943, p. 53).

**Habitat:** "I saw but one specimen of this frog and collected that on June 18 at the Machine Gun Range, twelve miles out from Camp [Houston, Tex.]. It was a half-grown frog and was hiding under a log at the edge of a pool" (P. H. Pope, Tex., 1919, pp. 97–98).

**Size:** Medium, length 2½–3½ inches (62–90 mm.).

**General appearance:** This is a stocky, medium to large, rather rough-skinned, brownish frog with round dark spots on back and sides, with reticulations of dotted light lines and with prominent dorsolateral folds.

"*Rana areolata*. . . . Appears to be closely allied to *R. halecina* [*pipiens*] and *utricularia*, but the head is larger and the spots of the back are smaller and more numerous Male with an external vocal vesicle on each side behind the angle of the mouth . . ." (G. A. Boulenger, Gen., 1882, p. 41).

According to Cope (Gen., 1889, p. 409), *R v. areolata* has "length of head to posterior tympana three times in total; tympanic disk round; dorsal spots well separated; nostril equidistant between end of muzzle and eye," whereas *R. v. circulosa* has "length of head one third of total; tympanic disk variable, dorsal spots so large as to leave only circles of the light ground-color; nostril nearer eye than end of muzzle in young."

Goin and Netting (Fla., 1940, p. 146) give these contrasting characters. "Head U-shaped in outline when viewed from above; dorsum often smooth, or nearly so; tibia length less than 40 mm. in adults; post-tympanic fold poorly developed; dorso-lateral folds narrow or only slightly raised, or both. . . . *Rana areolata areolata* Baird and Girard. Head orbiculate in outline when viewed above, dorsum rugose, tibia length more than 40 mm. in adults; post-tymphanic fold well developed; dorsolateral folds prominent. . . . *Rana areolata circulosa* Rice and Davis."

Bragg (Okla., 1942a, p. 18) of Oklahoma, which state has both *areolata* and *circulosa,* characterizes them as follows: "Dorsal surface smooth; dorsolateral folds narrow and usually not well developed; legs fairly short (tibiae 40 mm. or less). Distribution, southeastern Oklahoma. *Rana areolata areolata,* Southern Crayfish Frog. Dorsal surface often rugose; dorsolateral folds well developed; leg rather long (tibiae more than 40 mm.). Distribution northeastern Oklahoma. *Rana areolata circulosa* Rice and Davis (Northern Crayfish Frog)."

**Color:** Houston, Tex., from R. H. Vines through the kindness of A. C. Chandler, March 5, 1948. *Three males.* The background of the backs ranges from chalcedony yellow to olive-yellow. In the darkest one there are more speckles on the background, which is deep olive-buff. In two, the heads are much darker than the backs, and the larger spots are inconspicuous there. In one, the head is like the back, the spots clearly showing. The large collapsed vocal sacs are courge green to light-hellebore green. When one frog blew up his pouch to a diameter of ¼ inch, the pattern of spots showed in a dull and dusky manner. The concealed surfaces of hind legs and the groin are suffused with citron yellow to strontian yellow.

In the smallest and lightest frog, the background of back and head is dark olive buff except the snout, which is darker. On the back between dorsolateral folds are three irregular rows of spots of buffy olive, outlined by primrose yellow. On the side are three more irregular rows, but these spots are not completely encircled with light and hence are not so conspicuous. They are light brownish olive on a background of vinaceous-buff to wood brown, which is marked with conspicuous round spots of ivory yellow. The center of the tympanum is marguerite yellow, ivory yellow, or white. The bars on the legs are very prominent, 3 on tibia and 2 on thigh with 1 at the knee, and are colored and outlined like the spots of the back. On the tibia each interspace between bars bears a thin line of light brownish olive. On tarsus and outer edge of foot are 2 bars. The exposed surface of the femur is very spotted but the spots are not outlined and their color is olive-yellow. This spotted pattern is revealed on the venter and on the rear margin of the femur. The ventral surface of the femur is light vinaceous-fawn. The forelimbs are not conspicuously barred, being only irregularly spotted. The under surface is white. The edge of upper jaw from eye backward is mottled, and the rim of lower jaw bears a few dark spots. There is a spot on each eyelid and one on the interorbital space. The eye is large and bulging, the black iris bearing fine dots of zinc orange with the warm buff pupil rim notched below.

In the largest frog, the light spots of the sides are often centered with pin points of black and are raised warts on mounds. Similar wartlike spots cross the rear of the sacral region. The black pin points are so conspicuous on the back that this is a very speckled frog. Between the coastal folds are 5–7 low irregular broken rows of longitudinal folds.

**Structure:** Length of head contained in total length three times. Length of leg to heel equals length to eye or nostril. Tibia longer than femur.

"*Rana areolata,* B. & G. Head very large, sub-elliptical; snout prominent, nostrils situated halfway between its tips and the anterior rim of the eyes, which are proportionally large. The tympanum is spherical, and of medium size; its central portion is yellowish-white, whilst its periphery is black. The body is rather short and stout; the limbs well developed; the fingers and toes very long without being slender. The ground color of the body and head is yellowish-green, marked with dark brown. Besides there are from thirty to fifty brown areolae; margined with a yellowish line. The upper part of the limbs is of the same color as the body, but instead of areolae, transverse bands of brown are seen on the hind ones. The lower part of the head and body is yellowish, with small dusky spots along the margin of the lower jaw, and under the neck. A specimen three inches and a half long was found at Indianola [Texas], and a very small one on the Rio San Pedro of the Gila" (S. F. Baird and C. Girard, Gen., 1852, p. 173). This last frog might well be another form, or did *R. areolata* occur in Arizona? (Note suggestion on p. 516.)

"Skin rough, with elongated warts on back and sides. Lateral folds conspicuous. Tibia ridged lengthwise. No glandular fold along the jaw. A distinct fold over the ear from eye to shoulder. Under and posterior surface of femur granulated. Head large; unusually thick through. Muzzle long; space between eyes greater than width of eyelid; nostrils nearer to the end of the muzzle than to the eye; eyes large; ear half to two-thirds size of eye. Foot with a tarsal fold; webs short (three joints of fourth toe free); inner sole tubercle small, no outer tubercle, tubercles under toe-joints prominent" (M. G. Dickerson, Gen., 1906, pp. 192–193).

**Breeding:** February to June.

"As regards an easy way of capturing Texas gopher frogs, there is no such thing as an easy way in my limited experience with the species. In fact, I captured so few of them and those under conditions of unusual expenditure of energy that even at this date I can remember each individual capture. I have verified my memory by looking up my notes.

"The first is a male captured under circumstances which suggested the mating urge was upon him. The second was observed while feeding on insects under a street light on Main Street, just outside Hermann Park. It was captured after a merry chase that left me rather muddy. I was returning to the Institute when Dr. and Mrs. Chandler stopped their automobile by the curb for a little conversation. The remaining frogs were all captured on February 11, 1930, after a careful stalk of a breeding pool where the frogs were singing. In this case the stalk was performed so slowly that more than an hour was covered in approaching the pool where three clasping pairs were taken. The females extruded their eggs that night. Incidentally these frogs secreted a foamy, sour-smelling material that made my hands itch.

"I think the only means of capturing these frogs with any assurance of success would be to stalk the animals in the breeding pools. I made many unsuccessful attempts to capture these frogs before I approached sufficiently slowly and carefully to get them under the flash light. On land these frogs are very active. My experience suggesting they are even more difficult to capture on land than the southern leopard frog, but in the water they are very slow to move and can be seized easily. However, they are very shy and if one approaches the breeding pool at a normal pace, these frogs are nowhere to be seen when one arrives.

"The pool where I caught the mating pairs was located northwest of the chemistry building, but all that portion of the campus is now in cultivation and I dare say that the pool has been destroyed; the frogs dispersed to other areas. Breeding pools are easily located by the mating song, which is produced after each heavy rain in late January and February The mating song is easily learned, because so far as I could tell it is exactly like the mating song of the most common toad of Houston, namely, *Bufo valliceps*. However, the toad sings in May and June, while the gopher frog sings in the winter" (letter from P. D. Harwood to A. C. Chandler, June 12, 1946).

**Journal notes:** Northeast of Edinburg, Tex., Aug. 3, 1942. Ten or fifteen miles north of Raymondville a dead *Rana pipiens* or *areolata* in the road. Mesquite on either side. A many-spotted frog we could see, and little else. Another frog so crushed I could not tell it

**Authorities' corner:**

M. C. Dickerson, Gen., 1906, p. 193
C. E. Burt and M D. Burt, Tex., 1929a, p 6.
A. N. Bragg and C. C. Smith, Okla., 1943, p. 107.

## Northern Gopher Frog, Gopher Frog, Crayfish Frog, Hoosier Frog, Crawfish Frog, Ring Frog

*Rana areolata circulosa* Davis. Plate LXXXVI; Map 26.

**Range:** "From Rogers and Tulsa counties, Oklahoma, north through eastern Kansas, eastward across central Missouri and Illinois to Benton and Monroe counties, Indiana (possibly to Greene county, Ohio), and southward in the Mississippi Valley through western Kentucky and Tennessee to Pontotoc County, Mississippi" (L. Stejneger and T. Barbour, Check List, 1943, p. 54).

**Habitat:** Old burrows, commonly crayfish burrows in the vicinity of ponds.

In 1910, "Professor La Rue found the frogs in the mammal burrows along the shores of the ponds, as well as in crayfish holes, but it is probable that they were only temporarily occupying the former during the spawning season for we were unable to discover any mammal burrows, either in the vicinity of ponds or elsewhere inhabited by frogs" (C. Thompson, Ill., 1915, p. 6) "The old burrows occupied by crayfish were entirely without chimneys, and were

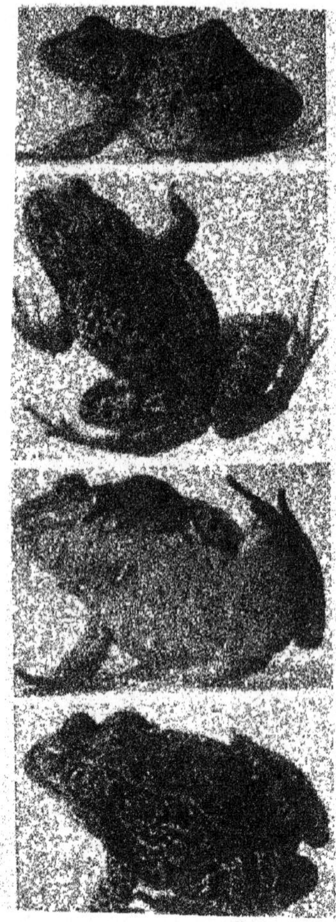

*Plate LXXXV Rana areolata areolata* (X½). Males

*Plate LXXXVI. Rana areolata circulosa.* 1,4. Females (X½). 2. Female (X⅓). 3. Male (X⅓).

approximately round at the entrance, which had a diameter of about three inches. The entrance was more or less overhung with grass, and at one side was a small bare space about six inches in diameter. . . . The burrows occupied by frogs differed but slightly from those just described" (same, p. 3).

"The habitat is, in general, low meadowland, which is sufficiently moist to harbor crayfishes. The burrows of the latter are necessary, apparently, for the well-being of this frog, which lives in them during the day. . . . Holes with funnels, of course, can be inhabited by nothing but crayfish; but frequently or

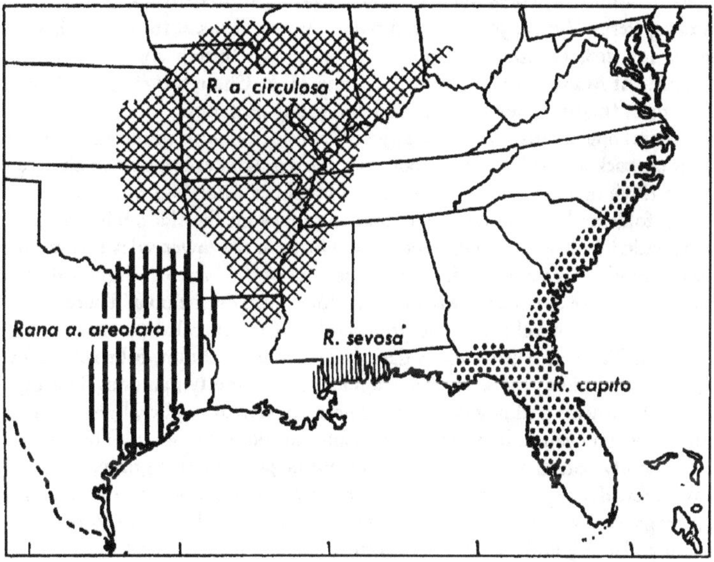


*Map 26*

usually they have nothing but the smooth platform in front—always in this case they are inhabited by frogs. These platforms serve to prevent grass from growing at the entrance and provide mounds upon which the frogs sit at night or early in the morning to catch stray insects" (H. M. Smith, Kans., 1934, pp. 480–481).

"During the postbreeding season *circulosa* resorts to crawfish burrows and, therefore, is not found in streams or ponds. Dr. Wilfred Crabb and Mr. George Wiseman collected four specimens on May 6, 1942 at Stockport, Van Buren County. The following habitat description is quoted from their field notes: 'The frogs were found sitting near the openings of holes into which they retreated when disturbed. They were extricated by fish hooks attached to the ends of slender sticks. The holes were apparently vacated crayfish burrows.

One was three feet deep with 18 inches of water in the bottom, another was 28 inches with 14 inches of water. Two frogs were usually present in the same burrow although the large one [adult male; snout to vent length 67 mm.] was alone. There were about 12 holes within a radius of 50 feet and all contained frogs. They were located on a short-grazed bluegrass pasture with a slope of 7 per cent. The day was cloudy and cool (about 40°F.) with a fresh west wind.' Another specimen taken in a similar situation the same day in an adjoining section was an adult female 101 mm. in length" (R. M. Bailey, Ia., 1943, p. 350).

**Size:** Adults, 2½–4½ inches. Males, 63–104 mm. Females, 75–113 mm. Among Percy Viosca, Jr.'s material from Ottawa, Kansas, from Gloyd, were males 105, 108, 111 mm. and one 92 mm., having thumb and sacs well developed. At Monroe, La., P. Viosca, Jr., and H. B. Chase had caught a female of 87 mm. (maturity not certain) and one young 46.5 mm.

**General appearance:** This is a large brownish frog with round dark brown spots on back and sides. These spots may vary in size, as large or small. They are in three or four rows between and sometimes extending onto the dorsolateral folds and several irregular rows or groups on the sides. The spots are surrounded with grayish white borders, which on the lower sides become the background color between the spots. The skin of the back is roughened with tubercles. There are one or two long glandular folds on the tibia. There is considerable greenish yellow in the groin and on the concealed portions of legs and feet. There is a prominent dark bar on the brachium, a broad, fleshy, spotted band along the jaw, and a light center to the tympanum. The light color on the arms and jaw is grayish. There are several smaller, light-rimmed, dark spots on eyelids, between the eyes and on top of the snout. The legs are prominently barred with brown and cream or gray. In this group, the frogs have a few dark spots just forward of the arm insertion. When cold and wet, the frogs were very dark. The vocal sacs of the males are large and conspicuous when collapsed, and bluish gray-green in color. When expanded they form large balls on either side above the arms. (When plowed out in early spring they are so dark as to be almost blackish.)

**Color:** Calhoun, Ill., from G. A. Nicholas, Feb. 27, 1930. *Male*. Down the back between dorsolateral folds are three rows of spots. Back of the hump mainly two rows. Spots mummy brown, raw umber, brownish olive, or clove brown. These are encircled by thin lines of ivory yellow or cartridge buff or marguerite yellow. This color merges into interstices between spots. These interstices are covered with small dots of the four browns given above for big spots, producing in effect a light grayish olive or grayish olive. This color on top of forearm becomes light mineral gray. It is grayish olive on hind legs. The femur, tibia, and tarsus have mummy brown or one of the other three browns in their conspicuous crossbars. The interspaces between bars are like interstices of back, but with small partial crossbars of the darker color. On sides are at least two rows of large spots; mummy brown bar on forearm insertion. Underside of forefeet and hind feet pale vinaceous-drab or light grayish vinaceous. Under parts, throat, breast, belly, and lower sides pale cinnamon-pink or cartridge buff (before molting it was colonial buff or deep colonial buff). Same color on fore half of venter of hind legs and underside of forearms. Underside of femur, down middle, pale vinaceous-drab or light grayish vinaceous. Top of foot and tarsus yellow ocher or honey yellow. Wash of picric yellow on rear of arm, axil, groin, front of thigh, and rear of tibia. On rear of thighs and somewhat in front of thighs the color becomes oil yellow. Edge of lower eyelid bluish gray-green or parula blue. Pupil horizontal, broken in middle below. Over pupil obscure longitudinal band of xanthine orange in front and rear or with considerable empire or pinard yellow. Pupil has rim of this yellow. Iris in general black. Vocal sacs tea green to celandine green.

*Female.* Encircling light lines around large dorsal spots, general interstices, interstices of hind legs, and light spot in tympanum, pale olive-buff or tilleul buff, on sides becoming even vinaceous-buff. The dorsolateral fold is tilleul buff or vinaceous-buff. This interstitial color is with many fine dots of olive brown or deep olive. The large dorsal spots, three rows forward and two backward of the hump, are clove brown or fuscous. These spots are smaller on sides and become natal brown. The crossbars on hind legs and spots on forelimbs are like spots of dorsum. Spot across arm insertion in front and one just beyond insertion on arm in axil. Side of head, edge of lower jaw, and venter ahead of arm insertion with small olive-brown or clove brown spots, giving side of head a speckled appearance Axil, rear of arm, groin, front of thigh, and rear of thigh greenish yellow or green-yellow. On reticulated rear of femur this becomes oil yellow or courge green. Dark color is fuscous Front of tibia and top of foot cream-buff. Under parts are pale pinkish buff or marguerite yellow. Thigh on underside has same light grayish vinaceous of male. Also same color on underside of foot and hand. Iris black or fuscous. Pupil rim vinaceous-tawny or vinaceous-fawn. Over pupil, a horizontal band or dash of these vinaceous colors. Same color in fine dots on lower iris and outer part of upper iris.

**Structure:** Large; skin warty on back and sides; head shorter, mouth smaller, and hind limbs longer than *R. capito;* males having prominent, collapsed, pleated vocal sacs resting outside like folds of skin and continuing along the sides as folds past the axil, the middle of the sac being back of the tympanum; thumb somewhat enlarged in the male; eye conspicuous, but small in relation to snout; fourth toe very long; a thickened or fleshy band along the edge of the jaw. On the breast, the arm insertion with the pectoral girdle is conspicuously indicated by a triangle of much thinner skin, the base at arm's insertion, the point at the pectoral region; waist slightly broader, thus making whole form less wedge-shaped than *R capito.*

In Jordan's *Manual of Vertebrates of the Northern United States . . .* (2d ed., rev. and enl., Chicago, 1878), page 355, we have this description: "*R. circu-*

*losa,* Rice and Davis (sp. nov.) Hoosier Frog. Head broad; body, head and sides with the ground color largely predominating, and with narrow rings of a greenish slate color, which becomes larger and more irregular posteriorly; hind legs black, crossed with irregular lines of yellowish slate color; fore limbs similarly marmorate; tympanum black with pale ring; below chiefly yellowish white; toes very long; size medium, L. 3½. Benton Co., Indiana, lately discovered by Mr. E. F. Shipman (abridged from Mr. Rice's Notes)."

"There is a strong dorsolateral glandular ridge on each side, and between these there are from six to eight narrow glandular folds not so much broken up as in the *R. a. aesopus,* but readily becoming indistinct in alcohol. The dorsolateral fold extends nearly to the groin. Below it the sides are crowded with longitudinal glandular folds, more or less broken up. . . .

"Since the above was written I have been able, through the kindness of Professor Forbes, of the university at Champaign, Ill., to examine the type specimen of Messrs. Rice and Davis. It differs considerably from the specimens above described, as follows: The muzzle is not protuberant, so that the nostril is equidistant between the end of the muzzle and the eye, as in the subspecies *areolata.* The tympanic disk is nearly round, and its long diameter is three-fourths that of the eye. This specimen has twice the bulk. In other respects it does not differ. A very strong glandular thickening of the skin extends from the eye above the tympanum, and then descends posterior to it. The eyelid also is thickened.

"Two specimens (No. 13828) from Olney, Ill., also received since the above description was written, explain these discrepancies. The larger of the two agrees with the type in all respects, but the smaller, which about equals the type in dimensions, has the elongate muzzle of the small ones that I have described above. In both the tympana are three-fourths the orbit, and in neither is it decidedly oval" (E. D. Cope, Gen., 1889, pp. 413–415).

**Voice:** "A loud trill, hoarser than that of the leopard frog and pitched somewhat higher than that of *Rana catesbeiana*" (C. Thompson, Mich., 1915a, p. 6). To Mr. Ackert, the call sounds "half-strangled" as if it had its mouth half out of water.

"The call, from near at hand, is of the general type of that of *Rana palustris,* but is much louder and quite distinct in timbre. It may best be described as a deep guttural, snoring sound, with a slight upward crescendo at the end. It is given at intervals of perhaps ten to fifteen seconds, though we did not time it" (H. P. Wright and G. S. Myers, Ind., 1927, p. 174).

"The song of *Rana areolata* was most often heard after dark although on one occasion several were singing and splashing in a roadside pond about an hour after sundown. The voice of these frogs does not have the prolonged resonance of that of the bullfrog, *R. catesbeiana,* although it is almost as deep and seems to have even more carrying power. The song most frequently heard is a low-pitched, drawn-out guttural note which may be suggested by the syllables "wurr-r-r-up" accented on the last. It is repeated several times, either from the surface of the water or from the shore, at more or less regular intervals, varying in frequency. The vocal sacs of the males are lateral and relatively much larger than those of *R. pipiens*. When singing they are distended until they resemble miniature balloons, each one almost as large as the head itself" (H. K. Gloyd, Kan., 1928, pp. 117–118).

"A deeply sonorous and resonant 'w-a-a-ah'; loud and of exceptional carrying quality. From mixed choruses this stands out above the others; clearly audible for over half a mile. The strong choruses are heard in April" (R. M. Bailey, Ia., 1944, p. 17).

**Breeding:** March to mid-May. The National Museum (no. 48697) has a ripe female of 103 mm. taken at Montgomery, Miss., on March 9, 1911, by Mr. Parker. (See Gloyd in "Authorities' corner.") We ourselves have not seen the egg masses, but they are doubtless plinthlike like those of *Rana capito*.

On April 11, 1926, near Bloomington, Ind., Herman P. Wright and George S. Myers found 17 egg masses of this species in a small pond not more than 90 feet in diameter.

"I have found these frogs singing in numerous choruses during the last of March and first of April in southeastern Kansas. Near Lawrence they were collected while breeding on April 27, 1931. In 1933 mated pairs were collected at the same locality on April 21. Gloyd . . . states that they were last heard singing in 1927 in Franklin county on April 9; the first specimens were taken March 11. . . .

"Temporary pools by roadsides and in pastures are chosen in which to breed and lay eggs. Males sing at the edge of the pools or out in the water, and, although they cease singing frequently upon the approach of a light, yet they will remain above water until splashing about or other noises cause them to duck beneath the water or to sidle back into their holes. In some pools it frequently was possible to capture them after they disappeared by passing the hands back and forth over the mud and grass at the bottoms of pools, where they remain hidden until further disturbed or danger is past. A number of specimens placed in a tank with three or four inches of water illustrate well this protective instinct. Upon being startled by some sudden activity outside, they duck to the bottom of the water, close their eyes, push their heads down against the bottom of the tank, and propel themselves blindly forward by slow alternate or coincident strokes of the hind legs, holding the front legs against the body. Such actions in pools on soft earth would very quickly cover them from sight" (H. M. Smith, Kans., 1934, pp. 479–480).

"Laid in large plinth-like masses about 5–6 inches in diameter in shallow water about stems of grass, etc. Probably about 7000 eggs are in each mass. Individual eggs are rather distinct. The outer membrane measures about 4.5–5.0 mm. in diameter, the inner about 3.15, and the vitellus about 2.46–2.50. The vitellus is considerably larger than in *pipiens*, and the space between the inner and outer membrane is greater than in the latter species" (same, p. 479).

The transformation time is the first week of July (H. P. Wright and G. S. Myers, Ind., 1927, p. 174). Size, 20–30 mm. Herman P. Wright and George S. Myers were to have described the tadpoles. We had tadpoles of this species from Antioch College, Yellow Springs, but they were without eyes, etc., i.e., experimental specimens. A number of tadpoles secured 4 miles north of Bloomington, Ind., April 12, 1940, by H. T. Gier were loaned to us by Mittleman. They measured 39.5–51.0 mm., the bodies being 20–22 mm. Most of them were approaching transformation. Three transformed and transforming ones were 20, 20, and 25.5 mm.

The Museum of Comparative Zoology has two specimens (no. 1478), collected in Michigan by J. G. Shute, 1863, which are slightly past transformation. They are 33 and 34.5 mm.

"Sexual maturity is apparently attained at an age of not less than three years. Three early spring collections of overwintering tadpoles show no sign of approaching metamorphosis, but since a unimodal size dispersion is evident . . . [a table gives overwintering tadpoles ranging from 31–63 mm.], transformation may be assumed to occur during the ensuing summer. Three frogs taken by Crabb and Wiseman on May 6 were immature; they have snout to vent lengths of 48 (♀), 49 (♀), and 51 (♂) mm., and are judged to be two years old, having transformed during the preceding summer. The adult male 67 mm. in length taken with them is presumably a year older; it is possible, however, that he transformed early in the summer of his first year and was mature at two years of age. Since this is easily the smallest adult taken it is believed the bulk of breeding specimens are at least four years old" (R. M. Bailey, Ia., 1943, p. 350).

**Journal notes:** Sept. 11, 1929. At 11 A.M. went with Dr. Fernandus Payne to the *Rana areolata* pond found near Bloomington, Ind., in 1926 by H. P. Wright and G. Myers. It is the only pond in that vicinity in which they have found this frog breeding. They discovered it by hearing the frog chorus. The pond is ¼ mile from the road. There are cultivated fields (cornfields) on one side of it and meadow on another. On one side is a hedgerow of a few willows and oaks, and near by are a few shrubs, but in the main the pond is open. It was dry in the summer and the bottom mud cracked into blocks. A recent rain formed a small pool in the center. We could not tell where in the surrounding country the *Rana a. circulosa* would be likely to have gone. We went on to Olney, Ill., and south to Calhoun to look at those habitats. There we looked up Lee Ackert, who went out as a young lad with the Thompson girls, when they were working on this form. He took us to their farm a mile or so east of Calhoun. Here in a field that contained an open pond we searched for the characteristic holes these frogs occupy. He said the holes were 2½–3 inches across. We found nothing promising in or near the pond. The fields were so thickly grown up to grass and pasture weeds that we found very few holes. The boy dug up two or three but had no luck. He said he has plowed them up and cut them in plowing. Thought possibly a field not worked this year would be better. Went to a pond a short distance north and showed us places there where the "girls" found them.

Mr. Nicholas reported plowing up several in the spring. We sought him 1½ miles southeast of Calhoun. He took us down his lane where 2 or 3 weeks ago he saw a *Rana a. circulosa* at the entrance of a 2–3-inch hole. We dug and dug; finally at about 4 feet we reached water level. He reached in several times and was nipped twice. Proved a crayfish. Did he drive out the frog? Went to house and field on opposite side of road. In a lower portion near woods, which he tells us is covered with water until late in April, we searched for likely holes. Found one but it was filled in. Mr. Nicholas told us that sometimes two or three frogs may be in one such hole with heads near the opening. Sometimes they appear to be in colonies when plowed up. They appear quite blackish when broken out and look almost the color of a catfish. They work down into the dirt again after being disturbed. They are large, heavy frogs, clumsy and slow-moving. His place is near the source of Sugar Creek. Sugar Creek Prairie, a known habitat, is southwest of him about 2½–3 miles toward Parkersburg.

During three warm days at the end of February, 1930, he caught and sent us four frogs, one male, three females, from this prairie. To secure one of these he told us he dug down 5 feet.

**Authorities' corner:**

G. E. Beyer, La., 1900, p. 37.
F. A. Hartman, Kans., 1907, pp. 226–229.
J. Hurter, Mo., 1911, pp. 116–117.
H. K. Gloyd, Kans., 1928, pp. 117–118.

## Oregon Red-legged Frog, Western Wood Frog

*Rana aurora aurora* (Baird and Girard). Plate LXXXVII; Map 27.

**Range:** British Columbia, Washington, Oregon, south along the coast of California to Eureka.

**Habitat:** "Oregon and Washington specimens were taken among the ferns and dense vegetation in the forests of the coastal belt" (J. R. Slevin, B.C., 1928, p. 129).

"This frog is abundant in the region of Portland throughout the year except in December, when all of our frogs are in hibernation. It is an inhabitant of the deep forests, resting under the cool sword ferns of this region during the day and often coming forth at night in search of food" (S. G. Jewett, Jr., Ore., 1936, p. 71).

"It is usually found in the ferns and vegetation of the woods, or in nearby wet areas" (K. Gordon, Ore., 1939, p. 62).

March 16, 1942, Clam Beach, Calif. In a pussy-willow pond took an *Ambystoma*-like mass of eggs. In a pond just back of beach dune behind a eucalyptus cover took several *Ambystoma* masses well along and one *Rana aurora* subsp. Saw two *Rana aurora* on logs and one gave a *Rana* catlike call when it leaped. They are not very fast but live among bad tangles of pussies and logs and tussocks.

**Size:** Adults, 1¾–3½ inches. Males, 44–63 mm. Females, 52–87 mm. Greatest size less than *Rana aurora draytonii*. Storer (Calif., 1925, p. 231) had males 50–58 mm. and females 57–76 mm. in length.

**General appearance:** Distinctly a wood frog, the mask is evident in many. It is medium in size, moderately stout, and smooth-skinned. The head is narrowly oval from above, the profile thin. The back is brownish or olive, frequently with inky spots. Sometimes a few of these spots have light centers. Frequently there is a dark bar across the upper arm. There is red on the sides of the body and on the concealed parts of the legs, feet, and underarms. The light line along the upper jaw ends in a fold at the corner of the mouth. Groin mottled.

March 31, 1942. J R. Slater compared three Ranas of Oregon and Washington.

Mottled red, yellow, and green in groin; *R. aurora aurora.*

Mottled somewhat in groin and lower sides yellowish, cream; *R. cascadae.*

Not mottled in groin; groin red; *R. pretiosa.*

April 2, Longview, Wash. Just east of Stella, at basaltic falls beside road, next the water's edge took one small *R. aurora aurora*. At west edge of falls in big cavities among large rocks and logs took five *R. aurora aurora,* not a fast frog nor hard to catch, yet it is

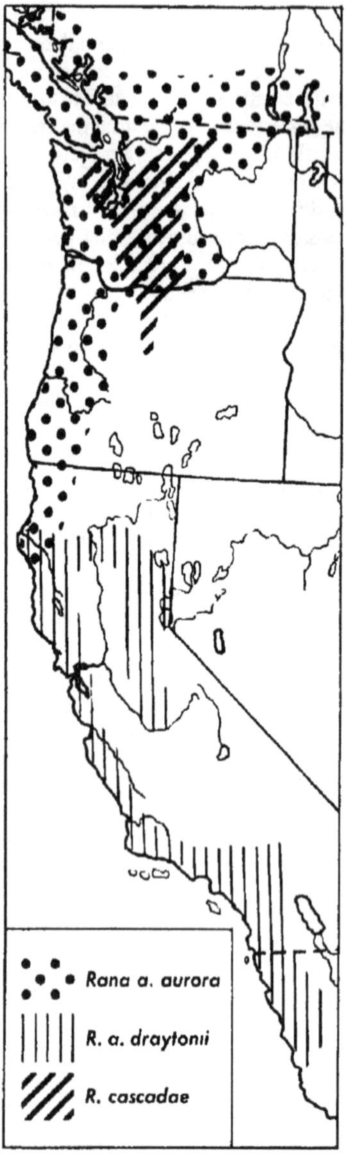


*Map 27*

more alert than *R. pretiosa pretiosa.* The groin is black marked with conspicuous spots of pale greenish yellow, which area extends slightly onto the belly.

"The Red-legged frog may be recognized by its slender form, smooth skin, dark patch behind the eye, and red colour on sides of body and under surfaces of legs" (G. C. Carl, B.C., 1943, p. 48).

**Color:** *Female.* Tacoma, Wash., from Prof. James Slater, April 21, 1930. Underside of tibia, front half of venter to femur and along sides from groin to axilla solid coral red, jasper red, or light jasper red. A wash of same color on hind toes and membrane of web. Top of back, snout, fore limbs, hind limbs brownish olive, light brownish olive, Saccardo's umber to umber. Sides below costal fold with considerable black, area back of eye more or less black but not a clear vitta. Deep colonial buff or deep olive-buff or Naples yellow line from shoulder insertion below tympanum to below eye is broken up on side of snout with many black dots. Throat heavily specked with smoke gray, pale olive-gray, or mouse gray. Breast and belly white but with much gray (of the shades listed above) on it, though not so uniformly overlaid as on throat. Groin has black and some light dull green-yellow spots. Eye barium yellow, iris border above ochraceous-orange or zinc orange on lower iris rim, which is broken in middle. In lower iris are specks of same color as lower iris border. In upper iris is a little ochraceous-orange. Bars on hind legs not very distinct, black with many ground color specks on them.

*Male.* Carbon River Valley, Rainier National Park, Wash., from J. R Slater, May 16, 17, 1930. Dorsal color sulphine yellow, citrine, dull citrine, or buffy citrine with few faint black specks. On brachium color becomes old gold. Hind legs and forelegs same color as dorsum. Stripe along upper jaw to over-arm insertion barium yellow to Naples yellow or cream color. Mask back of eye extends diagonally down to end of cream-colored upper labial stripe. Mask obscured by many minute oil yellow specks. Iris black with prominent lemon yellow or light greenish yellow bar across eye above pupil. Lower eye mainly black with few English red and xanthine orange spots. Upper eye with few specks above light greenish yellow bar. On sides more black specks. In groin several larger viridine green spots. Lower sides, undersides of tibia, and top of hind foot and femur slightly Etruscan red, old rose, Corinthian red, or deep vinaceous. Femur bone brown with white specks. Under parts dirty white or yellowish glaucous. In general venter cloudy. In the young the upper labial light line is particularly conspicuous. Iris golden yellow.

**Structure:** Frog medium in size; skin smooth; ridge from angle of eye to shoulder not prominent; dorsolateral folds indistinct; webs very well developed, greater in males than females; some males with inconspicuous groove across middle of thumb tubercle.

"The general aspect of this species differs greatly from all its congeners in North America. The length of the body and head together is three inches and a half, the head forming nearly one third of this length. The head itself is pyramidal, pointed, the nostrils situated midway between the anterior rim of the eye and the tip of the snout. Eyes of medium size, anterior limbs short; fingers rather long and slender. The body is orange red, with here and there black irregular patches. From Puget Sound" (S. F. Baird and C. Girard, Ore., 1852, p. 174).

**Voice:** Seldom recorded in the field. Like the wood frog it has a short breeding period so that few hear it to know it.

**Breeding:** These frogs breed from February to May. Eggs are 3.04 mm., outer envelope is about 12 mm. The tadpoles have not been described. They transform at $^{11}/_{16}$–$^{4}/_{5}$ inch (17–21 mm.), and the labial teeth are $^{3}/_{4}$.

"We collected a large series of adult and newly transformed *Rana aurora aurora* in April 1933, just north of Klamath, Del Norte County. It was raining and frogs were abundant on the sopping forest floor. On subsequent examination one of the supposed red-legged frogs turned out to be a female *Ascaphus*" (W. F. Wood, Calif., 1939, p. 110).

Wallace Wood's individuals that transformed in April interest us. We early recorded transformation at 17–21 mm. and observed: All this material (USNM no. 337) except two specimens, 26 and 44 mm., we interpret as recently transformed. The National Museum frogs were taken at the Columbia River on a United States exploring expedition, and Dr. Barnhart states that the expedition came to the Columbia River "late in April, 1841," and arrived two weeks later at Puget Sound. After our varied acquaintance with this form we conclude that these and Wood's transformees must have come from early breeders.

"Little is known of the life-history. The eggs are laid in masses during March and April in backwaters of lakes and streams. Tadpoles collected in a lake near Victoria, B.C. on May 9th, 1941, when about 1 inch in length, transformed in July of the same year" (G. C. Carl, B.C., 1943, p. 48).

"Eggs: The mosaic appearing masses are made up of large eggs with a volume of about 1.2 cc. each. The jelly is very transparent, loose, and viscid. Three envelopes are present in addition to the vitelline membrane, which is easily discernible in most cases. Although rather indistinct all envelopes can be seen without the aid of a lens when viewed in proper light. Most difficult to make out is the middle envelope, which is the thinnest. The fairly large vitellus is black at the animal pole and creamy white at the vegetal. Measurements are: vitellus 3.04 mm. (range 2.31 to 3.56 mm.); vitelline capsule 3.28 mm. (range 2.56 to 3.87 mm.); inner envelope 5.70 mm. (range 4.0 to 6.68 mm.); middle envelope 6.80 mm. (range 6.25 to 7.93 mm.); outer envelope 11.90 mm. (range 10.0 to 14.0 mm.).

". . . Several differences are noticeable between the eggs of *R. a. aurora* and its very near relation *R. a. draytonii*. In general, eggs of *R. a. aurora* are larger; the first thing to strike the eye, the vitellus, is perceptibly greater as is the dimension of the outer envelope. The outer envelope is also less distinct in *R. a. aurora*. Vitelline membranes are more easily seen in *R. a. draytonii*. With *R. a. draytonii* the three gelatinous envelopes become progressively greater in thickness from the inner to the outer, in *R. a. aurora* the middle envelope is the thinnest. The entire egg mass of *R. a. aurora* is from two to four inches greater in diameter than that of *R. a. draytonii*.

"*R. a. aurora* eggs somewhat resemble those of *R. sylvatica*. The looseness of the jelly and form of the mass are similar, but the lack of a middle envelope and usually smaller dimensions of individual eggs and masses readily separates *R. sylvatica* from *R. a. aurora*" (R. L. Livezey and A. H. Wright, Gen., 1945, pp. 702–703).

**Journal notes:** March 27, 1942. Stopped between Hoh and Borachiel rivers, Olympic Peninsula, Wash., beside a wonderland meadow, with spots of snow, *Ledum*, cranberry, etc. Here in ditch saw several fresh *R. a. aurora* egg masses. Saw one composite mass of frogs' eggs getting stranded, 2 ft. by 3 ft. in diameter. (Must have been 15 to 30 masses here. Mating congress in one place as in *R. sylvatica*.) In each egg envelope were green algae as in salamander eggs.

March 19, Oregon. From 11:00 A.M. to 12:30 stopped between Hauser and Lakeside. In a series of pools beside a road in a wood clearing recently cut off were several pussy-willow ponds. One has cattails; each has some sedge tussocks. All have some log entanglements. On these logs, along the banks, and in shallow mounds in the pond these frogs sometimes sit, not infrequently two in a place, either young or females. Lots of vegetation in bottom of ponds. Centers sometimes 3 feet deep. No eggs. All adults caught are females. Where are the males? The females all ripe. Some of the young are bright red under legs and even on sides of pectoral region. Throats much spotted. . . . Later took in a ditch, 1 foot wide but 2 feet deep, one female at least 20 feet from pond, on way to pond. These frogs surely look like wood frogs, and are wood frogs.

March 20. Up McKenzie R. with Ruth Hopson. . . . Caught little *R. aurora* and saw two adults. What is mass of *Ambystoma*-like eggs left high and dry?

March 27. Between Nolan Cr. and Hoh River found beside road a ditch at least 4 feet across, containing plenty of vegetation and with sedge clumps on its wooded side. Beside sedge clumps are *Ambystoma*-like masses. In shallow end of ditch Anna espied frogs' eggs, quite dark in color. The eggs are far apart in mass, at least ¾ inch from each other. The fresh mass is quite bluish in cast, and in water 6 inches deep. One mass at least 8–10 inches across! Another 6 inches across! Three good masses and a partial one; must be *R. a. aurora*. Where are the *R. a. aurora* males and females? Heard seven. Stopped beside another stream. Here found two *Rana,* one adult with much red and cloudiness and one small one, yellow below.

*Plate LXXXVII. Rana aurora aurora* 1. Male (×⅔). 2. Female (×½). 3 Female (×⅔).

*Plate LXXXVIII Rana aurora draytonii* (×½). 1,2,4. Females. 3 Male.

March 30. Went to Sparaway Lake with Mr. James Slater and later to another more brushy lake. Here he gets *R. a. aurora.* Found one mass of *R. a. aurora* eggs. The egg has two egg envelopes with a very visible vitelline membrane. The tadpoles have three rows of teeth on the upper labium and four rows on the lower.

**Authorities corner:**

H. S. Fitch, Ore., 1936, p. 640.
I. McT. Cowan, B.C., 1939, p. 48.
W. C. Brown and J. R. Slater, Wash., 1939, pp 17–18.

"Some previous collectors have placed specimens of this species [*Rana cascadae*] with *Rana aurora aurora.* . . . *Rana aurora aurora* and *Rana cascadae* overlap a little in distribution in the Canadian Zone" (J. R. Slater, Wash., 1939b, p. 149).

## California Red-legged Frog, Drayton's Frog, Bullfrog, Long-footed Frog, Bloody Nouns, Rocky Mountain Frog, Western Wood Frog, French Frog, Leconte's Frog

*Rana aurora draytonii* (Baird and Girard). Plate LXXXVIII; Map 27.

**Range:** Coastal California to Lower California. Few records in Sierras or east of them. Introduced in Nevada (Linsdale). "Inhabits chiefly the Upper Sonoran life-zone, but extends into Transition and Lower Sonoran" (J. Grinnell and C. L. Camp, Calif., 1917, p. 149).

**Habitat:** Ponds, lakes, or marshes. Large permanent pools or water courses. Linsdale in Lower California (L. C., 1932, p. 353) gives several habitats. "More than half the specimens in the series listed above were captured in or at the margins of streams. One individual was taken from a spring, one from a slough, one from the ground beneath willows near a creek, two in rat traps at the edge of a swamp, three from a marsh, and four from a lake. One of the frogs was captured by the use of a trout fly."

"It is known to occur in a number of water-storage reservoirs and other artificial ponds, and it has been cultivated with some degree of success in ponds of quiet water on one or more 'frog farms' within the State. . . . In general, the ponds and creek pools which are the haunts of this species are seldom frozen, and if they do freeze, the ice seldom lasts for more than part of one day" (T. I. Storer, Calif., 1925, pp. 236–237).

"This is the large frog which frequents the ponds and streams on both sides of the mountains. It is usually found where water is permanent and when disturbed takes refuge in the weeds at the bottom. It has been collected in Imperial County. It may be distinguished from the other frogs of the genus *Rana* in this territory (except the Leopard frog) by the ridges on the sides of the body, and from that frog by the absence of the conspicuous oval blotches which characterize the latter" (L. M. Klauber, Calif., 1934a, p. 7).

**Size:** Adults, 2⅓–5⅜ inches. Males, 63–100 mm. Females, 58–136 mm.

**General appearance:** This is a large, stout, rough-skinned frog with a thick broad head. It is the largest of California's native frogs. The leg bars on tibia and femur may be so prominent as to appear zebralike. The back is olive drab or buffy brown, spotted with light-centered spots; the groin, heavily spotted; the lateral fold, light pinkish cinnamon; the line on the upper jaw, cream buff or pale pinkish. The underside of the hind legs and the inner half of the tarsus and foot are pinkish to red. The young are apt to be conspicuously spotted.

**Color:** Sentenac Canyon, San Felipe Cr., Calif., from L. M. Klauber, March 25, 1928. *Female*. Upper parts isabella color, Saccardo's olive, drab, or buffy brown. Lateral fold light pinkish cinnamon. Line on upper jaw pale pinkish cinnamon or cream-buff. Brighter than in male. Around tubercles between lateral folds and on sides are black rings with light pinkish cinnamon in center on tubercle. On sides this becomes congo pink or dragon's blood red. Groin is dark purplish black and spotted with olive-buff or cartridge buff. Femur marked with dark purplish black and cartridge buff on dorsal surface. Underside of hind legs and inner half of tarsus and foot, pale pinkish cinnamon, congo pink to dragon's blood red. Iris orange.

*Male*. Upper parts citrine-drab or yellowish olive to light grayish olive on forearms; more uniform on back with few black spots or specks. Groin more spotted than in female, more yellow present. Ventral parts more heavily spotted and reticulated; otherwise as in female.

**Structure:** Thumb enlarged, slightly two-lobed; thumb base quite large in female and in some individuals would be mistaken for a male; prominent ridge from posterior angle of eye to shoulder; skin thick and roughened with many small papillae, even the eardrum may be so roughened; eardrum small; dorsolateral folds prominent; sacral hump prominent; back with regularly placed light-centered spots; male without visible vocal sac.

"This species resembles very much . . . [*R. aurora*] in its external appearance. It differs, however, in having a truncated snout, the nostrils consequently nearer to its tip than to the eyes. The eyes themselves and tympanum are proportionally larger than in *R. aurora,* the limbs more developed and the tongue much narrower. The ground color is olivaceous green, maculated with black on the upper region of the body and limbs, whilst underneath the hue is unicolor, except sometimes under the head, breast and hind legs, where the brown and white mingle in circular dots. Specimens were collected at San Francisco, California, and on Columbia River by Mr. Drayton himself, to whom we take pleasure in dedicating this species" (S. F. Baird and C. Girard, Ore., 1854, p. 174).

**Voice:** "A series of low tremulous or 'gurgling' notes, resembling somewhat the notes uttered by *Rana boylii*" (T. I. Storer, Calif., 1925, p. 238).

**Breeding:** This species breeds from January to March. The eggs are laid in overflow areas of permanent pools, the mass attached to vegetation. The jelly is soft and viscid; the outline of individual eggs is evident on the surface. The egg is 1/12 inch (1.8–2.1 mm.), the envelopes 1/8, 3/16, 3/8 inch (3.5 mm., 4.4 mm., 8.5 mm.), the eggs black and white. The dark brownish, mottled tadpole is 3 1/3 inches (83 mm.) and has tooth ridges 2/3. The larval period is 5–7 months. (Data from Storer, 1925.) The tadpoles transform from May to August at 3/4–1 1/5 inches (18–30 mm.).

This frog is one of earliest to spawn in California, the crest coming in January and February. The customary size at transformation is probably 22–30 mm. Of seven specimens taken by us Aug. 14, 1917, at Oceanside, Calif., none was smaller than 32 mm. and all were past transformation. In one set, that of the University of Michigan (no. 65203), appear nine transforming frogs 25–35 mm. in body length, with tail stubs from 13–48 mm. Two specimens just transformed are 31 and 32 mm. and 14 specimens are 29–37 mm.

In egg measurements one is not sure whether or not some other author interpreted the vitelline membrane as an envelope. We measured some of Storer's eggs from Thornhill, Calif., to be able to compare his statements with other material. We found eggs of 1.8–2.1-mm. vitelli, a vitelline membrane, and three envelopes, the outer of which was loose and the two inner much firmer. We therefore agree with Storer's diagrams and measurements.

**Journal notes:** Feb. 14, 1942, Hoover Ranch. Cook caught me an adult female *R. a. draytonii.*

March 10, Stanford. Anita Daugherty yesterday gave us *R. a. draytonii* eggs laid in lab from frogs taken at Los Trancos Creek March 1.

April 12. Out with Tracy and Ruth Storer. . . . After going along stream tributary to N. Fork Cosumnes River north of Plymouth, Calif., near the Amador-El Dorado County line, in the depressions of gold workings, saw a *R. a. draytonii* jump into a deep pool. It rested on the bottom. Brought net in front of it and poked it from rear as I pushed forward with net. Caught this one and three more. One was in grass; it leaped into a clump. Put net between clump and water. Then kicked from rear and in jumped my frog. These ugly deposits are from dredging or placer workings.

April 22. With Leo T. Hadsall and party stopped beside drainage ditch on level, near Fresno, Calif.; some three or four *R. a. draytonii* jumped in.

May 5, La Posta. At a creek beside a tule area saw some amphibian jump in. Had to know whether it was *Bufo californicus,* my search, or *Rana a. draytonii.* It proved the latter. Three and one-half to 4 miles south of Buckman's Spring at bridge below confluence of La Posta and Cottonwood Cr. took one *R. a. draytonii.* Saw no *Rana* tadpoles.

**Authorities' corner:**

M. C. Dickerson, Gen., 1906, p. 216.
T. I. Storer, Calif., 1925, p. 245.
J. M. Linsdale, Nev., 1938, p. 25.

## California Yellow-legged Frog, Thick-skinned Frog, Boyle's Frog

*Rana boylii boylii* (Baird). Plate LXXXIX; Map 28.

**Range:** Western Oregon, northern and central portions of California, chiefly west of the high Sierra Nevada.

"Life zones Upper Sonoran and Transition" (J. Grinnell and C. L. Camp, Calif., 1917, p. 146).

"Except for a small area in southwestern Oregon, the range of *Rana boylii boylii* seems to lie entirely within the state of California. It includes the northwestern part of the state, east to the McCloud River, Shasta County, and to the western foothills of the Sierra Nevada below 4100 feet altitude. The form occurs also at Mono Lake; in the Sierras it has been taken south to the vicinity of Walker Pass, Kern County; but where it meets the range of *R. b. muscosa* along the coast is not known. Specimens from the vicinity of Walker Pass show a more contrasted pattern of coloration, possibly indicating approach to the southern subspecies, described below" (C. L. Camp, Calif., 1917, p. 118).

**Habitat:** Margins of springs, streams, and fresh water lakes (J. Grinnell and C. L. Camp, Calif., 1917); gravelly streams (K. Gordon, Ore., 1939).

"It is confined to the immediate vicinity of permanent streams, at least those where water holes persist through the dry season. It is most common along streams having rocky beds, but occurs also in ones having mud buttoms" (H. S. Fitch, Ore., 1936, p. 640).

"This little frog inhabits the slow flowing streams of the coastal areas, and may be found in considerable numbers in the semipermanent pools, formed as the streams become low at the end of the rainy season" (J. R. Slevin, B.C., 1928, p. 139).

At Stevens Creek near Palo Alto, Calif., in shallow and quiet areas we found small *R. boylii*. Up one or two little runs bordered by *Rhus* (poison oak), saw four more.

T. I. Storer says: "The adult frogs of this species spend much of their time perched on rocks in the stream or on the bank, but in the latter place they never go more than two or three feet from the margin of the water. If approached, even from the direction of the stream, they invariably seek safety by leaping into the water, and immediately swim with swift strokes down to the bottom. In streams with silt on the bottom they hide in the mud and silt which their movements stir up; in clear waters they take refuge under overhanging rocks."

**Size:** Adults, 1⅗–3 inches. Males, 39–67 mm. Females, 40–75 mm. It is the smallest of the three subspecies of *Rana boylii*.

**General appearance:** This is a small frog with stout, broad body. The skin on the back, legs, and tympanum is thick and rough with small brownish papillae. The color of the back is black, light gray, greenish, or brownish with indistinct dark mottling. There is a patch of lighter color on top of the head with a darker area behind crossing the upper eyelids. The tympanic region is darker than the head. Red is never present in the coloration. The venter is white with pale yellow on the posterior part and on the hind legs. The throat and sides of the body are mottled with black.

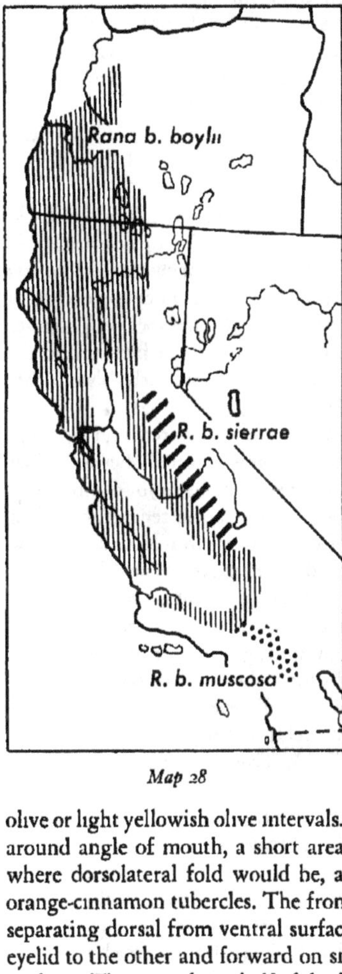


*Map 28*

Of four adult specimens of *R. b. boylii* taken April 2, 1942, only one, a male, had a tendency to be spotted in the groin. All had spotted throats. Three males had short, light tubercular ridges back of the angle of the mouth. It was either a continuous fold or two to four tubercles in a row; then came a hiatus and then another ridge or patch of one to three tubercles. The skin was rougher than in *Rana pretiosa* or *R. a. aurora*. Quite often they had a red line along the dorsolateral fold, the lower belly lumiere green, underside of femur mustard yellow, then primuline yellow, then yellow ocher, becoming in rear portion aniline yellow.

**Color:** *Female.* Mill Valley, Muir Woods, Calif., from John Needham, March 18, 1930. Dorsal color in general is buffy olive, light brownish olive, citrine-drab, or olive lake, coming to be, in the intervals between the leg and arm crossbars, isabella color, clay color, or honey yellow on the tarsus and outer edge of the foot. The crossbars are Saccardo's olive. On rear of femur and in the groin are several rather prominent black, olive, or deep olive areas. On the rear of femur the dark areas have ecru-olive or light yellowish olive intervals. A ridge from rear of upper labial margin around angle of mouth, a short area back of eye and irregularly along back where dorsolateral fold would be, and patches on either side of knee have orange-cinnamon tubercles. The front of the tibia bears an empire yellow line separating dorsal from ventral surface. The top of the head from front of one eyelid to the other and forward on snout is isabella color or old gold. Ventral surfaces: The central rear half of the femur is papillate, orange, or deep chrome, bounded behind by a more or less prominent black or deep olive band. In front of this orange area and on lower belly is a wash of picric yellow. Some of same color on groin, on rear of tibia, on venter of arm, and in axil of arm. The top of the foot has a wash of empire yellow. The throat and breast are white to pale pinkish buff with orange-cinnamon spots on throat and vaguely outlined on breast. These become verona brown spots on edge of lower jaw. Along side as back merges into belly are picric yellow spots among the deep olive. The eye is black, almost obscured by numerous specks of buff-pink or vinaceous-pink on lower portion giving place to light green-yellow and pale orange-yellow specks on the upper half. Pupil rim in lower half partakes of color of specks of that part, and so also the rim on the upper part.

**Structure:** Head broad and pointed; web of foot large, only slightly scalloped; toes blunt, tips slightly expanded; thumb of male enlarged, the swelling having two lobes; tympanum small, distinct.

"*Rana boylii*, Baird.—A broad depressed ridge of skin on each side of back. Skin finely tubercular above. Head broader than long. Tympanum scarcely evident, pustulated. Tibia more than half the length of body; hind foot less than half this length; webbed entirely to the horny tips; outer toe decidedly longer than the third. An elongated tubercle at base of inner toe, with another opposite to it. Above dull reddish olivaceous, with indistinct blotches on the back, and fascia on the legs. Beneath yellowish, mottled anteriorly. Two inches long. Hab. California (interior)" (S. F. Baird, Gen., 1856, p. 62).

"Those characters which pertain to this subspecies alone are: hind leg long, inside angle of bent tarsus reaching at least to nares and usually beyond when leg is advanced along body; tibia elongate, reaching usually beyond anus when flexed and held at right angles to axis of body; fourth toe on reflexed hind foot never reaching beyond end of knee and often not quite to fold of skin below knee; head broad and pointed when viewed from above, its width two and one-third to two and two-thirds times in body-length; skin on back, legs and tympanum, thick and rough with minute brownish spines; color dorsally varying from nearly uniform to black to light gray, greenish or brownish, with darker markings, if present, usually indistinct; there is always a patch of lighter color on top of head between nares and eyes, and behind this a darker area crossing posterior half of each eyelid and merging insensibly behind into the general dorsal coloration" (C. L. Camp, Calif., 1917, pp. 117–118).

"Size small; head broader than long, depressed; snout rounded, projecting beyond mouth; canthus rostralis distinct; loreal region concave; nostrils nearer to tip of snout than to orbit; distance between nostrils equals interorbital width. Interorbital width less than width of upper eyelid. Tympanum small, distinct, covered with small tubercles, about one-half diameter of eye. Fore limbs moderately robust; digits rather long, first and second equal, third much the longest; no lateral fold along sides of fingers; subarticular tubercles small or moderately large, rounded, prominent; outer metatarsal tubercles elongate, prominent, inner metatarsal tubercle rounded, somewhat obscure; web full, extending to tip of longest toe. Skin rugose, covered with warts or tubercles on back and sides; posterior surface of the thigh covered with small tubercles; dorso-lateral fold obscure; sacral hump rather prominent; a well developed fold from lip to side of neck or shoulder. Vomerine teeth in two oblique series, widely separated anteriorly, between and a little behind the choanae" (J. R. Slevin, B.C., 1928, p. 137).

**Voice:** No description of the call is recorded. The frog has internal vocal sacs.

**Breeding:** This frog breeds from the latter part of March to the first of May. The egg mass, in shallow water toward the margin of streams, is attached to sides of stones in the stream bed and is like a compact cluster of grapes, the individual eggs on the surface distinct, the jelly firm. The eggs are more closely set than are those in a *R. pipiens* mass.

"Three envelopes present. Outer envelope 3.88–4.47 mm., ave. 4.0 mm.; jelly firm. Middle envelope 2.58–3.35 mm., ave. 2.8 mm. Inner envelope 2.32–2.94 mm., ave. 2.5 mm. All envelopes distinct. Vitellus 1.93–2.48 mm., average 2.2 mm.; black above and white below. Mass 2 by 2 by 1⅕ to 2 by 4 by 2⅖ inches in dimensions. Eggs firmly attached to each other. 909–1037 eggs in a mass. Deposited in shallow water near the margins of streams, attached to stones in stream bed. Pick up much sediment" (R. L. Livezey and A. H. Wright, Gen., 1947).

The tadpole is medium, 2 inches (50 mm.), deep olive in color, and with tooth ridges ⅔, ¾, ¾. After 3 to 4 months, the tadpoles transform from June to September, at ⅘–1⅕ inches (20–30 mm.).

"Evans Creek (Oregon) on April 29, 1934. . . . Numerous egg masses attached to large pebbles and newly hatched tadpoles were seen. The spawning places were in pools four or five inches deep where slow currents or eddies caused constant circulation of water around the egg masses" (H. S. Fitch, Ore., 1936, p. 640)

A frog taken by J. C. Bradley, June 1907, Blue Lake, Humboldt Co., Calif., was 29 mm. and past transformation; and in a series of six from Marin Co. by J. C. Bradley, which were 22.5–30 mm., none had arm scars. Transformation of some of this group must have come at 20 mm. or smaller. H. C. Kellers, April 13, 1913, secured two specimens (USNM nos. 49874–5) 25 and 31 mm. These doubtless wintered over from the previous year. This same collector has taken this species in Calistoga, Napa Co., Calif., as small as 23 mm. Mr. Rutter, Oct. 17, 1899, in Mariposa, Calif., secured two specimens (nos. 38830–31) 29.0 and 25.5 mm. These might be of the season. The specimens (USNM nos. 20895–20903) secured by H. W. Henshaw Oct. 17, 1893, at Ukiah, Mendocino Co., Calif., ranging from 20–29 mm., may also be of the same season.

April 8, 1942. Ate at Trail, Ore. Went up the creek. In a spring area saw several *R. boylii boylii*. Took in side pools small *R. b. boylii*. They swim out into deep water and then generally back to edge or to shallow water. In the middle of stream riffles saw an adult *R. b. boylii* swimming. While waiting for Bert to search above the bridge for more snakes (*Thamnophis o. hydrophila*) I went to stream side near bridge. Across the stream I saw what I thought an adult *R. b. boylii*. This was a crossing place in the stream with flat rocks; just above were rapids and just below, deep pools with rapid current in water falling into pools. I waded across stream catching sight of two adult frogs. Then in a shallow side pocket with water flowing through but not rapidly, attached to a broken notch, was a mass of *R. b. boylii* eggs. The water was 3 to 4 inches deep. The egg cluster was somewhat plinthlike. Eggs were fresh and looked black. Bert came down and reported that this must be type locality for Fitch's *T. o. hydrophila.* No end of adult *Rana b. boylii* leaped into midstream ahead of him. It is interesting to see them helplessly carried over the shallow rock bottom by the current until they find a deep groove. They are shy frogs and you can't get within catching distance before they dash for the bottom under the edge of a near-by stone if there is a handy one.

**Journal notes:** Feb. 14, 1942. Trip to Theodore Hoover ranch, Calif. Went up steep side of small creek and in it Rodgers secured a yellow-legged frog. Around sawmill in little shallow pools found several small *R. boylii boylii.* During the day the boys got me one or two more.

March 15. Trip north. In Tuttle Ranch, Calif., took *R. b. boylii.*

March 18. Started at 10:30 along Smith River road toward Smith River village, Calif. It is the east segment of the triangle. Along a bank covered with ferns and oxalis in a rill where water goes under a road, Anna caught a male *R. b. boylii.* In pool at other end of pipe I took two more.

March 23. With Kenneth Gordon and group to Santiam River, Ore. In ponds beside stream under rock, Storm and Livezey took three *R. boylii boylii.* Under board, Anna found a female.

April 12. Out with Tracy and Ruth Storer. Region of dredging and placer working, north of Plymouth, Calif. Over in the stream Tracy and Ruth Storer and Anna kept seeing yellow-legged frogs leap into the water. This is a creek with plenty of riffly spots. In a fast-water stretch Tracy Storer found a mass of *R. b. boylii* eggs attached to stone 3 or 4 feet from bank in water 10 inches deep, a plinth. Before we got through we found five more masses—one very fresh and hardly expanded, this less plinthlike.

April 18. Went to Hasting's Natural History Reservation to see Jean Linsdale. He has *H regilla* and *R. boylii* there.

**Authorities' corner:**

C. E. and M. D. Burt, Ariz., 1929, p. 432.
J. Grinnell, J. J. Dixson, J. M. Linsdale, Calif., 1930, p. 143.
H. S. Fitch, Ore , 1936, pp. 640–641.
H. S. Fitch, Ore., 1938, p. 148.

"There is thus a good chance that on the desert slope of the San Gabriel

Mountains the frogs are *boylii* rather than *muscosa*" (C. L. Camp, Calif., 1917, p. 120). [A statement verified by Marr 26 years later.]

"In a herpetological collection made along the San Gabriel River, San Gabriel Mountains, Los Angeles County, August 11, 1940, I have four specimens of *Rana boylii boylii* and none of *Rana boylii muscosa*. . . . It is barely possible that this frog has been introduced by some chance into the San Gabriel River" (J. C. Marr, Calif, 1943, p. 56).

### Sierra Madre Yellow-legged Frog, Southern Yellow-legged Frog

*Rana boylii muscosa* Camp. Plate XC; Map 28.

**Range:** San Gabriel, San Bernardino, and San Jacinto Mountains of southern California. "This form inhabits stream cañons in southern California south of Tehachapi Pass. Localities of record extend from Pacoima Cañon near San Fernando eastward and southward along the southern and western slopes of the San Gabriel, San Bernardino and San Jacinto ranges as far as Keen's Camp, in the latter range. It has been found also at Little Rock Creek on the north slope of the San Gabriel Mountains. The range in altitude is from 1200 feet near Sierra Madre to 6500 feet on Fish Creek in the San Bernardino range" (C. L. Camp, Calif., 1917b, p. 119).

"Southern California south of Ventura County" (J. R. Slevin, Calif, 1934, p. 48).

"The previously recorded southern limit of this species has been Keen Camp in the San Jacinto Mountains, Riverside County, California. Recently it has been found to be plentiful in Pauma Creek, where it flows through Upper Doane Valley, Palomar Mountain, San Diego County, at elevation 5100 feet. The first specimens at this location were taken by Dr. E. H. Taylor of the University of Kansas during a collecting trip in which the writer participated" (L. M. Klauber, Calif., 1929, pp. 15–16)

**Habitat:** "Occupies the upper Sonoran and Transition life zones. Lives along streams in narrow rockwalled canons" (J. Grinnell and C. L. Camp, Calif., 1917, p. 148). "More or less common in streams throughout (Los Angeles) County" (C. M. Bogert, Calif., 1930, p. 5).

**Size:** Adults, 1⅘–3¼ inches. Males, 44–66 mm. Females, 47–85 mm. Our material taken in Santa Anita Canyon and Snow Creek in spring, 1942, falls into three classes: young 33–40 mm., males 49–56 mm., and females 49–64 mm.

**General appearance:** "Like *Rana boylii boylii*, but attaining much larger size, and (except in young) with no light patch in front of dark areas across upper eyelids. Dorsal ground color usually lighter than in *R. b. boylii*, light yellow to brown, contrasting with the darker mosslike patches on the back. Tips of toes more expanded than in *boylii*" (C. L. Camp, Calif., 1917, p. 119).

**Color:** *Male*. San Gabriel Canyon, Los Angeles region, Calif., from Berry

*Plate LXXXIX Rana boylii boylii* 1. Male (×⅔). 2,3 Females (×⅗).

*Plate XC. Rana boylii muscosa* (×⅘ 1,2. Females. 3,4. Males.

Campbell, April 11, 1930. Upper parts from tip of snout back between eyes and lateral folds to vent ecru-olive or deep olive-buff. Costal folds dark olive-buff. Interspaces on hind legs dark olive-buff instead of ecru-olive. Color below costal fold olive-buff or ivory yellow and same on under parts and front half of under part of hind legs. An oblique spot from eye to angle of mouth, one from tympanum obliquely backwards, colonial buff. On front of femur, top of foot, axilla, slightly on head and front edge of arm deep colonial buff. Throat cartridge buff with fine buffy olive spottings. Spot on top of head and back brownish olive. Same color also on hind legs and forelegs, on sides becoming buffy olive. Underside of head and hind ventral half of femur pale grayish vinaceous or pale vinaceous-fawn. Thumb excrescences clove brown, also underside of hand.

*Female.* Upper Doane Valley, Palomar Mt., San Diego Co., Calif., from L. M. Klauber and Dr. E. H. Taylor, Sept. 2, 1928. Upper parts from tip of snout back between eyes and two costal folds to vent grayish olive or citrine-drab (lighter than in male). Costal fold dark to deep olive-buff, color below costal fold pale olive-buff, and the same on under parts. An oblique spot from eye to angle of mouth, one back of angle, one over arm insertion and one in axilla primrose yellow or olive-buff. Under parts of legs like venter. Where lighter color joins upper color considerable of deep colonial buff or chamois. This color comes strongly into light intervals between crossbars on hind legs and somewhat on forelegs. Some wash of same color on throat, which is not as spotted as in male. Sides below costal folds heavily spotted with brownish olive. Spots on dorsum from tip of snout to vent smaller and often more or less olive-ocher encircled. Dark line from eye to nostril to labial margin. Black spot or bar below eye. Edge of lower jaw black or brownish olive and colonial buff or pale olive-buff. Top of fingers deep colonial buff or chamois. Dark bars of hind legs brownish olive or olive with some grayish olive spots in the dark color. Hind webs dark with some chamois. Horizontal bar of black or olive through eye; vertical bar of same below pupil; interspaces between the horizontal and vertical, isabella color or even primrose yellow; upper portion of eye colonial buff with black dot at the top. Sometimes at forward edge of eye occurs pale yellow-green.

**Structure:** Tips of toes more expanded than in *R. b. boylii,* dorsolateral fold indistinct, not pitted anteriorly; tympanum and area surrounding it very rough, covered with small tubercles; web of hind foot extending nearly to tips of toes, broader in expanse than in *R. b boylii;* swelling on thumb of male has two lobes, the constriction being diagonal not transverse.

"Vomerine teeth on two oblique ridges between nares; head pointed in outline as viewed from above, broad, its width entering body-length two and two-thirds times; hind limbs long, posterior side of bent tarsus reaching forward to snout; fourth toe on hind foot reaching forward not quite to knee-fold; dorsolateral fold indistinct, not pitted anteriorly; tympanum and area surrounding it very rough, beset with small tubercles, web of hind foot extending nearly to tips of toes; outer and inner metatarsal tubercles distinct; plantar tubercles very large; tips of toes expanded, disc-shaped; distal end of flexed tibia held at right angles to body reaching anus" (C. L. Camp, Calif., 1917, p. 119).

"Ground color above light gray or yellowish, with numerous black blotches or reticulation on head, body and limbs. Posterior surface of thigh rich yellow. Under surfaces yellowish or whitish, gular region slightly spotted or marbled with gray" (J. R. Slevin, Gen., 1928, p. 141).

**Voice:** Nothing on record.

**Breeding:** This species breeds during April. The eggs are not yet described. The tadpole is much like that of *R. boylii sierrae* and reaches 61 mm. in length. Its body is rather flat, the tail musculature heavy and almost uniform in width for about half the length of tail. Tooth ridges are variable, for example, ¾ in one, ⅔ in another, ¼ in another. Possibly they winter as tadpoles and transform in the spring. They transform at about ⅘ inch (20–24 mm.).

Two tadpoles, collected Sept. 5, 1922, in San Jacinto Mountains, Dark Valley, by Prof. J. C. Bradley are 41 and 43 mm., not fully grown. The crests remain about the same to the point where musculature tapers.

One specimen from near Claremont, Calif., 1907, is 30 mm., just beyond transformation. The two smallest in the National Museum (nos. 54899–54900), taken by E. J. Brown in San Gabriel Canyon, Los Angeles Co., Calif., in February, 1916, are 24 and 26 mm. Apparently they were transformed the season before. This seems to imply transformation in the neighborhood of 20 mm.

On June 20, 1928, Storer secured at Bluff Lake, 3400 feet elevation, San Bernardino Mts. and Co., a tadpole, 61 mm. long, body 23 mm. Its tail was rounded; apparently the tadpole was approaching transformation; its tooth formula was ¼. Other specimens had tails that were not broad, crests quite spotted. Some were practically transformed at 23 and 24 mm.

On May 1, 1909, C. L. Camp found specimens 20–28 mm.; on Feb. 17, 1918, J. Shaw took a 25-mm. specimen and on May 30, 1918, a 29-mm.; on Nov. 13, 1937, W. F. Wood took specimens from 24–36 mm. One wonders if they winter over as tadpoles.

**Journal notes:** April 26, 1942, Calif. Started for Santa Anita Canyon about 9:30 A.M., hazy over the mountains. Rode about 3 miles up canyon to public parking spot. Went down trail to the river, about ¾ mile down, and then a mile or so up the river. Near where trail went to ranger cabin crossed a very rocky, steep gorge with small amount of swift water. It was dark and shady at this point. We saw no frogs there. As we reached the river another side stream came in, White Creek. We went slowly up the river. At one spot beside the river but not connected with it was a pool, a rather scummy, dark-looking pool, small, perhaps 4 by 6 feet. Here Bert caught one male and one small *Rana b. muscosa* and some newts, *Triturus torosus*, and found quantities of beautiful newt egg clusters attached to sticks. More were under a board and some were attached to a board lying at the end of the pool. (Caught two *H. arenicolor*.) Much granitic rock here—light gray in color—almost no sediment in the stream. On our return, Bert stopped at White Creek and there caught three female *R. b. muscosa*, nice large ones. He carried them in a large wet bag. He had two newts with them. When we reached the car he put the bag into the thermos bottle with a little water. Either too much water or too much newt killed two of the females by the next day. A male *R. b. muscosa* leaped into a quiet algae-covered pool filled with brush. Took young *R. b. muscosa* in this pool. In a quiet cutoff saw a female leap into creek and go under a stone. I was too leisurely about it. Lost it. I was angry to lose the female; saw no more except two or three young.

On return came to Winter Creek. Here on a sandy bar was one female. It leaped into a quiet pool near the base of a falls. Another halfway up on falls leaped in and lodged under a stone part way down. Caught it. In a pool at top of this sloping granitic falls took another female in brushy edge. Many newts mating in this creek. A few trout in Winter Creek.

April 30. Trip to Idyllwyld. At mouth of Strawberry Creek in cattail area in one quiet pool saw two *Rana b. muscosa*. Took one in tules below bridge, and later above bridge there leaped in from a boulder a female *H. arenicolor*. Went to Idyllwyld—no luck. Tried several places.

May 9, Palm Springs. Went up Snow Creek 5 miles. Here road ends where water company's possessions are. The Sierra Club of Los Angeles was meeting here. Some eight to ten people were along the creek awaiting their leader's coming. A beautiful cool mountain stream. There used to be a fish hatchery in the stream. At once back of car—1850 feet elevation—we saw *R. boylii muscosa;* the first near weeds at edge leaped among some rocks but came up, as they frequently do, and was easy of capture.

May 9, Snow Creek. These frogs were most frequently seated on the rocks. I would flop the net flat on the rock and the frog would leap into the netting. Sometimes they disappeared before I reached close enough to catch them. Occasionally I could approach close and seize them with my left hand. We saw only two or three small ones. I collected about five females before I got a male. In the end there were seven females and two males in the lot. A fine grayish-white, bouldery, tumbling stream of cold water. No wonder these *muscosa* are much lighter than the *sierrae* and *boylii*. They are a shade-loving form and have a decided odor. They sat on damp rocks above the water line. The first male was darker than the rest.

**Authorities' corner:**

C. L. Camp, Calif., 1917, pp. 119–120.
L. M. Klauber, Calif., 1934a, p. 7

**Sierra Nevada Yellow-legged Frog, Western Frog, Pacific Frog, Stink Frog**

*Rana boylii sierrae* Camp. Plate XCI; Map 28.

**Range:** California. Southern half of Sierra Nevada, above 7000 feet altitude from Yosemite National Park on the north to southern Tulare County on the south.

**Habitat:** Meadows, streams, and lakes from 7000 to 10,500 feet in Yosemite Park, and to 11,500 feet near Mount Whitney.

"In some of the lakes it was found in great numbers, appearing as soon as the ice had melted in late June. The tadpoles were at this time of large size and must have been hatched from eggs of a laying not more recent than the previous year" (C. L. Camp, Calif., 1917b, p. 122).

**Size:** Adults, 1¾–3⅜ inches. Males, 44–72 mm. Females, 48–85 mm. The measurements of 19 males and 30 females in the California Academy, Stanford University, and University of California collections gave a range of 44–65 mm. for males and 52–85 mm. for females; average male 55.5, mean 56 mm.; average female 60 mm., mean 59, 66, 70 mm.

**General appearance:** This frog is like *Rana boylii boylii*, but lacks the light patch on the head. The back is slightly roughened, is dark olive in color with some darker spots showing when it is wet. The under parts are white on the throat, creamy or buff on the belly and the underside of the legs. The throat is marked with black spots. The sides are light, heavily mottled with distinct black blotches. The jaw is heavily mottled with light and dark. There is a distinct dark blotch on the upper part of the forearm. The inner surface of the arms is light, outer surface greenish, marked with dark blotches. The legs are marked with dark spots. The angle of the jaw forms a swollen light area marked with one or two dark spots, and back of this is another light tubercle or swollen area. The head is short and broad with the nostrils far apart, snout short, eyes small and widely separated. Costal folds low and inconspicuous. The young look something like newly transformed green frogs.

"With the general characters of *Rana boylii boylii*, but hind leg usually shorter and head relatively narrower; tympanum smoother; and light patch on top of head wanting" (C. L. Camp, Calif, 1917b, p. 120).

**Color:** *Female*. Yosemite Park, from C. A. Harwell, Oct. 12, 1929. (The frog was cold when described, hence dark.) Back deep olive, citrine-drab, light brownish olive, few black or dark spots centered with old gold between lateral folds from arm insertion level to vent. More heavily spotted on sides below lateral folds and spots sometimes light-centered there where belly color and spots are reticulate. Something of same spotting on front of dorsum of femur and rear of forelimb. Throat and upper and lower labial edge heavily spotted with black. A very light white or cartridge buff line begins below eye and extends across angle of mouth or just above it to arm insertion. Sometimes this is interrupted below tympanum, then resumed diagonally down from tympanum, then interrupted to appear as a swollen patch above arm insertion. The posttympanal and arm insertion cartridge buff patches may have two or three fine black spots on them and considerable black extending upward between them from arm insertion. Upper jaw and face pale olive-buff with numerous black spots. Tympanum clear, like background of dorsum or top of head. Background on hind legs and forelegs dark olive-buff or old gold; mottled or spotted with black or olive; lateral fold of same color. Underside of hind legs and forelegs pale chalcedony yellow, cream color, or seafoam yellow; a tinge of same color on lower belly. On tarsus old gold or aniline yellow. Throat and pectoral region white. Underside of forefeet and hind feet light brownish drab or hair brown; iris black dotted with citron to honey yellow, or strontian yellow; pupil rim broken in front and behind.

*Male.* Lake Alpine, 7300 ft., Alpine Co., Calif., from Tracy I. Storer, July 29, 1930. Back buffy olive, citrine-drab, or grayish olive. Under the lens it may look deep olive-buff. On sides interspace color is deep olive-buff, ivory yellow, or cartridge buff, becoming chamois on edges of belly. The interspaces of hind legs and of forelegs are light brownish olive or almost isabella color. Dorsolateral fold in front half isabella color or cinnamon-brown to tawny or sayal brown. Large spots of bister or auburn. Whole of interspaces and spots covered by spaced black points. On sides, dorsolateral fold, and top of femur these surmount larger papillae. Forearm, front of femur, rear of tibia, tarsus, and foot with transverse bars of same color as large dorsal spots. Lower rear half of femur with many papillae tipped with reed yellow or deep colonial buff. Throat to line of arm insertion and upper and lower labial fold heavily spotted with deep olive or citrine-drab. Middle belly reed yellow, its sides chamois. Underside of hind legs and forelegs colonial buff or cream-buff. Inside of tarsus and lower end of tibia chamois. Rear half of venter of femur vinaceous-drab or deep brownish vinaceous, each papilla tipped with deep olive-buff or, better, reed yellow or deep colonial buff. Underside of fingers and of toes like rear half of venter of femur. Cream buff or colonial buff fold from below eye to angle of mouth broken below tympanum, broken again, resumed as spot above arm insertion. Iris rim picric yellow or lemon yellow above. Iris mars orange or English red.

**Structure:** Hind legs shorter; head relatively narrower; tympanum smoother than in *Rana b. boylii;* web of hind foot very large, extending to tips of toes; tips of toes not much expanded; dorsolateral fold strongly pitted anteriorly; swelling on thumb of male bilobate.

"Vomerine teeth rudimentary, on two oblique ridges nearly meeting between and slightly behind nares . . . ; head viewed from above rounded in outline; head-width contained three times in body-length; hind limbs short, posterior side of bent tarsus reaching forward to anterior corner of eye; fourth toe on hind foot reaching forward to end of bent knee; dorso-lateral fold indistinct, strongly pitted anteriorly; tympanum nearly smooth, with scattered hispid points; web of hind foot very large, extending to tips of toes; outer metatarsal tubercle rudimentary, inner one small; plantar tubercles small; tips of toes not much expanded; distal end of flexed tibia, held at right angles to body, just reaching anus; color above, dark yellowish brown, obscurely marked with indefinite darker vermiculations; lower surface yellow, faintly dotted with brown beneath chin; upper lip below eye mottled; no dark cheek patch; hind limbs not distinctly barred with dark bands.

"This seems to be the subspecies of *boylii* which approaches most closely to the species *pretiosa*" (C. L. Camp, Calif., 1917b, pp. 120–122).

**Voice:** No data. No vocal sacs. Croaks not very loud in captive males.

**Breeding:** As soon as ice has melted in the mountain lakes, these frogs breed in June and July. The eggs are approximately like those of *Rana b. boylii* (T. I. Storer, Calif., 1925). The tadpole is fairly large, 2⅞ inches (72 mm.), its body flattened, the tail musculature wide for an inch or more, then, suddenly tapering, the tail tip rounded or spatulate. The crests are broader toward the tip than at the body. The tooth ridges are ⅓, ¾, or ⅔. The period of development is 1 year, the animal passing the winter as a tadpole. It transforms, during July and August, ⅞–1 1/12 inches (20–27 mm.).

In the summer of 1907, Prof. J. C. Bradley at Giant Forest, Calif., took transforming young measuring 21–26 mm. On Aug. 22-27, 1917, we took at Alta Meadows, Sequoia National Park, a series of transforming frogs which measured from 21 mm. to 27 mm., the average and mode being 23 mm. Of our twelve females, three had ripe eggs to be laid.

At Davis, Calif., we examined some of Professor Storer's material. He had males 54–72 mm. and females 58–82 mm. in length. He had a young specimen 36 mm. long July 14, and others, near transformation, 20, 21.5, 22, 22 mm. July 3, 1930. One tadpole of 54 mm. (body length 21.5 mm.) had a tail that tended to be rounded, even spatulate, at the tip. Its teeth were ⅓. Those of another were ¾. The eggs had three jelly envelopes; the vitellus was 2.0 mm.; and the egg was about 7 mm. across. Egg masses were attached to the banks of a small creek.

"One mass of eggs was collected by Osgood R. Smith on April 23, 1942 at Convict Creek, Mono County, California, at an elevation of 7,000 feet. This clutch was attached to stems of sedge and contained about 120 eggs. . . .

"Mass plinth-like, about 28 × 40 mm., individual eggs one-quarter to one-half inch apart. There are besides the vitelline capsule three gelatinous envelopes, all clear and transparent. The outline of the egg is distinct and the firm jelly does not collect much debris. All envelopes are quite distinguishable in good light without a lens, as is the vitelline capsule. Least in thickness is the middle envelope, the next in thickness is the inner, being about two times the thickness of the middle, and the thickest is the outer which is approximately twice that of the inner. The vitellus is black at the animal pole and grey-tan at the vegetal. Measurements are: vitellus 2.17 mm. (range 1.81 to 2.30 mm.);

vitelline capsule 2.58 mm. (range 2.25 to 2.75 mm.); inner envelope 3.93 mm. (range 3.75 to 4.81 mm.); middle envelope 4 60 mm. (range 4.25 to 5.00 mm.); outer envelope 7.19 mm. (range 6.43 to 7.87 mm.).

"Measurements on the eggs preserved before they had time to attain their full size showed the vitellus to average somewhat less (av. 1.88 mm.) than the other eggs taken from natural surroundings" (R. L. Livezey and A. H. Wright, Gen., 1945, p. 703).

**Journal notes:** Aug. 23, 1917, Alta Meadows, Calif. In the pools on the mats were plenty of ***Rana boylii sierrae***. They stink like minks or other weasels. They are very slow. One can run a net under them or put a net on the bottom in front and touch the back parts. They are very yellow underneath. The species is almost through transformation. The larvae look on the venter somewhat like large toad tadpoles. We found a few transformed individuals.

On June 5, 1930, C. E. Van Deman, while looking for ***Bufo canorus*** on Peregoy Meadows, Yosemite Park, found several frog egg masses in the stream flowing through the meadow. From his description (in 1931) it seems likely that they were this form.

July 23, 1934, Aspen Valley and White Wolf, Yosemite Valley. In a boulder-strewn stream found ***Rana boylii sierrae***. In a pool with brush saw a frog put out and stay poised. You are much impressed with the spotted condition and the stripe on upper jaw. The type of habitat is not unlike that of ***Rana tarahumarae*** except that this is high wooded country and a running mountain stream whereas ***Rana tarahumarae*** is in desert canyons. They surely belong in the same group.

Middle Fork crossing Tuolumne River, 8000 feet. In clear stream on riffles, in edges of pools, or among grassy clumps are Sierra yellow legs. They sit rather flattened close to stone or bottom. They permit close approach and are easy of capture. Some are quite light and then are very conspicuous, but if dark they may be hard to see on the bottom. Males have thumbs with two pads and throats clear or spotted. One male very brilliant orange or cadmium orange on belly and hind legs, becoming xanthine orange on rear of thighs and on the toes. In bag the males gave a low croak. Throat pale orange yellow. Females when held in hand may give a clicking or chuckling note. Under parts of females paler. When the male croaks, just the center of the throat swells out slightly. Tioga Pass—in one spot 50 tadpoles in one scoop, 25 in the next try.

April 22, 1942. Went up King's River road with L. T. Hadsall and party. In Sycamore Cr. in quiet portions of the stream we saw little ***R. b. sierrae***. The adults would leap from banks or gravelly strands into the very swift water and were often hard to catch, particularly if it was a bouldery portion of the creek. No eggs to be seen in the stream. We caught several small females and two males unbelievably small. These we put together in the fish pail. The very

*Plate XCI. Rana boylii sierrae.* 1,3 Females (×3/5) 2 Male (×4/5)

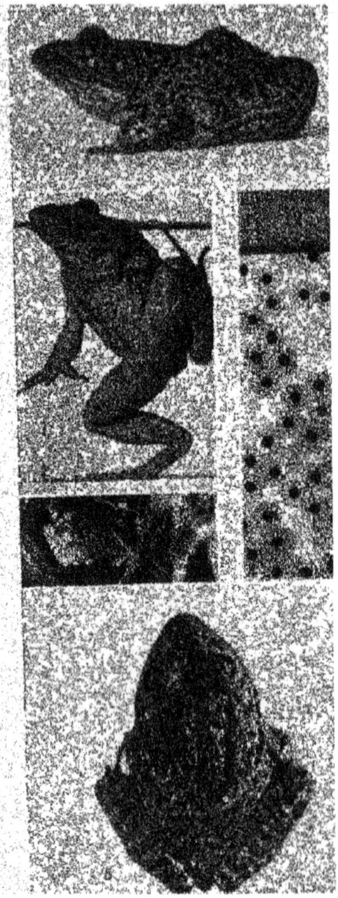

*Plate XCII. Rana capito.* 1,5. Males (×2/5). 2. Male (×2/5). 3. Male croaking (×1/5). 4. Eggs (×1).

little males mated, and one female through this last week (April 22–29) has laid a few eggs.

**Authorities' corner:**

C. L. Camp, Calif., 1917b, p 123.
J. Grinnell and T. I. Storer, Calif., 1924, p. 664.

## Florida Gopher Frog, Gopher Frog, Snake Frog, Southern Gopher Frog, Florida Frog

*Rana capito* Le Conte. Plates XCII; XV; Map 26.

**Range:** North Carolina to Florida.

"In the writer's possession is an adult male, collected in May 1919 by Charles E. Snyder near Pinelands, Hampton County, South Carolina, and it is quite likely that the species extends a good deal further north and east than even this locality" (R. F. Deckert, Fla., 1920, p 26). [Note Pineland, Jasper Co., is the locality in question?—E B. Chamberlain, S.C., 1939, p. 28]

**Habitat:** Almost solely in the burrows of the gopher turtle, which is common in the higher pine barrens and sandy hills. They breed in cypress and open ponds. We saw one go into a small opening which looked like a rat hole. The hole extended 18 inches into the ground and the end was only 9–12 inches below ground. There we found a female gopher frog. Near another turtle's burrow we saw a similar hole with a smooth worn spot about 8–12 inches away, the resting place of the frog.

The residents of Chesser Island, Ga., assured us that these frogs betake themselves to ratlike holes, hollow stumps, and holes beneath stumps, trees, and logs. Where gopher turtles are absent, they might resort to crayfish burrows, as Gaige tells us *Rana areolata,* a closely related species, does. Doubtless no other frog proves quite so typical of the higher pine barrens unless it be the oak toad. Occasionally the toad, the spadefoot, and the swamp cricket frog (*Pseudacris nigrita*) may be found in the same plant association.

"The specimen mentioned here was caught in a cage trap set among the sand hills to catch small rodents" (R. F. Deckert, Fla., 1920, p. 26)

"Moderately common on the oak ridges remaining in or near the burrows of *Gopherus polyphemus* (Daudin), going to ponds only to breed" (O. C. Van Hyning, Fla., 1933, p. 4).

"High pine, turkey oak ridges, and rosemary scrub. . . . Fairly common, but secretive and ungregarious; sometimes breeding in very large numbers in isolated ponds. . . . Nocturnal, but occasionally seen seated at the mouths of burrows on dark days. Although they occupy the holes of *Gopherus polyphemus* extensively, they are by no means confined to such retreats. Wright (1933) mentions finding them in small burrows which he took to be those of a rat. J. D. Kilby took one in the bottom of the burrow of a *Peromyscus polionotus;* I have twice found them in the burrows of the same mouse, and have also seen them frequently in stump holes and in the bottom of post holes, whence escape was apparently impossible. I caught one yearling in the mouth of a crayfish burrow at the edge of a cypress pond. They range some distance from their retreats in foraging at night, although Wright . . . believes they spend much time resting on 'a little clear place—a short distance from the hole.' I once saw one seated on a fallen pine log; looking about I located a gopher-hole some thirty feet from the frog; when I advanced and kicked one end of the log the frog hopped about wildly for a moment, then headed directly for the gopher-hole and disappeared down it. Since there was no other burrow in the immediate vicinity, and since the hole was not visible from the frog's original position, it seems to me justifiable to interpret this behavior as the result of homing instinct. Several observers have noticed the tendency of *capito* to crouch at the approach of an intruder. I found one which had been stepped on and killed by dogs running a fox" (A. F. Carr, Jr., Fla., 1940b, pp. 63–64).

**Size:** Adults, 2¾–4⅓ inches. Males, 68–101 mm. Females, 77–108 mm.

**General appearance:** This large, heavy-bodied gray frog is broad forward and has a slender waist. It has a cavernous mouth and prominent eyes. The gray of the back is finely speckled with black dots and marked with three or four rows of round dark spots between and often crossing the dorsolateral folds. There are many more along the sides. The arms and legs are conspicuously barred; and the throat, breast, and much of the underside of the hind legs are heavily dotted with dark. The males have yellow on folds, tubercles, iris, axilla, and groin, but the females have little or no yellow.

**Color:** *Male.* Okefinokee Swamp, Ga., July 20, 1921. Sides of head, dorsum of limbs and sides below the costal fold French gray or lilac gray. Between the costal folds about four rows of black spots. Fore and hind legs with numerous black bars, broken at times or speckled with French gray. Costal fold from honey yellow to mustard or buff (yellow to greenish yellow depending on degree of dark specking on it). Another similar stripe along upper jaw and over arm insertion. All the tubercles on the back with same color. Under parts white with hair brown, fuscous, or purplish; black spots on throat and chin. Posterior faces of hind limbs purplish vinaceous. Upper part of iris black then buff yellow or honey yellow over the pupil, black in front and behind the pupil, two light gray areas beneath pupil separated by black.

*Female.* Okefinokee Swamp, Ga., July 2, 1922. General color on sides French gray, cinereous, or pale purplish gray. Lateral fold, canthus rostralis, upper eyelid, beneath eye, and fold back of angle of mouth cream-buff or tilleul buff. Ground color of back a combination of colors of sides and lateral fold. On the back are four more or less irregular rows of black rounded spots, three such rows on the sides. Black crossbars on limbs. Spots on the throat bister to snuff brown. Those on sides of belly army brown. Underside of feet and hands and femur deep vinaceous-lavender. Iris black with prominent bar of colonial buff or tilleul buff above the pupil; below the pupil may be two small bars of French gray, cinereous, pale purplish, or pallid purplish gray. In another frog the two lower bars are united. Rest of eye black with a little dotting of the two colors.

**Structure:** Wedge-shaped body, wide in head and slender in waist; tubercles on back; thumbs of males somewhat enlarged and darkened; males with vocal sacs from angle of mouth halfway to the groin.

"Above very rough, dark grey or slate-color speckled with black with six rows of roundish spots on the back; side speckled and irregularly marked with spots of the same form and color; from the orbits to beyond the middle of the body runs a broad raised line or cutaneous fold; and another from the corner of the mouth to the insertion of the arm. Beneath smooth, yellowish white, speckled; spotted and varied with dusky; top of head coarsely punctured, back and sides tuberculous. Head very large, broad and blunt, a deep concavity between the nostrils and the eyes. Irides golden mixed with black. Tympanum of the color of the body. Lower jaw with a small protuberance or point resembling a tooth. Arms and legs above grey, speckled and barred with black, beneath yellowish spotted and varied with dusky, the yellowish color more decided at the axillae and groins. Hind part of the thighs granulate. Fingers slightly palmate at the base, the first longer than the second. The second toe twice as long as the first. Length 4.2 in., width of the head at the corners of the mouth 1.5 in., arm 1.87, leg 4.75, thigh 1.1 in., tibia 1.45, foot 2.2.

"Inhabits Georgia in the ditches of the rice-fields" (Le Conte, Gen., 1856, p. 425).

"This singular form may be known at once by the short and squat form of the body as compared with the size of the head, resembling in this some of the Australian Cystignathidae. . . . The only specimen of this subspecies which I have seen is the following: *Rana areolata aesopus* Cope. Catalogue number 4743, No. of spec. 1. Locality, Micanopy, Fla. From whom received: Dr. T. H. Bean. Nature of specimen: alcoholic" (E. D. Cope, Gen., 1889, pp. 412–413).

**Voice:** The call is a deep hollow roll, intermediate between a snore and a groan, *yawh h h h, yawh h h h h.*

The croaking is a very remarkable performance. A lateral pouch is inflated on each side of the neck and keeps swelling posteriorly until it extends halfway down the side of the body, attaining a size nearly equal to that of the frog's head. The creature's form is then strongly suggestive of a batfish. The note and likewise the inflation lasts for a second or so. At the start the intervals between notes may range from 10 seconds to nearly half a minute, but as the frog warms to its performance, a croak may be given every 2 or 3 seconds. The sound will probably carry a quarter of a mile. When we first heard the note, one of the residents thought it a woodpecker, but I recorded that it seemed more like *Rana sphenocephala* in tone, though the latter is a more rasping croak. The call of *Rana sphenocephala* is like a rattle compared with the uniform continuous roar of *Rana capito*. In chorus it sounded to Mrs. Wright and myself like the surf or a deep guttural roar (possibly a trill at times) like rolling *r*'s down deep in the throat. The chorus seemed to go in waves with decided crests.

"When the interior of the large glass jar in which it lives is sprinkled and after this certain noises are made like rustling papers or water running from a tap this frog 'sings.' The call resembles a loud snore similar to that of *Rana pipiens*, but much coarser and louder. During the calls, which are repeated about every two seconds and are of from three to five seconds' duration, the vocal vesicles over the arms are distended into hemispheres about the size of large hazel nuts" (R. F. Deckert, Fla., 1920, p. 26).

**Breeding:** This species breeds throughout the year. The eggs are in a large plinthlike mass about 6 by 8 inches and 1½ inches deep. The egg is 1/12 inch (2 mm.), the outer envelope ⅕ inch (5.2 mm.), the inner ⅛ inch (3.8 mm.). They hatch in 4–4½ days. The tadpole is large, 3⅜ inches (84 mm.), full and deep bodies, the venter strongly pigmented, the tail long. The color may be greenish, with yellowish on the top and side of the head, the belly yellowish. The tooth ridges are ⅔. After 85 to 100 days, the tadpoles transform from August to Nov. 1, at 1 1/12–1½ inches (27–38 mm.).

On Aug. 17, 1922, we found several egg masses laid in a cypress pond. On the north edge in water 6–8 inches deep and 30 feet from the edge of the pond, I found, 1 inch below the surface at the base of a small cypress (10 feet high) and among some brush, a mass attached to an upright twig. The black and cream eggs look larger and farther apart than are those of *Rana sphenocephala*. Near a large cypress stump in an open grassy area where pine cones were on the bottom, a large mass was attached to a sedge stem. Its top was level with the surface of the water. The water was 9 inches deep. The mass was 4 by 5 inches and 1½ inches thick. At first the mass impressed all of us as bluish, and two of us independently likened it to *R. sylvatica* in this respect. The lower pole may be cream at first, but it soon becomes white. The whole mass when turned over gives the same white mass impression that *R. sphenocephala* and *R. pipiens* egg masses give. Another mass was 6 by 8 by 1½ to 2 inches thick.

"The writer has also collected this species during its breeding season in February, near Jacksonville, Fla. in 1912" (R. F. Deckert, Fla., 1920, p. 26).

"March 13 to November 3 in grassy ponds. They must travel some distance to congregate at widely separated ponds, since I have found them a mile from water" (A. F. Carr, Fla., 1940b, p. 64).

**Journal notes:** Okefinokee Swamp, Ga. In its normal all-the-year habitat, the sand hills and turtle burrows, these frogs are seldom seen unless one deliberately seeks them. They usually rest at the mouth of the burrow, sometimes a foot or so down the decline; more rarely they may be a foot or more from the incline, on little, clear, smooth places 6 inches in diameter a short distance from the hole. One area we visited frequently. From midforenoon to midafternoon, they were seldom out. For example, on July 2, 1922, we visited this area at noon and 2:30 P.M. and found only one out, but at midnight we readily found eight. My journal reads, Called again at 12 midnight. Francis' special friend not to be seen. Anna's friend was under a log, the entrance a foot or more away because we had dug it back from under the log. Suddenly something tumbled from under the log into the hole before I realized what had happened. Francis found another at a hole near by. I found one and Miles saw three: one was 1–1½ feet from the entrance. This one I caught. It is a female. Tried for one or two more but did not succeed. They are not so strongly held by light as are most Anura.

July 11, 1922. At 7:15 P.M. we started for the gopher-frog area near Chesser School. Found seven or eight at entrances to holes or a foot or two away. At one hole Miles saw a cotton mouse (*Peromyscus gossypinus*). At another I saw a cotton rat (*Sigmodon*). We captured three frogs. I caught one by hand. Could have taken three or four more. Miles took the net without its handle, interposed it between frog and hole. Frog like a woodchuck makes for the hole and jumps into the net. Sometimes this works, sometimes it does not. At first I espied a frog at the entrance and tried to steal up on it from opposite the incline. It heard me. Wonder if one could catch them with baited hook and line. One was obliging and allowed us to take its picture. First one this year. It turned around twice during the process, then popped in. On Aug. 9, 1921, Mr. Harper stalked another, just north of MacClenny near the St. Mary's River on an oak ridge. In both instances a log rests over the entrance. This is a favorite cover for both frogs and turtles. The turtles seem at times to prefer to dig their hole under fallen logs and the frogs often apparently prefer such gopher-turtle burrows or burrows with saw palmettos near by.

July 17, 1921. About a dozen began croaking in a cypress pond on Chesser's Island, Ga., before darkness came on. When they began, one of the residents called it "the monster." At first while wading in the deeper water of the pond in the early evening, we would hear this mysterious note among the cypress trees, usually at their bases or on logs. The frog would espy us first, and all we could determine was a big splash, doubtless made by a large frog. Finally we heard one in shallow water in a tussock of sedge 2–3 feet across and 1 foot high, and another near the base of a cypress in deeper water. After 2 hours' work on *Hyla gratiosa* we sought out a group of gopher frogs we were hearing in the shallower western portion of the pond. One was beside a cypress tree in a depression of fibrous roots. After we had focused on it, it literally crawled around to a different position. I put the light on its nose and tried to push it back with my fingers. Then it leaped. At the base of a pine on a pile of chips 1½ feet above the surface was another croaker. After a time, it would "bat" its eye toward the bull's-eye. We secured two flashlight photographs of it. These frogs were not hard to catch when discovered, but they were shy. Often when first put under light they would sink back in the fibrous roots, depressions, and covers. One was spread out in the water among the spice bushes. The influence of near-by croakers seemed to stimulate this one as it does others. We caught several, put them in a bag, and induced these to croak. The sprawled-out specimen responded beautifully with his croaks.

August 17, 1922, Trail Ridge near Hilliard, Fla. (an oak ridge locality). After an excessively rainy period, we were detouring on the Dixie Highway when Mr. Harper heard spadefoots in some shallow pine barren ponds. Later, in the same place, after 5 P.M., I thought I heard frogs in the higher open places in the pine forest near the spadefoot pools. We suspected they were gopher frogs and queried whether they were in the ground, at the gopher-turtle burrows, or moving to their breeding places. We never found one, and one of the party thought it a ventriloquial effect from a near-by cypress pond. When darkness came on, this pond was suddenly resonant with gopher frog calls in chorus. These chose perches similar to those described in 1921. One was at the base of a stump and above the water. Another was in the notch of a floating log. A third was at the base of a cypress. A fourth was beside a stump and mostly sunk in the water. With all four of us searching we saw only one croak; the rest never responded when we were near.

**Authorities' corner:**

E. Loennberg, Fla., 1895, p. 339.
T. Barbour, Fla , 1920, p. 55.
T. Hallinan, Fla , 1923, pp. 19–20.
A. F. Carr, Jr., Fla., 1940b, p. 64.

## Slater's Frog, Slater's Spotted Frog, Cascade Frog

*Rana cascadae* Slater. Plate XCIII; Map 27

**Range and Habitat:** "Type—C. P. S No. 2883, an adult female from Elysian Fields, Rainier National Park, Washington. Elevation 5700 feet. Collected by the author June 19, 1938. On life zones *Rana cascadae* is typically a Hudsonian frog. I already have specimens in my collection from the high parts of the following counties of the State of Washington: Chelan, Clallam, Kittitas, Lewis, Mason, Pierce, Skagit, Skamania, Snohomish and Yakima; and one specimen from Potsville, Idaho. It will likely be found in Oregon, British Columbia, and possibly Alaska" (J. R. Slater, Wash., 1939b, pp. 146–149).

In 1942 Slater had it from thirteen instead of nine (1939) counties in Washington.

**Size:** Adults, 2–3 inches. Males 50–58 mm. Females, 52–74 mm. These measurements were taken from 21 males and 20 females in Slater's laboratory. The average of males was 53 3 mm., the mean 53 mm.; the average of the females was 63 mm., the mean 60 or 62 mm.—quite a difference in size. The frogs were taken April to October—April 10, May 15, 30, June 18, July 4, Aug. 29, Oct. 2.

**General appearance:** A medium-sized frog, somewhat similar to *R. pretiosa.* "General coloration dorsal surface slight greenish-brown with many black spots about three millimeters in diameter; dorsolateral folds light brown; sides green-brown mottled with black and fading to light yellow toward ventral surface; space behind eye including ear, and line under canthus rostralis, dark brown; ridge along upper jaw, yellowish; lips, mottled; throat and undersurfaces of body and limbs, very light yellow; upper surface fore limb, mottled and slight bar; hind limb with broken dark bands" (J. R. Slater, Wash., 1939b, p. 146).

**Color:** Tipso Lake, Pierce Co., Wash., from J. R. Slater, June 7, 1941. *Male.* Dorsal color and upper side of legs isabella color. On top of head and between costal folds and down to belly color are numerous irregular black or brownish olive spots, the largest 5 mm. across. These spots are in five or six bars on rear and front of tibia, being broken on middorsal tibial surface. There are three or four such indistinct bars on rear of tarsus and outer toe. There are two bars on antebrachium and a prominent vertical bar from insertion of brachium halfway to radius on front of brachium. The mask is brownish olive or Prout's brown, and from rear of mouth involves tympanum, extends forward as a prominent line past the nostril bordered below *with a prominent cream-buff line from snout to angle of mouth,* and incurves slightly along the infralabial margin of the rictus. The infralabial margin and throat are vermiculated with drab and ventral color. The throat is colonial buff, becoming deep colonial buff on belly and honey yellow on underside of legs The rear of femur is isabella color. Lower part of eye black with wash of drab and flecks of chamois. The lower portion of iris rim is chamois, but the upper part expands as a solid spot of reed yellow.

*Female.* Much the same as male but no spots or very few spots between dorsolateral folds, below which are a few scattered spots. The dorsum is buffy olive. The throat is clear and a bit yellow, perhaps amber yellow. The legs are much the same. The supralabial fold is primrose yellow rather sharply bordered below by brownish olive.

*Male.* Deer Lake, Sol Duc River, Clallam Co., Wash., north side Olympic Mts., from James R. Slater, June 7, 1930. Color of back a dark greenish olive with several rounded inky spots on dorsum and some below dorsolateral folds. Sides reed yellow to citron green with heavy black mottling. *Line on upper jaw reed yellow to primrose yellow.* Under surfaces primrose yellow, with some olive-ocher on under surfaces of legs. Legs with black bars. Mask is brownish olive. Eye as in the female.

*Female.* Back Saccardo's olive, mask Sanford's brown, dorsolateral folds conspicuous. Few to many black spots on dorsum and many along the sides on a pale yellow-green ground. The pale yellow-green conspicuous in axil and in groin. *Line along upper jaw is pale chalcedony yellow.* Ventral surfaces sulphur yellow. There is a touch of salmon-orange or orange-buff along underside of tarsus. Under surface of femur chamois to olive-buff. The iris is black with band of pinard yellow specks above and bordering pupil and light orange-yellow specks below. Around the outer edge is a broken band of light lumiere green.

**Structure:** "Form moderately slender; head broad; external nares halfway between tip of muzzle and orbit; canthus rostralis prominent; orbit moderate; interorbital space about two-thirds length of orbit; moderate ridge on upper jaw, beginning anterior to the orbit and extending posteriorly to fore limb; tympanum inconspicuous, round, diameter about one-half length of orbit, separated from orbit by about two-thirds of its diameter, foreleg stout; palm with three elongated tubercles; sesamoid tubercles very prominent; digits stout, in order of decreasing length, 3, 4, 1, 2; dorsolateral folds broad and prominent; hind limb slim; tibia nearly the same length as femur; tarsus greater than one-third length of foot; two metatarsal tubercles; toes stout, in order of decreasing length, 4, 3, 5, 2, 1; web moderate.

"Tongue narrow oval, posterior end with well developed lobes, attached by anterior one-half to floor of mouth; internal nares slightly overlapped by upper jaw; vomerine teeth mostly posterior to line joining centers of internal nares, two areas of which converge posteriorly and nearly join; maxillary and vomerine teeth small.

"Surfaces generally smooth with slight roughening on dorsal surface of body, posterior femur, and dorsal tibia" (J. R. Slater, Wash., 1939b, p. 145).

**Voice:** No record. Of the frogs from Tipso Lake (Pierce Co., Wash.), June 7, 1941, sent me by J. R. Slater this note was made: There are no external vocal sacs. While in captivity, they have croaked several times, especially when seized ahead of the hind legs. It is a low croak.

**Breeding:** Females shipped to us June 7, 1930, by J. R. Slater and collected at Deer Lake, Sol Duc River, Clallam Co., Wash., on north side of Olympic Mts. Enroute they laid eggs in the moss of the container. These may not have expanded normally but they appear to be far apart like *Rana sylvatica* eggs. They seem to have an inner envelope with the vitellus from 2.2–2.8 mm. or more in diameter.

"Eggs.—The different jelly envelopes average as follows: outer 11.3, middle, 5.8, inner 4.9, while the egg proper is 2.25. Color of egg is very dark on upper three-fourths and light cream below.

"Tadpoles.—The teeth are in two upper rows with a small gap in center of second row and four lower, three of which are nearly full length while the fourth is about one-fourth the length of the others. Tadpoles at hindlimb bud stage are 34 millimeters and when the toe buds show on hind limb they are about 40 millimeters.

"Life-history.—Spawning period is from May 20 to July 10 depending on how much snow there is to melt before the ponds appear; eggs deposited in small ponds in numbers up to 425 by single female, hatch in 8 to 20 days;

larval period 80 to 95 days, with very few tadpoles living over to following summer; transformation size for most of them 14 mm. or less; size at one year after transforming about 30 mm.; sexual maturity reached at end of three full years or possibly four" (J. R. Slater, Wash., 1939b, p. 149).

**Journal notes:** The last of March, 1942, we sought to see this frog, but Professor Slater told us that we were too early for this form of the higher elevations.

March 31–April 2. Worked over Slater's *R. cascadae;* measured for range of adults male and female and transformation. He says *R. cascadae* has no red underneath but is cream or straw color. Most of his records are above 4000 ft. He contrasts it with *R. aurora aurora.* He showed us two skins of *R. a. aurora* and *R. pretiosa* to show differences in coloration and color. *Aurora* is mottled black and yellow with some green in groin; *pretiosa* is red. Does *R. cascadae* run into *R. b. boylii* in Cascades? He has a number from Breitenbush Lake, Marion Co., Ore. Slater conceives of *R. cascadae* as closest to *R. a. aurora.* It is different from *R. b. boylii.* It is also different from *R. p. pretiosa.* What is its relation to *R. p. luteiventris?* (See *R. a. aurora*). Cursory notes on Slater's material follow:

1. He has many interesting young specimens. One lot just transformed measures 13, 13, 14, 15, 16, 17 mm. The tadpoles belong in wood frog group, a *R. temporaria* type. Longest tadpole is 70 mm., of which body is 22 mm., depth of body 14½ mm., and depth of tail crest 15 mm. The tail crest comes forward onto body almost to the vertical of spiracle; spiracle is nearer vent than tip of snout; eye is entirely dorsal. Another tadpole is 70 mm.

2. June 18, 1938. Two 23 mm. specimens just transformed; one young 28 mm.

3. June 18, 1938. Among the adults are three young, one 24 mm. and two 36 and 38 mm.

4. July 11, 1931. One transformed at 20 mm.; intermediate specimen 43 mm.

5. Aug. 5, 1937. Several transformed 23.5, 23.5 mm.; past transformation 25, 34 mm.

6. Aug. 16, 1930. One 21 mm. just transformed; one 32 mm.

7. Oct. 10, 1939. One just transformed 20.6 mm., another 22.6 mm., and one 36 mm.

8. We noted one specimen marked "male not strong" at 38 mm.; and one "female not mature" at 44 mm.

9. Random notes on specimens measured follow:

a. Young, 28 mm., has 2 prominent metatarsal tubercles.

b. Young, 36 mm., has 2 prominent metatarsal tubercles.

c. Young, 36 mm., heel goes to snout's tip.

d. Female, 44 mm., not mature. Hardly spotted at all; quite a few tubercles

*Plate XCIII. Rana cascadae* (×2/8). 1,2,3,5. Males. 4,6. Females.

*Plate XCIV. Rana catesbeiana.* 1,4,5. Males (×3/8). 2. Female (×3/8). 3. Tadpole (×3/8). 6. Eggs (×1/8). .

on back and side. Heel goes to nostril; there is a dark spot wherever there is a tubercle which serves as a light center.

e. Males, 56 mm., 56 mm ; female, 56 mm. One male very spotted; one male with heel almost to tip of snout. Male has web from tip of fourth toe convex and folded in one place, the web from fourth to third somewhat convex, from third to second about straight, but hind foot webbing is much more pronounced than in the female. In the female the web is concave between all toes. Tympanum same size but more oblique in male than in female. Thumb of male not as much bilobed as in some western frogs. All fingers of male are much thicker, also brachium and antebrachium.

f. Female, 68 mm. Internasal space broad, flat; interorbital space rather narrow and less than internasal; upper eyelid rather broader than interorbital space; dorsolateral folds rather flat but prominent, broader in the forward half. Skin between dorsolateral folds smooth, below folds quite a few tubercles; fore and hind limbs almost smooth above; dorsolateral fold starts below eye and then just below the tympanum doubles in width. It is light in color and this makes a prominent light wart back of corner of mouth. Rear of femur uniform. Two metatarsal tubercles, inner (opposite toe 5) is very slight. Prominent palmar tubercle at base of third and fourth digits. Tongue prominently or deeply notched. Vomerine patches between choanae almost meet on the meson. Articular tubercles on foot not very prominent. Specimen not much spotted.

**Authorities' corner:** There is as yet only one authority for this species, Prof. J. R. Slater, who kindly showed me all his material.

"Some previous collectors have placed specimens of this species with *Rana aurora aurora* while others have called them *Rana pretiosa* but it appears to me that *Rana cascadae* may be more primitive than these other two species. This species is named from the region in which I first found it which is the Cascade Range" (J. R. Slater, Wash., 1939b, p. 149).

## Bullfrog, Bloody Nouns, Bully, Jug-o'-Rum, North American Bullfrog, American Bullfrog

*Rana catesbeiana* Shaw. Plate XCIV; Map 29.

**Range:** From Laredo or the mouth of the Pecos River through the Panhandles of Texas and Oklahoma, extreme western Kansas, Nebraska to Minnesota, Lake Huron to Maine. Absent from southern half of Florida. Introduced in New Mexico, Colorado, Wyoming, Idaho, Arizona, Nevada, California, Oregon, Washington, and British Columbia.

**Habitat:** Strictly aquatic, these frogs seem to prefer millponds, hydraulic lakes, reservoirs, and kindred bodies of water.

The authors' best collecting grounds have been a clear glacial lake in a New

England kettle hole, with a slight suggestion of the sphagnous flora about it; a pond in a clear trout brook; a large reservoir for a hydraulic laboratory; a disused millpond; and a wooded lake whose shifting water level had made a fringe of overhanging dead trees, floating logs, and submerged roots and limbs. In every case the shores were more or less wooded, but more important are two factors: (1) shallows where the species can transform, and (2) brush, stumps whose roots are at the edge of the pond, driftwood along the bank, or matted roots of a fringe of willow trees.

When croaking begins, the males often take certain perches in which they keep a proprietary interest. About one pond the authors once located seven such places, each with its possessor, only once finding two in one place. The first frog was on a board in water filled with brush; another was perched on a log among brush beneath the float of a boathouse; the third was on the bank among some limbs extending into the water; the fourth was by an overturned stump whose roots were partly submerged; the fifth was among driftwood along the shore; the sixth was on a stationary float; and the last was at the base of a tree fallen into the pond. When, however, the males about a lake are numerous enough to make their night croaking a real chorus, it is not likely that any one individual holds a favorite site to the exclusion of the others. The bullfrog is a solitary form.

For migration and growth see E. C. Raney, N Y., 1940, pp. 733–745.

"Moderately common; frequents margins of ponds, ditches and swamps" (O C. Van Hyning, Fla., 1933, p. 4).

**Size:** Adults, 3⅝–8 inches. Males, 85–180 mm. Females, 89–184, possibly 200 mm. The species seldom breeds before it reaches 4 inches (100 mm.).

**General appearance:** The bullfrog is our largest frog. It is rather broad in body In the North it is usually a greenish drab on the back and yellowish white underneath. The skin may be roughened with fine tubercles. There is no lateral fold, except a short fold over and behind the tympanum. There are a few dusky spots on the legs. This frog in the Gulf region may be so dark as to be almost black on the back and heavily mottled beneath, and even the webs of the feet may be almost black.

**Color:** *Female.* Chopowampsic Swamp, Va., April 22, 1929. Head, before, below, and back of eyes, upper eyelids, and area from angle of mouth to tympanum are cosse green, calliste green, or courge green. Rest of upper parts same color or light yellowish olive, yellowish citrine, or oil yellow inconspicuously spotted with Saccardo's olive or light brownish olive. Rim on outer part of tympanum same color. Hind and fore limbs same color as back, or ecru-olive with yellowish olive or dark greenish olive crossbars on femur and tibia and same color in spots on fore limbs. Front of femur reticulated with grayish olive, also groin and undersides of hind legs partially reticulated or spotted with light grayish olive with white interspaces. Under parts white or pale olive-buff. Iris black spotted with rufous, apricot orange, or orange chrome. Pupil rim pale lemon yellow.

**Structure:** No ridges down either side of back; web of fourth toe extends to its tip; male with internal vocal sacs, when sacs inflated a flattened pouch beneath chin; male with tympana larger than eye; head narrow.

**Voice:** The sonorous bass notes have received countless characterizations, among which are the familiar *jug-o'-rum, more rum, blood 'n' ouns, br-wum, be drowned, knee deep,* and *bottle-o'-rum.* These notes have wonderful carrying power and are commonly heard in the evenings of early summer.

**Breeding:** In the North bullfrogs breed the last of June or in July when the air temperature is about 80° and the water has warmed up to 70°. In the South they breed much earlier. We found an egg mass in San Antonio, Tex., Feb. 12, 1925. The egg mass is a large surface film 2 by ½, 2 by 2, or 2 by 2½ feet; the eggs, black and white, are 1/20–1/15 inch (1.2–1.7 mm.) in diameter. There is no inner envelope and the outer merges into the jelly film. The tadpole is large, 4–6⅗ inches (100–165 mm), olive in color with fine speckings of black, and with the tooth ridges ⅔, rarely 3/3. In the North it spends two winters as a tadpole, and transforms from July 1 to Aug. 15, or in the South, from last of May onward, at 1¼–2⅜ inches (31–59 mm.).

See L. R. Aronson, N.Y., 1943, pp. 4–6.

**Journal notes:** McLean, N.Y. On June 16, 1913, when we discovered some seven or eight egg complements, considerably more light was thrown on the egg laying. More than ever are we of the opinion that in the expulsion of the eggs the two forms, green frog and bullfrog, agree. In several of the complements the egg masses were in brush near the bank's edge, and all of these either were of the film type or had originally been so. In one case the eggs had the spoiled appearance which green frogs' eggs sometimes have when they have been stranded high and dry. The fresh films, 1½ feet or more in diameter, we could easily detect because of the conspicuous air bubbles in the mass.

Along the east edge of this particular lake occurs the deepest water, and here for many years the tadpoles have often transformed. We could not understand this deep-water transformation site. Frequently the bullfrogs laid their films in midpond around stumps, or perchance attached the surface egg film to the tips of some dead elderberry stems reaching 8 feet out into the water. The strong western winds create waves on the water's surface, breaking up the disks into small packets. These drifted to the east side and we often detected them there among the algae, their position revealed by the foamy air bubbles. At this east edge they hatch, remain in the deep water, and hence transform here instead of in the usual transforming site, the shallows.

June 30, 1913, Otter Lake, Dorset, Ont. Evening. Bullfrogs in chorus. They are common here. In the grassy run west of Brennan's house, they are common and lie on the surface of the water. If frightened they dive and soon come up again a short distance away. The other day the boys caught 29 with a red flannel hook. The following evening with electric flashlight we caught 15. The next day, June 29, Charles and I in the daytime went up to the N. W. swampy corner of the lake, where untold logs and stumps are, and captured 20 more. When I cleaned them, none of the females had laid. They were still with eggs. Furthermore, we found no eggs in the field. Surely this is the wrong season to catch them. Their capture should not be allowed until the middle of July or beginning of August.

June 4, 1917. Camped at Broad River, S.C. In long shallow pools 2–3 ft. deep, where plenty of yellow water lilies grow, found three masses of bullfrog eggs. One fresh mass was 2½ by 1½ ft. in diameter and was at the surface around the stems of a yellow water lily. Another mass looked like cooked rhubarb and was more or less dirty. In another case, the egg mass was on *Chara* which surrounded the stems of the water lilies. Here there were plenty of adult bullfrogs.

Feb. 12, 1925, Brackenridge Park, San Antonio, Tex. Near a ford below the new swimming pool found two large films of eggs. Instinctively I called them *R. catesbeiana* but why February? The water was at least 55° to 60° at 3:30 P.M. The air according to the San Antonio weather bureau was 63° to 64°. One egg mass was 2½–3 ft. across. Film among algae and *Myriophyllum*-like plant. The inner edge of mass about one foot from bank in water 4–6 in. deep. A little below a camper said he had heard the bullfrogs croak, and in this locality were the large tadpoles of *R. catesbeiana*. Then at the place where the mass was, there were two bullfrogs with heads up, one a half-grown one and one a very large one.

*Introduction west of Rocky Mountains.* Several young naturalists have sent us strange frogs from the West. "Are they new?" "They do not agree with the descriptions of any frog of the Plateau or Pacific States." "What are they?" Usually the perplexing form is a young or half-grown introduced bullfrog.

To us as naturalists the presence in the extreme West of the bullfrog is undesirable. According to the following authorities this species has been introduced into Colorado (Ellis and Henderson), New Mexico and Arizona (Bogert), Idaho (Slevin), Washington (Slater), British Columbia (Carl), Oregon (Gordon), Nevada (Linsdale), and California (Slevin). Many who think of immediate results might proclaim it a blessing. It is a voracious, omnivorous, carnivorous species. We would hate to see it introduced in Myer's *Bufo exsul* colony. It is already in the restricted *R. fisheri* habitat. The following cursory notes of the summer of 1942 show how widepread it is:

March 8, 1942, California. Went to Searsbury Reservoir. Heard a bullfrog there. Saw no frogs.

March 30, Washington. Went on short trip . . . with Mr. James Slater to Sparaway Lake. There are no end of *R. catesbeiana* in the lake. In a man's pool near the pond saw several *R. catesbeiana.*

April 8, above Medford, Ore. Stopped on Rogue River east of Beagle. Here in a dug pond there were numerous bullfrogs leaping into the water. A short distance above Trail saw a series of brushy pools with immense bullfrogs.

April 11, Chico to Davis, Calif. Two miles north of Richvale, in bordering ditches filled with cattails, were bullfrogs.

May 15, Las Vegas, Nev. Went out toward Tonopah, 25 miles and returned after dark. Near a trailer camp bullfrogs calling in a large pond.

May 16, Las Vegas. At the U.S. Fish Hatchery springs found bullfrogs but no *R. fisheri.*

May 20, Moapa Indian Reservation (near Glendale, Nev.). Bullfrogs in their drainage ditches.

June 13, Arizona. Went out last night toward Florence Jct. Heard bullfrogs and Hammond's spadefoot in pool at Desert Wells.

July 21, LaPosta Lodge, El Paso, Tex. On road toward Smeltertown took one *Rana catesbeiana.*

**Authorities' corner:** "It is the General Belief of the People in Virginia that they keep the springs clean, and purify the Water, wherefore they never kill or molest them, but superstitiously believe it bodes them ill so to do.

"The Noise they make has caused their Name; for at a few Yards Distance their Bellowing sounds very much like that of a Bull a quarter of a Mile off, and what adds to the Force of the Sound, is their sitting within the hollow Mouth of the Spring" (M. Catesby, 1731–1743, p. 72).

"At Baltimore I first saw the fire-fly. . . . Mischievous boys will sometimes catch a bull-frog, and fasten them all over him. They show to great advantage, while the poor frog, who cannot understand the 'new lights' that are breaking upon him affords amusement to his tormentors by hopping about in a state of desperation" (G. T. Vigne, Gen., 1832, p. 140).

"The frogs were as great a source of amusement to us as the pigeons were of excitement. Wherever there was a spot of water, the double bass of the bullfrogs striking in every now and then amidst indescribable piping of the multitudes of their smaller brethren. It is very difficult to catch a sight of these bassoon performers, as they spring into the water at the slightest approach of danger; yet you may now and then come on them basking at the side of a pond or streamlet, their great goggle eyes and black skin making them look very grotesque. They are great thieves in their own element, many a duckling vanishing from its mother's side by a sudden snap of some one of these solemn gentlemen below. They are a hungry race, always ready apparently for what they can get, and making short work with small fishes, all kinds of small reptiles, and even, I believe, the lesser kinds of snakes, when they can get them. These fellows are the giants of the frog tribes, and portly gentlemen withal, some of them weighing very nearly a pound" (J. C. Geikie, Gen., 1882(?), pp. 216–217).

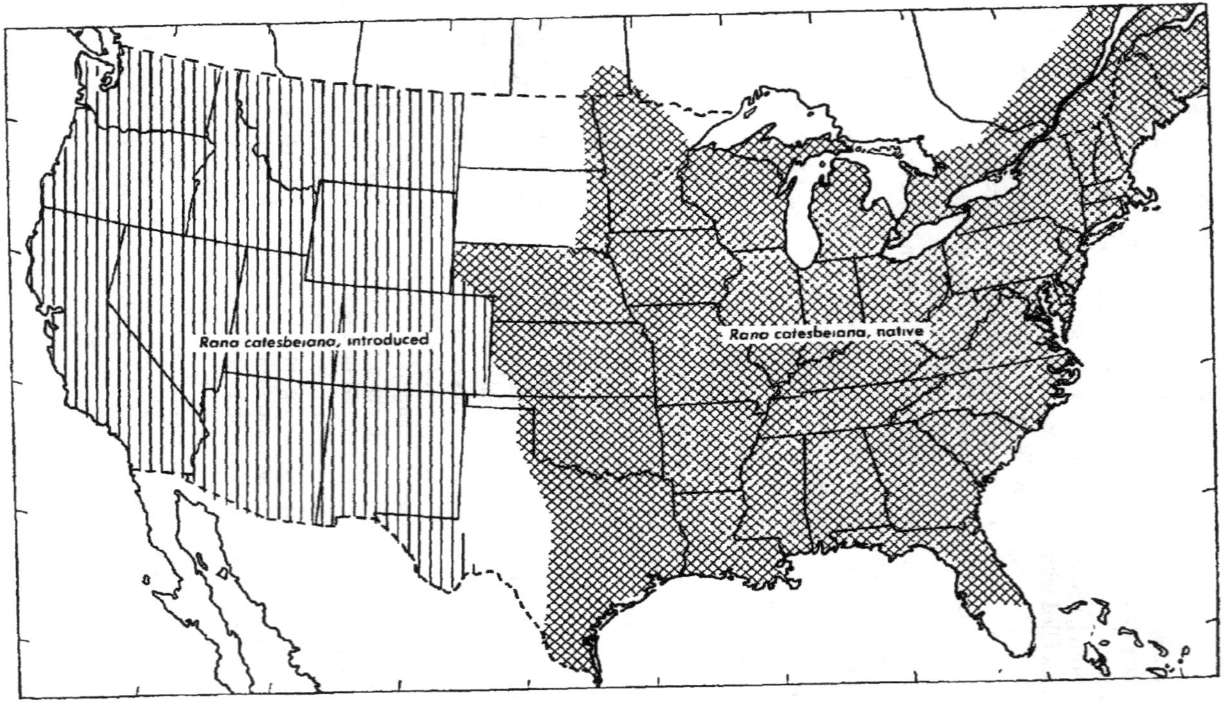


*Map 29*

## Green Frog, Pond Frog, Spring Frog, Common Spring Frog, Bullfrog, Bawling Frog, Yellow-throated Green Frog, Belly Bumper, Bully

*Rana clamitans* Latreille. Plate XCV; Map 30.

**Range:** Southeastern Texas to Louisiana, Arkansas, southeastern Oklahoma, eastern Kansas through Iowa, western Minnesota to Canada east to Gaspé Peninsula. Not in southern half of Florida.

**Habitat:** A solitary species. Like the bullfrog, it lives in swamps and in our deeper, larger ponds and reservoirs, but the green frog also lives in smaller ponds and pools. In fact, along watercourses there is hardly a small pond which cannot claim a green frog. Hibernates in the water.

"Bayheads and titi swamps; wet low hammocks, streams in mesophytic hammock; cypress swamps. . . . Not common . . ." (A. F. Carr, Jr., Fla., 1940b, p. 65).

**Size:** Adults, 2–4 inches. Smaller in the South. Males, 52–72 mm. in the South, and reaching 95 mm. in the North. Females, 58–75 mm. in the South, reaching 100 mm. in the North.

**General appearance:** This is a yellow-throated bullfrog. In the North the green frog is one of our largest frogs. It has a prominent dorsolateral fold with a branch extending almost at right angles downward toward the tympanum, which is large and conspicuous. The general color is a greenish brown with a bright green mask from the tympanum forward along the jaw. The skin may be slightly roughened with small tubercles. The legs have dusky bars. An occasional green frog has a few scattered black spots on the back. They are white beneath, the male having a yellow throat.

**Color:** *Male.* Westwood, N.J., from A. M. and C. C. Van Deman, April 30, 1928. Upper parts forward rainette green or parrot green. Below eye and forward, calliste green. Rear upper parts olive-citrine. Upper parts of fore and hind legs citrine or buffy-citrine. Tympanum Saccardo's olive, with center yellowish citrine. Barred with black on hind legs and feet. Side of body has sea-foam yellow interspaces between citrine-drab areas. Throat barium yellow. Rest of under parts white, groin with cream color cast. Under parts of hind legs dark vinaceous-brown. Front of hind legs with a line of Hay's brown. Line under tympanum neva green, becoming viridine yellow over shoulder. Line on upper jaw and lower jaw medal bronze. Front part of lateral fold blackish, a blackish bar back of tympanum, a raw umber line on front of foreleg. Iris black, pupil rim greenish yellow. Iris above and below pupil with much xanthine orange.

*Female.* Forward upper parts parrot green, or cedar green ahead of eyes; spinach green below eye and under tympanum. Rear parts Saccardo's olive, also upper part of fore and hind legs. Tympanum Saccardo's olive, center mummy brown. Top of hind legs with black spots and transverse bars. Rear of femur uniform Prout's brown or raw umber. Sides of body pale cendre green and black. Under parts white, heavily spotted with black except white throat. Lower jaw edge dotted white and olive Iris same as in male.

**Structure:** A large frog; skin smooth; broad short fold of skin on which is a yellowish white stripe extending from angle of mouth over arm insertion, dorsolateral fold ½–⅔ distance to hind limb; fourth toe free of webbing on last two phalanges; male with enlarged thumb and tympanum; male with ring of yellow in tympanum; male with throat a bright yellow; the swollen

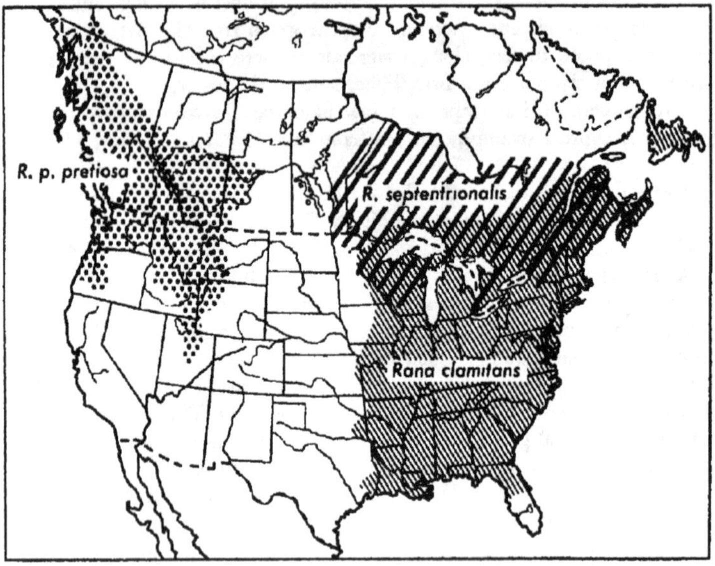


*Map 30*

throat of a croaking male is a flattened pouch, not a ball-like sac; the vocal sacs are internal.

**Voice:** The call is low-pitched, explosive. The note resembles the sound made by plucking the string of a bass viol or the twang of a rubber band slightly stretched over an open box. The male rests on a mat of vegetation or among grass or aquatic plants, or freely sprawls out on the water. Usually the hind quarters are slightly submerged.

**Breeding:** In the North they breed from the end of May to mid-August, but in the South they are late breeders. The black and white eggs are in a surface film usually less than a foot square and number 1000–4000. The egg is $\frac{1}{16}$ inch (1.5 mm.), the inner envelope elliptic, the outer merging into the jelly film. The olive green tadpole is large, $2\frac{9}{16}$ inches (64 mm.), its tail elongate, green mottled with brown, and with tip acute. The tooth ridges are ⅔, rarely ⅓. It spends one winter as a tadpole and transforms from April to September at ¾–1½ inches (23–38 mm.). Many transform at a smaller size in the South. We wonder whether the foregoing egg and tadpole measurements obtain with the smaller, browner, southern specimens of this species. Do they always winter over as tadpoles in the South? Does this long-extended summer breeder of the North have a long season of ovulation in the South?

**Journal notes:** June 21, 1907, Ithaca, N.Y. At the surface in the middle of the northeast slaughter house pond we found at 12:30 P.M. eggs laid by six pairs. In one case the complement was distributed in four groups about a foot apart. In other cases they were in one mass. They were readily distinguishable because of an excessive amount of air bubbles among them.

June 16, 1910, Ithaca, N Y., 5·10 P.M., air 82°. Heard *Rana clamitans.* In west stretch found one solid mat of waterweed. On top of this at surface a film 9 inches in diameter apparently fresh Water right at spot 82°. Little farther on two other films, irregular crescents, one on open water. In shallow water, two bunches 2 days old, one other bunch a composite of two, with diameter 15 by 10 inches. Another bunch in deep water, fresh but already distributed in little packets. Along the west side five fresh films, one 14 by 9 inches, but looks like two. Another bunch about hatched. Another on *Chara* at the surfaces as usual, a striking foamy mass.

Hellgate Ponds, Adirondacks, Onekio, N.Y., June 13, 1923. Pratt's *Manual* uses the character of spots or no spots on the back to separate the mink frog from the green frog. Imagine our surprise in finding practically all the green frogs of these parts distinctly spotted! Green frogs may have a few scattered dark spots, but not with the spotting all over the upper parts like these individual specimens. Some of these much-spotted frogs are of the general color of a green frog, some are very hard to distinguish from mink frogs, and one is a blue frog which we jokingly called our blue "green frog." This one was deep glaucous gray, deep bluish glaucous, or greenish glaucous-blue with small black spots all over upper parts.

June 16, 1924, Ithaca, N.Y. About 9 A.M. (sun shining brightly) along north side of my pond, a pair leaped in. In grassy corner saw spread out in water with head under water, an apparently exhausted or dead frog. Started to pick it up and another beneath it swam away. The upper one was a male. Suspect the lower one was a female. At 9:30 came to same corner and found a fresh mass which must have been laid soon after 9. Right where the supposed dead frog was, found another fresh mass just laid. Vegetative pole not turned down yet. Here I found a large male with a small male embracing it in the axils. The second male in turn was embraced by another male, making three males. Then the head of the first male was held by a fourth male whose nose touched the second male. The fourth male was embraced by a fifth one. The impulse must have been very great at the laying of the one female a while before. This

*Plate XCV. Rana clamitans.* 1. Male (×2/3). 2. Female (×1/2) 3. Hind foot (×1/2). 4 Eggs (×1/3) 5. Female (×2/3).

*Plate XCVI. Rana fisheri.* 1. Male (×2/3). 2,3,4. Females (×3/5).

is not exactly sex distinction. About 10:15 I returned to the spot. The first and second males were the same only turned around and the fourth male was still hanging on to the head. One of the other males, doubtless third or fifth, was near by, but not in embrace. The temperature of the water where the eggs are is 70°F.

**Authorities' corner:**

G. H. Loskiel, Gen., 1794, p. 89.
A. M. Banta, Ind., 1907, p. 22.
J. A. Weber, N.Y., 1928, pp 109–110

## Nevada Frog

*Rana fisheri* Stejneger. Plate XCVI, Map 34.

**Range:** Las Vegas, Nev.

**Habitat:** Spring basins or trickling streams in springy fields. Isolated in such spots because of surrounding desert.

"Inhabits the springs and short streams in the near vicinity of Las Vegas, close to 2000 feet elevation. These frogs are most active in spring and early summer; dates of capture range from early in March to August 13" (J. M. Linsdale, Nev., 1940, p. 210).

August 20, 1925, Las Vegas, Nev. Went out the Tonopah road to Tule Springs, a distance of about 16 miles. The springs are large and fine, but yielded us only water for our radiator. Then we turned back and about 3 miles from Las Vegas passed an artesian well pouring out a big stream of water, and then came to a low rather swampy area with quite a stream rushing on one side of it. No frogs seen here. We drove a short distance to a place where on both sides of the road small springs come out of the ground in basins perhaps 3–4 feet across, and run as trickling streams down into the field. These had been artificially ditched in places. The streams are flowing but covered with an alga. The region is grassy with a stiff grass. The immediate edges are sedgy. I first saw a frog jump into a tiny stream on the west side, just showing through a break in the algae We caught him. He is the game we came here for, *Rana fisheri* Then across the road we found a large male near the spring hole, and a little way down the stream another small one of the same species. We found tadpoles in the spring hole. Two hundred and fifty extra miles of desert for a frog seem worth it when you find your game. Followed one tiny stream back into the field and returned with the trophies, 6 *R. fisheri*, 4 *Hyla regilla*, 1 *Bufo compactilis*. These springs look marly or alkali. The second frog we caught was in one of the headwater springs and was resting against the bank with 1½ inches of head out. When I started to catch it, it swam only a short distance, didn't go into the bottom at all, just rested on top of the bottom. I moved away the scum over it and yet it stayed in position. Then with a pan we began to scoop the area along the edges. It came to the top. They are very easy to capture, not what I would call extremely alert.

The last one was in the west spring hole. He was deep in the center. The spring comes out here from a deep hole under a boulder. These males beneath the surface or resting with their heads out, when they have no spots, look much like small *R. catesbeiana* but deeper green. After we had caught the first three, I went up a stronger branch and began to get sedgy and bushy areas. There I found several *Rana fisheri* and *Hyla regilla*. This broad spring area, sedgy and shady, has been considerably cow punched. A little farther on in a heavy sedge clump beside flowing water, two frogs leaped out at once. I had to catch one with the right and one with the left hand at the same time. The water was very cool in these springs.

**Size:** Adults, 1¾–3 inches. Males, 44–64 mm. Females, 46–74 mm.

J. R. Slevin gives measurements for six adult specimens as 45, 48, 51, 56, 57, and 60 mm.

**General appearance:** This spotted frog with light stripes along the dorso-lateral folds is very similar to *R. pipiens*, *R. palustris*, or *R. septentrionalis*. The chamois or honey yellow of the hind limbs is very prominent in both male and female, reminding one of *R. palustris*. The females are more spotted than the males. The upper parts are olive green, the males showing a tendency toward uniform color in the forward part of body. This forward part may be a brighter green. In the groin and on the front and rear of the hind limbs are many reticulations of deep olive and pale olive-gray.

**Color:** Las Vegas, Nev. *Female* Upper parts dusky olive green, spots dark greenish olive, costal fold yellowish olive. Sides are light grayish olive with dark olive spots. In the groin and on front of hind legs, and rear as well, are vermiculations of deep olive and pale olive-gray. Throat light grape green or light turtle green with some pale pinkish cinnamon, clouded with dark grayish olive. Breast and belly pinkish cinnamon clouded like throat. The rear of tibia and some of foot with deep colonial buff or colonial buff. Another female has throat cartridge buff, and breast and forelegs the same with no clouding Females have more spots on the back than the males.

*Male.* They range in color from cedar green to dark greenish olive. The spots range from rainette green to pois green. The greatest difference between males and females is this tendency of old males to have spots obscured, being almost uniform like a bullfrog The forward part of the body may be methyl green. The tympanum may be like background or may be wood brown. Honey yellow or chamois color is present on underside of hind legs.

"Color above is brown, gray, olive, or green, with large or small discrete, dark brown spots on head, body and limbs. These spots usually are indefinitely bordered with light blue, gray, yellow, or green, and are irregularly rounded. They may form longitudinal rows, or the spots on their light borders may be nearly absent. The dorso-lateral fold may be light or dark as the general ground color. Posterior surface of thigh may be more or less clouded, spotted or marbled with brown or gray. Lower surfaces white or yellow, sometimes clouded, marbled or reticulated with gray or brown, especially on the throat" (J. R. Slevin, B.C., 1928, pp. 126–127).

**Structure:** Thumb enlarged in males; tympanic disk large, and larger in males than females. Old males may be smooth, but younger ones may be more warty than corresponding females. Fourth toe with two digits free.

Dr. Stejneger (Calif., 1893, p. 227) gives the following description: "Heel of extended hind limb reaching anterior eye canthus, falling considerably short of tip of snout, vomerine teeth between and projecting posteriorly beyond choanae; no black ear patch; vertical diameter of tympanic disk greater than distance between nostrils and eye; hind feet webbed for about two-thirds; one small metatarsal tubercle; one weak dorsolateral dermal fold, no dorsal folds between; posterior lower aspect of femur granular; back and sides with numerous small, distinct, dark spots, surrounded by lighter; no external vocal sacs. Habitat: Vegas Valley, Nevada. Type—U.S. Nat. Mus. No. 18957; Vegas Valley, Nevada, March 13, 1891; V. Bailey coll."

"Head as broad as, or broader than, long, slightly depressed; snout rounded, projecting more or less beyond mouth; canthus rostralis indistinct; loreal region concave; nostril nearer to eye than to tip of snout; distance between nostrils greater than interorbital width. Interorbital width less than width of upper eyelid. Tympanum large, distinct, nearly smooth, one-half to once diameter of eye. Fore limbs heavy, no rudiment of pollex; digits rather long, first as long as, or a little longer than, second, third much the longest; no slight fold along sides of fingers; subarticular tubercles small or moderately large, rounded, single. No tarsal fold; inner metatarsal tubercle elongate, fairly prominent; no outer metatarsal tubercle; digits moderately long; web moderately full, one or two phalanges of fourth toe free. Skin above smooth, or with a few tubercles or ridges on back and sides of body and dorsal surface of hind limbs; a strong dorso-lateral fold; a fold or series of warts from upper lip to side of neck or shoulder. Vomerine teeth in small, rounded groups or short oblique series between or a little behind the choanae" (J R. Slevin, B.C, 1928, p. 126).

**Voice:** These frogs have vocal sacs like *Rana pipiens*.

Aug 20, 1925, Las Vegas, Nev. When I picked up no. 10, he began tq swell out his sacs back of each ear like the sacs of *R. pipiens* and *R. virgatipes*. I had put the frogs in a bag and carried them on my belt. A few times they gave semicroaks which reminded me in some ways of *R. palustris*. Once or twice heard a very low croak. It must have been *Rana fisheri*. Occasionally in alcoholic males (MCZ no. 4840) one can clearly see between the ear and the shoulder the collapsed sac.

**Breeding:** This species probably breeds in the spring. The eggs are not known. The general color of the tadpole is dull citrine with the tail pale green-yellow, heavily mottled. The tail is elongate, its tip rounded, length to 85 mm., venter semitransparent. The largest tadpole we caught was probably not mature, being 1⅝ inches (42 mm.) and of the *R. clamitans* type. The tooth ridges are ⅔. We caught no specimens at transformation. The smallest frogs we saw were 1 9/16–1⅝ inches (39–42 mm.). J. M Linsdale secured transformation sizes of 28.0–30.5 mm., and from Las Vegas (May 1, 1913) J. R. Slevin has a 30-mm. transformed specimen.

**Journal notes:** Feb. 16, 17, 1942, Berkeley, Calif., MVZ. Worked on *Rana fisheri.*

May 16. What frog hunters we are! I thought I was good at it. I came here once with a golden spoon in my mouth. Seventeen years have gone since we were here last. Las Vegas has grown, but how? Thirty-five men sleeping on the Union Pacific lawn. Roads are changed. Took us most of the day to locate where the old artesian well and the springs were. At the U.S. Fish Hatchery found bullfrogs. The municipal golf course and possibly the hatcheries are where the springs were. Looked these over but no *R. fisheri.* Tried Las Vegas Creek upper stretches. Found a minnow and plenty of crayfish but no frogs.

May 17. Went out Main Ave. to U.S. Fish Hatchery. Looked around the big pond. No frogs. Walked from municipal golf course along water to main Tonopah road. Heard one jump in tules, probably my game. Went to Fifth St. crossing of Las Vegas Creek Looked it over. West of this crossing in tules heard one splash of frogs. Never saw them. This afternoon at 4·30 went to Main Street crossing and walked up to old artesian well, a mile or so. Some minnows in stream, lots of crayfish—heard four splashes in tules but never saw frogs. What a state! Men sleeping under trees, unemployed, unhoused and some unclean, one group quarreling.

Our *R. fisheri* may go with the old springs gone, the creek a mess.

**Authorities' corner:**

L. Stejneger, Calif., 1893, p. 227.

J. R. Slevin, B.C., 1928, pp. 126–127.

"For many years this form has been considered a synonym of *Rana onca* which was known from the single type specimen obtained by Yarrow in 1872 in 'Utah.' So few specimens have been available from southern Utah and southern Nevada that the relationships of the frogs in that area could not be studied satisfactorily. With the series now available from this region along with a study of the physiography of the area, I have been able to come to conclusions as follows: The population of frogs in Vegas Valley is sharply isolated from the closely related ones in the Colorado and Virgin River valleys. Although other colonies of *Rana* are isolated in eastern and southern Nevada, they have become less markedly differentiated from the common type of southwestern *Rana pipiens.* Whether the frogs of southern Utah and Nevada need separate recognition under the name *Onca* as a species or subspecies cannot be determined without a study of the whole species throughout its range, but it seems plain to me that the Vegas Valley ones should be recognized as distinct. Although entered here as a species, this form is obviously closely related to *Rana pipiens* and it might be well known as a race of that species. It contrasts most sharply with that frog in its peculiar shade of brown color, the reduction of dorsal spots, especially on the head, the enlarged tympanum and in the reduced hind legs" (J. M. Linsdale, Nev., 1940, pp. 210–211).

**Remarks:** Because of the precarious condition of the limited *Rana fisheri* habitat, we present this study of the fine collections of this species in the California Academy of Science, Stanford University, and the Museum of Vertebrate Zoology.

The California Academy of Science material was all collected in a small stream from a flowing well about a mile northwest of the town of Las Vegas. Among the young frogs secured May 1, 1913, by J. R. Slevin, there is a series 30, 32, 34, 35 mm., some having the transforming apron of the tadpole tail. In another group collected Aug. 10, 1913, by J. R. Slevin are males, all spotted, of 44, 45, 46, 47, 48, 48 mm.; the 44-mm. male has the heel reaching halfway between eye and tip of snout. Nineteen immature specimens 31–39 mm. all bear three to four rows of spots. The females range 48, 50, 51, 53, 56, 58, 64 mm., some very spotted on throat and on front of femur.

The Stanford University material coming from Tule Springs, north of Las Vegas, Nev., July 15, 1938, was collected by Alex Calhoun, Robert Miller, and Carl L. Hubbs. There are two tadpoles, one 83 mm. long; tail tips probably lost; labial teeth ⅔. The upper and lower tail crests are heavily mottled as in *R. clamitans,* much more heavily than in our eastern *R. pipiens,* but with intestines showing through as they do in the latter form, not concealed by pigment as in *R. clamitans* tadpoles. There is one transforming frog measuring 33.5 mm., and three females 51, 51, and 73 mm, the last with four rows of short folds between dorsolateral folds, and sides with many minute ridges

In the Museum of Vertebrate Zoology at the University of California, there are among the transformed frogs collected by J Linsdale one 28 mm. long, collected April 20, 1936, with a tail stub of 2 5 mm., with two irregular rows of spots on dorsum and two or three rows below dorsolateral folds, and with posttympanic folds and numerous tubercles. The fold of skin and light stripe on jaw are very obscure, but two folds forward from the vent between dorsolateral folds are evident. Another frog secured May 11, 1934, measures 30.5 mm., with stub of tail at least 5½ mm. long and three rows of scattered spots. One of April 19, 1936, is 31 5 mm. and another of May 11, 1934, is also 31.5 mm. Thomas Rodgers, R. Miller, and A. Calhoun found a very dark-colored one 36 mm., July 15, 1938, in which the tympanum is slightly inclined, two folds forward from vent are made up of tubercles, and the intermediate space ahead of these has four irregular rows of these tubercles appearing as small dots. A prominent thin white stripe from below the eye extends under the tympanum and onto the fold of skin back of the tympanum and is followed by an interrupted white mound at insertion of the arm. J. Linsdale collected one 38.5 mm. April 19, 1936, and a series 40, 44, 45.5, 47, 49, and 52 mm. May 1, 1934. The 44-mm. frog has prominent light ridges on tarsus with dark intervals; the 49-mm. one shows folds of the vocal sac but not in plaits. It has an enlarged and padlike thumb, a slight suggestion of two rump folds, three rows of spots between the dorsolateral folds and three below, but all small. The 52-mm. specimen is a male with light-colored vocal sacs between tympanum and brachium, which have rather deep valleys when not inflated. In the collection is a bright green female 50.5 mm. found by C. L. Camp March 23, 1923. J. Linsdale secured a series of larger adult females, April 24, 1936—62, 65, 68, 68.5, and 71 mm. The 68-mm. frog had two folds forward from vent for about ¾ of an inch; tympana obliquely inclined inward with a prominent curved fold from tympanum to arm insertion; and two rows of widely separated spots, five in each row being below the fold. In the 71-mm. female the tympanum was quite oblique mesad and a fold from the inner hand tubercle to tibia was present with a similar somewhat flattened fold from base of fifth toe to the tibia; numerous pebbly eminences, some longitudinal, are evident between dorsolateral folds; and fold from lower edge of tympanum toward shoulder is very prominent and unbroken. The very pebbled sides below dorsolateral folds are grayish with two rows of spots forward and spotting on sides scanty; reticulations in inguinal region and front of femur are prominent; a spot is present at insertion of arm and extending along brachium to beginning of the forearm. The last two joints of fourth toe are free of webbing.

### Southern Bullfrog, Joe Brown Frog, Pig Frog, Swamp Bullfrog, Bonnet's Frog, Lake Frog, Green Bullfrog, Florida Bullfrog

*Rana grylio* Stejneger. Plate XCVII; Map 31.

**Range:** Louisiana to Florida and southern Georgia.

**Habitat:** Aquatic. Open water-lily prairies, open ponds, or along deep-wooded, overflowed banks of southern rivers, among brush or similar debris, or among aquatic vegetation, like pickerel weed, and more especially near bushy edges. Exceedingly shy, hard to catch except at night with a light.

"Lakes and marshes; common. Our most aquatic frog" (O. C. Van Hyning, Fla., 1933, p. 4).

See F. Harper, Ga., 1935, p. 302.

"Bonnet and water-lily pads and prairies; in emergent vegetation (*Panicum hemitomon, Pontederia cordata, Sagittaria lancifolia*) along lake margins; among water-hyacinths in lakes and streams; cypress swamps. . . . Almost wholly aquatic; nocturnal, but occasionally fairly active on dark days. Various observers have commented on the extreme shyness of this frog . . . , but my observations do not confirm these impressions. On land it is unwary to the point of stupidity, while in the water I have caught as many as fifteen or twenty consecutively without allowing one to escape. The fact that it must be hunted in most cases in water two to four feet deep has no doubt contributed to its reputation for wildness. It is true that if regularly annoyed by intruders

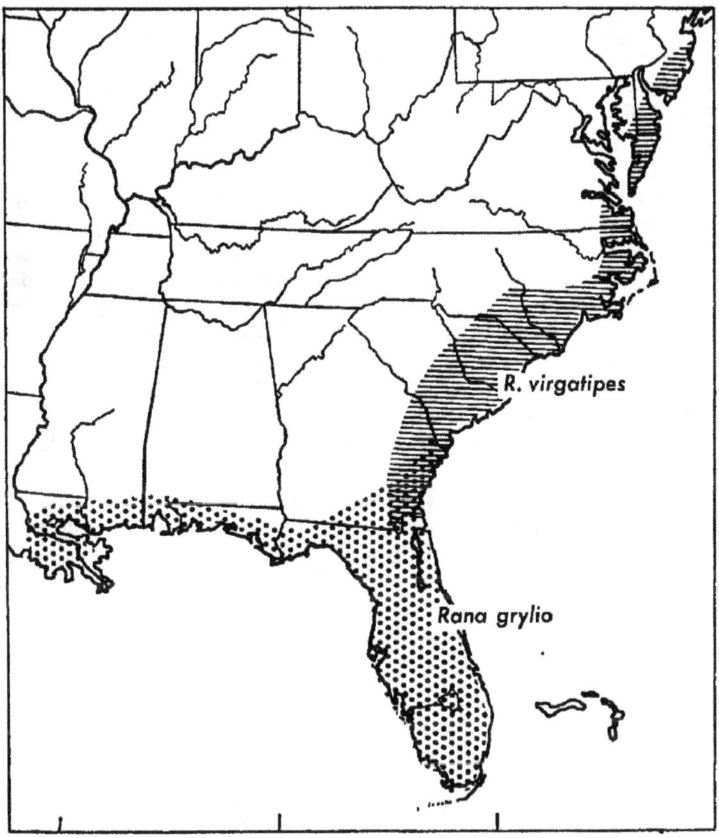


*Map 31*

*grylio* soon learns to avoid capture. . . . *R. grylio* is more buoyant in the water than *catesbeiana;* it usually floats with its head and shoulders well above the surface. I think that the difference in the degree of submergence of the tympanum may account for the fact that *catesbeiana* is much more difficult to approach" (A. F. Carr, Jr., Fla., 1940b, pp. 66–67).

**Size:** Adults, 3¼–6⅖ inches. Males, 82–152 mm. Females, 85–161 mm.

**General appearance:** This is a large frog similar to the common bullfrog and varies from brownish olive to blackish brown above, with some prominent, scattered black spots. The under parts often have a network of black, brown, and yellow, presenting a striking heavily mottled appearance. It has no dorsolateral folds.

**Color:** Okefinokee Swamp, Ga. *Male.* April 25, 1921 Upper parts rich brown with black spots obscured. Tympanum and outer circle deep brown, center green or dark green. Top of head dark green Belly creamy. Throat lemon yellow with dusky fine blotches on underside of fore and hind limbs. Lower belly blotched or reticulated with cream and brown. On sides of body and legs cream replaced by yellow. First finger of male much enlarged. In another male head deep bottle green. Tympanum center black, middle ring light brown, outer ring brownish black. Throat almost orange yellow on either side. On either side of breast between arm insertions a deep green area. On rear of femur the yellow extends as a yellow line with brown black on either side of it; this line golden or orange yellow, more intense than yellowish or cream of undersides of legs In some the black spots of the back are farther apart. Black spots of back surrounded by green with centers bronzy brown. Top of toes brown and yellow. Underside of toes brown. In half-grown male under color cream, slight wash of yellow. Femoral stripe cream, not yellow. Eardrum small, all brown. Two pectoral patches dusky, not green. (Non-Ridgway).

*Female.* June 21, 1921 Upper lip from tympanum to snout medal bronze, also top of head; upper parts olive-citrine with a few dark spots on the posterior back and groin. Upper part of legs Saccardo's olive with cross blotches. Throat baryta yellow or, better, straw yellow. Where dorsal color reaches light venter, also on fore and hind legs, there is some clear dull green-yellow or light dull green-yellow. Venter marguerite yellow, also same color on top of toes and fingers. Two patches on either side of throat and near pectoral region, so prominent in the male, are light yellowish olive, not pronounced as in male. No reticulations on venter except for faint ones on underside of hind legs and the slightest indications on the groin region Rear of femur with one lone band of seafoam yellow with line of quaker drab below and dark quaker drab or black above Iris with bright green-yellow ring around pupil. Iris black with lots of bright green-yellow spots. Green-yellow outer circle around the black.

**Structure:** Large frog; no dorsolateral folds; male with internal vocal sacs, the inflation forming a flattened pouch on throat with extra inflation on either side, giving the pouch a three-parted appearance; more pointed head and narrower snout than in *R. catesbeiana*, and with all the hind toes except the fourth proportionally longer; webs to the tips of toes.

"The most obvious difference between this species and the ordinary bullfrog (*Rana catesbeiana*) is the great length of the toes, except the fourth, the latter consequently projecting much less beyond the others than in *R. catesbeiana*, in which the third toe, measured from the inner metatarsal tubercle, is considerably less than three and one-half times the difference between it and the fourth toe. In fact, this difference is seldom more than one-fourth in the new species and seldom less than one-third in *R. catesbeiana*.

"In order to ascertain exactly the proportions of the first four toes in both species large series of both species were measured, viz.: 12 of *Rana grylio* and 50 of *R. catesbeiana*, the measurements, as well as their equivalents expressed in percentages of the fourth toe, being given at the end of this article. In order to get as stable a starting point as possible for these measurements the anterior edge of the inner metatarsal tubercle was chosen and the length of the toe in this case consequently means the distance from this point to the tip of the toe in question.

"The proportions obtained in this way may be expressed as follows:

| | *Rana grylio* Per cent of fourth toe | *Rana catesbeiana* Per cent of fourth toe |
|---|---|---|
| Third toe | 80 to 84 | 70 to 76 |
| Second toe | 55 to 61 | 47 to 51 |
| First toe | 34 to 39 | 27 to 33 |

There is consequently no overlapping or intergrading. The fourth toe has the same relative length in both species, but in the new one the other toes have become considerably lengthened, thus giving a much larger surface of web than in the ordinary bullfrog. . . .

"The range of the new species is as yet known but fragmentarily, as we have specimens only from southern Florida, Pensacola, Florida, and Bay St. Louis, Mississippi. The habitat of *R. grylio* is thus partly occupied by *R. catesbeiana*, which certainly occurs in northern Florida and on the Gulf coast reaches New Orleans. The overlapping of the two forms affords additional evidence of their specific distinctness, if such were needed. It may be mentioned in this connection that the most southern specimens of *R. catesbeiana* do not show the slightest tendency of a variation toward *R. grylio*, as is clearly proven by the measurements . . ." (L. Stejneger, Fla., 1901, pp. 212–213).

**Voice:** The call is a grunt like that of a pig or an alligator It is rough and guttural.

Dr. E. A. Mearns says it resembles "the grunt of a herd of pigs." To Dr. Barbour in 1920, "its call, which is heard at night, or on damp days, resembles the grunting of a pig, and consists of but one sound oft repeated." Dr. J. C. Bradley called its note "peculiar alligatorlike grunts."

In our journal under June 18, 1912, we wrote: We heard plenty of southern bullfrogs from 8–11 A.M. The water was waist deep and the bushes 8–12 feet above the water. One of their notes was very much like that of *Rana cates-*

*beiana* of the North. Another note frequently given in chorus was mournful, reverberating, prolonged, and deep, not at all like the regular bullfrog chorus note. There were a number in the chorus and it sounded like one continuous long deep roar. The following day, June 19, from 7–11 A.M., when the sun was very hot, we heard several along the tree-covered overflowed banks of Suwannee River. On June 13, while traveling through Minne Lake Run we heard the deep guttural notes of the "Swamp Bullfrog" all along the bonnet borders and through the cypress woods on either side.

The male frog has internal vocal sacs like *Rana clamitans* and *Rana catesbeiana,* but the inflation is greater than in these two species. There is a central inflation, but on either side of the middle is an extra inflation, giving the sac a three-parted appearance. The croak can be heard at considerable distance and a midnight chorus is loud. They call spread out on the surface of the water.

June 12, 1917, two miles from Theodore, Ala., we heard the croak or grunt (4 or 5 notes) of the southern bullfrog: hard to find, lost the first one. They are among cat briars (*Smilax*). Found a young one and later took a large male. To one member of the party there seemed something human in its voice.

**Breeding:** They breed from March 1 through September, generally in humid weather, with night temperatures of 65°–70° and day temperatures of 85°–90°. The crest is in June and July. The black and white eggs are in a surface film 12 by 12 inches to 12 by 25 inches, and attached to vegetation. The egg is $\frac{1}{16}$ inch (1.6 mm.), the outer envelope is $\frac{1}{6}$–$\frac{1}{4}$ inch (4–6 mm.), merging into the jelly mass. The greenish tadpole is quite large, 4 inches (100 mm.), with tail long and sharply acuminate. The tooth ridges are $\frac{2}{3}$ After a tadpole period of 1 to 2 years, the tadpoles transform from April 24 to July 19, at 1¼–2 inches (32–49 mm.). A young transformed *R. grylio* looks much like an adult or half-grown carpenter frog (*R. virgatipes*).

"They call every month of the year" (A. F. Carr, Jr, Fla., 1940b, p. 67).

**Journal notes:** 1912, Okefinokee Swamp, Ga. I will never forget my first capture of the swamp bullfrog. The prominent black or brown and yellow reticulations of the under parts are very conspicuous. Sometimes we succeeded in killing them with an oar or pole while pushing through the bonnets and occasionally the members of the party captured them when visiting set trap lanterns for insects.

On April 25, 1921, we went with flashlight after *Rana grylio.* On the vegetative carpet and lily pads were untold numbers of *Acris,* on the lily pads and on the bushes *Hyla cinerea,* and among the pickerel weeds different sizes of *Rana grylio.* In all, three of us secured only six adults and one transformed specimen. Later I found that they could be picked up rather easily with a flashlight. On May 6, Dave Lee went out on Billy's Lake at night with a torch to catch small fish for bait. With a small dip net he would scoop in front of a *Rana grylio* and usually catch it.

On May 10, 1921, we found one cypress pond with plenty of *Rana grylio* in all stages. Our comment is that they are easy of capture at night except for adults and even these can be taken. On May 11 we found many *R. grylio* at night along the edges of Billy's Lake. They usually were at the edge near the bushes or under them or among brush or in maiden cane. When one tried to take their pictures, they were too much surrounded with vegetation or sticks. We could approach closely, but in clearing away brush for the flashlight picture we would scare them. Often we heard them go skipping along across the lake or along the edges like *Rana catesbeiana*. Like most shy frogs they can be captured if females are around. In some cases the females led the way to where a male might be. Where we succeeded in flashlighting a croaking male, we were quite certain females were near because of eggs found there soon afterwards. On June 20 we found another method of capture. We never dreamed it would work for *Rana grylio*. We would pull in hurriedly masses of floating maiden cane, and in the corner at the bottom of the boat all kinds of life would drop. On this night we caught two *Rana grylio* specimens, one a fine ripe female. All in all, our main reliance was to wade about at night on the prairies or in open cypress ponds and to catch them by hand.

"Anent this species it might be interesting to include some comments of Percy Viosca, Jr., in a letter to Dr. H. F. Moore, U.S. Bureau of Fisheries. On July 11, 1923, he writes: 'It might also interest you to know that *Rana grylio* is abundant in this State [La.], but we have found it is a thoroughly aquatic species and not very hardy in captivity, and would not be suitable for frog culture even though it is a fine flavored species and we believe much superior to flesh of the *catesbeiana*. It would be only suitable for planting in shallow lakes of the lagoon type, but once established it would be difficult to collect, except by experienced night hunters. It would be a species very difficult to ship. Although we have shipped them successfully, the frogs need individual care'" (A. H. Wright, Gen., 1932, pp. 369–370).

**Authorities' corner:**

L. Stejneger, Fla., 1901, pp. 212–213.
R. F. Deckert, Fla., 1914,' pp. 3–4.
M. C Dickerson, Gen., 1914, pp. 226–227.
P. Viosca, Jr., La., 1918, p. 161
P. Viosca, Jr., La., 1923a, p. 39.
A. H. Wright, Gen., 1932, pp. 368–369.

"The largest frog known in Florida and on the sea coast of Carolina [mainly *R. grylio* but the Carolina ones may be also *R. catesbeiana*] is about eight or nine inches in length from the nose to the extremity of the toes; they are of a dusky brown or black colour on the upper side, and their belly or under side white, spotted and clouded with dusky spots of various size and figure; their legs and thighs also are variegated with transverse ringlets, of dark brown or black, and are yellow and green about their mouth and lips; they live in wet swamps and marshes, on the shores of large rivers and lakes; their voice is loud and hideous, greatly resembling the grunting of a swine, but not near as loud as the voice of the bullfrog of Virginia and Pennsylvania, neither do they arrive to half their size, the bull frog being frequently eighteen inches in length, and their roaring as loud as that of a bull" (W. Bartram, Gen., 1791, pp. 276–277).

"It has an enormous head, a thick-set body, and strongly formed limbs, much thicker in proportion than those of the common European frog. Its croak is spoken of as 'booming' and is very loud. It can sometimes be heard appearing to come from every part of an extensive district, and from a mile or more distant. I am not sure that the Okefinoke frog is not a distinct variety of the common bull-frog. It is larger than those which I have seen in streams running into the Mississippi and its tributaries, and in other places, and seems to differ in colour, though neither of these circumstances is of much importance. Size may depend on locality and abundance of food, and coloration certainly does. The following are the measurements of the largest specimen that I could find. Length of body from nose to base, 8 inches; breadth across, nearly 5 inches; girth, 14 inches; length of hind-limb, 12½ inches; weight, within a fraction of three pounds. The usual size is about seven inches in length, half as much more for length of hind-limb, and a weight of over two pounds" (P. Fountain, Ga., 1901, pp. 62–63).

### River-Swamp Frog, Greenback, Heckscher's Frog, Wright's Bullfrog, Alligator Frog

*Rana heckscheri* Wright. Plate XCVIII; Map 32.

**Range:** Coastal South Carolina to Oklawaha River, Fla., west to Biloxi, Miss., and possibly to Louisiana and North Carolina.

"To date this Lower Austral species, smaller than the common bullfrog, has been recorded as far north along the coast as Charleston County. W. W. Humphreys took several specimens from a flooded sand pit near the Edisto River at Pon Pon, Charleston County, June 1935" (E. B. Chamberlain, 1937).

"In July 1938, John C. Pearson presented the Charleston Museum with a number of strikingly marked tadpoles taken at Hail's Bluff, Edisto River, Dorchester County. Ivan R. Tomkins sent in two specimens from Canston's Bluff near Savannah, Georgia, in February 1935" (E. B. Chamberlain, S.C., 1939, pp. 30–31).

**Habitat:** Swampy edges of rivers and streams, a truly fluviatile species.

"I once took twenty adults together with eighteen *catesbeiana* in a swamp near the Santa Fe River (Columbia County). . . . Nocturnal, terrestrial. Where *heckscheri* and *catesbeiana* occupy the same major habitat they are found in essentially the same minor habitats, and apparently have very similar habits. Three or four individuals of each species are often found seated about residual pools along the course of an intermittent swamp stream near Gaines-

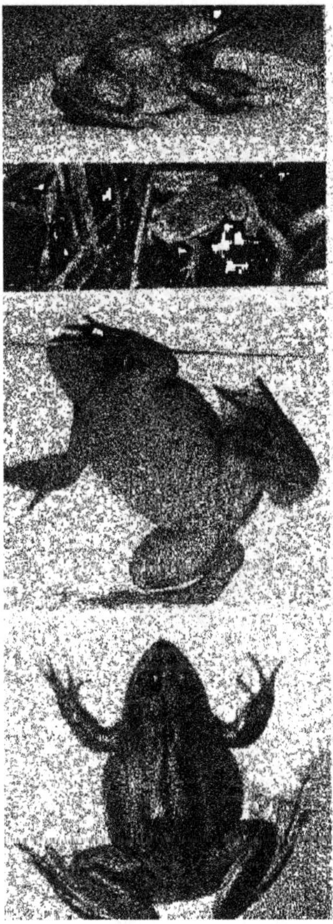

*Plate XCVII Rana grylio* 1 Female (×¼). 2 Male croaking (×⅛). 3,4. Females (×⅛).

*Plate XCVIII. Rana heckscheri.* 1,4 Females (×⅜) 2 Tadpole (×½). 3. Male (×⅜). 5. Hind foot (×¾) 6. Young tadpole (×½).

ville. The two show marked difference in their reactions to the presence of an intruder, *heckscheri* being much more phlegmatic in temperament; it is not alarmed easily and shows little shrewdness in eluding capture When

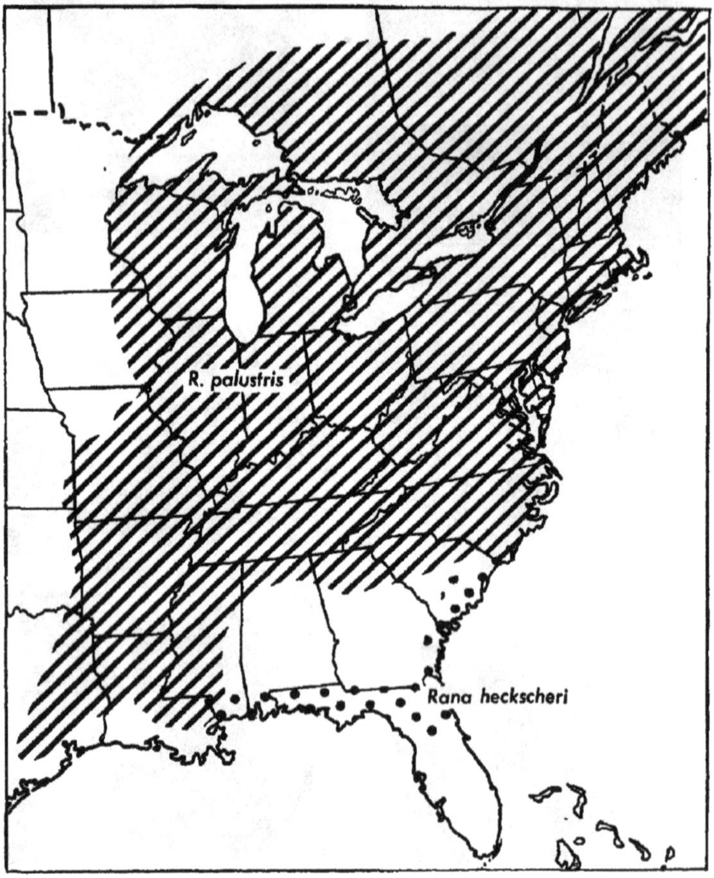


*Map 32*

caught, it hangs limp in the hand, never resorting to the vigorous kicks and contortions characteristic of *grylio* and *catesbeiana*" (A. F. Carr, Jr., Fla., 1940b, p. 66).

**Size:** Adults, 3¼–5 inches. Males, 82–131 mm. Females, 102–150 mm.

**General appearance:** This is a large greenish black, rough-skinned frog with the venter very heavily mottled with black. The throat of the male has a wash of yellow on a light grav background. The edge of the lower jaw with light spots of white, yellow, or buff, is similar to that of the green frog. The center of the eardrum is rough, light brown or greenish buff, with the remainder very dark, almost black. The webbing on the foot does not extend to the tip of the fourth toe, leaving about 1½ joints free. Rear of femur with prominent light spots; its color pattern not an alternation of light and dark parallel bars as in *R. grylio, R. virgatipes,* and *Acris gryllus.*

**Color:** Callahan, Fla. *Adult male* (95 mm.). Aug. 18, 1922. General dorsal color citrine-drab to grayish olive becoming on top and sides of head and center of tympanum dark olive-buff, isabella color, or cinnamon-brown. Eardrum except middle mummy brown. On back of body, on head, and on sides is some serpentine green. Under parts spotted white, with glaucous gray, light Payne's gray, or pale drab on throat and breast. Throat with a little citron green or deep chrysolite green. Spots on lower jaw rim four or five, seafoam yellow to deep colonial buff in the spot just back of the angle of the mouth. This spot except above surrounded by black. Black spot just below angle of mouth to and across the insertion of the brachium. Three black spots on the front edge of the antebrachium. Rear of forelegs black to tips of fingers and webs. Tops of the fingers with seafoam yellow or deep colonial buff spots. Narrow black bars across the dorsum of the femur, tibia, and hind foot. Rear of femur with white unconnected spots on the bone brown ground color. Rear edge of hind foot to tip of fourth and fifth toes black. Outside rim of iris bright green-yellow, inner rim capucine orange; interval black with orange-rufous spots.

*A younger specimen,* 65 mm. long, is dark olive or deep olive on entire upper parts and very warty. Throat is deep grayish olive.

*Another male.* June 10, 1928. When first caught this frog was very black, and white beneath, with throat washed with oil yellow on light mineral gray ground. The markings of the femur are in spots of white or pale vinaceous-fawn in contrast with the lines of white conspicuous in *Rana grylio.*

*Another male* is olive or dark greenish olive above.

*Adult female.* June 10, 1928. Much the same as male but upper parts much more spotted with black Head spotted Tympanum with blotches of black or olivaceous black (3). Half bars on femur. Bar across arm insertion. Throat with no or little oil yellow or sulphine yellow. White spots or pale vinaceous-fawn spots on rim of lower jaws prominent. Under parts not quite so spotted. Iris same as in male.

*Young transformed frogs.* June 10, 1928. A young transformed frog has a prominent eye. Sometimes brick red. Often mars orange predominates over black, and iris rim is orange-rufous or brighter. Entire under parts finely speckled white and deep olive-gray or deep grayish olive.

**Structure:** Upper parts sometimes very warty, no lateral fold; center of eardrum granular and light in color; males with tympanum much larger than eye; thumb enlarged, and throat darker and with yellow; back more warty in male.

"Like *Rana grylio* and *Rana catesbeiana* it has no dorsolateral fold and no phalanx of the fourth toe is totally free of web; third toe in 56 mm. specimens 1 to 3 mm. shorter in *Rana heckscheri* than in the other two species of bullfrog, or 3 to 6 mm. shorter in 82 mm. specimens or 6 to 9 mm. shorter in 95 mm. specimens; third toe 3.8 (95 mm.)–3.56 (82 mm.)–3.3 (56 mm.) in length (snout to vent) in *R. heckscheri* while 2.7 to 3.1 (95–56 mm.) in *R. grylio* and *R. catesbeiana;* third toe 1.6–1.7 in fourth toe in *R. heckscheri* while 1.2–1.5 in fourth toe in the other two species; first finger decidedly longer than second, while in the other two species it is usually shorter or sometimes equal; first, second, third and fifth toes shorter than corresponding toes of *R. grylio* and *R. catesbeiana;* fourth finger 8.6 (95 mm.)–8.2 (82 mm.)–8.0 (56 mm.) in length (snout to vent) while 6.0 to 6.3 (95 mm.)–6.8 to 7.4 (82 mm.)–5.6 to 7.1 (56 mm.) in the other two species; internasal space less than upper eyelid width, 1.07–1.43 in it while .85–1.0 in *R. grylio* and *R. catesbeiana;* tympanum in males is proportionally greatest in *R. grylio,* somewhat smaller in *R. catesbeiana* and *R. clamitans* and smallest in *R. heckscheri;* intertympanic width of 95 mm. males in length (snout to vent) 4.52 in *R. heckscheri,* 5.43 in *R. clamitans* and 6.3 in *R. grylio* (*R. catesbeiana* males of 95 mm. have tympanum poorly developed, but a 136 mm. male has it 4.85): in general, intertympanic width broadest in *R heckscheri* and *R. catesbeiana* and narrowest in *R. grylio,* distance from the rear corner of the eye to the same corner of the other eye much greater than the intertympanic width in *R. grylio,* somewhat greater in *R. clamitans,* about equal in *R. catesbeiana,* and equal in *R. heckscheri,* i.e., in the males.

"In spirits, four 95 mm. males of four species are as follows: bister or mummy brown on dorsum of *R. catesbeiana,* brownish olive in *R. grylio,* deep grayish olive in *R. clamitans,* and deep mouse gray in *R. heckscheri;* upper parts without very distinct dark spots in *R. clamitans* and *R. catesbeiana,* with prominent large black spots in *R. grylio,* and with many small dark spots in *R. heckscheri;* venter of *R. clamitans* clear white except for the yellow throat, venter of *R. catesbeiana* heavily blotched with black, so also in *R. grylio*—all three, however, with a white background color but in *R. heckscheri,* the deep mouse gray or dark color so prominent it becomes the background color and the white, scattering spots; light spots on upper and lower jaws more prominent than in *R. clamitans*" (A. H. Wright, Ga., 1924, pp. 143–144).

**Voice:** One call is a snore or snort, and another a peculiar, snarling, explosive grunt. The discovery of this frog came from his voice. On Aug. 18, 1922, we visited Alligator Swamp at Callahan, Fla., because of some curious large tadpoles with black borders on their tails that we had seen one month earlier. Mrs. Wright discovered a queer-looking green frog, as she supposed, and was calling to us when we were startled by a call unlike any other *Rana* we had ever heard.

For other notes see Harper, Gen., 1933, pp. 302–306.

"Intermittent croaks may be heard during the first warm rains in April (Alachua County), and spasmodically throughout the summer" (A. F. Carr, Jr., Fla., 1940b, p. 66).

**Breeding:** The eggs are probably a surface film. The tadpole grows large, 3⅞ inches (97 mm.). The young tadpole is black with a gold band across the body and the tail clear. The mature tadpole is dark in body with black-rimmed tail crests. The tooth ridges are ⅔ or ⅔. The tadpole period is probably 2 years. It transforms in June at 1⅕–1$\frac{9}{16}$ inches (30–39 mm.), sometimes at 2 inches (49–52 mm.). The small, transversely banded tadpoles were very numerous in June, 1921, July 17, 1922, and June 8–10, 1928. This seems to indicate spring and early summer as the breeding period—last week of April to July 8.

Young tadpole black with a gold band across the body and tail clear. When half grown this band disappears. The mature tadpole may become about as large (97 mm.) as a bullfrog tadpole. The black-rimmed crests of the tail and black bands on upper tail musculature and light color on lower half are the conspicuous and distinctive markings. Body dark greenish olive finely covered with pale greenish flecks. On the venter, vinaceous-fawn, vinaceous-cinnamon, or orange vinaceous. Clump of four to six large dark spots on throat. Lower belly pale forget-me-not blue, upper belly and breast jay-blue to grayish violaceous blue. Spots of back thicker on lower belly. Lateral line of pores conspicuous on head and body.

We started on this winding "tadpole trail" on our first trip to Okefinokee Swamp, Ga., in 1912. July 17, 1922, in a cut-off overflow pool at Thompson Landing (south of Folkston) on St. Mary's River we found an almost pure culture of a small black tadpole with a gold and white transverse band like those of June 16, 1912.

My journal reads: In one cut-off pool in a watercourse (which now is a succession of separated pools) we hauled the seine. It was covered with a wriggly mass which at first looked like water bettles to Miles (Dr. M. D. Pirnie). I must confess I would have seen them the same way if I had not had experience with them 10 years before. The tails being transparent were hardly in evidence. They have a band across the back. In another cut-off from St. Mary's River they were in immense numbers in shallow water and presented a very beautiful sight in the sunlight with their dark bodies and transverse bands. Were it not for the transverse bands, they would look like toad tadpoles. Then I provisionally placed them with the green tree frog, *Hyla cinerea,* which sometimes has somewhat the same appearance.

Three days later, July 20, we started for Jacksonville, Fla. Just north of

Callahan, near a large concrete bridge, a car was stuck on a smaller detour bridge and we had to wait. In the areas beside the new Dixie Highway were shallow ponds or overflowed areas. These were tributary to Alligator Swamp, which in turn is a part of Mills Swamp (U.S. Geol. Survey Quadrangle—Hilliard). At first I saw a few cross-banded forms of the Thompson Landing sort that I had taken to be *Hyla cinerea*. I began to suspect they might be *R. capito* or *R. virgatipes*, probably the former. We collected a few and went on. The larger ones were very conspicuous with black-rimmed crests and black bands on upper half of tail musculature and a light color on lower musculature. In one-third grown tads the crossbands show through faintly. When full grown they disappear. On July 21, on our return from Jacksonville, we stopped at Callahan (Alligator Swamp). The tadpoles of July 20 were abundant. They travel in big schools as no other big tadpoles do. They remind me of a school of mature *Bufo* tadpoles. Once in a while among the fair-sized ones were monsters almost as big as bullfrog tadpoles. And these monsters have no suggestion of hind leg buds. Does this species winter over 1 or 2 years as a tadpole?

We checked up our Thompson Landing (Ga.) and Alligator Swamp (Fla.) material and found them all of the same species, and the trail ended with the naming of the new frog *Rana heckscheri* Wright.

"The number of tadpoles produced in a given breeding site is astounding. Wright (1933) remarks on their abundance at Callahan. In Alachua County they transform consistently in April and May. H. K. Wallace and I found them emerging in tremendous numbers in a backwater of the Santa Fe River May 1, 1933; we probably could have collected a thousand with little difficulty. The disparity in relative abundance between the adults and the young of this species indicates an extremely low survival potential" (A. F. Carr, Jr., Fla., 1940b, p. 66).

"*Rana heckscheri* is very common in the vicinity of Silver Springs, Florida, in the streams and rivers and in the lakes connected by streams which flow into the Oklawaha River. The night of June 8, 1936, I caught three mating pairs and transferred them to my private, twenty acre, grassy lake. About five thousand eggs were laid in masses, in shallow water, among the water grasses; they were hatched in ten to fifteen days into black tadpoles. About ten per cent of the eggs failed to hatch. From then until September the tadpoles grew rapidly, attaining the length of four to five inches. The color changed to a lighter hue and showed a speckled appearance; the tail was bordered with black. The tadpoles stayed in shallow water and were always packed close together. They fed on meat thrown into the lake for the alligators, and seemed also to feed on plant life. Occasionally dead tadpoles were noted but I could not determine the cause of death.

"The growth was slower during the cooler months but the tadpoles remained very active. Banded water snakes fed on them occasionally. Sometimes the tadpoles came into shallow water so that their backs were exposed, but at night they went back into deep water. They were always found on the same side of the lake within an area of fifty yards. By March 1937, the hind legs appeared and growth was again noticeable. By April 1 the tadpoles were six to seven inches long and front legs appeared. On April 10 the transformation was well under way and the tadpoles were hopping out on the bank. During this time great numbers (about twenty per cent) died. By May 1 all had transformed, hopped out on the bank and scattered. On June 1, one was found hopping away about two hundred yards from the lake. Very few can be found now anywhere around the lake" (E. R. Allen, Fla., 1938, p. 50).

**Journal notes:** In August, 1922, at Callahan, Fla., we captured with a light eight or ten frogs of various sizes from 1-year frogs to full-sized adults. We found them in the shrubbery and on the banks about the bases of trees. More were captured than lost. They were rather awkward in their escape and would tumble off their perches.

June 8, 1928, Callahan, Fla. This afternoon went to type locality for *Rana heckscheri*. Saw lots of tadpoles among vegetation. Captured about 12 transformed ones. Can approach them when heads are out of water and can catch them. Some rest on mud of bank. Many here with four legs and long tail. Went along in pickerel weed on east side of bridge where is shady at 5 P.M. and finally saw a large one. Slowly approached from water side with net and came close enough to catch frog. Started skirting several edges. Soon saw another on bank among pickerel weed. Crawled upon it on my knees and caught it; it squealed as some frogs will do when caught. The children went along and scared another, which gave a startled note of the *R. catesbeiana* order. These two are the largest we have caught. They are bigger than any green frog. The transformed ones are somewhat like green frogs but with more intensified spotting on belly. These as transformed and adults have no costal fold.

June 9, Callahan. Went out last night at bridge which is type locality of *R. heckscheri*. Saw a female near edge of *Pontederia* bank. Later heard a big frog jump in. When I approached that area, found a male, a large one, on bank and among *Pontederia*, not at edge. Saw another female. Caught her. Later went over to Mr. Davis' brick-yard pools. Many transforming frogs here and countless tadpoles. Sometimes these tadpoles were so thick, one could reach in with hand and catch them. On the east side saw immense school of little black ones with the yellowish crossbands. Amongst them are some bigger ones about ½ inch in body. This means at least two lots have already bred. This is the first lot of young seen. These pools have water lilies, *Sagittaria*, water hyacinth, *Hydrocotyle*, and many other plants.

**Authorities' corner:**

M. J. Allen, Miss., 1932, pp. 10–11.
C. S. Brimley, N.C., 1941, p. 3.

## Utah Frog

*Rana onca* Cope. Plate XCIX; Map 34.

Are *Rana onca* and *Rana fisheri* one? Is *Rana onca, Rana pipiens*? Many collections in Utah, Nevada, and Arizona are needed to solve this possible *R. pipiens* derivative if it be such.

See L. Stejneger, Calif., 1893, p. 227, under *R. fisheri*.

In 1940 J. M. Linsdale re-established *Rana fisheri* Stejneger and retained *R. onca* Cope as distinct from *R. fisheri*. Excerpts from this author follow:

*Rana onca* "inhabits streams and springs in southeastern part of the state; localities are along the Virgin and Lower Muddy rivers. They range in altitude from about 1,200 feet up to around 2,000 feet.

"Recently collected series of specimens from several localities near the Virgin River indicate that this form is distinct from both *Rana pipiens* and *Rana fisheri*. From the former it differs by having smaller and fewer spots and these on a paler background and with less distinct gray borders, larger tympanum, and shorter legs It is nearer to *fisheri* which reaches the extreme development in these characters, having still fewer dorsal spots and much shorter hind legs. The characters of smaller size and absence of longitudinal folds between dorso-lateral ridges seem not to be diagnostic in the Nevada material" (J. M. Linsdale, Nev., 1940, pp. 210–211; see also his comments about *R. fisheri*).

"In 1928, I had an opportunity of examining the type specimen of this species described by Professor Cope in 1875. For a long time this species was questionable and the type was unknown; as a result Dr. Stejneger names the specimens taken in the Vegas Valley by members of the Death Valley Expedition *Rana fisheri*. The rediscovery of the type specimen which was so faithfully reproduced in 1875 places *R. fisheri* as a synonym" (V. M. Tanner, Utah, 1931, pp. 189–190).

**Range:** Along the Virgin River, southeastern Nevada, northwestern Arizona, and southwestern Utah.

**Size:** Linsdale collected 78 specimens. These measure as follows: adults 44–84 mm., males 44–68; females 51–84 mm. Rodgers took males of 44.0–53.5 mm. and females of 48.5–82.0 mm.

**General appearance:** Notes on Linsdale's, Rodger's, Smiley's, and Hall's specimens follow

1. Light line from below eye and under tympana to behind angle of mouth is prominent, this being absent in adults of *R. fisheri*. What is it in the leg that makes it possible for heel of *R onca* to go between eye and snout? Is it the femur? Dark spot from eye to nostril common in *R. onca*.

2. MVZ no. 19608, 47 5 mm., male, April 25, 1936. Seems to have tail apron long after transformation.

3. No. 20433, 47.5 mm., male, May 3, 1936. Big thumb.

4. No. 20662, 47 mm., male, June 10, 1936. Thumb not so well developed. Is it of breeding size?

5. No. 20660, 47.5 mm., male, June 10, 1936. Thumb not so well developed. Is it past breeding?

6. No. 19582, 48.5 mm., female, April 25, 1936. Is it breeding?

7. No. 13888, 52 mm., male, Sept. 30, 1931. Thumb pads not well developed.

8. No. 16571, 60 mm., female, April 25, 1936. Ripe.

**Color:** Spring 2 miles southeast of Overton, Nev., May 18, 1942. The general impression is brown in the forward dorsum and gray in the rear and upper forearms. The dorsal background color of top of head from front of snout, between nostrils, in front of eye, and upper eyelid is clear sudan brown or buffy brown. The tympanum is the same with a spot of cartridge buff or ivory yellow in the middle. The background color rearward becomes drab; rear of legs is smoky gray, forelegs are pale ecru-drab or ecru-drab on brachium. The sides are intermediate between color of hind legs and middorsum, with two lateral spots touching the dorsolateral folds and three more lower on the side. The costal folds are low, are tilleul buff or pale pinkish cinnamon. Between the folds are two irregular rows of dark spots with one spot between in middorsum and one extra in pelvic region. There is a touch of peacock green in middorsum and on outer edges of spots. The spots are cinnamon-brown or light brownish olive with tendency toward smoky gray margins. The bars on hind legs are light grayish olive in the center and grayish olive on margins. There is a little spot on heel, three bars on tibia, a prominent spot near femur-tibia articulation, and two to three bars on the femur. On fore limb there is an oblique band on antebrachium, one on elbow, and a prominent oblique brown bar from insertion halfway down on front of brachium. From front of nostril to eye is a band of light brownish olive or cinnamon-brown. The margins of upper and lower jaws are smoky gray. There is a thin line of peacock green under the eye, extending forward between the light brownish olive band above and the smoky gray upper labial region. From under the eye extending backward under the tympanum and downward on shoulder to arm insertion is a prominent light stripe like the dorsolateral folds. The under surfaces are white with the groin somewhat spotted and touched with yellow, which color is also toward the front. The iris is black with flecks and bands of orange-cinnamon.

**Structure:** "*Rana onca* Cope sp. nov. . . . Head oval, muzzle sloping to the lip. Diameter of tympanic membrane equal distance between nares and between nostril and orbit, and three-fourths the diameter of the orbit or the distance from nares to margin of lip in front. Vomerine teeth in vasciculi behind the line connecting the posterior borders of the choanae. A dermal fold on each side of the back, and a short one behind the angle of the mouth, with some scattered warts on the sides; skin otherwise entirely smooth. Toes obtuse, with wide webs reaching to the base of the penultimate phalange. One long metatarsal tubercle; no fold on the tarsus; a dermal border on outer toe. The heel extends beyond the end of the muzzle.

"Light brown above; below yellow. Three rows of rather distant solid black spots between the dorsal folds; two or three rows on each side; none of the spots yellow-bordered. Head unspotted; no band on the lip. A brown vertical band on the front of the humerus. Scattered spots on tibia and femur; clouded spots on the posterior face of the femur. Size of *Rana clamata*.

"This frog of which a female specimen was obtained, combines characteristics of different groups; its coloration resembles somewhat that of the eastern or typical form of *Rana halecina*, but the full palmation of the hind foot is that of *R. montezumae* and *R. catesbeiana*. It is also quite similar to the variety of *R. temporaria* from California, called *R. draytoni* by Baird and Girard and *R. longipes* by Hallowell. The feet are shorter, the hind feet being twice as long as the head to the posterior border of the tympanum, while in *R. t. draytoni* it is 2.5 times as long. The *R. onca* lacks the black cheek-patch of the *R. temporaria*. Specimen secured in 1872 in Utah by Dr. H. C. Yarrow. The plate affords view of the dorsum and mouth of this species" (H. C. Yarrow, Ariz., 1875, pp. 528–529).

This frog in snout and general appearance looks more like *R. sphenocephala* than *R. pipiens*. It is of *R. pipiens* class but smaller.

"This rare Utah species may be readily separated from all other native Batrachians except *R. pipiens* and from this species it differs in having no definite narrow longitudinal folds between the dorsolateral ridges, its smaller size, and habitat in the extreme southwestern corner of Utah along the Virgin River. The head is as broad as long and depressed; the nostrils are nearer the eyes than the end of the snout, canthus rostralis almost absent in the specimens before me. Tympanic membrane large and smooth. The limbs are well developed, digits long and webs well formed. Skin above smooth with a few warts and tubercles about the head and neck. The general color above is brown to olive green with spots that are bordered with grey. The noticeable dorsolateral fold is brown in the specimens examined. The undersurface is white over the belly and yellowish on the legs" (V. M. Tanner, Utah, 1931, p. 189).

**Voice:** Its call is not so long or loud as the call of the bigger *R. pipiens*.

**Breeding:** Most of the captures were late April. This is doubtless the height of its breeding season. It may breed March to May. Eggs and tadpoles are not of record. Transformation probably is from 25 to 30 mm or more in June. Were the specimens secured April 25, 1936, at Overton, sizes 36 to 42 mm., from the year before?

**Journal notes:** May 18, 1942, Glendale. Went to the ranger of Boulder Dam Museum. He said that "2 miles S. E. of Overton," where Linsdale and Rodgers caught the frog, must be a spring seep ½ mile beyond where the CCC boys were making a diversion dam on Muddy River. The museum is ¾ mile from Overton.

Went to seepage area, quite dry. Saw a frog leap into a clump of grass, missed it. My impression was gray. Went two steps farther and another (probably the same) leaped into brush. I whipped him out and he leaped into a pool. Got it. Later, lost another which leaped into rushes.

Beaver Dam Lodge, Ariz. We heard a low short croak—the frog we wanted. After a long effort I located it in the tules, but with one flashlight on right wrist and one in my hand and with a net and a bag at my waist, I missed in my grab at him. He looked like the one we captured at Overton.

**Authorities' corner:** "A search of several years, for this species, finally ended successfully when two specimens were taken in June, 1928, in a small stream south of St. George. While Dr. Yarrow does not give the exact locality for this species yet from his itinerary and subsequent collections we are reasonably sure in concluding that he captured his specimens somewhere along the Virgin River in Washington County [Utah]" (V. M. Tanner, Utah, 1929, p. 49).

"This species was first observed at the mouth of Boulder Wash, Colorado River, where the rising waters of the reservoir had submerged a small cat-tail swamp. Two specimens were seen clambering about on small bits of driftwood a few feet from the bank. One specimen was collected at Littlefield, Arizona, and five specimens were taken on the Muddy River at Glendale, Nevada. Although Woodbury (1930) has recorded *R. pipiens* from Zion Canyon on the Mukunteweap River, a tributary of the Virgin, it would seem improbable that two such closely related species as *onca* and *pipiens* would occur in contiguous regions of the same drainage system. More recently, Eaton has stated that specimens collected further eastward in Utah 'are intermediate' and he doubts the validity of *onca*. It is more probable that, if not valid species, the two forms may be subspecific" (R. B. Cowles and C. M. Bogert, Nev., 1936, p. 36).

## Pickerel Frog, Marsh Frog, Tiger Frog (DeKay), Leopard Frog (DeKay), Cold Swamp Frog, Swamp Frog, Spring Frog, Le Conte's Leopard Frog

*Rana palustris* Le Conte. Plate C; Map 32.

**Range:** From central plains to Atlantic seaboard; from the Gulf States to Hudson Bay.

"*Rana palustris* was not found (Northern Pontiac Co., Quebec) although it has been taken in the Laurentian Mountains (Lat. 46°N.). Cope (1889) assigned three specimens collected by Drexler from 'James Bay, N.B.' to *palustris*. The identification was confirmed by Preble (1902). The locality designated has been assumed by later authors to be James Bay proper, and since there is no James Bay in New Brunswick this is probably the correct interpretation. Since there are no other records of this species from high latitudes, Cope's record should not be accepted without confirmation" (R. Grant, Que., 1941, p. 153).

*Plate XCIX. Rana onca.* (×⅔). From 2 miles southeast of Overton, Nev.

*Plate C. Rana palustris.* 1,3 Males (×⅔) 2. Male croaking (×⅖). 4. Female (×⅔)

**Habitat:** Sphagnum bogs, marl ponds, cold streams, shallows of mill ponds, quiet water of bayous, rocky ravines. It is the most abundant frog in the rock-bottomed and rock-walled ravines of central New York, where it quite frequently breeds in the deep holes at the bases of waterfalls. It is also found in the sources of clear trout streams. After breeding time, the frog is found in meadowlands. Some individuals remain in ravines and similar places. They hibernate in water.

"The pickerel frog is usually restricted to flowing streams either cool or warm. Specimens have been taken in trout brooks, at 55°F. and in drainage creeks, at 80°F. In Glengarry County in late September we found specimens a considerable distance from any water" (G. C. Toner and N. de St. Remy, Ont., 1941, pp. 13–14).

**Size:** Adults, 1⅘–3⅙ inches. Males, 46–64 mm. Females, 49–79 mm.

**General appearance:** The pickerel frog at first glance looks much like the meadow frog. It is slender, smooth-skinned, medium in size, usually brown in color, with light raised ridges extending backward from the eyes. The dark spots are, however, square in shape and dark-bordered, regularly arranged in two rows with an occasional third spot between the dorsolateral folds, and covering more than one-half of that area. The spots on the sides also are square and arranged regularly, the upper row close to the dorsolateral fold. There is a dark streak from the eye to the nostril. Underneath it is glistening white on the forward part and yellow or orange on the underside of the legs, in the groin, forward along the sides of the belly, and on the underside of forearms. The legs are barred with dark bands.

**Color:** *Male*. McLean, N.Y., June 2, 1929. Ground color from back of snout to vent and between dorsolateral folds, ecru-olive, also same on interspaces of tibia and between crossbars of femur. Interspaces of forelegs and sides below dorsolateral folds avellaneous or vinaceous-buff. Snout and line over eye same or tawny olive. Dorsolateral fold citron yellow or ochraceous-buff, at times capucine yellow. Median spot ahead of eye, eyelid spot, stripe eye to snout, two rows down back, regular and smaller lower side spots, crossbars on legs, etc., brownish olive or black with lighter dots of light yellowish olive which give tibial crossbars and some others a rather "greenish" cast. Under parts of hind legs and forelegs, groin, and lower belly orange or cadmium yellow, becoming a narrow light orange-yellow band along side to axilla Rear of femur raw sienna or aniline yellow. Rest of under parts cream color. Tympanum wood brown. Iris black or clove brown dotted below with light russet-vinaceous flecks. Above pupil is a line of light green-yellow or empire yellow. Edge of eyelid with a little of neva green. Thumb pad blackish brown (1). Stripe on upper jaw extending almost to arm insertion is honey yellow at front, becoming cartridge buff at the rear, edged below by brownish olive. Prominent blackish brown (1) longitudinal spot at base of arm and in front.

*Female.* McLean, July 21, 1929. Ground color of back from snout to vent and the interspaces on fore and hind legs deep olive-buff or grayish olive. Below the dorsolateral folds and on the interspaces of forearms and hind legs the frogs have a tendency to become light drab or cinnamon-drab. The upper eyelid is vinaceous-fawn. The dorsolateral fold is light ochraceous-salmon or cinnamon-buff. One median spot ahead of the eye, eyelid spot, stripe from eye to snout, the two rows down the back, and a smaller row below the dorsolateral fold are buffy olive. So also the bars on the legs; the bars on the hind legs and the spots below the dorsolateral fold may be light brownish olive. The vermiculations on the rear of thighs and the margins to the spots, the oblique bar on the arm insertion, and the oblique stripe over tympanum from eye to arm may be black, olive, or brownish olive. As in the males, all of the dorsal spots and leg bars may have a greenish cast because of yellowish olive or light yellowish olive dots in their centers. In the groin and axilla is cadmium yellow, but the rear half of underside of femur, the whole underside of tibia, and the inner side of leg are raw sienna or mars yellow.

This is also true of vermiculations on the rear of femur. The rest of under parts, including some of the middle of the lower belly and some of basal half of femur, are cream-colored. The tympanum is wood brown. Stripe on jaw is cartridge buff with brownish olive edge below it. Eye as in the male.

**Structure:** Thumb much enlarged in breeding males; vocal sacs of males small lateral swellings between the tympanum and the arm; the skin has strong acrid secretion, irritating to the mouth of the dog who tries to eat one, a secretion which will kill other frogs put in the same jar of water.

"*Rana palustris,* or marsh frog; colour above pale brown, with two longitudinal rows of dark brown spots on the back, and the same number on the sides, hind part of the thighs yellow, spotted with black" (J. Le Conte, Gen., 1825, p. 282).

**Voice:** It has a low-pitched grating croak with little carrying power, shorter and higher than *Rana pipiens,* and more prolonged and lower than *Rana sylvatica.* These males frequently croak beneath the surface of the water, while in the embrace. Of our local frogs, this form and the rather silent wood frog make the least audible disturbance at the breeding season. The call is so characterless that the tendency is to link it with a subdued *Rana pipiens,* but the latter has not so short a note. The males occasionally answer each other with a croak totally different from the normal one. E. D. Cope (Gen., 1889, p. 408) says, "Its note is a low prolonged croak, somewhat resembling the sound produced by tearing some coarse material."

**Breeding:** These frogs breed from April 23 to May 15. They gather in large numbers, and often in a small area 6 feet square or less one finds 12 to 15 pickerel frogs mating or pairs laying. The brown and bright yellow eggs are submerged attached to twigs or grass stems, form a firm globular mass 3½–4 inches (87–100 mm.) in diameter, and number 2000–3000. The egg is 1/16 inch (1.6 mm.) in diameter, envelopes 1/9 inch (2.8 mm.) and 1/6 inch (4 mm.), a little smaller than those of *Rana pipiens*. The tadpole is large, 3 inches (75.8 mm.), greenish in color, the body and tail covered with fine black dots, the tail crests black or very clouded, and the belly cream. The tooth ridges are 2/3, 1/3. After 70–80 days, the tadpoles transform in August at 3/4–1 1/12 inches (19–27 mm.).

The species usually seeks the shallows for egg laying, though almost every year we find some egg masses in the middle of ponds where the water is 1–3 feet deep. Like *Rana sylvatica* and *Rana pipiens*, it frequently lays in special areas. In 1907 in an area 3 by 3 feet, 18 bunches were deposited; in another 12 bunches were recorded. In 1911, in another spot 3 by 3 feet, 31 bunches were found. All these areas gave excellent illustration of the building of bunches, one upon another. In one case four successive bunches upon one twig were recorded. The greatest number on one support was secured May 5, 1909, when seven were noted. Quite frequently, on tufts of grass or sticks one finds a bunch or more of spotted salamander eggs or meadow-frog eggs with one of two pickerel frog masses immediately above them, seldom below, because laid later.

**Journal notes:** April 28, 1911, Ithaca, N.Y. When I approached the *Rana palustris* egg area (just discovered today) there were within an area of 3 feet square 5 mated pairs and 21 unmated males. Of the mated pairs, the males were much lighter than the females A female will back up to a stem and clasp it with hind legs, then change position or back to another stem. Sometimes this will be a stem with one to three or four egg masses on it already. Her nervous leg movements and many changes often loosen or fray the former egg masses. In the area mentioned above there were already eight egg masses. Often when a pair took a position other males interfered. In such cases the female helped her consort to kick them away. While in the embrace, the male frequently gave his low grating note. Occasionally a pair put up for air. Finally one pair began to lay She was perfectly horizontal and flattened, her hind legs drawn up, the heels together, her front feet together; with his hind legs slightly within hers, he seemed to help push the eggs back. This egg laying occupied about 3 minutes in all, with about 10 to 12 fertilizations. I left the area after 10:50, returning at 11:00, and found another mass had been laid.

**Authorities' corner:**

D. H. Storer, Mass, 1839, p. 238.
H. C. Bumpus, R.I., 1886, pp. 7–8.
G. M. Allen, N.H, 1899, p. 69.
J. A. Weber, N.Y., 1928, p. 109.
H. M. Smith and B. C. Brown, Tex, 1947, pp. 47–50

Anita Daugherty's unpublished thesis (University of Rochester) may have pertinence in the understanding of the *Rana pipiens* complex.

## Meadow Frog, Leopard Frog, Shad Frog, Herring Hoppers, Common Frog, Berlandier's Frog, Spotted Frog, Grass Frog, Water Frog, Peeping Frog, Olive-colored Frog

*Rana pipiens pipiens* Schreber. Plate CI; Maps 33–34.

**Range:** Widespread and common over North America, east of the eastern edge of the Pacific Coast states, from the extreme north into Mexico.

Specifically on the west it extends from Mexico to the southeastern corner of California, up the Colorado River to Nevada, then to northeastern California, eastern edges of Oregon, Washington, and British Columbia to northern Alberta or even to Mackenzie, thence southeastward to Laurentian Mountains and Gaspé Peninsula, Labrador, and Newfoundland; thence along coast to northern New Jersey and along southeastern states in the Piedmont and the mountains mainly above the Fall line, i.e., western two-thirds of Virginia, western half of North Carolina, western South Carolina, northern Georgia and Alabama, eastern Tennessee and Kentucky; thence westward through northern Indiana, Illinois, and Missouri to Kansas and south through the Panhandle of Texas to extreme southern Texas and Mexico.

**Habitat:** In spring in swampy marsh lands, upland backwaters, overflows, and ponds. In summer in swamp lands, grassy woodland, or hay or grain fields in cultivated districts. They spend the winter in pools or marshes.

**Size:** Adults, 2½–4½ inches. Males, 52–80 mm. Females, 52–102 mm.

**General appearance:** These frogs are slender in form, smooth-skinned, medium in size, brown or green in general color, with two light raised stripes extending backward from the eye. Between these dorsolateral folds are two or three rows of irregularly arranged, rounded dark spots with light borders. On the sides are more rounded dark spots with light borders, irregularly arranged in three or four rows. There is usually a dark spot on the top of either eyelid. There is a light line along the jaw, below the ear, and over the arm, bordered below with a dark stripe The legs are barred with light-bordered dark bands. Beneath, it is a glistening white to yellow or orange under legs in Arizona (See *R. pipiens* complex.)

**Color:** *Male.* Ithaca, N.Y., from Harry Leighton, July 29, 1929. The back is Saccardo's olive to buffy brown with spots on back and sides of chestnut brown or olive-brown with black rims. The spots are surrounded by rings of apple green to yellow-green, which is the color extending from nostril to eye, over tympanum, and along the side just below the dorsolateral fold. There is a pale vinaceous-fawn to cartridge buff line along upper jaw to above arm insertion, bordered below by olive-brown, which in turn is margined on lower edge by cartridge buff or white. The dorsolateral folds are pale vinaceous-fawn to pale cinnamon-pink. The interspaces on forearms and lower sides are light vinaceous-fawn to ecru-drab. There is an olive-brown dash on front of brachial insertion. Upper parts of hind limbs are like the back, with interspaces on rear of femur viridine yellow or neuvider green spotted olive-brown to black. In the groin is a little bright green-yellow. The tympanum is vinaceous-buff or cinnamon with spotting of olive-brown Under parts are white or cartridge buff. The iris is black or olive-brown with an outside half-moon back and front of neuvider green; the lower part of iris and pupil rim are spotted with vinaceous buff and with a longitudinal band over the pupil and pupil rim of light greenish yellow. The thumb has basal pad of hair brown or dark grayish olive.

*Female.* Ithaca, N.Y., July 23, 1930. The dorsolateral folds, canthus rostralis, rear of upper eyelid, and supplementary folds between the dorsal folds are mikado brown to wood brown or avellaneous. The latter colors are the background of back, sides, and forelegs. On rear legs there is a little of this color on the distal cephalic portion of femur, on dorsal tibia, and on foot. The dorsal spots are Prout's brown or possibly bister. The borders of spots are neva green or calliste green. The lower lateral spots and spots of rear of femur are bone brown without light borders. The interstices of the groin and rear of femur are neuvider green. Some of the lower lateral spots and the spots on the arm and sometimes on foot are tilleul buff. The light stripe on upper jaw to arm insertion is tilleul buff becoming olive-buff or pale olive-buff over arm insertion. The tympanum is same color as dorsal folds. The iris is like the male's. Under parts are white.

**Structure:** Lateral folds prominent; head shorter than *R. p. sphenocephala;* snout medium, vocal sacs of males, lateral, between tympanum and arm, swelling out as round balls over the arms, with extensions down the sides; more spots below dorsolateral fold than in *Rana p. sphenocephala.*

**Voice:** The croak is a long, low guttural note, 3 or more seconds long, followed by three to six short notes each a second or less in length, or the short notes may precede or be interspersed. In early spring the leopard frogs form the second swamp chorus to arrest attention. Though not possessing loud voices individually, their concourses in our swamps, when most vociferous, cannot pass unnoticed. Usually the call is heard from males at the surface of the water, and before they are mated. Occasionally, when wading through an egg area, one hears croaks which at first puzzle; they come from the mated and mating frogs beneath the water and often reveal the game on the bottom.

**Breeding:** This species breeds from April 1 to May 15. The egg mass is a flattened sphere, 3–6 inches (75–150 mm.) by 2–3 inches (5–75 mm.). The eggs are black and white, 1/16 inch (1.6 mm.) in diameter, the envelopes 1/8 inch (3.4 mm.) and 1/5 inch (5 mm.). The tadpole is large, 3 3/8 inches (84 mm.), the tail lighter than the body, its crests translucent marked with fine spots and pencilings. The tooth ridges are 2/3, 3/3. After 60 to 80 days, the tadpoles transform in July at 3/4–1 1/4 inches (18–31 mm.).

These frogs have a tendency to congregate in large numbers at the breeding time and often 40 or more bunches of eggs are recorded within a small area. The egg masses are plinthlike and attached to submerged cattails, twigs, sticks, or grass, or even rest on the bottom unattached. They occur in the open, unprotected, marshy expanses, or in overflows where edges and bottoms have plenty of grass. Many of the egg masses are laid in very shallow water, and it does not require very much evaporation to leave them high and dry.

**Journal notes:** April 11, 1907, Ithaca, N.Y. In Bool's backwater, I found one bunch of *Rana pipiens* eggs. Just before I found them I heard a croak under my feet. There were two frogs trying to escape, a male and a female. . . . The dead-end stream running east furnished some good notes. I heard several croaks from frogs at the surface. It is a low croak. I captured a male *Rana pipiens*. Around were eight bunches of eggs. *Rana pipiens* eggs are not in the spherical masses that we find with *Rana sylvatica*. They are more flat; the longest diameter may be 5 or 6 inches, but seldom is the other diameter more than 1½ or 2 inches. *Rana pipiens* usually seeks places where the edges are grassy.

April 25, 1911, Dwyer's Pond, Ithaca, N.Y. Surface temperature 56°, bottom temperature 48°. I found several new bunches of *Rana pipiens* eggs, countless old bunches, immense *Rana pipiens* areas of 25–40 bunches, and several *Rana pipiens* croaking.

**Authorities' corner:**

P. Kalm, Gen., 1771, II, 88–90.
G. H. Loskiel, Gen., 1794, p. 89.
W. T. Davis, N.Y., 1898, p. 4.
B. W. Evermann and H. W. Clark, N.Y., 1920, p. 638.

## Plain Meadow Frog, Burns' Meadow Frog, Unspotted Meadow Frog

[Mutant] *Rana pipiens burnsi* Weed. Plate CII; Map 34.

**Range:** "The species seems to be confined to northern Iowa and southern Minnesota, with possibly some stragglers in western Illinois and Wisconsin. . . . This specimen (the type) and twenty paratypes, were received from New London, Kandiyohi County, Minnesota. There are about eighty other specimens of this species in the collections of Field Museum, from Spicer, Kandiyohi County, Minnesota; Okabena, Jackson County, Minnesota; Rothsay, Wilkin County, Minnesota; and Astoria, Deuel County, South Dakota" (A. C. Weed, Minn., 1922, pp. 108–109).

**Habitat:** Swampy stretches and meadows. (See "Journal notes" for this form and *Rana p. kandiyohi*.)

**Size:** "In size it is very little smaller than *Rana pipiens*. That is, the very largest individuals of the latter species are a little larger than the very largest ones of the former" (A. C. Weed, Minn., 1922, p. 108).

**General appearance:** These frogs are built like meadow frogs. They have the long snout of *R. p. sphenocephala*. Their general color and first appearance

*Plate CI. Rana pipiens pipiens.* 1. Female (×½). 2,5. Males (×½). 3. Egg masses on the bottom of a pond (×⅛). 4. Egg mass, plinth shaped (×⅓).

*Plate CII. Rana pipiens (burnsi)* (×⅗). 1–6. Males.

is like a bronzy wood frog (*R. sylvatica*) without the black mask. The costal folds are long, prominently raised, and frequently a light buff color. Some frogs are apple green, some wood brown. They have considerable green in axil and groin, and on rear of femur. Some have prominent black dash on arm insertion and black spot on elbow, and prominent black band on canthus rostralis. They are glistening white below. They are beautiful frogs and remind one of wood frogs.

Aug. 24, 1930, New London, Minn. We took two large males on Lower Florida slough. They are of equal size. We wonder whether this unspotted phase is a sexual color or one due to age. If this form is a variant of *Rana pipiens*, is it like albino or other heterochromatic or metachroistic phases in other groups? It is a fine breeding problem for some Minnesota student. (See J. A. Moore, Minn., 1942, in "Authorities' corner.")

"The brown color changes of *Rana burnsi* match almost exactly the similar changes of the Wood Frog, *Rana sylvatica*, the main difference being that the latter species seldom shows a strong green color and always has a black patch at the side of the head, which is lacking in *Rana burnsi*" (A. C. Weed, Minn., 1922, p. 108).

**Color:** Lake Florida, Spicer, Minn., Aug. 24, 1930. *Adult* The side of face, top of head, and down middle of back, apple green or dull green-yellow. On the sides below the costal folds, on rear of hind legs, courge green or deep chrysolite green. Top of forearms and hind legs to tarsus mignonette green. Groin and rear of femur deep lichen green or glaucous green. Rear of tibia bears slight indistinct dots or lines of black or light brownish olive. There are no spots on back except a few minute inky dots between the eyes and for an inch backward on middle of back. Costal fold, snout, and band on upper jaw extending backward to arm insertion is apricot buff to cinnamon-buff, the upper jaw tending toward mikado brown sometimes; on the rear of back between costal folds are two or three subfolds of orange-citrine or citrine. A small black spot on brachium near elbow is present on one arm and absent on the other. The green color of sides serves as center of tympanum surrounded by a cinnamon-brown circle Under parts white. The eye is black with outer circle of green yellow. Pupil rim baryta yellow, broken below. Iris particularly above the pupil ring with horizontal band of apricot buff or warm buff. The lower eye dotted with same color.

The general color of another frog is wood brown, the background being avellaneous to light cinnamon-drab, with raised folds of citrine-drab. The costal folds are olive-ocher to ecru-olive. This frog has no arm insertion spots.

"The color is extremely variable in each individual according to conditions of fear, etc., as well as in response to the color of the environment but is very uniform in the species as a whole. . . . The color of this species is usually some shade of green or brown, varying from the color of an old water-soaked board to a very light mist gray and to light apple green. About a third of the specimens have irregular black spots on arms or legs or both. These spots never approach the condition of regular cross-barring so often seen in *Rana pipiens*. They look more like blots of ink that might have gotten there accidentally" (A. C. Weed, Minn., 1922, p. 108).

**Structure:** "The web of the hind foot is quite variable. In the type it appears as a keel on the sides of about two and one half joints of the longest toe, but is clearly visible practically to the end of that toe. In some other specimens it is much larger and stretches almost directly across between the tips of the toes. There is every degree of variation between the two conditions" (same, p. 108).

**Voice:** When held just ahead of the hind legs, the males inflate lateral vocal sacs exactly like *Rana pipiens,* and do not sound unlike that species.

**Breeding:** *Eggs, Tadpoles, Transformation*. Nothing recorded.

**Journal notes:** Aug. 22, 1930. On the third floor of the Minneapolis Public Library, Mrs. Olive Wiley has a museum of reptiles and amphibia. One puzzle to her was a partly blue frog. It is the green frog (*Rana clamitans*). In one of her aquaria she had a *Rana* she alluded to as a wood frog It had the size and general appearance of a wood frog, but very manifestly it was the meadow frog we sought, *Rana burnsi* of Weed. It is a very bronzy, beautiful frog. Later Mr. O'Connor showed me another one which was green on the back. It too had no dorsal spots. The first one came from Coon Lake about 10 to 12 miles northeast of St. Paul. This extends the range of this species outside the Minnesota River drainage.

Aug. 23. Arrived at Spicer, Kandiyohi Co., Minn., at 5.30 P.M. Sought out Mr. M. F. Delaske, who told us that he sometimes had plain bait frogs with no spots. Mr. Oscar Hillman did not recall seeing meadow frogs without spots.

Aug. 24. Started for Lake Florida Jens Larson had in his bait box 15 frogs, two half-grown ones being *Rana burnsi*. Started for Mr. Carl Holm's place. We stopped in a meadow where fringed gentian, *Lobelia syphilitica,* smartweed, *Gerardia paupercula,* and other plants grew. Here took 1 *Rana burnsi* and 20 *Rana pipiens.*

We went down in the meadow with Mr. Carl Holm. The turkeys were there already. They eat frogs and grasshoppers. We caught many meadow frogs. We took in all about 5 or 6 *Rana burnsi,* or about 1 to every 50 *Rana pipiens.* Some of these *Rana burnsi* are brown, others plain green. Mr. Holm said he had found little meadow frogs without spots.

Went to South Florida sloughs. Here we found 6 or 7 *Rana burnsi* We must have seen 200 frogs. The ratio of *Rana burnsi* to *Rana pipiens* was 1 to 28 or 1 to 35. These were in sedgy grass. Most of the frogs are doubtless in the heavier and taller grasses Most of the *Rana burnsi* were half grown. We took two large males in quick succession. One was uniform green and the other brown. The next day, when we opened their can, they were still of the same colors.

Went to Sam Dilly's at Old Mill Inn 2 miles from New London. He had in his bait stock one *Rana burnsi*. *Rana burnsi* is a beautiful frog, brown or green when young, and equally variable when grown.

**Authorities' corner:**

A. C. Weed, Minn., 1922, p. 108.
A. C. Weed, Minn., 1930, p. 43.
L. Stejneger and T. Barbour, Check List, 1923, p. 4.
G. Swanson, Minn., 1933, p. 154.

An embryological and genetical study of this mutant was finally undertaken by J. A. Moore, who reached some interesting conclusions. From his paper (Minn., 1942, pp. 408–416), we take the following excerpts:

1. "A few years ago a shipment of *Rana pipiens* arrived from the middle west which included several *Rana burnsi*. This provided an opportunity for studying the early development of this non-spotted variety and for attempting to secure hybrids with typical *Rana pipiens*. Cross fertilization between *burnsi* and *pipiens* was successful, and a few tadpoles were kept until metamorphosis. In the controls, *burnsi* ♀ × *burnsi* ♂, three tadpoles transformed. These were of two kinds—one non-spotted like the parents, the other two spotted and indistinguishable from ordinary *pipiens*. The hybrids of *pipiens* and *burnsi* similarly gave rise to two types of offspring. Of the 24 transforming in this cross, 13 were non-spotted and 11 spotted. There was no evidence of blended inheritance. Seven controls, *pipiens* ♀ × *pipiens* ♂, differed in no way from their parents.

"These rather surprising results suggested that the non-spotted frogs that Weed had named *Rana burnsi* differed from the typical *Rana pipiens* by one dominant gene carried in the heterozygous state. Experiments with *Rana burnsi* were resumed the following year. The problem was assailed in two ways: (1) by a study of embryonic temperature tolerance and rate of development and (2) by breeding experiments to throw light on the inheritance of the pigment pattern."

2. "Morphologically the eggs of *pipiens* and *burnsi* are indistinguishable. The color and size of the eggs as well as the structure of the jelly membranes are identical. Wright and Wright (1933) have found characters of this nature useful in separating species in many cases."

"These observations on egg size, type of jelly, rate of development, and temperature tolerance do not reveal any difference between *Rana pipiens* and *Rana burnsi*. If *Rana burnsi* proved to be a 'good species' this would be surprising, but if the difference between the two is due to a single gene affecting pigmentation, as was suggested by the preliminary experiments, we would not necessarily expect embryonic differences of the type enumerated."

3. "Of the tadpoles originally classed as spotted, 90.3 per cent gave rise to *pipiens* and 9.7 per cent to *burnsi*. Of those classed as non-spotted, 93.7 per cent gave rise to *burnsi* and 6.3 per cent to *pipiens*. The adult pigment differences are thus heralded in the larval stage. The exceptions (*burnsi* from

spotted tadpoles and *pipiens* from non-spotted tadpoles) can be explained in part by incorrect classification of very young tadpoles."

4. "*Rana burnsi* differs from *Rana pipiens* by one dominant gene that influences pigmentation. Twenty-five animals have been tested and found to be heterozygous for the mutant in question. *Rana burnsi* should not have the status of a species or subspecies but should be reduced to synonymy with *Rana pipiens* and be referred to as the '*burnsi mutant.*'"

In general we accept Moore's study even though his *burnsi* did have a few small spots on the hind legs.

Breckenridge has recently discussed this form:

"Two color phases of this species that occur in Minnesota differ so widely from normal *R. pipiens* that they must be mentioned. These color phases were originally named as separate species (Weed 1922) *Rana burnsi* and *Rana kandiyohi*. These species were later reduced to subspecies and finally the terms were dropped entirely. Recent genetic work (Moore 1942) has proved that the former phase is a sport or mutant of the typical form and may be recognized simply as *R pipiens*, form *burnsi*. No similar work has been attempted with the other form but since it is probable that the case is the same, the form is here referred to as *R. pipiens*, form *kandiyohi*. Distinctions between the two are noted in the section on color phases" (W. J. Breckenridge, Minn, 1944, p. 82).

### Mottled Meadow Frog, Kandiyohi Meadow Frog

[Phase] *Rana pipiens kandiyohi* Weed. Plate CIII; Map 34.

**Range:** "The type, number 3066, Field museum of Natural History, was received from New London, Kandiyohi County, Minnesota. Two other specimens, paratypes, come from an unknown locality in Minnesota. About thirty other specimens were found in lots of frogs from Rothsay, Wilkin County, Minnesota, and from Astoria, Deuel County, South Dakota. . . .

"The name *Rana kandiyohi* is proposed with some misgivings because of the small knowledge we have of the form and its relation to other frogs and to its environment. Localities from which we have received it are, with one exception, in the southwest quarter of Minnesota. The other record is barely across the state line in South Dakota. It is to be hoped that careful field studies may be made of the frogs of the region within a hundred miles of Big Stone Lake in order that ecologic studies may supplement our present knowledge of the group" (A. C. Weed, Minn., 1922, pp. 109–110).

**Habitat:** Open meadows and pastures. The young and half-grown frogs remain throughout the summer in lowlands or along shores of lakes or streams.

**Size:** About same as the common meadow frog (*Rana p. pipiens*).

**General appearance:** "Typical specimens of this species show a color pattern which suggests a blending of *Rana pipiens* and *Rana septentrionalis*. It is as though the black spots of *Rana pipiens* had been superposed on the mottled color of *septentrionalis*. The spots are not as evenly rounded as in *pipiens* but show a tendency to fuse with the mottlings between them. The vermiculate mottlings are carried down on the legs and feet and are there combined with a dark barring like that of especially dark colored examples of *Rana pipiens*.

"The mottled color of the back is carried well down on the sides of this species and fades gradually into the white of the under parts. The light stripes along the glandular ridges are similar to those in *Rana pipiens* and sometimes in *Rana burnsi*.

"The ground color is represented by small spots and lines between the darker parts of the mottlings. It is about the same as in *Rana pipiens*. Sometimes the mottlings are as dark as the spots. At other times they are lighter" (A. C. Weed, Minn., 1922, p. 109).

**Color:** In August, 1930, we searched meadows and borders of lakes and small streams from Spicer, Minn., northward to Rainy Lake and westward to Walhalla, N.D., and then southward and eastward over a different route to St. Paul, Minn. We saw many, many meadow frogs of all sizes with a wide variation in their spotting. Some had few spots, even down to three or four small ones on the back, others had many. Some had long narrow spots, others had round ones. In some the spots were very weakly outlined so that they were much less conspicuous. In some there were many dark specks and dashes between the spots. In one large frog the bars on the tibia were entirely lacking, being replaced by many light spots on a dark background. Along a half-mile stretch of a canal at one end of Green Lake at Spicer, Minn., we saw along the shore 200 to 300 small meadow frogs. This was in the center of *Kandiyohi* country. There was wide variation in shape, size, number, and arrangement of spots, but all appeared to us as *Rana pipiens*

**Structure:** "The web of the hind foot is variable. In the type it is continued as a rather broad keel to the end of the longest toe. In one paratype it reaches about the middle of the distal joint of the longest toe. In the other paratype it extends on the next to last joint of longest toe as a very narrow keel" (A. C. Weed, Minn., 1922, p. 109).

**Voice:** "In conclusion it may be well to mention that males of *Rana kandiyohi* kept alive in the aquarium have been croaking vigorously for some weeks and that their note is quite distinct from that of some *Rana pipiens* from the vicinity of Chicago. The note of the Leopard Frog is more or less a succession of syllables and may be almost represented by striking stones together rather rapidly. That of *Rana kandiyohi* is more in the nature of a croak and might be represented by grinding two stones together under considerable pressure" (A. C. Weed, Minn., 1922, p. 110).

**Breeding:** *Eggs, Tadpoles, Transformation*. Nothing recorded.

**Journal notes:** Aug. 23, 1930. Arrived at Spicer, Kandiyohi Co., Minn., at 5:30 P.M. Sought out Mr. M. F. Delaske. He told us of Oscar Hillman and Sam Dilly at Old Mill Inn (2 miles from New London). He told us that frogs were shipped out of Spicer almost by the ton. Some made $100 in one night at frog catching. Next we went to see Mr. Hillman. He told us of the immense numbers caught. He said the mosquitoes got thick, the farmers protested, and "the law was put on frogs very tight." He suggested we go to Carl Holm's meadow at Lake Florida. More frogs were caught at Lake Florida than any other place. The land lies in such a way at Lake Florida that there is a lane leading to the lake, and here the frogs were caught in great quantities. Mr. Sam Dilly said, "It sounds fishy but people bring in frogs to Spicer like farmers drawing bags of grain. A man may bring in 8 or 10 such bags. They ship them in crates in tiers." The people in this vicinity shipped to F J. Burns of Chicago and to E. R. Neuenfeldt of Oshkosh. Many people not only collected but bought from others to ship. Many frogs were taken from Eagle Lake and Kandiyohi Lake near Willmar.

August 24. Started for Lake Florida. Drove into Mr. Carl Holm's place. He gave us a wealth of experiences about frog catching and frogs. Mr. E. R. Neuenfeldt came to his place at first and stayed for a time in his home. At first they were paid 3 cents a pound for frogs, later 10 cents, and once 17 cents. It takes about 10 to 12 frogs to make a pound Once he had 1000 pounds in burlap bags. A freeze came and they seemed dead. He hated to lose $400. He warmed some water to tepid temperature and put it into a barrel. He put one bag of stiffly frozen frogs into the water and, lo and behold! they all became active. He thus revived his whole thousand pounds.

When the first frosts come, the frogs begin to leave the lowland meadows for the lake, the young ones first, the adults later. Sometimes they delay so long that they get shut out of the lake by the formation of the ice. He has seen them moving in such numbers at this season as to form a band two rods wide and one-half mile long where no one could step without crushing frogs. They frequently put their frogs in milk cans. Sometimes they catch frogs by hand, sometimes with muslin fences and barrel or box traps. One night he and two other men picked up 750 pounds by hand. It was a cold night and the frogs were sluggish. They took out milk cans and could fill them within 3 inches of the top without their jumping out. One carried the can, two men caught frogs. When catching with traps, they buy muslin and cut it down the middle and stretch it one rod from the lake. The total run may be 600–700 yards, with a box every hundred yards. One spring they had the trap out and caught turtles, salamanders, and frogs in their boxes. They started collecting in 1909 and continued until the collecting season was closed by law.

We went down in the meadow with Mr. Carl Holm. These meadows are between two ridges of hills. The meadows form a narrow strip or lane, a capital place to catch the frogs in fall. We examined many meadow frogs. We caught five or six unspotted ones and some partially mottled. One meadow frog had tibia bands absent and tibia mottled. Am not yet satisfied I have seen a good *Rana kandiyohi*. What is *Rana kandiyohi*?

In 1944 a live frog of this phase came to Cornell with class material from Wisconsin. This showed plainly the broken tracery and fleckings between the usual spots and leg bars.

**Authorities' corner:**

A. C. Weed, Minn., 1922, p. 110.
A. C. Weed, Minn., 1923, p. 28.
A. C. Weed, Minn., 1930, pp. 43–44.

In a letter of Oct. 24, 1930, Dr. Weed wrote to us: "Preserved specimens of *kandiyohi* look much more like *pipiens* than the individuals did in life. The most conspicuous difference in the ones we have here is that the white border around the black spots is more or less definitely broken up into spots, which are matched in size and color by similar spots elsewhere. There seems also to be a definite tendency for black spots similar to those of the back to be found well down on the flanks or even on the sides of the belly. . . .

"Your failure to find *kandiyohi* at Florida Lake may be due to its absolute rarity in that region or (perhaps) to a difference in habitat. . . .

"In collections from farther west the condition was entirely different. The ratio of *burnsi* was about the same but *kandiyohi* tended to equal *pipiens* in numbers and, as I remember it, actually exceeded *pipiens* in one lot of several thousand from South Dakota. . . .

"In thinking over my experiences in collecting these frogs, it comes definitely in my mind that if I were looking for a large stock of *kandiyohi* I should start somewhere in the vicinity of Lake Traverse and Big Stone Lake and work westward toward the region where it becomes too dry for frogs to live. I should expect to find a region where *pipiens* is about as rare as *kandiyohi* is in some parts of Minnesota."

Since this letter only Swanson's (1933) and Breckenridge's (1944) contributions are pertinent.

"The vermiculated form (*kandiyohi*) Weed reports from Kandiyohi and Wilkin counties. It has not been noted in the Minneapolis region" (G. Swanson, Minn., 1935, p. 154).

"The dark color phase of the leopard frog, form *kandiyohi*, is characterized by a marked darkening of the interspaces between the black spots of normal *R. pipiens*. On the hind legs, the black spots are often much broken with coarse fleckings of black and greenish or yellowish. The result is a very dark frog, with the black spots of the normal pattern indistinctly outlined in broken light lines. The dorso-lateral ridges are often metallic in appearance. The few records of this dark, mottled form of the leopard frog are rather widely scattered over the prairie section of Minnesota, with one isolated record in Hennepin County in the eastern part of the state. . . . A fisherman's frog box containing

250 frogs was examined near Granite Falls and was found to contain five or 2 per cent of this dark form. On the basis of present data the author considers form *kandiyohi* to be much less common than form *burnsi* and more restricted in distribution" (W. J. Breckenridge, Minn., 1944, p. 84).

**Southern Meadow Frog, Southern Leopard Frog, Spring Frog, Spotted Frog, Water Frog, Shad Frog**

*Rana pipiens sphenocephala* (Cope). Plate CIV; Map 34.

**Range:** Southeastern states, north along the coast to Virginia or New Jersey; up Mississippi River to Indiana and Kentucky.

**Habitat:** Ponds, runs, canals, river swamps, and overflowed roads and ditches. In a large swamp it is ideally on the edge of cypress ponds and bays or small pools at an island's edge.

"Margins of streams and lakes, and marshy spots, common" (O C. Van Hyning, Fla., 1933, p. 4).

"When alarmed they usually make six or eight very long leaps, pivoting at each landing. Among thick palmettos I have seen them cover some distance in their precipitous retreats without ever touching the ground, each jump beginning and ending on one of the broad leaves Rarely one dives into the water when cornered, usually, however, reappearing at the water's edge and continuing the retreat on land" (A. F. Carr, Jr., Fla., 1940b, p. 67).

**Size:** Adults, 2–3¼ inches. Males, 49–78 mm. Females, 53–82 mm.

**General appearance:** It is like the meadow frog *R. p. pipiens*, but usually with a clear-cut, distinct white spot in the middle of the eardrum. It is an alert, active, long-legged, and long-snouted spotted frog.

It is usually glistening white below, but on the Florida Keys a form occurs that frequently has bronzy throat and clouded or mottled belly; and young there may have spotted throats and under parts. (See *R. pipiens* complex, p. 502.)

**Color:** *Male.* Okefinokee Swamp, Ga., July 3, 1921. Olive, jade, or grass green on back; pale chalcedony yellow on upper lip; pale dull green-yellow costal fold; center of tympanum chalcedony yellow. Some amber yellow or primuline yellow on underside of forearm, little on side of groin, on outer side of hind legs, and back of tarsus. Under parts white. Thumb with black swelling. Iris, back part chartreuse yellow; upper part vinaceous-buff; inner ring amber yellow or wax yellow; rest black.

*Female.* Okefinokee Swamp, Ga., June 21, 1921. Top of head to back of eye, cinnamon, Prout's, or snuff brown to bister, sudan, or brussels brown. Same color along inner and outer sides of costal fold, on upper jaw from snout to front of eye, on upper fore limb, and on ground color of back, at times becoming the predominant ground color. Background of back dark greenish olive to ivy green. Spots of back, sides, arms, and legs black. Those of back with

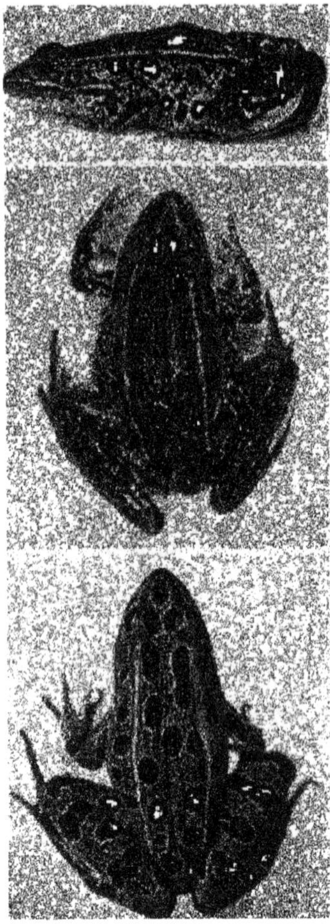

*Plate CIII. Rana pipiens (kandiyohi)* (×2/3) Females, from Wisconsin.

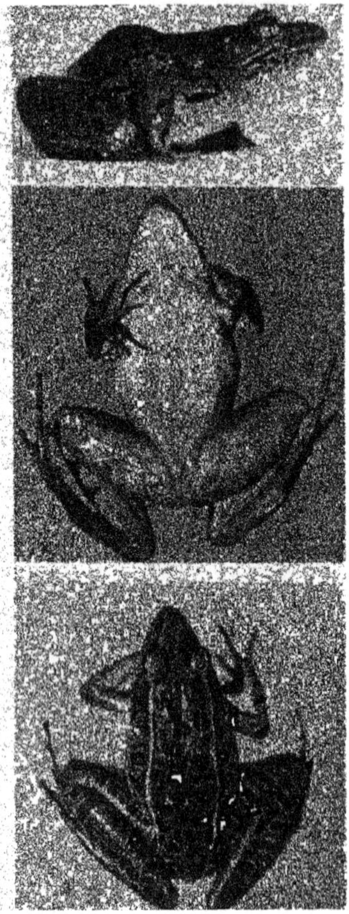

*Plate CIV. Rana pipiens sphenocephala.* 1. Male (×2/3) 2 Female (×2/3). 3 Female (×3/5).

a thin light green-yellow border. Under parts white. Throat and pectoral region dulled with blackish. Lower jaw rim marguerite yellow or seafoam yellow with black. Same color for upper jaw below the stripe from lower eye to arm insertion. Above the sudan brown of the side of snout and in front of eye through nostril is a blackish or greenish color. Two or three marguerite or seafoam yellow spots behind the eye. Stripe from under eye over angle of mouth and just beneath tympanum to over arm insertion marguerite yellow or seafoam yellow. Tympanum argus brown with marguerite yellow or seafoam yellow center. Iris in front, below, and behind pupil black with some pale vinaceous lilac or light pinkish lilac; rim pinard yellow; iris above pupil maize yellow; very top of eye with a small black area.

**Structure:** Head longer in proportion to body than in *R. pipiens;* snout acuminate or pointed; fourth toe shorter than in *R. pipiens* and more regularly placed; fewer spots and more vermiculations on sides of *R. p. sphenocephala;* dusky fleckings on the under parts more common in *R. p. sphenocephala;* lower lip with dark spots; vocal sacs on either side between arm and tympanum.

**Voice:** The call is three, four, or five guttural croaks with two or three clucks afterwards. The process may occupy 5 or 6 seconds. They are shy, croak at night, and even a big chorus is quickly stopped as one approaches the pond. They may croak from the surface, beneath the surface, or from perches on logs, sticks, or around the bases of bushes. The head and upper back are usually emergent. The croak itself comes from the swift inflation and deflation of the vocal sacs, which are on either side between forelegs and tympanum. At 11:20 P.M., May 16, 1921, we heard a *Rana p. sphenocephala* chorus. Strange we did not hear them when we were near the pond but distance had to sift out the calls. We had less success in photographing croaking males than with any other species encountered. July 13, 1922, at 12:30–1:00 A.M., we awoke and heard a great chorus northwest of our spring. Here in grassy borders of open spots were plenty of meadow frogs. In the same place Aug. 9, heard two immense choruses, one at 3:00 A.M., and another at 4–5 A.M. Went to the latter congress. Rarely, they are heard in the daytime before or after a storm passes.

**Breeding:** This species breeds from February to December, the crest coming from April to August. The egg mass is a plinth, 5–6 inches (125–150 mm.) wide, 1–2 inches (25–50 mm.) deep, attached to stems of plants or to sticks, submerged. The egg is 1/16 inch (1.6 mm.), the envelopes, 1/8 inch (3.2 mm.) and 1/5 inch (5.4 mm.). The tadpole is large, 3 inches (74 mm.), the tail with conspicuous black blotches as transformation approaches. The tooth ridges are 2/3 or 3/3. After 67 to 86 days, the tadpoles transform from April to October at 4/5–1 1/3 inches (20–33 mm.).

"They may breed every month of the year. The eggs are usually laid in masses of vegetation (algae, *Websteria, Persicaria, Hypericum,* etc.) at the water's edge or in the shallower portions of ponds and ditches" (A. F. Carr, Jr., Fla., 1940, p. 68).

"It is an early breeder, laying its eggs at Raleigh in February and March, usually starting a little later than the chorus frogs, but often the two are singing at the same time as their breeding largely coincides. However, the eggs are occasionally laid in late autumn" (C. S. Brimley, N.C., 1940, p. 27).

**Journal notes:** In 1921 we made these notes on places of ovulation. On April 24, we found them in a cypress pond. Center of pond is clear (alligator hole); then came a circle of *Pontederia* in which are toad and *Rana p. sphenocephala* eggs; a circle of sedges; next came bushes; a thin line of gums; and finally the pines. On April 29, Noah took me to where he had found frogs' eggs. They were about 8 feet from the edge of the pond in water 4–6 inches deep. This mass just hatching Noah found yesterday morning. Two more isolated masses found, each at or just below the surface and encircling the lizards' tail (*Saururus*) which is now in bloom. Water on the surface 90°.

On June 1 we remarked that *Rana p. sphenocephala* were hopping around the island after breeding, also that they were becoming browner when afield and as the season progressed.

Sept. 11, 1929. About dusk stopped near Lyons, Ind., near home of Gless J. Deckard. Heard many meadow frogs in a pond back of his place. Found many of them at edge of the pond in grass or in little depressions. At times, though not croaking, they kept sac inflated. They have more pointed snouts than our northern meadow frog and all have light centers to the tympanums. Is there another breeding period in the fall? Saw no females. Do supernumerary males or young males approaching breeding size croak the fall before, like young roosters learning to crow? One answer came the very next day Went on to Olney. Drove on the "slab road," about a mile south of the town lights. Here found a pond beside the road and, lo and behold! there were about ten egg complements of meadow frogs.

**Authorities' corner:**

W. Bartram, Gen., 1791, pp. 278–279.

J. D. Kilby, Fla., 1945, pp. 79–80.

Virginia. (M. K. Brady, 1927, p. 27.) "Leopard frogs in this locality [Dismal Swamp] have all the characteristics of *sphenocephala*. They suggest *pipiens* even less than the leopard frogs of the Potomac drainage do."

North Carolina. (C. S. Brimley, 1940, p. 27.) "Nearly allied to this is the Northern Leopard Frog (*Rana pipiens*) which grows to a larger size (maximum length head and body about four inches instead of about three in southern form), usually has a blunter snout, and generally does not have a white spot on the tympanum."

South Carolina. (E. B. Chamberlain, 1939, p. 32.) "Although Holbrook did not distinguish this southeastern form from the more northerly *pipiens* his plates of *'Rana halecina'* show the light spot at the center of the tympanum, usually considered as diagnostic of *sphenocephala.* An occasional specimen from the Upper Piedmont seems to show an approach to *pipiens,* but I have seen no typical example of the latter form from this state. . . ."

Georgia. (A. H. Wright, 1931, p. 434.) "This form seems a Lower Austral offshoot of *Rana pipiens* extending from New Jersey to Texas and up the Mississippi to Indiana." (Still our opinion after 14 years.)

Florida. (S. Springer, 1938, p. 49.) "In a recent paper on the status of the leopard frogs (Herpetologica 1, 1937: 84–87) Mr. Carl F. Kauffeld says that *Rana brachycephala* attains a greater size than either *pipiens* or *sphenocephala.* Over most of its range I have no doubt that *sphenocephala* is relatively small. In the area west of Myakka River on the west coast of Florida, however, *sphenocephala* attains a very large size. Specimens having a body length of four and one-half inches, measured from snout to anus, are quite common, and I have seen a few specimens with a body length of five inches. One of these weighed half a pound."

Mississippi. (M. J. Allen, 1932, p. 10.) "An examination of several hundred frogs leads to a conclusion that the majority of specimens agree with descriptions of *R. sphenocephala* with a few exhibiting tendencies toward intergradation, and a small percentage having some of the characters of *Rana pipiens.*"

Louisiana. (Viosca has consistently called his local forms different from northeast *R. pipiens.*)

Oklahoma. (A. N. Bragg, 1942a, p. 18.) "Some call this frog *Rana pipiens* Schreber; others believe both species occur in Oklahoma. It is the author's opinion that *R. sphenocephala* is the common leopard frog of the state but that some specimens in the northwestern part may be *pipiens.* The latter is a larger, broader-headed species."

Illinois. (D. W. Owens, 1941, p. 184.) "In order to test the relations of the Macoupin County specimens to the leopard frog of the Chicago Region and to specimens recorded as *Rana sphenocephala* from southern Illinois, I have measured the length of body and the tibia in all of the Illinois specimens available in Field Museum. . . . The tibia and body measurements expressed as the t/b ratio are as follows:

| | No. of specimens | Extremes | Average |
|---|---|---|---|
| Chicago Region—*pipiens* | 63 | .50–.61 | .55 |
| Southern Illinois—*sphenocephala* | 53 | .53–.62 | .58 |
| Macoupin County specimens | 10 | .54–.63 | .59 |

I concluded that the Macoupin County leopard frog should be referred to *sphenocephala,* the longer-legged and more sharp-snouted form of southeastern United States. . . ."

Indiana. (F. N. Blanchard, 1925, p. 372.) "All the leopard frogs collected are referred to this species rather than to *R. pipiens* because they look more like the southern than the northern leopard frogs. They are very different in appearance from the leopard frogs of Michigan. The spots on the back are very small and are without light outlines. The head averages a little longer than on leopard frogs from Michigan, its length being contained in the total length two and one-half to three times. The probability is that *R. sphenocephala* intergrades with *R. pipiens* somewhere north of Southern Indiana." (See also Swanson, Ind., 1939, pp. 688–689.)

Kentucky. (W. A. Welter, K. Carr, R. W. Barbour.) We have seen some of the material these workers identify as *Rana p. sphenocephala*.

In 1944 J. A. Moore (Gen., 1944, pp. 349–369) gave us a scholarly study of geographic variation in *Rana pipiens* of eastern North America. Some comments on Dr. Moore's article follow:

1. When Miss Dickerson (1906) of the American Museum featured *Rana sphenocephala,* there were young skeptics. Never have we been strong for it as a separate species. Probably *R. p. sphenocephala* is a better handle. But in spite of our (1906) skepticism, we soon began to recognize a southern leopard frog. In our 40 years' travels in the United States we have seen these frogs in their places, and we still recognize *sphenocephala,* call it species, subspecies, or race.

2. *Sphenocephala* sorts out the best of all the *pipiens* complex. Before we read Dr. Moore's paper or legends we sorted his *pipiens* and *sphenocephala* illustrations. Strange to say, we were over 90 per cent right on *sphenocephala* whether the frogs were facing, straight lateral, dorsal, or inclined toward or away from the photographer.

3. Much of Dr. Moore's tilting is with Kauffeld's establishment of three races along our Atlantic coast. We never indorsed that solution.

4. At times we have questioned Cope's use of external vocal sacs in separation of *R. pipiens* forms. It is strange that Moore finds that "from southern New York and south along the Atlantic coast the males possess well-developed external vocal sacs. . . . In the Mississippi Valley males from southern Indiana, Oklahoma, Arkansas and Mississippi have well developed external vocal sacs. . . ."

This reads much like our range characterization for *Rana p. sphenocephala.*

5. "Males from southern New York to northern Florida lack oviducts. . . . The same is true for males in Louisiana, Mississippi, eastern Texas and in the Mississippi Valley north to southern Indiana, Illinois and Missouri" (J. A. Moore, p. 362). Compare Moore's map of males without oviducts with our range map. One could substitute his map for ours if one eliminated southern peninsular Florida.

6. These characters (morphological and physiological) cannot be read out

of the picture. Still we call *R. p. sphenocephala* separate because of the "look of the beast." To return to these vocal-sac and without-oviduct males of *R. p. sphenocephala:* Could it be that *sphenocephala*—

(a) Matures smaller?

(b) Matures faster because it can grow the whole season. *R. p pipiens* does not and cannot because of northern winters?

(c) Breeds every month in the year, is a more active breeder?

## *Rana pipiens* complex

Plates CV–CXV; Map 34.

A comparison of Map 34, showing the hypothetical distribution of various *Rana* forms, with a geological map of the United States suggests that *Rana pipiens* frogs may find reasons for changing their coats in the chemical and structural changes of their habitats in the different sections of the country.

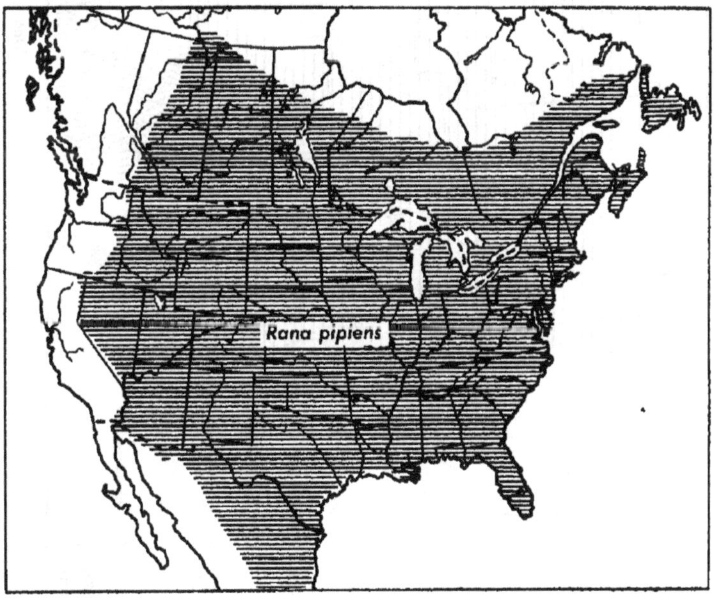


*Map 33*

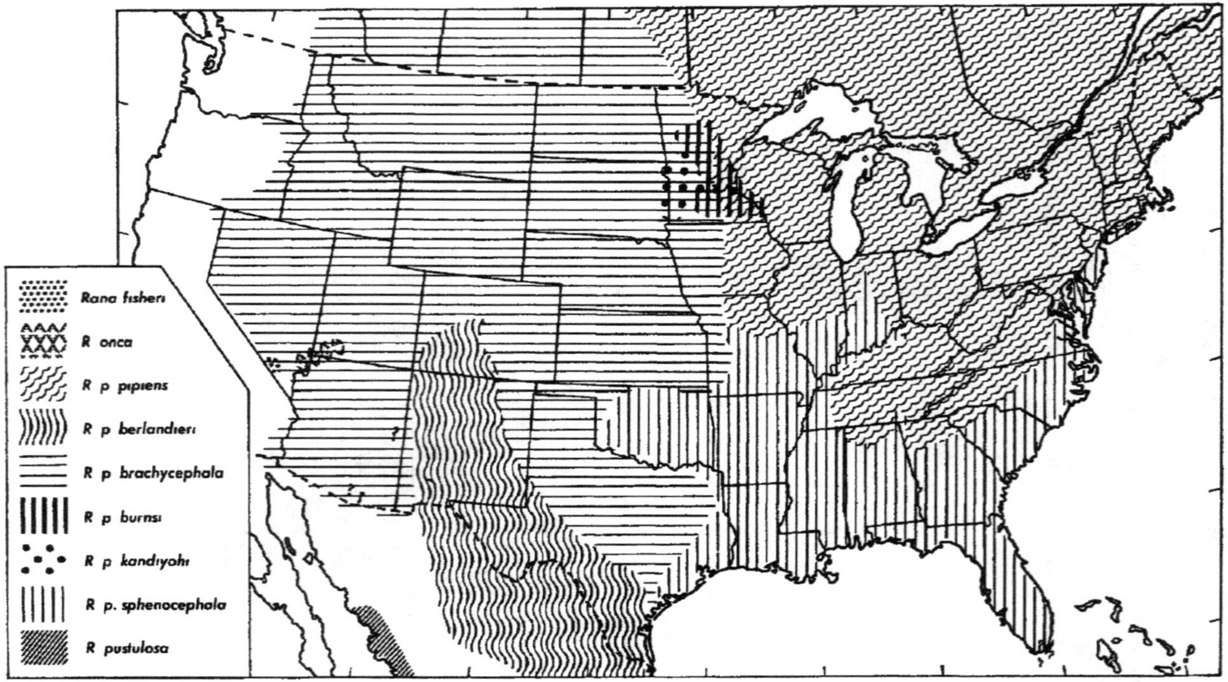
Rana fisheri
R onca
R p pipiens
R p berlandieri
R p brachycephala
R p burnsi
R p kandiyohi
R p. sphenocephala
R pustulosa

*Map 34*

Is *pipiens* one form, as Kellogg, Bogert, Moore, and others believe, or many subspecies? For many years, we were of the first school. Today, we are in balance, in suspended judgment. We feel that *R. p. sphenocephala* is as good a form as many forms in snakes, better than some in birds and mammals, and as good as some drainage forms in fishes. In 1925, we felt *R. fisheri* probably a good form, but at present, are the most striking specimens of this limited population gone? We present this rambling treatment to provoke thorough study—study of all the collections plus travel experience with these very forms, their eggs, tadpoles, and life histories. We are past appraisals of alcoholic specimens alone. Those began 75 years ago.

We hold the problems to be the isolated populations in the West and agree with Schmidt (Schmidt and Smith, Tex., 1944, p. 81), "The senior author is convinced that *Rana sphenocephala* can be distinguished, and that the essential problem lies in the Trans-Mississippian populations, in which characters distinctive of *pipiens* and *sphenocephala* in eastern North America appear in various mixtures."

A. The color phases or mutant forms, Plates CV; CVI; CVII.

1. *Burnsi* mutant. (See pages 483–488 for an account of this color phase.) We never considered this mutant and *kandiyohi* valid species or subspecies, but we included them in earlier editions of the *Handbook* to provoke some midwestern geneticist to drop *Drosophila* and work on an immediate backyard form, but it remained for someone in New York City to make the study. Many an American herpetologist on one specimen or a few specimens has made new species on as slender grounds as our old classmate, Weed.

In elementary class lots of many hundreds of frogs from Vermont and other parts we have occasionally seen unspotted *R. pipiens*, just as individual evittate *Hyla cinerea* appear in each southern state.

2. *Kandiyohi* phase. (See pp. 488–492 for an account of this form.)

B. Generally accepted form, *R. p. sphenocephala*. (See pages 492–498 for an account of this subspecies.)

Most herpetologists since Miss Dickerson have accepted this southeastern meadow frog as distinct and call it a race, variety, subspecies, or species.

It is true that Boulenger has written: "I am therefore unable to divide the species in minor groups with any precision, and must leave the matter in abeyance for the present." But he concluded his *R. halecina* account as follows: "A precise diagnosis of the var. *sphenocephala* is still a desideratum, as Miss Dickerson's definition . . . seems to me insufficient, in view of the variation in specimens referable to the typical form" (G. A. Boulenger, Gen., 1920, p. 439). Kauffeld accepts this form as a species but he would put the Piedmont specimens from "extreme southeastern New York, Long Island, southern Connecticut, New Jersey except the northwestern portion, southeastern Pennsylvania, Delaware, Maryland, south throughout the Coastal Plain and west into Texas" as *Rana pipiens* Schreber and the forms from the Fall line

*Plate CV. Rana pipiens* (×⅔). From Lake Florida, Minn.

*Plate CVI. Rana pipiens* (*burnsi*). (×⅔). From Lake Florida, Minn.

*Plate CVII. Left. Rana pipiens* (***kandiyohi***). From Wisconsin. ***Right. Rana pipiens*** (*kandiyohi*) intermediate From Lake Florida, Minn. (×⅔).

to the coast as *R. sphenocephala*. We are not of his school of interpretation, yet we thank him for his compact paper, which bravely touched off a sudden spurt of activity in *R. pipiens* study. In the same way, we admire the thoroughness of Moore's paper yet wonder whether some authors have had extensive field experience throughout the range of *R. p. sphenocephala*. For years we have been inebriated from alcoholic inspirations (the same thoughts some of the old masters had). Get out in the field of the species treated.

When Moore disagrees with Mittleman and Gier regarding their *R. berlandieri* (and we agree with Moore on this point), his clincher is: "In fact there are greater differences between species from Oklahoma and part of Texas than between the former and specimens from southern Indiana and parts of New Jersey." Of course he destroys *R. p. sphenocephala*, but we smile to recall that Oklahoma, southern Indiana, and New Jersey are within the range of *R. p. sphenocephala*, as is Lake Caddo (on the boundary of Texas and Louisiana) and possibly Belton, Tex. We have traveled over these areas several times. Before one discusses *Elaphe, Crotalus*, or the range of any form, well-recognized or debatable, one should travel over the area. Because we have rarely seen an unspotted *R. p. pipiens* from Vermont or Texas, we would not assert that a regular mutant population (*burnsi*) did not exist in Minnesota, without visiting the region in question. We need more of this type of investigation to reinforce the cloister of university and museum.

We append A. N. Bragg's (N. Mex., 1941, p. 116) trenchant remark: "After observing the two forms in the field, I feel certain that the frog about Las Vegas, New Mexico is very similar to, if not identical with, the grass-frog of New England (*Rana brachycephala*) of the recent checklist and the leopard frog of Wisconsin, and different from that of Oklahoma which I call *Rana sphenocephala* (Cope)."

C. Eastern puzzles.

1. Florida Keys.

On March 20 and 21, 1934, we made the following journal notes: Last night went along the railroad ditches. Saw *R. p. sphenocephala* on way to Key West. Looked in sinkholes, i.e., honeycombed rock, containing water and in them were meadow frogs. In a shallow covered well found several in holes along the sides. On a Key near Big Pine Key were numberless *R. p. sphenocephala*. The adults were bronzy on throat with belly much clouded and the entire under parts as cloudy as a Heckscher's frog or a young *R. clamitans*. The half-grown ones have very spotted throats and under parts. Someday someone with as close discrimination of details as now obtains in birds or snakes (scales to count) may make a new subspecies of this colored phase. We put the frogs in our covered fish can. Later when we photographed them we wrote in the photographic record: "The venter has already grown lighter but legs are still mottled. Big Pine Key." In a day or so some died. These looked almost exactly like ordinary *R. p. sphenocephala*.

2. Common northern form (*pipiens*).

In 1942 Moore (Gen., 1942a, VI, 201) reviewed the northeastern situation as follows: "Unfortunately taxonomists are not in agreement on the status of these frogs. Some years ago Cope (1889) divided *Rana virescens* (an old name for *Rana pipiens*) into three subspecies, *R v brachycephala, R. v. pipiens* and *R. v. sphenocephala.* Later workers for the most part did not recognize the subspecies *brachycephala* and called all individuals from the northern states and Canada *Rana pipiens.* The southern variety on the other hand was raised to specific rank, *Rana sphenocephala.* The differences between these two 'species' were so slight that many competent herpetologists would have difficulty in identifying a given specimen unless the locality was plainly indicated on the label. Kellogg (1932) examined an extensive series of frogs from many parts of the country and thought it best to lump them as *Rana pipiens.* Shortly after this Kauffeld (1937) suggested that all three of Cope's subspecies be raised to full specific rank—*Rana brachycephala, Rana pipiens* and *Rana sphenocephala.* The diagnostic characters given by Kauffeld have not been applied successfully by all taxonomists (Trapido and Clausen 1938; Grant 1941)."

C. F. Kauffeld certainly deserves special thanks for his two papers in *Herpetologica* (Gen., 1936, p. 11; 1937, pp. 84–87). He started a lot of writing if nothing more. He wrote:

"For some inexplicable reason, *Rana brachycephala* of Cope never gained the recognition it deserved although *sphenocephala* of the same author, a form much less distinct from true *pipiens* than *brachycephala,* has been universally accepted *Rana brachycephala* remained in complete obscurity from the time of its description (Cope 1889, pp. 403–406) No one, so far as I can find, even bothered to throw it into synonymy until Kellogg (1929, p. 203) placed *brachycephala* as well as *sphenocephala* in the synonymy of *pipiens.* There is no justification for treating either of these two forms in this way and *brachycephala* must be revived to supply a name for the leopard frog which has so often been erroneously figured and described as *pipiens* (Dickerson 1908, pl. 11; Wright and Wright 1933, pl. 71) "

Schmidt does not endorse the use of *R. brachycephala* for our northeastern meadow frog. "Kauffeld's remarks (1937, p. 84) about *Rana austricola, R. pipiens burnsi,* and *R. kandiyohi,* and his choice of *brachycephala* as the name of the northeastern '*pipiens*' are unintelligible to us" (K. P. Schmidt and T. F. Smith, Tex., 1944, p 81).

To quote Kauffeld again before we proceed to the discussion: "As the material which Cope had at the time he described *brachycephala* (which by the way, numbered 182 specimens and not 15 Kellogg loc. cit. mistakenly estimated) [Dr. Kellogg clearly says 2 adults, 1 young, and 12 tadpoles in the type lot no. 3363.—A. H. W.] this species occurs in the Transition Zone, particularly the Alleghanian Division, the southern extension of the Canadian, and the Upper Austral west of the Appalachian Highlands. Other material substantiates this distribution. . . . Schreber's type of *pipiens* was undoubtedly from the Carolinian of southern New York. We may define the range of *brachycephala* and *pipiens* as follows: *Rana brachycephala* (Cope), Southern Canada and New England except extreme southern Connecticut, New York except the southeastern portion, northwestern New Jersey, northern and western Pennsylvania, West to the Pacific Coast States. *Rana pipiens* Schreber, Extreme southeastern New York, Long Island, southern Connecticut, New Jersey except the northwestern portion, southeastern Pennsylvania, Delaware and Maryland, south throughout the coastal Plain and west into Texas" (Kauffeld, Gen., 1936, p. 11; 1937, pp. 84–87). [Neither his description nor his plate could be the frog Cope described as *brachycephala* because Cope's is western, Yellowstone River is the type locality, and Washington State is the illustration.]

Cope was indefinite in his definition of the ranges of these three forms Kauffeld gives us three forms in the Northeast. We suppose he thinks of his Piedmont *R. pipiens* much as we do of *Pseudacris n. feriarum, Hyla andersonii,* or *Rana virgatipes,* or Conant's *Lampropeltis e. temporalis.* The three frogs above range to South Carolina or Georgia and Conant's snake to North Carolina, but Kauffeld sends his *R. pipiens* "throughout the Coastal Plain and west to Texas." Why does he not have it going up the Mississippi Valley? If Cope was indefinite, Kauffeld is equally so, and particularly with *Rana sphenocephala.* He does not specify whether it is an Upper or Lower Austral or Gulf strip form. His arrangement sends three tongues of meadow frogs into the south, *brachycephala* in the high Allegheny Mountains, *pipiens* in the Piedmont, and *sphenocephala* probably in the Lower Austral or Gulf strip. This does not accord with our collecting experience of the last 35 years.

Trapido and Clausen (Que, 1938, pp 121–122) tested the head length and tibiotarsal lengths. "The remainder of the characters are equally unsatisfactory. . . . The material collected in Quebec, therefore, as well as specimens from widely scattered stations within the range which Kauffeld has assigned to *brachycephala,* fail to confirm his conclusions. It seems better for the present to refer the northern specimens to *pipiens,* until all the available material of this widespread and perplexing species can be studied."

R. Grant (Que., 1944, pp. 151–152) finds that his Quebec meadow frogs agree with Kauffeld's *R. pipiens* in head length, dorsal skin folds, and webbing of toes. They agree with his *R. brachycephala* in absence of tympanic spot, in extension of dorsolateral fold to supraocular region in one fourth of the specimens, and in the failure of the tibiotarsal joint to reach the snout in 16 out of 24 specimens.

For a discussion of Moore's extensive paper, see our account of *R. p. sphenocephala.* We do not differ with him on *pipiens* and *brachycephala* where his localities are certain, but his Vermont, Wisconsin, and, particularly, southern material is not so certain. His evidence, therefore, against *R. p. sphenocephala* is somewhat vitiated, and in his account (see *R. p. sphenocephala*) we see much to prove it a good form.

Some of us naturalists have existed for 35 years or more knowing *R. pipiens* and *R. p. sphenocephala* (*R. sphenocephala* to Miss Dickerson). Not until 1937 did *R. brachycephala* ever come out of the West and enter the eastern horizon. Moore's conclusion, we fear, is largely against the three-form conception instead of two forms for he writes:

"A study has been made of the taxonomic characters customarily employed in separating *Rana pipiens* Schreber, *Rana sphenocephala* (Cope) and *Rana brachycephala* (Cope). These diagnostic characters were found invalid when samples from many localities were studied. It does not appear possible to recognize *three* species or subspecies of meadow frogs on the basis of differences in body proportions or pigmentation. Therefore, the meadow frogs of eastern North America should be known as *Rana pipiens* Schreber. *Rana sphenocephala* Cope and *Rana brachycephala* (Cope) should be reduced to synonyms of *Rana pipiens* Schreber." The case for *R. pipiens* and a supposed eastern *R. brachycephala* as one may be proved by Moore; but probably nine of every ten naturalists who knew the meadow frogs of the East well have assumed this to be a fact. The case of *R. p. sphenocephala* as thrown into the scrap basket is not a frontal attack in his paper. It is a southpaw affair with dealer's material and as much proves *R. p. sphenocephala* good as bad. For example, in his argument against *R. p. sphenocephala*, Moore uses the tympanic spot: "Those with sharply defined circular spots are not restricted to the southern states . . . , and animals from this region may lack the spot entirely. . . . Thus a sharply defined white tympanic spot is not a constant feature of southern populations, as Kauffeld and others have suggested." This has not distressed field naturalists in the East for 20 years. Of course southern Indiana, southern Illinois, western Kentucky, and Oklahoma are in the range of *R. p. sphenocephala* Moore's observations help to prove the validity of *R. p. sphenocephala*. Our *R. p. sphenocephala* heresy regarding New Jersey has disturbed some of our naturalists of the Atlantic seaboard. That is north. But to push the case far toward the home of Moore's advisor, who may rightly believe all the western *pipiens* to be one, we quote E. H. Taylor (Kans., 1929b, p. 65). In speaking of the extreme southwestern corner of Kansas, Morton County (north not south, west not east) he remarks, "Specimens appear to approach the characters of the southern *Rana sphenocephala* (Cope)." It is not strange, if Bragg calls Oklahoma meadow frogs *R. p. sphenocephala*, to have frogs from this Kansas county at the tip end of the Cimarron River drainage (Arkansas River Basin) with *sphenocephala* tendencies. Let any physical geographer, life-zone enthusiast (life zones studied for 100 years), or ecologist observe Merriam's Lower Austral (map 1, p. 6), or Van Dersal's Coastal, Piedmont, and Ozark and Tennessee Valley districts (map 2, p. 8) of today, or Cooper's (1859)

Carolinian, Mississippian, Tennessean, and Floridian districts, and he has the natural range of *R. p. sphenocephala,* which follows up Mississippi tributaries.

D. Western puzzles.

1. *Rana fisheri.* Plate CVIII.

(See account pp 454-459.)

One cannot help wondering whether visitors to Las Vegas since Hoover Dam (Boulder Dam) came have ever seen fine big-eared males and other specimens like those Merriam and Stejneger had. Since fish ponds and a golf course have replaced the original springs, one queries whether what we saw in 1925 and what earlier workers saw are existent today. Even in 1925 the two or three specimens we collected in the creek near or in town seemed more like *R. pipiens,* but some of the spring's specimens were certainly different from our New York *R pipiens*. Nevertheless we must confess that it is of the *R. pipiens* complex. Those old 1925 specimens were more distinctive than the *Rana onca* as conceived by Tanner and Linsdale. Bogert and Oliver (Gen., 1945, p. 321) hold that "the relationships of leopard frogs, *Rana pipiens,* have been the subject of considerable debate, but no one has offered convincing evidence that more than one species is involved. . . . Nevertheless its failure to reach southern California (until introduced) and the fact that no well-defined races have evolved (recognition of the 'species' *Rana onca* and *Rana fisheri* to the contrary) indicate that its influx into the region west of the continental divide has been a recent one."

2. *Rana onca*. Plate CIX.

Shortly after we collected *R. pretiosa* with Wilmer W. Tanner at Provo, Utah, we saw Yarrow's illustration of *Rana onca*. His illustration looks like *R pretiosa*. We have never seen the type specimen. Certainly the figure looks little like the Virgin River specimens we saw or like those from the same region now in the University of California collection. We are not certain of *Rana onca* as a good species or subspecies. Strictly, we suppose we should dub it *R. pipiens onca.*

When we were mounting *Rana montezumae* original figures from the *U.S. and Mex. Boundary Survey* and *Mission Scientifique au Mexique* reports we noted for the first time that Boulenger in 1882 placed *R. onca* in the synonymy of *Rana montezumae*. We surely cannot blame him for this attribution when even today we do not understand the form very well and when the original *R. onca* figure is so uncertain.

3. *Rana pipiens berlandieri* (Baird). Plate CX.

In 1859 Baird described this form as follows: "117. *Rana berlandieri* Baird, Plate 36, Figs. 7-10. Sp. Ch.—Size large. Body stout, robust Eye distant not quite 1½ times its diameter from tip of snout, and contained 2⅔ times in the length of jaw from rictus. Tympanum two-thirds the diameter of the eye. A vocal vesicle on each side of the head. A glandular fold on each side the jaw, and another one broad and depressed on each side of the body. Between these

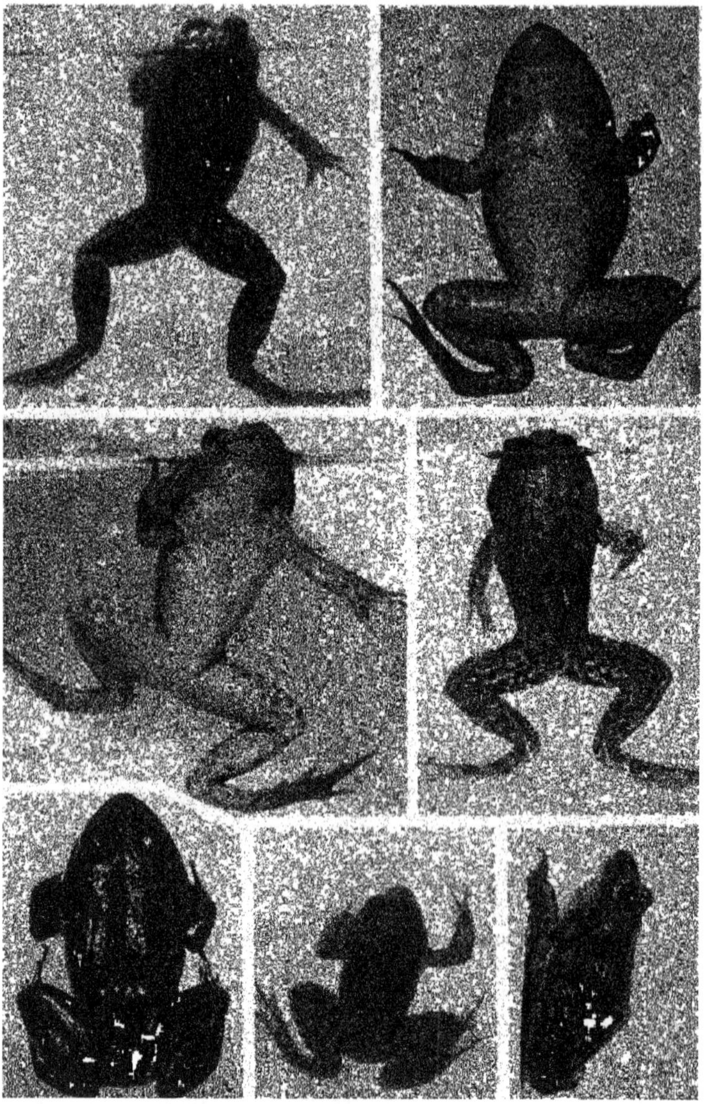

*Plate CVIII. Rana fisheri* (×⅘). From Las Vegas, Nev.

is one pair of ridges along the coccyx; several pairs more interrupted anterior to it. Skin corrugated and irregular, quite pustular in some specimens. Feet webbed from the bulb of the toes; excavated on the inner edges; last joint of longest free. Femur about half the length of body, shorter than the tibia. Color above greenish olive, with distant subcircular blotches of darker, scarcely areolated in the preserved specimens. Beneath yellowish white, with brown mottlings on the throat. An indistinct whitish line on the side of the head; especially in the young; the lateral ridges bronzed. Southern Texas generally" (*U.S. and Mex. Bound. Survey*, vol. II, pt. 2, pp. 27–28).

*Plate CIX Rana onca.* 1. From *Geog. Survey E of 100th Meridian*, Plate XXV. 2,3. From 2 miles southeast of Overton, Nev (×⅜).

For some time this form was quite universally used and its range interpreted as widespread, not southern Texas alone. Yarrow (Ariz., 1875, p. 527) had it from Provo, Ephraim City, and Beaver, Utah, to Denver, Colo., south to six localities in northern New Mexico (much of New Mexico and much of Colorado tributary to the Rio Grande River). In 1878 (Mont., p. 289), Coues and Yarrow (Dakotas and Montana) extended it to the Pembina Mountains with this disclaimer: "The common Western form is *Rana halecina berlandieri* which is only distinguished from *R. halecina* by its larger size and generally coarser and more pustulated skin The specimens represent *'berlandieri,'* but this we are disinclined to adopt without further investigation of its alleged distinctness."

In 1880 (Tex., 1880a, p. 24) Cope had "*Rana halecina berlandieri* Bd. Common at Dallas and on the first plateau; also in the low country near Washington on the Brazos"—i.e., in northern Texas outside the Rio Grande Valley. In fact, in 1879 Cope (Mont., p. 436) called *Rana halecina berlandieri* the abundant species on the plains, i.e., he had it 1879–1880 from the Rio Grande to Montana. But in 1889 he described *Rana virescens brachycephala* for meadow frogs from Provo, Utah, to Framingham, Mass., from Montana to Chihuahua, and the second frog on his list is from Brownsville, near or at the actual home of *R. berlandieri*.

If the name is employed, we would restrict it to southern Texas or the Rio Grande Valley until it is better described and understood. This position approaches that of Schmidt (1944, p. 81), who holds, "The name *berlandieri* appears available for the large form of *Rana pipiens* found at Brownsville, and it is reasonable to suppose that all the leopard frogs of the Rio Grande drainage are derived from this center. . . . In the present state of the *pipiens* problem, it is preferred to employ the earliest name available that is reasonably well associated geographically with our area."

Like K. P. Schmidt and T. F. Smith (Tex., 1944), M. B. Mittleman and H. T. Gier (Gen., 1942, pp 7–15) feel the emphasis should be on the western forms.

"Throughout the several discussions briefly mentioned above, there is only scant mention of Baird's *Rana berlandieri* (1859. 27) described on the basis of eleven specimens from 'Southern Texas generally.' We find in extensive series of leopard frogs from Texas, Kansas, Oklahoma and possibly certain adjacent States, characteristics which are not in accord with equivalent series of specimens from the Atlantic coastal plain, the Appalachian highlands or more northerly sections of the mid-western United States or from the Rocky Mountains and Pacific States. There is wide variation in the Texas-Kansas-Oklahoma series, as is natural with frogs of this group; none the less, it is comparatively easy to select specimens from these three states no matter whether they are mixed with examples from other areas or encountered alone Comparison of specimens from the three States mentioned, with the cotypes of Baird's *berlandieri*, shows immediately that they are syntypical" (Mittleman and Gier, Gen., 1942, p. 9).

In view of the fact that several Texas forms are now known to extend into Oklahoma (*Pseudacris streckeri* and *Scaphiopus h. hurterii*) or even into Kansas (*Microhyla olivacea* and *P. n. clarkii*), there is considerable evidence to suggest this grouping. In 1943 Stejneger and Barbour accepted this interpretation, but in 1943 A. N Bragg and C. C. Smith (Okla., 1943, p. 107) called all their Oklahoma meadow frogs *R. sphenocephala* Cope They stated: "We are not ready to express an opinion as to the correct name of this frog. Mittleman and Gier (1942) call it *R pipiens berlandieri* (Baird)." We will follow A. N. Bragg, who has seen specimens from all except nine counties of Oklahoma. Who knows but that Texas has three meadow-frog populations—northeastern, coastal, and forest *R. p sphenocephala;* Rio Grande Valley *R. p. berlandieri*, and a form showing northern influence found on a prairie central Texas tongue extending southward through the Panhandle. (See our *R. p berlandieri* plate.) Not until we are farther along in careful local state studies like Bragg's will we venture a positive opinion. Our inclination is to make the provisional *R. p. berlandieri* southern Texas to San Antonio, i.e., unite the Nueces, San Antonio, and possibly the Guadalupe rivers with the Rio Grande drainage—roughly San Antonio to the southeastern corner of New Mexico, most of that state to southern Colorado. One look at the original figure and our Beeville and our San Antonio pictures show considerable diversity, possibly three influences (Plate CX).

*Plate CX* 1 *Rana pipiens.* From Helotes, Tex 2 *Rana pipiens* From Beeville, Tex. 3,4,5. *R berlandieri* From *U S Boundary Survey,* Plate 36 (X⅔).

Mittleman and Gier consider Floridian and extreme southeastern states as *R. sphenocephala* (not the Mississippi Valley to the Wabash Valley and all of Oklahoma). For their comparisons with their Texas-Oklahoma-Kansas *R. berlandieri* they use all the rest except *"the debatable coastal strip from Southern Quebec to southern New Jersey"* as *R. brachycephala.* We do not know any such *coastal* strip. Bragg's *R. p. sphenocephala* cuts in two their *R berlandieri* range. If one were to recognize a northeastern race of *pipiens,* a western and northwestern race of *brachycephala,* a southern and Mississippi Valley race of ***sphenocephala,*** and a Rio Grande Valley race (to southern Colorado), he would have in these populations elements of all four to compare with their Kansas-Oklahoma-Texas race.

Moore (1944, p. 349) wrote: "Recently Mittleman and Gier (1942) have suggested that the meadow frogs of 'Texas, Kansas and Oklahoma and possibly certain adjacent States' are distinct from other populations and propose to call them ***Rana pipiens berlandieri.*** Their evidence was given careful consideration, but no support for their contention could be gathered from the living and preserved material used in this report."

4. ***Rana pipiens brachycephala.*** Plate CXI.

*Plate CXI R. pipiens* (***brachycephala***) *Left* From Larry Flower, Elko, Nev. *Right.* From Deeth, Nev

In 1889 Cope described *R* ***pipiens brachycephala.*** In his 69 lots of 188 specimens his second number, 3293, consisted of 7 specimens from Brownsville, Capt. S. Van Vliet, United States collector. This may mean he considered ***R. berlandieri*** Baird of 1859 as a synonym. He put it in the synonymy as ***Rana halecina berlandieri*** Cope Check List Batr Rept N. Amer., p. 32; ***nec. Rana berlandieri*** Baird. The only specimens of ***Rana virescens virescens*** Cope had from Texas were a Dallas specimen and one lot of 10 from Matamoros, Mexico. These may have been in the collection bought from Berlandier at Matamoros. Did they come from Matamoros? Cope's type no. 3363 came from the Yellowstone River and he figured a Fort Walla Walla, Wash, specimen no. 10922. Of his 69 lots, 63 came from Illinois or Wisconsin westward, or 181 of the 188 specimens. Of these 181 specimens only 3 came from Iowa, 2 from Illinois, 2 from Wisconsin, and 1 from Minnesota. This means only 4 east of the

Mississippi. These 4 frogs with 6 lots (7 specimens) from east of Mississippi make 11 individuals of the 188 The 6 lots are: 2 Maine, 1 Massachusetts, 1 Connecticut, 1 Quebec, 1 South Carolina, 1 Michigan.

Said Cope (Gen., 1889, p. 405): "This is the common and only species of *Rana* found between the eastern part of the Great Plains and the Sierra Nevada Mountains. It is common wherever there is sufficient water to supply its necessities. In some of the Western towns it is eaten in the restaurants, and I have not infrequently found it excellent food when the larder of my expeditions in search of fossils has run low."

Before we give you his original description we cannot resist the observation that we believe *R. p. brachycephala* is western if it is anything at all.

"The muzzle is less elongate, and the extended hind leg brings the heel to its apex, but not beyond The tympanic disk is two-thirds the diameter of the eye. The head is shorter, entering the length of the head and body three and a half times. The dorsal dermal plicae are thicker and there are but two between the dorsolaterals; usually, however there are four, as in the other subspecies. First finger longer than second. Web leaving two free phalanges of the fourth digit, but so repand as to give the antepenultimate phalange only a wide border. The inner cuneiform tubercle is rather small, but has a rather prominent compressed edge External tubercle, none. A thick tarsal fold. There are no large warts on the skin, but there are occasionally minute warts and folds on the superior face of the tibia.

"In life the color of the superior surfaces is green. The dorsolateral ridges are light yellow, and so is a stripe from the end of the muzzle, which passes above the lip and below the eye and tympanum to above the middle of the humerus. There are two rows of large rounded dorsal spots between the dorsolateral ridges, which are edged with greenish-yellow. There are two similar rows on each side, of which the inferior is the smaller, which are not regularly arranged. There is a spot on each eyelid and one on the end of the nose above There is a light band, frequently broken into spots near the edge of the upper lip. There is a brown spot on the elbow and one on the front of the cubitus. The band seen on the front of the humerus in *R. v. virescens* is here an illy defined spot. On the superior face of the femur there are three brown spots, but there is no longitudinal brown band in front of these spots, as is usual in the two other subspecies of the *R. virescens*. There are three complete wide brown cross-bands on the femur, and sometimes four. Frequently there are one or two spots on one or both faces of the tibia besides the three bands. The posterior face of the femur is greenish llow, coarsely marbled with brown. All the spots and bands are narrowly y w-edged. Inferior surfaces are light yellow, unspotted" (E. D. Cope, Gen., ), pp. 403-404).

Note the last sentence.

Two years after this description appe d, Dr. Stejneger (Calif., 1893, p. 228) used *Rana pipiens brachycephala* for aranagat Valley, Nev., material. The same year (Ind., 1892, p. 474) O. P. Hay characterized this form, ending, "Maine to Oregon and Mexico, but mostly western U.S . . . The variety *sphenocephala* is chiefly southern in its range, *pipiens* (*virescens* of Cope) eastern and northern, and *brachycephala* western. Neither is confined, however, to these limits. With us the common form is *pipiens,* and it is everywhere abundant. *Sphenocephala* is in the National Museum from Wheatland, Ind., and to this I refer one specimen from Lake Maxinkuckee, which I find in the collection of the State Normal School One specimen in the same collection and taken at Camden, Carroll County, had some of the characteristics of *brachycephala.*"

Kellogg has written about *R. h berlandieri* Cope as follows: "Until the publication of Cope's 'Batrachia of North America,' the subspecific name *brachycephala* was strictly a *nomen nudum,* inasmuch as the characters that distinguished this subspecies from supposed typical *halecina* (*virescens* Cope, 1889) were not indicated. Cope's diagnosis of the subspecies *brachycephala* published in 1889 is seemingly based upon one specimen, and this inference is drawn from his introductory remark that 'I select as typical a specimen from the Yellowstone River (no. 3363).' There are, however, 15 specimens catalogued under that number, although Cope mentions only 5 in his list of specimens examined, all of them were collected by Dr. F. U. Hayden in 1857 along the Yellowstone River in Montana. This lot consists of 2 adults, 1 young and 12 tadpoles. Inasmuch as it is now impossible to recognize the actual individual upon which Cope based his description, all of these specimens have been designated as the cotypes of the subspecies *brachycephala.* The following notes apply to the largest cotype: Head-and-body length, 86; transverse diameter of tympanum, 6; transverse diameter of eye, 8; anterior edge of eye to nostril, 5.4 mm ; the hind limb being carried forward along the body, the tibio-tarsal joint reaches to the anterior margin of eye" (Kellogg, Gen., 1932, pp. 208–209).

If, sometime in the future, students prove that the western and northwestern form is different from the northeastern, then we would recommend *R. p. brachycephala.* We must confess that in 1925, 1934, and 1942, we did not note any surprising differences from *R pipiens* proper in the northern Nevada, Utah, or Wyoming meadow frogs. In 1942, for example, we made these notes:

May 22, 1942, Deeth, Nev. Short distance beyond is pool with bushes. Bert caught meadow frogs here, two females ripe, much bigger than Virgin River frogs and dorsal spots larger and very light-margined

May 23, Elko, Nev. Went to Maggie and Susie creeks at Carlin. On way back saw near Humboldt River in overflow six *Rana pipiens* with numerous dorsal spots and these light-encircled. Caught three, one male and two half-grown.

May 30. With Wilmer Webster Tanner, went 1 mile west of Provo to a spring. Beside the stream took a *R. pipiens.*

June 5, north of Kanab. A fine pond, fish in it—very quagmirelike. Saw four meadow frogs. Caught three. Meadow frogs out of water were in a meadowlike area.

These notes reveal no feeling of differences on our part. We are reminded that in 1915 Ruthven and Gaige in northern Nevada held, "The specimens show little variation from Dickerson's (*The Frog Book*, 171) description."

Recently, almost everyone has called this form *Rana pipiens*. We are glad to see that when A. and R. D. Svihla (Wash., 1933, p. 125) do use a subspecies term they employ *R. p. brachycephala*.

5. Arizona problems.

After studies in the Navaho country or Painted Desert region T. H. Eaton, Jr. (Ariz., 1935, p. 150) wrote, "The great variability of *pipiens* in the southwest, appears ample reason for doubting the validity of *onca*, since numerous intermediates occur." This is true not only of southern Nevada and southern Utah but also of all Arizona. Witness the following notes made at various places in Arizona where it seemed as if each spring or moist area had a different form.

a (1). Arivaca and Pena Blanca Springs

June 17, 1934, went with Prof. and Mrs. L. P. Wehrle and family to Arivaca. Here is a fine stream with water now in pools—all along it are willows and huge cottonwoods. In one pool found tadpoles of *R. pipiens* and some transformed ones. Secured a fine male and female of *Rana pipiens*. They are so different from ours in Ithaca, New York!

June 18, Pena Blanca Spring. Came here Monday. Arrived at dusk In the overflow of the spring one meadow frog and one *Hyla arenicolor*—one meadow frog in cow trough. They are much spotted and *yellow under legs* like the Arivaca ones.

June 21, Pena Blanca. Went with Mr. G. W. Harvey. In the shallower pools found some *R. pipiens* adults, young, and tadpoles as well. Most of the big rocky pools had only *R. tarahumarae* adults and tadpoles, while the more shallow ones had *R. pipiens*.

June 25, 1942. Today we went to Arivaca. Went the length of this creek and along irrigation ditch. Saw plenty of meadow frogs.

a (2). Fauna of Pajaritos Mts.

". . . Of batrachians, a toad (*Bufo*) and a frog (*Rana virescens brachycephala* Cope) were found at Warsaw Mills; and at Buenos Ayres, at the beginning of the summer rains . . ." (Mearns, Ariz., 1907, p. 113).

(This locality like Arivaca and Pena Blanca Springs is close to the Mexican boundary and just northwest of Nogales.)

b. Sabino Canyon.

July 2, 1934. We went about 5 to picnic spots where there were two pools. The upper pool was filled with *Rana pipiens*. They would often climb up on slanting rocks, some 8–10 feet, possibly for insects. They are *very orange on underside of legs*.

When we observed the decided orange color on the ventral surface of the hind legs, we did not know that King had anticipated us by 2 years. He had written:

"Leopard frogs were common along the stream in Sabino Canyon. One large individual was also found under a bunch of hay on University Farm, at least two hundred yards from any permanent water. The young were transforming the latter part of July. All individuals examined showed very bright orange coloration on backs of thighs and on flanks. The dorsal spotting is irregular; the tympanum may or may not have a light spot; the spot on the snout is also variable; the legs are barred. The general coloration is grayish with many showing green or brown as a dominant color" (F. W. King, Ariz., 1932, p. 176).

c. Carr Canyon, Huachuca Mts Plates CXII; CXIII.

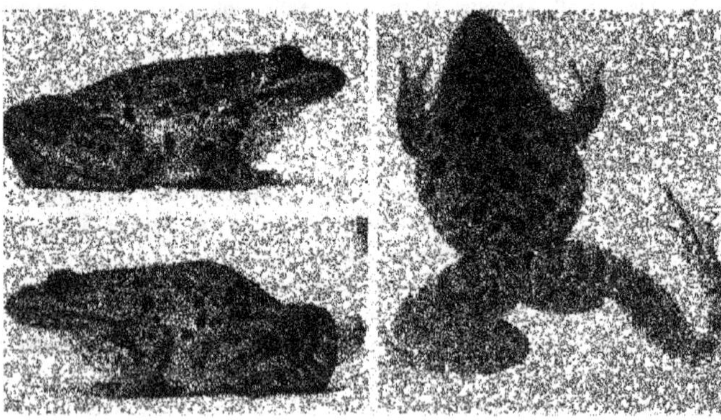

*Plate CXII Rana pipiens* (×½). Females, from Carr Canyon, Ariz.

July 1, 1942. On a bank of the reservoir I espied four fat spotted frogs. I made a pass at one and it slipped out of my hands. The others were frightened. It was a precarious spot. Then Anna suggested I try the fish pole noose on them. One was out of water on the bank. In spite of the fact that the noose could be brought only to the shoulders we were both amazed at the results. The first one leaped through the noose, the next one on the bank was captured, and how Anna did laugh at the success of the method. The third stuck its head and the forepart of its body out of the water and I draped the noose around its neck with no concern on its part. This one I also caught. These are large frogs.

*Color:* The ground color of back is drab-gray or light drab. The spots are black or fuscous with centers of drab and slight thread of pale vinaceous-fawn outlining them. The sides are avellaneous, the groin marbled The dorsolateral folds are drab-gray or light drab. There are five or six broken folds on back between the dorsolateral ones and also one or two on leg. The bands on legs and tarsus are drab The lower jaw is mottled. There is no pronounced light center in tympanum. Under parts are in part white or ivory yellow, with the underside of legs, femur, tibia, and top of tarsus and foot antimony yellow, with a slight wash of same in axil of arm, on brachium, lower belly, and groin.

The measurements in millimeters of two males follow: length (snout to vent) 88, 89; head (tympanum) 28, 27; head (angle of mouth) 26, 25; width of head 29, 29; snout 13, 13; eye 14, 14; interorbital space 4, 4 5; upper eyelid 5, 5.5; tympanum 7.5, 6; intertympanic space 20.5, 19.5; internasal space 7, 11; fore limb 32, 45; first finger 13, 13; second finger 12, 12.5; third finger 19.5, 18.5; fourth finger 14, 14 5; hind limb 124, 134; tibia 48, 47; foot with tarsus 60, 60; foot without tarsus 41, 41; first toe 11, 13; second toe 20, 22; third toe 28, 32; fourth toe 39.5, 42; fifth toe 27, 29 5; hind limb from vent 134, 135.

When we came to the deep pool 6–10 feet below us in Carr Canyon, we beheld what did not look like *R. pipiens.* Were we seeing *R. forreri* or *R. omiltemana* of the Biologia Centrali-Americana figures or the predecessors of *R. areolata* of the United States or *Rana montezumae* or *R. p. berlandieri*? We could get them alive only by noosing.

By Boulenger's 1920 key the frog traces to *Rana montezumae.* With Kellogg (1932) we get the same result. If by these two conservative authors we arrive at *R. montezumae,* it is apparent that the Huachuca Mountain frogs need to be carefully examined with a larger series. We have not compared it with good new *R. montezumae* material from mid-Mexico. We keep this form in the *R. pipiens* complex until more data appear. By measurements and white stippling, however, it appears to be *R. montezumae.*

In their description of the type of *R areolata,* S F Baird and C. Girard (Gen , 1852, p 173) remarked that they had "a very small one on the Rio San Pedro of the Gila." We wonder what their frog was.

d. Lakeside, Ariz., Plate CXIV; CXV.

July 9, 1942. Show-Low, Ariz. Stopped at 1.30 at Carrizo Creek, Gila Co., Ariz. Saw a meadow frog near edge of pool Caught it. Two more jumped in. Near another pool three more leaped in. In *Chara* found fish, damsel fly, and meadow frog tadpoles. Seemingly straight *R. pipiens.*

July 9. Lakeside, Ariz., on the edge of Mogollon Mesa. One mile north of Lakeside, Ariz., saw an interesting pool beside the road with no end of meadow frogs. Put up at Lake-O-Woods Lodge. Went down to a swampy area below the swimming pool dam, and found countless puzzling meadow frogs. Went to a drainage or irrigation ditch which goes off from the swimming pool pond. Here along the steep walls saw some frogs which at first looked like bullfrogs or *Rana tarahumarae,* and some were surely *Rana pipiens* in appearance. Tonight early in evening heard no frogs.

July 10. In the irrigation ditch cut through rock we noosed several of the large frogs. One was brown with no spots; another, a male, was green with very little indication of spots; and another was quite *R. pipiens*-like. These frogs are a queer lot Are they all one? Some were quite wary and would sink into vegetation as the end of pole and noose approached. We went down to lower pond Caught frogs from transformation to full grown Many were caught with the noose. How they would leap at the line! As we came along the edge of the lake and waded out to catch frogs out of the floating mat with our fish pole noose we discovered four masses of eggs near the bank.

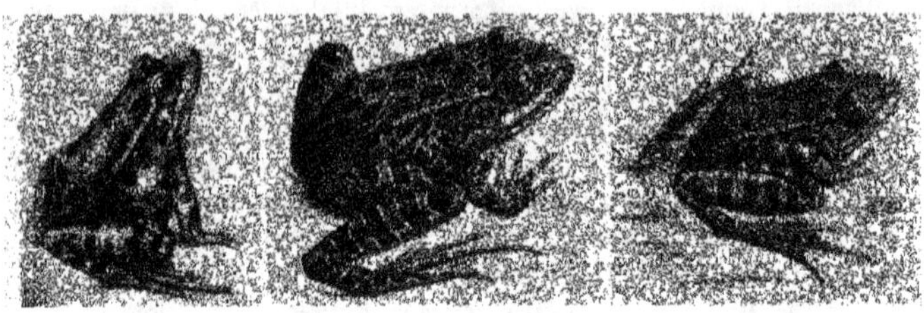

*Plate CXIII Left Rana lecontei* From *Mission Sc. du Mexique*, Plate 4, Fig. 1. *Center Rana forreri* From *Biol Centr Amer.*, Plate 60, Fig. A *Right. Rana omiltemana.* From *Biol Centr Amer.*, Plate 61, Fig. A

*Plate CXIV.* 1 *Rana pustulosa Biol Centr Amer*, Plate 61, Fig B 2,3. *Rana montezumae* From *U S and Mex Boundary Survey*, Plate 36, Figs 1,5

They are plinths attached to milfoillike plants. Presently near bank found a fresh mass. Were they laid when rain threatened last night? The other four masses were approaching hatching. A few days ago, about Thursday of last week, a small rain came. The uniform frog now has spots on its back like *R pipiens* The green bullfroglike one has a few spots.

July 11 Today Anna and I went along the drainage ditch west of the lower pond. Here saw many snakes. Plenty of frogs in the ditch. Saw no tadpoles.

July 13. At 8,500-ft. elevation, east of McNary, 20 miles or more, on Eager side of crest found a fine spring with many *Rana pipiens* They look different from Lakeside frogs, so also the tadpoles.

*Color* Lakeside, Ariz. *Large female* The background between costal folds

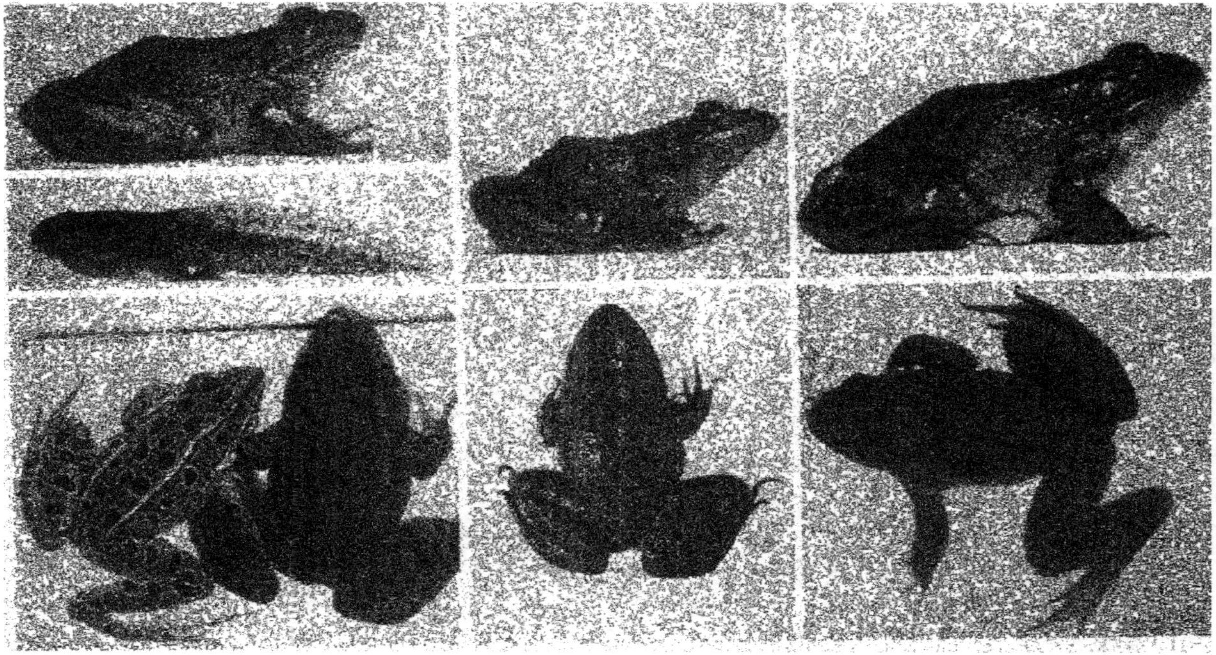

*Plate CXV. Rana* ———— (×½). From Lakeside, Ariz.

is grass green, sides sayal-brown or mikado brown with rear of eyelid the same, and upper jaw grass green. Between the dorsolateral folds are bare suggestions of other folds. The top of fore and hind limbs is bister. Down the back are 3 rows of large but obscure cinnamon-brown spots. Below the lateral folds are 2 or 3 rows of very small spots and here also are many tubercles. The rear of back has same, also rear of fore limbs, and top of hind limbs. The tibia has suggestion of 3 or 4 tubercular ridges. One tibial ridge of tubercles runs along foot almost to tip of fifth toe, and an inner tarsal ridge goes to metatarsal tubercle. The groin is mottled with cinnamon-brown or black and antimony yellow. There are 4 half-bars on femur and 2 full and 3 broken bars on tibia, 2 prominent bars on tarsus, and 6 on foot counting down the fourth toe. The rear of femur is black, spotted with rough tubercles, which are antimony yellow or yellow ocher. The underside of hind legs and top of foot are mustard yellow. The under parts of body bear wash of same or of naples yellow. The throat and underside of fore limbs are pale ochraceous-buff. The iris is bister with light vinaceous-cinnamon streaks and clear dull green-yellow on outer edge of eye.

*Male.* The back is olive-green, becoming on the sides pyrite yellow. Spots are very obscure, barely showing, black. The upper jaw from snout to tympanum is lettuce green. There are prominent tubercles below the lateral folds and some between them. The whole rear of legs and back of fore limbs are tubercular, the tibia with 3 or 4 tubercular ridges. The belly is white, with underside of throat cream color clouded with lettuce green, thus reminding one of the bullfrog. Under legs and groin are mustard yellow as in female. This frog has no lateral vocal sacs.

*A young frog* (smaller than typically spotted *pipiens*) has a bright-green mask and green back and is colored just like the male described above.

*Small frog.* Background of back fawn, becoming below dorsolateral folds vinaceous-fawn. Very few tubercles are apparent. There are four prominent ridges between the dorsolateral folds These folds and the one on upper jaw are deep olive-buff or olive-buff. The dorsal spots of body and legs are black outlined with tilleul buff. Upper side of fore limbs is vinaceous-fawn. Under parts are entirely white except for a little yellow on groin and foot.

*Comments.*

(1) Except for their much greater size these frogs at first reminded us of our 1925 impressions of *R. fisheri* at the original springs of Las Vegas, Nev.

(2) Some specimens at first and at a distance suggested *Rana clamitans.*

(3) Are they a part of the unstable population (northern Arizona and southern Utah) from which Tanner's and Linsdale's *R. onca* came?

(4) Were the frogs of the lower pond (*Rana pipiens*) the same as the forms from the rock-walled, canyonlike irrigation ditch? The tadpole tails with heavier spots (although of the *R. pipiens* class) suggest *areolata* tadpole coloration.

(5) Were these colorations somewhat akin to our northeastern dark *R. pipiens* just out of hibernation, and were these frogs only a short time out of hibernation?

## Western Spotted Frog, Western Frog, Pacific Frog, Spotted Frog

*Rana pretiosa pretiosa* (Baird and Girard). Plate CXVI; Maps 30, 35.

**Range:** Northern California to southeastern Alaska, and east to Waskesiu Lake, Saskatchewan, Montana, and western Wyoming. Through central Utah to northern Arizona (Tanner and Hunt).

"In southern British Columbia *Rana pretiosa* and *Rana aurora* occupy geographically complementary ranges. Thus *pretiosa* is recorded from many localities east of the coast range and reaches the coast north of Prince Rupert, while *aurora* is known only from the coast of extreme southwestern British Columbia and the adjacent islands. Logier . . . cites a record of *pretiosa* on Sumas Prairie in the center of the area occupied by *aurora*. It is significant to record the capture of two recently transformed specimens of *pretiosa* on Nicomen Island, in the Fraser River some 50 miles east of Vancouver, on October 20, 1941. The occurrence of these two species on the same general territory provides an opportunity to investigate their ecological relations" (G. C. Carl, B.C., 1945, p. 53)

**Habitat:** Aquatic. In pools and marshes along permanent streams, in lakes or springs of mountainous sections.

"Common along streams, but nowhere plentiful. A stupid frog, easily caught; neither a strong jumper nor a fast swimmer. The salmon color of the underside is absent from the newly transformed adult; it increases in extent and brilliancy with increase in size, occasionally overspreading nearly the entire under surface in a large adult. About one hundred specimens secured" (F. N. Blanchard, Wash., 1921, p. 6)

"*Rana pretiosa* is found abundantly in the high mountain streams and small ponds left by the melting snow. It is strictly an aquatic frog and is seldom found any distance from water" (J. R. Slevin, Calif., 1928, p. 136).

"In the vicinity of Pullman the first amphibian to appear in the spring is the long toed salamander, *Ambystoma macrodactylum* . . The spotted frog emerges a few weeks later, usually late February or early March. By the middle of March and early April the breeding season is in full swing, and mating pairs as well as eggs in all stages of development can be found. The breeding season extends into the middle of April. After this time it is usually impossible to find eggs or even adult frogs" (A. Svihla, Wash., 1935, p. 119).

"Common along the sloughs of the Willamette and Columbia rivers. It is mainly aquatic, seldom leaving the water" (S. G. Jewett, Jr., Ore., 1936, p. 72).

"It is found in or near pools, ponds, slough, marshes or springs" (K. Gordon, Ore., 1939, p. 64).

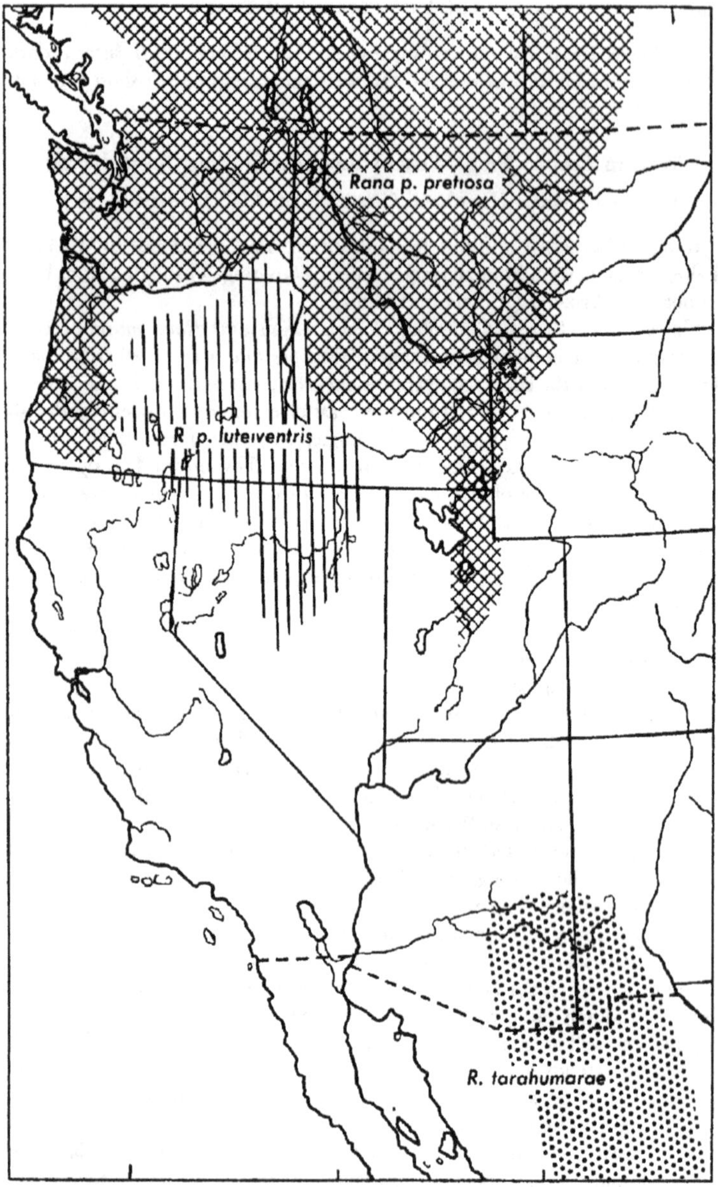


*Map 35*

"This is a race of the Pacific northwest which occurs in the Rocky Mountains in Montana and Wyoming. It is most abundant in the higher mountain lakes" (T. L. Rodgers and W. J. Jellison, Mont., 1942, p. 11).

"Two specimens of this species were taken in the grasses at the edge of Jorn Lake, where this form apparently meets the following [*R. p. luteiventris*]" (F. G. Evenden, Jr., Ore., 1943, p. 252).

**Size:** Adults, 2⅗–3⅘ inches. Males, 44–75 mm. Females, 46–95 mm. (These measurements are of *R. p. pretiosa* and *R. p. luteiventris*.) We doubt if males and females under 50 mm. breed to any great extent. We have seen records of 100 mm. or more for these frogs, but such large specimens must be rare. In Dr. Storer's material we saw females from 46–90 mm., males from 48–62 mm. In Mr. J. R. Slater's collection we have females 39–99 + mm. and males 33–68 mm., but one 36 mm. we call young (very warty, probably not mature, going to be a male). A male of 44 mm. we think perhaps mature, thumb enlarged. We did not determine the sex of a University of Michigan Zoological specimen of 44 mm. Specimens below 44 mm. are doubtless immature.

**General appearance:** This is a medium-sized frog, light or dark brown with finely roughened skin on the dorsal parts; the back and top of head have inky black spots, which at times may be very large and irregular. Occasionally these dark spots have light centers like the ones in *R. a. draytonii*. It usually has a prominent dorsolateral fold, but in some even this disappears. Sometimes the throat and the entire under parts are spotted. The under parts are yellowish to salmon red, clouded or marbled with gray. The limbs have crossbars. Preserved specimens may approach the appearance of *R. s. cantabrigensis*, or with few or no spots may suggest the green frog, *R. clamitans*. Groin not mottled as in *R. a. aurora*.

"The Western Spotted frog can be recognized by its stout form, rough skin and by the presence of dark spots with light centers on the back and salmon or red colour on the under parts only" (G. C. Carl, B.C., 1943, p. 50).

**Color:** Near west edge of Provo at springy area. *Female*. The back is serpentine green or Saccardo's olive, becoming on upper part of fore limbs and sides yellowish citrine or olive lake. The dorsum of this individual bears no dark spots and has no costal folds, so that it reminds one of a young bullfrog. On the sides are a few flat tubercles with chamois or pinkish cinnamon tops. There is a fold of the same color above the arm insertion that passes under the tympanum but there becomes very faint. The groin is somewhat mottled. There are three crossbars of olive on femur and tibia, two on tarsus, and one on foot. The eye is almost black with just a slight touch of citron yellow spots and a very thin pupil rim of the same color. The underside of throat is cream-colored as is also the venter. Underside of fore limbs, forward half of femur, underside of tibia, and top of tarsus onto inner side of foot are zinc orange, apricot orange, or orange chrome in solid color. The pectoral region and belly are thickly spotted with the same.

*Male.* The dorsum is yellowish citrine or olive lake, the same on fore limbs and top of head. The back bears numerous inky black spots with a few of the rear ones light-centered. The barring of the legs is like that of female. There is not quite so much zinc orange on the belly, but on the legs it is more intense becoming scarlet. The underside of fore limbs and hind limbs is scarlet, and there is spotting of same color on breast and belly. The throat is cream. The eye is like the female's. The dorsal fold is practically absent. Another male is almost uniform warbler green or serpentine green on the back, almost like a bullfrog. These two males are from Wilmer W. Tanner.

British Columbia. "Specimens were taken in small streams near Watson Lake, Meadow Lake, and Clinton. Following is a description of a 2.75 inch female specimen from Meadow Lake. Hind leg to heel equals length of body forward to ear. Skin everywhere rough. Lateral folds distinct. Ground color yellowish-brown on head, back, and upper surface of legs. Irregular roundish spots on head, back (including lateral folds), and front legs are black, and the majority have raised reddish-brown centres. Indistinct leg bars formed by black specks. Irregular black spot above each eye. Lateral folds, reddish-brown. Vertebral stripe, light yellowish-brown showing only on pelvis. Irregular line from eye across nostril to end of muzzle, black sprinkled with yellowish-brown. Reddish-cream streak from muzzle to arm, interrupted at end of jaw. Sides whitish, mottled with yellowish-brown. Throat white, mottled with salmon-red. Belly white, marked with salmon-red in shape of thick U. Legs salmon-red on lower surface. Feet salmon-red on inner half (hidden when sitting). Soles of feet, purplish-brown with lighter tubercles. Of five specimens 1.15 inch in length, only one shows slight traces of salmon-red on lower surfaces of femur, all other under surfaces being immaculate white" (C. L. Patch, B.C., 1922, p. 78).

**Structure:** Male with thumbs enlarged and webs of hind feet tending to become convex as in *Rana sylvatica;* tip of fourth toe free; no dark cheek patches; no red on sides.

"Female. Body thick and stout; head short, broader than long. Tympanum not two-thirds the length of the eye. Tongue large. Palatine teeth minute, posterior to the inner nares. Skin leathery, covered with asperities, except on inner surfaces, even on the sole of the foot. A depressed ridge of skin on each side, none intermediate; a glandular ridge along the upper jaw. Femur not half the length of the body; tibia about equal to it, but shorter than the hind foot. Terminal joint of longest toe free, next margined, and web generally extending between the tips of the toes on one side, and the last articulation on the other. Shortest toe rather more than one-third the length of the hind foot, both measured from the tarsus. Above yellowish brown with rounded dark blotches. Sides dusky; dorsal ridge lighter; a light line along the posterior ridge of the upper jaw. Faint indications of a dark area about the tympanum; a few spots about the nostrils. Beneath yellowish white, obsoletely marmorated with brown. About two and a half inches long. Syn. *Rana pretiosa* B. & G., Proc. Acad. Nat. Sc. Phila. VI 378. Hab. Washington Territory" (S. F. Baird, Gen., [1854] 1856, p. 62).

**Voice:** The male is without lateral vocal sacs.

"While endeavoring to escape from the hand, a young specimen 1 45 inch in length opened the mouth and emitted squeaks resembling those made by a mouse" (C L. Patch, B.C., 1922, p. 78).

"Soon after the spotted frog makes its appearance in the spring, mating commences, and the ponds are resonant with their deep bass calls. Their short bass notes are easily distinguishable from the almost constant high shrill song of the tree frog and can be heard for at least a quarter of a mile. On several occasions pairs of spotted frogs brought into the laboratory while in amplexus were observed to drop to the bottom of the aquarium in which they were kept and there emit their call. Although the sound was greatly dampened by the water, the note could still be heard distinctly for some distance within the room. When emitting their call notes only a slight tremor at the sides of the throat is visible. The vocal sacs are evidently poorly developed for they do not protrude as they do in other ranas" (A. Svihla, Wash., 1935, pp. 119–120).

**Breeding:** This species breeds from March to May. The egg mass is about a pint in bulk. The egg is 1/12 inch (2 mm.), the outer jelly envelope 2/5–3/5 inch (10–14 mm.) (adapted from Dickerson, 1906, p. 219). The envelopes are large and the eggs appear far apart. The tadpoles, 2¼–2⅘ inches (56–70 mm.) with tooth ridges 3/3, sometimes 2/3, transform from June to August at ⅝–⅞ inch (16–23 mm.). Like our eastern wood frog, many frogs of this species apparently breed before summer, particularly in March to April.

"A female of 61 mm. taken at Cottonwood Creek on June 6, 1928, had rather large ovaries with enlarging eggs. Two females of 46 and 74 mm. taken at Six Mile lake on June 19, two of 58 and 60 mm. taken at Lytton, July 1 to 8, 1925, had only minute eggs in their ovaries. Two females of 89 and 93 mm. taken at Brent's lake on July 1, and four of from 73 to 78 mm taken at Summerland on July 6, 1928, contained ripening eggs Another specimen of 51 mm. taken at Summerland on July 20, 1928, had small ovaries with minute eggs. Dickerson (1906, p. 219) gives the month of March as the spawning season for this frog at Puget Sound. The above limited data would suggest that in the interior country it occurs in June and July" (E. B. S. Logier, B.C., 1932, p. 323).

Tadpole: The National Museum has the following material:

No. 21484 B. W. Evermann and C. Gilbert, Natches R. near N. Yakima, Wash.—1 tadpole with 4 legs, total length 59 mm., body 22 mm.; 1 tadpole—66 mm., body 24 mm ; 1 tadpole—68.5 mm., body 25.5 mm., hind legs showing, rather far advanced, but with three rows of teeth on upper jaw.

No. 17615: B. W. Evermann, Silver Bow, Brown's Gulch, Mont., July 27, 1891—1 tadpole 56 mm., body 23 mm.

No. 17616—1 tadpole 53 mm., body 25 mm. Mouth parts possibly not normal but teeth $\frac{3}{4}$. (Also see account by Helen Thompson, 1913, under *R. p luteiventris*.)

Transformation Time, June–August, the bulk of transformation apparently in July and early August. Size, 16–23 mm. July 19, 1908, Prairie Hill, Selkirk Mts., British Columbia, J. C. Bradley secured transforming and transformed individuals from 16 to 22 mm. Others in the same lot of 23, 25, 28 mm. were past transformation.

The National Museum has the following significant records:

No 32663–6. June 1, 1898—21, 23, 23.5 mm. Lake Bennet, B.C. A. Seal.

No. 53142. Aug. 2, 1915—20 mm. Riverside, Matthews Co., Ore. E. A. Preble.

No. 17622–4. Aug. 8, 1891—22, 21, 22 mm. just past transformation. Cañon Cr. Nat. Park, Wyo. B. W. Evermann.

No. 16793. Aug. 20, 1890—23 mm. Salmon River, Idaho. V. Bailey and Butcher.

In Storer's collection are transformees 18, 18.5, 18.5, and 21 mm. In Slater's material a series of transformed specimens range from 13 to 18 mm.; another series 17 to 27 mm.

"Nineteen tadpoles were taken in Brent's Lake on July 1, 1928. They ranged in length from 43 to 76 mm. In two of them, all four limbs were functioning; in two more the front limbs were well developed and could be seen folded beneath the skin; in seven others the hind limbs were from one quarter to half grown. . . . There would seem to be little doubt that the mature and transforming tadpoles taken at Brent's lake on July 1, with an average body length for all of 21 98 mm , and for the eleven larger specimens of 27.63 mm., belonged to the brood of the preceding year and had wintered over as tadpoles, and consequently were ready to begin transformation earlier in the summer than those nearer the coast (Puget Sound) which go through their metamorphosis in the same year in which they are hatched" (E. B. S. Logier, B.C., 1932, p. 324).

The best account of its breeding is given by A. Svihla (Wash., 1935, pp. 119–122):

"In the vicinity of Pullman the egg masses are deposited in shallow water among the grasses at the edges of ponds, although the egg masses themselves are not attached to blades. . . . Two egg masses were measured and the number of eggs estimated. One mass contained 1500 cc. and the other 1100 cc. Since each egg measures more than 1 cc the number of eggs in these masses would approximate 1500 and 1100 respectively.

"Each egg including its jelly coats measures from 10 to 15 mm. in diameter, the egg proper being only 2 to 2.8 mm. in diameter. There are two jelly coats present, an inner one measuring from 5 to 6 mm. and an outer varying from 10 to 15 mm. . . . The inner coat is rather hard to see but is apparent when viewed obliquely or when the egg becomes infected with a fungus growth or bacterial growth, which is usually found in the inner coat. The newly deposited egg is black in color at the animal pole and creamy white at the vegetal pole. The vegetal pole varies in size from a mere point to half of the egg. The vitelline capsule closely circumscribes the egg.

". . . At the time of hatching the young tadpoles are sooty brown in color and measure 7.3 to 8.7 mm. in length. The adhesive discs, dextral anus, and external gills are apparent at this time.

"The tadpoles grow very rapidly for in about thirty days the hind limb buds appear and the total length has increased from about 8 mm. to 36 mm. At this time the head and body are 15 mm. in length and the tail 20 mm. The depth of the body is about 10 mm. and the greatest width 7 mm. The tail is 1.4 to 1.6 times the combined length of head and body. The eyes are dorsal, well up on the head, and rather close together, the interorbital distance being about 2 mm. The external nares are situated almost midway between the eyes and the tip of the snout but are slightly closer to the eyes. The interorbital distance is contained 7.5 times in the length of the head and body. The anus is dextral and spiraculum sinistral, being directed upward and backward as in other Ranidae. The greatest depth of the tail (over fins) is contained 2.5 times in the length, while the greatest depth of the muscular portion is contained approximately 7 times in the length of the tail

"At the age of the appearance of the hind limb buds the mouth parts appear as follows: on the upper lip there is but a single row of labial teeth which is divided medially into two very short sets situated near the ends of the upper jaws. On the lower labium there are three long rows of teeth, the second or middle row the longest, the first and third about equal in length A single row of labial cirri extends along the sides and bottom of the lips. . . .

"The mouth parts of *R. p pretiosa* tadpoles differ from those of *R. p. luteiventris*. In *pretiosa* there are four rows of labial teeth, one very short upper row and three lower rows. In *luteiventris* there are five rows, two long upper rows and three lower, as figured by Thompson (1913). The first lower row in *luteiventris* is longer than the analogous one in *pretiosa*.

"By the middle of June the tadpoles metamorphose into frogs. At this time the newly transformed frogs are 60 mm. in total length with a head and body length of 26 mm There is no indication of the reddish coloration on the underside of the thighs and abdomen of these young frogs.

"Since spotted frogs of two very divergent sizes, one about half the size of the other, can be found during the springtime, it seems reasonable to conclude that at least two years are required for this frog to reach mature size" (A. Svihla, Wash., 1935, pp. 120–121).

**Journal notes:** March 30, 1942. Went on short trip with Mr. James Slater to Sparaway Lake. Here he finds *R. pretiosa.* (Sparaway Lake is near old type locality of *R. pretiosa.*) Went to head of Sparaway Lake and traveled along the drainage ditches. Saw two frogs leap before we got to them. Finally espied one, but as I tried to catch it, I went in deep. We came back later and caught it. They are sluggish, slow frogs.

April 1. With Slater. See *R. aurora* for key characters.

In one conversation with Slater he remarked:

| | |
|---|---|
| "No mottling in groin | *R. p. pretiosa* |
| Slight mottling in groin | *R. cascadae* |
| Always mottling in groin | *R. a. aurora*" |

May 30, Utah. With W. W. Tanner went 1 mile west of Provo to a spring. Here we found one female *Rana p. pretiosa* and one young. In another spring took five young *R. p pretiosa.*

**Authorities' corner:**

F. C. Test, Mont., [1891] 1893, p. 58.

J. Grinnell, J. Dixon, J. M. Linsdale, Calif., 1930, p. 144

## Nevada Spotted Frog

*Rana pretiosa luteiventris* Thompson. Plate CXVII; Map 35.

**Range:** Southeastern Washington, eastern Oregon, northeastern California, northeastern Nevada, and probably other interior parts. Camp (Calif, 1917, p. 124) holds that it "seems to be represented in the Museum of Vertebrate Zoology by two specimens (Nos. 2098, 2099), collected by Dr. H. C Bryant at Alturas, Modoc County, California." Gordon (Ore., 1939, p. 64) assigns specimens to it from Klamath Lake, Harney, Crook, Grant, Umatilla, Union, Wallowa, and Linn counties and Dechutes River, Ore. Storer, 1925, assigns Fort Walla Walla, Humpeg Falls, and Butte Creek specimens from eastern Washington to this form.

Do we have *R p pretiosa* to the Cascades, a tongue of *R. cascadae* down the Oregon Sky Line, and *R. p. luteiventris* eastward of the Cascades? The specimens we collected at Lapine, Ore., we interpret as *R. p. luteiventris.*

In order to be satisfied that these Oregon frogs were like those of the type locality, we sought frogs from the Owyhee-Snake River drainage of northern Nevada. We finally secured several handsome highly colored frogs of this species from a boy, Larry Flower, of Elko, Nev., who collected them in Taylor Canyon, Elko Co., Nev, July 22, 1945. These were as flame scarlet to apricot orange on the belly as were ours from Lapine.

**Habitat:** Irrigation ditches, streams, ponds, lakes.

"It is quite aquatic, although the stomach contents, consisting of ants and water insects, indicate that at least part of the hunting is done on land. A few young specimens were taken a short distance from water on the banks of Anne

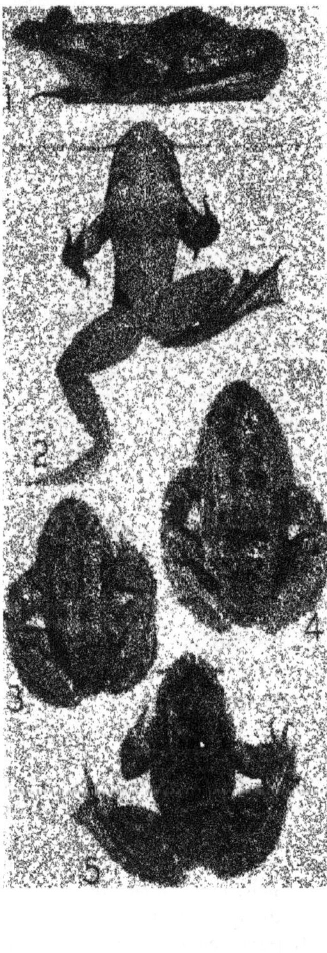


*Plate CXVI. Rana pretiosa pretiosa* (×¾). 1,2,3,4. Males. 5. Female

*Plate CXVII Rana pretiosa luteiventris* (×¾) 1,2. From Deeth, Nev 3 Enlarged thumb of male, from Lapine, Ore. 4. From Lapine, Ore.

Creek, but the adults were usually found along the edges of swiftly flowing streams or with only the head projecting from the vegetation of stagnant pools. When disturbed, they slipped quietly under the surface, but quickly reappeared, usually in the same place. Although they were almost as common as *Rana pipiens*, the two species were seldom found in the same pond" (H Thompson, Nev, 1913, pp. 53–55).

**Size:** (See *R. p. pretiosa*) $1\frac{3}{4}$–$3\frac{1}{2}$ inches (44–87 mm.).

**General appearance:** "Color above grayish brown. . . . In the brighter colored specimens the lateral folds are lighter than the ground color. There is occasionally a trace of a dark cheek patch, and the spots on the back may be obscure or distinct and few or many in number. The bright color on the ventral surface varies from a faint yellowish tinge on the feet of the young specimens to orange yellow (141, 156, 161, 171) [Klincksieck et Valette, *Code des Couleurs*, Paris] in adults, and it may be present on the thighs, may extend in a more or less U-shaped blotch on the belly, or may cover the entire ventral surface to the shoulder girdle" (H. Thompson, Nev., 1913, p 54).

**Color:** *Male*. Deeth, Nev., May 22, 1942. Back and dorsum of hind limbs dark greenish olive or deep olive, fore limbs citrine-drab or yellowish olive. There is band on upper jaw of pale ochraceous-salmon from near tip of snout to arm insertion, with a touch of same on lower jaw; margins of both jaws marbled. The spots of the back are few (8) and very indistinct, with light tubercle in center. This frog when first caught showed no spots because it was so dark. There is no dark mask. The tympanum is smooth, smaller than eye. The iris is black with flecks of ochraceous-orange above and below pupil rim, which is pale chalcedony yellow. The very front of eye bears a slight crescentic bar of veronese green.

*Female* Deeth, Nev., May 24, 1942 The back is dark olive, with a few light tubercle-centered black spots which are not very evident. There is a prominent bar on forward half of brachium, but otherwise bars on fore limb are practically lacking, and bars on hind limbs are obscure The costal folds are broad and rounded but quite conspicuous An avellaneous jaw stripe extends to the arm insertion. The upper labial margin is fuscous with specklings of light green-yellow, the lower fuscous interrupted by the pale olive-buff of the throat. On the rear of thigh each tubercle is apricot yellow. There is apricot yellow on the sides of belly and back of arm insertion and a touch of it on pectoral region. The background of throat and belly is pale olive-buff to white with fuscous black spotting on the belly and fuscous mottling on the throat. The iris of eye is black or dark olive heavily punctuated with bright green-yellow. The skin is rough.

Lapine, Ore, April 5, 1942 *Adult male*. The top of head, face, and dorsal background are Saccardo's umber or snuff brown becoming on arms and legs light brownish olive. There is heavy black spotting on the back and spots on top of head and back of head across the neck in this individual The spots between costal folds and below them have light pinpoint tubercles as centers. The tympanum is light brownish olive; the costal folds and slight suffusion over shoulder back of tympanum are warm sepia. The brachium has one half and one full black crossband, the antebrachium has two full and two broken bands. In the hind limbs, the front half of femur bears three half black bands less prominent than ones on tibia. tarsus, and toes, which are prominently banded. The intervening area is grayish olive. The membranes of hind foot are suffused with vinaceous-brown or purplish vinaceous. A jaw stripe starts at snout, not prominent ahead of eye, enlarging below eye, and continues to insertion of arm as pale salmon color stripe, which then extends backward as a body-colored fold of skin forming a half moon back of axil. The edge of the lower jaw is marked with a series of spots. The eyes stand up prominently and are black with a light green-yellow bar above the pupil and a suffusion of the same below. The color on the belly is flame scarlet to apricot orange with a few cephalic mid-belly mottlings of apricot buff. This color extends up the sides and, mingling with dorsal color, gives an English red cast to the lateral areas. This scarlet to orange is most pronounced in the groin, which is not mottled. The flame scarlet to apricot orange appears also on the underside of arms and forward half of femur. The lower third of femur and tibia is Brazil red washed out to peach red on the upper tarsus. These oranges are not solid but interlaced or mottled with light buff or cream color. The mottling most prominent on the ventral body color becomes dots on femur. The same kind occurs on upper pectoral and throat region, but there the intense oranges are replaced by light grayish olive.

*Young.* Upper part citrine-drab with no dark spots below dorsolateral folds, but between folds are about three spots, wide but not regular and with light central tubercle. The venter is unmottled cream-colored, with slightest touches of orange on belly and orange on underside of limbs, but lacking in groin.

*Second young.* Just a touch of orange on fore limb and wash on femur, which becomes bright on tibia, tarsus, and foot.

**Structure:** "Form stout. Head broader than long; snout rounded; external nares small and round, nearer end of snout than eye; eye small; tympanum small, three-fifths the size of the eye; tongue large and fleshy, strongly notched behind; vomerine teeth extending back in two oblique patches from the inner edge of the internal nares. Skin roughly tubercular; sides, outer surface of leg and lower surface of foot covered with small pointed granules; lateral folds inconspicuous; glandular ridge along the jaw, interrupted at the angle of the jaw and at the shoulder by a ridge curving behind the tympanum; fold of skin across the chest. Fingers not webbed, first slightly longer than second, palmar tubercle indistinct. Legs massive, length to heel equalling that of body forward to anterior corner of eye; foot broadly webbed; terminal joint of fourth toe free; small inner metatarsal tubercle, no outer tubercle" (H. Thompson, Nev., 1913, pp. 53–54).

**Voice:** Not on record.

**Breeding:** Probably from March or April onward. Labial tooth rows of tadpole $\frac{2}{3}$. Miss H. Thompson described a tadpole collected July 10 which was nearing transformation.

"One mass of 260 cc. volume contained about 2,400 eggs spaced one-quarter to three-quarters of an inch from each other. The jelly of the eggs is not firm thus giving the mass a loose, flowing appearance when agitated.

"Only one clear transparent gelatinous envelope is present; its outline is fairly distinct, but merges slightly with the jelly of the adjacent eggs. The vitelline capsule is close to the vitellus and is seen best with the aid of a lens. The vitelli are black at the animal pole and tan at the vegetal pole.

"Eggs at late cleavage to crescentic groove stage gave the following measurements: vitellus 1.97 mm. (range 1.81 to 2.12 mm.); vitelline capsule 2.06 mm. (range 1.93 to 2.25 mm.); envelope 6.33 mm. (range 5.0 to 7.12 mm.).

"*Affinities: R. p. luteiventris* eggs are much smaller in the diameter of the envelope than those of *R. p. pretiosa,* which Dickerson (1906, p. 219) gives roughly as being one-half inch across. Svihla (1935, p. 120) gives ten to fifteen millimeters as the diameter and also notes that there is an inner envelope five to six millimeters in diameter in *R. p. pretiosa* eggs. No such envelope could be demonstrated in our eggs of *R. p. luteiventris.* Sizes of the vitelli are apparently the same" (R. L. Livezey and A. H. Wright, Gen., 1945, pp. 704–705).

**Journal notes:** July 29, 1934, Welcome Motor Park, Wells, Nev. Went up one of the streams that is supposed to be one source of Humboldt River almost to the fish hatchery. The water is cold. No luck. Returned to station and found Anna had one of the prizes we sought. When she first saw it, it was sitting just at the edge of the pond in the water. When we caught it, it was resting on a mat of algae. It ducked beneath the algae and slowly swam out and rested on the muddy bottom with its head in the mud. They are rather slow. They have considerable orange or yellow. When held in hand they sometimes give a very interesting squeal but not the mercy cry of the bullfrog.

Easter, April 5, 1942, Lapine, Ore. Clear at 11:00 A.M. Frosty last night. Shallow weedy end of irrigation overflow ditch beside road. Anna saw something move in the grassy vegetation. She called to me. Just then I espied a frog egg mass in ditch on opposite side. I came to her. We walked along ditch. About 1½ feet from edge of water 3 inches deep is a mass 6 by 3½, another 3 by 3 in water 4 inches deep. Anna and I came to a little pool where there were three masses. Here poised in water was an adult *R. pretiosa.* Tried to get it with net. Never should have lost it. Some of these masses at surface were 8 by 5 or 6 inches. Saw one mass in shallow water almost high and dry. While I was easing an egg mass out of water, Anna espied a frog on opposite bank among grassy tussocks. Egg masses gather a lot of dirt. One was in center of ditch. Fresh ones are quite bluish.

In one pool were three egg masses at surface. Here was an adult. Lost it. Later came back to area and caught it, a beautiful male. Color on belly different from Washington (Tacoma) *R. pretiosa.* Has one metatarsal tubercle. If one loses one of these frogs, he reappears, like *R. pretiosa* of Tacoma, in the same place poised on water or in weeds. This is flat land, open, partly cultivated, partly meadows, and with trees.

May 22, 1942, Wells. Have had only two or three nice days here. Snowed considerably last week. Went in creek below Welcome cabins, 8 miles west of Wells, but no frogs.

At Deeth are many sloughs more or less tributary as overflows of Mary's River. One shallow pond only slightly connected with sloughs from river had clumps of sedges slightly out from shore. As I walked along shore saw quite a stirring movement in one clump. Bert came over, placed the net, tramped in the clump, and the frog came out moving to one side. Bert swung net around and caught it. Saw another movement in near-by clump. Bert thought he saw a larger frog but lost it. We made several dips at the spot but had no more luck.

When Anna told me a movement was in a certain clump, I stomped it out toward the net. Was lucky to get a male *Rana p. luteiventris.* Soon saw another movement and for an instant a bigger one than that captured appeared but went back into vegetation. Never got it.

May 23, 1942, Elko. Went to Maggie and Susie Creeks at Carlin. Streams too muddy, Humboldt River too high, winter snows not yet gone long enough to make hunting satisfactory.

In afternoon, late, we went to Deeth to our favorite pond. Anna for an instant saw two little bubbles in a tussock of sedge, but when the two bubbles went back into the water she knew it was a frog. We never saw it. Later returned and here was her "bubble frog" Approached slowly and with quick sweep of net I had it, a half-grown *R. pretiosa luteiventris.* Spring has barely arrived and several fields are yellow with the dandelions in bloom.

On way to Salt Lake City stopped at 9:30 at our Deeth pond. Thought I saw a movement. Took off my shoes and stockings. As I approached pond, something leaped in. Placed my net with idea of driving the frog in the clump into it. Just then saw a little one in next clump and he was facing the shore. Caught it by hand, then tromped the other clump and didn't look in net at once. Then to my surprise here was a small female in my net. What luck! Our only captures have been from this one small pond.

**Authorities' corner:**

A. Svihla, Wash., 1935, p. 119. J. M. Linsdale, Nev., 1940, p. 212.
K. Gordon, Ore., 1939, p. 64. F G. Evenden, Jr., Ore., 1943, p. 252.

Dr. Gordon and his Oregon group interpret *R. p. pretiosa* as entering Cascades from west and *R. p. luteiventris* from high Cascades eastward to northern Nevada. In the very early spring of 1942 our student, Miss Ruth Hopson, at Eugene, tried to take us to Mackenzie Pass, but snow stopped us. She described from the "Three Sisters" a frog such as Evenden records on the Oregon Sky Line, immediately north of Mt. Washington. Later Slater showed us his *R. cascadae* which he collects at Breitenbush area just north of Mt. Jefferson. These suggest a meeting in ranges of *R. p. luteiventris* and *R. cascadae* in northern Oregon.

We are following Mrs. Gaige and employ Dr. Gordon's interpretation that the *R. pretiosa* from Cascades in Oregon eastward into northern Nevada is *R p. luteiventris.*

### Mink Frog, Northern Frog, Hoosier Frog, Rocky Mountain Frog

*Rana septentrionalis* Baird. Plate CXVIII; Map 30.

**Range:** Northern New England and northern New York south to Peterboro (G. S. Miller, Jr.), west to Minnesota, north in Canada to Hudson Bay, and eastward to Gaspé Peninsula, Prince Edward Island, and Nova Scotia.

**Habitat:** This is an aquatic frog, found in peaty or sphagnaceous lakes or ponds or in inlets or outlets of such lakes or ponds, particularly where water lilies are growing.

**Size:** Adults, 1⅞–3 inches. Males, 46–71 mm. Females, 48–76 mm. "The smallest mature female captured was 48 mm. in length and the smallest mature male 46 mm It seems probable, therefore, that *R. septentrionalis* females mature at the same age as the males, whereas *R clamitans* females mature at a considerably larger size than do males and probably at least one year later" (R. Grant, Que., 1941, p. 152).

**General appearance:** This frog is a small representative of the bullfrog-green-frog group. The sides are heavily mottled, the rear of the femur is heavily reticulated. The back is buffy or brownish olive, almost uniform, or mottled with large dark areas set off by a tracery of light lines around or among them, or spotted with widely separated spots. Sometimes the forward part of the back is uniform and quite green, and the rear part spotted (much like some *R. fisheri*). The upper jaw is green. The legs are spotted or with a few bars. The mottling on the femur is suggestive of the *R. virgatipes-R. grylio* group. In young specimens the sides may be speckled and the throats mottled. In the largest males, the entire under parts are maize yellow.

"These frogs are variable in color and pattern, but are distinguished from young *R. clamitans* by the less prominent dorso-lateral folds, smooth skin, more extensive webs and strong odor when handled" (R. Grant, Que., 1941, p. 152).

**Color:** *Male.* On back, buffy olive or light brownish olive to olive, marked with wavy lines or spots of oil yellow or yellowish citrine. On the middle of the back are two irregular rows of round or elongated black spots, widely separated. Back, ahead of tympanum, is without black spots and with cosse

*Plate CXVIII. Rana septentrionalis.* 1. Female (×⅔). 2 Male (×½). 3. Egg mass (×⅙) 4 Head of male (×½). 5. Male (×½). 6. Male (×⅔).

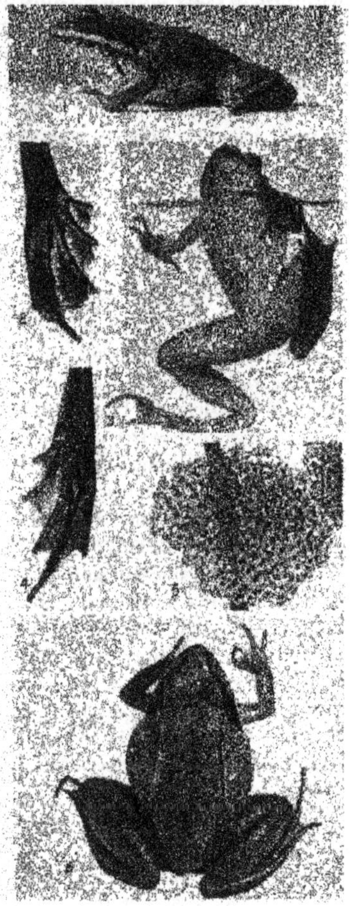

*Plate CXIX Rana sylvatica sylvatica.* 1. Female (×⅔). 2. Foot of male with convex webs (×1). 3 Female (×⅗) 4 Foot of female with concave webs (×1). 5 Egg mass, spherical in shape (×½) 6. Male (×⅔).

green or lettuce green interspersed with the buffy olive. This green is a solid color on upper jaw. Courge or yellow-green in region of tympanum, which is tawny-olive to buffy brown. Mixture of yellow-green, black, and hazel along sides. Throat, and on some of largest males entire under parts, maize yellow.

*Female.* Clear Lake, Adirondack Lodge, N.Y., from S. C. Bishop, July 14, 1923. Several seem more spotted on under part of hind legs than are males. Some have spots on either side of the throat, hazel of back more prominent and more hazel on sides, usually more spots on the head. Underneath, females are white or whitish except for the throat, which may be pale chalcedony yellow or seafoam yellow.

**Structure:** No lateral folds, or folds interrupted; webs large, but leaving one joint of fourth toe free; head narrow, snout pointed; eyes close together; tympanum conspicuous, in males much larger than the eye.

"Body stout, depressed. Skin not tuberculated, but uneven. A broad depressed ridge on each side of back; none intermediate; a branch of same round the tympanum, meeting a thickening from the jaw. Hand much longer than forearm. Femur and tibia nearly equal, about half the length of the body, and less than the hind foot. Foot large; terminal joint of middle toe free; that of the others free only on the inner side. Above light greenish olive, vermiculated with lighter, and with a few large dark blotches posteriorly. Beneath yellow, unblotched. No line on sides of the jaw. Two inches long. Hab. Northern Minnesota" (S. F. Baird, Gen., [1854] 1856, p. 61).

**Voice:** This species has a *chant d'amour* which at chorus season can be heard one-third or one-half mile away. A. H. Norton of Maine considered the call similar to that of the green frog, but higher and slightly metallic. He thinks it resembles "closely the sound produced by striking a long nail on the head with a hammer in driving it into heavy timber." S. C. Bishop described the call as a "Cut-cut, with sometimes a 'burred' gh-r-r-r." J. H. Garnier calls it a "rapid squeaking croak." The croaking sac is similar to that of *Rana palustris,* being the throat and sides of head below the corners of the mouth; it is not so well developed as in the sphagnum frog (*R. virgatipes*).

**Breeding:** This species breeds from June 24 to July 30 or possibly Aug. 16, the crest coming in July. The egg mass is a plinth, 3–5 inches (75–125 mm.) by 2 inches (50 mm.) thick. The egg is brown to black and buff to yellow, the envelope ¼ inch (6–7 mm), becoming 5/16–3/8 inch (8–9 mm.) as development proceeds. The olive tadpole is large, 4 inches (99 mm.), its tail elongate with acute tip. The tooth ridges are 2/3. After a period of 1 year or slightly more, the tadpoles transform from June 24 to Aug. 30, the bulk in July, at 1 1/16–1 3/5 inches (29–40 mm.).

"Some of the female mink frogs taken on July 20 to 22 had laid their eggs. *Rana clamitans* and *R. septentrionalis* thus occupy the same habitats and breed at the same time. Metamorphosing mink frog tadpoles were caught along with metamorphosing green frogs on July 22" (R. Grant, Que., 1941, p. 152).

**Journal notes:** Near Dorset, Ontario, from July 2–14, 1913, we heard at night along the shore of Otter Lake the peculiar note which is the croak of the mink frog. On the fifteenth of July at 10 P.M. we heard several frogs and started with flashlights for Peat Lake where the species was in chorus. The air temperatures ranged from 52° to 55°F., but the water of Otter Lake at its surface registered 69°F.

In this peaty lake with a clear sphagnaceous border we found several *R. septentrionalis*. On July 16 and 17 we examined the place closely. All along the north edge of the lake were white water lilies, yellow spatterdocks, and water shields. These three made a perfect carpet on the water's surface. On these plants during the day the frogs rested. In the outlet to Otter Lake (Ten Mile Creek between Lake of Bays and Otter Lake) we found them common, July 24, on muddy bottoms where water lilies were abundant. Another habitat we discovered Aug. 31 was a beaver lake where *Cassandra* and all the associated heathlike plants grew. Finally in Fletcher Lake, Sept. 1, we found them in the shallow, sandy shores among pipeworts (*Eriocaulon articulatum*).

On June 14, 1923, we found most of our frogs at Hellgate Ponds, Onekio, N.Y. Here in driftwood pools below a beaver dam, we took several *R. clamitans, R. catesbeiana* young, and *R. septentrionalis*. Later took several more mink frogs in muddy pools among granite boulders.

**Authorities' corner:**

A. G. Ruthven, Mich., 1910, p. 59.
P. H. Pope, Me., 1915, pp. 1–2.
J. A. Weber, N.Y., 1928, p. 110.
I. Hoopes, Me., 1938, pp. 4–6.
L. R. Aronson, N.H., 1943, pp. 242–244.

Field notes of Dr. S. C. Bishop, made at Clear Lake, Adirondack Lodge, N.Y.: "July 2, 1923. Many *Rana septentrionalis* in Clear Lake. 24 taken, of which 23 were males, 1 juvenile female, swimming and floating in open water 3 or 4 rods from shore or resting on pads of yellow cow lilies—croaking at 8:30 A.M. in broad sunlight, at midday and in the evening.

"July 13, P.M. Day mostly bright and windy. Found three egg masses of the mink frog, *Rana septentrionalis* Baird, fastened to the stems of the yellow cow lily. They were attached about 8, 12, and 18 inches below the surface, in globular masses from 4–5½ in. in diameter. The lilies were about 4–6 rods from shore in 6–8 feet of water. Took one egg mass. The egg mass is slightly heavier than the water and sinks slowly when detached. The individual eggs have 3 envelopes visible with a hand lens. First closely surrounds egg—2d about 5 mm. diameter—last (3d) ⅜ inch. The upper half in freshly laid eggs black, the lower half creamy white. Division of color being about equal. Frogs croaked just at daybreak and during morning, rarely in afternoon. . . .

"July 14th. Frogs croaked all night, males on lily pads in lake and a few immature females near shore. . . . Found 2 egg masses . . . 1st about 16 to 18 in. below surface, the embryos already hatching; 2d lot, 2 feet below surface, freshly laid. . . . During middle of day many males left the open lake to hide along shore. The male croaking expands the throat and sides of head below ears. . . . Eggs are apparently laid at night—at least we could find no females in act of laying during the day or early night when using a light, nor in the early morn at 5:30 A.M.

"July 15. Dark and rainy. Only a few frogs croaking during the night and *very* infrequently in the daylight. Three egg masses found. One lot 4½–5 feet below the surface; 2d with embryos ready to leave egg mass, 3 feet below the surface, was 6 in. in diameter, the jelly ready to disintegrate. 3d mass, 18–20 inches below surface. . . .

"July 15, P.M. Two egg masses, one about 4 feet below surface in 7 feet water was 6 in. in diameter and fastened to two stems of yellow lily—*Nymphaea variegata*. The mass (with well developed embryos) was longer than wide with the supporting stems running through one side. 2d egg mass was smaller, about 3 x 4 inches and 3 feet below the surface."

## Dusky Gopher Frog, Dark Gopher Frog

*Rana sevosa* Goin and Netting. Map 26.

**Range:** "The known range of *sevosa* extends along the Gulf coast from St. Tammany Parish, Louisiana, to Mobile County, Alabama. . . . The easternmost station for *sevosa* is three hundred miles west of the westernmost *capito* locality; the ranges of *sevosa* and *areolata* are separated by about two hundred miles" (C. J. Goin and M. G. Netting, La., 1940, p. 156).

**Habitat:** Gopher turtle and other holes.

**Size:** Adults: "The largest male *sevosa* among 22 specimens was 84 mm. long, and the largest of 29 females was 92.5" (C. J. Goin and M. G. Netting, La., 1940, p. 146). We ourselves have seen males 71–85 mm. and females 82–105 mm.

**General appearance:** "Of the three species *Rana sevosa* has the darkest dorsal coloration and the least amount of contrast between ground color and dorsal spots. Many of the paratypes are uniform black above, a condition that appears to be more characteristic of males than of females. The lightest specimens have a gray or brown ground color and dorsal spots that range from red brown to dark brown but are not black. The dorsal color and pattern are continued over the folds, which are never distinctively colored. The preserved specimens offer no indication that yellow was present on any part of the body in life. Metachrosis has not been reported in this species but may be expected to occur within a narrow color range.

"In *sevosa* the entire anterior half of the lower surface is thickly covered with spots and dusky markings; in males the remainder of the lower surface, except for a small pubic area, is spotted, whereas in females the central lower thigh surfaces and the posterior portion of the belly are usually immaculate" (C. J. Goin and M. G. Netting, La., 1940, pp. 150–152).

**Structure:** "A dark, medium-sized Rana with a very warty dorsum and a heavily spotted venter. Its dorsal spots are frequently indiscernible from the dark ground color, but when distinct they are irregular in shape and are not outlined with a light color. *Rana sevosa* can be distinguished from both races of *areolata* by its spotted venter, lack of circular, light-bordered dorsal spots, warty dorsum with broad dorsolateral folds, and broad head. *Rana sevosa* differs from *capito* in having a darker ground color, heavier and more extensive ventral markings, broader waist, narrower dorsolateral folds, wartier dorsum, and dark hind limb bars which are broader than the light spaces between the bars" (same, p. 138).

"Head triangular in outline, dorsolateral folds high and relatively narrow; dorsum with numerous prominent warts; dorsal spots poorly differentiated from gray, brown, or black ground color; venter always spotted at least from chin to midbody; dark bars on hindlegs separated by interspaces that are never wider than the bars" (same, p. 146).

**Voice:** Little of record. See next paragraph.

**Breeding:** "Fortunately, while this description was in course of preparation, Stewart Springer visited Pittsburgh and contributed additional information upon the habits of *sevosa* from memory. He recalled finding these frogs breeding in the water in southern Mississippi concurrently with *Hyla gratiosa* and *Hyla cinerea cinerea;* Allen . . . reports the former breeding near Biloxi on April 18 and 19, and the latter 'as soon as the weather becomes warm and settled.' Mr. Springer further reported that the eggs, in masses about the size of two fists, are laid under water at a depth of approximately one foot and are attached to plant stems. He stated that *sevosa* is less restricted to cypress swamps for breeding sites than is *gratiosa,* since the former occurs also in pine barren ponds, even those of temporary character. The call, as he remembered it, is less snore-like than is that of *capito.* He found that frightened individuals dive and swim along the bottom of the pond" (same, pp. 142–143).

**Journal notes:** Most of our knowledge of this form comes from Goin and Netting. We revert to their original designation *R. sevosa* We have known more or less about it since our visits to *R. areolata* territory in Illinois. In 1930 we wrote: "*Rana aesopus* (*capito*) South Carolina to Florida to Louisiana (North Slidell, May 3, 1926, P. Viosca, Jr, and H. B. Chase et al.)." When we visited Stewart Springer and Morrow J. Allen at Biloxi we saw their *Rana sevosa.* On June 10, 1930, we started from New Orleans, La., for the north country, Pearl River, and the pine barren parishes of Louisiana with Percy Viosca, Jr., and H. B. Chase. They tell me that they find *R. aesopus* (*sevosa*) in holes under stumps. First found it breeding in a mayhaw pond. In general our luck with this elusive form has been failure. One has to be in their region at certain periods for success.

We have these two notes: (1) Biloxi, Miss., Caribbean Biol. Lab., 1930.

Males, 71, 85, 87, 90, 92 mm. Females, 82, 82, 84, 86, 90, 90, 105 mm. Male 78 mm. from 12 miles south of Vestry near Harrison-Jackson County line, Miss., M. J. Allen. (2) The sizes of these frogs are: 82 mm. male, very rugose, with triangle from arm inward on venter conspicuous; 75 mm. male, vocal sacs beginning to enlarge; 74 mm. male, thumb enlarged, vocal sacs partially developed. Other males 75, 82, 82, 82, 83, 83, 83.5, 85, 85, 90 mm. Females, 82 mm., spent; 85 mm., ripe; 88 mm., not ripe; 89 mm., ripe.

**Authorities' corner:** "Practically all extant specimens of *sevosa* were collected by Morrow J Allen, Stewart Springer, or their associates, in southern Mississippi. Neither they nor any other collectors have secured either *capito* or *areolata,* as now restricted, in this area" (C. J. Goin and M. G. Netting, La., 1940, p. 142).

The observations of Morrow J. Allen (Miss. 1932a, p. 9) are: "This species has been abundantly found throughout the months of October, November and December in the burrows made by *Gopherus polyhemus.* When the temperature rises, these frogs become active and may be seen sitting in the openings of the tunnels down which they disappear at the least indication of danger. In colder weather they are never at the surface and can only be taken by digging to the bottom of the gopher hole, where never more than one is found in company of one or two turtles."

"At the time of publication of our description of *Rana sevosa* (1940, Ann. Carnegie Mus. 28: 137–168) we had not seen any Alabama specimens of this species, but we referred Loding's record (1922, Alabama Mus. Nat. Hist., paper no. 5:20) of *Rana areolata* from Dog River, Mobile County to the synonymy of *sevosa* on grounds of geographic probability. The apparent correctness of this action was confirmed by Mr Loding, who wrote under date of February 12, 1941, as follows:

" 'There can be no doubt that the *Rana sevosa* described is the same thing as the three frogs I took years ago under drift logs on the beach of Mobile Bay just south of the mouth of Dog River, and which I identified as *areolata* from Dickerson's Frog Book; later Hurter agreed that while it differed in some respects from *areolata* as he knew it from Missouri it must be that species. The triangular head, dorsal warts, and color agree entirely with your description and the plate is a dead ringer of these specimens. This frog must be very secretive for I have never seen specimens since, but Viosca identified the sound of what he called *aesopus* from a swamp in the same neighborhood. Two of the specimens in the Chas. Mohr Museum were lost some years after, but if I remember right, Hurter got the third one.'

"Mr. R. W. McFarland, of Fairhope, Alabama, recently sent us, for determination, a gopher frog (Alabama Museum of Herpetology No. 218), which he collected on the evening of June 2, 1941, as it was hopping across a road, 8 miles southeast of Fairhope, Baldwin County, Alabama. This specimen is clearly referable to *sevosa,* and thus constitutes the first record of the species east of Mobile Bay. It is an adult female, 99 mm. in snout-to-vent length, and the largest known *sevosa:* The maximum size of 29 Mississippi females previously reported, was 92.5 mm. It agrees with typical *sevosa* in morphology and in ventral markings, but differs somewhat in dorsal pattern; the ground color is lighter gray, and the dark spots superimposed upon it are somewhat larger and less numerous than in most *sevosa.* This variation probably indicates only that *sevosa* is variable in number and size of dorsal spots, as are other representatives of the *areolata* group. It is possible that the atypical dorsal pattern of this specimen may indicate some *capito* tendencies in the population east of Mobile Bay, and that *sevosa* and *capito* may be found to intergrade somewhere in the area between Baldwin County, Alabama, and Berrien County, Georgia, although no gopher frogs are as yet known from that region.

"Upon the basis of its structure and relationships we postulated (*op. cit.:* 154) that *sevosa* was both batrachophagous and insectivorous. The latter of these suppositions has now been confirmed, for Mr. McFarland's specimen contained the remains of three large beetles; namely, a carabid of the genus *Pasimachus,* and two scarabaeids belonging to the genera *Canthon* and *Ligryus.*

"At the Gainesville meeting of the Society, Mr. Percy Viosca, Jr., exhibited two *sevosa,* an adult collected at Pearl River, St. Tammany Parish, Louisiana, on December 29, 1936, and a juvenile collected 'ten miles out of Picayune, Mississippi' (Pearl River Co.?) in August, 1935. These specimens provide two additional localities for the species" (M. G. Netting and C. J. Goin, Ala., 1942, p. 259).

### Wood Frog, Woods Frog

*Rana sylvatica sylvatica* Le Conte. Plate CXIX; Map 36.

**Range:** From southern Minnesota and Wisconsin south to Arkansas, Tennessee, and northern South Carolina, through Appalachians to Maryland, north to Nova Scotia, thence westward through Quebec to Sault Sainte Marie.

**Habitat:** Wooded areas. Breeds in leaf-laden ponds and transient pools of wooded districts. Hibernates in logs, stumps, under stones in wooded ravines, or beneath boards near woods, never in the water.

**Size:** Adults, 1⅜–3⅓ inches. Males, 34–60 mm. Females, 34–68 mm. One female from Linville, N C. (USNM no 55159), measures 82.5 mm.

**General appearance:** The wood frog is medium in size, either light or reddish brown above, with a darker brown streak or mask on either side of the head and a dark line from the eye to the tip of the snout. There is a light line along the upper jaw continuing to the shoulder. Underneath, it is a glistening white with a dark bar on the upper arm. The legs are long, marked with dark crossbars. It has prominent dorsolateral folds. When caught in the breeding pools, the body seems broad, flat, rather soft, and dark in color, but when caught later in the woods, the form is compact, more slender, and the frog has a very alert appearance Some individuals have inky dashes on the sides and occasionally on the back.

**Color:** *Male.* Girl Scout Camp, Ithaca, N.Y., Aug. 21, 1929. The dorsolateral folds are buff-pink to light vinaceous-cinnamon or vinaceous-cinnamon.

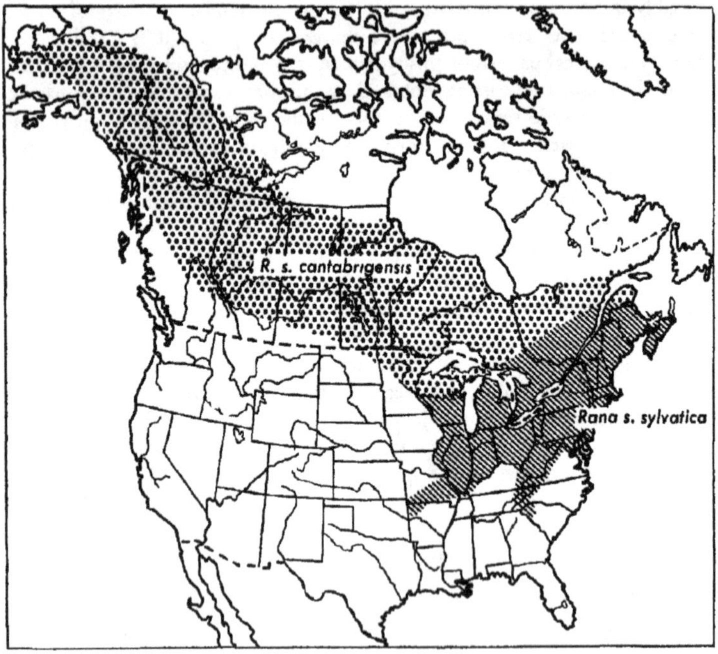


*Map 36*

The upper back may be onion-skin pink or vinaceous-fawn. This becomes on top of head and in front of eye vinaceous-buff. The face mask and the line from eye to nostril are olive-brown. The face mask in the rear is bordered by clove brown. The rear of the femur, tibia, and top of foot are russet-vinaceous or vinaceous-russet. The dark bar on the hind foot and on to the tip of the fifth toe is black. The dorsolateral fold has a few spots of black or clove brown Across the arm insertion on the ventral side is a black or clove brown bar. The lower jaw has bars of army brown or russet-vinaceous or vinaceous-russet. The upper jaw margin is a more or less entire line of the same color with a very prominent line above it, from the nostril to below the rear of the face mask, which is cartridge buff to pale cinnamon-pink. The under parts are white. The rear half of under parts of femur may have some pale orange-yellow or buffy yellow, soon yielding to the rear color of the femur, tibia, and upper side of foot. Upper portion of iris is vinaceous-cinnamon. Band through center eye is black or color of preorbital stripe. Pupil rim citron yellow, broken below.

**Structure:** Head pointed; legs long; webs of hind feet of males very convex at breeding season; hind leg long (0.53–0.62 in length of body while 0.62–0.74 in *R. s. cantabrigensis*). Tibia more than half the length of the body (1.67–1.88 in the length of body).

"Colour above . . . [varies] from light to dark brown, with two interrupted longitudinal lines of black, a dark brown stripe extending from the tip of the nose through the eyes, and covering the auricles" (J. Le Conte, Gen., 1825, p. 282).

See K. P. Schmidt's suggestive article (Gen., 1938d), "A Geographic Variation Gradient in Frogs," for a discussion of wood frogs.

**Voice:** The wood frog's note is very short, a sharp, snappy *clack*. At times 2, 4, or 6 notes are given in rapid succession; and when close at hand, they sound high and grating in character. It can be heard only a short distance from the pond. In chorus, it is more of a rattle than that of any other frogs It has often been likened to the quacking of ducks.

"The note of *sylvatica* peculiar to the mating season I have only seen or known to be given by the males, and only when in the water; it consists of a repeated croak or quack, and may be heard at any time of day or night when the temperature is favorable. The mouth remains closed and each time the sound is uttered the side of the body over each lung is distended into an oblong sac. This clamor has often been mistaken for ducks quacking, but when near enough one finds it more liquid in tone. In 'Early Spring in Massachusetts' p. 228, Thoreau describes the note, 'Wurrk wurrk wurr r k wurk.' During the mating season the males will give voice in confinement, under favorable conditions of water and temperature. In addition to the notes already described, I have heard the young frogs reared in captivity give a single musical 'chip,' not unlike the call note of the song-sparrow. The note was uttered at intervals, in the excitement of capturing flies on which they were fed. Owing to the frog's extreme shyness I have never been able to detect the sound in the field" (M. H. Hinckley, Mass., 1884, p. 86).

**Breeding:** This species breeds from March 19 to April 30 (Ithaca, N.Y.), at a temperature of about 50°F. The egg mass is globose, 2½–4 inches (62–100 mm.) in diameter, the individual eggs appearing larger than in *R. pipiens* and freer, and the outer envelope of each egg keeping its spherical form. The egg is 1/14–1/10 inch (1.8–2.4 mm.), the inner envelope faint, 1/7–1/4 inch (3.6–5.8 mm.), the outer, distinct 1/5–2/5 inch (5.2–9.4 mm.). The egg complement is 2,000–3,000. The deep olive tadpole is medium, 2 inches (49.8 mm.), its tail long, acuminate, and with dorsal crest very high. The tooth ridges are ¾.

After 44 to 85 days, the tadpoles transform from June 8 to Aug. 1, mostly before July 15, at ⅝–¾ inch (16–18 mm.).

"The eggs are deposited near the shore where the frogs first congregate and the temperature of the water is most favorable. They are of a deep chocolate-brown color on the upper surface, and whitish beneath. When first laid they are held closely together by a gelatinous substance, which, after a few hours in the water, begins to increase in size, and gradually changes from a bluish to greenish tint. These masses of eggs are attached to grasses, weed stalks, or branches under water. It is not uncommon to find two or more bunches laid closely together, giving, as soon as the gelatinous portion enlarges, the appearance of one large bunch. This season I found in a swamp within a space of about ten by eighteen inches, sixteen bunches, evidently laid about the same time, attached to the reclining grasses of a submerged tussock. The masses of eggs vary little in size. On counting a bunch of average size the day after it was laid, which measured about four inches long by three wide, I found it numbered 1380 eggs, each of which was enclosed by two transparent, membranous shells. The time in which the eggs develop depends chiefly on the temperature of the water; those laid early in March are rarely hatched before the first week in April here, while those laid at the latter date, in an average season, hatch in from ten to fourteen days. This year, eggs laid March 23, and April 2, hatched at the same time, April 16. In this locality the period of egg-laying is usually over about the twentieth of April" (M. H Hinckley, Mass., 1884, pp. 86–87).

L. W. Wilson (W. Va, 1946, pp. 39–41) found these frogs breeding as early as Feb. 20 in West Virginia.

**Journal notes:** Southeast Slaughter House Pond, Ithaca, N.Y., April 6, 1908. As I approached the pond I heard the greatest chorus of low grating croaks I ever recorded from wood frogs. This was at 11:30 A.M. From the south I crawled upon them (bellywise using elbows to move along slowly). At times used my opera glasses. In this way was able to reach the edge of pond without disturbing croakers. In this pond, there were at least 200 males croaking It resembled a small toad concourse. The same scrabbling and zeal of mating. The water temperature was 58°. Where yesterday there was only one *Rana sylvatica* bunch, there are now 17 bunches of eggs laid April 5–6. When I arose, the frogs all disappeared simultaneously, and to go through the pond one would little realize 200 males were there, to say nothing of the females. One pair was captured. One male taken. Near the sedge with 17 bunches, found another pair. There were about 15 eggs about the vent of the female. Was she laying on the sedge when I rushed into the pond?

Since many of the egg masses are laid near the edges of shallow ponds, many egg masses are left high and dry. A far more serious source of danger is freezing. Most of the bunches are laid from ½ to 2 inches beneath the water's surface. In many instances, long before the hatching period approaches, the tops of these complements appear at the surface because of the reduction of water level by rapid evaporation. In 1907 on April 11 the tops of exposed masses in two ponds were frozen in a crust of ice and spoiled. The following year, on April 17, in another pond, a thin transparent crust formed, which was sufficient to kill the upper part of several bunches. In all cases observed, however, the lower portions not caught within the sheet of ice have progressed nicely.

This silent species is not often recorded in autumn. Our late records are mostly in the month of October, the latest being Oct. 30, 1905. Through midsummer (including the first weeks of September) one occasionally comes upon this form in the woods in much lighter livery than in the early spring. Thereafter, it begins to think of its winter quarters, and by the last of September or the first of October it seeks cover.

**Authorities' corner:**

M. H. Hinckley, Mass., 1884, pp. 87–88.
A. M Banta, Gen., 1914, p. 172.

## Northern Wood Frog, Cambridge Frog

*Rana sylvatica cantabrigensis* Baird. Plates CXX; CXXI; Map 36.

**Range:** Alaska and Mackenzie across northern British Columbia, Alberta, and Saskatchewan to Red River of the North, northern Minnesota, Wisconsin, and Michigan. From Sault Sainte Marie eastward between Hudson Bay and Great Lakes drainages to Saguenay River and to Gaspé Peninsula, and into northeastern Maine. Northern border from Mackenzie and Alaska to Hudson Bay to Labrador.

We are not believers in three forms (*sylvatica, cantabrigensis,* and *latiremis*). Rather are we close to the Patch school, although we have drawn the southern border of *R. s cantabrigensis* considerably south of where Patch ostensibly would place it. He quite likely is right.

The paper by R. H. Howe, Jr., on North American wood frogs (Gen., 1899) upon which we were brought up says that the so-called Cambridge frog type "has been lost to all intents and purposes, although it may be an old, shrunken and unlabeled specimen found with a lot from Saskatchewan, Can., in the collection of the Museum of Comparative Zoology." Howe recognized three forms *R. sylvatica, R. cantabrigensis,* and *R. c. latiremis*. He was helped by S. Garman, G. M. Allen, and F. W. True.

**Habitat:** Terrestrial except at breeding periods, living in woods among dead leaves or moss.

**Size:** Adults, 1⅔–2¼ inches. Males, 36–50 mm. Females, 37–56 mm.

**General appearance:** This is a short-legged northern form of the wood frog, with a dark vitta or mask from the eye over the tympanum, and with a light line along the jaw. Many of these small wood frogs are grayish in color with an

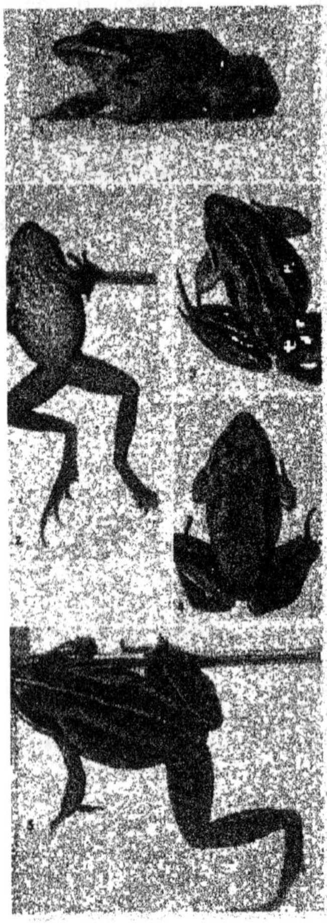

*Plate CXX. Rana sylvatica cantabrigensis* (×⅘). 1,4,5. Females. 2,3 Males.

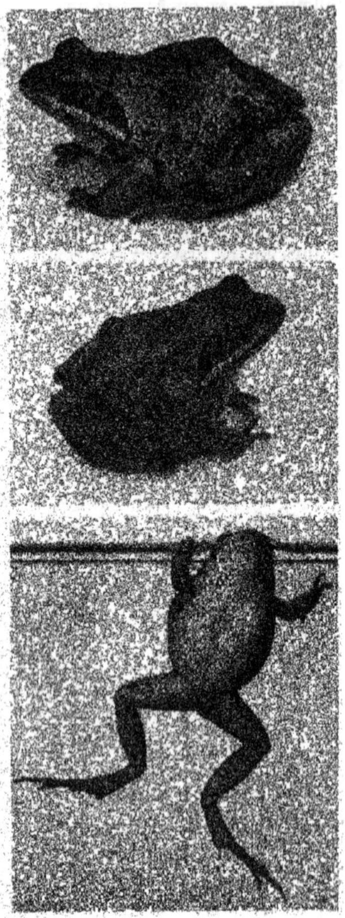

*Plate CXXI. Rana sylvatica cantabrigensis* Adults, from Clinton, B.C. Negatives of National Museum, Canada. Kindness of C. L. Patch.

irregular dark brownish band on the back and a light median dorsal stripe. In some, this stripe extends from snout to vent; in others, to varied distances or is entirely lacking. There is a prominent dark brown stripe on the snout joining the dark mask back of the eye. This is bordered below by a light yellowish or buffy stripe. The costal fold is bronzy. In many frogs there may be dark spots bordering the costal fold below, on the dorsum, or on the sides. Some are almost free of dark spots. The throat and breast are usually speckled.

We are deeply grateful for a beautiful series of wood frog photographs from Clinton, British Columbia. The prints were loaned to us by Clyde S. Patch of the National Museum of Canada, which kindly permits their use in our second plate for this form.

**Color:** The majority of wood frogs from Pembina, N D., seem to possess the light median dorsal stripe, although it is by no means universal. Those of Itasca Park, Bemidji, and points further south are more inclined to brown without the light median stripe; the hind legs average shorter than do those of the typical *R. s. sylvatica;* and the frogs attain breeding characters at a much smaller size than do *R. s. sylvatica.*

From examination of material in the National and other museums, we observed that, sometimes in the same lot, there may be individuals of the same sex, one with middorsal line, one without it. In the same way, the light tibial stripe may be absent or present in the same lot

Pembina, N.D., August, 1930. *Male.* This frog has much the same color as the female, but the median dorsal stripe extends only from snout to point halfway to vent. The costal folds are more evenly bordered below by mummy brown spots. In the same way, the dark grayish olive dorsal band is at times edged with or dotted with mummy brown spots. The eye is much the same as in the female.

*Female* The median stripe extends all the way down the back from tip of snout to vent. It is tilleul buff in color. There is a broader band of darker color on either side of this light stripe that is drab or grayish olive. Between this area and costal fold is a pale smoke gray stripe extending backward from the upper eyelid. The costal fold is avellaneous. The costal fold is interrupted in the rear but continued to the hind leg. Below the costal fold, just back of the arm insertion and above the groin, are two large mummy brown spots. There are a few scattered spots of the same color on the sides. The mask is mummy brown, bordered below by an ivory yellow or seafoam green line, which extends to the snout. The margin of the upper jaw is buffy olive The lower jaw has a series of prominent buffy olive spots interrupted by seafoam green and pale cinnamon-pink of the chin color. This same green color is on entire venter of frog. The breast and throat are spotted with an indefinable gray. The under surfaces of hind legs are russet-vinaceous. The hind legs have 3 or 4 transverse bars on front half of femur; 4 or 5 on tibia, about 3 on tarsus, and 2 or 3 on foot. There is mignonette green or deep chrysolite green in groin.

The eye is the same color as the mask except for the upper pupil rim, which is strontian yellow with an ochraceous-orange band above it. There is a black band on front of brachium near arm insertion.

*Male.* Manitowish, Vitas Co., Wis., Oct. 12, 1929, from Carolyn Weber. Back sayal brown, on sides cacao brown. Lateral fold, fore limbs, and some of hind limbs vinaceous-tawny. Prominent black spot or spots along lower edge of lateral fold at its rear end. Throat, breast, and sides heavily spotted with drab or grayish olive spots. Sides with heavy spots of hair brown or black.

The following frog came from Presque Isle, Maine, from Glenn D. Chamberlain, May 15, 1946, collected by Carroll B. Knox, May 3, at the edge of a grassy field adjoining a cedar swamp that concealed two small ponds where wood frogs were breeding.

The top of head, upper eyelid, back between middorsal stripe and dorsolateral ones are orange-cinnamon or mikado brown to cinnamon-rufous or tawny. This color is also on top of forearm and hand and tops of femur, tibia, and tarsus. The middorsal stripe is chamois, cinnamon-buff, or warm buff, outlined from vertical of shoulder backward by a few black spots. The under edge of costal fold is edged with black and the sides bear numerous prominent black spots. The hind legs bear three broken black bars on tibia; less conspicuous ones on femur and three on tarsus. There is a light stripe on inside edge of tibia, a similar one on outer edge of tarsus, and one on femur which extends halfway to vent like the middorsal one. The mask is mummy brown, as are also the spots on rear of brachium, underside of tarsus, stripe from eye to snout, and bar on insertion of brachium. The stripe on jaw below mask extending to tip of snout is barium yellow. The eye is flecked below with ochraceous-orange and above with salmon-buff. The underside is white except for underside of femur, which is pale ochraceous-salmon. The groin and front and under edge of femur are strontian yellow. There are slight touches of barium yellow on edges of lower jaw and on underside of brachium.

"Specimen No. 1. A female with the dorsal stripe entirely present and with noticeable stripes on the tibia. Throat heavily speckled with black. When this frog was collected, it was mated with a male *Rana sylvatica*. Collected May 3 at a small pond ¾ of a mile north-west of Presque Isle.

"Specimen No. 2. A female, fitting the description of the one above except for the speckled throat which was lacking. This specimen was also mated with a male *Rana sylvatica* at the time of collection and it laid a bunch of eggs in the school laboratory the next night. Collected May 3 at the same pond.

"Specimen No. 3. A male frog with only about half of the dorsal stripe present. The stripes which were present on the tibia of the females are lacking and there are only slight traces of the speckling on the throat. Collected May 4 at the same pond" (letter from Carroll B. Knox, May 13, 1947).

The above is one of several justifications for the practice of Logier and Toner (forthcoming check list) in placing all the wood frogs in *Rana sylvatica* without subdivision into subspecies.

**Structure:** Body stout; legs shorter and stouter than in *Rana sylvatica;* heel reaching tympanum or eye; tibia 3–4 times as long as broad; tibia ½ or less than ½ the length of body; back, flanks, and lower belly smooth; tympanum smooth; thumb of male enlarged; greater webbing in hind foot of males. The most apparent difference between males and females is the presence of greater webbing in the hind foot of males. In some males the web from fifth to fourth toes is almost straight, but in all it is convex between third and fourth. In one specimen, the webs between first and second toes are also convex. In the females, the edge of web is concave. The thumb of the males is enlarged, although not to the same extent as in the green frog and meadow frog groups.

"Above yellowish brown. A dark vitta through the eye, margined below by whitish. Lateral fold of skin light colored, as is also a median dorsal line extending from the snout to the anus. A narrow light line along the posterior faces of the thigh and leg. Tibia half the length of body. General appearance and size of *R. sylvatica*. Hab. Cambridge, Mass. (Collection of Prof. Agassiz.)" (S. F. Baird [1854] 1856, p. 62.)

"*Rana cantabrigensis* has been separated from *R. sylvatica* as a species because of certain color differences and different relative measurements. It is a smaller and more stocky frog than typical *R. sylvatica*. This is shown by a comparison of the length of the tibia with the total length, the diameter of the tibia with its length, and other measurements. Typical *cantabrigensis* is remarkable for a light median dorsal stripe and sometimes a similar light stripe on the thigh and tibia. Schmidt and Necker (Ill., 1933) have revived the name *latiremis* for the short-legged, stocky frogs from the north, while, on a basis of the color characters, they have referred wood frogs from Illinois, Indiana, and Michigan to *R. c. cantabrigensis* despite the body proportions, which are those of *R. sylvatica*. The color characters, as Wright and Wright (1934) have already pointed out, are not constant. We find this inconstancy to be true not only for wood frogs from the north central states, but also for those from the region of Hudson Bay. The Hudson Bay frogs which lack the striping do not differ structurally from the striped ones. Color characters can not, therefore, be considered as absolute criteria for the separation of the two forms.

"Since series of measurements of frogs from various localities in the ranges of *R. sylvatica* and *R. cantabrigensis* demonstrate that there is no sharp break between the two populations, it seems evident that these forms are best regarded as subspecies. For their differentiation, we prefer the comparative structural characters which show some north to south geographic correlation, rather than color characters, which are apparently variable over the entire range of *R. cantabrigensis*. Schmidt (1938) has independently come to a similar realization of north to south variation in body form of these frogs. We prefer to give nomenclatorial recognition only to this variation in body form, which has some geographic correlation, and not to color variations which apparently lack such correlation.

"*R. cantabrigensis* is usually separated from *R. sylvatica* by the length of the tibia, which is less than half the total length in the former and greater than half in the latter. The heel extends beyond the snout in *sylvatica,* but does not reach the snout in *cantabrigensis.* Specimens from Gaspé Peninsula and from the north shore of the St. Lawrence in eastern Quebec are somewhat intermediate in these arbitrary characters, but are here referred to *S. cantabrigensis*" (H. Trapido and R. T. Clausen, Que., 1938, p. 123).

"Wood-frogs are variable in color and markings. For example, some individuals from western Canada, eastern Canada and Georgetown, Maryland have spotted breasts, while others from the same localities have no breast markings. The upper surface is also variable, as mentioned by Wright and Wright (1934) and Trapido and Clausen (1938). It would appear that the feature distinguishing *cantabrigensis* from *sylvatica* is length of hind leg in comparison to body length. The table shows specimens (*Rana sylvatica cantabrigensis*) from Yukon to James Bay and Natashkwan Quebec (north of Anticosti Island), have the hind leg shorter than the body, and specimens (*Rana sylvatica sylvatica*) with the hind leg equal to or longer than the body occur in Nova Scotia, New Brunswick, Gaspé Peninsula, southern Quebec, and southern Ontario westward around Lake Superior. Trapido and Clausen (1938) refer specimens from Gaspé Peninsula, north shore of the St. Lawrence and eastern Quebec to *R. s. cantabrigensis*" (C. L. Patch, Ont., 1939, p. 235).

"Common both in the forest and at the water's edge The 12 specimens collected were intermediate between typical *R. sylvatica sylvatica* and typical *R. sylvatica cantabrigensis* Baird, the heel reaching a point varying from the anterior border of the orbit to the tip of the snout. None show the mid-dorsal pale line commonly found in *cantabrigensis.* Wood-frogs from the Montreal area are similar but have slightly longer legs. Authorities agree in separating the three subspecies of *Rana sylvatica* (*sylvatica, cantabrigensis, latiremis*) mainly on the ratio of leg length to body length. Data given by Patch (1939), Schmidt (1938), Boulenger (1920), and others indicate that when this criterion for separating *sylvatica* from *cantabrigensis* is taken (leg length to heel equal to or greater than body length in *sylvatica*) the territories occupied by the two subspecies are separated by the St. Lawrence River and the Great Lakes. But Preble (1902) and Schmidt (1938) have noted that there is a progressive decrease in the relative length of the legs in the wood frogs with increasing latitude, so that it is possible that the differences between the three supposed subspecies of *R. sylvatica* may be due to the influence of environment upon the expression of similar genetic potentialities, *R. s. sylvatica* of the southeast merging into *cantabrigensis* to the northwest and the latter into *latiremis* in the far north. Until further studies have been made it seems advisable to withhold subspecific rank from these forms of the wood frog" (R. Grant, Que., 1941, pp. 152–153).

"Many seen and some specimens taken in Ashland County, one specimen seen in Bayfield County about 8 miles south of Ashland. Eggs were found in ponds at Camp McLean in April in 1943. The t/b ratio of the single male taken at Ashland is .53; in five females it varies from .54 to .57, mean .55; and in four juveniles from .50 to .53, mean .51" (R. A. J. Edgren, Wis., 1944, p. 497).

"The proportions suggested by Wright and Wright (1942) would place St. Croix Valley material as well as scattered individuals from all over Minnesota as belonging to *R. s. sylvatica*. Patch (1939) has suggested dividing the species into only two forms, *R. sylvatica* and *R. s. cantabrigensis* distinguishing them on the basis of whether the leg, minus the foot, is longer or shorter than the body. On this basis all Minnesota material would be referred to *R. s. cantabrigensis*" (W. J. Breckenridge, Minn., 1944, p. 91).

We have always thought of northern Minnesota wood frogs as within the southern border of *R. s. cantabrigensis*.

**Voice:** The call is a hoarse clacking. It has no external vocal sac and calls from the surface of the water.

"In the early spring it makes the ponds resound with its short, harsh, quacking notes" (E. T. Seton, Man., 1918, p. 82).

**Breeding:** This species breeds from March to July depending upon the portion of range, March–April in Michigan, May–July in Mackenzie region. Like *R. sylvatica* the eggs are in masses attached to vegetation. The tadpoles are like those of *R. sylvatica*. They transform from May 25–Sept. 15 at ¾–⅞ inch (18–22 mm.).

E. A. Preble in "A Biological Investigation of the Athabaska-Mackenzie Region" (1908) said of *Rana cantabrigensis latiremis* Cope: "This is the common frog throughout the region north to Great Bear Lake and the lower Mackenzie. In the course of our journeys we collected a large series. . . . Richardson records frogs, undoubtedly of this species, from Fort Franklin, where he says they croak loudly in the beginning of June. . . .

"In the spring of 1904 H. W. Jones heard the notes of this frog beside the Mackenzie above Fort Simpson on April 22. I heard the first ones in the vicinity of the post April 28, when I took three specimens. At this time the ponds were still frozen to the bottom in most places, but had thawed in the more exposed parts."

Preble has taken ripe females from April 28 to July 19. There are records, however, as late as Aug. 7. Spent females have been collected in May, June, and July.

The tadpoles are very similar to *Rana sylvatica* We have material from Ontario collected by Toner and Logier, but are awaiting tadpoles from the extreme north before stating their characters. The period is probably as variable as for *Rana sylvatica,* depending upon early or late ovulation, and upon northern or southern location in the range.

There are records of transformation from May 25 to Sept. 15. The May and June transformations coming in the same lots with ripe females suggest that possibly some tadpoles winter over, or some individuals transform in the fall and appear in the spring with little increase in size.

"*Rana cantabrigensis latiremis* Cope. Northern Wood Frog. The most abundant and widespread amphibian of the Peace River district. Spawning started at Tupper Creek on May 9th. On this date the low-pitched croaking, of remarkable intensity and carrying quality, was heard at our camp a mile from the spawning pond. The species 'swarms' during breeding activities. We found several aggregations of from twenty to sixty individuals in areas of not more than ten square feet of water surface. There was no apparent reason for the choice of these particular spots on an homogeneous lakeshore, but at these points the egg masses covered the bottom, lying one upon the other in the shallow water, quite unattached to the substratum. After spawning the frogs left the water under the protection of the first rain and spread out over the surrounding country.

"At Swan Lake and in Tupper Creek these frogs were very seldom seen along the margins of the main lake and the lower reaches of the river while at Charlie Lake they were abundant in the grass along Stoddart Creek and adjoining the lake. Possibly the large numbers of pike in the first locality and the absence of this fish from the latter water bodies serve to explain the different behaviour of the frog population" (I. McT. Cowan, B C, 1939, pp. 92–93).

In some of Trapido and Clausen's Quebec material (August, 1937) we have transformation at 14, 16, 16, 16, 17, 17.5, 19, 20, 20 mm. and one possibly past at 24 mm. In some of the Minnesota material (August, 1930) appear transformees at or just past transformation—21.5, 22, 23, 23, 24, 24, 24.5, 25, 26, 26 mm. long. In some tadpoles from Laurentides Park, Quebec, we find tadpoles 47, 48, 50, 50 mm. long, with bodies 19.5, 20, 20, 19 mm. The tooth rows are ¼, ⁴⁄₁, ¾. One had three upper rows on one side and four on other side, and only three rows below with faint indication of the fourth row. This tadpole was not approaching transformation.

**Journal notes:** Aug. 26, 1930, Long Lake, near Brainerd, Minn. Tramped where grass comes to sandy shore. The frogs leaped out onto sand or piles of old sedge stalks. Thought I saw *Pseudacris septentrionalis*. Later concluded it was a little northern wood frog (*R. s. cantabrigensis*). In the piles of wet sedge stalks along shore found several small *Bufo*. By working grass hard found two *Hyla crucifer,* several small *Rana s. catabrigensis,* and three *Rana s. cantabrigensis* half grown. One of the half-grown northern wood frogs has a beautiful median stripe. Just what we want. It also shows that the stripe is not exclusively a mature coloration. The bulk of the frogs which leaped out were *Rana pipiens*. There is a yellow *Utricularia, Potamogeton,* sedges, etc., along the lake shore edge.

Aug. 27, Itasca Lake, Minn. Went to inlet of Itasca Lake in low-lying birch woods. Thought I'd found an ideal *R. s. cantabrigensis* habitat—dwarf cornel and all—but took only one small one. About 6:30 went with Mr. Olin Coan to a spot 7 miles away where a well had been dug among hardwood trees. It was at the edge of a bog some distance back from Lake Mallard. There had once been cranberries here, but with the drilling it was drying up. Here next a roadway and low ridge, we caught several young *R. s. cantabrigensis* and one large one. We caught about 15 small ones, three being with median stripes. One of the 12 without median stripe had a light stripe or area along either lateral fold. We caught one adult—the first yet taken. The vegetation consisted of many hummocks or clumps among which were buck bean, purple cinquefoil, wild calla, grass of parnassus—really a bog situation. Around this area were many alders (*Alnus*).

Aug. 28. Toward Bemidji went through a tamarack woods. Ditches either side of the road, took several adult *R. s. cantabrigensis* and young. In tamarack woods noticed bunchberry, *Dalibardia repens,* mountain maple, buckthorn, *Chiogenes,* and other bog forms. Later along road found spot where road had sunk into the swamp. Here took a good male northern wood frog. It is surely the form of these ditches along these highways of the tamarack region. Only one or two had the median dorsal stripe.

Aug. 30, Pembina, N.D., Red River of the North. Late in the afternoon went down to the river. The river is low with a zone of 6 feet of mud inclined and exposed. This is broken into blocks ½–1½ feet and is clear of vegetation Cracks 1–3 inches wide. Blocks 6–9 inches deep. Then comes a zone of low weeds, dandelions, some small amaranthlike plant, and very low grasses. Then area of dense low willows up bank for 2 rods or more, very dry and baked. Then upland meadow or cultivated field. Here by walking along moist edge of vegetation wood frogs and meadow frogs leaped out onto the mud blocks. Took several median-striped northern wood frogs For the first time found the median stripe predominant. Took adult male with median stripe halfway to vent, a male without median stripe, a female with median stripe from snout to vent, and a female without median stripe. Several young with and several without median stripe. All quite spotted on breast. Dark pattern on back quite conspicuous. This is the finest series of northern wood frogs we have taken or seen alive.

**Authorities' corner:**

G. A. Boulenger, Gen., 1891, p. 453.
R. H. Howe, Jr., Gen., 1899, p. 374.
E. A. Preble, Keewatin, 1902, pp. 133–134.
G. A. Boulenger, Gen., 1920, pp. 457–458.
C. L. Patch, B.C., 1922, p. 77.

## Mexican Frog

*Rana tarahumarae* Boulenger. Plate CXXII; Map 35.

**Range:** "Sierra Tarahumarae, N. W. Mexico about 3000 feet" (Boulenger, Gen., 1919, p. 415); Peña Blanca Spring, Santa Cruz Co., Ariz.; 1 mile above the XSX Ranch, east fork of the Gila River, Socorro Co., N. Mex. (J. M. Linsdale, N. Mex., 1933, p. 222).

"Mesilla Valley, N. M." (Little and Keller, N. Mex, 1937, p. 221). "Rose Creek, Roosevelt Reservoir Area, Ariz. 1940" (E. L. Little, Jr., Ariz., 1940, p. 262).

**Habitat:** "The colony was clustered around a series of pot-holes in a canyon, . . . and no running water could be found in the region. Besides the twenty or so adults seen in these pot-holes, a group of probably half that number was found in an old tumbled-in mine which had filled with water" (B. Campbell, Ariz., 1931, p. 164).

"All [were] in small pools bordered by willows and cottonwoods along Rio Grande near Mesilla Dam" (E. L. Little, Jr., and J G. Keller, N. Mex., 1937, p. 221).

"A series of 22 specimens was taken out of about 100 observed in pools of water shaded by alders and sycamores along Rose Creek, elevation about 5400 feet, at the low border of the pine-fir zone, on August 22, 1936" (E. L. Little, Jr., Ariz., 1940, p. 262).

**Size:** Adults, 2⅓–4½ inches (58–113 mm.). "The resemblance of the adults to *Rana boylii* is very noticeable, but the size is distinctive—the three specimens on hand measuring 81, 91 and 113 mm. (head and body)" (B. Campbell, Ariz., 1931, p. 164).

"One specimen 70 mm. long was caught on August 11, 1934 and 9 smaller ones averaging 50 mm. in length were taken November 4, 1934" (E. L. Little, Jr., and J. G. Keller, N. Mex., 1937, p. 221).

**General appearance:** This is a large dusky-olive frog, with a few black spots on the back and broken crossbands and dark spots on the legs, chunky of body and broad in the head with rounded snout.

**Color:** *Female*. Peña Blanca Spring, Ariz., June 19, 1934. The upper parts are lincoln green or dusky olive-green There are four black or dusky olive-green transverse bars on femur to the knee, four, sometimes broken, bands on tibia and two on tarsus, and several on outer edges of foot and toes; these all distinct. Back is marked with many small, round, black or olivaceous black spots. These also show on top of head to level of eyes. Top of head and face is buffy olive with numerous round spots of isabella color. The tympanum has color of back. On one side is quite a prominent olive-ocher or ecru-olive band from in front of eye to angle of mouth, becoming back of **V** of mouth honey yellow. On other side it is almost absent, being olive-ocher just in front and underneath the ear. Side of body is largely olive-ocher. Under parts white, except for throat which is heavily clouded. Rear of femur has some clay color among the dark spots. Underside of tibia and front of foot with some honey yellow. Iris ring citron yellow. Iris olivaceous black with spottings of light russet-vinaceous.

**Structure:** The male has a swollen thumb with a slight tendency toward a diagonal oblique depression across its middle like *R. boylii* subspecies.

"Vomerine teeth in small groups close together behind the level of the choanae.

"Head broader than long, much depressed; snout rounded, feebly projecting beyond the mouth, as long as the eye; canthus rostralis indistinct; loreal region very oblique, slightly concave; nostril equidistant from the eye and from the tip of the snout; distance between the nostrils equal to the interorbital width, which is equal to or a little less than that of the upper eyelid; tympanum distinct, without or with a few small asperities, ⅔ to ½ the diameter of the eye, once to once and a half its distance from the latter.

"Fingers moderate, the tips feebly swollen, first longer than the second, third longer than the snout; subarticular tubercles large, prominent.

"Hind limb long, the tibio-tarsal articulation reaching the tip of the snout, the heels meeting when the limbs are folded at right angles to the body; tibia 4 to 4½ times as long as broad, 1⅚ to 2 times in length from snout to vent, shorter than the fore limb, as long as or slightly longer or shorter than the foot. Toes with the tips swollen into small disks, the base of which is involved in the very broad web; outer metatarsals separated nearly to the base; subarticular tubercles rather large and prominent; no tarsal fold; inner metatarsal tubercle elliptic, feebly prominent, ⅓ to ⅔ the length of the inner toe; no outer tubercle.

"Skin smooth, or upper parts with small pustules; a feeble, curved glandular fold from the eye to the shoulder" (G. A. Boulenger, 1920, p. 468).

**Breeding:** "The breeding season is evidently after the heavy summer rains which begin in July" (B. Campbell, Ariz.. 1931, p. 164).

The tadpole is quite large, 3½–4 inches (88–101 mm.), and the tooth ridges are ⅔, ¾. On June 21, 1934, with Mr. G. W. Harvey we took many mature tadpoles at Alamo Canyon, Peña Blanca, Ariz., and some at transformation. The tadpoles averaged between 70–88 mm. and transformed at 30–35 mm. B. Campbell found them transforming June 18, 1931.

In general appearance the tadpole is deep green with very close-set small spots on the body. These become much larger and prominent on tail musculature and tail crests. The body is buffy citrine or yellowish olive to dark greenish olive. The spots may be black, brownish olive, or olive. In some tadpoles the ground color is so dark that no dorsal spotting is revealed. In lighter-colored tadpoles the small spots are quite prominent on sides and top of body and top of head; the face usually has less spotting. The belly and throat are white with the lateral spots encroaching on either side. That color may be like the background color or bone brown. There is a wash along the sides of olive lake, as one gets toward the developing hind legs. Occasionally in the tadpole there is a reminder on rear upper edge of the labial of an olive-ocher line suggestive of the yellow line of the jaw of the adult. The tail has much of same background color as the back, being conspicuously spotted with large black or brownish olive spots. The upper and lower tail crests are as conspicuously spotted as the tail musculature, except the basal third or fourth of lower tail crest, which is free of spots. Toward tip of tail strongly washed with Hay's russet, apricot buff, or ochraceous buff in interspaces. The ventral side of musculature on either side of clear portion of under tailcrest is without spots, but the paired veins on either side stand out prominently. The iris is dark olive with citrine yellow rim, dotted with apricot buff and olive lake. Teeth $\frac{5}{3}$. Hind legs, on upper portions, one shade lighter than ground color.

When we first glanced at the tadpoles they did not impress us as of the *R. boylii* group, but somehow (possibly irrelevantly) like the *R. grylio–R. virgatipes–R. heckscheri* group. Of course they are not marked like *R. heckscheri* but the tadpoles are marked as conspicuously in a different way.

**Journal notes:** June 19, 1934, Peña Blanca Spring, Ariz. Last night saw a *Rana tarahumarae* on weight stone of the spring's concrete tank. Saw another near the outlet. Caught one near overflow pipe. Yes, it is Berry Campbell's *R. tarahumarae.*

June 21, 1934 Went at 6 A.M with Mr. G. W. Harvey through Aqua Fria Canyon to Alamo Canyon where he first showed Campbell the frogs. It is a narrow canyon. Did not try tumbled-in mine. In first pool saw a large one and no end of striking spotted tadpoles. Took several with dip net; we could bring it in water right up to the frog, and he would jump into it Could see large ones on bottom and bring net up to them. One large male in the water looked to have bronzy or brick red casts on the legs and elsewhere. Their webbed fourth toe indicates they are quite aquatic. In shallower pools *R. pipiens* adults and tadpoles. Most of the bigger pools had only *R. tarahumarae.* Took a series from tadpole to transformation and secured ten adults. Could have taken many They certainly are *Rana boylii*-like. Are they nearest to *R. b. sierrae* or *R. b. muscosa*? The males have clouded throats. When Campbell was here the water was much higher.

Campbell's largest adult with its uniform color, cloudy throat and venter, fully webbed hind feet (almost straight from tip of fifth toe to fourth toe) looked as much a member of the *Rana heckscheri, R. catesbeiana, R. virgatipes* type as of the *R. boylii* group. Examination of the smaller examples bring out better the *R. boylii* resemblances.

**Authorities' corner:**

B. Campbell, Ariz , 1931, p. 164.
J. M. Linsdale, N. Mex., 1933, p. 222.
E. L. Little, Jr., and J. C. Keller, N. Mex., 1937, p. 221.
E. L. Little, Jr., Ariz , 1940, p. 262.

## Sphagnum Frog, Carpenter Frog, Cope's Frog

*Rana virgatipes* Cope. Plate CXXIII; Map 31.

**Range:** New Jersey to Okefinokee Swamp, Ga. Delaware (Conant). South Carolina (Chamberlain, 1939).

**Habitat:** This species may be in the sphagnum edge of open ponds, in sphagnum mats in deeper parts of ponds or lakes, in wooded edges of some of the coastal rivers, in branch swamps of the Southeast, in wooded inlets or outlets of open ponds, cypress bays, or strands of islands in southern swamps, or at times in the open water-lily prairie.

**Size:** Adults, 1⅝–2⅝ inches. Males, 41–63 mm. Females, 41–66 mm.

**General appearance:** This small frog has a long, narrow head, back brownish with four yellowish or golden-brown, longitudinal stripes. The under parts are yellowish white with dark brown or black spots. The rear of the femur has alternating dark and light stripes. The sides also are marked with blackish spots.

In coloration *R. virgatipes* looks most like *R. grylio*. In adult size it is more like *R. septentrionalis* but smaller, or is possibly like a small *R. catesbeiana*. At Lakehurst Lake it reminds one of the water prairie form, *R. grylio*, in the sphagnum strands and thickets of the Okefinokee it reminds me of the peat-lake species of Canada or beaver-lake thicket form of the Adirondacks, namely, *R septentrionalis*. In egg mass it is most like *R. septentrionalis*, but in individual eggs unlike *R. septentrionalis*, *R. clamitans*, and *R. grylio* because it has no inner jelly envelope. The individual eggs are more like the eggs of the film species *R catesbeiana*, but the jelly is firmer. The tadpole reminds one most of *R. grylio* in coloration, but it is more of the *R clamitans* type. Like all of the *R. clamitans* and *R. catesbeiana* type it winters over as a tadpole. It transforms at a size near that of *R. clamitans* and may have a larger tadpole than that species. Therein it approaches *R. catesbeiana*, *R. grylio*, and *R septentrionalis*.

**Color:** *Male*. Okefinokee Swamp, Ga., July 15, 1921. Back natal brown or chestnut brown with black spots. Natal brown on dorsum of fore and hind legs. Stripe down either side from eye to hind leg hazel or fawn color. Smaller stripe of light or pale ochraceous-salmon from angle of mouth halfway down side. This stripe continues over angle of mouth and on to upper jaw as pale greenish yellow. Throat sulphur yellow with indefinite deep brown spots. Rest of under parts cartridge buff to pale chalcedony yellow with beautifully marked bone brown or almost black spots on venter and sides. Back and forward parts of iris neva green, rim green yellow. Iris proper spotted black and empire yellow.

*Female*. Okefinokee Swamp, Ga., July 22, 1922. Back olive-brown. Back stripe and side stripe buffy brown. Throat sulphur yellow, also inner edge of fore limb. This yellow also from angle of mouth to over arm insertion. Spotting on under parts not so prominent as in male nor so clear-cut, but it is

*Plate CXXII. Rana tarahumarae* ($\times \frac{1}{3}$). 1,3,5,7. Males. 2. Tadpole. 4. Female 6. Transformed frog.

*Plate CXXIII Rana virgatipes* 1,3. Females ($\times \frac{4}{5}$). 2,5. Males ($\times \frac{4}{5}$). 4. Male croaking ($\times \frac{1}{3}$).

conspicuous. Females in general look white on under parts, while males have washes of yellow on throat, on sides, and slightly on other parts. Eye as in the male.

**Structure:** Tympana enlarged in the males, but not so striking as in *Rana grylio, R. catesbeiana, R. clamitans,* or *R. fisheri* (except in very old males), nor is the thumb quite so large proportionally; no dermal folds; two joints of fourth toe free; males with vocal pouch on either side; these being perfectly round vesicles when inflated, and the throat not inflating.

"*Rana virgatipes,* sp. nov.—Vomerine tooth patches between the choanae, and extending posteriorly to their posterior border. Hind legs short, the heel extending from the middle of the tympanum in some to near the eye in other specimens. Webs rather short, two phalanges of the fourth toe free. Praehallux small, but quite prominent; no external solar tubercle. Skin of upper surfaces of body and posterior limb covered with minute tubercles; no longitudinal dermal folds. Males with, females without, external vocal vesicles. Interocular width one-half that of each eyelid. Tympanic disk distinct, equaling the eye in longest diameter. Head (to posterior border of tympanic disk) about one-third length of head and body. End of muzzle oval-acuminate, projecting moderately beyond mouth border. Nostril opening vertically equidistant between border of orbit and end of muzzle. First and second fingers subequal and longer than the fourth.

"Length of head and body, 60 mm ; width of head at posterior borders of tympana, 21.5 mm.; length of fore limb from axilla, 28 mm ; length of hind limb from vent, 76 mm.; length of hind foot, 39 mm.; of tarsus, 15 mm.; of tibia, 23 mm." (E. D. Cope, N.J , 1891, pp. 1017–1018).

**Voice:** The call is like the blow of a hammer, usually repeated three to six times in rapid succession, or like wood choppers.

W. T Davis (1907) said, "Its note sounds much like the blow of a hammer on a board. It is a quickly uttered *Chuck-up, chuck-up* and the frog usually hammers three or four times." Fowler likens it to "the noise produced by wood choppers cutting trees a short distance back in the forest." Harper calls it "a rather loud, incisive, distinctive, clucking-croak." The croak is four to seven notes in rapid succession, all alike. Each part occupies a second or less in duration. Besides this, the species has another call of two notes lower, in pitch. The chorus starts about dusk or sometimes before and gathers strength as midnight approaches At 3 or 4 in the morning they go strong. At daybreak one to several may be heard and these may continue until 8·30 to 9:00 A.M. Once in a while it is heard by day during cloudy weather.

"The clack, clack, clack, clack, clack of this frog could be heard about the Rancocas Creek above New Lisbon, in Burlington county, on May 12th, 1907. It occurred at intervals, interrupting the stillness of a backward spring. Though loud and not often uttered, in comparison with those found at Mare Run, their croaking could be heard at quite a distance. Sometimes the animals must have been quite close, for we could hear them when but a few feet away without seeing them. It may have been that the weather was too cold, for their croaking was always located as coming from among the submerged and overgrown vegetation along the banks. In such places the temperature was considerably higher by midday than elsewhere. When Mr. Hunt visited this place just a year previously, the frogs were very numerous. The weather at that time, however, though about the same time in May, was much warmer. In the evening, during the night, and in the early morning, they were very noisy, but during the day were more or less quiet, only an occasional croak being heard at intervals, or as noted above" (H. W. Fowler, N.J., 1908, p. 194).

**Breeding:** This species breeds from late April to mid-August. The egg mass is a plinth 3–4 inches (75–100 mm.) by 1½ inches (38 mm.), or it may be globular. The complement is small, 200–600 eggs. The black and creamy-white eggs are large and far apart. The egg is 1/16 (1.5–1.8 mm.), the envelope ⅛–¼ inch (3.8–6.9 mm.). The tadpole is large, 3⅝ inches (92 mm.), dark in color with a few black spots, its tail grayish with a row of large spots in the upper crest. The tooth ridges are ⅔ or ⅓. After a tadpole period of 1 year, the tadpoles transform in early spring at 15/16–1¼ inches (23–31 mm.).

This frog passes the winter as a tadpole and transforms in early spring before May 15, a few stragglers going along to mid-July. C. S. Brimley in North Carolina, W. T. Davis and we at Lakehurst, N.J., in May, and T. and F. K. Barbour at Lakehurst in July have taken specimens 33–37 mm. just beyond transformation.

**Journal notes:** On May 22–23, 1924, we heard a few males croaking on the south side of the west point into the lake at Lakehurst, N.J. It was noon and the sun was shining. Here in the sphagnum-heath edge, we caught four adults, two females and two males. As we waded along we would see them sometimes wholly out of water or at the lake's edge. Usually they leaped into the water and hid under the vegetation mat or quickly came up under a water-lily leaf or swam some distance and then poked out their heads. Most of the males were out in the deeper water.

On Black Jack Island, July 28, 1921, we had one of the hardest rains I ever experienced. In the morning, July 29, with a temperature of 73°, I heard a carpenter frog chorus. They were scattered in among the small cypress where there was an undercarpet of *Woodwardia* and a little sphagnum. They seemed to be around the bases of the cypress trees and on the cypress knees. I saw none of them. In the daytime they are shy.

In 1922 we camped the night of June 9 on the north side of Everett's Pond (about 5 or 10 min. ride by auto from the N.C.–S.C. state line), N.C. In the wooded sections where streams flowed into the lake in dense thickets of *Smilax* (briar) and other plants were several *Rana virgatipes* croaking. In 1922 on June 21 in the prairie just north of Lake Sego in the Okefinokee Swamp, heard seven or eight *R. virgatipes*. Found one in a grassy place with water lilies.

On a water-lily pad was the one I captured. They like grassy places near the edge of a head (islet) which is bordered with sphagneous strand. Also seem to like some timbered parts.

June 8, 1929. Needed a male and female *Rana virgatipes* for photographs. Boarded a train at Ridgewood for Lakehurst and without collecting kit or proper clothes. It rained until midafternoon. With every handicap, we waded the edge of the lake with no success. The same result along the west point of landing extending into the lake. The vegetation mats have not reached the surface to any appreciable degree. Mr. Shinn and his boys have a cottage at the base of the point. They informed us that locally the frogs have long been called "carpenter frogs."

Some new visitors beside the lake can hardly sleep at night when the species is in full chorus. Mr. Shinn sent the boys out in a canoe to get some on the mats in mid-lake and along the east side. We went to Emslie's Pond. When we returned the boys had four males, one female, and one recently transformed frog. Several they had thrown back. They approached lily pads and with a scoop of a long-handled dip net caught the frogs. The lily pad and mid-lake habits suggest *Rana septentrionalis* of the Adirondack Mountains and the North.

**Authorities' corner:**

W. T. Davis, N.J., 1907, pp. 49, 50.
H. W. Fowler, N.J., 1908, pp. 191–195.
C. S. Brimley, N.C., 1927a, p. 12.
E. B. Chamberlain, S.C., 1939, p. 34.
R. Conant, Del., 1945, p. 4.

# FAMILY BREVICIPITIDAE

## Genus *HYPOPACHUS* Keferstein

Map 37

The best recent discussion of the genus, that by E. H. Taylor (Tex., 1940c, pp. 515–516), makes any other evaluation useless. Following his remarks on the genus, Taylor describes five new forms, prefacing them with a good appraisal of *Hypopachus cuneus cuneus* (pp. 517–528). Before Taylor three more had been recognized, making at least 13 now known in the genus.

### Taylor's Toad

*Hypopachus cuneus* Cope. Plate CXXIV; Map 37.

**Range:** Southern Texas southward, Tamaulipas, Mexico (Smith-Dunkle).

**Habitat:** Subterranean form. We do not know whether or not it breeds in such transient pools as *Microhyla*. Our own field experience is restricted to tadpoles and transforming frogs.

"Adults driven from under mesquite trees during irrigation were found to have been feeding on termites and minute dipterous insects. Specimens in captivity likewise fed readily upon termites. Even though buried several inches underground, while in captivity, the placing of termites upon the surface readily brought them into the open. In the natural state, however, they do not come into the open except when driven out by excessive rains. They invariably are to be found in burrows, among the trash of pack rats, and in the hollows under trees. As humidity decreases, they apparently seek out deeper and more moist situations, or burrow backwards into the soil, where they are not subjected to rapid drying out" (S. Mulaik and D. Sollberger, Tex., 1938, p. 90).

**Size:** Adults, 1–1⅝ inches. Males, smaller, 25.0–37.5 mm. Females, 29–41 mm.

**General appearance:** The conspicuous mark is the light yellow or orange thread stripe down mid-back. A similar white line extends length of gray-mottled venter with a branch to each arm. Broad constant oblique white mark from eye to angle of mouth, thence to the arm insertion. This line bordered by black spots. An irregular line of black dots may extend from middorsal line near head to upper groin on either side. The sides, groin, rear of femur,

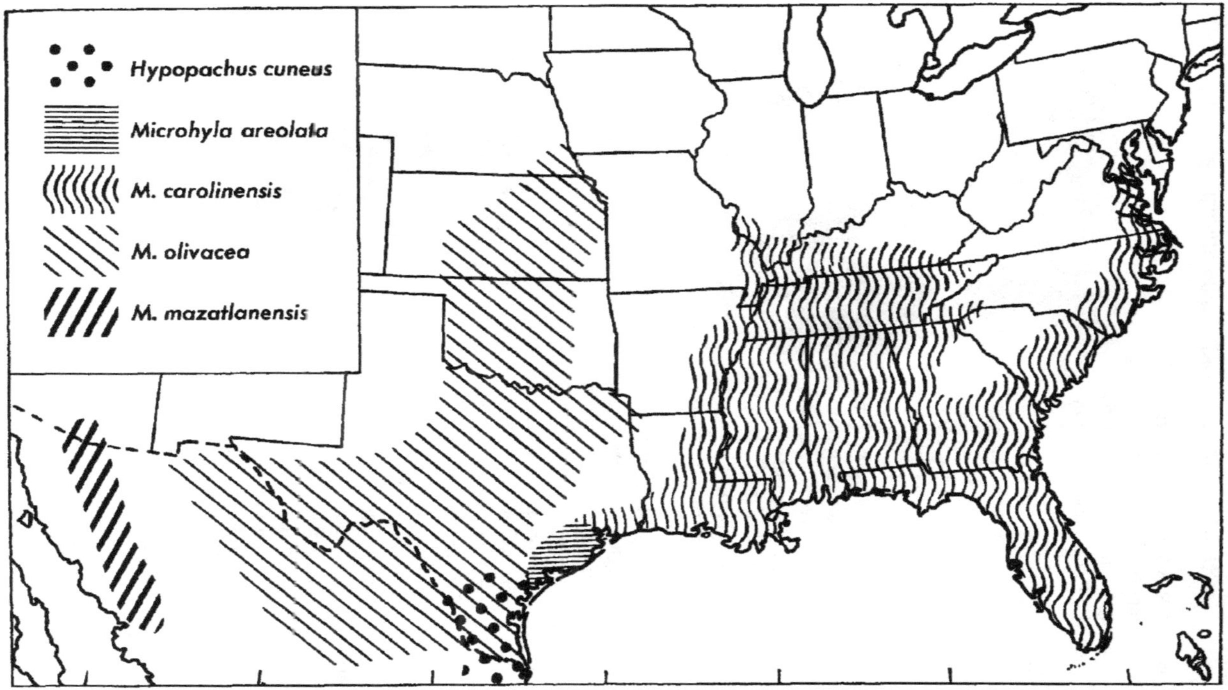
Hypopachus cuneus
Microhyla areolata
M. carolinensis
M. olivacea
M. mazatlanensis

Map 37

and sides of legs are heavily marked with inky spots. There is a cinnamon, fawn, or orange tinge in the groin, on the femur, and on the upper arm.

**Color:** One female and five males, Kingsville, Texas, from C. L. Reed, August, 1931.

*Female.* Upper parts of back brussels brown or snuff brown with same color on top of head, upper surface of tibia, rear edge of tarsus, and hind foot to base of fifth toe. Beginning ¼ inch from transverse head fold, there goes off from dorsal line a row of black dots, which extend irregularly to the upper groin. The light line down middle of back is orange-buff. Just above vent is a very narrow transverse orange-buff line leading to rear angle of knee, then broken, to be resumed later halfway down on rear of tibia and on to the tarsus, where it becomes whitish. From the point where these lines meet the dorsal line, the dorsal extends caudad to vent as a white line. The tip of snout and canthus are olive-buff or deep olive-buff, with a black border from the eye to tip of snout below this color. This snout color breaks the continuous dorsal line. On the ventral side of snout, this median line resumes as a short white line. Broken by the mouth, it continues as a white line down middle of venter to end of belly. On the pectoral region a diagonal white line goes to the axilla and continues on the rear of fore limb to the base of the hand. The dorsal color is bordered back of eye to groin and on either side of hind legs by a more or less broken string of irregular black blotches, which are particularly prominent in the groin and on rear of femur. The black spots of groin, hind legs, and forelegs are

*Plate CXXIV Hypopachus cuneus* 1,3. Female (×1¼). 2. Male (×1¼)

interspersed with rufous, flesh ocher, onion-skin pink, or light vinaceous-cinnamon tinges. The stripe from eye obliquely down to an area intermediate between forearm insertion and mouth is white, irregularly bordered on either side with black spots. That portion between eye and level of mouth is tinged with cinnamon-buff. The sides from white oblique stripe to groin are almost solid smoke gray or light grayish olive. On the belly this becomes pale smoke gray mottled with drab-gray, while the throat becomes more light drab than smoke gray. Iris of one side brazil red or flame scarlet heavily speckled with black. Iris rim is pale green-yellow. Iris of other side green-yellow heavily spotted with black with iris rim sulphur yellow. Pupil round.

*Male.* The dorsal color is Saccardo's olive to citrine-drab with an oblique line of obscure black dots from median line at shoulder to groin. The groin, rear and front of femur, and sides are more heavily spotted with black than in female, although the lateral black band is more prominent in the female. The white mid-ventral, pectoral, brachial, and antebrachial stripes are less prominent than in female. The stripe down back is very prominent, but the dorsofemoral lines are less prominent. The light dorsal lines are buff-yellow or light orange-yellow. The bright color of groin and concealed surfaces of hind legs is not so bright in the five males in hand as in the one female that we have. This bright tinge is cinnamon to tawny-olive. The color of top of forearms and hind limbs of two is isabella color. In one, the light diagonal band is wholly cream-buff; in another, upper end cream-buff and lower end cartridge buff. The mottling of the venter is much heavier and more strongly contrasted than in female. The throat is blackish slate, plumbeous-black, or dark quaker drab. From end of light oblique stripe across to other end is the rear margin of this dark area. Behind this dark area is an area of light grayish vinaceous or vinaceous-buff. The rear of this area is about on a line with front line of arm insertion where fold comes when head is withdrawn. When head is withdrawn, the fold across top of head from rear of one eye to rear of other eye is prominent. In the same way, another fold appears on the venter just in front of arm insertion. Eye is like that of female, one individual having eye with reddish cast, other having green-yellow eyes like the female.

Two other males sent by H. C. Blanchard from Brownsville, Tex., in August, 1931. These two are Saccardo's olive on back. The bright color on legs ranges from orange-cinnamon to ochraceous-salmon. The black along the side of one is a heavy unbroken line, of the other a band of broken spots. The stripe from vent to hind legs is not so prominent as in our toads from Kingsville.

**Structure:** Toes and fingers slender, feet with very short webs; tubercles under joints of toes prominent; inner and outer sole tubercles large, each with a cutting edge; legs short; short fifth toe in contrast to the third toe; skin smooth, loose, and leathery. Fold across head prominent or almost lacking; eyes prominent and beadlike.

"Head small, body large. Limbs short. Muzzle scarcely longer than diameter of eye, projecting a little beyond mouth border. A dermal groove across head at posterior borders of eyelids, and one from below posterior canthus of eye to shoulder. Another across the thorax from the inferior origin of one humerus to the other. Skin everywhere smooth. Tympanic drum invisible. When the anterior limb is extended the end of the fore-arm reaches the end of the muzzle. The distal end of the tarsus reaches the anterior base of the humerus, and the end of the second toe reaches the end of the muzzle when the hind limb is extended. The third finger is rather elongate, and the lengths of the fingers are in order, beginning with the shortest, 1–2–4–3, the second and fourth being equal. In the posterior foot the lengths are, beginning with the shortest, 1–2–5–3–4, the second and fifth being about equal, and the third a good deal shorter than the fourth. The palmar tubercles are not very distinct. At the distal end of the tarsus there are two large subequal sharp-edged tuberosities The edge of the internal is oblique, that of the external transverse. Distinct small tubercles under the articulations of the phalanges. The femur is almost entirely inclosed in the integument of the body.

"The tongue is large, and forms an elongate flat ellipse. The interior nostrils are anterior, and are a little farther apart than the external nostrils. The latter are nearly terminal in position.

| *"Measurements* | *Meters* |
|---|---|
| Length of head and body | .041 |
| Length of head to rictus oris | .006 |
| Length to axilla, axially | .015 |
| Length of fore limb from front | .022 |
| Length of fore foot | .0095 |
| Length of hind limb from anus | .046 |
| Length of hind foot | .023 |
| Width of head at rictus oris | .010 |
| Width of extended femora | 031 |

Rather abundant" (E. D. Cope, Tex, [1888] 1889, p. 396).

**Voice:** "The call of *Hypopachus cuneus* is a bleat about three or four tones lower than that of *Gastrophryne olivacea* but much more resonant. Calls last about two seconds and are seldom repeated at less than 15 second intervals, often at much longer intervals. Whereas *Gastrophryne* prefers to support itself by some vertical object, *Hypopachus* generally floats at the surface, and from these positions the calls are made. After the rains cease *Hypopachus* becomes silent long before *Gastrophryne*" (S. Mulaik and D. Sollberger, Tex., 1938, p. 90).

**Breeding:** This species breeds from March to September in periods of heavy rain. The tadpole is small, 1 1/12–1 1/6 inches (27–30 mm.), wide, and flat, like *Microhyla*. It has a broad middorsal band of grayish olive, with scalloped edges. There are no labial teeth, no horny mandibles, no papillae. The tadpoles transform from April to October, at ⅖–½ inch (10–12 mm.).

June 16, 1930, San Benito, Tex. Went to the breeding pond of five years ago. Heard no frogs and took a very few tadpoles with hind legs well developed. With early heavy rains of 1930 the species probably finished by June 1 or earlier.

The independent shipments of live *Hypopachus cuneus* in August, 1931, by C. L. Reed and H. C. Blanchard might imply an August breeding after heavy rains. The females from Brownsville were gravid.

We secured transformed frogs April 22, 1925, at San Benito, Tex. They probably transform through the summer and fall. Size, 10–12 mm.

On June 15, 1930, at the same pond as in 1925, found transformed frogs (37) which measured from 11.0 to 13.5 mm., one 16.0 mm.; average, 12.3 mm., and two means, 12.0 mm. and 12.5 mm.

Notes on seven of these transformed frogs follow:

1. 16 mm. This was the only one of the 37 that had a light, narrow line down middle of the back. This same specimen had a light median line on the throat, the belly blotched with white spots, and fingers and toes tessellated or alternately light- and dark-banded. Pectoral girdle outlined in front by black line which goes in front of arm to eye.
2. 13 mm. Black border to white face-line-to-be goes almost to meson or breast in front edge of pectoral girdle outline.
3. 12.5 mm. Black line from eye to front of arm to pectoral meson. One of each side meets on meson in a **V**, then continues caudad on meson of breast and upper belly to spiracle.
4. 12 mm. Tail 13 mm., tadpole mouth, white beak. Spiracle scar halfway from pectoral region to hind legs.
5. 12 mm. Tail 15 mm. Tail tip "purplish black." Looks as if area under eye to shoulder is white or gray.
6. 12 mm. Tadpole mouth. Beak made of two trough ridges ending in beak Each corner of mouth with clear white area outlined with black. Basal tail musculature clear white or gray. Tail crests heavily blotched with black; tail tip or caudal half of tail crests and musculature almost all black.
7. 12 mm. Viewed from above back seems to have two white areas bordering dorsal black region, which extends back onto tail, with musculature on either side white.

"The senior author has observed the eggs being laid 24 hours after the beginning of heavy rains from April to October. These hatched in approximately 12 hours and the tadpoles transformed in about 30 days. The gills disappeared within approximately 30 hours after hatching. . . . A complement of approximately 700 eggs was taken from a copulating pair of *Hypopachus cuneus* at Edinburg, Texas, on Sept 24, 1935. They are black and white and measure with the single envelope 1.5 to 2 mm. Without the envelope they measure about 1 mm. The eggs float on the surface of temporary pools in rafts loosely held together. These eggs resemble those of *Gastrophryne* in that the envelope is truncate and they float with this flattened surface upward" (S. Mulaik and D. Sollberger, Tex., 1938, p. 90).

**Journal notes:** April 22, 1925, San Benito, Tex. One mile or more south of town at Highland found on east edge of a fine blue water-lily pond one *Hypopachus* just transformed. It was in the wet edges where *B. valliceps* transformed were hopping about. *Pseudacris* transformed were in water's edge. Found two or three more. Found no mature tads in this pond; must be species is through transforming here. One had a long tail and a dark dorsal band with concave scalloped edges. In a fully transformed one the tail stump looks "bronzy." Under parts speckled whitish and gray.

June 15, 1930, San Benito, Tex. Same pond, opposite Highland School. As I approached heard a note I thought a frog, but soon saw it came from black-necked stilts. Found in the grass *Pseudemys elegans*. Does it feed on young *Bufo valliceps* and *Hypopachus cuneus*? Found a riband snake (*T. s. proximus*). When I stepped on it, it regurgitated three transformed *Hypopachus cuneus*. Then I made it give up more. Had nine or ten of these little narrow-mouthed toads. This started me to working the edge of the pond. Found several transformed ones and a very few tadpoles. A few *Bufo valliceps* transformed. Saw another riband snake. Made it disgorge. One of these narrow mouths had the light line down the middle of the back. Others do not have it. No cover around pond. Snakes collect these tiny toads. I must find them; once in a while see a transformed *H. cuneus* in grass or in a cow-punched hole. There being no apparent cover, in my desperation I resorted to turning over dried cow dung. Under the first one found six little transformed frogs. Under an old shoe found several Also under a clump of matted and cut weeds. No adults anywhere. Waited for darkness. None heard.

**Authorities' corner:**

E. H. Taylor and H. M. Smith, Gen., 1945, p. 604.

## Genus *MICROHYLA* Tschudi

(Formerly *Engystoma* and *Gastrophryne*) Map 37

Recently (April 1, 1946) the Hechts—Max K. and Bessie L. Matalas—reviewed this group. Their conclusions which we more or less anticipated are:

1. *Microhyla carolinensis, M. olivacea,* and *M. mazatlanensis* apparently interbreed and therefore are subspecies.

2. *Microhyla areolata* is an intermediate between *carolinensis* and *olivacea.*

3. The Key West population is 29 per cent *olivacea*-like, 48 per cent Key Westian, and 23 per cent *carolinensis*-like—therefore not described as new.

We follow the old pattern yet awhile until more field work can be done even though we agree with the Hechts that *M. areolata* is supported by very weak evidence. Their paper is a fine paper, conservative on Key West, and they recognize the need of more field work ("apparently interbreed") in their first conclusion.

### Mitchell's Narrow-Mouth Toad

*Microhyla areolata* (Strecker) Map 37.

**Range:** Southeastern Texas. Known only from Victoria and Calhoun counties (J. K. Strecker, Jr., Tex., 1915, p. 47). More recent specimens from Houston to western Louisiana have been so identified by some authors.

**Habitat:** Under logs and similar shelter.

**Size:** Adults, ⅞–1⅕ inches. Males, 24–28 mm. Females, 23–29 mm. (From 5 accessions totaling 14 specimens in USNM.)

**General appearance:** It is like *Microhyla carolinensis,* but the back is areolated, the posterior parts even pustular (in alcohol). One is light gray with darker markings or marblings, which are heaviest in the dorsal region. The limbs are heavily marked. Another is dark, the limbs marked with blotches of brownish olive, a dark line from orbit to orbit along the muzzle, and a V-shaped mark between the orbits. No dark line extends along the sides as in *M. carolinensis* (data from J. K. Strecker, Jr., Tex., 1909a, pp. 118–119).

J. K. Strecker, Jr., refers the following notes of Dr. Stejneger to this form: "No. 35,942 (USNM) Victoria, Texas. J. D. Mitchell, collected in 1897. Skin of back areolated. Four specimens (Victoria High School Collection, No. 52), collected by Mitchell under timber in Spring Marsh, Well Camp, Alligator

Head, Calhoun County, Texas, March 1902, also have the back areolated, the posterior parts even pustular. Metatarsal tubercles rather large and hind feet short."

**Color** (in alcohol): "Above, light gray, with darker markings which are heaviest in the dorsal region. Style of markings might be termed 'marbling' on account of their irregular outlines and light colored interspaces. Limbs heavily marked. Under surfaces, light gray with closely placed lightish spots. Skin of back areolated, even pustular on the posterior part. Pustules very uniformly distributed. . . . Another is 'rather dark' and the back and upper surface of the limbs are marked with closely placed blotches of brownish olive. In the type a dark line extends along the muzzle from orbit to orbit and there is a small dark broad V-shaped mark between the orbits. No dark line along the sides as in *carolinense*" (J. K. Strecker, Jr., Tex., 1909, pp. 118–119).

**Structure:** "Smaller than *E. carolinense*. . . . Body stout, more uniform in width than *E. carolinense*. Muzzle shorter than in examples of *E. carolinense* and *E. texense* of the same size. Canthus rostralis not prominent. Hind limbs short. Hind foot unusually short. Inner sole tubercle large. . . . It resembles *E. texense* in size and in the shortness of the hind limbs but in no other characteristic" (J. K. Strecker, Jr., Tex., 1909a, p. 119).

Because of its restricted distribution and the presence of the other two species in the same place, we wonder if this species has any connection with Duméril and Bibron's *Engystoma rugosum* (Parker, 1934, suggests *M. rugosum* as a possible synonym), which Boulenger reduced to *G. carolinensis*. And is it by any chance the roughened "hotter and more dry season" form which Girard intimates might exist for *G. olivacea?* Relative measurements have been given a prominent place in separating the three species of *Microhyla*. We find these differences slight and append here a table of a few measurements of the three in sizes 20 mm. and 28 mm. taken from specimens in the National Museum, and one set from a frog in the Cornell University collection.

| Name | *carolinensis* | | *olivacea* | | *areolata* | *carolinensis* | | *olivacea* | | *areolata* |
|---|---|---|---|---|---|---|---|---|---|---|
| No. | *37063* | *37064* | *23744* | | *38999* | *57688* | *48893* | *52296* | *1306* | *42334* |
| Sex | M | F | M | F | Type | M | F | F | M | M |
| Length | 20.0 | 20.0 | 20.0 | 20.0 | 20.0 | 28.0 | 28.0 | 28.0 | 28.0 | 28.0 |
| Head to fold | 5.5 | 5.5 | 5.0 | | | 5.0 | 5.0 | 6.0 | 4.8 | 6.5 |
| Head to angle of mouth | 5.0 | 4.5 | 4.0 | 5.0 | 4.0 | 5.0 | 5.5 | 5.0 | 5.0 | 5.5 |
| Snout | 3.0 | 3.0 | 3.0 | 3.5 | 2.5 | 3.5 | 3.5 | 3.5 | 3.2 | 3.5 |
| Fore limb | 11.0 | 9.5 | 11.0 | 9.0 | 10.0 | 12.0 | 11.0 | 11.5 | 11.5 | 12.5 |

| Name | *carolinensis* | | *olivacea* | | *areo-lata* | *carolinensis* | | *olivacea* | | *areo-lata* |
|---|---|---|---|---|---|---|---|---|---|---|
| Hind limb | 26.0 | 23.5 | 23.0 | 22.5 | 21.0 | 29.0 | 29.0 | 31.0 | 27.0 | 26.0 |
| Hind foot with tarsus | 14.5 | 13.0 | 13.0 | 13.5 | 12 0 | 16.0 | 17.0 | 16.5 | 14.0 | 15.5 |

The pustulate or areolate character of *M. areolata* does not impress us as noteworthy when we consider the pustulate character in the posterior region or whole dorsum of some *M. carolinensis* specimens in the Southeast. In fact, we have seen there some individuals more pustular than any specimen of *M. areolata* revealed to date.

Furthermore the types and some of the other specimens were of young or half-grown individuals.

**Voice:** See "Journal notes" and "Authorities' corner."

**Breeding:** See "Journal notes."

**Journal notes:** June 13, 1925. Arrived at Victoria at noon Rained just before we arrived. Ought to be *Microhyla areolata* in railroad ditches. No frog notes.

June 14. Went along railroad right of way. Turned over cover. Saw *Cnemidophorus* but no *M. areolata,* which we consider a debatable form.

April 17, 1934, Spring Creek near Houston, Tex. Prof. A. C. Chandler of Rice Institute took us to the bottom lands where he and Harwood first found the *Microhyla* which they considered *areolata.* We searched under and in logs but did not succeed in catching any. Much rain came last night and on days before, and soon in a shady overflow of the woods we heard a chorus of narrow-mouths. We also heard a few *Rana catesbeiana.* Many *R. clamitans,* a few *Acris,* and no end of *Microhyla* At the base of a tree would be driftwood and a mass of needles. In these masses, usually beneath, we would hear the little chorister, but we could never locate one and we had no net. The note sounds like that of *M. carolinensis.* Later, beside the edge of the overflow in trash Anna found little packets of 5–12 eggs. They were very scattered. Either the pair moved or the masses had broken. These small masses suggest *M. texensis* (*olivacea*) in packet size and inconspicuousness of eggs. There were many of these in the dumbbell form of development.

April 18. Stopped at W. A. Bevans' reptile garden, Houston, Tex. Found he had a *Microhyla* in the snake cage for food. He gave it to me He said they were common around the reptile house and he feeds these frogs to his coral snakes and other snakes.

**Authorities' corner:** "In Texas . . . I heard it in the streets of Houston and San Antonio. In the former city it was abundant, in copula, in the ditches that border some of the streets, in September. The cry is loud for the size of the animal, and is similar to that of *Bufo americanus,* except in being higher pitched and more nasal (in the vulgar sense). The animals are extremely shy, and become silent on the approach of human footsteps; and as only the tip of their nose projects above the water-level they disappear beneath it without leaving a ripple" (E. D. Cope, Gen., 1889, p. 386).

"June 15, 1918. A heavy thunder shower brought out the Narrow-mouthed Toads. Found them abundant and noisy in a large rain pool about ten o'clock at night. The call is harsh and grating, almost a bleat. It is repeated frequently, but not as rapidly as that of the Hylas. The males sit in the water in the thick grass that fringes the pools, and are almost impossible to find with a light, although they are not at all shy. Collected six specimens by treading down the grass into the water and catching them as they swam. They swim slowly with their short legs and webless feet and do not dive when disturbed as frogs and toads do. From this date until the middle of August I heard them frequently, but seldom in any abundance. After a rain could be heard now and then in a pool or roadside ditch before sunset as well as at night" (P. H. Pope, Tex., 1919, p. 94).

Frankly we never have believed very strongly in this form. We have retained it partly because of attachment for its author and partly because this volume should be conservative and suggestive.

### Narrow-Mouth Toad, Narrow-Mouth Frog, Narrow-mouthed Frog, Narrow-mouthed Toad, Nebulous Toad, Toothless Frog

*Microhyla carolinensis* (Holbrook). Plate CXXV; Map 37.

**Range:** Maryland to Florida to Texas. North to Nebraska, Illinois, southern Indiana, and Kentucky.

**Habitat:** Nocturnal, a lover of rain, cover, and moist situations. It is a subterranean species. Hides in or beneath decaying logs or under haycocks or other shelter.

One would never find it during the day if he did not hear it bleat during a rainstorm or cloudy weather, or if he did not unearth it from beneath its cover. They may appear by day during a drenching rain. Sometimes the din is incredible. They apparently do not have far to migrate when the call of the rain comes.

"Found under rocks, boards, and debris; moderately common" (O. C. Van Hyning, Fla., 1933, p. 4).

"Apparently this species has not been recorded from the state. We heard several calling from thick grass in a cattail swamp a few hundred feet from Cove Point lighthouse. The water was slightly brackish but *Hyla cinerea* and *H. versicolor* were present. Several other *Gastrophryne* were collected in a fresh water swamp between Cove Point and Solomon's Island. These were also calling from thick tussocks of grass with usually the rear part of the body submerged. The call seemed to us to resemble that of *Bufo fowleri* but was more explosive, shorter and higher pitched" (G. K. Noble and W. G. Hassler, Md., 1936, p. 63).

"Males were heard calling on May 8 at the time of the earliest spring appearance The call resembles the bleat of a kid. They appear to spend much time in the vicinity of the pools probably waiting favorable conditions of high humidity and heavy rains to begin breeding. On July 3 many were found hidden under pine needles in the vicinity of 'low ground.' After heavy rains in early August they were in the puddles and ponds, calling and clasping in tremendous numbers. They utilized the edges of permanent ponds as well as the most temporary puddles. Active individuals were taken on the night of November 6" (B. B Brandt, N.C., 1936, p. 222).

"Little affected by major habitat boundaries; under rocks, logs, and piles of debris; usually, but not always, in moist soil. Abundance.—Solitary and secretive, but common in all parts of its Florida range. The breeding choruses are sometimes very large. Habits.—Lucifugous; I have never seen one in the open in the daytime. Despite its rotund belly and short legs *Microhyla* is nimble and active when frightened. I have seen several dive into the mouths of crayfish burrows when the logs under which they were hiding were overturned; in loose leaf-mold they rapidly burrow out of sight. In Key West they occur in old lumber and trash piles with the geckos and skinks" (A. F. Carr, Jr., Fla., 1940, p. 68).

**Size:** Adults, ⅘–1⅖ inches. Males, 20–34 mm. Females, 22–36 mm.

**General appearance:** This frog is small, dark-colored, and relatively smooth-skinned. A fold of skin extends across the head just back of the eye. The head is small, the snout pointed. As one child remarked, its head looks like a tiny turtle head. The fold of skin accentuates this. There is no tympanum. The hind limbs are proportionally stout. The fingers and toes are without webs. The back may be black, brown, or gray, the under parts dusky gray or brown speckled or mottled with light.

**Color:** *Male.* Top of head and upper eyelids mineral gray, pale smoke gray, or with yellowish cast. Back dusky with fine bluish white spots or dots. Under parts dusky and bluish white. Throat with fine dots not blotches, therefore looks blacker in male. Pupil circular.

*Female.* Lighter, larger. Practically no spots on pectoral region. None on throat. Throat same color as belly. Practically no rusty spots. Ground color of the dorsum more greenish, i.e, olive-gray, mineral gray, or grayish olive.. Sometimes at breeding season males and females may be alike in color; for instance, on April 24, 1921, several pairs were alike, some reddish, one gray. Most of the pairs, however, were diverse.

**Structure:** Skin usually smooth or finely tuberculate; upper jaw projecting beyond the lower; a fold of skin extending from one arm insertion to eyes, thence to other arm insertion; tongue broad, only caudal border free; inner metatarsal tubercle present.

**Voice:** The call is a bleating *baa* that might well deceive anyone. They usually call from the water with rear parts submerged and fore feet planted on the bank or on some other support such as trash on the water's surface. Occasionally they are out on the bank or in a grassy tussock. The throat swells out like the light bubble of a toad or spadefoot. The call lasts 1.0–2.0 seconds. Though he had never caught the frog and did not know which one it was, Le Conte (Gen., 1856, p. 431) gave a very good description of *Microhyla's* call: "There is in the waters of ponds and ditches a small frog whose note exactly resembles the bleating of a lamb, so truly as to deceive anyone." As a general rule, one must be within 20–60 yards to hear *Microhyla's baaa.* At times the male has one or two other notes not of this order. The frog becomes vertical or bent backward with the effort of calling. On May 21, 1921, F. Harper and I counted the intervals and periods of calls. The record of thirty-seven intervals ranged from 3–58 seconds, at least 20 lasting 30 seconds or more. The actual call in most instances occupied 1.5–2.0 seconds. The intervals of another calling frog were from 1–60 seconds with only one below 10 seconds.

**Breeding:** This species breeds from May 1 to Sept. 1. The egg mass is a surface film, or smaller packets of 10–90 eggs; the complement is 850 eggs. The black and white eggs are firm and distinct like glass marbles, making a fine mosaic; the envelope $\frac{1}{9}$-$\frac{1}{6}$ inch (2.8–4.0 mm.) is a truncated sphere, flat above. The egg is $\frac{1}{25}$–$\frac{1}{20}$ inch (1.0–1.2 mm.). The tadpole is small, 1 inch (26.5 mm.) flat, wide, and elliptical in shape; the snout is truncate; the dorsal and ventral sides of the head are flattened; and the eyes are visible from the ventral aspect. The tail is medium, obtuse or rounded, sometimes with a black tip. The spiracle is median, closely associated with the anus, and its separation apparent as the hind legs appear. There are no teeth, no horny mandibles, no papillae. After a period of 20 to 70 days, the tadpoles transform from mid-June to mid-October, at $\frac{5}{16}$–$\frac{1}{2}$ inch (8.5–12 mm.).

"April 1 to September 3. They breed during or after heavy rains in puddles or the inundated margins of ponds and ditches. The singing males usually conceal themselves in grass or trash at the water's edge. On July 14, 1935, I saw a small chorus in a rain puddle in bare white sand on the banks of Weekiwachee Spring Run; here the males had all wriggled their bodies into the wet sand and were calling with only the snouts protruding; this puddle could not possibly have lasted more than a few hours after the cessation of the rain" (A. F. Carr, Jr., Fla., 1940, p. 68).

"A nocturnal species very hard to find except in the breeding season, which may be exemplified by the fact that although I caught forty the first time I ever found them breeding, I have only seen two or three at Raleigh apart from the breeding season.

"The breeding season is from May to August and these frogs seem to prefer a night when a warm drizzle is falling. The cry is loud, easy to recognize but hard to describe, and the only description I have ever seen that seemed to fit was the one that compared it to an electric buzzer. The tadpoles are dark colored and transform to tiny frogs the same season" (C. S. Brimley, N.C., 1941, p. 3).

**Journal notes:** May 21, 1921, Okefinokee Swamp. Went to old and new hog hole and heard a *Microhyla,* a bleat like a lamb or calf. Came home pell-mell and heard *Microhyla* in ditch in Negro quarters. We started at 8 P.M. Air 70°F. We stopped to find them in ditch. Throat like *Bufo* throat, black in color.

May 22, Okefinokee Swamp, Ga. In the ditches were *Microhyla* eggs. Each egg stands out distinctly. We found the water blackish, trashy, and oily with floating packets of eggs. Some masses were 1 by 1 inch (25 by 25 mm.) in diameter; others 2 by 1 inches (50 by 25 mm.); others 2 by 2 inches (50 by 50 mm.); some round masses, others square. Each jelly envelope abuts that of the next in pentagonal or hexagonal fashion. In proper light a mass of eggs makes a mosaic. Some egg masses along banks in weeds may be 1 foot 10 inches (550 mm.) long and 3 or 4 inches (75 or 100 mm.) wide. One mass in the middle of ditch was among chips and was 4 by 7 inches (100 by 175 mm.). There are few such in mid-pond. We believe they lay large masses along the edges or among the brush, and the wind scatters them.

In a clean pond (20 by 3 feet) along its edges among grass was one packet of eggs, 100–125. They are brown and yellowish, more eggs in a mass than in a film of *Hyla versicolor.* Insects get into the fresh masses.

**Authorities' corner:**

J. E. Holbrook, Gen., 1842, p. 24.
E. Loennberg, Fla., 1895, p. 338
J. A. Ryder, N.C., 1891, p. 838.
R. Barbour, Ky., 1941, p. 262.

## Taylor's Microhyla

*Microhyla mazatlanensis* Taylor. Map 37.

**Range:** "The third race, *Microhyla c. mazatlanensis,* probably is generally distributed in the foothills of northwestern Mexico (Sinaloa and Sonora) barely ranging into southern Arizona; roughly its range may be said to occupy the eastern portion of the Sonoran and Sinaloan biotic provinces, as mapped by Dice. . . . If our belief concerning the identity of the type is correct, *mazatlanensis* is known from the following localities: Mazatlán, Sinaloa (type locality); 10 miles north of Pilares, 5 miles north of Noria, and from Guirocoba in Sonora; and Peña Blanca Springs, in Santa Cruz County, Arizona" (M. K. Hecht and B. L. Matalas, Gen., 1946, pp. 5–6).

**Habitat:** A lowland form; under rocks, in piles of stones, at edge of and in pools, boggy areas, and overflow areas.

**Size:** Adults smaller than *M. olivacea,* 7/8–1 1/5 inches. Males, 22–28 mm. Females, 22–30 mm.

**General appearance:** "Toes without webs, the outer metatarsal tubercle absent. Related to *Microhyla olivacea* but distinctly smaller in size, the head a little narrower, the snout projecting more, a little more flattened above and rounding at the tip; eye smaller proportionally; choanae smaller, largely concealed by the shelf from the maxilla when seen from below; toes and fingers more rounded without a lateral ridge. An indistinct black stripe behind eye to some distance on side. Brown above" (E. H. Taylor, Ariz., 1943, p. 355).

"From the diagnosis given little can be found that warrants the description of a new form although the form appears to be recognizable on the basis of pattern characters. . . . Presumably the series is composed of small adults, and it is for this reason that the head appears to be narrower and the snout longer. It has been observed that smaller specimens of both *carolinensis* and *olivacea* tend to have more acute snouts and relatively narrower heads than adults approaching full maturity and maximum size. Perhaps the most useful data given are those in the color pattern" (M. K. Hecht and B. L. Matalas, Gen., 1946, p. 4).

"Ventrum immaculate or with scattered melanophores. A blotch or spots on the femur and tibia which form a bar or continuous line when the limb is folded; dorsum with dark spots. *Mazatlanensis*" (M. K. Hecht and B. L. Matalas, Gen., 1946, p 7).

**Structure:** (Omitted. See "General Appearance," "Color," and "Authorities' corner.")

**Color:** "Above nearly uniform brown with some black spots tending to form a pattern medially; a broken black line begins behind the eye and continues to some distance on the side; trace of an inguinal spot, which together with a single bar or spot on the femur, the tibia and foot, form a continuous line when the limb is folded. Venter cream, with a very slight peppering of pigment on the chin; sides slightly mottled with lighter and darker; underside of the feet purplish brown, and the hands similarly colored, but to a lesser extent" (E. H. Taylor, 1938, p. 356).

"Taylor's *mazatlanensis* is virtually identical with the specimens from Peña Blanca Springs, Santa Cruz County, Arizona (U. M M. Z. Nos. 75737, 75738, totaling 15 specimens), and those from Sonora 10 miles north of Pilares (U. M. M. Z. No. 78333), Guirocoba (A. M. N. H. Nos. 51244–51247) and Noria (U. M. M. Z. Nos. 72174–72177) which have these same markings . . ." (M. K. Hecht and B. L. Matalas, Gen., 1946, p 4).

**Voice and Breeding:** Our only evidence comes from B. Campbell's first collection of this form and from J. W. Hilton's notes for Bogert and Oliver.

Considering it *Gastrophryne olivacea* (Hallowell) B. Campbell wrote:

"Adults: Peña Blanca Springs, 15, July 11 and 20. Larvae: Peña Blanca Springs, Aug. 2. After one of the first heavy rains of the season at Peña Blanca Springs, we heard strange noises coming from a boggy spot at the overflow of the reservoir. We stalked the source with a flashlight and were surprised to find narrow-mouth toads, which have been reported but once (Sonora, Mexico) west of Texas. They were squatting in the half inch or so of water between the hillocks of grass and calling at approximately twelve-second intervals, mostly in unison. One was heard from a pool down the canyon but was not collected.

"On the evening of July 20, we went up the canyon to investigate a chorus of *Hyla arenicolor* which we had heard for several nights. A number of *Gastrophryne* were found in the pools, croaking. Curiously enough, they seemed to be limited to the pools at the bases of trees; possibly they remained among the roots in the daytime. Several pairs were found in amplexation, both in the pools and just out of the water. The males have round blackish voice pouches which swell, in croaking, to the size of a small marble. Some males were sprawled out on the water after the manner of *Scaphiopus,* but most of them were standing upright in the water next to the roots of trees or near the bases of large rocks, with their heads emerging. These toads were heard in a small pool in a gully near the top of the canyon wall on the evening of July 22. About seven miles east and somewhat north of Patagonia, at a little station named Vaughan, I heard them croaking on the evening of August 23.

"We found no eggs of this species, but collected the larvae from the canyon pools at Peña Blanca Springs" (B Campbell, Ariz., 1933, pp. 6–7).

"Three males and one mature female, with well developed eggs, were collected by Hilton [at Guirocoba, Sonora]. The largest male measures 28.7 mm. in snout-vent length; the female measures 29.6 mm.

"Both Allen ([Ariz.,] 1933, p. 3) and Taylor (1938b, p. 516 [Gen. 1936a]; 1940b, p. 531) have suggested the possibility that Sonoran and Sinaloan specimens represent an unrecognized form. Sufficient material is not at hand to verify this.

"Hilton says in his field notes, 'This is one of the noisiest amphibians in the arroyos but difficult to locate. They sit under dead leaves and twigs along the bank and make a shrill call that sounds more like that of a bird. This frog is called "rana Pajanto" and is not easy to capture' " (C. M. Bogert and J. A. Oliver, Gen., 1945, pp. 343–344).

**Journal notes:** The three times we have been at Peña Blanca Springs have been of short duration and not in a rainy season, and we therefore whôlly missed this form.

**Authorities' corner:** The first record of this form came in Allen's capture of four at Noria, Sonora.

"The specimens are all males, with a head and body length of 25 to 30 mm. Further collecting in Mexico will be necessary before the status of this *Gastrophryne* is clearly understood. It differs distinctly from *G. usta* in coloration and in having only one metatarsal tubercle and from *elegans* in coloration and proportions. The coloration is that of *texensis,* and the proportions are about the same, though slight differences not evident in proportional measurements seem apparent to the eye. The Sonoran specimens will have to stand as *texensis* for the present, in spite of the wide gap in the known range. Found about the same pools as *Pternohyla fodiens*" (M. J. Allen, Ariz. and Sonora, 1933, p. 3).

In July 15, 1936, E. H. Taylor gave us his first record of this species: "*Microhyla olivacea.* . . . I have tentatively associated with this species three small microhylids (Nos. 1236 to 1238) collected about two miles east of Mazatlán under rocks at the base of a small clay hill. When compared with Texas specimens of equal size they differ in having a narrower head, the snout a little more projecting and more flattened. They are somewhat darker and on the side, from snout to groin, the pigment tends to form a darker broken line. There is a slight difference in the shape of the foot and the metatarsal tubercle is slightly more salient. They differ somewhat less from a series of specimens collected by Hobart Smith and David Dunkle at Conefos, Durango. None of the three specimens approaches the maximum size of *olivacea.* A larger, more representative series may demonstrate that these and perchance other characters warrant a specific designation for the coastal form. If properly associated with *olivacea* these records extend the known range some 200 miles farther to the southwest" (E. H. Taylor, Gen., 1936a, p. 516).

In 1943 Taylor in describing this form as a new species remarked: "These small specimens were obtained from a pile of rocks near a small temporary rain pool. In the same pile of stones I obtained the type of *Bufo mazatlanensis.*

"These specimens were originally associated with *Microhyla olivacea,* although the differences were recognized at that time. . . . Since then I have examined large series of this genus from Mexico and have a better idea of the amount of variation that may be expected. This has caused me to regard this lowland form as distinct from *M. olivacea.*

"The species differs from *Microhyla elegans,* in lacking the heavy pigmentation of the ventral surfaces, and the broad lateral stripe which begins on the tip of the snout. *Elegans* has well-developed lateral ridges or fringes on the sides of most of the digits, and the tips are flattened and somewhat widened. The inguinal spot is strongly defined.

"*Microhyla usta* has been reported from Presidio in the southern part of Sinaloa and may also occur in this locality. This may be separated easily by the fact that *usta* has a very large inner metatarsal tubercle, and also a strongly developed outer one, while the described form has a small inner and no outer" (E. H. Taylor, Gen., 1943, p. 357).

## Texas Narrow-Mouth Toad, Texas Toothless Frog, Western Narrow-mouthed Frog

*Microhyla olivacea* (Hallowell). Plate CXXVI; Map 37.

**Range:** Western Missouri and eastern Nebraska and Kansas through Oklahoma and central Texas to Coahuila (Taylor-Smith, Schmidt and Owens), Chihuahua (Taylor and Smith), and Durango (Smith and Dunkle).

**Habitat:** Nocturnal in habit. Seek protection under logs or dead stumps sunken in the ground; in the far southern tip of Texas under fallen trunks of Spanish bayonet. Breed in ponds, roadside ditches, or temporary rain pools.

"Fairly common in damp soil, under pieces of limestone or sandstone. The earliest spring date is April 1" (E. R. Force, Okla., 1930, p. 27).

"As Dice (1923), who found this species on the Rocky-ground community and Hillside forest community of Riley county, indicates, this species of frog in Kansas is far more characteristic of terrestrial than of aquatic habitats. Of the numerous specimens I have collected or seen collected near Manhattan, all were from communities mentioned by Dice. . . . The usual cover is rocks" (H. M. Smith, Kans., 1934, p. 503).

"The Texas narrow-mouthed toad is common and numerous in all parts of Oklahoma. It is especially abundant in the prairies and in the oak-hickory savannah areas" (A. N. Bragg, Okla., 1941a, p. 52).

**Size:** Adults, ⅘–1½ inches. Males, 20–33 mm. Females, 19–38 mm.

**General appearance:** This is a small, usually dark-colored, smooth-skinned "frog-toad" with small, pointed, flattened head. The under parts are uniformly white, the head and body depressed, the limbs slender in appearance. The back has black spots. The eyes are small and beadlike.

**Color:** March 27, 1925, Beeville, Tex. *Male.* Grayish olive, or citrine-drab on back. Spots on back black. Color on side wood brown, buffy brown, or olive-brown. Rear of thighs with some spots of the three browns above. Throat violet-slate, rim of lower jaw like back or sides. Pectoral region and front half of breast whitish with seafoam green cast. Abdominal region and underside of thighs with some pinkish vinaceous cast. Pupil round. Iris spotted, grayish olive or yellow-green with wood brown or other browns. Fingers cartridge buff. Foot like upper parts of limbs but with whitish tips.

*Female.* Throat light. Fingers, forefeet white. Underside of hind feet grayish. Upper parts grayish olive or light grayish olive Irregular lateral stripe of light vinaceous-drab or brownish drab.

**Structure:** Body more depressed than in *M. carolinensis* and head appearing more pointed, because of depressed body; limbs more slender in *M. olivacea.*

Three characters often emphasized prove neither constant nor absolute points of difference between the two species.

1. Girard held that the cleft of the mouth does not extend as far back in

*Plate CXXV. Microhyla carolinensis* ($\times 1$). 1,2,6,7 Females 3. Male croaking Tadpole 5. Egg mass.

*Plate CXXVI. Microhyla olivacea.* 1,7. Females ($\times 1\frac{1}{4}$). 2,6 Males ($\times 1\frac{1}{4}$) 3 Eggs ($\times \frac{2}{3}$). 4,5. Transforming frogs ($\times 1$).

*M. olivacea* as in *M. carolinensis.* Sometimes specimens of exactly the same length have it farther back in *M. olivacea* than in *M. carolinensis.*

2. Miss Dickerson stated that the head to shoulder length is one-third the total length in *M. olivacea* and one-fourth in *M. carolinensis.* Some relative measurements of *M. olivacea* from Beeville, Tex., and *M. carolinensis* from Okefinokee Swamp, Ga., are as follows:

HEAD TO SHOULDER CONTAINED IN LENGTH

| | *M. olivacea* | | *M. carolinensis* | |
|---|---|---|---|---|
| Males | 2.4 | 2.5 | 2.3 | 2.6 |
| Females | 2.8 | 2.95 | 2.5 | 2.9 |

The difference is much less than was stated by Miss Dickerson.

3. Strecker holds that the greatest width of body in *M. olivacea* is usually less than one-half the length. A few random comparisons of the same Beeville and Okefinokee Swamp materials show:

WIDTH IN LENGTH

| | *M. olivacea* | *M. carolinensis* |
|---|---|---|
| Males | 1.65–4.0 av. 2.16 | 1.7–3.1 av. 2.2 |
| Females | 2.46–3.1 av. 2.7 | 1.83–2.3 av. 2.0 |

The female *M. carolinensis* is certainly wider in body than *M. olivacea.* For example: A ripe female of the former 30 mm. long is 16 mm. wide, one of the latter 30 mm. long is 12 mm. wide; or a ripe female of the former 27 mm. long is 14.5 mm. wide, whereas a similar one of the latter is 11 mm. But apparently width into length is not a good distinguishing character for the males. The most constant character that we have found is Girard's depressed form of the body. This is certainly a flattened frog. Our measurements are:

THICKNESS INTO LENGTH

| | *M. olivacea* | *M. carolinensis* |
|---|---|---|
| Males: | 3.0–5.6, av. 3.7 | 2.5–3.35, av. 2.85 |
| Females: | 4.0–4.3, av. 4.2 (in 2 ripe females, 4.2, 4.0) | 2.65–3.4, av. 2.9 (in 2 ripe females, 2.7, 2.65) |

In the field in March, 1925, we wrote that we believed they had more pointed heads than *M. carolinensis* We now find that this impression is due to the more depressed head.

Limbs are more slender in *M. olivacea.*

TIBIA WIDTH INTO LENGTH

| *M. olivacea* | *M. carolinensis* |
|---|---|
| 3–4 | 2½–3 |

The latter has thicker tibia and femur.

"Slate gray upper parts, usually with some indefinitely outlined small black spots concentrated on middorsal region and hind quarters; ventral surfaces white, immaculate, occasionally with very faint reticulations in gular region and on sides; skin smooth.

". . . From *carolinensis, olivacea* differs largely in color, the southeastern species being usually brownish above, sometimes reticulated with darker brown, and at other times with an indistinct broad band on the back extending from the post-orbital region to the hind legs, about as broad as the interorbital distance anteriorly, gradually widening posteriorly until at the groin it covers ¾ of the back. This particular marking is very suggestive of *Gastrophryne elegans* of Mexico and Central America. The ventral surfaces of *carolinensis* are distinctly reticulated with light brown" (H. M. Smith, Kans., 1934, pp. 501–502).

"*Engystoma olivaceum* nob. There is a single specimen of *Engystoma*, one inch one line in length by seven lines in breadth; the anterior extremities 6; the posterior 1 inch 10 lines in length. The general color above is olive, with dark colored spots posteriorly; these are observed in considerable number upon the posterior part of the body and upper parts of the thighs; a few also are seen over the shoulders; the sides are obscurely marbled with brown; under surface yellow, immaculate; a well marked fold passes across the head behind the eyes, extending down alongside the head.

"This specimen is larger than any of those in the collection of the Academy, and the coloration is quite different from that of Dr. Holbrook's figure . . . and the specimens from Georgia in the collection presented by Maj. Le Conte. These are all more or less mottled with brown beneath and brown and chestnut colored above Dimensions· As above, length of tarsus and toes 9 lines; of leg 4 lines; of thigh 4; of arm 2, or forearm 2. Structure: II. *Engystoma texense.*—Head constituting the third of the total length. Snout forming an acute triangle rounded at the summit. Gape of the mouth horizonal, its cleft extending to a perpendicular line drawn posteriorly to the pupil Limbs slender; three carpal callosities, and one metatarsal tubercle. Palm of hands and sole of feet smooth. Skin smooth also Color above light olivaceous brown, with a few black dots posteriorly; beneath uniform whitish.

"This species is allied to *E. carolinense,* and differs from it by a more depressed and flattened head, a more truncated snout, which, as usual, protrudes beyond the lower jaw. The body itself is likewise more depressed, and the limbs assume a slender appearance.

"The head is continuous with the body, and constitutes about the third of their combined length. The cleft of the mouth does not extend as far back as in *E. carolinense,* since it corresponds to a perpendicular line drawn behind the pupil. The longitudinal diameter of the eye is equal to the distance between the orbit and the nostril. The interocular space measured across the anterior rim of the orbits, is greater than the rostral space from the orbits forwards. The symphysis of the lower jaw presents the same structure as in the species just alluded to.

"The skin is perfectly smooth throughout in all the specimens which we have examined; they were collected in April, and are, no doubt, liable to assume a rougher appearance during the hotter and more dry season of the year.

"Gen. Remarks. Duméril and Bibron describe five species of *Engystoma*—two from N. America (*carolinense* and *rugosum*), two from S. America (*ovale* and *microps*), and one from Malabar (*ornatum*). Habitat. According to Dr. Holbrook, *Engystoma carolinense* has never been found north of Charleston, its range extending westward to the lower Mississippi" (E. Hallowell, Gen., 1856a, VIII, 252).

"The ground color of the upper region of the head, body, and limbs, is of a light olivaceous brown tint, anteriorly uniform, posteriorly besprinkled with small black spots or dots especially over the coccyx and thighs. A whitish tint pervades uniformly throughout the inferior regions Specimens of this species were procured in Texas, by Capt. John Pope" (C. Girard, Gen., 1859, 169–170).

**Voice:** This frog begins its call with a pleasant little whistle and then runs into its bleat. It opens something like *whee.*

When we first heard these frogs 8:30–9:30 P.M., we thought their call different from that of our eastern ones, a much lower and less carrying note than that of *M. carolinensis.*

"The breeding call is a high, shrill buzz of some 2–3 seconds duration, and of such slight volume that a single call cannot be heard more than fifty to a hundred feet away. A full chorus sounds like a band saw in operation" (H. M. Smith, Kans., 1934, p. 503). "The note of this species is a shrill long-drawn 'quaw, quaw,' repeated at intervals of several seconds duration. This note is quite different from the loud explosive 'quack' of *Bufo compactilis*" (J. K. Strecker, Jr., Tex., 1926f, p. 12).

**Breeding:** This species breeds from March 15 to September in heavy rain periods. The egg mass is a surface film, the complement 645, the eggs, black and white The egg is 1/30–1/25 inch (0.8–0.9 mm.); the envelope 1/9–1/8 inch (2.8–3.0 mm.), loose and irregular, possibly merging in the film mass. The grayish olive tadpole is small, 15/16 inch (23 mm.), flat and wide, the tail tip black, the eye just visible from the ventral aspect. There are no teeth, no horny mandibles, and no papillae After 30 to 50 days, the tadpoles transform from April 15 to October at 2/5–1/2 inch (10–12 mm.). Amplexation as in *M. carolinensis.*

April 15, Beeville, Tex., cattletank area. *Microhyla* tadpoles are at the surface among brush. Some are mature, some with tails getting short, some with hind legs well developed. They ought to transform in a week or two. In the dirty water, when one comes to rest at the surface, his circular body and black tail tip are very prominent. They seem to have more speckled tails than *M. carolinensis*. They seem to be more or less localized in the brushy areas.

"Little seems to have been recorded of the breeding habits of this frog. Dickerson (1913, p. 169) remarks that they were found breeding during late June in 1905 near Brownsville, Texas. In early September of 1932 I heard large choruses in the same region. The season in Kansas may be extremely late, as a female collected during August of 1926 in Montgomery County near Independence retained large numbers of eggs in her abdomen. Other females collected as late as June 16 near Manhattan contained eggs" (H. M. Smith, Kans., 1934, p. 503).

"Again, hatching in *Microhyla olivacea* is more like *Hyla v. versicolor* than any other so far observed, although these forms belong to different families" (A. N. Bragg, Okla., 1944, p. 234).

**Journal notes:** March 24, 1925, Beeville, Tex. In a roadside ditch, *Microhyla* are at the edge, above the water, croaking. We approached one slowly, didn't see him croak, but the instant the light was put on him, he began to crawl up the bank and through the grass, mouselike, going very fast.

June 15, 1930, Beeville, Tex. Heard only one or two. Took me an hour to locate one of three croaking. Much less volume than in *M. carolinensis*. Not so much bleat in its note. They must be over breeding in this region. Can find no eggs or tadpoles in old places of 5 years ago.

July 10, 1925, Fort Davis Mts., Tex. In a large permanent pool 2 miles south of Fort Davis, we were much surprised to find one lone narrow-mouthed toad tadpole, a mature one. This was the only one we caught. Strecker credits the Texas narrow-mouth to east-central, central, and southern Texas. We know of no record of *Microhyla* this far westward. In the present state of our knowledge of *Microhyla* tadpoles, it looks to be similar to *M. olivacea* larvae which we took at Beeville and San Antonio. This seems to justify Stejneger and Barbour in giving the range of *M. olivacea* as Texas.

July 22, 1942, Toyahvale, Tex. Night trip west on highway. In this pond heard one lone *Microhyla olivacea*. Farther on heard plenty of *Microhyla*. Then I began to question in my mind whether they were all this species. (See *Bufo insidior*, p. 185.)

**Authorities' corner:**

H. W. Parker, Gen., 1934, pp. 1–208.
W. F. Blair, Okla., 1936, p. 115.
G. A. Moore and C. C. Rigney, Okla., 1942, p. 78.

# Bibliography

## I. GENERAL WORKS

1768 Laurenti, J. N. *Specimen Medicum, Exhibens Synopsin Reptilium.* Vienna. Pp. 24–35.

1770–1771 Kalm, P. *Travels into North America. . . .* Tr. by Forster. London. Vol. II (1771), pp. 88–90.

1791 Bartram, W. *Travels through North and South Carolina, Georgia, East and West Florida. . . .* Philadelphia.

1794 Loskiel, G. H. *History of the Mission of the United Brethren among the Indians of North America. . . .* Tr. by La Trobe. London.

1800 Bomare, J. C. Valmont de. *Dictionnaire raisonné universel d'histoire naturelle.* Lyons. Vol. IV, pp. 258–280; Vol. XII, pp. 150–156.

1801–1803 Daudin, F. M. *Histoire naturelle, générale et particulière des reptiles. . . .* Paris, 8 vols.

1801 Sonnini, C. S., and P. A. Latreille. *Histoire naturelle des reptiles. . . .* Paris, 4 vols.

1802 Shaw, G. *General Zoology: Amphibia.* London. Vol. III, pt. 1, pp. 97–176.

1802 Kerr, R., tr. *The Natural History of Oviparous Quadrupeds and Serpents.* Arr. and pub. from the papers and collections of the Count de Buffon by Count de la Lacépède. Edinburgh. Vol. II, pp. 191–320.

1803 Bosc, L. A. G. *Nouveau dictionnaire d'histoire naturelle.* Paris. Vol. VI, pp. 481–492; Vol. X, pp. 126–136.

1810 Oppel, M. *Annales du Museum d'Histoire Naturelle.* Paris. Vol. XVI, pp. 394–407, 409–410, 415–418.

1811 Oppel, M. *Die Ordnungen Familien und Gattungen der Reptilien.* Munich. Pp. 82–86.

1812 Sutcliff, R. *Travels in Some Parts of North America in the Years 1804, 1805 and 1806.* Philadelphia. Pp. 213–214.

1815 Gmelin, C. C. *Gemeinnussige systematische Naturgeschichte für gebildete Leser.* Pt. 3. "Amphibien." Mannheim. Pp. 28–53.

1819 Say, T. *Amer. Jour. Sci. and Arts,* $1^{3}$, 265.

1820 Merrem, B. *Tentamen Systematis Amphibiorum.* Marburg. Pp. 169–183.

1823 Duncan, J. M. *Travels through Part of the United States and Canada in 1818 and 1819.* Glasgow and London. Vol. I, pp. 89–90.

1825 Le Conte, J. *Annals Lyc. Nat. Hist. N.Y.,* **1**, pt. 2, 278–282.

1826 Fitzinger, L. J. *Neue Classification der Reptilien.* Vienna. Pp. 37–40, 63–65.

1826 Harlan, R. *Amer. Jour. Sci. and Arts.,* **10**, 53–65.

1827 Harlan, R. *Jour. Acad. Nat. Sci. Phila.*, 5, pt. 2, 334–345. Read Dec. 12, 1826.

1829 Gravenhorst, J. L. C. *Reptilia Musei Zoologici Vratislaviensis Lipsiae.* Pp. 23–72.

1830 Duméril, A. M. C. *Eléments des sciences naturelles.* Paris. Vol. II, pp. 241–246. (1st ed., 1804.)

1831 Griffith, E., *et al.*, tr. *The Animal Kingdom.* By Baron Cuvier. London. Vol. IX, pp. 388–404, 414–464.

1831 Gray, J. E. *A Synopsis of the Species of Reptilia of the Class Reptilia.* In Griffith, *Animal Kingdom.* Vol. IX, pp. 99–105.

1832 Vigne, G. T. *Six Months in America.* London. Vol. I, p. 140.

1835 Harlan, R. *Medical and Physical Researches.* Philadelphia. Pp. 100–110.

1836–1842 Holbrook, J. E. *North American Herpetology.* 1st ed. 1836–1838. Philadelphia, 3 vols. (There is a scarce fourth volume.) 2d ed., 1842, 5 vols.

1839 Tschudi, J. J. *Classif. der Batrachier. . . . Mem. Soc. Neuch.*, 2, 1–7, 27–55, 70–90.

1839–1841 Wied, Prinz Maximilian zu. *Reise in das innere Nord-America unden Jahren 1832 bis 1834.* Coblenz. Paris, 1840–1843, 3 vols. London, 1843, 1 vol.

1841 Duméril, A. M. C., and G. Bibron. *Erpétologie générale ou histoire naturelle complète: Des reptiles.* Paris, 8 vols. and atlas.

1844–1883 Leunis, J. *Synopsis der drei Naturreiche.* 1st ed., Hanover, 1844. 2d ed., 1853. 3d ed., 1856, "Frogs," pp. 334–339. 4th ed., 1883, "Frogs," pp. 607–622.

1845 Ruppell, E. *Cat. d. Amph. Senck. Museums.* Frankfurt. Vol. III, pp. 313–316.

1849 Baird, S. F. *Jour. Acad. Nat. Sci. Phila*, 2d ser., 1, 281–294.

1852 Baird, S. F., and C. Girard. *Jour. Acad. Nat. Sci. Phila.*, 6 (1852, 1853), 173.

1854–1859 Baird, S. F. (Several papers and reports published by the Academy of Natural Sciences of Philadelphia and by the U.S. Government, Washington, D.C.)

1856 Baird, S. F. *Proc. Acad. Nat. Sci. Phila.* (1854), 7 (1854, 1855), 59–62.

1856 Girard, C. *Proc. Acad. Nat. Sci. Phila.* (1854), 7 (1854, 1855), 86–88.

1856a Hallowell, E. *Proc. Acad. Nat. Sci. Phila.*, 8, 252.

1856 Le Conte, J. Same (1855), 7 (1854, 1855), 423–431.

1857 Chenu, J. C., and M. E. Desmarest. *Encyclopédie d'histoire naturelle: Reptiles et poissons.* Paris. Pp. 155–170.

1858 Gunther, A. *Catalogue Batrachia Salientia.* Brit. Museum, London. Pp. 1–160, 12 pls.

1859 Girard, C. *Proc. Acad. Nat. Sci. Phila.*, 11, 169–170.

1865 Muller, J. W. von. *Reisen in den Vereinigten Staaten, Canada und Mexico.* Leipzig. Vol. III, pp. 615–618.

1870 Dugès, A. *La naturaleza*, 1, 144–145.

1876+ Jordan, D. S. *Manual of the Vertebrates of Northern United States.* Chicago. Pp. 187–190. (1878 ed, pp. 187–190; 1894 ed., pp. 181–186.)

1877 Cope, E. D. *Proc. Amer. Phil. Soc.*, 17, 90.

1879 Brocchi, P. *Bull. Soc. Philomath.* (Paris), 7th ser., 3, 13–24 ff.

1879 Smith, W. H. *Science News*, pp. 263–265.

1880b Cope, E. D. (see *Texas*).

1880–1883 Duncan, P. M. *Cassell's Natural History*. London, Paris, New York, and Melbourne. Vol. IV (1883), pp. 342–368.

1881–1883 Brocchi, P. *Etudes des batraciens de l'Amérique Centrale: Mission scientifique au Mexique et dans l'Amérique Centrale*. Paris.

1882(?) Geikie, J. C. *Adventures in Canada, or Life in the Woods*. Philadelphia. Pp. 216–217.

1882 Boulenger, G. A. *Catalogue Batrachia Salientia*. 2d ed. Brit. Museum, London. Pp. 1–503.

1882–1884 Brehm, A. E. *Thierleben*. . . . Leipzig, 10 vols. (esp. vol. III, part 1).

1885 Cope, E. D. In J. S. Kingsley, *The Standard Natural Hist.*, vol. III. "Batrachia," pp. 317–344.

1885–1902 Gunther, A. *Biologia Centrali-Americana*. London. Pp. 326, pls. 76.

1889 Cope, E. D. *The Batrachia of North America*. (*Bull. U.S. Nat. Mus.*, no. 34, pp. 1–525. Review, *Amer. Naturalist*, **23**, 793–796.)

1890 Herrara, A. L. *La naturaleza* (Mexico City), 2d ser., $1^{7, 8}$, 330, 338, 339.

1891 Boulenger, G. A. *Ann. Mag. Nat. Hist.*, 6th ser., **8**, art. LIII, 453–456.

1891 Dugès, A. *La naturaleza* (Mexico City), 2d ser., 1, 136–141.

1896 Cope, E. D. *Amer. Naturalist*, **30**, 886–902, 1002–1026.

1897 Shufeldt, R. W. *Chapters on the Natural History of the United States*. New York Pp. 100–107, ch. vii.

1897 Bateman, G. C. *The Vivarium*. London. Pp. 294–357.

1899 Howe, R. H., Jr. *Proc. Boston Soc. Nat. Hist.*, $28^{14}$, 369–374.

1899 Mocquard, F. *Bull. Soc. Philomath.* (Paris), 2d ser., $1^{4}$ (1898 and 1899), 154, 158–169. (Collections of M. L. Diguet in Mexico 1896, 1897.)

1899 Test, F. C. *Proc. U.S Nat. Mus.*, **21**, 477–492.

1900 Sampson, L. V. *Amer. Naturalist*, **34**, 687–715.

1901 Gadow, H. *Amphibia and Reptilia. Cambridge Nat. Hist.* Macmillan Co. Vol. VIII, 1–668.

1903 Hay, W. P. *Forest and Stream*, $60^{22}$, 425–426.

1905 Gadow, H. *Proc. Zool. Soc. London*, **2**, 191–244.

1906 Dickerson, M. C. *The Frog Book*. New York. Pp. 1–253. (Review in *Science*, **26**, 546–547.)

1908 Brown, A. E. *Proc. Acad. Nat. Sci. Phila.*, no. 60, pp. 125–126.

1908 Gadow, H. *Through Southern Mexico*. London. Pp. 75–76.

1910 Gadow, H. *Zool. Jahrb.* Jena. Pp. 689–714.

1912 Richardson, C. H., Jr. *Amer. Naturalist*, **46**, 605–611.

1912 Ruthven, A. G. *Zool. Jahrb* (*Syst. Abtheil.*). Vol. XXXII, pt. 4, 310, 311.

1914 Banta, A. M. *Biol. Bull.*, $26^{8}$, 171–183.

1914 Boulenger, E. G. *Reptiles and Batrachians*. London. Pp. 1–278.

1917 Deckert, R. F. *Science*, new ser., $45^{1158}$, 113–114.

1919 Boulenger, G. A. *Ann. Mag. Nat. Hist.*, 9th ser., **3**, 408–416.

1920 Boulenger, G. A. *Proc. Amer. Acad. Arts Sciences*, **55**, 413–480.

1920 Wright, A. H. *U.S. Bur. Fisheries*, doc. no. 888, pp. 1–44.

1922 Noble, G. K. *Bull. Amer. Mus. Nat. Hist.*, **46**, 1–89.

1922 Werner, F. *Brehms Tierleben von Alfred Brehm· Die Lurche und Kriechtiere*. Vol. I, pp. 164–328.

1923 Noble, G. K. *Amer. Mus. Novitates*, no. 70, pp. 1–6.

1923 Pratt, H. S. *A Manual of Land and Fresh Water Vertebrates of the United States*. Philadelphia. Pp. 144–187.

1923–1926 Nieden, F. *Anura: Das Tierreich*. Berlin. Vol. I (1923), pp. i–xxii, 1–584; Vol. II (1926), pp. i–xvi, 1–110.

1924 Wright, A. H., and Wright, A. A. *Amer. Naturalist*, **58**, 375–381.

1924 Haber, V. R. *Jour. Parasit.*, **11**, 1–32.

1926 Berridge, W. S. *Marvels of Reptile Life*. London. Pp. 221–237.

1926 Barbour, T. *Reptiles and Amphibians: Their Habits and Adaptations*. Boston and New York. Pp. 1–125. (Rev. ed., 1934.)

1927 Myers, G. S. *Copeia*, no. 163, pp. 50–53.

1927 Slevin, J. R. *Proc. Calif. Acad. Sci.*, 4th ser., $\mathbf{16}^{9}$, 231–259.

1928 Schmidt, K. P. *Sci. Survey P. R. and V. I., N.Y. Acad. Sci.*, **10**, pt. 1, 1–160.

1929 Jordan, D. S. *Manual of the Vertebrate Animals of the Northeastern United States* Yonkers, N.Y. Pp. 1–446. (1st ed., Chicago, 1876. Pp. 1–342.)

1929 Patch, C. L. *Copeia*, no. 4, p. 235.

1929 Barbour, T., and A. Loveridge. *Bull. Mus. Comp. Zool.*, $\mathbf{69}^{10}$, 205–360.

1929 Wright, A. H. *Proc. U.S. Nat. Mus.*, **74**, art. XI, 1–70.

1930 Metcalf, Z. P. A. *Textbook of Economic Zoology*. Philadelphia. Pp. 1–392.

1930 Netting, M. G. *Papers Mich. Acad. Sci. Arts Letters* (1929), pp. 437–443.

1931 Ahl, E. In *Amphibia (Lurche) Reptilia (Kriechtiere) Tabulae Biologicae*, ed. W. Junk. Berlin. Suppl. 2 (1930), pp. 598–715; Tab. biol. period 1 (1931), pp. 346–384.

1931 Noble, G. K *The Biology of the Amphibia*. New York and London. Pp. 1–577.

1932 Wright, A. H. *Life Histories of the Frogs of Okefinokee Swamp, Georgia*. New York. Pp. 1–497.

1932 Kellogg, R *Bull U.S. Nat. Mus.*, no. 160, pp. 1–224.

1933a Burt, C. E. *Amer Midl. Naturalist*, $\mathbf{14}^{4}$, 350–354.

1933 Villiers, C. G. S. de *Nature*, $\mathbf{131}^{3316}$, 693–694

1934 Villiers, C. G S. de. *Studies . . . Ascaphus truei. . . . Bull. Amer. Mus. Nat. Hist*, **77**, 1–18.

1934 Parker, H. W *A Monograph of the Frogs of the Family Microhylidae*. British Museum, London. Pp. 1–208

1935 Burt, C E *Amer Midl. Naturalist*, $\mathbf{16}^{3}$, 311–319.

1935 Harper, F. Same, $\mathbf{16}^{1}$, 275–310.

1935 Liu, C. C. *Jour. Morphol*, **57**, 131–142. (See Schmidt, K P., *Copeia*, no. 4, 1938, p. 99.)

1935 Wright, A. H. *Proc Nat. Acad. Sci.* (Washington), $\mathbf{21}^{6}$, 340–345.

1936 Bragg, A. N. *Amer. Naturalist*, **70**, 459–466.

1936 Kauffeld, C. F. *Herpetologica*, $\mathbf{1}^{1}$, 11.

1936a Taylor, E. H. *Kans. Univ. Sci. Bull.*, $\mathbf{24}^{20}$, 505–516. (*Bull. Univ. of Kans*, $\mathbf{37}^{14}$, issued Feb. 16, 1938.)

1937 Gaige, H. T., N. Hartweg, and L. C. Stuart. *Occ. Papers Mus. Zool. Univ. Mich.*, no. 357, pp. 1–6.

1937 Gaige, H. T. *Univ. Mich. Studies Sci. Ser.*, **12**, 301–302 (Tamaulipas).

1937 Kauffeld, C. F. *Herpetologica*, $\mathbf{1}^{3}$, 84–86.

1937 Oliver, J. A. *Occ. Papers Mus. Zool. Univ. Mich.*, no. 360, pp. 1–8.

1938 Brownell, L. W. *Amer. Photography*, **32**, 353–354.
1938 Burt, C. E. *Trans. Kans. Acad. Sci.*, **41**, 331–360.
1938 Gloyd, H. K. *Turtox News*, $16^{3}$, 49–53, 66–67.
1938 Schmidt, K. P. *Copeia*, no. 4, p. 199.
1938a Schmidt, K. P. *Field Mus. Nat. Hist.*, Zool. ser., $20^{20}$, 377–382.
1938 Taylor, E. H. *Bull. Univ. of Kans.*, $39^{11}$. (*Kans. Univ. Sci. Bull.*, $25^{17}$, 385–405.)
1939 Bushnell, R. J., E. P. Bushnell, and M. V. Parker *Jour. Tenn. Acad. Sci*, $14^{2}$, 209–215 (Chromosome study.)
1939 DeSola, R. *Reptiles and Amphibians, an Illustrated Natural History*. (Federal Writers' Project, W.P.A, New York City.) Chicago.
1939 Dunn, E. R *Proc. Acad. Nat. Sci. Phila.*, **90**, 153–154.
1939 Eaton, T. H., Jr. *Copeia*, no. 2, pp. 95–97.
1939 Janes, R. G. *Copeia*, no. 3, pp. 134–140.
1939 McClung, C. E. *Tabulae Biologicae*, ed. W. Junk. Vol XVIII, pt. I, 39–47.
1939 Morgan, A. H. *Animals in Winter*. New York. Pp. 331–369.
1939 Tanner, V. M. *Great Basin Naturalist*, $1^{1}$, 3–26.
1940 Babcock, H. L., and I. Hoopes. *New Eng. Naturalist*, no. 6, pp. 7–9.
1940 Cochran, D. M. *Nature Magazine*, **33**, 324.
1940 Cott, H. B. *Adaptive Coloration in Animals*. London. Pp 1–508.
1940 Devoe, A. *Amer. Mercury*, $51^{199}$, 365–368.
1940 Dunn, E. R., and M. T. Dunn. *Copeia*, no. 2, pp. 69–74 (esp. pp. 71–72).
1940 Harper, F. *Amer. Midl. Naturalist*, $23^{3}$, 692–723.
1940 Moore, J. A. *Amer. Naturalist*, **74**, 89–93.
1940 Necker, W. L. *Chicago Acad. Sci.*, Leaflet no 15, pp. 1–2.
1940 Necker, W. L. Same, no. 16, pp. 1, 2.
1940 Rugh, R., and I. Exner. *Proc. Amer. Phil. Soc.*, no. 5, pp. 607–619.
1940 Smith, A. L. *Jour. Biol. Photog. Assoc.*, $9^{1}$, 11–17.
1940 Stejneger, L. *Copeia*, no. 3, pp. 149–151.
1941 Illingworth, J. T *Proc. Ent. Soc* (1940), **11**, 51.
1941 Moore, J. A. *Jour. Exp. Zool*, $86^{3}$, 405–422.
1941 Raney, E. C, and W. M Ingram. *Amer. Midl. Naturalist*, $26^{1}$, 201–206.
1941 Rugh, R. *Proc. Amer. Phil. Soc*, $34^{5}$, 617–631.
1941 Smith, C. C., and A. N. Bragg. *Anat. Rec.*, $81^{4}$, suppl. p. 111.
1941a Smith, C C., and A. N. Bragg. Same, p. 53.
1942g Bragg, A. N. *Anat. Rec.*, $84^{4}$, 507.
1942 *Collier's*, Feb. 7, 1942, pp. 60–61.
1942 DeVoe, A. *Amer. Mercury*, $54^{220}$, 491–495.
1942 Driver, E. C. *Name That Animal . . . Amphibians and Reptiles*. Northampton, Mass. Pp. 293–413.
1942a Moore, J. A. *Biological Symposia*. Lancaster, Pa. Vol. VI, pp. 189–213.
1942 Goin, C. J. *Copeia*, no. 3, pp. 183–184.
1942 Mittleman, M. B., and H. T. Gier. *Proc. N. E. Zool. Club*, **20**, 7–15.
1942 Moore, J. A. *Biol. Bull*, no. 83, pp. 375–388.
1942 Noble, G. K., and L. R. Aronson. *Bull. Amer. Mus. Nat. Hist.*, **80**, art. V, 127–142.

1942 Schmidt, K. P. *Copeia,* no. 1, pp. 53–54.
1943a Blair, A. P. *Amer. Midl. Naturalist,* pp. 615–620.
1943 Lynn, W. G., and J. N. Dent. *Copeia,* no. 4, pp. 234–242.
1943 Preble, E. A. *Nature Magazine,* $36^{3}$, 137–139.
1943 Pusey, H. K. *Quart. Jour. Micros. Sci.,* new ser., $84^{331-335}$, 105–185.
1943 Taylor, E. H. *Bull. Univ. of Kans.,* $29^{8}$, pt. 2, 343–361.
1944 Lynn, W. G. *Copeia,* no. 3, pp. 189, 190.
1944 Marr, J. C. *Amer. Midl. Naturalist,* $32^{2}$, 478–481.
1944 Moore, J. A. *Bull. Amer. Mus. Nat. Hist.,* $82^{8}$, 345–370.
1944 Palmer, E. L. *Nature Magazine,* $37^{6}$, 305–312.
1945 Bogert, C. M., and J. A. Oliver. *Bull. Amer. Mus. Nat. Hist.,* **83**, art. 6, 301–425.
1945 Brownell, L. W. *Amer. Photography,* $39^{4}$, 34–37.
1945 Ely, C. A. *Copeia,* no. 4, p. 256.
1945 Livezey, R. L., and A. H. Wright. *Amer. Midl. Naturalist,* $34^{3}$, 701–706.
1945 Mittleman, M. B *Copeia,* no. 1, pp. 31–37.
1945 Smith, H. M. *Ann. Carnegie Mus.,* **30**, 89–92.
1945 Taylor, E. H., and H. M. Smith. *Proc. U.S. Nat. Mus.,* **95**, 521–623.
1946 Blair, A. P. *Amer. Mus. Novitates,* no. 1327, pp. 1–3.
1946 Bragg, A. N. *Herpetologica,* **3**, pt. 3, 89–97.
1946 Hecht, M. K., and B. L. Matalas. *Amer. Mus. Novitates,* no. 1315, pp. 1–21.
1946 Mittleman, M. B *Herpetologica,* **3**, pt. 2, 57–60.
1946 Netting, M. G , and C. J. Goin. *Copeia,* no 2, p. 107.
1947a Blair, A. P. *Amer. Mus. Novitates,* no. 1344, April 15, 1947.
1947b Blair, A. P. *Copeia,* 1947, p 67.
1947 Harper, F *Proc. Biol. Soc. Wash.,* **60**, 39–40.
1947 Livezey, R. L., and A. H. Wright. *Amer. Midl. Naturalist,* $37^{1}$, 177–222.
1947 Richmond, N D (see *Virginia*).
1947 Smith, H. M. *Herpetologica,* **4**, 7–13.

## II. GENERAL CHECK LISTS OR CATALOGUES

1875b Cope, E. D. *Bull. U.S. Nat. Mus.,* no. 1, pp. 1–10, 29–32, 55–104.
1882 Yarrow, H. C. Same, no. 24, pp. 1–249.
1883 Davis, N. S., Jr., and F. L Rice. *Bull. Ill. State Lab Nat. Hist.,* no. 5, pp. 15–25.
1884 Garman, S. *Bull. Essex Inst.,* $16^{1-3}$, 41–46.
1886 Cope, E. D. *Proc. Amer. Phil. Soc.,* **23**, 514–521.
1917–1943 Stejneger, L., and T. Barbour. *A Check List of North American Amphibians and Reptiles.* Cambridge. 1st ed., 1917. 2d ed., 1923. 3d ed., 1933. 4th ed., 1939. 5th ed , 1943.
1945 Taylor, E. H., and H. M. Smith. *Proc. U.S. Nat. Mus.,* **95**, 521–623
1947 Logier, E. B. S , and G. C. Toner. *Check List of Canadian Amphibians and Reptiles.* Manuscript
1948 Smith, H. M., and E. H. Taylor. *An Annotated Checklist and Key to the Amphibia of Mexico. Bull. U.S. Nat. Mus.,* no. 194, pp. 1–118.

## III. STATE AND PROVINCE LISTS

### CANADA

**Alberta**

1908 Preble, E. A. *North Amer. Fauna,* no. 27, pp. 501–502. Washington, D.C
1929 Patch, C. L. *Can. Field Naturalist,* **43**, 137–138.
1931 Harper, F. Same, **45**, 68–70.
1931 Logier, E. B. S. Same, **45**, 90.
1939 Patch, C. L (see *Ontario*).
1942 Logier, E. B. S., and G. C. Toner. *Can. Field Naturalist,* **56**, 15–16.
1942 Slater, J. R. (see *Washington*).
1943 Slipp, J. W., and G C. Carl (see *British Columbia*)
1946 Williams, M. Y. *Can. Field Naturalist,* **6**, 47–49.

**Athabaska**

1908 Preble, E. A. *North American Fauna,* no. 27, pp. 501–502.
1931 Harper, F. (see *Alberta*).

**British Columbia**

1894 Cope, E. D. *Proc. Acad. Nat. Sci. Phila* (1893), **45**, 181–184.
1898 Fannin, J. *A Preliminary Catalogue of the Collections of Natural History and Ethnology in the Provincial Museum.* Victoria, B.C P. 58.
1922 Patch, C. L. *Copeia,* 1922, pp. 76–78.
1926 Hardy, G. A. *Rept. Prov. Mus. Nat. Hist B.C.* (1925), pp. C23–C24.
1927 Hardy, G A. Same (1926), pp. C25, C39.
1928 Hardy, G. A. Same (1927), pp. E17, 19.
1928 Slevin, J. R *Occ. Papers Calif. Acad. Sciences,* **16**, 1–152.
1929 Newcome, W. A. *Rept. Prov Mus. Nat. Hist. B.C.* (1928), p F24.
1929 Patch, C. L. (see *Alberta*).
1930 Newcome, W. A. *Rept. Prov. Mus. Nat. Hist. B.C.* (1929), p. F22.
1931 Newcome, W. A. Same (1930), p. C19.
1932 Logier, E. B. S. *Trans. Roy. Can. Inst.,* **18**, pt. 2, 311–315, 319–324.
1933 Williams, M Y. *Rept. Prov. Mus. Nat. Hist. B.C.* (1932), p. C22.
1935 Ricker, W. E., and E. B. S. Logier. *Copeia,* no. 1, p. 46.
1937 Cowan, I. McT. *Rept. Prov. Mus. Nat. Hist. B.C.* (1936), pp. 16–25.
1937 Cowan, I. McT. Same (1936), pp. K18–20.
1939 Cowan, I. McT. *Occ Papers Brit. Col. Prov. Mus.,* **1**, 92–93.
1939 Patch, C. L. (see *Ontario*).
1941 Cowan I. McT. *Copeia,* no. 1, p. 48.
1942 Carl, G. C. *Copeia,* no. 2, p. 129.
1942 Slater, J R. (see *Washington*).
1943 Carl, G. C. *Brit. Col. Prov. Mus. Handbook,* no. 2, pp. 1–62.
1943 Slipp, J. W., and G. C. Carl. *Copeia,* no. 2, p. 127.
1945 Carl, G. C., and I. McT. Cowan. *Copeia,* no. 1, p. 43.
1945a Carl, G. C., and I. McT. Cowan. *Copeia,* no. 1, pp. 52–53.

**Keewatin**

1902 Preble, E. A. *North Amer. Fauna,* no. 22, pp. 133–134.

**Labrador**

1925 Speck, F. G. *Copeia,* no. 138, pp. 5–6.

1938 Schmidt, K. P. (see *Illinois*).

**Mackenzie**

1908 Preble, E. A. (see *Alberta*).
1931 Harper, F. (see *Alberta*).

**Manitoba**

1918 Seton, E. T. *Ottawa Naturalist*, **32**, 82–83.
1921 O'Donoghue, C. H. *Can. Field Naturalist*, **35**, 121–128, 129–131.
1938 Schmidt, K. P. (see *Illinois*).
1939 Patch, C. L. (see *Ontario*).

**Newfoundland**

1926 Johansen, Frits. *Can Field Naturalist*, **40**, 16.

**New Brunswick**

1873 Adams, A. L. *Field and Forest Rambles*. London. Pp. 197, 303.
1898 Cox, P. *Nat. Hist. Soc. New Bruns.*, **4**, pt. 1, art. VI, 64–66.
1899a Cox, P *Trans. Roy. Soc. Can.*, 2d ser **5**, sec. IV, art V, 152, 153.
1899b Cox, P. *Ottawa Naturalist*, **13**, 194, 195.
1939 Patch, C. L. (see *Ontario*).

**Nova Scotia**

1865 Jones, J. M. *Proc and Trans. Nova Scotia Inst. Sci.*, **1** (not **2**), pt. III (1864–1865) Halifax. Pp. 116, 122–126.
1896 Mackay, A. H. *Proc. and Trans. Nova Scotia Inst. Sci*, **9** (2d ser., **2**), xli–xliii.
1899a Cox, P. (see *New Brunswick*).
1899b Cox, P. (see *New Brunswick*).
1939 Patch, C L. (see *Ontario*).

**Ontario**

1850 Agassiz, A. *Lake Superior*. Boston. Pp. 378–380, 382.
1858 Agassiz, A. In *The Handbook of Toronto*. Toronto, 1878. Pp. 60–61.
1878 Yarrow, H. C., and H. W. Henshaw (see *Nevada*).
1881 Garnier, J. H. *The Canadian Sportsman and Naturalist*, $1^5$, 38, 39.
1883 Garnier, J H. *Amer. Naturalist*, $\mathbf{17}^9$, 945–954.
1884 Small, H. B., and William P. Lett. *Ottawa Field-Naturalist's Club Trans., No. 5*, $\mathbf{2}^{I}$, 148, 149.
1885 Small, H. B., and William P. Lett Same, *No. 6*, $\mathbf{2}^{II}$, 282–283.
1899 Meek, S. E. *Field Columbian Mus*, Pub. no 41, $1^{17}$, 331.
1902 Meek, S. E, and H. W. Clark. Same, no. 67, Zool. ser., $3^7$, 139–140.
1908 Nash, C. W. In *Vertebrates of Ontario* (Dept. of Education, Toronto). "Batrachians and Reptiles of Ontario," pp. 7–10.
1913 Piersol, M. H. In J. H. Faull, *Natural History of the Toronto Region*. Toronto. Ch. xviii, "Amphibia," pp 244–248.
1915 Wright, A. H. *Copeia*, no. 23, pp. 46–48.
1918 Patch, C. L. *Ottawa Naturalist*, $\mathbf{32}^8$, 53.
1920 Williams, M. Y. *Can. Field Naturalist*, $\mathbf{34}^7$, 125.
1920 Wright, A. H., and S. E. R. Simpson. Same, **34**, 144.
1922 Klugh, A. B. *Copeia*, no. 103, pp. 14, 15.
1925 Logier, E. B S. *Can. Field Naturalist*, $\mathbf{39}^6$, 91–93.
1928 Brown, J. R. *Can. Field Naturalist*, **42**, 126.

1928 Dymond, J. R. *Cont. Roy. Ont. Mus. Zool.*, no. 2 (reprinted from *Univ. Toronto, Studies Biol.*, ser. 32), pp 35–36.
1928 Logier, E. B. S. *Trans. Roy. Can. Inst.*, $16^{2}$, 279–291.
1931 Coventry, A. F. *Can. Field Naturalist*, 45, 109.
1931 Logier, E. B. S. *Trans. Roy. Can. Inst.*, 18, pt. 1, no 39, 229–232.
1932 Gaige, H. T. *Copeia*, no. 3, p. 134.
1934 Logier, E. B. S. In R. D. Black's "Chas. Fothergill's Notes . . . ," *Trans. Roy. Can. Inst.*, $20^{43}$, pt. I, 160.
1937 Logier, E. B. S. *Handb 3, Roy. Ont. Mus. Zool.*, pp. 1–16 (see *School*, Apr., May, June, 1937).
1938 Toner, G. C, and W. E. Edwards. *Can. Field Naturalist*, 52, 40–43 (esp. 42).
1939 Patch, C. L. *Copeia*, no. 4, p. 235.
1940 Allin, A. E. *Trans. Roy. Can. Inst.*, 23, 83–118.
1941 Logier, E. B. S., *Univ. Toronto, Studies Biol. Ser*, 48, pp. 93–101.
1941 Toner, G. C, and N. de St. Remy. *Copeia*, no. 1, pp 10–13.
1942 Logier, E. B S *Cont Roy. Ont Mus. Zool.*, no. 21, pp. 154–163.
1942 Williams, M. Y. *Can. Field Naturalist*, 56, no. 6, p 93.
1943 Logier, E. B S, and G C. Toner. *Can. Field Naturalist*, 57, 104–105.

**Prince Edward Island**

1899a Cox, P. (see *New Brunswick*).
1899b Cox, P. (see *New Brunswick*).

**Quebec**

1874–1875 Provancher, L. *Nat. Can.*, 6, 273–278; 7, 10–20, 42–46, 65–73, 289–298, 321–330, 353–370.
1899a Cox, P. (see *New Brunswick*).
1899b Cox, P. (see *New Brunswick*).
1937 Ball, S. C. *Copeia*, no. 4, p 230.
1938 Trapido, H., and R. T. Clausen. *Copeia*, no. 3, pp. 117–125
1939 Moore, J., and B. Moore. *Copeia*, no. 2, p 104
1939 Patch, C. L. (see *Ontario*).
1941 Grant, R, *Copeia*, no. 3, pp. 151–153.
1941 Vladykov, V. D., *Can. Field Naturalist*, $55^{6}$, pp. 83–84.

**Saskatchewan**

1908 Preble, E A. (see *Alberta*).
1931 Harper, F. (see *Alberta*).
1938 Schmidt, K. P. (see *Illinois*).
1939 Patch, C. L. (see *Ontario*).
1946 Williams, M. Y. (see *Alberta*).

## THE UNITED STATES

**Alabama**

1910 Brimley, C. S. *Proc. Biol. Soc. Wash.*, 23, 9–18.
1920 Dunn, E. R. Same, 33, 129–130, 135–136.
1922 Löding, H. P. *Geol. Survey, Alabama* (*Mus. Paper no. 5, Ala Mus. Nat. Hist. Univ. Ala.*), pp. 16–21.

1924 Holt, E. G. *Copeia,* no. 135, p. 95.
1931 Haltom, W. L. *Mus. Papers, Ala. Mus. Nat. Hist.,* 11, 1–145.
1938 Viosca, P. *Copeia,* no. 4, p. 201.
1939 Cahn, A. R. (see *Tennessee*).
1940 Penn, G. H., Jr. *Jour. Tenn. Acad. Sci.,* $15^3$, 353–355.
1942 Netting, M. G., and C. J. Goin. *Copeia,* no. 4, p. 259.

**Alaska**

1898 Van Denburgh, J. *Proc. Amer. Phil. Soc.,* 37, 139
1920 Dice, L. R. *Occ. Papers Mus. Zool. Univ. Mich.,* no 85, pp. 7, 11.
1925 Williams, M. Y. *Can. Field Naturalist,* $39^4$, 72.
1928 Slevin, J. R. (see *British Columbia*).

**Arizona**

1859 Baird, S. F. (see *Texas*).
1866 Cope, E. D. *Proc. Acad. Nat. Sci. Phila.,* 18, 301, 310–314.
1875 Coues, E. In G M. Wheeler's *Rept Geog. Explor. West of 100th Meridian.* Washington. Vol. V, "Zoology," 627–631.
1875 Yarrow, H. C. In same, pp. 520–529.
1890 Stejneger, L. *North American Fauna,* no. 3, art. 5, pp. 116–118.
1907 Mearns, E. A. *Bull. U.S. Nat. Mus.,* no. 56, pt. 1, pp. 110, 113, 117, 118, 125.
1907 Ruthven, A. G. *Bull. Amer. Mus. Nat. Hist.,* 23, art. XXIII, 483–511.
1913 Van Denburgh, J., and J R. Slevin, *Proc. Calif. Acad. Sci.,* 4th ser., 3, 391–396.
1917 Engelhardt, G. P. *Copeia,* no. 39, pp. 5–7.
1924 Cowles, R. A. *Jour. Ent. & Zool. Pomona Coll.,* $16^4$, 107–110.
1925 Engelhardt, G. P. *Copeia,* no. 149, pp. 91–92.
1925 Ortenburger, A. I. *Univ. of Okla. Bull*, new ser, no 322, Univ. Studies no 21 (*Proc Okla. Acad. Sci.,* 4 [1924], art. VI, 19–20.)
1926–1927 Ortenburger, A. I., and R. D. Ortenburger. *Univ. Okla. Bull.,* new ser., no. 348, Jan. 1, 1927. (*Proc. Okla. Acad. Sci.,* 6 [1926], pt. I, 101–103.)
1928 Slevin, J. R. (see *British Columbia*).
1929b Burt, C. E., and M. D. Burt. *Jour. Wash. Acad. Sci.,* 19, 428–434.
1930 Musgrove, M. E., and D. M. Cochran. *Copeia,* no. 173 (Oct.–Dec. 1929), Jan. 16, 1930, pp. 97–99.
1931 Campbell, B. *Copeia,* no. 4, p. 164.
1931 Slevin, J. R. *Copeia,* no. 3, pp. 140, 141.
1932 Hobbs, K. L. *Copeia,* no. 2, p. 104.
1932a Kellogg, R. *Bull. U.S. Nat. Mus.,* no. 160, pp. 1–224.
1932 King, F. W. *Copeia,* no. 2, p. 99.
1932 King, F. W. *Copeia,* no. 4, pp. 175–176.
1932 Klauber, L. M. (see *California*).
1932a Klauber, L. M. *Zool. Soc. San Diego,* Bull. 9, p. 77.
1932 MacCoy, C. U. *Occ. Papers Boston Soc. Nat. Hist.,* 8, 11–15.
1933 Allen, M. J. *Occ. Papers Mus. Zool. Univ. Mich.,* no. 259, pp. 1–3.
1933a Burt, C. E. (see *General Works*).
1933 Campbell, B. *Copeia,* no. 2, p. 100.
1934 Campbell, B. *Occ. Papers Mus. Zool. Univ. Mich.,* no. 280, pp. 1–9.

1934 McKee, E. D., and C. M. Bogert. *Copeia,* no. 4, p. 178.
1935a Eaton, T. H., Jr. *Copeia,* no. 3, p. 150.
1935b Eaton, T. H., Jr. *Rainbow Bridge Monument Exped. (1933),* Bull. 3 (June, 1935), pp. 3–8.
1935 Quaintance, C. W. *Copeia,* no. 4, pp. 183, 184.
1935 Wood, W. F. (see *Utah*).
1936 Cowles, R. B., and C. M. Bogert (see *Nevada*).
1937 Dunn, E. R. *Proc. Acad. Nat. Sci. Phila.* (1936), **88**, 471–472.
1937 Gloyd, H. K. *Bull. Chicago Acad. Sci.,* **5**, 79–136.
1938 Dodge, N. N. *Grand Canyon Nat. Hist Assoc., Nat. Hist. Bull.,* no. 9, pp. 1–15.
1938 Taylor, E. H. *Bull. Univ. of Kan.,* $39^{11}$, 421–445.
1939 Chapel, W. L. *Copeia,* no. 4, pp. 225–227.
1940a Gloyd, H. K. *Chicago Naturalist,* $3^{3-4}$, 67–78, 111–124 (esp. 111–113).
1940 Little, E. L., Jr. *Copeia,* no. 4, pp. 260–265.
1940 Tanner, W. W. (see *Utah*).
1940 Taylor, E. H., and I. W. Knobloch. *Proc. Biol Soc. Wash.,* **53** (Oct. 7, 1941), 125.
1943 Arnold, L. W. *Copeia,* no. 2, p 128.
1943 Kauffeld, C. K. *Amer. Midl. Naturalist,* $29^{2}$, 342–359.

**Arkansas**

1859 Baird, S. F. *Explor. and Surveys R. R. Route from Miss. River to Pacific Ocean 1853–56,* **10,** Zool. Rept. no. 4, 37–45.
1890 Cope, E. D. *Amer. Naturalist,* **24,** 1204, 1205.
1903 Stone, W. *Proc. Acad. Nat. Sci. Phila ,* **55,** 538, 539.
1908 Strecker, J. K., Jr. *Proc. Biol Soc. Wash.,* **21,** 88.
1909 Hurter, J., and J. K. Strecker, Jr. *Trans. Acad. Sci. St. Louis,* **18,** 11–15, 18–20.
1924 Strecker, J. K., Jr. *Baylor Univ. Bull ,* $27^{3}$, pt. 3, 29–34.
1929a Burt, C. E., and M. D. Burt. *Amer. Mus. Novitates,* no. 381, pp. 1–7.
1929a Ortenburger, A. I. (see *Oklahoma*).
1933 Black, J. D. *Copeia,* no. 2, pp. 100, 101.
1934 Perkins, R. M., and M. J. R. Lentz. *Copeia,* no. 3, pp. 140, 189.
1935 Burt, C. E. (see *General Works*).
1935 Taylor, E. H. *Kans. Univ. Sci. Bull.,* **22,** 207–218.
1938 Black, J. D. *Copeia,* no. 1, pp. 48, 49.

**California**

1853 Baird, S. F., and C. Girard. *Proc. Acad. Nat Sci. Phila.,* **6,** 301, 302.
1854 Baird, S. F., and C. Girard (see *Oregon*).
1854 Hallowell, E., *Proc. Acad. Nat. Sci. Phila.,* **6,** 238.
1856 Hallowell, E. Same, **7** (1854, 1855), 96, 97.
1859 Baird, S. F. (see *Texas*).
1859 Borland, J. N. *Proc. Boston Soc. Nat. Hist.* (1856–1859), **6,** 193. Read May 6, 1857.
1859 Hallowell, E. *Explor. and Surveys Pacific R. R. Route 1853–56* Washington, D.C. Vol. X, Sen. Ex. Doc. no. 78, 33d Congress, 2d session, no. 1, 1–23.

1868 Cronise, T. F. *The Natural Wealth of California*. San Francisco. Pp. 485, 486.
1869 Cooper, J. G. *Proc. Calif. Acad. Sci.*, **4** (1868–1872). San Francisco, 1873. Pp. 61–81. Read Sept. 6, 1869.
1869 Cooper, J. G. *Amer. Naturalist*, $3^{9}$, 478, 480.
1875 Yarrow, H. C. (see *Arizona*).
1878 Yarrow, H. C., and H. W. Henshaw (see *Nevada*).
1879 Lockington, W. N. *Amer. Naturalist*, $13^{12}$, 780.
1883 Stearns, R. E. C. Same, $17^{9}$, 982.
1884 Cope, E. D. *Proc. Acad. Nat. Sci. Phila.* (1883), **35**, 15, 25–27, 32–35.
1888 Cope, E. D. *Proc. U S. Nat. Mus.* (1887), **10**, 241.
1893 Stejneger, L. *North Amer. Fauna*, no. 7, pp. 159–161, 219–228.
1907 Mearns, E. A. *Bull. U S. Nat. Mus.*, no. 56, pt. I, pp. 133, 138.
1912 Hurter, J. *First Ann Rept. Laguna Marine Lab.* Claremont. P 67.
1912a Van Denburgh, J. *Proc. Calif. Acad. Sci.*, 4th ser., **3** (Jan. 17, 1912), 149.
1916 Camp, C. L. *Univ. Calif. Pub. Zool.*, $12^{17}$, 503–512.
1916a Camp, C. L. Same, $17^{6}$, 59–62.
1916 Ruthling, P. D. R. *Lorquinia* (Los Angeles), $1^{1}$, 6.
1917b Camp, C. L *Univ. Calif. Pub. Zool.*, $17^{9}$, 115–125.
1917 Grinnell, J., and C. L. Camp. Same, $17^{10}$, 127–208.
1919 Hall, H. M., and J. Grinnell. *Proc. Calif. Acad. Sci.*, 4th ser., $9^{2}$, 47, 54.
1922 Van Winkle, K. (see *Washington*).
1923 Marimon, S. *Jour. Ent. & Zool.*, $15^{2}$, 27–31.
1923 Storer, T I. *Copeia*, no. 114, p. 8.
1924 Dunn, E. R. *Copeia*, no. 133, pp. 75, 76.
1924 Grinnell, J., and T. I. Storer. *Animal Life in the Yosemite*. San Francisco. Pp. 1–741.
1925 Storer, T. I. *Univ. Calif. Pub. Zool.*, **27**, pp. 1–342.
1928 Klauber, L. M. *Zool. Soc. San Diego*, Bull. no. 4, pp. 1–8. 2d ed., 1930, no. 5.
1928 Slevin, J. R. (see *British Columbia*).
1929 Burt, C. E., and M. D. Burt (see *Arizona*).
1929 Klauber, L. M. *Copeia*, no. 170, pp. 15, 16.
1930 Bogert, C. M. *Bull. S. Calif. Acad. Sci.*, $29^{1}$, 1–14.
1930 Grinnell, J., J. Dixon, and J. M. Linsdale. *Univ. Calif. Pub. Zool*, **35**, 139–144.
1930 Klauber, L. M. (see *Klauber, 1928*, above).
1930 Myers, G. S. *Copeia*, **43**, 61–64.
1930 Myers, G. S. *Proc. Biol Soc. Wash.*, pp. 73–77.
1930 Pickwell, G., E. Smith, and K. Hazeltine. *Western Nature Study* (San Jose), $1^{1}$, 1–55.
1931 Myers, G. S. *Copeia*, no. 2, pp. 56, 57.
1932 Brues, C. T. (see *Nevada*).
1932 Klauber, L. M. *Copeia*, no. 3, pp. 118–120.
1934 Eckert, J. E. *Copeia*, no. 2, pp. 92–93.
1934a Klauber, L. M. *Zool. Soc. San Diego*, Bull. no. 11, pp. 1–28.
1936 Fitch, H. S. (see *Oregon*).

1936 Grinnell, J., and J. M. Linsdale. *Carnegie Inst. Pub.*, no. 481, pp. 35–39.
1936 Miller, L., and A. H. Miller. *Copeia*, no. 3, p. 176.
1937 Shapovalov, L. *Copeia*, no. 4, p. 234.
1938 Schmidt, K. P. (see *Illinois*).
1939 Wood, W. F. *Copeia*, p. 110.
1940 Smith, R. E. *Science*, $92^{2391}$, 379, 380.
1940 Stanton, K. *Copeia*, no. 2, p. 136.
1941 Twitty, V. C. *Copeia*, no. 1, pp. 1–3.
1941 Vestal, E. H. *Copeia*, no. 3, pp. 183.
1942 Myers, G. S. *Occ. Papers Mus. Zool.*, Stanford Univ, no. 460, pp. 1–13 (plus 8 pp. of plates).
1942 von Bloecker, J. C., Jr. *Bull. So. Calif. Acad. Sci.*, 41, pt. 1, 29–38.
1943 Marr, J. C. *Copeia*, no. 1, p. 56.
1943 Myers, G. S. *Copeia*, no. 2, pp. 125–126.
1943 Wiggins, I. L. *Copeia*, no. 3, p. 197.
1944 Miller, R. R. *Copeia*, no. 2, p. 123.
1944 Myers, G. S. *Copeia*, no. 1, p. 58.
1945 Pequegnat, W. E. *Jour. Ent. & Zool.*, $37^1$, 1–7.

**Colorado**

1875 Yarrow, H. C. (see *Arizona*).
1910 Cockerell, T. D. A. *Univ. Colo Studies*, $8^2$, 130.
1911 Cary, M. *North Amer. Fauna*, no. 33, pp. 24, 27, 40.
1913–1915 Ellis, M. M., and J. Henderson. *Univ. Colo. Studies*, $10^2$, pt. 1, 39–61; $11^4$, pt. 2, 253–259.
1924 Gilmore, R. J. *Colo Coll. Pub*, gen. ser. no. 129, science ser, $13^1$, 1–12.
1926 Burnett, W. L. *Occ. Papers Mus. Zool. and Ent.* (Colo. State Coll.), $1^1$, 1–4.
1927 Cockerell, T. D. A. *Zoology of Colorado*. Boulder. Pp. 112–113.
1929b Burt, C. E., and M. D. Burt (see *Arizona*).
1933a Burt, C. E. (see *General Works*).
1935 Burt, C. E. (see *General Works*).

**Connecticut**

1844 Linsley, J. H. *Amer. Jour. Sci and Arts*, 1st ser., 46, 47–48.
1898 Sherwood, W. L. *Proc. Linn. Soc. N.Y. 1897–1898*, no. 10, pp. 9–24.
1904 Henshaw, S. *Fauna of New England. Occ. Papers Boston Soc. Nat. Hist.*, $7^2$, 10–17.
1905 Ditmars, R. L. *Amer. Mus. Jour.*, $5^4$, 184–206.
1921 Babcock, H. L. *Copeia*, no. 90, p. 8.
1926 Babcock, H. L. *Bull. Boston Soc. Nat. Hist.*, no. 38, pp. 11–14.
1932 Babbitt, L. H. Same, no. 63, pp. 25–26.
1933 Ball, S. C. *Anat Rec* 47 (4 Suppl.), p. 101.
1936 Ball, S. C. *Trans. Conn. Acad. Arts Sci.*, 32, 351–359.
1937 Babbitt, L. H. *State Geol. and Nat. Hist. Survey* (Conn.), Bull. no 57. Hartford. Pp. 50, 20 pls.

**Delaware**

1906 Stone, W. *Amer. Naturalist*, 40, 162–164.
1925 Fowler, H. W. *Copeia*, no. 145, pp. 57–59.

1940 Conant, R. *Herpetologica*, **1**, 176–177.
1945 Conant, R. *Soc. Nat. Hist. Dela.* (Wilmington), Feb., 1945, pp. 1–8.

**District of Columbia**

1899 Miller, G. S., Jr. *Proc. Biol. Soc. Wash.*, **13**, 75–78.
1902 Hay, W. P. Same, **15**, 127–131.
1915 Grönberger, S. M. *Copeia*, no. 24, pp. 54–55.
1918 Dunn, E. R. (see *Virginia*).
1918 McAtee, W. L. *Bull. Biol. Soc. Wash.*, no. 1, pp. 44–46.
1937a Brady, M. K. (see *Maryland*).
1937b Brady, M. K. *Proc. Biol. Soc Wash.*, **50**, pp. 137–139.

**Florida**

1857 Hallowell, E. *Proc. Acad. Nat. Sci. Phila.* (1856), **8**, 141, 142, 143.
1871 Cope, E. D., *2nd and 3rd Ann. Rept. Peabody Acad.* Salem. Pp. 182.
1877 Cope, E. D. *Amer. Naturalist*, **11**[9], 565.
1877a Cope, E. D. *Proc. Amer. Phil. Soc.*, **17**, 87–88.
1888 Cope, E. D. *Proc. U.S. Nat. Mus.* (1887), **10**, 436.
1895 Cope, E. D. *Proc. Acad. Nat. Sci. Phila.* (1894, 1895), **46**, 429, 437, 438.
1895 Loennberg, E. *Proc. U.S. Nat. Mus* (1894), **17**, 338–339.
1901 Stejneger, L. Same, **24**, 212–213.
1905 Stejneger, L. In G. B. Shattuck, *The Bahama Islands.* New York. Pp. 329–343.
1906 Fowler, H. W. *Proc Acad. Nat. Sci. Phila*, **58**, 109.
1910 Barbour, T. *Proc. Biol. Soc Wash*, **23**, 100.
1910 Brimley, C. S. (see *Alabama*).
1910 Barbour, T. *Mem. Mus. Comp. Zool.*, **44**[3], 209–359.
1914 Deckert, R. F. *Copeia*, no. 5, pp. 2–4; no. 9, pp. 1–3.
1915 Deckert, R. F. *Copeia*, no. 18, pp. 3–5.
1915a Deckert, R. F. *Copeia*, no. 20, pp. 21–22.
1917 Fowler, H. W. *Copeia*, no. 43, p 39.
1920 Barbour, T. *Copeia*, no. 84, pp. 55–56.
1921 Deckert, R. F. *Copeia*, no. 92, pp. 20–23.
1922 Deckert, R. F. *Copeia*, no. 112, p. 88.
1923 Hallinan, T. *Copeia*, no. 115, pp. 19, 20.
1923 Van Hyning, T. *Copeia*, no. 118, p. 68.
1926 Dunn, E. R. *Copeia*, no. 157, pp. 154–156.
1931 Barbour, T. *Copeia*, no. 3, p. 140.
1933 Van Hyning, O. C. *Copeia*, no. 1, pp. 5–7.
1934 Carr, A. F., Jr. *Fla. Naturalist*, **7**[2], 19–23.
1935 Barbour, T. *Zoologica*, **19**[3], 78, 79, 89–91, 96.
1935 Brady, M. K., and F. Harper. *Proc. Biol. Soc. Wash.*, **48**, 107–110.
1935 Harper, F. *Proc. Biol. Soc. Wash.*, **48**, 79–82.
1935 Harper, F. (see *General Works*).
1938 Allen, E. R. *Copeia*, no. 1, p. 50.
1938 Goin, C. J. *Copeia*, no. 1, p. 48.
1938 Springer, S. *Copeia*, no. 1, p. 49.
1939 Allen, E. R. *Copeia*, no. 1, p. 53.
1939 Campbell, G. R., and W. H. Stickel. *Copeia*, no. 2, p. 105.

1939 Harper, F. (see *Georgia*).
1939 Skermer, G. A. *Copeia,* no. 2, pp. 107–108.
1940 Allen, [E.] R., and M. P. Merryday. *Nat. Hist.,* $46^{1}$, 234.
1940 Blair, A. P., C. C. Hargreaves, and K. K. Chen *Proc Soc. Exp Biol. Med*, $45^{1}$, 209–214.
1940a Carr, A. F., Jr. *Copeia,* no. 1, p. 55.
1940b Carr, A. F., Jr. *Univ. Fla. Pub. Biol. Sci.,* ser. 3, no. 1, pp. 1–118.
1940 Goin, C. J., and M. G. Netting (see *Louisiana*).
1940 Stejneger, L. *Copeia,* no. 3, pp. 149–151.
1941 Moore, J. A. (see *General Works*).
1943 Goin, C. J. *Proc. Fla. Acad Sci.,* $6^{1,4}$, 148–149.
1944 Goin, C. J. *Copeia,* no. 3, p. 192.
1945 Allen, E. [R.], and R. Slatten. *Herpetologica,* 3, pt. 1, 25.
1945 Kilby, J. D *Quart. Jour. Fla. Acad Sci*, 8, no. 1, 71–104.
1945 Myers, G. S. *Copeia,* no. 1, p. 44.
1945 Netting, M. G., and C. J. Goin. *Proc. Fla. Acad. Sci* (1944), $7^{2-3}$, 181–184.
1945 Shreve, B. *Copeia,* no. 2, p. 117.
1947 Goin, C. J. *Univ. Fla. Studies, Biol. Sci*, ser. 4, no. 2, 1–66.

**Georgia**

1849 Holbrook, J. E. In George White, *Statistics of Georgia.* Savannah. App., p. 15.
1857 Le Conte, J. *Proc. Acad. Nat. Sci. Phila.* (1856), 8, 146.
1901 Fountain, P. *The Great Deserts and Forests of North America* London, New York, and Bombay. Pp. 62–64.
1908 Allard, H. A. *Science* (*n.s.*), $28^{723}$, 655–656.
1910 Brimley, C. S. (see *Alabama*).
1923 Wright, A. H. *Copeia,* no. 115, p. 34.
1926 Wright, A. H. *Ecology,* $7^{1}$, 81–83.
1930 Harper, F. *Copeia,* pp. 152–154.
1931a Harper, F. *Copeia,* pp. 159–161.
1931 Harper, F. *Sci. Monthly,* 32, 176–181.
1932 Wright, A H. (see *General Works*).
1933 Brandt, B. B., and C. F. Walker (see *North Carolina*).
1934 Carter, H. A. *Copeia,* no. 3, p. 138.
1935 Harper, F. (see *Florida*).
1937 Harper, F. *Amer. Midl. Naturalist,* $18^{2}$, 260–272.
1939a Harper, F. Same, 22, 134–149.
1939b Harper, F. *Notulae Naturae* (Phila.), 27, pp. 1–4.
1942 Stewart, L. *Nature Magazine,* $35^{2}$, 128–130.
1948 Neill, W. T. *Herpetologica,* $4^{3}$, 108–109.
1948 Neill, W. T. Same, $4^{4}$, 158.
1948 Neill, W. T. Same, $4^{5}$, 175–179.

**Idaho**

1869 Cooper, J. G. (see *Montana*).
1872 Cope, E. D. (see *Montana*).
1884 Cope, E. D. (see *California*).
1884 Cope, E. D. *Proc. Acad. Nat. Sci. Phila.* (1883), 35, 17.

1891 Stejneger, L. *North American Fauna,* no. 5, pp. 112–113.
1895 Van Denburgh, J. *Bull. U.S. Fish Commission,* 14, 207.
1912 Van Denburgh, J. *Proc. Calif. Acad. Sci.,* 4th ser., 3, 158, 159.
1921b Van Denburgh, J., and J. R. Slevin. Same, $11^{3}$, 39, 42.
1928 Slevin, J. R. (see *British Columbia*).
1933 Linsdale, J. M. *Copeia,* no. 4, p. 223.
1940 Tanner, W. W. (see *Utah*).
1941a Slater, J. R. *Occ Papers Dept. Biol., Coll Puget Sound* (Tacoma), no. 14, pp. 78–108.
1941 Tanner, W. W. *Great Basin Naturalist,* $2^{2}$, 87–90.
1942 Slater, J. R. (see *Washington*).
1944 Knowlton, G. F. (see *Utah*).
1946 Evenden, F. G. *Copeia,* no. 4, p. 257.

**Illinois**

1883 Davis, N. S., Jr., and F. L Rice. *Bull Chicago Acad. Sciences,* $1^{3}$, 25, 27, 28.
1889 Roberts, H. L. *Amer. Naturalist,* $23^{267}$, 74.
1890a Garman, H. *Bull. Ill. State Lab. Nat Hist.,* 3, 133, 134.
1890 Garman, H. Same, 3, 188–190.
1892 Garman, H. Same, 3, art. XIII, 316–352.
1892 Hay, O. P. (see *Indiana*).
1893 Hurter, J. *Trans. Acad. Sci. St Louis,* $6^{11}$, 251–254.
1902 Garman, H *Bull Ill State Lab Nat. Hist ,* 3, 335–339.
1914 Gaige, H. T. *Copeia,* no. 11, p. 4.
1915 Thompson, C. *Occ. Papers Mus Zool. Univ Mich ,* 9, 1–7.
1917 Hankinson, T. L. *Trans Ill. Acad. Sci., Tenth Ann. Meeting,* 10, pp. 324–325.
1918 Hubbs, C. L. *Copeia,* no. 55, pp. 40–43.
1919 Pope, P. H. *Copeia,* no. 74, pp. 83, 84.
1923 Weed, A. C. *Copeia,* no. 116, pp. 45–46, 48, 49
1924 Ridgway, R. *Copeia,* no. 128, p. 39.
1925 Blanchard, F. N. *Papers Mich. Acad. Sci. Arts Letters,* pp. 534–535.
1926 Cahn, A. R. *Copeia,* no 151, pp. 107–109.
1929a Burt, C E , and M D Burt (see *Arkansas*).
1929b Burt, C. E., and M. D. Burt (see *Arizona*).
1929 Schmidt, K. P. *Field Museum Nat. Hist. Zool. Leaflet,* no. 11, pp. 1–15.
1933 Davis, D. D. *Copeia,* no. 4, pp. 223–224.
1935 Burt, C. E. (see *General Works*).
1935 Schmidt, K. P , and W. L. Necker. *Bull. Chicago Acad. Sci ,* $5^{4}$, 57–61, 64–67, 76–77.
1938 Necker, W. L. *Chicago Acad. Sci.,* Leaflet no. 1, p. 2.
1938 Schmidt, K. P. *Field Mus. Nat. Hist ,* Zool ser , $20^{20}$, 377–382.
1939 Necker, W. L. *Bull. Chicago Acad. Sci.,* $6^{1}$, 1, 2, 4–6.
1941 Cagle, F. R. *Cont. So. Ill. Norm. Univ., Mus. Nat. and Soc. Sci.* Carbondale. IV. 32 pp.
1941 Owens, D. W. *Copeia,* No. 3, pp. 183, 184.
1942 Cagle, F. R. *Amer. Midl. Naturalist,* $28^{1}$, 164–200.

1942 Gloyd, H. K. *Trans. Ill. Acad. Sci.*, $34^{1}$, 220.

1942 Peters, J. A. *Copeia*, no. 3, p. 182.

1944 Pope, C. L. *Amphibians and Reptiles of the Chicago Area.* Nat. Hist. Mus., Chicago. Pp. 1–275.

1945 Elder, W. H. *Copeia*, no. 2, p. 122.

1946 Conant, R. *Copeia*, no. 2, p. 109.

**Indiana**

1886 Hughes, E. *Brookville Soc. Nat. Hist.*, no. 2, p. 43.

1887 Butler, A. W. *Jour. Cinc. Soc. Nat. Hist.*, $10^{3}$, 147–148.

1887 Hay, O. P. Same, $10^{2}$, 59, 62–63.

1887 James, J. E. (see *Ohio*).

1889 Hay, O. P. *Amer. Naturalist*, $23^{9}$, 770–774.

1891 Blatchley, W. S. *Jour. Cincinnati Soc. Nat.*, 14, 27–28.

1891–1892 Butler, A. W. Same, 13, 175.

1892 Hay, O. P. *Ind. Dept. Geol. and Nat. Res.*, 17th Ann. Rept. (1891), pp. 456–481, 585, 586.

1895a Kirsch, P. H. *Bull. U.S. Fish Commission* (1894), 14, art. 6, 41.

1895b Kirsch, P. H. Same, art. 20, p. 333.

1896 Atkinson, C. *Proc. Ind. Acad. Sci.* (1895), pp. 258–261.

1900 Blatchley, W. L. *Ind. Dept. Geol. and Nat. Res.*, 24th Ann. Rept. (1899), pp. 542, 543, 551.

1901 Ramsey, E. E. *Proc. Ind. Acad. Sci.* (1900), p. 222.

1907 Banta, A. M. *Carnegie Inst. Pub.* Washington.

1907 McAtee, W. L. *Proc. Biol. Soc. Wash.*, 20, 15, 16.

1909 Hahn, W. L. *Proc. U.S. Nat. Mus.*, 35 (Dec. 7, 1908), 545–548, 557–562.

1918 Hubbs, C. L. (see *Illinois*).

1920 Evermann, B. W., and H. W. Clark. *Lake Maxinkuckee, Ind. Dept. Conservation Pub.*, 1, 631–644.

1921 Ortenburger, A. I. *Copeia*, no. 99, pp. 73–75.

1926 Blanchard, F. N. *Papers Mich. Acad. Sci. Arts Letters* (1925), pp. 371–373.

1926 Myers, G. S. *Proc. Ind. Acad. Sci.* (1925), 35, 281–286.

1927a Myers, G. S. *Proc. Ind. Acad. Sci.*, 36, 338–339.

1927b Myers, G. S. *Copeia*, no. 163, pp. 50–53.

1927 Wright, H. P., and G. S. Myers, *Copeia*, no. 159, pp. 173–175.

1928 Springer, S. *Proc. Ind. Acad. Sci.* (1927), 37, 492.

1931 Grave, B. H., *Proc. Ind. Acad. Sci.* (1930), 40, 339.

1931 Piatt, J. Same, pp. 362, 363, 365.

1935 Burt, C. E. (see *General Works*).

1935 Schmidt, K. P., and W. L. Necker (see *Illinois*).

1936 Grant, C. *Proc. Ind. Acad. Sci.*, 45, 323–333.

1938 Necker, W. L. (see *Illinois*).

1938 Schmidt, K. P. (see *Illinois*).

1938 Swanson, P. L. *Amer. Midl. Naturalist*, $20^{3}$, 713.

1939 Miller, D. C. *Proc. Ind. Acad. Sci.* (1940), 49, 209–214.

1939 Necker, W. L. (see *Illinois*).

1940 Swanson, Paul L. *Amer. Midl. Naturalist*, $22^{8}$, 684–695.

1941a Blair, A. P. *Proc. Nat. Acad. Sci.*, **27**[1], 14–17.
1942 Vogel, H. H., Jr. *Proc. Ind. Acad. Sci.*, **51**, p. 266.

**Iowa**

1878 Aldrich, C. *Amer. Naturalist*, **12**[7], 473–474.
1892 Osborn, H. *A Partial Catalogue of the Animals of Iowa.* Ames. P. 10.
1910b Ruthven, A. G. *Proc. Iowa Acad. Sci.* (1910), **17**, 198–205.
1912e Ruthven, A. G. Same (1912), **19**, 207.
1919 Ruthven, A. G. *Occ. Papers Mus. Zool. Univ. Mich.*, no. 66, pp. 1–2.
1923 Blanchard, F. N *Univ. Iowa Studies in Nat. Hist.*, new ser. no. 67, **10**[2], 19–22.
1929a Burt, C. E., and M. D. Burt (see *Arkansas*).
1929b Burt, C. E., and M. D Burt (see *Arizona*).
1935 Burt, C. E. (see *General Works*).
1941 Bailey, R. M., and M. K. Bailey. *Iowa State Coll. Jour. Sci.*, **15**, 169–177.
1943 Bailey, R. M. *Iowa Acad. Sci*, **50**, 347–352.
1944 Bailey, R. M. *Iowa Conservationist*, **3**[3], 17–20; **3**[4], 25, 27–30.
1945 Abbott, R. L. *Nat. Hist*, **54**[3], 114–117
1948 Loomis, R. B. *Herpetologica*, **4**[4], 121–122.

**Kansas**

1857a Hallowell, E. *Proc. Acad. Nat. Sci. Phila.* (1856), **8**, 250–252.
1857b Hallowell, E. (see *Texas*).
1881 Cragin, F. W. *Trans. Kans. Acad. Sci*, **7**, 121–123.
1885 Cragin, F. W. Same, **9**, 136–140.
1894 Cragin, F W. *Colo. Coll Studies*, **5**, 39.
1907 Hartmann, F. A. *Trans. Kans. Acad. Sci.* (1906), **20**, pt. 2, 227–229.
1925 Dice, L R. *Ecology*, **4** (Jan., 1923), 40–53.
1927 Burt, C E. *Occ Papers Mus. Zool. Univ. Mich.*, no. 189, pp. 1–3.
1927 Linsdale, J. M. *Copeia*, no. 164, pp. 75–77.
1928 Gloyd, H. K *Trans. Kans. Acad. Sci*, **31**, pp. 116–119.
1929a Burt, C. E., and M. D. Burt (see *Arkansas*).
1929b Burt, C. E., and M. D. Burt (see *Arizona*).
1929 Gloyd, H. K. *Science*, **69**[1776], 44
1929b Taylor, E. H. *Kans. Univ. Sci. Bull.*, **19**[6], 65.
1931 Burt, C E. *Proc. Biol. Soc. Wash.*, **44**, 11–14
1932 Gloyd, H. K. *Papers Mich. Acad. Sci.* (1931), **15**, 389–400.
1932 Smith, H. M. *Trans. Kans. Acad. Sci.*, **35**, 93–96.
1933 Smith, H. M. *Copeia*, no. 4, p. 217.
1934 Brennan, L. A. *Trans. Kans Acad. Sci.*, **37**, 189–191.
1934 Smith, H. M *Amer Midl. Naturalist*, **15**[4], 377–390, 427–528.
1936 Hibbard, C. W., and A B. Leonard. *Copeia*, no. 2, p. 114.
1936 Youngstrom, K. A., and H. M. Smith. *Amer. Midl. Naturalist*, **17**[3], 629–633.
1937 Brenkelman, J. P., and A. Downs. *Trans. Kans. Acad. Sci.*, **39**, 267–268.
1937 Grant, C *Amer. Midl. Naturalist*, **18**, 370–372.
1938 Brennan, L. A. *Trans. Kans. Acad. Sci.*, **40**, 341–347
1938 Tihen, J. A. Same, pp. 401–409.
1939 Tihen, J. A., and J. M. Sprague. Same, **42**, 499–512.

1944 Marr, J. C. (see *General Works*).

1945 Mittleman, M. B. *Herpetologica*, **3**, pt. 1, 20–21.

1946 Breukelman, J., and H. M. Smith. *Univ. Kans. Pub. Mus. Nat. Hist.*, $1^{5}$, 103–105.

1947 Smith, H. M. *Herpetologica*, **4**, 13–14.

**Kentucky**

1894 Garman, H. *Bull. Essex Inst.*, **26**, 36–37.

1901 Garman, H. *Ky. Ag. Expt. Stat. Bull.*, no. 91, pp. 62–64.

1926 Bishop, S. C. *Copeia*, no. 152, pp. 118–120.

1926 Blanchard, F. N. (see *Indiana*).

1929a Burt, C. E., and M. D. Burt (see *Arkansas*).

1933b Burt, C. E. *Amer. Midl. Naturalist*, $14^{6}$, 669–679.

1934 Bailey, V. Same (1933), $14^{5}$, 594–596.

1935 Harper, F. (see *General Works*).

1936 Giovanolli, L. *Copeia*, no. 1, p. 69.

1937 Hibbard, C. W. *Trans. Kans. Acad. Sci.*, **39**, 277–281.

1939 Parker, M. V. (see *Tennessee*).

1939 Welter, W. A., and K. Carr. *Copeia*, no. 3, pp. 128–130.

1940 Dury, R., and W. Gessing, Jr. *Herpetologica*, **2**, pt. 2, 31, 32.

1941 Barbour, R. W., and E. P. Walters. *Copeia*, no. 2, p. 116.

1941 Barbour, R. W. *Copeia*, no. 4, p. 262.

1942 Barbour, R. W. *Copeia*, no. 2, p. 128.

1946 Barbour, R. W. *Copeia*, no. 1, p. 44.

**Louisiana**

1900 Beyer, G. E. *Proc. La. Soc. Naturalists* (1897–1899), Appendix, 1, 35–37.

1918 Viosca, Percy, Jr. *Bienn. Rept. La. Dept. Conservation* (Apr. 1, 1916), pp. 160–162.

1920 Schmidt, K. P. *Copeia*, no. 86, pp. 84–85.

1923a Viosca, P., Jr. *Copeia*, no. 115, pp. 35–44.

1923b Viosca, P., Jr. *Copeia*, no. 122, pp. 96–99.

1926 Strecker, J. K., Jr., and L. S. Frierson, Jr. *Cont. Baylor Univ. Mus.*, no. 5, pp. 4–5.

1926 Viosca, P., Jr. *Ecology*, **7**, 307–314.

1928 Viosca, P., Jr. *Proc. Biol. Soc. Wash.*, **41**, 89–92.

1929a Burt, C. E., and M. D. Burt (see *Arkansas*).

1935 Burt, C. E. (see *General Works*).

1935 Harper, F. (see *General Works*).

1938 George, I. D. *Proc. La. Acad. Sci.*, 4, 255–259.

1939 Schmidt, K. P. (see *Illinois*).

1939 *La. Dept. Conservation, Div. Fisheries*, Bull. 26.

1940 Blair, A. P., C. C. Hargreaves, and K. K. Chen (see *Florida*).

1940 George, I. D. *Copeia*, no. 2, p. 134.

1940 Goin, C. J., and M. Graham Netting. *Ann. Carnegie Mus.*, **28**, 137–168.

1942 Palmer, M. E. *Proc. La. Acad. Sci.*, **6**, 73–74.

1944 Marr, J. C. (see *General Works*).

1944 Viosca, P., Jr. *Proc. La. Acad. Sci.*, **8**, 47–62.

1945 Burt, C. E. *Trans. Kans. Acad. Sci.* (1945–1946), $48^{3}$, 423–425.

1947 Orton, G. L. *Ann Carnegie Mus.* **30**, 363–383.

**Maine**

1832 Williamson, W. D. *History of the State of Maine.* Hallowell. Vol. I, sect. V, p. 169.

1862 Fogg, B. F *Proc. Portland Soc Nat. Hist.*, **1**, pt. I, 86.

1863 Verrill, A. E. *Proc. Boston Soc. Nat. Hist.* (1862, 1863), **9**, 197–198. Boston, 1865 (Read Feb. 4, 1863.)

1873 Adams, A. L. (see *New Brunswick*).

1873 Hill, T. *Amer. Naturalist,* **7**[11], 660–662.

1904 Henshaw, S. (see *Connecticut*).

1915 Pope, P. H *Copeia,* no. 16, pp. 1–2.

1918 Pope, P. H. *Copeia,* no. 64, pp. 96–97.

1926 Babcock, H L (see *Connecticut*).

1938 Hoopes, I. *New Eng. Naturalist,* no 1, pp. 4–6.

1939 Manville, R. H. *Copeia,* p. 174.

1942 Fowler, J. A. *Copeia,* no. 3, pp 185–186.

**Maryland**

1902 Hay, W. P. (see *District of Columbia*)

1914 Keim, T D. *Copeia,* no 2, p. 2

1915 Fowler, H. W. *Copeia,* no. 22, pp. 38–39.

1918 McAtee, W. L. (see *District of Columbia*).

1925 Fowler, H. W. *Copeia,* no. 145, pp. 61–63.

1932 Walker, C. F. (see *Ohio*).

1936 Noble, G. K., and W. G. Hassler. *Copeia,* no. 1, pp. 63–64.

1937a Brady, M. K , *Proc. Biol Soc. Wash* , **50**, 190–191.

1937b Brady, M. K. Same, pp. 137–138.

1937 Kelly, H. A. *Snakes of Maryland,* Baltimore. Pp. 1–103.

1939 Robertson, H C. *Bull. Nat. Hist. Soc. Md.*, **9**[10], 89–93

1940 McCauley, R. H., Jr , and C. S. East. *Copeia,* no. 2, pp 120–123.

1940 Mansueti, R. *Bull. Nat. Hist. Soc. Md.*, **10**[10], 88–96.

1941 Mansueti, R. *Proc. Nat. Hist. Soc. Md.*, **7**, 1–53.

1942 Mansueti, R. *Bull. Nat. Hist. Soc Md.*, **12**[4], 33–43.

1946 Littleford, R. A. *Copeia,* no. 2, p 104.

1947 Fowler, J. A., *Maryland,* **17**, 6, 7.

**Massachusetts**

1833 Smith, D. S. C. H. In *Rept. Geol. Min. Bot. Zool.*, by E. Hitchcock, pt. IV, p. 552.

1839 Storer, D H. *Repts. Mass. Commissioners 1838, Zool. Survey* Boston. Pp. 235–245.

1840 Storer, D H. *Boston Jour. Nat. Hist.*, **3**[1–2], 40–53.

1852 Nichols, A. *Jour. Essex Co. Nat. Hist. Soc.*, **1**[3], 113–117. (Read June 17, 1853.)

1865 Putnam, F. W. *Proc. Boston Soc. Nat. Hist.*, **9**, 229–230.

1867 Putnam, F. W. *Amer. Naturalist,* **1**, 107–109.

1868 Allen, J A. *Proc. Boston Soc. Nat. Hist.*, **12**, 185–198, 249.

1870 Allen, J. A. Same, **13** (1869–1871), 261, 263 March 16, 1870.

1873 Fowler, S. P. *Amer. Naturalist,* **7**[4], 239.

1880 Hinckley, M. H. *Proc. Boston Soc. Nat. Hist.*, **21** (1880–1882), 104–107. Nov. 17, 1880.
1882 Hinckley, M. H. *Amer. Naturalist*, **16**, 636–639.
1883 Hinckley, M. H. *Proc. Boston Soc. Hist.*, **21**, 307–315.
1884 Hinckley, M. H. Same (1882–1883), **22**, 85–95.
1888 Hargett, C. U. *Amer. Naturalist*, **22**, 536, 537.
1897 Kirkland, A. H. *Hatch Expt. Stat., Mass. Ag. Coll. Bull.*, no. 46, pp. 1–29.
1904 Henshaw, S. (see *Connecticut*).
1926 Babcock, H. L. (see *Connecticut*).
1930 Dunn, E. R. *Bull. Boston Soc. Nat. Hist.*, no. 57, pp. 5–6.
1936 Driver, E. G. *Copeia*, no. 1, pp. 67, 68, 69.
1941 Moore, J. A. (see *General Works*).
1944 Sweetman, H. L. *Amer. Midl. Naturalist*, **32**[2], 499–501.
1947 Blair, A. P. (see *New Jersey*).
1947 Hoopes, I. *Copeia*, no. 2, pp. 138–139.

**Michigan**

1861 Miles, M. *Geol Survey Mich.*, First Bienn. Rept., p. 234.
1865 Cope, E. D. *Proc. Acad. Nat. Sci. Phila.*, **17**, 84–85.
1879 Smith, W H *Science News, Supplement*, 1[23], i, v, viii
1895 Gibbs, M. *Amer. Field*, pp. 179, 203, 228, 251, 273, 274, 299, 325.
1895b Kirsch, P. H. (see *Indiana*).
1904 Clark, H. L. *Mich. Acad. Sci*, Fourth Ann. Rept. (1902), p 192.
1906 Ruthven, A G. *Geol. Survey Mich*, Ann. Rept, 1905, pp. 109–110.
1908 Hankinson, T. L. *State Board Geol. Survey Mich. 1907–1908, Rept.*, pp. 235–236.
1909 Ruthven, A. G. *Geol. Survey Mich, Rept.*, pp 329–333.
1909a Ruthven, A. G. *Mich. Acad. Sci.*, Eleventh Rept., p. 116.
1910 Ruthven, A. G Same, Rept., **12**, 59.
1911a Ruthven, A. G. *Mich. Geol. Biol. Survey Pub.*, 4, Biol. ser. 2, pp. 257–263.
1911b Ruthven, A. G. *Mich. Acad. Sci.*, Thirteenth Rept., p. 115.
1911 Thompson, C. Same, pp 105–106.
1912 Ruthven, A. G., C. Thompson, and H. Thompson. *Mich. Geol. Biol. Survey Pub.*, 10, Biol ser., pp. 1–166.
1912 Thompson, C., and H. Thompson. *Mich. Acad. Sci.*, Fourteenth Rept., pp. 156–157
1912 Thompson, H. Same, p. 189.
1912 Thompson, C Same, p. 190.
1913 Thompson, C., and H. Thompson. Same, Fifteenth Rept., pp. 215–216.
1915a Gaige, H. T. *Copeia*, no. 14, p. 2.
1915b Gaige, H. T. *Occ. Papers Univ. Mus. Univ. Mich.*, no. 17, pp. 1–4.
1915 Thompson, C. *Occ. Papers Mus. Zool. Univ. Mich*, no 18, pp. 1–4.
1915a Thompson, C. Same, no. 9, pp. 1–7.
1916 Thompson, C. *Mich. Geol. Biol. Survey Pub.*, 20, Biol. ser. 4, pp. 62, 63.
1916 Evans, A. T. *Proc. U.S. Nat. Mus.*, **49**, 351–354.
1917 Ellis, M. M. *Mich. Acad. Sci.*, Nineteenth Rept., pp. 45–48.
1917 Ruthven, A. G. *Occ. Papers Mus. Zool. Univ. Mich.*, no. 47, pp. 1–5.

1918 Hubbs, C. L. (see *Illinois*).
1920 Potter, D. *Copeia,* no. 82, pp. 89–90.
1924 Hatt, R. T. *Papers Mich. Acad. Sci.,* pp. 374, 385.
1928 Blanchard, F. N. *Copeia,* no. 167, pp. 45–47.
1929a Burt, C. E., and M. D. Burt (see *Arkansas*).
1933 Blanchard, F. N. *Copeia,* no. 4, p. 216.
1933 Force, E. R. *Copeia,* no. 3, pp. 128–131.
1935 Schmidt, K. P., and W. L. Necker (see *Illinois*).
1937 Allen, D. *Copeia,* no. 19, no. 3, pp. 190, 191.
1938 Allen, D. L. *Ecol. Monog*, 8³, 430, 431.
1938 Necker, W. L. (see *Illinois*).
1939 Necker, W. L. (see *Illinois*).
1940 George, I. D. (see *Louisiana*).
1941 Moore, J. A. (see *General Works*).
1942 Edgren, R. A., Jr. *Copeia,* no. 3, p. 180.
1944 Creaser, C. W. *Papers Mich. Acad. Sci. Arts Letters* (1943), **29,** 229–249 (esp 234–236).

**Minnesota**

1922 Weed, A. C. *Proc. Biol Soc. Wash.,* **35,** 107–110.
1923 Weed, A. C. *Copeia,* p. 28.
1930 Weed, A. C. *Turtox News,* **8,** 43.
1935 Swanson, G. *Copeia,* no. 3, pp. 152–154.
1938 Breckenridge, W. J. *Copeia,* no. 1, p. 47.
1941 Moore, J. A. (see *General Works*).
1942 Moore, J. A *Genetics,* **27,** 408–416.
1944 Breckenridge, W. J. *Minn. Mus. Nat. Hist. Univ. Minn.,* Univ. Minn. Press. Pp 1–202.

**Mississippi**

1901 Stejneger, L. (see *Florida*).
1910 Brimley, C. S. (see *Alabama*).
1920 Potter, D. *Copeia,* no. 82, p. 82.
1927 Corrington, J. D. *Copeia,* no. 165, pp. 98–100, 102.
1932a Allen, M. J *Amer. Mus. Novitates,* no. 542, pp. 1–2, 6–11.
1932b Allen, M. J. *Copeia,* no. 2, p. 104.
1935 Harper, F. (see *General Works*).
1938 Springer, S (see *Florida*).
1940 Goin, C. J., and M. G. Netting (see *Louisiana*).
1942 Netting, M. G., and C. J. Goin (see *Alabama*).

**Missouri**

1893 Hurter, J. (see *Illinois*).
1894 Test, F. C. *Bull U.S. Fish Commission,* **12** (1892, 1894), 122.
1897 Hurter, J. *Trans. Acad. Sci. St. Louis,* **7,** 503.
1903 Hurter, J. Same, **13,** 80.
1911 Hurter, J. Same, **20,** 96–127.
1921 Danforth, C. H. Same, **24**³.
1925 Blanchard, F. N. (see *Illinois*).
1929a Burt, C. E., and M. D. Burt (see *Arkansas*).

1933 Burt, C. E. *Amer. Midl. Naturalist,* $14^2$, 170–173.
1934 Boyer, D. A., and A. A. Heinze. *Trans. Acad. Sci. St. Louis,* $28^{3-4}$, 185–200.
1935 Burt, C. E. (see *General Works*).
1938 Henning, W. L. *Copeia,* no. 2, pp. 91–92.
1942 Anderson, P. *Bull. Chicago Acad. Sci.,* $6^{11}$, 203, 205–207.
1945 Anderson, P. Same, $7^5$, 272–273.
1946 Peter, J. A. *Copeia,* no. 1, p. 44.

**Montana**

1869 Cooper, J. G. *Amer. Naturalist,* 3, 125.
1872 Cope, E. D. In *U.S. Geol Survey of Mont. and Adjacent Territories,* Prelim. Rept. (1871), by F. V. Hayden. Pp 468–469.
1874 Allen, J. A. *Proc. Boston Soc. Nat. Hist,* 17, 70
1875 Hayden, F. V (see *Nebraska*)
1878 Coues, E., and H. C. Yarrow. *Bull. U S. Geol. and Geog Survey,* 4, art XI, 288–290.
1879 Cope, E. D. *Amer. Naturalist,* 13, 435–438.
1893 Test, F. C. *Bull U S. Fish Commission,* 11, art I, 57–59
1895 Van Denburgh, J. (see *Idaho*).
1932 Kellogg, R. *Copeia,* no 1, p. 36.
1932 Smith, H. M. *Copeia,* no. 2, p. 100.
1934 Donaldson, L. R. *Copeia,* no. 4, p. 184
1942 Rodgers, T. L., and W. J Jellison. *Copeia,* no 1, pp. 10–11.
1943 Slipp, J. W., and G. C. Carl (see *British Columbia*).

**Nebraska**

1857a Hallowell, E. *Proc. Acad. Nat. Sci. Phila.* (Oct 28, 1856), 8, 250–252.
1875 Hayden, F. V. *Rept. Engineer's Dept. U.S. Army,* p. 105.
1929a Burt, C. E., and M. D. Burt (see *Arkansas*).
1929b Burt, C. E., and M. D. Burt (see *Arizona*).
1931 Burt, C E. (see *Kansas*).
1935 Burt, C E. (see *General Works*).
1942 Hudson, G., *Univ. Neb. Conservation and Survey Div, Neb. Conservation Bull.,* no. 24, pp. 1–32, 105–124.
1944 Marr, J. C. (see *General Works*).
1945 Loomis, R *Herpetologica,* $2^{7-8}$, 211–212

**Nevada**

1878 Yarrow, H. C., and H. W. Henshaw. *Geog. Surveys Territory of U S. West of 100th Meridian,* App. Ann. Rept., pp. 206–210.
1884 Cope, E. D. *Proc. Acad. Nat. Sci. Phila.* (1883), 35, 14, 18.
1893 Stejneger, L. (see *California*).
1912 Taylor, W. P. *Univ. Calif. Pub. Zool.,* $7^{10}$, 340, 342–346.
1913 Thompson, H. *Proc Biol. Soc. Wash.,* 26, 53–56.
1915 Ruthven, A G., and H. T. Gaige. *Occ. Papers Mus. Zool. Univ. Mich.,* no. 8, pp. 1–34.
1920 Snyder, J. O. *Copeia,* no. 86, pp. 83–84.
1921a Van Denburgh, J, and J. R. Slevin. *Proc. Calif. Acad. Sci.,* 4th ser., $11^2$, 27–30.

1928 Slevin, J. R (see *British Columbia*).
1932 Brues, C. T. *Proc. Amer. Acad. Arts Sciences,* $67^{7}$, 281–283.
1932 Klauber, L. M. (see *California*).
1933a Burt, C. E. (see *General Works*).
1936 Cowles, R. B., and C. M. Bogert. *Herpetologica,* $1^{33-42}$.
1938 Linsdale, J M. *Amer. Midl. Naturalist,* $19^{1}$, 20–25.
1940 Linsdale, J. M. *Proc. Amer. Acad. Arts Sciences,* $73^{8}$, 197–257.
1942 Rivers, I. L. *Jour. Ent. & Zool. Pomona College,* $34^{3}$, 52–56.

**New Hampshire**

1899 Allen, G M. *Proc. Boston Soc. Nat. Hist.,* **29,** art. 3, 69–72.
1904 Henshaw, S. (see *Connecticut*).
1918c Evermann, B. W. *Copeia,* no. 61, pp. 81–83.
1919 Speck, F. G. *Copeia,* no. 70, pp. 46–48.
1926 Babcock, H. L. (see *Connecticut*).
1939 Oliver, J., and J. R. Bailey. In *Surv. Rept. N.H. Fish and Game Dept.* Concord. Vol. IV, pp. 195–217.
1943 Aronson, L. R. *American Midl. Naturalist,* $29^{1}$, 242–244.

**New Jersey**

1868 Abbott, C. C. *Geology of New Jersey.* Newark. App. E, pp. 804–805.
1882 Abbott, C. C. *Amer. Naturalist,* **16,** 707–711.
1884a Abbott, C C. *A Naturalist's Rambles about Home.* New York. Pp. 312–340, 476.
1884b Abbott, C. C. *Amer. Naturalist,* **18,** 1075–1080
1884 Davis, W. T. *Proc. Nat. Sci Assoc. Staten Is*, **1,** 13.
1889 Peter, J. E. *Amer. Naturalist,* **23,** 58–59.
1890 Abbott, C. C. Same, **24,** 189.
1890 Nelson, J. *Geol. Survey N.J., Final Rept. State Geol.,* **2,** pt. 2. Zoology, pp. 649–652.
1891 Cope, E. D. *Amer. Naturalist,* **25,** 1017–1019.
1904 Davis, W. T. Same, **38,** 893.
1905 Davis, W. T. Same, **39,** 795, 796.
1905 Ditmars, R L. (see *Connecticut*).
1906 Fowler, H. W. *Amer. Naturalist,* **40,** 596
1906 Stone, W. (see *Delaware*).
1907 Davis, W. T. *Amer Naturalist,* **41,** 49–50.
1907 Fowler, H W *Ann. Rept N.J. State Mus.* (1906), pp. 1–408.
1908 Davis, W. T. *Proc. Staten Is. Assoc. Arts Sciences,* **2,** pt. II, 48–50.
1908 Fowler, H. W. *Ann Rept. N J. State Mus* (1907), pp 191–195.
1909 Fowler, H. W. Same (1908), pt. III, no 2, pp. 395–400.
1910 Miller, W. DeW., and J. Chapin. *Science* (N.A.), $32^{818}$, 315–317.
1914 Street, J. F. *Copeia,* no. 4, p. 2
1916 Barbour, T. *Copeia,* no. 26, pp. 5–7
1916 Miller, W. D. *Copeia,* no. 34, pp. 67, 68.
1921 McAtee, W. L. *Copeia,* no. 96, pp. 39, 40.
1923 Noble, G. K., and R. C. Noble. *Zoologica,* $2^{18}$, 414–455.
1927 Breder, C. M , Jr., R. B. Breder, and C. Redmond. *Zoologica,* $9^{3}$, 201–229.
1927b Myers, G. S. (see *Indiana*).

1929 Myers, G. S. *Copeia,* no. 170, p. 23.
1930 Klots, A. B. *Copeia,* no. 173 (Oct.–Dec., 1929; Jan. 16, 1930), pp. 108–111.
1931 Burt, C. E. *Jour. Wash. Acad. Sci.,* $21^{9}$, 198–203.
1936 Conant, R., and R. M. Bailey. *Occ. Papers Mus. Zool. Univ. Mich.,* no. 328, pp. 1–5.
1940 Moore, J. A. (see *General Works*).
1943 Aronson, L. R. *Copeia,* no. 4, pp. 246–249.
1947 Blair, A. P. *Amer. Mus. Novitates,* no. 1343, pp. 1–5.

**New Mexico**

1854 Hallowell, E. *Proc. Acad. Nat. Sci. Phila.* (Oct. 26, 1852), 6 (1852, 1853), 181–182.
1875 Yarrow, H. C. (see *Arizona*).
1875 Coues, E. (see *Arizona*).
1884 Cope, E. D. *Proc. Acad. Nat. Sci. Phila.* (1883), 35, 10, 14, 15.
1896 Cockerell, T. D A. *Amer. Naturalist,* 30, 327.
1903 Stone, W., and J. A. G. Rehn. *Proc. Acad. Nat. Sci. Phila*, 55, 34.
1907 Ruthven, A. G. (see *Arizona*).
1913 Bailey, V. *North American Fauna,* no 35, p. 35.
1917 Ellis, M. M. *Copeia,* no. 43, p 39.
1924b Van Denburgh, J. *Proc. Calif. Acad. Sci.,* 4th ser., $13^{12}$, 189–191, 194–199.
1932 Mosauer, W. *Occ. Papers Mus. Zool Univ. Mich*, no. 246, pp. 1–5.
1933a Burt, C. E. (see *General Works*).
1933 Linsdale, J. M. *Copeia,* no 4, p 222.
1935 Burt, C. E (see *General Works*).
1937 Little, E. L., Jr., and J. G. Keller. *Copeia,* no. 4, pp. 216–222.
1938 Taylor, E. H. (see *Arizona*).
1941b Bragg, A. N. *Great Basin Naturalist,* $2^{8}$, 109–117.
1941c Bragg, A. N. *Wasmann Collector,* $4^{3}$, 92–94.
1946 Koster, W. J. *Copeia,* no. 3, p. 173.

**New York**

1842 DeKay, J. E. *Zoology of New York, or New York Fauna.* Pt III, "Reptiles and Amphibia," pp. 59–72. Pt. IV, plates 19–22.
1851 Gebbard, J., Jr. *N.Y. State Cabinet Nat. Hist.,* p 23.
1852 Hough, F. B. Same, fifth ann. rept., p. 19.
1852 Hough, F. B. Same, p. 24.
1853 Gebbard, J., Jr. Same, p. 23.
1878 Monks, S. P. *Amer. Naturalist,* 12, 695.
1879 Gilbert, E S. *Science News,* p 336.
1882 Bicknell, E. P. *Trans. Linn. Soc. N.Y*, 1, 124.
1898 Davis, W. T. *Proc Nat. Sci. Assoc. Staten Is.,* $7^{2}$, 4.
1898 Mearns, E. A. *Bull. Amer. Mus. Nat. Hist.,* no. 10, art. XVI, pp. 324–326.
1898 Sherwood, W. L. (see *Connecticut*).
1899 Mearns, E A *Proc. U.S. Nat. Mus.,* 21, 345. (Read Nov. 4, 1898.)
1902 Paulmier, F. C. *N.Y. State Mus. Bull.,* no. 51, pp. 403, 414.
1903 Britcher, H. W. *Proc. Onondaga Acad. Sci.,* 1, 120–122.
1904 Gage, S. H. *Cornell Nature-Study Leaflet,* no. 16, pp. 185–205; *Teachers' Leaflet,* no. 9 (May, 1897).

1905 Ditmars, R. L. (see *Connecticut*).
1908 Wright, A. H., and A. A. Allen. *Amer. Naturalist,* **42,** 39–42.
1910 Miller, W. DeW., and J. Chapin (see *New Jersey*).
1912 Davis, W. T. *Proc. Staten Is. Assoc. Arts Sciences* (Oct. 1909–May 1911), pp. 66–67. Read Apr. 16, 1910.
1914 Overton, F. *Mus. Brooklyn Inst. Arts Sciences, Science Bull.,* **$2^8$,** 23–40.
1914 Wright, A. H. *Carnegie Inst. Pub.,* no. 197, pp. 1–98.
1915 Overton, F. *Copeia,* no. 20, p. 17; no. 24, pp. 52–53.
1917 Nichols, J. T. *Copeia,* no. 45, pp. 59–60.
1918 Evermann, B. W. *Copeia,* no. 56, pp. 48–51.
1918 Latham, R. *Copeia,* no. 62, p. 88.
1919 Wright, A. H., and J. Moesel. *Copeia,* no 74, pp. 81–83.
1920 Fisher, G C. *Copeia,* no. 85, pp. 76–77.
1923 Bishop, S. C. *Copeia,* no. 120, pp. 83–84.
1923 Green, H. T. *Copeia,* no. 122, p 99
1924 Frost, S. W. *Jour. N.Y. Ent. Soc.,* **32,** 173–185
1927 Bishop, S. C., and W. P. Alexander. *N.Y. State Museum Handbook,* no. 3. Albany. Pp. 60–76.
1927 Heller, J. A. *Copeia,* no 165, p. 116.
1927b Myers, G. S. (see *Indiana*).
1828 Weber, J. A *Copeia,* no 169, pp. 106, 108–110.
1930 Hamilton, W J., Jr. *Copeia,* no. 2, p. 45.
1930 Myers, G S. (see *New Jersey*).
1931 Burt, C. E. (see *New Jersey*).
1932 Frost, S. W. (see *Pennsylvania*).
1934 Hamilton, W. J , Jr. *Copeia,* no. 2, pp. 88–90.
1934 Maynard, E. A. *Copeia,* no. 4, pp. 174–177.
1935 Frost, S. R. (see *Pennsylvania*).
1936 Kauffeld, C. F. *Herpetologica,* **1,** 11.
1939 Janes, R. G. *Copeia,* no. 3, pp. 134–140.
1939 Moore, J. A. *Ecology,* **$20^4$,** 459–478
1940 Raney, E. C., and W. M. Ingram. *Bull. Ecol. Soc. Amer.,* **$21^4$,** 30.
1940 Raney, E C. *Amer. Midl. Naturalist,* **$23^3$,** 733–745.
1940 Moore, J. A. (see *General Works*).
1941 Moore, J. A. (see *General Works*).
1941 Pratt, J. *Copeia,* no. 4, p. 264.
1941 Raney, E. C., and W. M. Ingram *Amer. Midl. Naturalist,* **$26^1$,** 201–206.
1941 Raney, E. C., and W. M. Ingram (see *General Works*).
1942 Gilbert, P. W. *Copeia,* no. 3, p 177
1942 Vogel, H. H., Jr. *Proc. Ind. Acad. Sci.* (1941), p. 266.
1943 Aronson, L. R. *Amer. Mus. Novitates,* no. 1224, pp. 1–6.
1943 Clausen, R. T. *Amer. Midl Naturalist,* **$29^2$,** 360–364.
1943 Ingram, W. M., and E. C. Raney. Same, **$29^1$,** 239–241.
1944 Aronson, L. R. *Amer. Mus. Novitates,* no. 1250, pp. 1–15.
1944 Moore, C. B. *Science Digest,* **$15^1$,** 75, 76; also, *Nat History,* **50** (1942), 191–192.
1945 Eaton, T. H., Jr. *Copeia,* no. 2, p. 115.

1947 Blair, A. P. (see *New Jersey*).

1947 Evans, H. E. *Herpetologica*, **4**, 19–21.

1947 Raney, E. C, and E. A. Lachner. *Copeia*, 1947, pp. 113–116.

**North Carolina**

1870 Cope, E. D. *Amer. Naturalist*, **4**, 397.

1878 Coues, E., and H. C. Yarrow. *Proc. Acad. Nat. Sci. Phila.*, **30**, 28.

1879 Humphreys, J. T. *Science News*, p 304.

1891 Ryder, J. A. *Amer. Naturalist*, **25**, 838–840.

1896 Brimley, C. S. Same, **30**, 501.

1907–1927 Brimley, C. S. *Jour. Elisha Mitchell Sci. Soc*, **23**$^{4}$, 157–160; 2d ed., 1926, **42**$^{1-2}$, 80–83.

1908 Brimley, C. S., and F. Sherman, Jr. Same, **24**, 14–22.

1909 Brimley, C. S. *Proc. Biol. Soc Wash.*, **22**, 129–131, 133.

1910 Brimley, C. S. (see *Alabama*).

1917 Dunn, E. R *Bull. Amer. Mus. Nat. Hist.*, **37**, 593–597, 620–623.

1920 Dunn, E. R. (see *Alabama*).

1921 Metcalf, Z. P. *Copeia*, no. 100, pp. 81–82.

1922 Brimley, C. S. *Copeia*, no 107, p 48.

1923 Breder, C M., Jr., and R. B. Breder. *Zoologica*, 4, 3–9, 18–20.

1923 Brimley, C S. *Copeia*, no. 114, p. 4

1924 Myers, G. S. *Copeia*, no 131, pp. 59–60

1925 Brimley, C. S., and W. B. Mabie. *Copeia*, no. 139, p. 15.

1927a Brimley, C. S *Copeia*, no. 162, pp. 11–12.

1927b Myers, G. S. (see *Indiana*).

1928 Andrews, E. A. *Science*, new ser., **67**, 269–270.

1928 Bishop, S. C. *Jour Elisha Mitchell Sci. Soc.*, **43**, 167.

1933 Brandt, B. B. *Copeia*, no. 1, p. 39.

1933 Brandt, B. B., and C. F. Walker. *Occ. Papers Mus. Zool. Univ. Mich*, no. 272, pp. 1–7.

1935 Harper, F. (see *General Works*).

1936a Brandt, B. B. *Copeia*, no. 4, pp. 215–223.

1936b Brandt, B. B. *Ecol. Monog.* (Durham, N.C ), **6**, 491–532.

1939 King, W. (see *Tennessee*).

1941 Gray, I. E. *Amer. Midl. Naturalist*, **25**$^{3}$, 652–658.

1940–1941 Brimley, C. S. *Carolina Tips*, 3 (April, 1940), 10–11; (June, 1940), 14, 15; (August, 1940), 18–19; (Sept., 1940), 22–23; (Nov., 1940), 26–27; (Jan., 1941), 2–3.

1942 Engels, W. L. *Amer. Midl. Naturalist*, **28**, 293–294.

**North Dakota**

1874 Allen, J. A. (see *Montana*).

1878 Coues, E., and H. C. Yarrow (see *Montana*).

1887 Ballou, W. H. *Amer. Naturalist*, **21**, 388.

1944 Telford, H. S. *N.D. Ag Expt. Stat. Bimonthly Bull.*, **6**$^{1}$, 33–35.

1944 Telford, H. S. Same, **6**$^{4}$, 35–37.

**Ohio**

1838 Kirtland, J. P., "Rept. on Zoology of Ohio." In W. W. Mather, *Second Ann. Rept. Geol. Surv. Ohio*. Columbus. P. 168.

1882 Smith, W. H. *Rept. Geol Survey Ohio*, **4**, pt. I, Zool. sect. III, pp. 701–713, 733, 734.
1887 James, J. F. *Jour. Cincinnati Soc. Nat. Hist.*, **10**$^{1}$, 35–36.
1891 Wilcox, E. V. *Otterbein* (Ohio) *Aegis*.
1895a Kirsch, P. H. *Bull. U.S. Fish Commission* (1894), **14**, art. 20, 333.
1901 Morse, M. *Ohio Naturalist*, **1**$^{7}$, 114–115.
1903 Morse, M. Same, **3**$^{3}$, 360, 361.
1904 Morse, M. *Proc. Ohio State Acad. Sci.*, **4**, pt. 3, Special papers no. 9, 102, 116–122.
1932 Walker, C. F. *Ohio Jour. Sci.*, **32**$^{4}$, 379–384.
1933 Walker, C. F. *Copeia*, no. 4, p. 224.
1937 Conant, R. P., and W. M. Clay. *Occ. Papers Mus. Zool. Univ. Mich.*, no. 346, pp. 1–9.
1945 Gier, H. T. *Copeia*, no. 1, p. 50.
1946 Walker, C. F. *Ohio State Arch. Hist. Soc., Ohio State Mus. Bull.*, **1**$^{3}$, 1–109.
1947 Wood, J. T., and W. E. Duellman. *Herpetologica*, **4**, 3–6.

**Oklahoma**

1894 Cragin, F. W. (see *Kansas*).
1894 Cope, E. D. *Proc Acad Nat. Sci Phila.* (1893), **45**, 386.
1903 Stone, W. (see *Arkansas*).
1919 Schmidt, K. P. *Copeia*, no. 73, p. 71.
1924 Ortenburger, A. I. *Proc. Okla. Acad. Sci.*, **4**, 19–20.
1925 Force, E. R. *Copeia*, no. 141, p. 25.
1926 Force, E. R. *Proc. Okla. Acad. Sci.*, **5**, 80–82. *Univ. Okla. Bull.*, new ser., no. 330, Univ. Studies no. 22.
1926a Ortenburger, A. I *Copeia*, no. 155, pp. 137–138.
1926b Ortenburger, A. I. *Copeia*, no. 156, p. 145.
1927a Ortenburger, A. I. *Proc. Okla. Acad. Sci.*, **6**, pt. I, 89–93. *Univ. Okla. Bull.*, new ser., no. 348.
1927b Ortenburger, A. I. *Copeia*, no. 163, pp. 46–47.
1928 Force, E. R. *Proc. Okla. Acad. Sci.*, art. XVII, pp. 78, 79 *Univ. Okla. Bull.*, new ser., no. 410, Univ. Studies no. 30.
1929a Burt, C. E., and M. D. Burt (see *Arkansas*).
1929a Ortenburger, A. I. *Copeia*, no. 170, pp. 8–10.
1929b Ortenburger, A. I. *Copeia*, no. 170, pp. 26–27.
1930 Force, E. R. *Copeia*, no. 2, pp. 25–27, 38, 39.
1930 Ortenburger, A. I., and Beryl Freeman. *Pub. Univ. Okla.*, **2**, Biol. Survey, no. 4, 176–178.
1930 Ortenburger, A. I. *Copeia*, no. 173 (Oct.–Dec. 1929, Jan. 16, 1930), p. 94.
1931 Burt, C. E. (see *Kansas*).
1933 Smith, H. M. (see *Kansas*).
1934 Smith, H. M., and A. B. Leonard. *Amer. Midl. Naturalist*, **15**, 190–196.
1935 Burt, C. E. (see *General Works*).
1936 Blair, W. F. *Copeia*, no. 2, p. 115.
1936 Bragg, A. N. *Copeia*, no. 1, pp. 14–20.
1937 Bragg, A. N. *Copeia*, no. 4, pp. 227–228.

1937a Bragg, A. N. *Amer. Midl. Naturalist*, $18^{2}$, 273–284.

1937 Moore, G. A. *Copeia*, no. 4, pp. 225–226.

1937 Trowbridge, A. H. *Copeia*, no. 1, pp. 71–72.

1937 Trowbridge, A. H. *Amer. Midl. Naturalist*, $18^{2}$, 284–303.

1937 Trowbridge, A. H. and M. S. Trowbridge. *Amer. Naturalist*, $71^{796}$, 460–480.

1939 Bragg, A. N. *Proc. Okla. Acad. Sci.* 19, 41–42.

1939a Bragg, A. N. *Copeia*, no. 3, p. 173.

1939 Jones, R. W., and G. E. Derrick. *Proc. Okla. Acad. Sci.* 19, 39.

1940a Bragg, A. N. *Amer. Naturalist*, 74, 322–349, 424–438.

1940b Bragg, A N. *Wasmann Collector*, 4, 6–16.

1940c Bragg, A. N. *Proc. Okla. Acad. Sci.*, 20, 71–74.

1940d Bragg, A. N. Same, pp. 75–76.

1940e Bragg, A. N. *Observations on the Ecology of Natural History of Anura II and III. Amer. Midl. Naturalist*, $24^{2}$, 306–335. (Observation II, pp. 301–321; Observation III, pp. 322–335.)

1940 Bragg, A. N., and R. E. Kuntz. *Proc. Okla. Acad. Sci.*, 20, 77.

1941 Bragg, A. N. *Key to the Toads (Bufo) of Oklahoma.* Same (1940), 21, 17–18.

1941a Bragg, A. N. *Copeia*, no. 1, pp. 51–52.

1941b Bragg, A N. (see *New Mexico*).

1941d Bragg, A. N. *Turtox News*, $19^{1}$, 10–12. (Observation VIII.)

1941 Smith, C. C., and A. N. Bragg (see *General Works*).

1941a Smith, C. C., and A. N. Bragg (see *General Works*).

1941 Trowbridge, M. S. *Trans. Amer. Micros. Soc.*, $60^{4}$, 508–526.

1942 Bragg, A. N. *Proc. Okla. Acad. Sci.*, 22, 16–17.

1942a Bragg, A. N. *Proc. Okla. Acad Sci.*, 22, 18.

1942c Bragg, A. N. *Turtox News*, $20^{1}$, 12, 13.

1942d Bragg, A. N. Same, $20^{11}$, 154.

1942e Bragg, A. N. *Science*, new ser., 95, 194–195.

1942f Bragg, A. N. *Anat. Rec.*, $84^{4}$, 506.

1942g Bragg, A. N. Same, $84^{4}$, 507.

1942h Bragg, A. N. *Wasmann Collector*, $5^{2}$, 47–60.

1942i Bragg, A. N. *Proc. Okla. Acad. Sci.*, 22, 73–74. (Observation XI.)

1942 Bragg, A. N., and C. C. Smith *Great Basin Naturalist*, $2^{2}$, 33–50. (Observation IX.)

1942 Moore, G. A., and C. C. Rigney. *Proc. Okla. Acad. Sci* (1941), 22, 77–80.

1942 Trowbridge, M. S. *Trans. Amer. Micros. Soc.*, $61^{1}$, 66–83.

1943 Blair, A. P. *Amer Naturalist*, $77^{7}$, 563–568.

1943 Bragg, A. *Great Basin Naturalist*, $4^{3,4}$, 62–80. (Observation XV.)

1943a Bragg, A. N. *Proc. Okla. Acad. Sci.* (1942), 23, 37–39.

1943b Bragg, A. N. Same, pp. 39–40.

1943c Bragg, A. N. *Wasmann Collector*, $5^{4}$, 129–140. (Observation XVI.)

1943 Bragg, A. N., and C. C. Smith. *Turtox News*, $21^{5}$, 107.

1944 Bragg, A. N. *Copeia*, no. 4, pp. 230–241. (Observation XIII.)

1944a Bragg, A. N. *Proc. Okla. Acad. Sci.* (1934), 24, 13–14.

1944b Bragg, A. N. *Amer. Naturalist,* **78**, 517–533; **79**, 52–72. (Observation XII.)

1944 Marr, J. C. (see *General Works*).

1945 Bragg, A. N. *Proc. Okla. Acad. Sci.* (1944), **25**, 27.

1945 Bragg, A. N. *Wasmann Collector,* $6^{3, 4}$, 68–78.

1946 Bragg, A. N. *Proc. Okla. Acad. Sci.*, **26**, 16.

1946a Bragg, A. N. *Proc. Okla. Acad. Sci.*, **26**, 19.

1946b Bragg, A. N. *Herpetologica,* 3, 89–97.

1946 Dundee, H., and A. N. Bragg. *Proc. Okla. Acad. Sci.*, **26**, 18.

1945 Smith, H. M. *Univ. Kans. Pub. Mus. Nat. Hist.*, $1^{2}$, 88–89.

1947 Blair, A. P. (see *New Jersey*).

**Oregon**

1854 Baird, S. F., and C. Girard. *Proc. Acad. Nat. Sci. Phila.* (Oct. 26, 1842), **6**, (1852, 1853), 174–175.

1854 Hallowell, E. Same, p. 183.

1884 Cope, E. D. Same (1883), **35**, 19, 20, 23.

1895 Van Denburgh, J. (see *Idaho*).

1899 Washburn, F L. *Amer. Naturalist,* $33^{386}$, 139–141.

1912a Van Denburgh, J. (see *Idaho*).

1917 Camp, C. L. *Copeia,* no. 40, pp. 13, 14.

1922 Van Winkle, K. (see *Washington*).

1928 Brues, C. T. *Proc. Amer. Acad. Arts Sciences,* $63^{4}$, 205–206.

1928 Slevin, J. R. (see *British Columbia*).

1934 Brooking, W J. *Copeia,* no. 2, pp. 93, 94.

1936 Fitch, H. S. *Amer. Midl Naturalist,* $17^{3}$, 634–652.

1936 Jewett, S. G., Jr. *Copeia,* no. 1, pp. 71, 72.

1938 Fitch, H. S. *Copeia,* no. 3, p. 148.

1939 Gordon, K. *Oregon State Coll. Monog.*, no. 1, pp. 1–82.

1939 Graf, W., Stanley G. Jewett, Jr., and Kenneth Gordon. *Copeia,* no. 2, pp. 101–104.

1942 Slater, J. R. (see *Washington*).

1943 Evenden, F. G., Jr. *Copeia,* no. 4, pp. 251–252.

1945 Schonberger, C. F. *Copeia,* no. 2, pp. 120–121.

**Pennsylvania**

1843 Haldeman, S. S. In Trego, *Geography of Pennsylvania.* Philadelphia. P. 78.

1844 Haldeman, S. S. In Rupp, *History of Lancaster County.* Lancaster, Pa Appendix.

1857 Hallowell, E. *Proc. Acad. Nat. Hist. Phila.* (1856), 8, 141–142.

1869 Stauffer, J. In Mombert, *History of Lancaster County.* Lancaster, Pa. P. 576.

1879 Rathvon, S. S. *Science News,* p. 368.

1903 Reese, A. M. *Science,* new ser., $17^{425}$.

1906 Stone, W. (see *Delaware*).

1908 Palmer, T. C. *Proc. Delaware Co.* (Pa.) *Inst. Sci.*, $4^{1}$, 12–22.

1913 Surface, H. A. *Pa. Dept. Ag., Div. Zool., Bimonthly Zool. Bull.*, 3, 66–152.

1914 Palmer, T. C. *Proc. Delaware Co.* (Pa.) *Inst. Sci.*, **7**, 15–17.
1915 Dunn, E. R. *Copeia*, no. 16, p. 3.
1915 Fowler, H. W. *Proc. Delaware Co.* (Pa.) *Inst. Sci.*, $7^{2}$, 41, 42.
1915 Keim, T. D. *Copeia*, no. 24, pp. 51–52.
1917 Fowler, H. W. *Copeia*, no. 40, pp. 14, 15.
1917 Mattern, E. S., and W. I. Mattern. *Copeia*, no. 46, p. 65.
1918b Evermann, B. W. *Copeia*, no. 58, p. 67.
1924 Frost, S. W. (see *New York*).
1928 Netting, M. G. *The Cardinal*, $2^{9}$, 2.
1932 Frost, S. W. *Amer. Naturalist*, **66**, 530–540.
1933 Burger, J. W. *Copeia*, no. 2, pp. 94.
1933 Netting, M. G. *Proc. Pa. Acad. Sci.*, **7**, 1, 7–11.
1935 Frost, S. R. *Copeia*, no. 1, pp. 15–18.
1936a Netting, M. G. *Proc Pa. Acad. Sci.*, **10**, 26–28.
1936b Netting, M. G. *Carnegie Mus. Pa. Herpetology Leaflet*, no. 1.
1939 Mohr, C. E. *Proc Pa Acad. Sci*, **13**, 76–78.
1939 Pawling, R. O. *Herpetologica*, **1**, 165–169.
1940 Mohr, C. E. *Frontiers*, $4^{1}$, 142–146.
1940 Yoder, H. D. *Proc. Pa. Acad. Sci.*, **14**, 90–92.
1941 Freyburger, W. A., Jr. Same, **15**, 180–183.
1941 Knepp, T. H. Same, p. 164.
1942 Conant, R. *Amer. Midl. Naturalist*, $27^{1}$, 161–163.
1943 Baldauf, R. J *Mengel Nat Hist Soc Leaflet*, no. 1, pp. 1–8.
1945 Smith, A. G. *Proc. Pa. Acad. Sci.*, **19**, 77.

**Rhode Island**

1884–1886 Bumpus, H. C. *Random Notes of Natural History*, $1^{10}$, 4, 5; $3^{7}$, 52.
1904 Henshaw, S. (see *Connecticut*).
1905 Drowne, F. P. *Roger Williams Mark Mus. Monogr.*, no. 15, pp. 1–24.
1921 Babcock, H. L. (see *Connecticut*).
1926 Babcock, H. L. (see *Connecticut*).

**South Carolina**

1920 Deckert, R. F. *Copeia*, no. 80, p. 26.
1924b Schmidt, K. P. *Copeia*, no. 132, p. 68.
1924 McManus, I. *The Anura of the Columbia, S C. Region*. M. A. Thesis, Columbia.
1927a Pickens, A. L. *Copeia*, no. 162, pp. 25–26.
1927b Pickens, A. L. *Copeia*, no. 165, pp. 106–110.
1929 Corrington, J. D. *Copeia*, July–Sept., pp. 58–67.
1935 Harper, F. (see *General Works*).
1937 Chamberlain, E. B. *Copeia*, no. 2, p. 142.
1939 Chamberlain, E. B. *Charleston Mus. Leaflet*, no. 12, pp. 1–38.
1940 Jopson, H. G. M. *Herpetologica*, **2**, pt. 2, 39–43.
1940 Stejneger, L. (see *Florida*).
1946 Obrecht, C. B. *Copeia*, no. 2, pp. 71–72.
1947 Blair, A. P. (see *New Jersey*).
1948b Neill, W. T. (see *Georgia*).

**South Dakota**

1874 Allen, J. A. (see *Montana*).

1874 Coues, E. (see *Montana*).

1875 Hayden, F. V. (see *Nebraska*).

1908 Reagen, A. B. *Zoologischer Anzeiger*, **32**, Band Nr. I, 31; also in *Rept. State Geol., S D. Geol. Survey Bull.*, no 4, p. 164.

1914 Visher, S. S. *S.D. Geol. Survey Bull.*, no. 6, p. 93.

1923 Over, W. H. *S.D. Geol.,Nat. Hist. Survey Bull*, 12, *Bull. Univ. S D* ser XXIII, no. 10, pp. 11–15.

1929a Burt, C. E., and M. D. Burt (see *Arkansas*).

1935 Burt, C. E. (see *General Works*).

1943 Larsen, N. P. *Jour. Econ. Ent* **63**, no. 3, 480.

**Tennessee**

1844 Troost, G. *Seventh Geol. Rept. Tenn.*, p. 40.

1896 Rhoads, S. N. *Proc. Acad. Nat. Sci. Phila.*, **47** (Nov. 15, 1895), 376–383, 395–399, 405, 407.

1920 Dunn, E. R. (see *Alabama*).

1922 Blanchard, F. N *Occ. Papers Mus. Zool Univ. Mich*, no. 117, pp. 4–6.

1927 Dunn, E. R. *Copeia*, no. 162, p. 19.

1934 Necker, W. *Bull. Chicago Acad. Sci.*, **5**[1], 1–4.

1936 Bailey, J. R. *Copeia*, no. 2, p. 115.

1937 Cagle, F. R. *Jour. Tenn. Acad. Sci.*, **12**[2], 179–185.

1937 Endsley, J. R. *Copeia*, no. 1, p. 70.

1937a Parker, M. V. *Jour. Tenn. Acad. Sci.*, **12**, 169–178.

1937b Parker, M. V. Same, **12**[1], 60–86.

1939 Cahn, A. R *Copeia*, no. 1, pp. 52–53.

1939 King, W. *Amer Midl. Naturalist*, **2**[3], 531–582.

1939 Parker, Malcolm V. *Jour. Tenn. Acad. Sci.*, **14**[1], 72, 73, 76–81.

1940 Shoup, C. S., and J. H. Peyton. *Jour. Tenn. Acad Sci*, **15**, 114.

1941 Gentry, G. *Tenn. Dept. Conservation, Div. Fish and Game, Misc Pub*, no. 4, pp. 329–331.

1944 King, W. *Copeia*, no 4, p. 255.

**Texas**

1854 Baird, S. F., and C. Girard. *Proc. Acad. Nat. Sci. Phila.* (1852), **6** (1852, 1853), 173.

1857b Hallowell, E. Same (1856), **8**, 307–309.

1859 Baird, S. F. "Reptiles of the Boundary." In W. H. Emory, *U.S. and Mex. Boundary Survey*. Vol. II (1858), 25–29.

1859 Baird, S. F. (see *Arkansas*).

1865 Cope, E. D. *Proc. Acad. Nat Sci. Phila.*, **17**, 194, 195, 197.

1878 Cope, E. D. *Amer. Naturalist*, **12**, 186; **12**[4], 252, 253.

1880a Cope, E. D. *Bull. U.S. Nat. Mus.*, no. 17. pp. 8, 24–29, 42–47

1880b Cope, E. D. *Proc Amer Phil. Soc.*, **18** (June 20, 1879), p. 263.

1888 Garman, S. *Bull. Essex Inst.*, **19** (1887), 134, 138.

1889 Cope, E. D. *Proc. U.S. Nat. Mus.* (1888), **11**, 317–318, 395–396.

1893 Cope, E. D. *Proc. Acad. Nat. Sci. Phila.* (1892), **44**, 333, 337.

1893 Cope, E. D. *Amer. Naturalist*, no. 314, pp. 155–156.

1894 Test, F. C. *Bull. U.S. Fish Commission*, 12 (1892, 1894), 122.
1899 Mocquard, F. (see *General Works*).
1902 Strecker, J. K., Jr. *Trans. Tex. Acad. Sci.* (1901), $4^5$, pt. II, 6–7.
1903 Stone, W. (see *Arkansas*).
1905 Gadow, H. *Proc. Zool. Soc.* London, 2, 193–194, 205–208, 230–231.
1907 Mearns, E. A. *Bull. U.S. Nat. Mus.*, no. 56, pt. I, p. 81.
1908a Strecker, J. K., Jr. *Proc. Biol. Soc. Wash.*, 21, 80–83.
1908b Strecker, J. K., Jr. Same, pp. 51–52.
1908c Strecker, J. K., Jr. Same, pp. 56–61.
1908d Strecker, J. K., Jr. Same, p. 88.
1908e Strecker, J. K., Jr. Same, pp. 199–206.
1909 Strecker, J. K., Jr. *Baylor Univ. Bull.*, $12^1$, 9, 15.
1909a Strecker, J. K., Jr. *Proc Biol. Soc. Wash.*, 22, 115–120.
1910a Strecker, J. K., Jr. Same, 23, 115–122.
1910b Strecker, J. K., Jr. *Baylor Univ. Bull.*, $13^{4,5}$, 1–4, 17–21.
1910c Strecker, J. K., Jr. *Trans. Acad. Sci. St. Louis*, $19^5$, 73–82.
1915 Stejneger, L. *Proc. Biol. Soc. Wash.*, 28, 131–132.
1915 Strecker, J. K., Jr. *Baylor Univ. Bull.*, $18^4$, 45–54, 61–82.
1919 Pope, P. H. *Copeia*, no. 76, pp. 93–98.
1920 Schmidt, K. P. (see *Louisiana*).
1922 Strecker, J. K., Jr. *Bull. Sci. Soc. San Antonio*, no. 4, pp. 1–5, 9–16, 45.
1926a Strecker, J. K., Jr. *Cont. Baylor Univ. Mus.*, no. 2, pp. 1, 2.
1926b Strecker, J. K., Jr. Same, no. 3, p. 3.
1926c Strecker, J. K., Jr. Same, no. 6, pp. 1, 8, 9.
1926d Strecker, J. K., Jr. Same, no. 7, pp. 3–11.
1926e Strecker, J. K., Jr. Same, no. 7, pp. 8–11.
1926f Strecker, J. K., Jr. Same, no. 8, pp. 7–12.
1927a Strecker, J. K., Jr. Same, no. 10, pp. 13, 14.
1927b Strecker, J. K., Jr. *Copeia*, no. 162, p. 8.
1927 Strecker, J. K., Jr., and W. J. Williams. *Cont. Baylor Univ Mus*, no. 12, pp. 1–8, 13, 16.
1928 Strecker, J. K., Jr., and W. J. Williams. Same, no. 17, pp. 3–19.
1928b Strecker, J. K., Jr. Same, no. 15, pp. 3–5, 7.
1928c Strecker, J. K., Jr. Same, no. 16, pp. 1–21, 3–6, 9–10.
1929a Burt, C. E., and M. D. Burt (see *Arkansas*).
1929b Burt, C. E., and M. D. Burt (see *Arizona*).
1929 Strecker, J. K., Jr. *Cont. Baylor Univ. Mus.*, no. 19, pp. 1–15.
1930 Strecker, J. K., Jr. Same, no. 23, pp. 2–4, 6–8.
1931 Gaige, H. T. *Copeia*, no. 2, p. 63.
1932 Burt, C. E. *Copeia*, no. 3, p. 158.
1932a Burt, C. E. *Bio-Log*, $2^1$, 1, 2.
1932 Mosauer, W. (see *New Mexico*).
1932 Taylor, E. H. *Univ. Kans. Sci. Bull.*, no. 11, pp. 243–245.
1932 Taylor, E. H., and J. S. Wright. Same, no. 12, pp. 247–249.
1933 Martin, F. *Aquar.* (Berlin), pp. 92–93.
1933 Smith, H. M. *Copeia*, no. 4, p. 217.
1933 Strecker, J. K., Jr. *Copeia*, no. 2, pp. 77–79.

1934 Piatt, J. *Amer. Midl. Naturalist,* **$15^{1}$**, 89–91.
1935 Strecker, J. K., Jr., and J. E. Johnson. *Baylor Univ Bull.*, no. 38, 3, pp. 17–23.
1935 Williams, W. J. *Baylor Bulletin,* Vol. 38, no. 3, pp. 17–19, 32–36.
1936 Burt, C. E. *Amer. Midl. Naturalist,* **$17^{4}$**, 770–775.
1936 Parks, H. B., V. R. Cory, and others. *Biol. Survey East Tex. Big Thicket Area. Tex. Acad. Sci.*, pp. 18–20.
1937 Mulaik, S. *Copeia,* no. 1, pp. 72–73.
1937 Smith, H. M. *Herpetologica,* **$1^{4}$**, 104–108.
1938 Burt, C. E. *Papers Mich. Acad. Sci. Arts Letters* (1937), **23**, 607–610.
1938 Mulaik, S., and D. Sollberger. *Copeia,* no. 2, p. 90.
1938 Wright, A. H., and A. A. Wright. *Trans. Tex. Acad. Sci.*, **21**, 5–35.
1939 Murray, L. T. *Cont. Baylor Univ. Mus.*, no. 24, pp. 4–16.
1939 Taylor, E. H. *Kans. Univ. Sci. Bull.*, **$26^{15}$**, 515–518, 529–531, 550–551.
1940 Taylor, E. H., and I. W. Knobloch (see *Arizona*).
1941 Gunter, G. *Copeia,* no. 4, p. 266.
1942 Baker, R. H. *Texas Game Fish and Oyster Com* , Bull. no. 23, pp. 1–7.
1942 Gloyd, H. K., and H. M. Smith. *Bull Chicago Acad. Sci.*, **$6^{11}$**, 231, 232.
1944 Marr, J. C. (see *General Works*).
1944 Schmidt, K. P., and T. F. Smith. *Field Mus. Nat Hist.*, Zool. ser., **$29^{5}$**, 75–96.
1944 Schmidt, K. P., and D. W. Owens. Same, **$29^{6}$**, 97–115.
1945 Smith, H. M., and L. E. Laufe. *Trans. Kans. Acad. Sci* , **$48^{3}$**, 325–329.
1946 Glass, B. P. *Copeia,* no. 2, p. 103.
1946 Glass, B. P. *Herpetologica,* **3**, pt. 3, 101–103.
1946 Netting, M. G , and C. J. Goin. *Copeia,* no. 4, p. 253.
1946 Smith, H. M., and B. C. Brown. *Herpetologica,* **3**, pt. 3, 73.
1947 Blair, A. P. *Copeia,* 1947, p. 137.
1947 Smith, H. M., and B. C. Brown. *Proc Biol. Soc. Wash.*, **60**, 47–50.
1947 Smith, H. M., and H. K. Buechner. *Bull. Chicago Acad. Sci.*, **$6^{1}$**, 1–16.
1948 Livezey, R. L , and H. M. Johnson. *Herpetologica,* **$4^{5}$**, 164.

**Utah**

1875 Yarrow, H. C. (see *Arizona*).
1884a Cope, E. D. *Proc. Acad. Nat. Sci. Phila.* (1883), **35**, 15, 16.
1884b Cope, E. D. (see *California*).
1912a Van Denburgh, J. (see *Idaho*).
1915 Van Denburgh, J., and J. R. Slevin. *Proc Calif Acad. Sci.*, 4th ser., **$5^{4}$**, 99–102.
1918 Engelhardt, G. P. *Copeia,* no. 60, pp. 77–79.
1920 Pack, Herbert J. *Copeia,* no. 77, p. 7.
1922 Pack, Herbert J. *Copeia,* no. 102, p. 8.
1922b Pack, Herbert J. *Copeia,* no. 107, pp. 46–47.
1927a Tanner, V. M. *Copeia,* no. 163, pp. 54–55.
1927b Tanner, V. M. *Utah Acad. Sci.*, 21st meeting, pp. 6–7.
1928 Tanner, V. M. *Copeia,* no. 166, pp. 23–25.
1928 Slevin, J. R. (see *British Columbia*).
1929a Burt, C. E., and M. D. Burt (see *Arkansas*).

1929b Burt, C. E., and M. D. Burt (see *Arizona*).
1929 Tanner, V. M. *Copeia,* no. 171, pp. 46–52.
1930 Tanner, V. M. *Copeia,* no. 2, pp. 41–42.
1931 Tanner, V. M. *Proc. Utah Acad. Sci.* (Provo), pp. 159–198.
1932 Ruthven, A. G. *Occ. Papers Mus. Zool. Univ. Mich.,* no. 243, pp. 1–2.
1932 Taylor, E. H., and J. S. Wright. *Kans. Univ. Sci. Bull.,* $20^{12}$, 247–249.
1933a Burt, C. E. (see *General Works*).
1935 Wood, W. F. *Copeia,* no. 2, pp. 100–102.
1935 Wood, W. F. (see *Lower California*).
1935a Eaton, T. H., Jr. *Copeia,* no. 3, p. 150.
1935b Eaton, T. H., Jr. (see *Arizona*).
1936 Burt, C. E. *Amer. Midl. Naturalist,* $17^{4}$, 770–775.
1936 Cowles, R. B., and C. M. Bogert (see *Nevada*).
1938 Hardy, Ross. *Utah Acad. Sci. Arts Letters,* 15, 99, 102.
1940 Tanner, W. W. *Great Basin Naturalist,* $1^{3,4}$, 138–139.
1944 Knowlton, G. F. *Copeia,* no. 2, p. 119.

**Vermont**

1842 Thompson, Z. *History of Vermont, Natural, Civil and Statistical.* Burlington. Pt. I, pp. 112–113, 119–123.
1904 Henshaw, S. (see *Connecticut*).
1926 Babcock, H. L. (see *Connecticut*).
1931 Loveridge, A. *Bull. Boston Soc. Nat. Hist.,* no. 61, p. 15.
1938 Fowler, J. A., and H. J. Cole. *Copeia,* no. 2, p. 93.
1940 Trapido, H. *New England Naturalist,* no. 7, pp. 11–14.
1941 Moore, J. A. (see *General Works*).

**Virginia**

1899 Miller, G. S., Jr. (see *District of Columbia*).
1915a Dunn, E. R. *Copeia,* no. 18, p. 56.
1915b Dunn, E. R. *Copeia,* no. 25, p. 63.
1916 Dunn, E. R. *Copeia,* no. 28, pp. 22, 23.
1918 Dunn, E. R. *Copeia,* no. 53, pp. 16–22.
1918 Fowler, H. W. *Copeia,* no. 55, p. 44.
1920 Dunn, E. R. (see *Alabama*).
1925 Fowler, H. W. *Copeia,* no. 146, pp. 65, 66.
1925 Brady, M. K. *Copeia,* no. 137, p. 110.
1927 Brady, M. *Copeia,* no. 162, pp. 26–28.
1929a Burt, C. E., and M. D. Burt (see *Arkansas*).
1931 Trautman, M. B. *Copeia,* no. 2, p. 63.
1933 Brandt, B. B., and C. F. Walker (see *North Carolina*).
1937 Brady, M. K. (see *Maryland; District of Columbia*).
1938 Richmond, N. D., and C. J. Goin. *Ann. Carnegie Mus.,* 27, 301–304.
1940 Netting, M. G., and L. W. Wilson. Same, 28, 1–8.
1944 Bartsch, Paul. *Copeia,* no. 3, p. 187.
1945 Hoffman, R. L. *Herpetologica,* $2^{7-8}$, 199–205.
1946 Ackroyd, J. F., and R. L. Hoffman. *Copeia,* no. 4, pp. 257–258.
1946 Hoffman, R. L. *Herpetologica,* 3, pt. 4, 141–142.
1947 Richmond, N. D. *Ecology,* $28^{1}$, 53–67.

**Washington**

1854 Baird, S. F., and C. Girard (see *Oregon*).
1869 Cooper, J. G. (see *Montana*).
1895 Van Denburgh, J. (see *Idaho*).
1899 Meek, S. E., and D. G. Elliot. *Field Columbian Mus. Pub.*, no. 31, Zool, ser., 1[12], 232–234.
1899 Stejneger, L. *Proc U.S Nat. Mus*, **21**[1178], 899–901.
1912c Van Denburgh, J. *Proc. Calif. Acad. Sci.*, 4th ser., **3**, 259–264.
1916 Dice, L. R. *Univ. Calif. Pub. Zool.*, 16[17], 293–348.
1918 Ruthven, A. G *Copeia*, no. 53, p. 10.
1920 Gaige, H. T. *Occ. Papers Mus. Zool. Univ. Mich.*, no. 84, pp. 1–9.
1921 Blanchard, F. N. *Copeia*, no. 90, pp. 5–6.
1922 Van Winkle, K. *Copeia*, no. 102, pp. 4–6.
1928 Slevin, J. R. (see *British Columbia*)
1931 Noble, G K, and P. G. Putnam. *Copeia*, no. 3, pp. 97–101.
1931 Slater, J. R. *Copeia*, no. 2, pp. 62–63.
1933 Svihla, A. *Copeia*, no. 1, p. 39.
1933 Svihla, A., and R. D. Svihla. *Copeia*, no. 1, pp. 37–38.
1934 Slater, J. R. *Copeia*, no. 3, pp. 140–141.
1935 Svihla, A. *Copeia*, no. 3, pp. 119–122.
1939 Brown, W. C., and J. R Slater. *Occ. Papers Dept. Biol., Coll. Puget Sound* (Tacoma), no. 4, pp. 6–31.
1939a Slater, J. R. Same, no. 2, pp. 4–5.
1939b Slater, J. R. *Herpetologica*, **1**, 145–149.
1940 Tanner, W. W. (see *Utah*).
1941 Slater, J. R., and W. C. Brown. *Occ. Papers Dept Biol., Coll. Puget Sound* (Tacoma), no. 13, pp. 74–77.
1942 Slater, J. R. *A Checklist of the Amphibians and Reptiles of the Pacific Northwest.* Tacoma, Wash.. Biol. Dept., College Puget Sound. Mimeographed. P. 2.
1943 Slipp, J. W., and G. C. Carl (see *British Columbia*).
1945 Schonberger, C. F. (see *Oregon*).

**West Virginia**

1929a Burt, C. E., and M. D. Burt (see *Arkansas*).
1931 Bond, H. D. *Copeia*, no. 2, p. 54.
1932 Walker, C F. (see *Ohio*).
1935 Strader, L. D. *Proc. W. Va. Acad. Sci.*, **9**, 32–35.
1936 Green, N. B. Same, **10**, 80–83.
1936 Netting, M. G. Same, pp. 88–89.
1937a Green, N. B. *Herpetologica*, **1**, 113–116.
1937b Green, N. B. *Mag Hist. and Biog.*, pp. 1–8.
1938 Green, N. B. *Copeia*, no. 2, pp. 79–82.
1939 Richmond, N. D., and G. S. Boggess. *Proc W. Va. Acad. Sci.*, **12**, 57–60.
1940 Green, N. B. Same, **14**, 13.
1940 Green, N. B. Same, p. 145.
1940 Green, N. B., and N. D. Richmond. *Copeia*, no. 2, p. 127
1940 Llewellyn, L. M. *Proc. W. Va. Acad. Sci.*, **14**, 148–150.

1940 Netting, M. G., and L. W. Wilson. *Ann. Carnegie Mus.*, **28**, 1–8.
1945 Wilson, L. W. *Proc. W. Va. Acad. Sci.* (1944), *W. Va. Univ. Bull.*, no. 10–1, pp. 39–41.

**Wisconsin**

1853 Lapham, I. A. *Trans Wis. State Ag. Soc* (1852), **2**, 366.
1883 Hoy, P. R. *Geol. Survey Wis., 1872–1879*, **1**, pt. II, 425.
1889 Higley, W. K. *Trans. Wis. Acad. Sci Art Letters, 1883–1887*, **7**, 167–169, 175.
1914 Jackson, H. H. T. *Bull. Wis. Nat. His. Soc.*, new ser., **12**$^{1,2}$, 17–20, 22, 28–29, 35–36.
1915 Nelson, T. C. *Copeia*, no. 19, pp. 13–14.
1926 Schmidt, F. J. W. *Copeia*, no. 154, pp. 131–132.
1928 Pope, T. E. B., and W. E. Dickinson. *Bull. Pub. Mus. Milwaukee*, **8**$^{1}$, 1–138.
1929 Cahn, A. R. *Copeia*, no. 170, pp. 4–6.
1929 Pope, T. E. B. *Yearbook Pub. Mus. Milwaukee* (1928), **8**, pt. I, 177–179, 181.
1930 Pope, T. E. B. *Trans Wis. Acad. Sci. Arts Letters*, **25**, 273, 275, 276, 278, 279.
1935 Schmidt, K. P., and W. L. Necker (see *Illinois*).
1938 Schmidt, K. P. (see *Illinois*).
1940 Hawkins, A. S. *Trans. Wis. Acad. Sci. Arts Letters*, **32**, 63.
1941 Moore, J. A. (see *General Works*).
1944 Edgren, R. A. J. *Amer. Midl. Naturalist*, no. 2, pp. 495–498.

**Wyoming**

1872 Cope, E. D. (see *Montana*).
1893 Test, F. C. (see *Montana*).
1917 Cary, M. *North American Fauna*, no. 42, pp. 19, 27, 33.
1932 Brues, C. T. (see *Nevada*).
1938 Necker, W. L. (see *Illinois*).
1939 Necker, W. L. (see *Illinois*).

## MEXICO

See *Arizona, New Mexico, Texas, and General*

**Lower California**

1861 Cope, E. D. *Proc. Acad. Nat. Sci. Phila.*, p. 305.
1866 Cope, E. D. Same, **18**, 312–314.
1877 Streets, T. H. *Bull. U.S. Nat. Mus.*, no. 7, p. 35.
1887 Belding, L. *The West American Scientist*, **3**$^{24}$, 99.
1895 Van Denburgh, J. *Proc. Calif. Acad. Sci.*, 2d. ser., **5**, pt. I, 556–560.
1896a Van Denburgh, J. Same, pt. II, 1004, 1008.
1899 Mocquard, F. *Nouv. arch. Mus. d'hist. natur.* (Paris), 4th ser., **1**, 297–299, 334–344.
1905 Van Denburgh, J. *Proc. Calif. Acad. Sci.*, 3d ser., Zool., **4**$^{1}$, 1–5, 23.
1914 Van Denburgh, J., and J. R. Slevin. *Proc. Calif. Acad. Sci.*, 4th ser., **4**, 132, 144.

1921c Van Denburgh, J., and J. R. Slevin. *Proc. Calif. Acad. Sci.*, 4th ser., $11^4$, 49–50, 53–54.
1922 Nelson, E. W. *Mem. Nat. Acad. Sci.*, $16^1$, 113.
1922 Schmidt, K. P. *Bull. Amer. Mus. Nat. Hist.*, 46, art. XI, 607–634.
1931 Klauber, L. M. *Copeia*, no. 3, p. 141.
1932 Linsdale, J. M. *Univ. Calif. Pub. Zool.*, $38^6$, 345–354.
1935 Wood, W. F. (see *Utah*).
1936 Mosauer, W. *Occ. Papers Mus. Zool. Univ. Mich.*, no. 329, pp. 1–4, 19–21.
1944 Tevis, L., Jr. *Copeia*, no. 1, pp. 6, 7.
1948 Smith, H. M., and E. H. Taylor (see *General Check Lists*).

# Index

[Numbers in boldface refer to the pages of the species account.]

CPSIA information can be obtained
at www.ICGtesting.com
Printed in the USA
LVHW042108280323
742726LV00014B/665

9 781376 979794